Dramaturgy in American Theater

A Source Book

Dramaturgy in American Theater

A Source Book

EDITED BY

SUSAN JONAS
CLASSIC STAGE COMPANY (CSC)

GEOFFREY S. PROEHL
UNIVERSITY OF PUGET SOUND

CONSULTING EDITOR
MICHAEL LUPU
THE GUTHRIE THEATER

Harcourt Brace College Publishers

Fort Worth   Philadelphia   San Diego   New York   Orlando   Austin   San Antonio
Toronto   Montreal   London   Sydney   Tokyo

Publisher	•	Christopher P. Klein
Acquisitions Editor	•	Barbara J. C. Rosenberg
Development Editor	•	Terri House
Project Editor	•	Matt Ball
Art Director	•	Don Fujimoto
Production Manager	•	Jane Tyndall Ponceti
Product Manager	•	Ilse Wolfe West

Requests for permission to make copies of any part of the work should be mailed to: Permissions Department, Harcourt Brace & Company, 6277 Sea Harbor Drive, Orlando, Florida 32887-6777

Address for orders:
Harcourt Brace College Publishers
6277 Sea Harbor Drive
Orlando, FL 32887
1-800-782-4479 or 1-800-433-0001 (in Florida)

Address for editorial correspondence:
Harcourt Brace College Publishers
301 Commerce Street, Suite 3700
Fort Worth, TX 76102

Harcourt Brace College Publishers may provide complimentary instructional aids and supplements or supplement packages to those adopters qualified under our adoption policy. Please contact your sales representative for more information. If as an adopter or potential user you receive supplements you do not need, please return them to your sales representative or send them to:

Attn: Returns Department
Troy Warehouse
465 South Lincoln Drive
Troy, MO 63379

ISBN: 0-15-502586-4

Library of Congress Catalog Card Number: 96-79351

Printed in the United States of America

6 7 8 9 0 1 2 3 4 5   066   9 8 7 6 5 4 3 2 1

IN MEMORY OF

MICHAEL LOWELL QUINN

JANUARY 31, 1958—AUGUST 27, 1994

Preface

What is a dramaturg? A dramaturg might help select a season at Lincoln Center, write a program note for a production of *Misalliance,* collaborate with a director on a new approach to *Midsummer Night's Dream,* work with a playwright such as Tony Kushner on the germination and creation of a new play, lead an after-show discussion at the Goodman Theatre, fill a wall with images for an acting ensemble, or prepare a new translation of a play by Marivaux. She or he might work at a regional theater in Washington, D.C., in a midwestern high school, or with a dance company in Germany. Even some filmmakers and puppeteers have employed their expertise. Students study for the position in graduate programs at Yale, SUNY–Stony Brook, and many other schools. (More than forty theater departments offer degrees, programs, or coursework in dramaturgy.) Others might step into the field from a background in journalism or Asian studies. At an increasing rate, dramaturgy is becoming part of theater education at all levels from the introductory survey course to the graduate seminar. As a role or function, dramaturgy often traces its origins to eighteenth-century Germany but it has antecedents throughout theater history (East and West); the function itself is probably as old as theater and fundamentally inseparable from it. Some of the best dramaturgs are actors, directors, designers, playwrights, and producers, even though they might not use this word to describe what they do. Dramaturgy might be performed by an individual or by an entire production ensemble. Its close cousin is the literary manager.

Few terms in contemporary theater practice have consistently occasioned more perplexity. Individuals who find themselves listed as dramaturgs on theater programs often grow tired of explaining just what it is they do, whether to someone who has never been in a play or to one of their fellow professionals. Although the days of forever needing to explain what a dramaturg does are coming to an end, many who pick up this book will be just beginning this search for definitions. If you are new to this topic, you might first read Anne Cattaneo's excellent overview at the beginning of section one, "Precedents and New Beginnings." Other material in this first section will also help you get started, along with articles in section two, "Toward a Dramaturgical Sensibility," particularly those by Oscar Brockett and Richard Pettengill. Geoff Proehl's piece at the beginning of section three also serves as a good beginning point: as co-editor of this book, he surveys the topical literature, explores several ways of thinking about the role of the dramaturg in American theater, and offers extensive cross-references to other articles within this volume. His piece serves as a second introduction to the materials gathered here.

The editors believe that injecting the idea of the dramaturg and dramaturgy into American theater and the effort to come to terms with how it might influence the ways in which we make plays is one of the most significant developments in American theater in the last quarter of the twentieth century. It has created a space where academic and professional theater makers (too often opposed to one another) can meet and exchange energies. Within the university itself, it has provided a contact point for practitioners and historians, for directors and theoreticians. The introduction of dramaturgy has opened the door for an influx of materials into the production process: critical, historical, sociological, ideological, imagistic. It has raised stimulating questions about models for the rehearsal process, particularly with regards to the roles of playwright and director, and even about various aspects of the self that we bring to the rehearsal room. It has spurred educational programs and community initiatives. And yet, dramaturgy is far from a panacea for the problems of American theater: some regard it with mistrust, others with animosity and even contempt.

For all of these reasons, we have recognized a need for a book that introduces students, teachers, lay people, and professionals to current conversations and presentations on the role of dramaturgy, to the experiences of university and professional dramaturgs and literary managers in American theater. We want to share with others the vital and far-reaching series of dialogues that we've been reading and hearing.

Dramaturgy in America: A Thumbnail Sketch

In Germany, the dramaturg's role has been institutionalized by a two-hundred year tradition, unlike the profession's brief history in America. Theatrical practice here is quite a different animal, and the profession itself is only as old—or as young—as the regional theater movement, some thirty years. Just as Gotthold Ephraim Lessing took issue with the taste of his contemporary audience, which tended toward neoclassicism and bourgeois sentimental drama, so was there consensus in the sixties in America that the public deserved better fare than it was currently offered. Until then, the commercial theater had been localized in one corner of the Eastern seaboard, New York, which made it relatively inaccessible to the rest of the country. In *Hamburg Dramaturgy,* Lessing championed the development of an indigenous national repertoire and of the plays of the ancients and of Shakespeare, which were virtually unstaged in Germany at that time. In the same way, America witnessed a renewed interest in the canon and a vigorous advocacy of a new American repertoire.

With the advent of a multiplicity of regional venues came the call for hybrid minds that could marry theory and practice. Increased production also brought a ravenous hunger for new work, but theaters had no system in place to nurture a legion of burgeoning playwrights, nor to administer a deluge of new plays. Developing regional theaters looked to traditional Western and Eastern European theatrical practice, and imported the notion of the dramaturg, refashioning after their own interests.

At first, dramaturgs and literary managers were culled from scholars and critics, but as the profession took root, and the dramaturg became a familiar presence in the rehearsal hall, training programs evolved that groomed professionals in the history, theory, criticism *and* practice of theater.

Dramaturgs assisted artistic directors in selecting plays for the season, drawing from their extensive knowledge of international plays, and ability to commission or render lively American translations. Directors, who now often had the overwhelming task of mounting a four-hour Shakespearean tragedy in three and a half weeks of rehearsal, often working with strangers in an unfamiliar town, now had the support of dramaturgs, who provided research, constructive criticism, and collaboration. Institutional dramaturgs often served as the liaison between visiting directors and artistic directors.

Dramaturgs and literary managers also became invaluable in the fostering of new playwrights. While the commercial theater had its eye on the hit play, the dramaturg had his or her eye on the promising playwright. Unlike Broadway's play-doctor, brought in at the eleventh hour to salvage a production with the sole purpose of achieving popular and remunerative success, the dramaturg had to serve the theater's artistic mission. (In fact, in order to incorporate as nonprofit institutions and receive public funds, each theater had to articulate and commit to a specific mission.) Through workshops, play festivals, staged readings—all of which were propagating in abundance—dramaturgs helped provide opportunities for playwrights to develop not just individual plays but individual talents. The feedback and encouragement they offered, formally and informally, reassured writers and the theater-at-large that the playwright was valued and indispensable. As the financial and administrative demands of artistic directors enlarged along with their theaters, the dramaturg and literary manager were expected to have a finger on the pulse of the talent of the times. Toward this end, they read (and read and read) monumental stacks of solicited and unsolicited scripts; supervised other readers; attended local, regional, and national productions and conferences; maintained relationships with agents, playwrights, translators, foreign producers, and other dramaturgs and literary managers.

Part of the mission of the regional theaters was to become vital to their communities, which often showed little habit of theater attendance. Theaters developed audiences through public education. Working with the artistic director, the dramaturg's task was to articulate and communicate the goals of their institution to the community. The dramaturg aided advertising, marketing, publicity, and public relations efforts by supplying background, description, and copy. This also helped educate local reviewers and critics, who often came from journalistic rather than theater backgrounds. The educational mission was also served by compiling, writing, and editing substantive play programs, and creating study guides, which accompanied efforts to reach out to area schools and organizations. As arts education dwindled in the school curriculum, dramaturgs often designed and supervised advocacy programs, bringing students to the theater and theater to the students, and sometimes providing teachers with training and materials. Education initiatives extended beyond the audiences of tomorrow, and invited veteran theatergoers to learn more; dramaturgs organized lectures and post-show discussions to recruit more active audience participation and offer some behind-the-scenes perspective on the making of productions. All of these strategies shared one goal: to increase the esteem in which communities held their theaters.

Scarcely more than a century ago, the role of the director had yet to be imagined. In barely three decades, the profession of dramaturgy has established itself. It is still young enough, however, to provoke controversy. We are still arguing about its definition, its best use, the best training, even the correct spelling of the word. (The preferred spelling in the United States is "dramaturg," from the German, rather than the French "dramaturge," meaning playwright. Canadians favor the French spelling.) This anthology will resolve few of these arguments; it will, like a good dramaturg, ask questions. It will demonstrate in a variety of ways that dramaturgy is both the frontier of theater and a permanent part of its landscape.

Not only are dramaturgs routinely on the theater payroll, but they are frequently on the masthead. It bodes well that around the country dramaturgs are also being appointed to run theaters such as Portland Stage (Portland, Maine), Trinity Rep (Providence, Rhode Island), The Magic Theatre (San Francisco), and Playwrights Horizons (New York City). Dramaturgs have also become an increasingly common feature in other media, such as opera, dance, puppetry, folklore, and anthropology. As already noted, dramaturgs have credits on films, such as *The Age of Innocence*, and television programming, from "American Playhouse" to daytime soap operas. Perhaps the ultimate assurance of the dramaturg's durability is the ribbing they've taken in a recent *New Yorker* cartoon and in one of Robert Parker's Spencer mysteries.

Where the practice and profession of dramaturgy will go is as difficult to predict as the future of the arts in America. The regional theater movement is experiencing its most serious growing pains since its inception. Politicians have brought into question the very notions of public support for the arts and freedom of expression. At this writing, elimination of the National Endowment for the Arts and federal funding for public television are being seriously contemplated. The average age of our audience is increasing, while our potential younger audiences have been decimated by television. While video becomes increasingly accessible and affordable, the cost of theater attendance becomes increasingly prohibitive. We pursue our honorable intentions of producing theater that better reflects our nation's diversity and changing demographics, but we have not yet found ways to reach new audiences. All in all, it's difficult to tell what theater will look like when the dust settles. One thing we can venture to guess, however, is that the inevitability of change will provoke thought—serious, passionate philosophical and practical inquiry into the value of theater in our time. Who better to lead that discussion than dramaturgs? Who better to plan for the future and execute the plan?

Dramaturgy and the Liberal Arts

Though this book is intended primarily for the student of dramaturgy, we strongly believe that it is useful to all students of drama and recommend its use in classes on directing, playwriting, and acting, as well as theater history and criticism. Furthermore, we see in the structure of dramaturgical inquiry a promising application to other subjects such as history, philosophy, cultural studies, and aesthetics.

Although the best means to provide a liberal arts education has always been and should always be a matter for heated debate, the assumption of its value remains an article of faith in higher education. In the main, we continue to agree that the best preparation for all pursuits—personal and professional—is well-rounded education that introduces students to a variety of disciplines and fosters familiarity with a broad canon of ideas and contexts, as well as critical and associative thinking. The foundation we help lay is like an exercise program meant to get the mind in shape for life-long learning. Liberal arts pedagogy teaches curiosity, the delight of learning for its own sake, the ability to recognize and desire to seize the infinite opportunities to pursue knowledge. Our aspiration is to have our students graduate with the realization of how much more there is to know and how capable they are of learning.

Theater education could be a dazzling conduit for all of these lofty aims. By its nature collaborative, it requires interdisciplinary thinking and a consonance of skills that honor the parts and whole equally. Its repertoire introduces a variety of periods, and relates to the study of literature, history, sociology, philosophy, politics, aesthetics, and so on. By its nature, production requires the translation of theory to practice, and is inherently comparative. What better paradigm for liberal arts education?

Too often we merely pay lip service to our desire for this kind of education, and sabotage the opportunity this and other models suggest. We stress particularization, and encourage the development of "specialists" (such as Tesman in *Hedda Gabler*) within our institutions of higher learning, our theater training, our theaters. In teaching subjects discretely, we position ourselves as pieces in the great puzzle rather than view ourselves as great puzzlers.

Consider theater training. Performance is at the core of the curriculum and extracurricular production. We emphasize technical development over liberal arts education. Typically, acting students take three years of acting and voice classes, but only two semesters of theater history or literature or both. Often they slop through their requirements without mustering even a genuine competency in writing or critical analysis. We are not teaching actors, or most theater students for that matter, to be thinking people. Actors' Equity claims a one percent employment rate for their members, and that does not reflect an even greater number of nonunionized actors, yet we remain acting-centric. This serves neither the actor, who becomes a disempowered cog in the wheel (and unemployed, to boot) nor the beacon of liberal arts education. It certainly does nothing for our theater. We could better serve all by training our students to become generalists, conversant with all aspects of our collaborative art and diversely capable. After all, the trend toward specialization is relatively recent in the scheme of theater history. One need only think of Sophocles, Molière, and Shakespeare to remember that it was expected that they combine abilities in acting, writing, directing, dramaturgy, producing, and public relations. Even now, unable to find their niche in the extant theater world, artists such as Spalding Gray, John Leguizamo, Anna Deavere Smith, and Claudia Schear have become viable by adding to their performance skills other skills in playwriting, dramaturgy, directing, and producing. These solo performance artists have redefined the mainstream by becoming "people of the theater." Their routes suggest a new feasible model for empowerment through multidisciplinary training, the centerpiece of which is dramaturgy.

For the best of reasons and the worst—progressive and financial considerations—interdisciplinary learning is the wave of the future. In this, theater can look to its most ancient traditions to find its path to the forefront. And at the zenith of its already interdisciplinary nature is dramaturgy.

Our purpose here is not to prescribe specialization. We hope that exposure to the university of ideas herein will excite students to become inveterate generalists, mentally acquisitive in all subjects. Theater, like humanity, must hold up its mirror not only to its own aspect, but also to the world.

How to Use This Book

This anthology surveys the current practice and theory of dramaturgy in America and begins to investigate the depth and breadth of the field. An anthology is not unlike a good play, full of paradoxes, ambiguity, and contradictions. We sought to preserve such elements, borrowing our editorial principle from dramaturgical philosophy. Our contributors include practitioners from university and professional settings, institutional and free-lance dramaturgs, those who rode in on the first training wave and are now senior in the practice, and those early in their careers. Among these dramaturgs are translators, directors, adapters, scholars, playwrights, literary managers, historians, and artistic directors. The book is a rich resource, containing myriad opposing points of view, all authoritative and "right." That is to say that the field is no less complicated than its spectrum of constituent minds, hearts, and visions.

We have preserved not only the divergence of opinion, but also of format and style. Here you will find philosophical pieces complemented with the more hands-on, nuts-and-bolts kind. Some articles are descriptive, some are intimate, some are highly theoretic. Some are written as essays, some as interviews, some as poems. The cohesion here is of subject. Consequently, the book comes with a warning: If you are hoping to find a single article that will define or explain the dramaturg or dramaturgy, you are out of luck. Knowing one recipe does not mean you can cook. To gain a sense of the scope, variety, and potential of this field, you'll have to read the whole book.

This anthology is not meant to be read straight through, cover to cover, but to be a kind of library through which the reader can wander. The paths are oriented toward new play development, institutional practice, rehearsal methodology, collaboration, research, personal histories, and multiculturalism. At the beginning of each section we suggest some possible groupings of articles that speak to these different areas, but expect that students and teachers will designate their own combinations. The previews preceding each article and section help alert readers to focus, and suggest some interesting comparisons and contrasts. In this way the reader becomes a participant, navigating interactively—to borrow a term from computer language—rather than passively or sequentially. There is no one way to chart a course through this material, just as there is no one way to do dramaturgy. We expect the reader to be compelled by tastes as individual as those of the authors.

The final section contains comprehensive bibliography, as well as Internet resources, a brief glossary, information about the Literary Managers and Dramaturgs of the Americas organization, and a compendium of quotes. These, too, are intended to be provocative rather than prescriptive. Prescription is lethal to original thinking and art. This is the only credo to which all dramaturgs subscribe, and the philosophy that underlies the design of this book.

In sum then, we suggest these six strategies for students who use this collection:

1. Look for continuities among these pieces, for those ideas, images, and metaphors that surface again and again.

2. Look for and enjoy the contradictions between various positions and approaches.

3. Listen for the variety among these voices. Look both for those that resonate with your own and those that seems most distant from yours.

4. Question everything.

5. Let these authors and their endnotes lead you to other books, writers, topics, and plays.

6. Read these selections not in isolation but as elements of a comprehensive and rigorous education in dramaturgy (in the broadest sense of the word) that will include extensive study in theater history (performance and playscript), dramatic theory and criticism, and the whole range of the liberal arts completed by intensive experience in theatermaking itself—in acting, directing, design, and technical theater.

Let this book be one of your beginning points.

SUSAN JONAS AND GEOFF PROEHL

Acknowledgments and Thanks

To Anne Cattaneo (dramaturg, Lincoln Center Theatre) for outstanding leadership that has greatly contributed to the work of dramaturgs and literary managers both in professional and university theater. Without the support of Anne Cattaneo, Literary Managers and Dramaturgs of the Americas (LMDA)—its officers and its members—this anthology would not exist today.

To Lisa Fabian, Gretchen Haley, Donna Maria Mattia, Rachel Stires, and Chris Wight for help in preparing this manuscript.

To Matt Ball, Terri House, Barbara J. C. Rosenberg, and Laura Miley of Harcourt Brace College Publishers for their patience and expertise over the course of this project. And to Karen Keady for her copyediting.

To Melanie Deas, Jean Detre, Mona Heinze-Barreca, James Leverett, Stanley Levin, and the theatre history/dramaturgy students of the University of Puget Sound for editorial advice at different stages in this manuscript's preparation. Thanks also to Leon Katz and Richard Gilman for years of guidance. The strengths of this manuscript owe much to their patient efforts.

To the Association for Theatre in Higher Education, East Central Theatre Conference, Southeastern Theatre Conference, and again Literary Managers and Dramaturgs of the Americas, for providing places at which dramaturgs, literary managers, and teachers can gather to exchange ideas and share their work.

To Princeton Univeristy, Stanford University, the University of Puget Sound, Villanova University, and the Yale School of Drama. These schools—their teachers, students, and administrators—have nurtured this work financially, intellectually, and emotionally.

From Geoff Proehl: To Joshua Proehl, Kristen Proehl, and Morlie Proehl, and Mercedes and Darrold Proehl for your patience, love, and encouragement.

From Susan Jonas for support in various ways: To Isabella Blake, Paul Bolduc, Norma Bowles, Wayne Brusseau, David Copelin, Shavonne Dowd, Keller Easterling, Rufus T. Firefly III, Donald Hull, Michelle Kahane, Betty Kronsky, Gladys Levy, Eric Lister, Jennifer McCray, Alan McVay, Brighde Mullins, and Leah Pitell-Jacobs. And above all to Barbara Levin.

Contents

Section 1

PRECEDENTS AND NEW BEGINNINGS

"Precedents and New Beginnings" introduces the role of the dramaturg in American theater and explores its antecedents. Anne Cattaneo, one of America's most distinguished dramaturgs, begins this volume by noting American and European precursors to today's dramaturgs and then moves on to a detailed discussion of the role of the dramaturg in American theater. She examines work with classical plays, creating texts from existing materials, research, production books, in-house criticism, new play development, and commissioning. For her, however, the primary job of a theater's production dramaturg is in long-range research and development. Joel Schechter takes the reader even more deeply into the history of dramaturgy as a profession from Gotthold Ephraim Lessing in eighteenth-century Germany to Bertolt Brecht and Heiner Müller in the twentieth century. He argues for a vision of the dramaturg as a person actively involved in the cultural and political affairs of the day.

Martin Esslin, who has had extensive experience in both European and American theater, has spent much of his career mediating between various cultures and languages. Here he compares the function of the dramaturg in contemporary Europe, particularly in German-speaking countries, with its

American counterpart. Writings on dramaturgy often emphasize the need to learn rehearsal decorum, but for Esslin, the ideal dramaturg would be "a kind of court jester, licensed to be as rude as possible."

While at Yale, Robert Brustein established the first graduate program to educate dramaturgs as such in the United States. Jonathan Marks, who worked closely with Brustein, notes the latter's considerable leadership in this field, leadership shared with individuals such as Arthur Ballet of the University of Minnesota, Felicia Londre of the University of Missouri, and many others from George Pierce Baker to the present who may not have adopted the term but certainly performed or taught the function: professors, producers, agents, play-doctors, and critics.[1] Brustein's piece itself recounts a transition at Yale that transformed critics from an adversarial position outside the rehearsal process to a collaborative role within it.

Jonathan Kalb's short note concludes this section. He uses dramaturgy and the future as a basis for comment on the current state of cultural affairs.

Other works in this volume also explore the historical lineage of this field and might well be read alongside these pieces. For example, Mark Bly in section two ("Toward a Dramaturgical Sensibility") offers insight into the ongoing history of the Yale program, almost thirty years after events described by Marks and Brustein. Art Borreca, also in section two, examines in detail the history of two major theater programs as paradigms for fundamental approaches to dramaturgy. Allen Kuharski looks at the role of the dramaturg in Joseph Chaikin's work; Norman Frisch and Marianne Weems do the same for the Wooster Group. Steven Weeks (section five: "Developing New Works") gives historical perspective to notions of what constitutes craft in playwriting and discusses the implications of those notions for contemporary dramaturgy. Finally, the articles in this volume are historical documents in and of themselves: they provide snapshots of dramaturgy and theater making in late twentieth-century American theater. The goal of these snapshots is, of course, not to freeze the discipline but to provide an image to which it can react and from which it can continue to grow.

Dramaturgy: An Overview

by Anne Cattaneo

ANNE CATTANEO is the dramaturg of Lincoln Center Theater in New York and a three-term past president of Literary Managers and Directors of America (LMDA). As a dramaturg, she has worked widely on classical plays with directors such as James Lapine, Robert Wilson, Adrian Hall, Robert Falls, Mark Lamos, and JoAnne Akalaitis. As the director of the Playworks Program at the Phoenix Theater in New York during the late 1970s, she commissioned and produced plays by Wendy Wasserstein *(Isn't It Romantic)*, Mustapha Matura *(Meetings)*, and Christopher Durang *(Beyond Therapy)*. For the Acting Company she created the Chekhov short story project *Orchards,* which presented seven stories adapted for the stage by Maria Irene Fornes, Spalding Gray, John Guare, David Mamet, Wendy Wasserstein, Michael Weller, and Samm-Art Williams.

Although G.E. Lessing is acknowledged as the father of the profession of dramaturgy, the field only established itself in the twentieth century—first in the large German institutional theaters and then in England, France, and America. The functions of the dramaturg existed well before the profession itself had a name. Directing for the stage has a similar history. The fifth-century BC Greek *choregus* functioned as an early kind of stage director, as did the medieval town clerks who organized the passion play cycles. The profession of stage director is relatively new—a creation in many ways of the nineteenth century. In Shakespeare's time, plays were staged by the acting company members without a "specialist" to guide them.

During the eighteenth and nineteenth centuries, English actor/managers, from John Philip Kemble to Harley Granville-Barker, functioned as dramaturgs. They reinvented the classical repertory and interpreted and adapted plays (often in ways amusing to the modern reader) to reflect the taste of the times: plays in the English repertory were traditionally bowdlerized by inserting musical interludes, inventing happy endings, and adding scenes for the audiences' favorite subplot characters. Many great plays of the canon mutated (or were mutilated) to conform to the whims of popular actors as well as the needs of the box office. For example, Launce returns in the last act of *Two Gentlemen of Verona,* and Cordelia doesn't die at the end of *King Lear.* Most of these eighteenth and nineteenth century alterations reflect a sensibility that is foreign to us, but the stagecraft that informed these changes is remarkable. In the tradition of Shakespeare, these actor/managers were men of the theater with a profound understanding of acting, writing, and how plays work in front of audiences. Often they came from long lineages of actors, and knew a wealth of anecdotal information about Shakespeare and his plays. Their work as editors and interpreters of these classic texts offers a fascinating glimpse of dramaturgy during this time.

At the beginning of our own century, American commercial theater producers such as David Belasco and organizations such as the Theatre Guild and Hedgerow Theatre also pioneered innovative dramaturgical ideas such as commissioning new plays and presenting classical revivals reinvented for American audiences. Like Lessing one hundred fifty years before, influential American men of letters such as Francis Ferguson, the great theoretician and critic, participated in a dialogue about what might constitute their country's ideal repertory. In his 1928 "Letter to the Administration of the American Laboratory Theatre," Ferguson, then the playreader of that theater, urged Richard Boleslavsky, Maria Ouspenskaya, and their colleagues working in the shadow of the Moscow Art Theatre, to abandon the romantic tradition of art for art's sake and Gordon Craig's theater of pure form and to acknowledge that "the dramatist, as the mouthpiece of the best thought and taste of the time, should rule the theatre."

Both Ferguson and Arthur Ballet, the two Americans who presage the advent of the dramaturgy profession in America, were early advocates of American playwriting. During the 1960s, from his base in the Office of Advanced Drama Research (OADR) at the University of Minnesota, Arthur Ballet tirelessly read and recommended new American plays to his theater colleagues who were working around the country establishing the regional theater movement. Ballet's work—a sort of national dramaturgy office—is often credited as the spark that began the major playwrights' movement of the 1970s.

In England during the sixties, the work of Jan Kott and Kenneth Tynan began to define the parameters of the newly emerging dramaturgy profession. In his influential book *Shakespeare Our Contemporary,* Polish scholar Jan Kott reinvented Shakespeare in the view of Beckett and the postwar existential world. Kott's interpretation of *A Midsummer Night's Dream* and *King Lear* provided the springboard for Peter Brook's legendary productions of these plays, perhaps the greatest Shakespearean productions of our era.

After many years as a leading English theater critic, Kenneth Tynan served as dramaturg of the National Theatre during the administration of Sir Lawrence Olivier, often guiding the theater's artistic policy into controversial waters. His important work there has been widely documented in his own memoirs and those of his wife and his artistic collaborators, such as Olivier and Peter Hall. Tynan, who held the title of literary manager after the National board refused his request to work under the title of dramaturge, brought plays and projects into the repertory and extended his influence to the press and marketing offices. How the theater presented its repertory to the public and the press—in press releases, programs, and advertising—became as central to Tynan's concerns as the play selection itself.

The German-speaking theater—with its well-established resident theater movement dating from the nineteenth century and before—has the richest tradition of dramaturgy. By the turn of the century, many companies had need of artistic administrators willing to provide translations, new plays, and ideas for the repertory. Groundbreaking directors such as Erwin Piscator employed brilliant dramaturgs. Playwright Bertolt Brecht worked as a dramaturg throughout his life, and his dramaturgy office at the Berliner Ensemble was a model of creative collaboration. Brecht gathered his dramaturgs, directors, and writers in the office to brainstorm about programming and season planning. Their task was to interpret and respond to the events of the day through the choice of repertory. The office was asked to commission, translate, and finally adapt plays to exemplify and realize the Berliner Ensemble's Marxist political mission. This dramaturgy office kept detailed logs and rehearsal notes, which are now published and provide an important window into the work of Brecht, the Berliner Ensemble, and the profession itself. Today, hundreds of dramaturgs work in the German-speaking theater. The resident theaters of every major German city have two- to four-person dramaturgy staffs that organize and plan the repertory for these important state-subsidized institutions. During the 1970s, Botho Strauss and Dieter Stürm, two dramaturgs from Peter Stein's Schaubühne in Berlin were widely credited with creating a model of what a creative dramaturgy office should be. Their work in interpreting and conceiving productions with Stein and other directors such as Klaus Michael Grueber, helped to make the Schaubühne Company one of the most renowned theaters in Europe during this time.

One reason that dramaturgy has become so well established in Europe, especially in Germany, is that resident theaters have existed there for centuries. In the United States, we date our large theater institutions and the regional theater movement from the pioneering Ford Foundation grants, starting in 1959, and the initial authorization of the National Endowment for the Arts in 1965. The not-for-profit theater movement is itself scarcely thirty-five years old.

The late sixties were devoted to building the theaters and exploring the classical repertory. By the early seventies, an American playwriting movement began. The O'Neill Theater Center had been founded by this time, creating an atmosphere where playwrights could develop new work. Arthur Ballet's OADR sent new plays around the country. By the mid-seventies, the administrative staffs of newly established theaters such as the Guthrie (Minneapolis), Goodman Theatre (Chicago), American Conservatory Theater (San Francisco), Mark Taper Forum (Los Angeles), Arena Stage (Washington, D.C.), Seattle Rep, Lincoln Center, and The Alley Theatre (Houston) began to expand. As writers such as Sam Shepard, David Mamet, Maria Irene Fornes, David Rabe, John Guare, Terrence McNally, and Lanford Wilson heralded a new age of American playwriting, dramaturgs were soon added to the staffs of these theaters to read the tide of incoming material and organize the developmental arms of these growing institutions. Today, the job of production dramaturgy is performed by many people holding a variety of official titles : dramaturg, literary manager, literary adviser, artistic associate, playwright-in-residence, director, and often artistic director. Production dramaturgy is a set of tasks, and these tasks can be carried out by any member of the theater's artistic team who is qualified and interested in taking responsibility for them.

What are the tasks of a production dramaturg? In his book about city and community planning, *The Experience of Place* (Vintage Paperback, 1990), *New Yorker* author Tony Hiss devotes several chapters to the history, current situation, and future plans for Times Square. He expresses a wish for another voice to be added to the chorus of business developers, city planners, conservationists, and other parties interested in the discussion: someone who will be a "vigilant guardian of the experience of a public area," "a watchdog," "the conscience keeping watch over a place." He mentions the dramaturg's role in the theater as one who "looks out for the play itself." A dramaturg for Hiss, in architecture or theater, is "someone who keeps the whole in mind."

The primary job of a theater's production dramaturg is to focus his or her energies and those of the artistic director on long-range research and development and on artistic planning. The dramaturg must ask important questions— of both the theater and his or her artistic collaborators. These questions will determine what lines the theater plans along and what kind of plays the theater will eventually develop and produce. These important questions begin with the most fundamental ones: Who are we as artists? What are our theatrical or extratheatrical models and our ideals? What kind of work do we respond to? Who is our work for? What is our theater's community in terms both of artists and audience? How do we identify and involve our community of artists and audience? As these questions are discussed and addressed, an artistic philosophy will be shaped and discerned. In the end, artistic policy is of course defined by the repertory itself. It may or may not be stated in programs or grant applications, but it is always evident on the stage.

The production dramaturg's role is to develop repertory material that will express the theater's artistic purpose. The dramaturg will need to find, develop, and possibly even create plays by contacting writers, commissioning plays, researching lost or little-known plays in libraries or archives, and occasionally compiling texts as an editor would from other existing literary or nonliterary sources. The aim of this work is to present the artistic director with a slate of plays for inclusion in the season that embody the theater's artistic purpose. The creation of this slate of plays requires experience in two areas of the repertory: the first includes classical plays and revivals, and the second area comprises work on new plays.

CLASSICAL PLAYS AND REVIVALS

In working with classical plays and revivals, the job of the production dramaturg is to recommend the play, prepare and edit the text, and collaborate with the director on how the piece is interpreted. It is therefore critical that a dramaturg know the classics inside and out. But a knowledge of the plays as literature is not sufficient. A knowledge of theater history is equally important. The production dramaturg must also consider how the plays were produced and published in their own time, how the theater functioned, and who acted in the play. How did the play interact with its audience? What role did this theater play in the community? How does the play's structure work? Where does this play structure come from? These matters are central to any investigation of how to make a classical play work today.

To begin to answer these questions, a good production dramaturg needs to have access to original source material: letters, illustrations, documentation, historical references. Good dramaturgs have highly developed research skills and an often secret network of reference librarians to help them in their quests. Many collect reference books and photocopy information from literary and visual sources.

To stage a classical play for an audience today, the dramaturg must get together with a director to examine and rethink the play. A dramaturg's first contribution to this discussion is to know how the play functioned in its own time. What type of stage was the play written for? What kind of acting? Who were its audiences? More importantly, what was the play's function? To entertain? Was there another aim (as there was an additional civic purpose in, say, Greek or medieval drama)? In early discussions with the director—well before the play is designed or cast—a concept or a way "into" the play should emerge that embraces and adjusts the heart of the play for a twentieth-century production. How can a modern production honor and preserve the way the play worked in its own time and yet allow it to speak to a society that is vastly different? Answering these questions may result in a production that remains in period setting with little textual alteration. Or it may result in moving the play into altogether new territory. Peter Brook's reading of Jan Kott's *Shakespeare Our Contemporary* led him to discover a circus world for *A Midsummer Night's Dream,* and a Beckett landscape for *King Lear.* Lee Breuer's more recent *Gospel at Colonus* at The Brooklyn Academy of Music reinvented Sophocles' *Oedipus at Colonus* as a modern-day gospel church service. Breuer found a modern equivalent for Greek drama's choral elements, sense of community, and its audiences' knowledge of the play's outcome.

The dramaturg then prepares the text for the production, choosing the text of the play selected, editing or translating it, or commissioning or supervising a translation. A strong speaking knowledge (or at least reading knowledge) of one or two other languages is important to the job. With Shakespeare, an investigation into the variants of the play, its various folio and quarto editions, will result in a script that supports the interpretation of each specific production. A dramaturg should discuss with the director the modernization of individual words, obscure references, and unclear or obscure scansion, along with any other textual irregularities. On the first day of rehearsal, the actors should be presented with a finished text, incorporating cuts, emendations, and changes.

The reasons behind the choice of a classical play may shape its adaptation, or interpretation. At the Berliner Ensemble, as Brecht's work with Shakespeare was motivated by strong political goals, his adaptations were created in response to the current events of 1950s East German politics. Brecht's version of *Coriolanus,* for example, focuses on class struggle with the crowd of citizens as protagonist. The play was cut and lines were reassigned to underscore this interpretation. Other plays created for intensely specific theater environments—or perhaps plays that were never realized in their own time—may need substantial cutting, reordering or reworking to make them "producable" in the theater today. Certain texts of Musset, Kleist, or Maeterlinck for instance, which call for extreme physical production elements might require rethinking.

ASSEMBLING AND CREATING A TEXT FROM EXISTING MATERIAL

A director's vision might dictate the creation of a new text comprised of selections from preexisting material. At the Guthrie Theater, director Garland Wright's desire to stage the complete story of Clytemnestra led the dramaturgy office to create a text comprised of scenes from Aeschylus, Sophocles, and Euripides for presentation together in one evening. In the 1993 New York Lincoln Center Theater revival of Jane Bowles' *In the Summer House,* directed by JoAnne Akalaitis, we on the artistic team read intensively about Bowles in biographies and letters, and spoke with many of her colleagues from the 1950s. We came to believe that the only published text of her play represented a version that she, as a novice to Broadway, had rewritten unwisely under the pressure of opening the play in such a high-powered commercial venue. As a result, LCT located all the early drafts of the play from Bowles' friends, biographers, and library archives around the country. We began to see how the play had developed during several years in the early 1950s in the course of workshops and out-of-town productions and try-outs. With the permission and encouragement of the executor of her estate, her husband Paul Bowles, LCT restored several passages that had been removed from the Broadway version and did some minor rearranging of sections of scenes. In doing this, we believed we were returning to a "truer" version of *In the Summer House,* and one that Bowles herself would have wanted to see. LCT corresponded with Paul Bowles in Tangiers, with Oliver Smith, the play's original producer and designer, as well as with Bowles' scholars and biographers to find confirmation that our changes would not damage the play.

As the dramaturg and director sit down some months prior to the beginning of rehearsals and go over the text line by line (having the design team present at this stage makes for an ideal collaboration), the production dramaturg's job is to convey a detailed knowledge of the text and its variants; an understanding of the way the play was originally performed; biographical information about the writer; a past production history of the play throughout history; and an overview of literary and dramatic criticism of the text. Play reviews, however, often offer little value, because the insights and level of writing are so meager. After Shaw, there's little to be learned from them.

RESEARCH

All kinds of historical research are needed once rehearsals begin. Information on professions (What is a "joiner," "provost," or "Amazon?") can be provided to the actors playing these roles. The setting, such as the Elizabethan prison in *Measure for Measure,* can provide the occasion to see how prison incarceration differs today. How criminals lived in prison, brought in their own possessions, received visitors, who their fellow prisoners were—all may inform the design, staging, and acting. Information on madness and its treatments during Shakespeare's time may shed light on Malvolio's fate in *Twelfth Night.* Brecht's *Galileo* contains references to scientific discoveries and theorems and to nuances of social class distinctions of the period—important details because they clarify the plot and illuminate Brecht's own interest in the class system as well. The production dramaturg's job is to have this information at hand for the director and cast.

Illustrations and detailed historical facts are especially useful. In 1982, I worked with director James Lapine on a New York Shakespeare Festival production of *A Midsummer Night's Dream* in Central Park. In early discussions about the play I mentioned that the professions of the Elizabethan playwrights' families were closer in class to the play's mechanicals, than to its highborn lovers. Shakespeare's father was a glover, Webster's a coachmaker, Ben Jonson worked as a bricklayer. Lapine came to see the mechanicals not as buffoons, but as regular citizens and eventually the heart of our production. Titania's seduction of Bottom was not ridiculous but became an almost plausible dream of emancipation, and the production allowed Theseus at the end to recognize Bottom for a moment as an equal. Because Lapine's interpretation centered on a Jungian interpretation of the play and its symbols, the production team visited New York's Jung Library to look at imagery of fairies, oak trees, and asse's heads. We later brought the actors there to look at additional material and discuss transformation myths. While researching past productions of *Midsummer,* I discovered an amusing addition of Titania-Oberon dialogue from *Two Noble Kinsmen* that Granville-Barker had used in a late nineteenth-century London production. We needed more text toward the conclusion of our production to add time before the epilogue, and so we followed his lead and incorporated it.

PRODUCTION BOOKS

Each play has its own special world that embraces not only its historical period and its literary affiliations but also a world of ideas. Some production dramaturgs share their journey of discovery about the play with the audience through playbills or programs that incorporate material that has inspired the director and cast during the rehearsal process. This shares the director's approach to the play and highlights ideas important to this specific production. German theaters actually publish a book for major productions that documents the text and how the artistic team arrived at their interpretation. The original foreign-language text might appear across the page from the translation, or the original German across from the edited text. Essays, historical research, and literary criticism might be included along with art or photography that inspired the design. During the 1970s, for Botho Strauss's *Big and Little,* which chronicled the spiritual wasting away of a contemporary woman, the Phoenix Theatre in New York published a slim production book that included reproductions of Giacometti sculpture. The sculpture was not used in the production or referred to in the play, but reflected to the author and to us a similar state of mind.

IN-HOUSE CRITIC: WATCHING OUT FOR THE PLAY IN REHEARSALS

After information has been shared with the cast during the early weeks of rehearsal, a production dramaturg's job changes. As the director needs to work more intensely and closely getting the play on its feet, the dramaturg often begins to establish some physical distance from the rehearsal process. The dramaturg needs to view run-throughs of scenes, acts, and finally the entire play, with a more objective eye to what is and isn't "working." Knowing firsthand what the director was aiming for, the dramaturg can offer an informed second opinion and suggest solutions to specific problems. At the Phoenix, during the 1970s, in late rehearsals for the world premiere of Wendy Wasserstein's *Isn't It Romantic,* the play's balance began to shift from the two women protagonists to the supporting character of the handsome doctor, played in this production by Peter Riegert. Wasserstein was happy to write Riegert new material when he thought he needed to better clarify his journey in the play, but while interesting, this sidetracked the main plot and had to be cut.

During the crucial time of dress rehearsals and early previews, the production dramaturg looks at how the whole is coming together, seeing where and how the play's interpretation can be strengthened. Functioning as what has often been called an "in-house critic," a dramaturg can anticipate audience reponse and alert the director to possible problems well before opening night.

WORKING ON NEW PLAYS

In a new play, a production dramaturg's work most closely resembles the job of an acquisitions' editor in publishing. In fact, new-play dramaturgs can learn much from book editors. Courses in editing, practical experience in publishing jobs, or at least a familiarity with books about editors will aid an aspiring dramaturg seeking to learn how to work with living writers. As Scott Berg's biography of Maxwell Perkins details, the Scribner's editor's work with Thomas Wolfe, Hemingway, and Fitzgerald is a model of how to discover, sustain, and edit major writers.[2] His encouragement and shaping hands helped transform Wolfe's *Time and the River* from shopping bags filled with loose pages into a cohesive novel. Following Perkins' model, it is most productive when an editor or dramaturg can work regularly with a writer, who ideally becomes over time a trusted and intimate friend.

The way to these creative collaborations is paved by the sound and responsible organization of the dramaturg's office. At the most basic level, a theater's literary or dramaturgy office is the mail room for all scripts that come into the theater. These manuscripts need to be handled with the utmost care. Each one is the product of months and years of hard work and deserves to be treated with respect. Scripts should be "logged in" using a simple and efficient system. Play synopses should be promptly read and responded to. The manuscripts should be read, a written report circulated to the artistic director, and the plays then accepted for workshop, reading or production, or returned. Theaters should make an effort to return or respond to all scripts within eight weeks of receipt. Caution is also needed in the use of readers. It may seem a simple task to weed out substandard work, but in fact it is far from easy. All material that truly breaks new ground will not "look like a play" when it first appears. Play reading is best done only in-house by staff members who are most familiar with the theater's artistic mission.

Beyond the mechanics of administering a literary office, the challenge and reward for a dramaturg (as it is for any editor) is getting to know and supporting writers one admires. Here dramaturgs are only as good as the writers they discover and bring into the theater. A good eye and an open mind are critical. The ability to recognize work that stretches the definition of theater can help establish a whole new generation of writers. If a new play interests a dramaturg, the dramaturg should contact the writer, get to know the writer's other work, and initiate a relationship between the writer and the theater. The dramaturg can offer feedback and encouragement or provide leads and letters of recommendation for grants or residencies. Dramaturgs not only urge their own theaters to produce plays or commission new material from the writer, but also call colleagues at other theaters to introduce them to the author's work. Brecht's work in this area as a dramaturg is inspirational: he championed unknown contemporary German playwrights such as Marie Luise Fleisser and fought to get their plays produced and published.

COMMISSIONING AND CREATING MATERIAL

In most theaters, the dramaturg oversees any commissioning programs and is instrumental in suggesting candidates to the artistic director. During the early 1980s, during my tenure as literary manager at New York's Phoenix Theater, I ran a commissioning and play development program that produced the new works of several gifted then-emerging Off-Broadway playwrights. Christopher Durang's *Beyond Therapy,* Wendy Wasserstein's *Isn't It Romantic,* and William Hamilton's *Save Grand Central* began in this program. After a developmental process of a year or two, which consisted of regular meetings with the writers, the Phoenix did readings of the plays-in-progress, hired directors, and eventually produced them.

Similarly, in the mid-eighties, at the Acting Company, I conceived a new play–classical play commissioning hybrid called *Orchards.* The theater approached seven contemporary playwrights (Maria Irene Fornes, Spalding Gray, John Guare, David Mamet, Wendy Wasserstein, Michael Weller, and Samm-Art Williams) with seven short stories by Chekhov that I had selected. The authors' adaptations, which were developed through readings with Acting Company members, were produced and toured the country.

Although a production dramaturg will want to get to know the work of the country's leading playwrights, it is just as important to read writers who are still unknown. All theaters and artists throughout history have established themselves by building peer-level relationships with a new generation of writers. Early in a dramaturg's career is a good time to start finding and producing the work of playwrights who will change the theater in years to come. A dramaturg's new play work should revolve around strong and well-established relationships with playwrights. The blind-date system, where writer meets dramaturg at the first rehearsal, rarely works. If the dramaturg is instrumental in bringing the writer to his or her theater's attention, and if the dramaturg works on many plays with one writer, a peer relationship will develop naturally.

Once a script is identified and contact is established with the writer, the dramaturg's job is to identify with the writer what the script needs as the next phase of its development. In cases where the script is finished and the play might be ready to go into production, it is the dramaturg's job to suggest the play as a candidate for the theater's season, and to begin discussions with the writer and the artistic director about who will direct the play.

In new play rehearsals, the production dramaturg's job is to keep a protective eye on the script. Working with both writer and director, the dramaturg sees that the demands of production (especially a premiere production) do not push the author to alter the script in harmful ways. Strong or weak performances in key roles, or inappropriate or awkward design elements might tempt an author to rewrite to accommodate them. Such rewrites should be watched carefully. The director, once attached to the play, must know everything the dramaturg intends to communicate to the writer. Directors will often delegate to dramaturgs details to be discussed with the writer, or dramaturgs will suggest ideas of their own, but under no circumstances should the author receive different or mixed messages from the director and dramaturg.

The editorial side of new-play production dramaturgy is potentially problematic: there is always a real danger of harming the play. Many playwrights have had bad experiences with dramaturgs—as they have with directors and producers—but dramaturgs (as the playwright's advocate) must be especially cautious that they are serving and not hurting the play. As in the publishing world, long-standing relationships result in the most fruitful and least coercive collaborations. A dramaturg's job is not to "fix" the play, or offer specific solutions to problems in the text. This is the job of the playwright. Instead, a dramaturg can offer the writer a highly personal but well-informed reading of the play: "To me, this plot point is unclear," "I lose this character during this section of the play," or perhaps "For me, the play changes stylistically between acts one and two." Written notes that an author can take away are often helpful, because this allows more time for the dramaturg to formulate thoughts, and the writer to consider the response. It's important to be sensitive to what the writer is trying to do and what the writer is capable of doing. A dramaturg has no business pushing the play in any direction. The goal is to realize the author's objectives—not the dramaturg's.

Some dramaturgs find it helpful to communicate to the author a short list of what appeals to them in the play, (interesting subject matter, energy in the writing, a compelling character, original syntax or wit, playable dialogue, and such) followed by a short list of what they find confusing. Listing the play's strong points first, followed by the play's weaknesses phrased as a list of questions that the author should not answer, but which merely indicate places the dramaturg feels bear investigation, focuses the meeting in a positive way. Experienced writers who have mastered their craft may require far less feedback than writers who are entering their first rehearsal period.

Today, more than three hundred dramaturgs work in American theaters, and many more in university settings. A national service organization, Literary Managers and Dramaturgs of the Americas (LMDA), serves the field. That some dramaturgs have moved into positions such as artistic director and associate artistic director may be seen as a sign of the profession's success, but it also points to some of the challenges and difficulties of keeping a creative dramaturgy office open. Moving into associate or artistic director positions removes a dramaturg from a gadfly position into a job with countless pressing practical responsibilities. Thus is gained the ability to present work the artistic director wants, but lost may be a vision of an institution with a pioneering research and development arm—an institution with the ability to spend time looking at the community and the world we live in—anticipating which artists should be engaged to speak to our coming concerns.

When the job of production dramaturg bogs down in a daily routine of script reading, script sorting, program editing, research, and rehearsals, the more important roles of thinker and advocate can get lost. But Kenneth Tynan, Jan Kott, and Arthur Ballet are not remembered primarily as script readers. As dramaturgs, they looked at the world and at the theater and sought to expand the way in which we now see plays. The real job of all good dramaturgs is to extend and explore territory that the theater has not yet made its own. This may mean finding, interpreting, or translating plays, or encouraging company actors to undertake different kinds of roles, or suggesting a classical play to a fine new-play director, or urging an artistic director to explore a new part of the repertory or a new kind of writing.

In all periods of history—and ours today is no exception—theaters are inclined to stay with a conservative, familiar repertory. Lessing's *Hamburg Dramaturgy* always has a contemporary ring. A glance in the back of the magazine *American Theatre* shows the uniformity of much of the programming of American theater—in both new plays and the classics. As in many areas of American life, theater moves away from an investment in research and development, and toward material that already has a track record with consumers and audiences. As a theater staff member, the dramaturg must of course understand the need to maintain the financial viability of the institution. But with an eye to the history books, it's clear that only pioneering change will be remembered. These are the tensions that inform the job.

Even in new play development, change is swift. During the first heady years of the new play movement of the 1970s, many structures for developing plays were created, including protected venues where plays could be read aloud or rehearsed and presented in a one- to two-week rehearsed workshop settings for invited audiences. Play development is by now an established part of most institutional theaters, as well as most professional training programs. But as the theater continues to evolve, institutions continue to grow, and a new generation of writers seeks to gain a foothold, the method of developing plays pioneered in the seventies is becoming out-of-date. What began at the O'Neill Theater Center, or at Circle Repertory Company with Lanford Wilson, or at the Magic Theatre with Sam Shepard, was a hardworking but informal atmosphere in which playwrights and their colleagues could work together as peers. Today most emerging writers are a generation younger than the artistic staffs at the theaters in which they seek to work, and many are given reading after reading without ever having the experience of rehearsing for production. This situation creates many unfortunate consequences. Playwrights feel pressured to rewrite in specific ways to gain a production. They have little chance to work with actors creating characters over a regular four- to five-week rehearsal period. They may subtly conform to an existing definition of what theater is, instead of with their peers creating something new—of their own definition. From decade to decade, artists and theaters may need to fundamentally revise and rethink their ways of working.

The production dramaturg is probably the most intellectual or academic position in the theater, and the best dramaturgs are usually the most involved in the world. Knowing the city in which you live, reading widely in other fields, cultivating colleagues and contacts in other neighborhoods and other walks of life—can help the dramaturg keep the theater in touch with real life.

Theater in every age has had to reinvent itself. As we enter the twenty-first century, we find ourselves ensconced for the first time in new American theater institutions. It will be the dramaturg's challenge to keep the artists center stage in the mainstream of American culture.

In the Beginning There Was Lessing . . . Then Brecht, Müller, and Other Dramaturgs

by Joel Schechter

JOEL SCHECHTER, Professor and Chair of Theatre Arts at San Francisco State University, is the author of several books on satire, including *Satiric Impersonations: From Aristophanes to the Guerrilla Girls* and *Durov's Pig.* He previously served as a dramaturg at the Yale Rep and the American Place Theatre in New York, and as editor of *Theater* magazine at Yale's School of Drama.

The dramaturg's profession began in eighteenth-century Germany, and reached American shores considerably later. Many American theaters now call their literary associates and critics-in-residence "dramaturgs," although the German title may require some explanation for visitors who read the staff list, and even for some of the staff itself.

Several prominent German playwrights advanced the profession and made the term dramaturg better known to their country's artists when they served as dramaturgs at prestigious theaters. The history of dramaturgy, beginning with Gotthold Ephraim Lessing (1729–1781) in the eighteenth century and continuing with Bertolt Brecht and Heiner Müller in the twentieth century, reveals quarrels and innovative collaborations that continue to surface—like the term "dramaturg" itself—with variations, in American settings as well as German ones.

LESSING'S *HAMBURG DRAMATURGY*

Gotthold Ephraim Lessing was so financially impoverished by January 1767, that he agreed to serve as a resident critic at the Hamburg National Theatre. He would have preferred to be a librarian at the Royal Library in Berlin, but Frederick the Great denied him that opportunity in 1766 by hiring a Frenchman instead. Lessing had to settle for a position in Hamburg. In this casual, almost accidental manner, the dramaturgical profession began.

While at the Hamburg National Theatre, Lessing wrote *Hamburg Dramaturgy,* a collection of essays on theater which popularized dramaturgy as a word and a practice. Today, many of Lessing's successors—resident theater critics throughout the world—are called "dramaturgs." Lessing, like some modern dramaturgs, was a playwright who advised his theater's management on play selection, and offered his theater continuous, sometimes adverse criticism of its productions. Since Lessing's day, dramaturgs have also been known to direct plays, translate foreign drama, commission works, prepare essays for inclusion in theater programs, assist stage directors and actors in background research, and usher. Many dramaturgs are also play readers for their theaters, and go through manuscripts in search of material for future seasons. One notable exception in this last area is the dramaturg in Brecht's *Messingkauf Dialogues;* he stays out of his office because "it would mean sitting under the reproachful eyes of all those scripts I ought to have read."[3] Difficulties that present-day American dramaturgs encounter at regional theaters have antecedents in Lessing's career. The German playwright and critic found his dramaturgical advice ignored when art had been, in his words, "degraded to the level of a trade."[4] As Lessing's career suggests, salable theater and dramaturgs are often at odds. This and other problems Lessing encountered two centuries ago in his role as first dramaturg still trouble the profession. The new profession gave rise to controversies that can now be "considered proverbial for the fate of the man of letters who rashly interferes in the business of the theater," as Edwin Zeydel notes in his biography of Germany's second major dramaturg, Ludwig Tieck.[5]

Lessing's reputation as a man of letters in the theater rests on several well-received plays and a few volumes of criticism. *Hamburg Dramaturgy,* written between April 1767 and April 1769, has been carefully analyzed by Lessing scholars and historians. Their analyses usually focus on the German critic's preferences for Aristotelian theory and for Shakespearean plays over French neoclassic theory and drama. The book's relevance to the origins of the dramaturgical profession deserves closer attention. While the *Dramaturgy* offers no detailed reports or complaints about Lessing's professional role at Hamburg, it includes numerous clues about his dramaturgical influence, or lack of it. From the book, an intriguing if incomplete biography of the theater's first dramaturg can be reconstructed.

Lessing's dramaturgical career began when he was asked by a consortium of twelve Hamburg businessmen and their theater's managing director, J.F. Löwen, to serve as theater poet. The consortium of financial backers expected Lessing to write new plays for them and to lend their enterprise the prestige of his already respected name. Lessing initially balked at the invitation; he could not promise to write plays on a regular basis. Löwen, who had once been a theater critic himself, then thought of paying Lessing to publish criticism of National Theatre performances in a consortium-sponsored journal. Lessing accepted this offer, and in April 1767 he began writing biweekly sheets of criticism, which sold for two shillings per copy, and by subscription for five Hamburg marks yearly. While the journal's contents and its title, *Hamburg Dramaturgy,* were wholly Lessing's creations, the consortium's sponsorship of the journal invites suspicion. Why would the National Theatre publish Lessing's commentary on its plays, and pay the critic, unless it expected favorable notices? Lessing's employers undoubtedly thought that, besides acquiring the prestige that his reputation as playwright and critic already carried with it, they would attract an audience through his printed commentaries.

Instead of inviting the public to Hamburg's National Theatre, Lessing's essays occasionally attacked the taste of spectators already there, comparing eighteenth-century Germans unfavorably to ancient Athenians. Far from seeing himself as a publicity agent, Lessing assumed the role of public educator; he wrote, as he declared any good author would write, to "enlighten the mass and not confirm them in their prejudices or in their ignoble mode of thought."[6] Lessing issued further installments of the *Dramaturgy* after his break with activity at the National Theatre, but these later essays were less a running commentary on performances than an exegesis of Aristotle's *Poetics* and obituaries for a failing repertory theater. Objections from actresses compelled Lessing to record virtually nothing about acting at Hamburg after the twenty-fifth of his one hundred and four essays in the *Dramaturgy*. The journal reported on most productions long after they had opened, and only the first fourteen weeks (fifty-two nights) of the theater's productions were covered by the *Dramaturgy* in two years.

A dramaturg who does not confirm the public in its prejudices, and instead challenges popular taste, invites a decline in attendance and risks becoming, in Zeydel's phrase, "the man of letters who rashly interferes with the business of the theater."[7] But Lessing argued that criticism never discourages a serious playgoer; he was "firmly convinced that criticism does not interfere with enjoyment and that those who have learned to judge a piece most severely are always those that visit the theater most frequently."[8] Unfortunately, not many Germans visited the Hamburg National Theatre with frequency. Subsidies ran out, company tours were insufficiently remunerative, and the permanent repertory company was bankrupt by March 1769.

It is doubtful that Lessing's adverse criticism dissuaded any readers from seeing Voltaire or Corneille. Most of his essays were published long after the plays under discussion had opened. Still, Lessing clearly had preferences that differed from those of both the Hamburg management and the public, and he said so in print. Dissatisfaction is strongly evident in his reference to Hamburg's staging of "wretched stuff" by Corneille, and in his unequivocal advice "to leave all existent Christian tragedies [including the one by Cronegk under discussion] unperformed. This advice . . . deprives us of nothing more than very mediocre plays."[9] Another Christian tragedy, Voltaire's *Zayre,* was performed five days after Lessing published his advice against the genre, which may indicate how little his remarks altered policy. Lessing wrote only about the plays, however, not about Hamburg management, even when it began hiring jugglers and acrobats to draw spectators.

Lessing's final essay in the *Dramaturgy,* written when he knew that the Hamburg enterprise had failed financially as well as aesthetically, includes one strong blast at the German public's Francophilia:

> Out on the good-natured idea to procure for the Germans a national
> theater, when we Germans are not yet a nation! I do not speak of our
> political constitution, but only of our social character. . . . We are still the
> sworn copyists of all that is foreign, especially are we still the obedient
> admirers of the never sufficiently admired French.[10]

"That a German should . . . have the audacity to doubt the excellence of a Frenchman, who could conceive such a thing?"[11] asked Lessing while conceiving such a thing in his *Dramaturgy*. To counteract the excessive German admiration for French drama, the *Hamburg Dramaturgy* repeatedly disputed the aesthetics of Voltaire and Corneille, contending that "no nation had more misapprehended the rules of ancient drama than the French."[12] Ironically, while he condemned fellow countrymen for admiring French drama, Lessing himself admired mainly Shakespeare, Diderot, and the ancients. Neither he nor his contemporaries could admire German playwriting when much of it was inferior to or clumsily derived from foreign drama. Goethe, Schiller, Lenz, Tieck, Grabbe, Büchner, Kleist, and Hebbel had not yet arrived. To a small extent, Lessing's admiration for Shakespeare, which the great German Romantic and Post-Romantic playwrights subsequently shared, inspired many important German plays.

Small as Lessing's influence at the Hamburg National Theatre may have been, his effect on later criticism and on the dramaturgical profession was far from negligible. Publication of others' volumes of dramaturgy followed soon after his. In 1775, von Gemmimgen, a playwright associated with the state-supported theater in Mannheim, wrote *Mannheimer Dramaturgie*. Von Knigge published *Dramaturgische Blatter* in 1789. Albrecht completed *Neue Hamburgische Dramaturgie* in 1791. The word "dramaturgie" seems to have been in vogue among German critics after Lessing. (Incidentally, this German word should not be confused with the French term for playwright, which is "dramaturge.") The hiring of dramaturgs continued despite objections to the profession raised by Lessing's associates at Hamburg. Dramaturgs brought to theaters not only the prestige of having a "Lessing" on the staff, they also possessed a knowledge of playwriting and dramatic theory with which new plays could be expertly screened prior to production, assuming that the management was interested in new plays. Löwen, having vowed initially to produce new German plays at Hamburg, knew that a man with Lessing's background could both locate the plays and write them. As the number of subsidized repertory theaters in Germany increased, more productions of untried plays could be risked by managements no longer wholly financially dependent on popular taste or box-office success.

The Age of Enlightenment missionary stance, which underlay Lessing's Hamburg essays and caused most of his difficulties with actors at Hamburg, was not his alone. At least in theory, Löwen, the managing director of the theater, also planned to educate German audiences, first by having Lessing publish in his journal information about plays and their authors, along with a running commentary on performances. Löwen further proposed to develop the country's first permanent repertory company by offering prizes for new German plays and by staging the new drama in repertory with standard, already popular French works. As it turned out, however, the prizes were not awarded; the theater's managing committee, of which Lessing was a member, chose to mainly produce well-established plays by Frenchmen. Perhaps the National Theatre, with its avowed aim of producing German plays, was misnamed. Certainly it was mismanaged. The "permanent repertory company" lasted about two years, ending in bankruptcy, and Löwen and Lessing resigned from their positions in the summer of 1768.

Lessing also advocated the advancement of the then new and emerging genre of bourgeois tragedy (see his essay #14), which later became quite popular in German. He wrote plays and essays favoring this genre that Diderot had promoted in France.

Later dramaturgs exerted more influence than Lessing over play selection, but it should not be thought that Lessing's disputes with actors, audience and management taste were simply the birth pangs of the dramaturgical profession. The same disputes recurred a half century later during Ludwig Tieck's term as dramaturg, and echoes of the disputes can still be heard in German theater today. Edwin Zeydel's account of Tieck's tenure at Dresden practically sums up Lessing's dramaturgical career as well. Tieck was appointed dramaturg at Dresden in 1824. Then, as Zeydel reports,

> it soon developed that his strong opposition to the prevailing low standards of taste would make his position very difficult. . . . The bureaucrats in the theater were deaf to his suggestions. The public resented the 'despotic' manner in which he foisted his taste upon them. The actors . . . grumbled about the unabbreviated performances of Shakespeare's plays, and were indignant over his plain-spoken criticism of their work. . . . And the Dresden playwrights could not forgive him the severe judgment of their feeble efforts. . . . It is clear, then, that Tieck was not spared the indignities and intrigues which have always been the lot of men with exquisite literary taste who venture to oppose with their own artistic standards, the indolence and commercialism of the existing stage, the public's witless love of pleasure, and the venal criticism of the day.[13]

BRECHT'S EPIC DRAMATURGY

Artistic standards as high as Lessing's or Tieck's, along with almost comic arrogance, led one twentieth-century dramaturg to demand that the theater management transfer all its decision-making power to him. Bertolt Brecht (1898–1956) made this demand in 1928, while he was one of several literary editors and advisers at Berlin's Deutsches Theatre. According to Carl Zuck-mayer, Brecht asked the management to cede its control so that he could shape the repertoire entirely according to his own ideas and rename the Rein-hardt theaters [such as the Deutsches Theatre] epic smoking theatres, for he thought people might be more inclined to think if they were allowed to smoke in the theater. As these demands were rejected, he confined his activ-ity to occasional appearances to collect his salary.[14] Brecht, like Lessing, had a far longer and more active career as playwright than as dramaturg.

Brecht served as a dramaturg first at the Munich Kammerspiele from 1923–24, then in Berlin at Max Reinhardt's Deutsches Theater from 1924–25, and at the Piscator Stage from 1927–28. While in these positions, he collabo-rated on rewritings of Marlowe's *Edward the Second* (1924), *Camille* (1925), Tolstoy's *Rasputin* (1927), *The Good Soldier Schweik* (1928), and Leo Lania's *Konjunktur* (1928). He also completed a number of his own plays during this period with assistance from Emil Burri, Slatan Dudow, Caspar Neher, and his sec-retary, Elizabeth Hauptman, all members of the "Brecht Collective." When the group completed *Man Is Man* in 1925, Brecht told Elizabeth Hauptman that "piecing together the manuscript from twenty pounds of paper was heavy work; it took me two days, a half bottle of brandy, four bottles of soda water, eight to ten cigars, and a lot of patience, and it was the only part I did on my own."[15]

Collective authorship of plays is not uncommon, but it is frequently unac-knowledged. Broadway "play doctors" who receive a salary for writing scenes credited to someone else have their noncommercial counterparts in the pro-fession of dramaturgs. Dramaturgs who rewrite a classic or adapt a novel as Brecht did a number of times may create a virtually new play: the distinctions between playwright and dramaturg then become tenuous. Brecht, the collec-tive playwright, was sometimes inseparable from Brecht, the dramaturg in a collective. But even in his most thorough collaborations, Brecht's personal identity remained prominent. The intellectual property of others became his as much as it was theirs. Most of the collective theater activity in which Brecht engaged meant group realization of his politics, his aesthetics, and his reputa-tion. In his dramaturgical career and elsewhere, Brecht's private self continu-ally surfaced. At Reinhardt's and Piscator's theaters, Brecht evidently spent less time working as a dramaturg than as a playwright; he was busy attending rehearsals of new plays such as *Man Is Man,* and new productions of slightly older plays such as *Jungle of the Cities* and *Baal.* Even so, his dramaturgical experience had a lasting influence on the profession in Germany. Volker Ca-naris suggests that under Brecht's leadership at the Berliner Ensemble:

> The dramaturg became the director's most important theoretical collab-orator. Dramaturgy in Brecht's sense comprises the entire conceptual preparation of a production from its inception to its realization. Accord-ingly, it is the task of dramaturgy to clarify the political and historical, as well as the aesthetic and formal aspects of a play, and to convey the sci-entifically researched material to the other participants.[16]

Prior to Brecht's alteration of the dramaturgical profession, dramaturgs were not necessarily people with practical stage experience, unless they were playwrights. Brecht had served as critic, dramaturg, playwright, and director prior to founding the Berliner Ensemble, and had all these roles performed by dramaturgs at his own theater. In a sense, he moved the dramaturgical staff out of its script-reading library and into rehearsal halls. This move led to a strong emphasis on dramaturgy in production, with dramaturgical advisers attending rehearsals to help directors follow through on textual interpretation and rewrite plays.

Although it may have been implemented during Brecht's lifetime and earlier, the concept of "production dramaturgy" only entered the German theater vocabulary in the 1970s. The dramaturg and critic Ernst Wendt said that the name and idea of production dramaturgy arose around 1970, when the desire for ideology grew immensely. Since then there have been directors who would "not even stage *Charley's Aunt* without the help of a dramaturg."[17] Wendt had become wary of production dramaturgs serving as supertheoreticians of productions in which the ideological superstructure does not show up in the visual appearance.

MÜLLER'S POST-BRECHTIAN DRAMATURGY

Heiner Müller (1929–1995), one of Germany's most innovative playwrights after Brecht, served as dramaturg at the Berliner Ensemble before his ascent to the position of artistic director at the Ensemble. Although his reputation as author and stage director far exceeded his renown as dramaturg, it was to discuss his lesser-known career as dramaturg that I met with him some years ago in East Berlin (before the Berlin Wall was removed and East and West Germany were reunited). When I met Müller in his apartment, he began by cheerfully saying that while he held the title of dramaturg at the Berliner Ensemble from 1972 on, the Ensemble paid him primarily for writing plays. In this regard he seemed to be upholding Brechtian tradition at the theater Brecht founded. Few of the East German dramaturgs whom Müller met impressed him. He joked that the concept of dramaturg was invented by Joseph Goebbels when the Nazi minister of propaganda appointed a "Reichsdramaturg" to oversee the political acceptability of all Third Reich theater.

Under Marxist government the East German political scene changed, but political criteria still heavily influenced the work of dramaturgs and directors. Every director had to submit his production plans (explaining why he chose the play and how he would stage it) to the Ministry of Culture of the DDR (East German government) months before rehearsals began. Directors relied on their dramaturgs to develop and present production plans for the ministry's approval. Rather than submit their plans to the Ministry of Culture, a few of East Germany's best directors and dramaturgs chose to work in France and Switzerland, but most acquiesced to the government's rule because, as Müller said with a hint of irony, "They are German." Dramaturgs also prepared program notes, usually a series of quotations and pictures related to the play, for approval and printing six months before a play opened. (American theaters' management might welcome dramaturgs who meet deadlines this far ahead of an opening.)

When he first became a dramaturg at the Berliner Ensemble in 1972, Müller persuaded the Ensemble to stage an unconventional production of Brecht's *Baden Learning Play,* which resulted in extremely interesting post-play discussions between Müller and young audience members. Müller regretted that the Ensemble did not subsequently stage other, similarly lively productions. In 1995, the year of his death, the most provocative theater at the Berliner Ensemble was occurring offstage, in disputes over the Ensemble's future between Müller and the prominent playwright Rolf Hochhuth, a former West German. Hochhuth purchased ownership of the Berliner Ensemble's main theater after tracing deeds back to pre-Nazi owners and their relatives and paying earlier owners for the property rights that were theirs before the Nazis forcefully transferred the title papers. After this fantastic purchase, Hochhuth, the new theater owner, vowed to choose the repertoire of the Berliner Ensemble himself and ensure that at least one of his plays *(The Deputy)* is staged there each year. Under such circumstances, advice from dramaturgs might be superfluous.

Despite the opposition Lessing, Brecht, Müller, and other dramaturgs have encountered, or perhaps *because* of it, these writers and critics-in-residence played an active role in their country's intellectual and theater life. It could be argued that in America, too, the increasing prominence of literary advisers and dramaturgs has enhanced the life of the nation's theaters.

Today, Lessing, Brecht, and Müller are remembered far more for their plays than their dramaturgical advising. For this very reason, their examples deserve attention. From its inception, dramaturgy was not an end in itself, but part of a full and varied life in the arts practiced by men (and a few women) of letters. Now, we live in an age of specialization, and risk losing artists and dramaturgs who previously have engaged in a wide range of activities, as did Brecht, Lessing, and Müller.

CONFESSION: I AM NOT LESSING, NOR MEANT TO BE

Nearly two decades ago, when I first read about the dramaturgical activities of Lessing and Brecht, their work as literary advisers served as a model for my own. Within their advocacy of plays (middle-class drama and epic theater, respectively) I saw an antecedent for my own efforts to promote new, post-Brechtian political theater and satire. I have now written several books on political satire; taught workshops and seminars on the subject; published editions of plays by Dario Fo, the San Francisco Mime Troupe, and others whose work I admire, so that they will be more widely read. Outside the world of theater, or, rather, in a world of theatrical politics, I also ran for elected office a few times, and began writing satiric columns for newspapers. In these later activities, I identified with Lessing's and Brecht's extratheatrical activities in the culture of their country, and their less-than-full commitment to a lifetime of dramaturgy. I still see dramaturgy as an opportunity to encourage new play creation, to confer with outstanding directors, to learn from all the theater's collaborators. These experiences have enhanced other endeavors I made as teacher, writer, producer, and satiric political candidate.

Although dramaturgs tend to influence theaters through their meetings with directors, writers and actors, I think they may also effect changes in culture outside the playhouse, through theater education, writing, and political activism. I am particularly eager to see dramaturgs write essays and books that will reach audiences beyond the confines of their own theater. When Jan Kott wrote *Shakespeare Our Contemporary,* he influenced a whole generation of theater directors; some of those directors (including Peter Brook) subsequently asked him to advise them on productions, but Kott's book on Shakespeare *was* his dramaturgy at its best—much as Lessing's series of essays on Hamburg was *his* best dramaturgy.

I would like to see more writers consider themselves as "dramaturgs without theaters." If their writing is persuasive, the theaters will find them. These dramaturgs might write proposals for productions and theater companies that do not yet exist. They might also turn their attention to the immense theatricality of events outside traditional theater—political, sports, and religious rallies, for example—which contain vitality and enthusiastic audiences often absent from conventional playhouses. Let the realm of dramaturgy be as large as life itself. We need dramaturgs who are citizens as well as artists.

The dramaturgical profession has already demonstrated that critics, besides selling plays through reviews, can also collaborate on stage productions: by advising the playwright or director during rehearsals; by recommending to producers plays that challenge both actors and audience; by offering theater companies standards of achievement based on past theater history and criticism, and imagined future works; by helping companies to surpass and build on earlier achievements; and by leaving their positions as dramaturgs to become editors, teachers, essayists, playwrights, producers or arts patrons. All of this will help to create the Utopian theater of which Lessing wrote in his *Dramaturgy:* a theater where even the lighting technician (or "candle-snuffer," in Lessing's words) is a Garrick.

Acknowledgments: I am grateful to Stanley Kauffmann, Alois Nagler, John Newfield, and the editors of this volume for their advice. Sections of this essay first appeared in different form in yale/theatre *and* Theatre *and are used with permission.*

Towards an American Dramaturg
Adapting the function of dramaturgy to U.S. conditions
by **Martin Esslin**

MARTIN ESSLIN joined the BBC in 1940 and was head of Drama (Radio) from 1963–1977. He is author of books on Pinter, Brecht, and Artaud and of a seminal book on modern drama, *The Theatre of the Absurd*. He has published two collections of essays: *Brief Chronicles: Essays on Modern Drama* and *Meditations: Essays on Brecht, Beckett and the Media*. His critical articles have appeared regularly in *Plays and Players, Encounter,* and many other periodicals. He is also a well-known translator of plays, particularly by German-speaking dramatists.

In the German-speaking world (and those parts of Central and Eastern Europe that follow its basic pattern in theatre organisation) the function of the "Dramaturg" (or rather the "Dramaturgien"—well-staffed dramaturgical departments) is firmly embedded in an elaborate structure.

Its basis is formed by a network of some 200 highly subsidized municipal or state theatres in the major cities, with large permanent ensembles, presenting plays in repertoire—that is: with several different productions being shown each week to audiences motivated by the convention that theatregoing is evidence of social status in the community; audiences kept up-to-date and educated in their taste by a well-informed body of highly literate critics.

The dramaturgy departments of these theaters are fed by a large number of *"Theaterverlage"* (theatre publishers). These are a cross between literary agent and publisher: their main task is to find new plays, by reading what authors send them, scouting for, and commissioning translations of, foreign material and nurturing their own stable of established authors. The scripts they take on are printed—but "as manuscripts for internal use only" and distributed to all the "Dramaturgien".

In this structure the "Dramaturgie" has a well-defined and varied function; the members of its staff read all incoming scripts, report on them and file them; the "Chef-Dramaturg" in consultation with the artistic director or "Intendant" selects the repertoire; dramaturgs work on adaptation and cutting of scripts revising translations etc.; the Dramaturgie provides the editors of the elaborate and scholarly programme booklet which contains essays and other explanatory material about the play, and also distributes public relations material to

---

Editor's note: At author's request we have retained European usage for punctuation and spelling.

the press. And as the theatres usually have more than one auditorium and often also a company out on tour in neighbouring cities, the Dramaturgie also has to piece together the elaborate jig-saw of the actual schedule, so that acting assignments don't overlap; and members of the Dramaturgie travel widely to see performances in other theatres to scout for new acting talent. As the making of the repertoire greatly depends on the available acting-strengths in the company the Dramaturgie often also plays the part of casting director: "we must find a really good part for X, our outstanding middle-aged character actress next season, or we shall lose her . . . etc. etc."

And, in recent years members of the Dramaturgie have also increasingly been used as "Produktions-Dramaturgen" who stand by the director throughout rehearsals and render him every possible assistance with research on the play's background, cutting, rewrites, revisions of the text in the case of translations, etc. Young people who aspire to join these well-structured—not to say bureaucratically rigid—organisations, usually are the products of the theatre departments of universities (which, unlike American theatre departments, do not try to produce plays, but concentrate on theatre scholarship). They enter upon a clear-cut career structure, starting in smaller, provincial theatres, advancing to larger houses in bigger cities, and up the ladder leading to "Chef-Dramaturg" of a major theatre, or even beyond that to becoming artistic director or "Intendant".

In this organisational pattern the inter-action between the dramaturgy departments and the theatre publishing houses produces a very useful creative tension. The leading theatres are in intense competition to secure premieres of important new work. When I was translator of Pinter's plays into German, the moment it became known that a new play was finished, my phone in London never stopped ringing with theatres trying to find out about it; the theatre publisher, Rowohlt, then negotiated the premiere with the theatre that could promise the most prominent cast and the best director. It is obviously in the theatre publisher's interest to maximise the chances of success of the first production, so that a large number of other theatres would want to produce the play. Moreover it is not unknown that a powerful theatre publisher like Rowohlt will let a leading theatre have the first production of an important new play as part of a package—"if you do this play you are so keen on, will you also do one or two plays by our new and relatively unknown authors. . . ."

New plays that get done in this way, and are a success, have a very good chance of being picked up by numerous other theatres; that is how new authors often get launched. All this is very different from conditions in the English-speaking world, particularly the United States, where the theatrical landscape is infinitely more complex, not to say chaotic, where the commercial sector is geared to long runs of plays produced as distinct commercial ventures, and where, even in the so-called "repertory", non-commercial sector genuine repertoire theatres are largely unknown, and woefully undersubsidised in a much more complex and anarchic pattern from public, foundation, corporate, and private sources.

I can only speak from my relatively restricted experience as an unpaid, consultant dramaturg of the Magic Theatre in San Francisco from 1977 to 1989, and from my work over many years as a dramaturg of the National Playwrights Conference at Waterford, Connecticut in the seventies and eighties. It was during this period that the function of the dramaturg gradually took shape in the world of "non-profit" theatres in the United States and made its way onto the syllabus of some university drama departments.

It is clear that the function of the dramaturg could not just be taken over unchanged from the German model. Much more than the German dramaturg who operates in a well-established structure, and above all, in a culture in which the theatre performs a well-defined and important social, cultural and political role, the American dramaturg not only has to do the basic job of finding and nurturing scripts, but has also to work hard on helping to create that basic cultural atmosphere in which a healthy theatre can operate. In the German-speaking world the theatre acts not only as a status symbol for individuals—you are not regarded as "gebildet" (educated and socially acceptable) if you are not a regular theater-goer and can be relied upon to be able to discuss theatre with your friends and acquaintances—it is also a powerful status symbol for its community: a city without its own municipal theatre is definitely second-class, "in the sticks". A civil servant who has misbehaved is transferred to a smaller town, and everybody will comment that he has been exiled to "a place that does not even have a theatre!" The theatre there plays a role analogous to that of a nationally prominent football or baseball team in the United States.

As the resident literary person and "intellectual" in his organisation the dramaturg in the United States will have an increasingly important role to play in the gradual establishment of such an accepted status in the community for his theatre, and the theatre as a cultural force in general. One facet of this must surely be the widening of knowledge, critical acumen and taste for the drama, the art of acting and its appreciation, the problems of directing, etc.

One of the greatest handicaps in such an endeavour is the woeful state of theatre criticism in the press in the United States. This is not just the fault of the individual critics (some of whom are splendid people) but of the low status of theatre criticism in the editorial policy of newspapers. Far too little space is available to most theatre critics, so that hardly more than the synopsis of the plot and a few words about leading actors can find mention in the short reviews allowed. And what is even worse: there is no space at all for preliminary material about the authors and backgrounds to forthcoming plays which form an essential part of newspaper coverage of the theatre in continental Europe. The dramaturg must seek—and find—ways to compensate for this lack, be it by himself trying to place articles of this kind, by lectures and discussions on related topics, etc., by arranging for discussions with authors and actors after performances—and by generally making the work of the theatre and its repertoire genuinely newsworthy, the object of heated discussion and sensational controversy.

And, of course, in the absence of effective press criticism, the dramaturg must act as its chief critic within the theatre. (It is significant that Lessing's famous *Hamburgische Dramaturgie,* one of the basic texts of the profession, the theoretical groundwork of modern theatre, was written as such internal criticism for the first German national theatre in the late eighteenth century). In present-day conditions in the United States the dramaturg must be the critical and artistic conscience of his or her theatre: it is he/she who must apply the most rigorous yardsticks to the texts, the performance of directors, actors and designers, and to the policy of the organisation in general.

Clearly, this cannot be done in full view of everybody concerned—too many egos would be offended. The dramaturg must convey these criticisms to the artistic director, be his constant gadfly, or even perhaps a kind of court jester, licensed to be as rude as possible, to preserve his boss from complacency. In conveying these criticisms, the dramaturg must be truly ruthless and severe towards everyone (including himself as regards choice of plays, etc.). One of the greatest dangers of organisations operating in a critical vacuum is that they deteriorate into mutual admiration societies. The dramaturg must be the counselor who is able to tell the artistic director the full truth, however hurtful it might be about the true artistic status of his organisation. He must have sufficient standing to be able to confront his artistic director fearlessly. That is by no means an easy task. I frequently could prevent disastrous choices of repertoire at the Magic only by threatening to resign if a particular play was taken on. Not every dramaturg has sufficient prestige to make this a real threat. All the more reason for him to acquire it by the quality of his work and his standing in local public opinion.

It is clear that the choice of plays to be performed must be the basis for the regional theatre's maximum impact on its community. The dramaturg must, among many other things, be an expert on the problems, demography, prejudices and prides of the community he serves, to have his or her finger on its pulse.

The repertoire of individual theatres is, moreover, often governed by the terms under which they were established. The Magic Theatre, for example, was mainly, officially, dedicated to the performance of new, American material. The subsidies from certain quarters depended on the fulfillment of this remit. Hence it was impossible to perform classical plays or foreign material, unless it lent itself to translation into the local idiom and milieu. Other theatres labour under similar restrictions. The best way out here, it seems to me, is not to wait for suitable scripts to land on one's desk by chance, but to originate material oneself: pin-point a local concern or problem and get the right local author, or group of authors, to create a tailor-made product. Even if the resultant drama is not a master-piece, at least it will cause a stir by tackling a local concern.

One of the greatest drawbacks to a rational dramaturgical policy in the non-profit sector of the American theatre is the fundamentally flawed philosophy behind the granting of subsidies. Due to the basically commercially oriented ideology of funding bodies, it is always assumed that a subsidy is merely there to "prime the pump", that, after a start having been made the project will come into its own and become commercially viable. As this is evidently impossible in repertoire-theatre, new subsidies have constantly to be applied for, for three-year projects under separate headings, such as, fostering new female, black, Hispanic, gay or lesbian playwrights etc., while it is quite clear that none of these projects will ever result in a diminution of the need for financial assistance. I have always felt that this plunges the theatres into a sea of fantasy and conscious mendacity—and an enormous amount of energy is spent by the dramaturgs on having to think up ever new such projects to keep the funds flowing from arts councils and foundations all of whom seem constrained to subscribe to the clearly unrealistic basis of this type of subvention policy, which, moreover, once a project is approved and embarked upon, distorts the general policy of the theatre and even compels it to use inferior material just because it falls within the parameters of that particular remit. In Europe a theatre, if judged worthy, is simply given an annual subsidy and is then free to shape its policy and repertoire—only if major flaws in these policies become obvious, do the subsidizing bodies—state or municipal—intervene, change the management or close the operation down—after a period of due warning during which the situation can be improved has elapsed.

Of course, the shaping of each theatre repertoire and policy depends on the particular circumstances of its area, funding, history and tradition (if any). Nevertheless the task of designing a season is greatly hampered, as against the situation in the German-speaking world, by the absence of a structured system of distribution of new material. In my experience the American literary or theatrical agent is not particularly interested in getting a new play that seems promising placed in a small theatre—and contracts are hedged round with innumerable safeguards in case the property becomes a success and might be taken up by other media. The Theatre Communications Group does make valiant efforts to circulate likely scripts, but on the whole new material appears in an extremely chancy and haphazard fashion. I used to bring interesting material to the Magic Theatre from my own work as a (production) dramaturg at the National Playwrights Conference where scripts were being developed in rehearsed readings. Enterprises of this type (mostly modeled on the NPC) are a very useful substitute for the widely lacking opportunity new playwrights have in Europe to see their work done professionally as they learn their craft. But, of course, these are very limited opportunities.

The result I, for one, frequently observed is a great deal of overwriting and sheer lack of theatrical craft one finds in the work of even the most talented new playwrights, a tendency greatly increased in a generation that has grown up exposed to immense quantities of television situation comedy and police series. Here the dramaturg can do important work in revising and, above all, cutting and slimming—scripts with the author.

What, then, is the profile of the successful dramaturg in the conditions prevailing in the American theater landscape—in which regard the United States must still be regarded as a severely "underdeveloped country"?

Clearly the dramaturg must be a highly knowledgeable individual, widely read and cultured, familiar with the demography, sociology, and psychology of his environment. But, above all, he or she must be a person of authority, able to command the respect of writers and directors, able to stand up to his or her artistic director, able to tell even established authors where they might improve their scripts, capable of influencing the local press and to contribute to it articles on forthcoming productions of the theatre involved. A reputation as a working and successful playwright, translator or adaptor, or as a respected critic will be an immense advantage in establishing this type of status and visibility in the community as well as within the organisation itself.

Clearly, therefore, the ideal starting-off point must be previous, visible success in the theatrical profession itself. In the commercial sector the nearest equivalent to dramaturgs were the "play-doctors" called in to remedy defects of shows during their pre-Broadway tours. Those usually were playwrights or directors of established success and fame. A background as author of successful plays, or as a leading critic (Edith Oliver of *The New Yorker* was a most successful dramaturg at the National Playwrights Conference) will be of immense help in convincing playwrights that the advice offered is valid and based on real experience. I should also posit a knowledge of foreign languages as an important qualification: one of the greatest drawbacks of the American theatre scene is its insularity, its ignorance and neglect of foreign plays. This is largely due to the fact that hardly anybody can read plays—or theatrical magazines reporting on plays—in the main languages—French, German, Spanish, Russian—among the professionals in the theatre.

One of the most important tasks of the new breed of dramaturgs in the United States must be an effort to broaden the subject matter of the plays offered. One of the main weaknesses of American playwriting to me—as an outsider—always seemed the almost exclusive concentration on family and emotional subjects, to the virtual exclusion of politics, ideology, philosophy and other wider cultural thematic concerns. There have been exceptions to this general impression, but even seemingly "political" themes, like the spate of plays about AIDS, or feminism, basically approached these matter as an emotional, personalised issue, rather than as grounds for serious thought and debate. An injection of foreign material dealing with such wider subjects would perhaps induce local playwrights to regard drama as a vehicle for "concrete thought" rather than as emotional steambaths.

Of course, the public must be brought to appreciate such drama and it is notorious that they shrink from anything that seems too "intellectually demanding". Here we are back with what I regard as the main mission of the dramaturg in this country—the mission of making the theatre accepted as a major cultural, social, and ideological factor in the community.

It is a vast mission, and an uphill task, but one of immense importance.

On Robert Brustein and Dramaturgy

by Jonathan Marks

JONATHAN MARKS, a reformed dramaturg, is Associate Professor of Theatre and Head of Directing at Texas Tech University. He was Literary Manager of the Yale Repertory Theatre and Literary Director of the American Repertory Theatre (Cambridge, Massachusetts), and has worked at the Berkeley Repertory Theatre, Magic Theatre (San Francisco), American Conservatory Theater (San Francisco), Playhouse in the Park (Cincinnati), and the O'Neill Theater Center (Waterford, Connecticut). He has taught at Yale, Harvard, Stanford, and San Francisco State, holds bachelor of arts, master of fine arts, and doctor of fine arts degrees from Yale, and was a Fulbright Fellow in Nancy, France, where he trained in acting.

I was Robert Brustein's dramaturg for a dozen years or so. In that time under his aegis I developed my own definition of a dramaturg: a person who mediates between the intellectual, literary, and aesthetic aspects of the theater, on the one hand, and its practice on the other; a person who sits, however uncomfortably, on the nonexistent stool between the professional and the professorial, attempting to speak the languages of thought and action simultaneously, to translate from drama to theater and back again.

I realize now that, even though he has never called himself a dramaturg, this definition perfectly describes Robert Brustein: professor and professional, enduring contributor to the life of the American theater and the life of the American mind: actor, director, playwright, and, most saliently, producer; and critic, teacher, and intellectual force, all at the same time.

Think of the playwrights he has introduced, coaxed to do their best work, and advanced. Think of the directors, the actors, the designers he has taught, goaded, challenged, and presented. Think of the critics he has influenced, and the dramaturgs who have trained in his shop.

Some dramaturgs productively confine themselves to working with playwrights; others take it as their mission to work with all the aspects of the theater. Such a one is Brustein. If the dramaturg is, as he says below, "the humanist in the woodpile," then how can he deny that he is one, and one of the foremost?

I first heard the ugly "turg-word" in 1967, when I was an undergraduate at Yale. A friend of mine who was a student in the doctoral program in Dramatic Literature and Criticism enthused to me about the opportunities it presented to combine the intellectual and the practical in order to be trained as a critic, a teacher (if you were so inclined), or even, as Michael Feingold was doing, a dramaturg. (Whazzat?) After a year on a Fulbright in France, I entered the program.

The model before us was Feingold, who soon became the Yale Rep's first Literary Manager. A classmate, Rocco Landesman said, "Take everything I know—about baseball, football, the track, the market, theater, and everything else—and Michael knows more than that about the theater." Yet behind this prodigious model, for all their differences and periodic squabbles, was Bob: the model's model.

In my first year I started editing the theater's program notes. After three years, I graduated, joined the faculty, acted with the company, and became Michael's Assistant Literary Manager, and soon his successor. From him I learned the full gamut of functions a dramaturg could perform, supporting each production and helping to nurture the organism of the theater.

After a few years, Bob decided that the department needed a new focus; it should openly concentrate on training literary managers for the nonprofit theater movement. There was some hesitancy on the part of the critics who comprised the senior faculty, but as usual, Bob had his way. The new name of the department was a point of contention; it was cruising toward "Criticism, Dramatic Literature, and Literary Management Department" when I proposed an alternative that I thought would encompass all the elements: "Dramaturgy Department." One of my colleagues patiently—and correctly—explained that the word referred to the art of dramatic composition, and not to what a dramaturg does, but my neologistic suggestion won the day, and seems to have stuck.

A new course in dramaturgy was instituted, and each student was detailed to work under me on one production during the course of the year, as well as to evaluate manuscripts submitted to the theater. Many of these playreaders and student dramaturgs went on to make important contributions to the development of the American dramaturg—and to this volume. I was honored to have a hand in their training, and to serve as their conduit to the formative influence of Robert Brustein.

Dramaturgy thrived and developed elsewhere, too. A distinction arose between the functions of dramaturgs and literary managers quite apart from Brustein's influence, and the modesty and discretion of Yale dramaturgs was modified elsewhere, as they began to assert their independence, and to get their names published right under the director's. Nonetheless, the rise of the dramaturg at Yale and throughout America owes a debt to its true founder, patron, and model, Robert Brustein. And it's time that we—and he—recognize his membership and place of honor in the fellowship.

From "The Future of an Un-American Activity"[18]

by **Robert Brustein**

As founding director of the Yale Repertory and American Repertory Theatres (Cambridge, Massachusetts), **MR. BRUSTEIN** has supervised close to two hundred productions, acting in eight and directing twelve (including his own adaptations of *The Father, Ghosts, The Changeling,* and the trilogy of Pirandello works: *Six Characters in Search of an Author, Right You Are (If You Think You Are),* and *Tonight We Improvise.* Most recently he adapted the A.R.T.'s world premier musical *Shlemiel the First.* He is the author of eleven books on theatre and society, including *Reimagining American Theatre, The Theatre of Revolt, Making Scenes,* a memoir of his Yale years when he was Dean of the Drama School; and *Who Needs Theatre,* a collection of reviews and essays for which he received his second George Jean Nathan Award for dramatic criticism. His latest book *Dumbocracy in America,* has just been published. Mr. Brustein is also Director of the Loeb Drama Center, Professor of English at Harvard, and drama critic for the *New Republic.* He is a recipient of the George Polk Award in journalism, the Elliot Norton Award for professional excellence in Boston theatre, the New England Theatre Conference's 1985 Annual Award for outstanding creative achievement in the American theatre, and the 1995 American Academy of Arts and Letters Award for Distinguished Service to the Arts. His play, *Demons,* was broadcast on WGBH radio in April 1993, and had its stage world premiere as part of *A.R.T.'s New Stages.* In addition to his work at Yale and Harvard, Robert Brustein has taught at Cornell, Vassar, and Columbia.

The hostility to the dramaturg partly reflects America's historical anti-intellectualism, and partly a traditional antagonism between the humanist and the artist, who normally regard each other as two mutually aggressive carnivores. In the university, for example, there is no scorn more contemptuously expressed than that of the English faculty towards the Theatre department, and no new appointment more fiercely resisted than that of a creative writer or a practicing artist. How can we account for this? One explanation is that people who consider themselves custodians of the past sometimes have an impulse to preserve the past in formaldehyde. Plays are considered forms of literature, which stage interpretations can only stale and violate. I suspect the relationship between the scholar of dramatic literature and the practitioner is not much different than that between the art historian and the painter, or between the musicologist and the composer. Those engaged in practice often seem to threaten those engaged in pedagogical, analytical tasks.

It's hardly surprising, therefore, that analytical minds should in turn constitute a threat to artists. And the greatest hurdle of the dramaturg in trying to gain acceptance in the professional theatre is to convince the people engaged in practice that he or she is there to help the enterprise rather than to criticize, ridicule, or scorn it. Most dramaturgs began their careers as university humanists, remember—some even did time as theatre critics—so it is not unexpected that actors and directors, even those considered close friends and colleagues, should welcome them with the rapture and cordiality of a Grant gazelle being stalked by a cheetah.

For the sake of some historical perspective on this relationship, allow me to recount how we evolved the Dramaturgy program at the Yale School of Drama. In 1966, when I became Dean, the only vaguely literary degree was a Doctor of Fine Arts in Directing or Playwriting, presumably for those who desired careers in college theatre departments. The new Drama School regime, however, was trying to improve the quality and aspiration of the profession rather than provide teachers for educational theatre, and this, we thought, meant trying to develop well-informed, intelligent drama critics. Thus, at the same time we were professionalizing the training in acting and directing, we introduced a new program in Criticism and Dramatic Literature, offered in place of the old Directing/Playwriting DFA.

I suppose this was an inevitable development considering that the Dean of the School had been a critic, the associate Dean (Gordon Rogoff) was a critic, and two more critics, Richard Gilman and Stanley Kauffmann, were about to join the faculty. Since none of us was known for mild or temperate writings, it was also inevitable that the model for these DFA's should be a SuperCritic in the role of Samson slaying the Philistines, which may explain why they began cutting down actors before they had even cut their first teeth. We had a training procedure at Yale which gave each critic-in-training an opportunity to address the school regarding a recent production, including those of the recently formed Yale Repertory Theatre. This quickly became known as the Blood Bath. I remember Michael Feingold making his critical debut as a student by announcing publicly, to the student body and professional company alike, that the Rep had effectively massacred *Three Sisters,* a play he doubted was worthy of production in the first place, and that the performers were in need of basic acting training.

This left not only blood, but ruptured spleens, chewed intestines, and smashed kidneys on the floor, so henceforth we decided that the DFA critiques should be written rather than spoken, and deposited in the library for interested readers. (I suspect that few if any members of the professional acting company were numbered among the curious.) The criticism students couldn't understand why they were no longer permitted to express their views in public forums, and were upset with me for failing to be as frank about our work at Yale as I had been about theatre in New York. They had a point, insofar as they still regarded me as a practicing critic. What they failed to realize was that I had now assumed another persona—artistic director of a company—and that it was also my job to protect the morale and spirit of a developing ensemble of sensitive actors.

They also failed to realize that they, too, had other personas. They were not only embryonic critics, but also the colleagues of those whose work they were evaluating, both students and professionals, and for these young savages to sharpen their teeth on the flesh of their friends was to invite suspicion, mistrust, and even hatred. For a while the DFA's found themselves isolated from most of the activities of the School, scorned as self-regarding pariahs more infatuated with expressing their opinions than with learning about the theatre, and therefore outside the boundaries of the process.

As an antidote, we invented a variety of methods to bring them inside the process, the most successful being dramaturgical assignments. Before long, the DFA's were writing program material, reading new scripts, translating foreign plays, doing research for directors and actors, giving lectures on the texts, designing special series, and leading Wednesday seminars for the audiences. Many of them began to act, direct, and write as well. The first Literary Director of the Rep was the original SuperCritic himself, Michael Feingold, who by that time had found a telephone booth and changed himself into the mild-mannered Clark Kent, an infallible source of scholarly, textual, aesthetic, and artistic support for all who availed themselves of his learning. He, in turn, was succeeded in the position by a number of graduates of the DFA program, after each of them had trained as student dramaturgs on a series of Rep and School shows—and many of these, in turn, found places in American resident theatres.

For we had decided to substitute for the existing Criticism program a new program in Dramaturgy. With very few exceptions—Feingold was one, when he left Yale to begin writing regular reviews for the *Village Voice*—our graduates were not having much success in finding positions as theatre critics on magazines or newspapers. Editors were still drawing their reviewing talent from the foreign desk or the sports department or the dance area, and the incumbents were showing no particular willingness to resign their sinecures to these upstarts from Yale. We also concluded it had probably been a mistake to install a Criticism program in a School of Drama where to practice the traditional critical virtues—disinterestedness, detachment, ruthless honesty—was to invite the kind of reception the misanthrope Alceste enjoyed when he assessed the poetic abilities of Clitandre. Those trained in Dramaturgy could always function as critics if the opportunity arose, especially since such people would have gained considerably more experience of the theatrical process than the majority of those who now pass judgments only on results. And knowing the process, such people would be less likely to subject theatre artists to the kind of abusive and savage personal attacks they often suffer today at the hands of our more brutal reviewers.

Yale, therefore, became one of at least two places—the University of Iowa was another—training dramaturgs for positions in resident theatres. Iowa primarily drew its recruits from the ranks of playwrights, Yale from a nexus of critics, writers, scholars, and translators. Now there is a third place for training dramaturgs—at the A.R.T. Institute for Advanced Theatre Training at Harvard.

Those who fill these posts today are able to speak with more authority than I about what special qualities best serve which dramaturgical function, but I think we can all agree that the more deeply engaged they are in the process of production, the more generally accepted they are by colleagues and collaborators. It would seem, therefore, that the most delicate and difficult function of all remains that of internal critic—finding a way to communicate your views about particular productions, and about the conduct of the theatre, without arousing the defensiveness of the artistic director or hurting the feelings of the company. This requires extraordinary discretion, but it is a necessary, indeed critical aspect of the job, and it can be accomplished so long as the dramaturg is perceived to be concerned with the improvement of the institution rather than with the satisfaction of vanity or the enhancement of ego. For the dramaturg is potentially the artistic director's Good Angel—a corrective necessity in his dealings with Board members exhorting him to take the safe way, with Managers asking him to toe the bottom line, with audiences proving unresponsive to challenging works, and even with reviewers displaying impatience with the laborious process of building a company or developing a playwright. As the humanist in the woodpile, it is the dramaturg who must act as the conscience of the theatre, reminding it of its original promise, when it threatens to relax into facile, slack, and easy paths.

Notes for a Definition
by Jonathan Kalb

JONATHAN KALB is the author of *Beckett in Performance* and *Free Admissions: Collected Theater Writings.* He writes for the *Village Voice,* teaches at Hunter College and the CUNY Graduate Center, and is currently completing a book on Heiner Müller.

Dramaturgy is a profession that doesn't exist yet in the United States, conceived, here, by a tiny circle of intellectuals dedicated to the metaphysical project of inspiring itself with the final breaths of another profession, dramatic criticism. The ideal is: when the last forum for respectable publication disappears, the theater itself could then provide its own sanctuary for those with the imagination to take it seriously. Barring that, dramaturgy becomes an interesting lost cause. It is the dream of a better future: of an American culture that has broken out of its arrested adolescence, an American theater that looks mistily back at the void of indifference that once surrounded it, and an American society that no longer regards rapacious individualism as a moral imperative. In a hundred years, let's say, today's American dramaturgs will be revered as extremists among the last Enlightenment Quixotes, their history taught by an even smaller group of very last Enlightenment Quixotes working adjunct at racially segregated private colleges. The new Lessing, if there ever could be one, will be one of their students.

NOTES

1. See, for example, Laurence Shyer's article, "America's First Literary Manager: John Corbin at the New Theatre" in *Theater* 10.1 (1978): 8–14. Anne Cattaneo also discusses dramaturgical precursors in her article for this section.
2. Andrew Scott Berg, *Max Perkins: Editor of Genius* (New York: Dutton, 1978).
3. Bertolt Brecht, *Messingkauf Dialogues,* trans. John Willet (London: Eyre Methuen, 1956) 11.
4. G. E. Lessing, *Hamburg Dramaturgy,* trans. Helen Zimmern (New York: Dover, 1962) 2.
5. Edwin H. Zeydel, *Ludwig Tieck, The German Romanticist* (Princeton: Princeton University Press, 1935) 261.
6. Lessing 8.
7. Zeydel 261.
8. Lessing 64.
9. Lessing 9.
10. Lessing 262.
11. Lessing 92.
12. Lessing 264.
13. Zeydel 259–60.
14. Carl Zuckmayer, *A Part of Myself,* trans. Richard and Clara Winston (New York: Harcourt Brace, 1970) 275–76.
15. Bertolt Brecht quoted in the introduction to Brecht, *Collected Plays,* ed. Ralph Manheim and John Willet, vol. 2 (New York: Vintage, 1977) 250.
16. Volker Canaris, *Style and the Director in The German Theatre,* ed. Ronald Hayman (London: Oswald Wolff, 1975) 250.
17. Ernst Wendt, quoted in *yale/theatre* interview, *Dramaturgy in Berlin,* 10.1 (1978): 51.
18. "The Future of an Un-American Activity" was originally delivered as an address at a conference sponsored by Theatre Communications Group at Columbia University in the early 1980s and later published in the TCG newsletter, *Theatre Communications.*

Section 2

TOWARD A DRAMATURGICAL SENSIBILITY

The idea of a dramaturgical sensibility suggests that dramaturgy is not so much a matter of how to do it as it is about the development of an interconnected set of ideas, attitudes, feelings, skills, and behaviors: in short, an education. Such an education takes time, talents, and practice: with luck, it never ends. These articles approach the development of a dramaturgical sensibility from a variety of perspectives. Theater historian Oscar Brockett begins with an introduction to the role of dramaturgy in the university, with a particular emphasis on its relationship to the role of the director in American theater.

Mark Bly focuses in particular on the importance of a "questioning spirit." Drawing analogies from physics and Darwin, he warns against simplistic solutions or easy codifications that might shut off future possibilities.

Art Borreca analyzes two of the oldest centers of dramaturgical activity on the university scene: Yale University and the University of Iowa. He finds in these two influential programs contrasting images of the dramaturg's identity: one aligned with the critic; the other with the playwright. He uses these differences to draw distinctions about ways we might enter the rehearsal process and suggests an alternate model for consideration. Borreca's piece addresses several key issues: collaboration, the dramaturgical sensibility, new play development, and the history of dramaturgy in the United States.

This section takes its title from Jane Ann Crum's article. Crum describes exercises and activities she has developed to nurture qualities she finds essential to the practice of dramaturgy. Her piece will, of course, be helpful to teachers in the field and to students devising independent study projects. Even more importantly, by considering how to teach a new discipline, this article clarifies many of its emergent features. She concludes her piece with a consideration of how best to begin a dialogue between directors and dramaturgs.

The second half of this section offers contrasting personal statements about what it means to think of oneself as a dramaturg. Arthur Ballet speaks from years of experience in the field, as someone who was doing dramaturgy before it had that name. His image of the dramaturg is far from that of the "resident intellectual," closer to that of con man and magician.

Dramaturgy is finding increasing application outside of traditional theater: in opera, in film, in puppetry, in dance, in interactive technology. Heidi Gilpin is a leader in both of these latter areas. In her piece, she introduces her pioneering work with William Forsythe and the Frankfurt Ballet. She also articulates a sensibility critical to her work as a dramaturg, taking off from the work of contemporary choreographers and the Renaissance notion of *sprezzatura* (seamless effortlessness).

Mark Lord's essay/poem challenges readers to reconsider the assumptions that underlie their work in the theater. Lord attacks the status quo, but not without presenting his own alternate vision of a kind of theater and the sensibility that would inform it.

In turn, Richard Pettengill takes readers on the journey that brought him from a doctoral program in literature at the University of Chicago to his position as dramaturg and director of arts in education at the Goodman Theatre in Chicago, a journey representative of the paths taken by a number of first generation dramaturgs who did not major in theater at the undergraduate or graduate level but who found in dramaturgy an outlet for their skills and an important place in the theatermaking process. In doing so, he offers insights into the daily work of a dramaturg at a major American theater and the kinds of skills and qualities that work demands.

Michael Lupu, senior dramaturg at the Guthrie Theater in Minneapolis and consulting editor for this volume contrasts dramaturgy as a perhaps dispensible profession with dramaturgy as a fundamental function of theatermaking. Chekhov is his favorite dramaturg, and Lupu tells the reader why.

Finally, Leon Katz, one of the country's most influential teachers of dramaturgy, gives a concise overview of those characteristics that he feels best describe the "compleat dramaturg."

These, of course, are not the only pieces that contribute to the notion of a dramaturgical sensibility (or sensibilities) in this volume: the theme runs throughout. This section, in particular, blends over and into section three, "Models of Collaboration," in that collaboration is central to the dramaturg's work. Other pieces that might be effectively compared and contrasted with the above would those by Royston Coppenger and Travis Preston, Tori Haring-Smith, Norman Frisch and Marianne Weems, and Jayme Koszyn.

Dramaturgy in Education
Introduction
by **Oscar G. Brockett**

OSCAR G. BROCKETT, Professor of Theatre and holder of the Z. T. Scott Family Chair in Drama at the University of Texas, received his Ph.D. from Stanford University and has taught at several universities, including the University of Iowa, Indiana University, the University of Southern California, and Bristol University in England. He is the author of several books, including *History of the Theatre* and *The Essential Theatre,* and numerous articles. He has served as president of the American Theatre Association and editor of the *Educational Theatre Journal,* has held Guggenheim and Fulbright Fellowships, and has received career achievement awards from four theater organizations. He is a member of Literary Managers and Dramaturgs of the Americas (LMDA) and is active in the Dramaturgy Forum of the Association for Theatre in Higher Education (ATHE).

Although dramaturgy is a relative newcomer as a field of study and training within universities, most of its foundational elements are not. Theater history, dramatic literature, theories of drama and theater, dramatic structure and play analysis, and other theatrical skills pertinent to dramaturgy have been included in university curricula during most of the twentieth century. Until recently, however, many of these subjects were characterized as "academic" studies, distinct from those such as directing, acting, and design—the "practical" elements of theatrical performance. These two types of study were often polarized as "reading and talking about" versus "doing." Although these perceived distinctions have not disappeared, the boundaries between them have blurred considerably during the past two decades. Much of the credit for this change goes to the introduction of dramaturgy into the curriculum.

One of dramaturgy's primary goals is to promote integration of the knowledge and perception learned from theater history, dramatic literature, and theory with the skills and expertise needed to realize the potential of a particular script in a particular production in a particular time and place for a particular audience. It discourages the isolation from each other of specialized areas of study and skills, and perhaps more importantly it raises penetrating questions about what is being done, why it is being done that way, and whether the processes being applied are achieving the desired results. Overall, dramaturgy, by drawing together what all too often have been isolated strands of theatrical thought and practice, has become a significant means of integrating theatrical training and practice.

Nevertheless, one cannot claim that dramaturgy was wholly absent in universities before that term came into common use in the United States and courses in dramaturgy were introduced. That aspect of dramaturgy that has to do with developing new scripts (new play dramaturgy) has a long history in

American universities. The pioneering programs at Harvard, Yale, and the University of Iowa are described in this volume by Art Borreca, Steven Weeks, and Robert Brustein. Plays written in these and other programs went through readings, critiques, revisions, and productions. These processes, or variations on them, have continued to be typical as master of fine arts programs in playwriting have profilerated. Only recently, however, has "dramaturgy" been much used to describe these processes.

Early in the century, there was a strong belief that the principles of effective playwriting were clear, and consequently much of the work with playwrights was directed toward bringing plays into conformity with those principles. (See the essays in this volume by Weeks and Katz.) Since the advent of writers such as Samuel Beckett, however, belief in the reliability of received principles has steadily eroded. Today, though traditional structures still are often emphasized, the more common aim is to help writers clarify what they have set out to do and to assess where they have succeeded in accomplishing these aims. This approach respects the vision of the individual playwright and the need to help the playwright realize that vision, however much it may deviate from traditional structural patterns. Script readings and performances allow writers to see their work; teachers, fellow playwriting students, and others often are called upon to describe what they saw in the play, what they understood or did not understand; playwrights then assess performances and responses and use whatever they consider useful in making revisions. (See the essay by Cummings in this volume.) Perhaps the most important innovation is the specialized attempt to train new play dramaturgs who can work closely with the playwright—asking questions, giving reactions, responding to the writer's queries—all with the goal of assisting the writer in clarifying the play's action and overall effectiveness.

Prior to the advent of university dramaturgical training, significant functions of production dramaturgy were performed by directors. In the American theater the director has been seen as the primary decision maker, artistic guide, and final authority on all things having to do with a production, especially interpretation and performance style. Under this system, many productions have been staged efficiently without the assistance of a dramaturg. What, then, was missing that the production dramaturg and production dramaturgical training could supply?

Some longstanding assumptions about directors can illuminate this question. One assumption is that directors are sufficiently educated to bring to all productions an adequate historical, critical, and theoretical base. Another is that, even without such a foundation, directors can discover all they need to know quickly while coping with all the other demands made by production planning. Still another assumption is that directors have such clear vision that they need no help in assessing the effectiveness of productions as they develop. Indeed, there was in the past, and sometimes still is, an unspoken assumption that to question any of these premises is to doubt the director's competence and to undermine directorial authority.

These assumptions about the director have been the greatest stumbling blocks to the acceptance of dramaturgy into university training. To accept assistance with historical, critical, and theoretical preparations has often been interpreted as a challenge to the director's competence. Viewing dramaturgs as threats, some directors have sought to convert them into research assistants or errand runners who provide no input that is not specifically requested, thereby reducing the dramaturg to a position of indisputable inferiority. The production dramaturg's work also has tended to raise questions about the adequacy of preparation undertaken in the past under the typical production timetable, thereby suggesting that the director might be accustomed to relying on insufficient preparation. And the desire of the dramaturg to discuss production concept, interpretation, difficulties encountered during the rehearsal process, and similar matters often has made directors feel that dramaturgs are trying to usurp directorial functions.

Yet it is in those places where directors may feel most threatened that dramaturgs can be most helpful—if they have the director's full cooperation. Directors usually are not trained in depth in theater history, dramatic literature, and theory; there rarely is time during the production process for the director to undertake all the desirable research and analysis; and the director is often too close to the production to recognize when certain scenes are not effective or do not fit the interpretation or concept that supposedly is guiding and unifying the production.

If dramaturgs are to be of significant help, they must learn to ask the right questions, not only for their own enlightenment but also as a guide about how to proceed in working on a production. One effect of dramaturgy should be to orient discussions toward process and not merely toward product. Perhaps the most basic question is: Why this play, at this time, for this audience? Answers to this question provide a focus for interpretation and implementation. They lead to clearer understanding about the goals of the production, which in turn serves as a guide for judging both what is needed and what is effective. Without answers to this question, everything may be partially arbitrary or unfocused and far less meaningful to the participants.

The dramaturg, then, can provide what was missing in previous assumptions about directors: meaningful questioning, information, and discussion, all designed not only to provoke thoughtful consideration of the text but also of the most effective means of achieving the director's vision for this particular production. The dramaturg should be able to:

- bring to any production a broad spectrum of information and critical concerns that can facilitate thoughtful directorial decisions
- raise questions with the director about the proposed directorial concept or interpretation of the script, and
- suggest contextual or critical writings that illuminate the text and interpretational possibilities.

Dramaturgs should also be able to attend rehearsals, regularly or at intervals, and talk to directors about what they have seen, thereby initiating discussions of choices that may more adequately articulate directorial intentions. In this way, dramaturgs become not intruders but partners.

Discussions of the dramaturg's function usually concentrate on work with the playwright and the director, although they should encompass other members of the production team, especially designers and actors. Explorations with designers about imagery, iconography, symbology, space, and the role of each in realizing the production concept, can be as helpful as parallel work done with directors and playwrights. Similarly, discussions with actors about characterization, motivation, the function of each role within the dramatic action, and similar topics can open paths of exploration for actors if the dramaturg is allowed to pursue them.

Although the dramaturg's potential value in the production process can be stated with relative ease, how dramaturgs should be trained and how they are to achieve maximum effectiveness is problematic. How to attain adequate knowledge and how to attain adequate experience, both difficult to define, are major considerations. Nevertheless, there is wide agreement that an effective dramaturg should have a broad education, encompassing not only theater history, dramatic literature, dramatic and theatrical theory, and research and critical methodology but also other fields. Additional knowledge and skills that are useful include foreign languages, literature, philosophy, psychology, history, sociology, music, visual arts, and electronic media (a list not meant to be exhaustive or essentialist). Familiarity with (and preferably experience in) theatrical practice is also essential.

Perhaps most important is knowing how to find out what one wishes to know, because no one can ever master everything that will be needed in dealing with the wide range of playwrights, directors, designers actors, and productions one is apt to encounter as a dramaturg. One cannot begin from scratch on each production. The ideal educational base for the dramaturg is probably summed up in what used to be touted as the goal of a liberal education—to prepare the student for continuous lifelong learning. (See the essay by Bly in this volume.)

Obviously, not all that is pertinent can be learned simultaneously and instantaneously. Like any other, dramaturgical training is gradual and incremental. Just as one does not expect skills to be fully developed and ready for expert practice after the first course in acting, directing, playwriting, or other theater arts, so one must accept that dramaturgical training takes time. It is a combination of accumulated knowledge and practice of the component skills. How long this process takes and precisely what its components should be are matters of debate. Perhaps the best answer would be that the process never ends, for the practicing dramaturg is faced with new problems with each new production.

One of the issues in training dramaturgs is how to provide experience without handicapping a director, playwright, or production. Working as an assistant dramaturg can provide significant experience without involving excessive re-sponsibility for the beginner. Not all those who serve as dramaturgs have had dramaturgical training in the technical sense but may nevertheless perform well within the parameters of a single production. Professors or students spe-cializing in the work of a particular period or dramatist are sometimes asked to serve as dramaturgs on productions of plays about which they are thought to have expert knowledge. This can be highly rewarding and may cement re-lations across departmental boundaries. The implication of this practice is that one might do well to seek out specialized scholars to serve as dramaturgs rather than use dramaturgs trained in a more comprehensive manner. But even if such an arrangement proves positive, the theater's association with the spe-cialist usually ends after one production and the range of services it receives tends to be limited. The specialist may supplement but cannot replace the work of an ongoing, more comprehensively-trained dramaturg.

This truth reflects the wide range of services a dramaturg must be prepared to perform as part of a theater's total program. One service concerns the se-lection of plays for an entire season. Dramaturgs, in addition to assessing the potential of new scripts submitted directly to the theater, are often expected to keep abreast of new and revived plays being performed elsewhere. They should be encouraged, therefore, to read newpapers, magazines, journals, and books about what is going on in other theaters, both in the United States and abroad, which can alert them to plays that might be considered for their own theaters. To make informed recommendations for a theater's season, dra-maturgs must not only be familiar with a wide range of plays from many peri-ods and countries but also be able to assess the potential effectiveness of scripts for their own theaters and audiences.

Dramaturgs may assist in creating production scripts. If a script is in a lan-guage other than English, translation becomes an issue. (See the essays by Weber and Magruder in this volume.) Even if lacking the ability to read the original language, the dramaturg may be expected to assess the relative effec-tiveness of various translations of a script or to secure a new translation. Some-times the dramatic or theatrical conventions that shaped a play are barriers to present-day production and may require limited or extensive alterations. The chorus in Greek tragedy, for example, almost always creates difficulties for modern productions. If the answer is to adapt the script, the dramaturg may undertake that task. (See the essays by Ramírez, Jonas, and Niesen in this vol-ume.) Such problems should be addressed in the dramaturg's training.

Other training may concern educating the audience. Dramaturgs often are asked to supply information about the play, its past, this production, or other matters that will help those who provide publicity to make the play more at-tractive and accessible to an audience. They may also have some responsibil-ity for the printed program, especially if it includes materials that support and elaborate on the interpretation of the script. If the theater has an outreach program that takes productions to specialized audiences or brings audiences to the theater, the dramaturg may be responsible for creating materials used to prepare the audiences for these theatrical experiences. The dramaturg may also be responsible for "talk back" sessions following performances. (See the essays by Pettengill and Kennedy in this volume.)

Most of these responsibilities can be addressed tangibly in preparing students for dramaturgical work. Some of the most important components of success, however, are much more difficult to teach, although students can be alerted to them. One may learn what dramaturgs ideally should offer a production, but what one cannot so easily predict are dynamics of interpersonal relationships between the dramaturg and the director or with other members of a production team. Negotiating the working relationship is perhaps the most crucial element in effective dramaturgical work and one that must be undertaken with each new production unless the relationship is ongoing. How a question is phrased and when it is asked can be as risky as walking through a mine field if the director and dramaturg have not achieved mutual trust. The production dramaturg can do no more than the director is willing to accept, and a new play dramaturg can do no more than the playwright is willing to accept. Trust and respect can be built with the right approach, but how to achieve this is difficult either to teach or to learn. Here, experience probably becomes the best teacher. Nevertheless, dramaturgs in training can be alerted to possible areas of conflict and made aware of potential solutions through class discussions and experienced supervisors.

Interpersonal issues may also be addressed from several angles in dramaturgy courses if they are team-taught (for example, by a dramaturg and a playwright; by dramaturg and a director; or by a dramaturg, a director, and a designer) or include students from areas other than dramaturgy—especially directing, playwriting, and design. Promoting understanding of the problems and needs of each production area and about how cooperation and mutual support can enhance the effectiveness of each may be the greatest service such courses can perform. (See the essays by Crum, Haring-Smith, and Coppenger/Preston in this volume.)

Dramaturgy has now been long enough taught in universities that effective approaches have been developed by many teachers, several of whom have been willing to share their methods with others. The Literary Managers and Dramaturgs of the Americas (LMDA), the primary professional organization for this field, has collected syllabi used by teachers of dramaturgy in various universities and has made them available to all those interested. (On LMDA, see the essay by Abrash in this volume.) The Association for Theatre in Higher Education (ATHE) also has recognized a forum (interest group) among its members for the exploration of dramaturgy and its teaching within the university setting. Members of these organizations have contributed the essays that follow. Together, they do much to explore the potentials and pitfalls of dramaturgy. These essays also clarify how dramaturgy has and is serving as a unifier of scholarship and production in the theater.

Bristling with Multiple Possibilities

by **Mark Bly** *(Copyright 1996 Mark John Bly)*

MARK BLY has just finished his fourth season as Associate Artistic Director of the Yale Repertory Theatre and co-chair of the playwriting, dramaturgy, and dramatic criticism programs at the Yale School of Drama. In the past fifteen years, he has been a dramaturg on more than fifty productions at the Guthrie Theater (Minneapolis), Arena Stage (Washington, D.C.), Seattle Rep, and Yale Repertory Theatre (New Haven, Connecticut), working with directors such as Liviu Ciulei, Garland Wright, Daniel Sullivan, JoAnne Akalaitis, Stan Wojewodski, Jr., Liz Diamond, and Peter Sellars. In 1986, he served as the dramaturg for Emily Mann's Broadway production of *Execution of Justice.* Bly has written for the *Dramatists' Sourcebook* and *Theatre Journal,* and for Yale's *Theater* as a contributing editor and advisory editor. He did his graduate work at Yale, and he created and now heads the Production Notebooks Project for the Literary Managers and Dramaturgs of the Americas. The first volume of *The Production Notebooks: Theatre in Process,* which he edited, is scheduled to be published by Theatre Communications Group in 1996.

During the past twenty years, the near frenetic impulse to define the role of the dramaturg in North American theater has led to an inquiry as impishly elusive as the search for a Grand Unified Theory by contemporary physicists. Our fundamental profile, our *raison d'être,* has been triumphantly proclaimed over the years with whispered "Eurekas" at conferences and in theater boardrooms, but each newly minted nomenclature has been superseded inevitably over the years by yet one more all-encompassing, but ludicrously inadequate, taxonomic gesture. As a theater artist who has helped to pioneer the profession in the United States, I believe such attempts to codify the behavior of dramaturgs and to circumscribe the sphere of their influence have been not only counterproductive and limiting, but also harmful to our collective evolution as artists.

None of this is to say, however, that I cannot—when pressed—describe what I do, envision a collective future, or profess a philosophy of how dramaturgy might be practiced and taught today. But most of my ideas focus on the opening up of possibilities for artistic expression rather than limiting or narrowly defining them.

In my more whimsical moments, I like to imagine we dramaturgs have more in common perhaps with electrons or other inhabitants of the subatomic world than we might readily divine. I encountered recently an essay entitled "Quantum Consciousness" by the contemporary science writer David

---

An earlier version of this essay was delivered at the Literary Managers and Dramaturgs of the Americas Conference in Atlanta in June 1994. That version was subsequently published in Theatre Symposium *3 (1995): 12-17.*

H. Freedman, who, in describing the life of a subatomic particle, serendipitously characterized the life of a dramaturg in the "unrelentingly strange" realm of theater:

> Quantum mechanics is an unrelentingly strange theory. Among other things, it tells us that an electron or another denizen of the subatomic world tends to exist in a multitude of states all at once: it is simultaneously here and there, moving fast and slowly, spinning one way and the other. But at the moment the electron interacts with ordinary matter or energy—when it smacks into the molecules in a detector, for example, or is bombarded by a beam of light—the disturbance somehow causes the electron to "choose" a single state.[1]

In my professional life during the past fifteen years, I have had to respond to narrow definitions of my position, especially after "smacking into" the egos of other members of a production team. I have had to live with restrictive "creative givens" and known what it means to be "bombarded" by a concept that forces an artist to "choose" prematurely a "single state" or approach to a classic or a new play. It has been at such moments that I have felt my voice was limited, static, most muted, devoid of any real power, and yet, ironically, most needed.

The fundamental impulse behind all of my work as a dramaturg can be described by the phrase, "I question." Years ago, I read an interview, "Utopia as the Past Conserved," which has been critical to my evolution as an artist and continues to inform whatever dramaturgical voice I bring to my work today. Peter Stein and his dramaturg, Dieter Stürm, noted in the interview that the "doubting process" was a central maxim of all of their rehearsal work in the 1970s at the Schaubühne in Berlin. For them, this doubting entailed "a destruction of illusionary knowledge *(Scheinwissen)* and the questioning of precipitous analyses."[2]

When pressed for a definition of what it is that I do as a dramaturg, both in a rehearsal hall and in the theater at large, I generally answer, "I question." I also believe as the contemporary French writer Hélène Cixous observes in her essay on Rembrandt, "The Last Painting or The Portrait of God," that true understanding comes only to that artist who achieves a "second innocence, the one that comes after knowing, the one that no longer knows, the one that knows how not to know."[3]

In my role as a teacher and dramaturg at Yale, I offer a course, Principles of Dramaturgy, which has been taught during the past two decades by other professors with divergent philosophies. I have designed the class to expose students to the diverse skills and the creative thinking required to practice dramaturgy both in production and on a larger institutional level. The first-year dramaturgy students are required to take the two-semester course, but other students, particularly playwrights and directors, may attend as well. The class is connected directly to the first-year classical and new play projects.

The work of the individual dramaturg assigned to each project is discussed in class throughout the production's different stages. These projects are supervised by the resident dramaturg and me, as we attend rehearsals regularly and conduct weekly tutorials with the students.

A major aspect of their training centers on the creation of production casebooks. The students are taught to create in advance of rehearsal, during the planning stages of a production, a casebook that opens with a letter to the director. This letter is often one of the first manifestations of the dramaturg's "questioning spirit," helping to challenge fixed notions about the play to be staged. The dramaturg's letter to the director should reflect initial discussions on the text, casting and design; major directorial, stylistic, and imagistic approaches; character interpretations; and thematic explorations from past productions. Copies of primary research materials are included in the casebook.

The letter also discusses fundamental questions raised by the act of staging the play. The dramaturgy students are urged to avoid using the term "concept" in the letter and to question overly conceptual productions that strive for a "perfect fit," shoehorning the play and blistering it beyond recognition. I encourage the students to stay away from such reductive impulses and to embrace alternatives that amplify instead. They are told to concentrate on asking thought-provoking questions: What drew you as a director to this play? What images or sounds did you encounter reading the play? How do you think these sensory elements will feed or inform your staging? What questions does the play raise for you about our culture? About our society today? As an audience encounters your production, *what might lodge in their brains?* What would be so essential in your staging of this classic or new play that if an audience missed it you would be disappointed?

The casebook should contain, after this letter, a diversity of resource materials. It might offer, but not be limited to the following elements, depending upon whether the project is a classic or a new play: (1) pertinent cultural, historical, and social background of the play; (2) significant biographical information on the playwright that may help to illuminate critical issues in the play; (3) commentary by the playwright in the form of interviews, letters, or passages from other works by the writer; (4) relevant criticism or commentary by other artists or critics; (5) images from painters, sculptors, and photographers that can feed, complement, and challenge the work of the director and other artists on the project; (6) a listing and brief commentary on related films and music and their direct or associative value for the stage production; and (7) a highly selective production history of the play. The emphasis is placed on making the casebook a tool for exploration, rather than a prescriptive, formulistic guide to staging a particular play. For inspiration and enlightenment, we examine the existing production casebooks of some of the United States's leading dramaturgs.

This year-long class also focuses on a wide range of other topics related to dramaturgy: (1) the history of the dramaturgical profession; (2) the emergence of modern art forms; (3) principles of comedy and tragedy; (4) theater in relation to its community; (5) contemporary issues in dramaturgy and playwriting; (6) the reading and evaluation of new scripts; and (7) the art of cutting classical texts and new plays.

The students are exposed to Lessing's *Hamburg Dramaturgy,* of course, but much else, too: Aristotle's *Poetics;* Mikhail Bakhtin's *Rabelais and His World,* which focuses on the carnival impulse of laughter and anarchic irreverence; George Meredith's "An Essay on Comedy," and its companion essay, "Laughter," by Henri Bergson, which investigates the notion that "laughter is an exposure of our ready-made gestures and values"; Oscar Wilde's "The Decay of Lying," with its exploration of art that does not rely on reality for its efficacy; Elinor Fuchs's essay "The Death of Character," chronicling the influence of the Post-Modern movement in American theater; "Lamia" by John Keats, in which the poet rages against the obsessive desire to dissect all reality, admonishing those who would dare to "unweave a rainbow"; excerpts from Gertrude Stein's *Picasso* and *The Making of the Americans,* focusing on cubism and her use of the "continuous present" in her writing; Kenneth Tynan in his role as Olivier's dramaturg at the National Theatre; Jan Kott's *Shakespeare Our Contemporary* and how he became a dramaturgical "animus" outside of the rehearsal hall; Francis Fergusson's book *The Idea of the Theater* and his discussion of the need for theater to be at the center of a community; Alan Lightman's *Einstein's Dreams,* an imaginative exploration of alternative views of time and space; the plays and writing strategies of Peter Barnes, Caryl Churchill, Maria Irene Fornes, John Guare, Len Jenkin, Eric Overmyer and Suzan-Lori Parks. During the year we watch a few selected films: Buster Keaton's *Sherlock, Jr.,* which gives insights into the workings of comedy; and Joel and Ethan Coen's *Blood Simple* and Dennis Potter's *The Singing Detective,* both of which play imaginatively with linear and nonlinear narrative strategies.

We also discuss a wide spectrum of art perspectives and movements, dipping into selected interdisciplinary chapters of Sandro Sproccati's *Guide to Art* and Arnold Hauser's four-volume survey, *The Social History of Art.* The students pore over the work of artists such as Bacon, Beckmann, de Chirico, Clemente, Delvaux, Dix, Ernst, Friedrich, Giotto, Goya, Grosz, Kahlo, Lindner, Magritte, Munch, Rauschenberg, Schiele, Schwarzer, Serov, and Tooker. This emphasis on visual artists has grown out of my desire to make the students more aware of such resources. As part of a casebook, this visual art can be used to "feed" directors, designers, and actors in their creative work. And it can provide images and inspiration for dramaturg-created theater programs that go beyond columns of deadly copy.

And once a year, I bring to class a forty-pound limestone rock from the Middle Ordovician period (475 million years ago). This rock, which I found at the base of an outcrop near the Mississippi River in east central Minnesota, contains a one-inch "death layer" of marine fossils. I use this sedimentary rock as a geological tool to debunk the prevailing myths surrounding the comparative values of objectivity and subjectivity in the dramaturg's process, leaving the students with a greater awareness of how difficult it is to interpret adequately an event by merely observing its precipitate.

Early in the dramaturgs' first semester, I conduct a series of classes explicitly entitled The Questioning Spirit and the Creative Process, which is obviously germane and central to this discussion. As mentioned previously, I urge the students to question "creative givens" and to avoid "precipitous analysis" in their work as dramaturgs. As a way of illustrating the need for such an approach, we read and discuss Julian Barnes's essay, "Shipwreck," in his book, *The History of the World in 10 1/2 Chapters,* in which the author looks at Gericault's painting *The Raft of the Medusa* and what the artist chose not to paint; two essays by Mac Wellman that question our obsession with Euclidian, linear playwriting and what he unaffectionately calls "geezer" theater: "The Theater of Good Intentions" and "A Chrestomathy of 22 Answers to 22 Wholly Unaskable and Unrelated Questions Concerning Political and Poetic Theater"; and, finally, the most enlightening dramaturgical tool I have encountered in recent memory, Stephen Jay Gould's essay, "Full of Hot Air," on the biological evolution of swim bladders and lungs, and redundancy as a creative principle.

For those who are not familiar with Stephen Jay Gould and his free-ranging monthly column in *Natural History* magazine, he is a professor of geology at Harvard with an interest in the history of science, population biology, racial biases, "flamingos' smiles," and why there are no .400 hitters in baseball today. Gould's essay focuses on what he calls an "instructive error" that Charles Darwin made in his revolutionary work, *The Origin of Species by Means of Natural Selection.* Darwin made an error of "thoughtless convention," or what Gould describes as "passive repetitions of standard cultural assumptions stated so automatically, or so deeply (and silently) embedded within the structure of an argument, that we scarcely detect their presence."[4] I usually point out to my students that perhaps there is more than a superficial kinship between these "passive repetitions of standard cultural assumptions" and the German *Scheinwissen* or "illusionary knowledge."

The error Darwin made was to decide that lungs evolved from fish swim bladders, based on his false assumptions about biological progress. Gould diagnoses the error: "What can be wrong with Darwin's claim? The two organs are homologous, right? Right. Terrestrial vertebrates evolved from fishes, right? Yes, again. So lungs must have evolved from swim bladders, right? Wrong, dead wrong. Swim bladders evolved from lungs."[5]

Gould goes on to point out the basic fallacies behind Darwin's "intuitively obvious" assertions:

> . . . first, the false assumption of progress, which makes the lung a
> "higher" organ than a swim bladder and thus unfit for creatures on the
> bottom; second, and more seriously, the confusion of ladders and

bushes, or sequences and branching orders. Fish—amphibian—reptile—mammal is not *the* road of change among vertebrates; it represents only one pathway among thousands in the complexly branching bush of vertebrate evolution. . . .[6]

This is a critical distinction for dramaturgs to remember. Too often we intuitively, reflexively perceive art or the human experience as behaving or moving in a tidy, linear fashion. It is not unlike one of those misleading anthropological "Hominoids on Parade" posters where a series of hominoids are depicted as slowly, but inexorably shedding their primitive characteristics until *"he"* is walking erect and confidently into a biologically inevitable future as the pinnacle of the evolutionary ladder. However, neither evolution nor art moves in such an efficient, directed pattern. For that matter, neither should the profession of dramaturgy be viewed as merely evolving along a single, inevitable evolutionary path.

Gould goes on to make yet one more observation that I insist on sharing with my students: *redundancy* as a source of creativity. He alludes to why Darwin devoted so much attention to swim bladders and lungs in *The Origin of Species.* Darwin cites these organs as examples of his "one-for-two principle" (often single organs perform more than one function); and the "two-for-one principle" (vital functions can be performed simultaneously by more than one organ).

Gould is fascinated by Darwin's argument concerning these two principles, for as he notes with great enthusiasm:

> Neither situation is rare, and the two phenomena—one-for-two and two-for-one—are not really separate at all. Both are expressions of a deeper, and profoundly important, principle—*redundancy* as the ground of creativity in any form. . . .
>
> . . . evolution is a messy process brimming with redundancy. An organ might be molded by natural selection for advantages in one role, but anything complex has a range of other potential uses by virtue of inherited structure. . . .
>
> . . . rules of structure, deeper than natural selection itself, guarantee that complex features must bristle with multiple possibilities and evolution wins its required flexibility thanks to messiness, redundancy, and lack of perfect fit. . . .
>
> How sad then that we live in a culture almost dedicated to wiping out the leisure of ambiguity and the creative joy of redundancy.[7]

In this age of ubiquitous specialization, the dramaturg can become a model of redundancy, "bristling with multiple possibilities," and not limited to a single task or one evolutionary path. On individual projects, the dramaturg can be that artist who functions in a multifaceted manner helping the director and other artists to develop and shape the sociological, textual, directing, acting, and design values. In this way dramaturgs are perfect illustrations of Darwin's one-for-two principle, for the more gifted ones may perform more than a single function on a production.

Alternately, a dramaturg may appear to overlap with other artists in their duties, especially in interpreting the play and shaping the production, so that an apparent redundancy may be manifested. But it is a redundancy that often leads to an increased creativity, and it is an example of Darwin's two-for-one principle. Redundancy, in both cases, can be a creative fount in service of a larger artistic impulse underlying the production's development.

I believe that attempts to codify the role of the dramaturg in the United States are simply premature. We need to suppress those urges to limit, to define for all time the rules, behavior, and goals of this seemingly elusive profession. Let us not yield to the temptation to slavishly justify our existence or to deny our mutative powers. We should remember, perhaps with a prescient grin, that the dramaturg's function in the theater now is in an embryonic stage not unlike the role of the director nearly two centuries ago, when actors and playwrights wondered why this strange creature should be allowed to exist within their magic circle. Finally, in our more reflective moments, let us envision a time in the not too distant future when Darwin's closing words of wonder in *The Origin of Species* may apply to this profession "bristling with multiple possibilities":

> ... from so simple a beginning endless forms most beautiful and most wonderful have been, and are being evolved.[8]

SELECTED BIBLIOGRAPHY

Bakhtin, Mikhail. *Rabelais and His World.* Trans. Hélène Iswolsky. Bloomington: Indiana University Press, 1984.

Barnes, Julian. *A History of the World in 10 1/2 Chapters.* New York: Vintage International, 1990. 113–139.

Bharucha, Rustom, Janice Paran, Laurence Shyer, and Joel Schechter. "Directors, Dramaturgs, and War in Poland: An Interview with Jan Kott." *Theater* 14.2 (1983): 27–31.

Bly, Mark. "American Production Dramaturgs: An Introduction and Seven Interviews." *Theater* 17.3 (1986): 5–6. See also pp. 7–62 of this issue, for which Bly served as special editor.

Cixous, Hélène. "The Last Painting or the Portrait of God." Trans. Sarah Cornell, Susan Sellers, and Deborah Jenson. *"Coming to Writing" and other Essays.* Ed. Deborah Jenson. Cambridge, Massachusetts: Harvard University Press, 1991. 104–131.

Darwin, Charles. *The Origin of Species.* New York: Random House, 1993.

Fergusson, Francis. *The Idea of a Theater: The Art of Drama in Changing Perspective.* Garden City, New York: Doubleday Anchor Books, 1954.

Fuchs, Elinor. "The Death of Character." *Theatre Communications* 5.3 (1983): 1–6.

Gould, Stephen Jay. "Full of Hot Air." *Natural History* (October 1989): 28–38.

Hauser, Arnold. *The Social History of Art.* 4 vols. New York: Vintage Books, 1951.

Keats, John. "Lamia." *English Romantic Writers*. Ed. David Perkins. New York: Harcourt Brace Jovanovich, 1967. 1188–1197.

Kott, Jan. *Shakespeare Our Contemporary*. Trans. Boleslaw Taborski. New York: W.W. Norton & Company, Inc., 1974.

Krajewska-Wieczorck, Anna. "Still Contemporary: A Conversation with Jan Kott." *Theater* 25.3 (1995): 85–89.

Lessing, Gotthold Ephraim. *Hamburg Dramaturgy*. Trans. Helen Zimmern. New York: Dover Publications, 1962.

Lightman, Alan. *Einstein's Dreams*. New York: Warner Books, 1994.

Meredith, George and Henri Bergson. *Comedy*. Garden City, New York: Doubleday Anchor Books, 1956.

Schechter, Joel. "Lessing, Jugglers and Dramaturgs." *Theater* 7.1 (1975/76): 94–103.

Sproccati, Sandro, ed. *A Guide to Art*. New York: Harry N. Abrams, 1992.

Stein, Gertrude. *The Making of the Americans*. Normal, Illinois: Dalkey Archive Press, 1995.

—*Picasso*. New York: Dover Publications, 1984.

Tynan, Kenneth. "The Critic Comes Full Circle." *Theatre Quarterly* 1.2 (1971): 37–48.

Wellman, Mac. "A Chrestomathy of 22 Answers to 22 Wholly Unaskable and Unrelated Questions Concerning Political and Poetic Theater." *Theater* 24.1 (1993) 43–51.

—"The Theater of Good Intentions." *Performing Arts Journal* 8.3 (1984): 59–70.

Wilde, Oscar. "The Decay of Lying." *The Complete Works of Oscar Wilde*. London: Hamlyn, 1986. 825–843.

Dramaturging New Play Dramaturgy:
The Yale and Iowa Ideals
by **Art Borreca**

ART BORRECA is Assistant Professor of Theatre History, Literature, Theory, and Dramaturgy at the University of Iowa, where he serves as dramaturg to the Iowa Playwrights Workshop. He has worked as a dramaturg on projects at the Yale Repertory Theatre, New York Theatre Workshop, O'Neill Theater Center (Waterford, Connecticut), and other theaters, and in the University of Iowa's Partnership-in-the-Arts program, which develops new works for the theater through professional residencies. His scholarly and critical writing has appeared in *TDR, Modern Drama, Theatre Journal,* and several collections, including *What is Dramaturgy?* (Peter Lang, 1995). He is currently completing a book, *Remaking History: British Historical Drama since 1956,* for Southern Illinois University Press.

The Yale School of Drama and the University of Iowa share a progressive history in theater education, especially in the training of playwrights. In the past thirty years, dramaturgy has become an important part of that history. In the process, Yale and Iowa have developed different, if overlapping, answers to the question of how dramaturgy might move scholarship, criticism, theory and the creation of new theater closer together. In its basic form, the history of new play dramaturgy at Yale and Iowa is that of the individuals—Joel Schechter, Leon Katz, Mark Bly, Oscar Brownstein, and others—who have taught and practiced it, and of the diverse models of dramaturgical practice they have presented to their students. Despite variations in these models, however, Yale and Iowa have repeatedly aspired to certain ideals of new play dramaturgy: those of the Yale critic who is brought inside the theatrical process to help improve the artistic and intellectual quality of the play or the production, and of the Iowa playwright/dramaturg—and, more recently, scholar/dramaturg—who serves as an empathic facilitator of the playwright's and director's process and vision.

Both ideals run up against the kinds of problems that arise from any attempt to translate theory into practice. As a critical resource, Yale dramaturgs can help protect the play and the production from misguided textual interpretation and superficial theatrical thinking, yet they can also find that their critical evaluation of the work-in-process suppresses their empathy for artists engaged in that process. In contrast, the Iowa ideal can lead dramaturgs to empathize with the playwright's and director's creative struggles at the expense of encouraging what is best for the play or production.

As a former Yale dramaturgy student now on the faculty at Iowa, I have worked in both the Yale and Iowa traditions, alternately thriving on and struggling with the tasks of distinguishing the process from the product, the artist's ego from the work, and my own ego from my dramaturgical function. If I had to draw a single lesson from my experience, it would be that the operational conditions of university-based new play dramaturgy (curricula, dramaturgical guidelines, and so on) have ideals inscribed within them, and that contradictions arising from those ideals must be confronted for effective dramaturgy to take place. These contradictions have special relevance now, when theater departments across the country have been revising their history, literature, and criticism programs to include dramaturgy, and when dramaturgy has become a subject for theses, dissertations, and books such as this one. Dramaturgs need to be vigilant about the invisible assumptions underlying their practice, so that they can effectively "dramaturg" their own teaching and programs as well as the work of student playwrights and dramaturgs. A critical step toward that kind of dramaturgy is to historicize the traditions in which one works.

THE YALE CRITIC/DRAMATURG

The tradition of the Yale critic/dramaturg has two beginnings. The first occurred in 1925, when George Pierce Baker moved from Harvard to Yale in order to head its new Department of Drama in the School of Fine Arts. At Harvard, Baker had demonstrated that the training of playwrights was the legitimate object of universities; at Yale he placed his famous 47 Workshop—a new-play production workshop that grew out of his playwriting course—at the center of the first drama department in the country to offer a master of fine arts degree (MFA).[9] (For more detail on Baker, see Stephen Weeks's essay in this collection.) Without being known as such, Baker was Yale's first critic/dramaturg: the first in a line of Yale playwriting instructors—Baker, John Gassner, Richard Gilman—who were primarily critics rather than creative writers. Despite the national proliferation of playwright-teachers in the past thirty years, Yale has regularly employed critics as well as playwrights to set the theatrical standards to which playwriting students should aspire. And today the 47 Workshop (known as Drama 47) remains at the center of the Yale School of Drama's new play activity.

The second beginning for the Yale critic/dramaturg was the founding in 1966 of the Yale Repertory Theatre (Yale Rep) as the professional training ground of the Yale School of Drama. That year the School of Drama also introduced the doctor of fine arts (DFA) program in dramatic literature and criticism. As Robert Brustein explains in this collection and elsewhere, he designed the program to train professional critics; however, the Yale Rep soon employed DFA students to carry out such dramaturgical tasks as script evaluation and the writing of program notes, and also hired graduates of the program as literary managers.[10] (See Brustein's excerpt in this collection from "The Future of an Un-American Activity.") In 1974 the School of Drama initiated a scheme by which all literature/criticism students were required to serve as dramaturgs on Yale Rep productions; in 1977 Brustein and the DFA faculty reworked the literature/criticism program into an MFA/DFA program in dramaturgy and dramatic criticism.[11]

The new program had, in Robert Brustein's words, the explicitly stated objective to turn "alienated critics" into "helpful and creative associates."[12] Jonathan Marks, literary manager of the Rep at the time of the program's founding, explains the rationale for this objective in his 1977 "Dramaturg's Guide: A Handbook for Student Dramaturgs at the Yale School of Drama and Yale Repertory Theatre:"

> [The Yale Repertory Theatre and the Yale School of Drama] are imbued with the philosophy that the theater must participate in the intellectual life of its age, and that the intellectual aspect of the theater, too often scorned by American theater professionals, must be ever present and sound. . . .
> The goals of the program [are] . . . to resolve the antipathy between the intellecual and the practical, and to fuse the two into an organic whole.[13]

The question the Yale program has repeatedly faced is: How can critical skills be employed to effect such fusion? In 1977 a partial answer came from the artistic goals and practical needs of the Yale Rep. The Rep aspired to the repertory ideal of the European municipal theaters; accordingly, the dramaturgy/criticism program would follow the German tradition of dramaturgy as "in-house criticism." In addition to evaluating scripts and writing program notes, critic/dramaturgs would conduct research for directors and designers, write articles for subscriber newsletters, compose study guides for student groups, and serve as liaisons between productions and the press and box offices. They would also be assigned to productions for which they would observe rehearsals and make themselves available as critical resources for directors, actors, and designers.[14]

Less clear was exactly *how* the in-house critic's observations of the process would contribute to—and make a difference in—productions; or conversely, how the Rep would make in-house criticism a regular part of its production process, such that research, program notes, study guides, and newsletter articles would be fundamental rather than ornamental to that process. Marks's "Guide" exhorts student dramaturgs to attend rehearsals as much as possible and to be always available for consultation with their directors. However:

> You and your critical skill are there as a resource, ready in case the director feels he needs your opinion. Anything is possible: he may need you, call upon you, and use your advice to stunning effect; he may call upon you and ignore you; he may need you and not know it; or he simply may not need you. . . . Whether he will call on you or not depends

> largely on his personality and work method, yours, the relationship you
> have established—in short, on chemistry. . . . He will let you know if he
> wants to hear from you.[15]

In other words, although the program was founded on the principle that students can be trained as critic/dramaturgs who serve a purpose necessary to all theater, they were in fact being trained as *critics* who needed to soften their *critical* voices when performing their dramaturgical roles.

As dramaturgs came to establish themselves within the American theater in the 1970s and '80s, the dramaturgy/criticism program developed a more systematic approach to production dramaturgy at the Rep. Yet the system continued to be driven by the need for students to adapt their critical instincts to the working methods of professional directors and playwrights who might see dramaturgs as unnecessary or fear having criticism students in the rehearsal room. In his version of the "Dramaturg's Guide," Leon Katz, cohead (with Richard Gilman) of the program from 1983 to 1988, explains when, where, and how student dramaturgs should participate in the production process. For example, student dramaturgs should hold preproduction meetings with the director, in which they should present him or her with research and learn about his or her approach to the play; they should take notes at read-throughs, early blocking rehearsals, run-throughs, and dress rehearsals; and they should skip technical and work rehearsals in order to maintain a critical distance from the production. Despite their copious note taking, however, dramaturgs should provide their notes not to the director but to the artistic director (at the time, Lloyd Richards).[16] Furthermore:

> For the Dramaturg to avoid not being consulted at all, he must win the
> Director's respect for his judgment and his understanding of the rehearsal
> process, and the Director's confidence in his supportive intent.[17]

Clearly, such guidelines arose from a need to rethink criticism in terms of how it might function inside the process, and to devise a sensible and respectful decorum for dramaturgy students consulting with professional directors. Dramaturgs were new to the American theater—they still are—and many directors and playwrights were unused to and resistant to having dramaturgs around. However, what is striking in both Marks's and Katz's guidelines is the degree to which the dialogue between student dramaturgs and professional directors is made to depend on the students, who have to prove their integrity as creative collaborators, rather than on a principle and method of integrating critic/dramaturgs into the production process. The proof was necessary because the Rep perceived dramaturgy students primarily as potentially destructive critics rather than as constructive collaborators; the institution could not or did not develop regular procedures for enabling students to synthesize their critical sensibilities with dramaturgical practice. Although the Rep's actors, directors, and designers were expected to serve as mentors to MFA students in those fields, it was assumed that the Rep's directors would not perform a similar role in relation to dramaturgy students. And while the Rep's resident literary managers and dramaturgs, including Marks, Schechter, Michael Cadden, and Gitta Honegger, served as mentors to student dramaturgs, such mentoring itself took place in an institution that viewed dramaturgy as a secondary function of critics.[18]

Ultimately Marks's and Katz's guidelines reflected the need to rethink the attitudes and practices of a program founded to train critics in the tradition of Brustein, Gilman, and Stanley Kauffmann, all of whom have been members of the Yale faculty. These critics are, in Brustein's words, "[SuperCritics] in the role of Samson slaying the Philistines."[19] They take an adamantly adversarial stance in relation to the theatrical status quo. They are "cruel in order to be kind": they decry aesthetically unfruitful practices in order to more forcefully praise what are, in their view, the highest aesthetic achievements. Despite several revisions of the dramaturgy/criticism curriculum since the 1970s, its one unchanging element has been a series of workshops in critical writing taught by Gilman, Kauffmann, and, more recently, Gordon Rogoff and Erika Munk. The editions of the "Dramaturg's Guide" were designed to caution student dramaturgs from taking the kind of adversaral stance they were cultivating in those workshops. As Marks wrote:

> A "pure" critic must be disinterested, impartial, frank and unfettered; an "in-house" critic must be interested, partial, discreet and loyally bound to his production. . . .
>
> Richard Gilman has written of the necessity for destructive criticism and the fallacy of the inherent notion of constructive criticism and, in the domain of published criticism, he is right; for the purposes of the dramaturg, however, opposite standards obtain.[20]

Thus, while the Dramaturgy and Dramatic Criticism program sought "to resolve the antipathy betwen the intellectual and the practical," the resolution was left to the *chance* that the intellectual (the student dramaturg) and the practitioner (the director or playwright) *might* find a way of working together.

The antipathy has shown up not only in the program's guidelines for decorum but in such required dramaturgical tools as production logs and protocols. The tradition of keeping logs at Yale was begun in 1977—one reason students had to attend reherasals regularly was to keep thorough logs—and has been revived there recently by Mark Bly, who became Associate Artistic Director of the Yale Rep and cohead (with Richard Gilman) of the dramaturgy program in 1990. A log is a regular diary of observations about the production process and a running critique of the production; it may contain "observations, judgments, gossip, jokes—anything goes."[21] Ideally the log serves as a source of critical insight for the dramaturg, and might become an invaluable record of the process, including the dramaturg's contributions to it. In contrast to the log, a protocol is a set of materials prepared in advance of rehearsals for the director, designers, and actors. According to Leon Katz, these materials should include historical and sociocultural background on the play; relevant biographical information about the playwright and an examination of the play's place in his or her work; a critical history of the play and its production; and an extensive analysis of the play in terms of how and why it might be produced.[22] Like the log, the protocol has an ideal function: to serve as the basis for the dramaturg's dialogue with the director and playwright. In fact, it should be designed to serve the particular research and analytical needs of the production, whether of an old or new play.

In a context in which dramaturgs are primarily critics, however, the function of logs is to enable students to exercise their critical engagement with the work and the process, whatever their role in that process; similarly, the function of protocols is to guarantee that student dramaturgs provide directors with research and criticism, whatever their influence on the production. Although it is undeniably important for student dramaturgs to develop their skills in research, analysis, and the documentation of productions, in a program that distinguishes criticism from dramaturgy logs and protocols can merely reflect and even reinforce the practical divorce between the critic/dramaturg and the process. Their value can remain predominantly critical and historical without becoming authentically dramaturgical.

During my enrollment in the MFA program (1983–86), Leon Katz had recently added protocol, translation, and bibliography requirements to the program, as well as an intensive six-semester survey of Western theater history and literature. The new requirements were designed to knit the critical and the dramaturgical together more tightly and to train what Katz calls the "compleat dramaturg."[23] However, Katz's efforts could not break down the separation between critic and dramaturg written into the program's history and its relationship to the Rep; his new requirements enhanced the scholarly element within the unsynthesized compound of criticism/dramaturgy. Many students found themselves having to negotiate a truce among the demands of Katz's history and literature courses, the criticism workshops, and production dramaturgy assignments, and even to choose whether they were primarily scholars, critics, *or* dramaturgs. Upon Katz's retirement from Yale in 1989, the separation among these areas was institutionalized in a system of curricular tracking, in which students elect to focus on either history/literature, criticism, or production dramaturgy.

The divorce between the critical and the dramaturgical (or the intellectual and the practical) has had several ramifications for the training of new play dramaturgs at Yale. In the 1970s and 1980s, the divorce was written into the relationship between the dramaturgy and playwriting programs. Although they shared faculty—Gilman in the 1970s, Katz in the 1980s—they operated independently of each other, with separate missions and curricula. The programs interacted with each other on the common ground defined by those missions, but not in the spirit of concerted integration. After their first year of the program, students who preferred to work on classic texts could avoid living playwrights altogether. An exception to this was a course in collaboration, the first semester of which was taken by all first-year actors, directors, dramaturgs, playwrights, and stage managers. (The second semester was taken only by directors and dramaturgs, who collaborated in preparing classic verse plays for production in the second year.) In the first semester, playwrights, directors, and dramaturgs were assigned to collaborate with one another in developing and staging a one-act play based on a short piece of prose fiction, and to present it—through further collaboration with first-year actors, designers, and stage managers—in a workshop production. The dramaturg's work might include research; discussions with the playwright and director of the original story and the playwright's various drafts of the play; and taking notes at readings and rehearsals. The course created stable conditions for playwrights and directors to begin to draw on dramaturgs as critical resources.

Nevertheless, although Katz used this course to impart his methods of dramaturgical analysis and consultation, the course initiated but did not facilitate playwright/director/dramaturg collaborations. Student dramaturgs could learn only by chance how to translate a critical and analytical vocabulary into terms that would help artists fulfill their visions; the kinds of questions they might use to "jump-start" a stalled playwright's process; what their roles should be in conflicts between directors and playwrights; or how to turn their most destructive critical assessments of a play into constructive dialogue. Students had to find their own ways of working as in-process critics and of dealing with the often explosive "chemistry" of playwright/dramaturg/director collaborations. In encountering the intricacies of the process, the only thing they could rely on was, to borrow a phrase from W. H. Auden, "the chameleon's discretion." Yet it was difficult to exercise such discretion when one was at the same time being trained as an uncompromising advocate of high critical standards. One could find oneself advocating such standards and alienating one's collaborators, supporting one's collaborators psychologically and emotionally yet lacking the means to facilitate their work; or trying both to advocate standards and stimulate the process but ending up doing neither. The critical training at Yale was essentialist and aestheticist: it taught dramaturgy students that their primary responsibility was to the aesthetics of the text and its "truest" possible representation on stage. But the program provided few ways to look at a play or production outside the traditional means of examining it as if it were already finished, or as if it could become only one ultimately-to-be-analyzed and -evaluated thing.

In 1990 Mark Bly and Stan Wojewodski, Jr., the new dean of the Drama School and artistic director of the Yale Rep, combined the school's playwriting and dramaturgy programs into a single program in order to create a context in which the tensions between criticism and dramaturgy could be examined and made part of the theatrical process. According to Bly, combining the programs has placed a new emphasis on collaboration between playwriting and dramaturgy students as well as their shared training as theater practitioners. Wojewodski, Jr. and Bly have reconceived the first-year course in collaboration as well as created two new courses in which playwrights and dramaturgs work together. In the first semester of the old collaboration course, directors, designers, dramaturgs, and playwrights collaborate on full studio productions of classical projects. According to Bly, this course makes the rethinking of the classics the foundation for students' later work on both classical and new plays. The two new courses are designed to reinforce this foundation, and to "break down the barriers" between playwrights and dramaturgs even further. In one course, first-year dramaturgy and playwriting students examinine their concurrent work and working process in the collaboration course, and then collaborate with first-year directors on the development and production of new plays. In the other course, actors, directors, playwrights, and dramaturgs cross the practical boundaries of their disciplines—for example, dramaturgs and playwrights act and direct, actors and directors work as dramaturgs, and so on—while working on nontraditional theatrical projects.[24]

These new courses are intended to cultivate the role of the dramaturg as an integral figure in the collaborative process. Bly explains that he teaches dramaturgs to provide "descriptive commentary of a play rather than destructive criticism of it"; to isolate a play's strengths; to help playwrights who reach an impasse to get back to their original sensory impulses; and to protect aspects of the play essential to its performance.[25] The question is: Can such courses reconceive the program so that the impulses of critics-in-training can be reconciled—or placed in creative tension—with those of dramaturgical collaborators, and in a manner that doesn't leave the reconciliation to individual experience, chance, and chemistry? Can the courses break down the historically entrenched assumption that the best dramaturgs are adversarial critics who temper the expression of their critical perceptions for their collaborators?

FROM PLAYWRIGHT/DRAMATURG TO SCHOLAR/DRAMATURG AT IOWA

In 1929, the University of Iowa appointed E. C. Mabie, a professor in the Department of Speech, to head a newly founded Department of Speech and Dramatic Art, which established as one of its main objectives the nurturing of young playwrights and the production of new plays.[26] At Iowa, dramaturgy and dramaturgy training, which possess a less rich history than at Yale, have always been linked directly to this objective. In the 1970s Oscar Brownstein established a course in dramaturgy within the MFA program in playwriting, known as the Iowa Playwrights Workshop. He also initiated a program by which student playwrights worked regularly with student, faculty, and visiting directors on the production of classical plays. According to Brownstein, the program encountered some resistance from faculty and professionals.[27] The playwright/dramaturg's job was to serve, in Brownstein's words, as a "surrogate for an absent playwright," someone who provides a playwright's perspective on the text and its interpretation; contributes to the director's analysis of the play for production; and finds translations, makes cuts in the script, and deals with other textual matters. Playwright/dramaturgs also attended rehearsals to provide an "inside/outside" perspective on the development of the production's concept.[28] On the production of new plays, playwright/dramaturgs had the same responsibilities, only their role became "advisory and mediative."[29] Thus, Brownstein conceived of playwright/dramaturgs as empathic facilitators of artists' work, whose empathy arises from their special knowledge of the writing process.

Although the University of Iowa had a prestigious Ph.D. program in theatre history during Brownstein's tenure, a course in dramaturgy became part of the playwriting curriculum, and only playwrights worked as dramaturgs on productions in the department. Under Robert Hedley, who served as both chair of the department and head of the Playwrights Workshop from 1982 to 1988, the department phased out its Ph.D. and concentrated its resources on its MFA programs in acting, directing, design, and playwriting.[30] After Brownstein's departure, the regular use of playwright/dramaturgs waned; however, the phasing-out of the Ph.D. program guaranteed that the dramaturgy course would remain in the playwriting area, and that on occasion department productions would benefit from playwright/dramaturgs completing projects for the course.

Three other developments have sustained a dramaturgical tradition within the Playwrights Workshop in the 1980s and '90s. First, in 1985 the department hired Shelley Berc, a playwright who trained as a dramaturg at Yale and whose best-known work is as an adaptor of classical plays in collaboration with director Andrei Belgrader. From 1985 to 1989 Berc taught the dramaturgy course with a special emphasis on adaptation and new play advocacy. Second, the playwriting program regularly employed guest directors, playwrights, and dramaturgs to respond to student work in the department's annual Playwrights Festival, a week of readings, workshops, and presentations by Iowa playwriting students; dramaturgs attended these festivals as often as directors and playwrights.

Third, my own personal history—and my training as a Yale critic/dramaturg—intersected with the history of the department in 1989. I was hired as Assistant Professor of Theater History, Dramatic Literature, and Dramaturgy, filling a position that had previously been designed for an Assistant Professor in Theater History, Dramatic Literature, and Performance Theory. The department had to make a special case to the College of Liberal Arts for hiring a critic/dramaturg rather than a theater historian; while supportive of the department, the college cherished the memory of the theater history program. Since 1989 I have served as dramaturg within the core course of the playwriting program, called Playwrights Workshop, in which students present staged readings of works-in-progress and receive feedback on the work from their colleagues and instructors. I have also worked as production dramaturg on selected mainstage productions of student work and have participated dramaturgically in the preparaton of the Playwrights Festival. In 1993 Iowa admitted its first student into a pilot MFA program in dramaturgy, which I conceived in collaboration with my colleague, theater historian Kim Marra. The program focuses on new play dramaturgy.

From a limited perspective, my function in the Playwrights Workshop has not been different from that of Mark Bly in relation to Yale playwriting students: I have had the luxury of working as a dramaturg with the authority of a faculty member. And yet, a crucial aspect of my dramaturgical role has been that I have never been viewed, by the department, the playwriting instructors, or the students, as *another* playwriting instructor. Since Berc joined the faculty, there have always been two playwriting instructors, both of whom have been playwrights (or, in the case of Hedley, a director who has worked extensively with new plays). I was invited to participate in the Playwrights Workshop in order to add the perspective of a critic/dramaturg to those of the playwriting instructors. The pedagogy and procedures of the workshop, which were longstanding, included a freewheeling postreading critique in which the students and instructors subjected the play to intense criticism, both destructive and constructive. The peculiar dynamics of this critique gradually shaped my dramaturgical function into that of providing a critical perspective not only on the play but also on the perspectives of the students and other instructors. This was partly the result of my own sense of how I could best help the students, but it was also the product of departmental and program needs. In the workshop critiques, I could either contribute "objective" critical analysis to an already intensive scrutiny of the work or, following the dramaturgical impulse to maintain distance from the process, contribute such analysis *and* help the playwright sort out all the feedback.

Partly by way of the workshop's dynamics, then, I came to aspire to an ideal which I have come to think of as the scholar/dramaturg. With this term, I do not refer to the scholar who serves the theatrical process solely as scholarly expert, although this can certainly be part of the scholar/dramaturg's function. I refer instead to dramaturgs who maintain a scholarly role *in relation to* the process according to the original meaning of that term: "learned." Scholar/dramaturgs seek to learn as much as possible about the play's origins, sources, and evolution; others' criticisms of the play, the playwright's interpretation of them, and the effects of the feedback session on the playwright's process and plans. They use this knowledge to determine what would be most helpful to the playwright at the current stage of his or her process. If the scholarly knowledge of critic/dramaturgs informs their critical responses, the scholarly instincts of scholar/dramaturgs shapes the very manner in which they enagage in the playwright's process. They view it as something to be carefully investigated, and to be intervened in with a special restraint that comes of fully respecting the writer's way of working and of the effort to determine how and when one's knowledge and criticism would best serve the process.

Scholar/dramaturgs are not the opposite to critic/dramaturgs: the scholar/ dramaturg ideal synthesizes the Yale critic/dramaturg with Brownstein's "surrogate author," turning the critic/dramaturg into an empathic facilitator who combines (ideally) the empathy of a surrogate author and the investigative acumen of the scholar. The scholar/dramaturg is in a unique position to defamiliarize, in the Brechtian sense, other feedback playwrights have received: to explore the aesthetic and ideological biases from which it arises, and to use this exploration as a means of clarifying the playwright's next step in the writing process. In the Playwrights Workshop, for example, playwrights typically leave the postreading critique feeling overwhelmed by criticism. Usually these critiques open with the playwright being invited to say a few words about the play—about its origins, how fully developed it is, and questions that need to be addressed. Then there's an open discussion of the play, with the playwright/instructors presenting their opinions at some point. I participate in that discussion and take extensive notes on others' comments; in the ensuing week I hold an extensive conference with the playwright to discuss the critique. This discussion proceeds partly on the basis of my critical response to the play, but mainly it is a scholarly session in which I try to "read" the playwright's creative, emotional, and psychological relationships to the play, the writing process, and others' feedback; and to ascertain as much as possible where the play is in relation to what the playwright hopes and wants it to be. Then I draw on my own critical assessment of the play, and my own reading of what it might become, to offer suggestions. Yet I make suggestions only as they become appropriate to the discussion, and I try to defamiliarize my own comments as much as I can, to "foreground" their own aesthetic and ideological biases. Frequently this leads playwrights to clarify their own thinking about the play, in comparison to mine.

These conferences have two main objectives: first, to help playwrights toward a perspective from which they can rethink, restructure, and rework their plays on their own aesthetic terms and vis-à-vis the playwright's hopes for the work; second, to help the playwright attain a psychologically and creatively secure state—or a state of secure insecurity—for further writing. Because students will always be writing within a system of power relations and of ideas about how theater *should* be made—of which the university theater department is but one instance—they need to build trust in themselves and their work. The only way to help them to do this is to ask questions, questions, and more questions, in order to establish that they are proceeding from their own instincts, interests, ideas, and images, and to help establish what makes these ideas the students' own.

There are risks in asking these questions; some of them might seem obvious, uncritical, and unscholarly: What draft is this? What interested you in this subject? Why did you make this character the central character? What are your sources? What plays, other reading, and works of art have played a role in your thinking and writing? How much further do you feel you have to go? What did you find useful in the feedback session? What feedback would you absolutely not use?

As the playwright answers such questions, I learn a great deal about the play's original impulses; what the play aspires to dramatically; and where it is in relation to the playwright's aspirations for it. I try as much as possible to understand internal obstacles (psychological, emotional) to the writing process. A second set of questions usually emerges from the discussion—questions about dramatic idea, structure, action, character, imagery, and all their possible manifestations in this play. As we discuss them, I offer tentative critical answers, especially when they seem to facilitate the playwright's ideas about the play, and when they help the playwright begin to see a way past the obstacles. I also describe, from a variety of perspectives, what the play might become; this often stimulates playwrights to see both what they do and do *not* want the play to do. The discussion then focuses on the playwright's sense of what remains to be done and, more importantly, what to do next.[31]

The fall 1994 University of Iowa Theatre Arts Department production of *Out* by Ellen Melaver, a 1994 Playwrights Workshop graduate, can serve to illustrate my working process. The production process, and my dramaturgical feedback to the director, does not fundamentally alter my work with playwrights, although it heightens and focuses it. Everything is speeded up: questions of whether staging problems are script problems, and vice versa, place special pressure on the playwright. Throughout, I continue to make the play and the playwright the focus of my work, concentrating on the play in terms of what the production reveals about it. In the case of *Out*, which explores the social and personal dimensions of gay "outing," the playwright, director Carol McVey, and I all believed that the play had not achieved its potential in an Iowa Playwrights Festival production directed by a different director the previous spring. In order to facilitate the playwright's revisions, I helped her sort through the criticism of festival guests, audience members, and her two directors. I also retraced some of the research she had done on outing and conducted my own research, which formed a basis for questioning not only the play's authenticity but also its ideological implications.

In this respect, traditional scholarly questions (What is outing? What are its historical origins? What ideological arguments has it provoked?) became the basis for questions about the play (Does it take a side in the outing debate? Does it want to take a side? If not, how does it seek to represent the arguments for and against outing? How does it represent outing as a social phenomenon?

How does it represent the gay male subculture? For what dramatic purposes does it do all of these things? How are those purposes realized dramatically and theatrically?). Drawing upon this research, others' criticism, and my own response to the play, I questioned the play extensively with the director and playwright and, later, with the playwright alone. We met repeatedly until she came up with specific plans for restructuring and rewriting. This process extended into the rehearsal period, in which questions about the play's double plot lines, their development of separate lines of action, and their interplay became the primary focus of our discussions. Eventually we dealt with the line-by-line dynamics of crucial scenes in much the same way that we had worked through the play as a whole.

The scholar/dramaturg ideal is at the heart of Iowa's embryonic dramaturgy program: Iowa dramaturgs are no longer Brownstein's surrogate authors, but neither are they critics brought inside the process; instead they are playwrights' (and directors') scholarly allies, interested in learning everything there is to know about the play and the process, and committed to applying a (growing) breadth of knowledge to them. Students' programs of study are independently designed, although all programs combine coursework in dramaturgy, theater history, dramatic literature, and performance theory—all of which are taken with MFA directors, designers, playwrights, stage managers, and actors—with electives in acting and directing and, more important, other liberal arts departments such as English, Comparative Literature, and languages. Students work regularly on new plays; because the program is small (as of 1996 it enrolled only three students), student dramaturgical work is closely supervised with respect to the dynamics of collaboration. Thus, the program seeks to combine three elements: a solid foundation for the dramaturg's lifelong study of theater history, dramatic literature, and performance theory; scholarly breadth, the capacity of the student to see both theater and the world from a variety of critical, historical, and theoretical perspectives; and highly individualized dramaturgical work, with an emphasis on collaboration with playwrights and their directors and designers.

If I have written critically of Yale and enthusiastically of Iowa, it is because my work at Iowa has sought to resolve the contradictions of my Yale training. However, seeking to put a different ideal into practice, I am aware of new contradictions. For example, if I believe a play to possess little hope of becoming stageworthy, do I encourage the playwright to abandon it? Or do I engage the playwright in the process I've described with the hope that it will help him or her find a way to writing a better version of the play? The scholar/dramaturg ideal calls for the latter, encouraging a loyalty to people that can ultimately be harmful to them, if they are being encouraged in hopeless enterprises. On the other hand, whereas the critic/dramaturg might suggest that the playwright abandon his or her play, elaborating on why it is unworkable, the scholar/dramaturg does not assume to possess ultimate solutions of this kind. The scholar/dramaturg is more inclined to encourage the playwright to make a start on a new work that plays to his or her strengths, and to engage in a dialogue that might get that work going. Although the critic/dramaturg might come to the same conclusion, his or her criticism might discourage the playwright so much as to shut down dialogue altogether. The critic/dramaturg might believe that art matters more than people, whereas the scholar/dramaturg is committed to people, and to art as a crucial aspect of their lives, rather than to art in, of, and for itself.

THE IDEAL DRAMATURG?

In the final analysis, the ideal dramaturg would be a brilliant critic, a scholar of great breadth, *and* an empathic facilitator of the creative process. Yale and Iowa have provided different historical variations on this ideal. Having evolved out of a criticism program, the Yale program embodies the idea that dramaturgy is the practical application of criticism, and that to possess critical and analytical tools is to have most of what a dramaturg needs to be successful. The answers to the questions of how one might apply criticism—especially evaluative criticism—to theatrical practice, and how one might apply it to diverse creative processes and forms can be learned only through experience and in retrospect. At Iowa, dramaturgy, having evolved from Brownstein's concept of the surrogate playwright, is founded on the idea that dramaturgical work requires an empathic, learned sensibility, which extends the playwright's own process of self-questioning into a playwright-dramaturg dialogue about the play and its process of creation.

The Yale and Iowa ideals show that dramaturgy, that ambiguous profession, may be ambiguous partly because its products are invisible. Dramaturgy contributes criticism and scholarship as well as emotional, moral, and psychological support to the theatrical process, but its products and effects are not as visible to the naked eye as the work of directors, actors, and designers. The invisibility of dramaturgy creates problems for dramaturgy training; these problems become particularly thorny in conceiving and teaching new play dramaturgy. Still, although dramaturgs might not always be able to articulate precisely what dramaturgy is or how to teach it, in their teaching and practice they betray their dramaturgical ideals. And they create contradictions that demand constantly to be examined.

Toward A Dramaturgical Sensibility

by Jane Ann Crum

JANE ANN CRUM teaches dramaturgy and dramatic literature and works as a free-lance dramaturg, most recently at Baltimore's Center Stage *(The Taming of the Shrew)* and the McCarter Theatre in Princeton, New Jersey *(Random Acts '95)*. Her essays have been published in *Theater, Before His Eyes: Essays in Honor of Stanley Kauffmann, George Bernard Shaw: The Neglected Plays, Notable Women in the American Theatre, Sam Shepard: A Casebook,* and *Rereading Shepard.* She is a member of Literary Managers and Dramaturgs of the Americas (LMDA).

Tangibles of the dramaturg's craft are eminently teachable, for example, skills in research, the communication of ideas, translation and adaptation, theater history, dramatic literature and criticism, and studies in music, art, dance, film, and foreign languages. Intangibles are more difficult not only to teach, but to describe, for how does one describe a state of mind? One of Leon Katz's phrases seems eminently applicable: "exquisite sensibility," the ability to know what to say and more importantly, when to say it. Few would argue that practical experience in theater production is essential to a dramaturg's training. Without it, we run the risk of breeding what James Magruder calls "the killjoy dramaturg,"[32] who, ignorant of the process of making theater, may know what to say, but says it two weeks too early or three weeks too late. Timing is everything, as are subtlety, irony, and wit. Dramaturgical training offers the student what is in many ways the essence of a liberal arts education, namely, a **synthesis** of theory and practice, an opportunity to test the ideal in the fiery furnace of the real.

Although a dramaturgical sensibility may or may not be teachable, I am of the opinion that it can and must be encouraged. Toward that end, I propose a teaching model developed for the purpose of training student dramaturgs,[33] including suggestions for improving communication between directors and dramaturgs, especially in the context of first conversations. Interested students might adapt this format for purposes of pursuing independent study in dramaturgy; teachers might adapt it for use in new or already existent courses; departments without specialty programs in dramaturgy might consider adding dramaturgical studies to current curricula.

THE IDEAL THEATRE PROJECT AND THE
DIRECTOR/DRAMATURG TEAM

The most levelheaded description I ever heard of how a dramaturg should be trained goes something like this:"Train them ideally; acquaint them with reality."[34] As a result, this course was designed to ensure that dramaturgs and directors collaborate on both theoretical and practical levels.

The seminar focuses on production dramaturgy and writing, with the first four weeks of the class (the Ideal Theatre Project) devoted to the formation of a mutually acceptable aesthetic. Out of that aesthetic is born the play to be produced during the remainder of the semester, which also becomes the focus of all writing assignments. Although the course culminates in performance, my objective for it was to emphasize process over product, collaboration over compromise.

Part I: The Ideal Theatre Project

Working in tandem, a student director and student dramaturg create a hypothetical theater. The scope of that theater is unlimited—it may be collective, nonprofit, or commercial; it may take a particular political or aesthetic stance, may explore a particular type of dramatic literature or reject plays altogether in favor of developing theater pieces from nondramatic sources.

As their artistic aims emerge, students are asked to define their audience. (A working-class community in east Baltimore? The Latino community of a major metropolis? Suburban shoppers in a mall in Northern Virginia?) They also must determine the physical theater space best suited to their artistic aims and projected audience. (A converted warehouse or a parking garage? A high-tech "room" to be converted as necessary? An outdoor theater? A site-specific approach similar to En Garde Arts?)[35]

Once these decisions are made, the student director and dramaturg's next task is to write a manifesto,[36] which should include a philosophy of performance as it relates to the audience, the artistic staff, and the greater community of theater artists. A premiere season must be proposed, including an explanation of how each play or event supports their artistic vision, that is, what they hope to communicate to their audience and how each particular play offers challenges to their team(s) of artistic collaborators.

A mock budget form is circulated, and they are asked to produce an operating budget allocating monies for production, salaries, royalties, publicity, and so on. The point of the exercise is to take a finite amount of money and establish priorities as to how it should be spent. For purposes of the exercise, they are allowed to omit rent, utilities, and plant maintenance.

This part of the exercise culminates in the third and fourth week of class, when each team is given time in which to present their hypothetical "ideal" theater to their instructors and classmates. For purposes of the exercise, they are encouraged to think of their classmates and instructors as potential members of the collective, potential producers, or members of their fundraising board. Copies of premiere seasons and operating budgets are distributed, and the presentations begin.

Part II: Production Dramaturgy

Concurrent with their discussions concerning the Ideal Theatre Project, the artistic team is actively selecting a play for production. They are encouraged (but not required) to choose something from the premiere season of their "ideal" theater. The fifth week of class is devoted to another set of presentations as the team presents their play choice to the class, covering such issues as preparation of the playtext, questions of translation and cutting, design, and casting. Once the play choice is approved, the actors cast, and the rehearsal schedule set, the student dramaturg assumes the duties of a professional production dramaturg.

Each week I hold hourly seminars on such topics as: translation and adaptation, the new play, the dramaturg's protocol, rehearsal procedures, note taking and note giving. Remaining class time is spent attending rehearsals. Dramaturgs are required to keep a journal and to supply me with copies of all production notes. The journal provides an admittedly subjective account of the rehearsal process by the student dramaturg, serving as a place to record contributions to the collaboration, successes and failures, points of friction, questions—resolved and unresolved—and at the end of term, a thoughtful evaluation of the play in performance.

One of the most visible functions of the production dramaturg is that of writer. In regional theaters, the dramaturg supplies the majority of writing for publication, including play descriptions for brochures, newsletters, program notes, and study guides. For purposes of the exercise, student dramaturgs prepare a play description for a brochure to be mailed to the general public, a newsletter article for theater subscribers, program notes for the audience, and a study guide for teachers.

To prepare students for this exercise, we analyze and critique brochures, newsletters, and program notes from theaters throughout the United States and Canada. Two days before individual writing assignments are due, dramaturgs must circulate photocopies of their writing so that members of the seminar can study their classmate's work before class time.

Explanations and Elaborations

The first four weeks of the class were devoted to forming a mutually acceptable aesthetic between pairs of student dramaturgs and directors. Their first task: to compose an **individual** first draft of a mission statement. Because all students had taken a course in the twentieth-century avant garde, they were familiar with the manifestos of Tristan Tzara, André Breton, Antonin Artaud,

Richard Foreman, Charles Ludlam, and others. The final mission statement, whether written jointly or by one member of the team, was to be mutually acceptable.

We stressed the idea of suiting the theater to the community it would serve. At the same time, the project was to be developed under "ideal" circumstances (that is, a healthy initial budget, a rent-free theater space of their own design, a generous arrangement with Actors' Equity), we wanted them to address a "real" audience. Not surprisingly, two groups chose Washington, D.C., as their projected performance site. One project was designed specifically for an already existent theater that stands empty on a Marine base on the southeastern shore of North Carolina. Another was designed to serve a primarily working-class community surrounding a well-known liberal arts college in Ohio.

Finally, we asked that in their conversations (which occurred during the next three weeks) they consider issues of cultural and gender diversity from the standpoint of play selection, audience development, and casting, as well as the formation of the artistic staff.

During the next three weeks, four pairs of directors and dramaturgs met for approximately eighteen hours of conversation. During class meeting times, Jackson Phippin and I wandered from group to group, sometimes observing, sometimes entering into the discussion in progress. In several cases we were approached for advice, especially when a pair was at loggerheads or (in my case) when suggestions were needed as to a particular "type" of play. Budget forms were supplied by a former business manager of The Great Lakes Shakespeare Festival (Cleveland) now on the Catholic University of America (CUA) staff. One student made an appointment to speak with a member of the artistic staff at D.C.'s Arena Stage; another journeyed to New York City to talk to a representative of Actors' Equity. Copies of stage configurations were requested of several university theaters and one regional theater. The governmental offices of the District of Columbia supplied breakdowns of ethnic populations and statistics on family incomes. Playscripts were exchanged manifestos written and rewritten, presentation strategies discussed.

We agreed that presentation of the projects should be formal in nature, an exercise in communicating ideas to a civilian audience. As a result, we asked that the pair who were presenting consider us (Jackson, myself, other members of the class) as either an advisory board or prospective financial sponsors. A full sixty minutes were accorded each group for their presentations, with another fifteen minutes reserved for questions and answers. Although the presentations were primarily oral, two of the four groups supplied extensive packets of information.

While all the projects possessed individual merit, one of them, The Inter-Cultural Theatre Project, proposed a plan whereby various embassies based in Washington would become one-year sponsors of a season devoted to that country's particular theatrical traditions. Embassy representatives would serve as board members, with the artistic leadership of the project made up of bilingual dramaturgs and imported guest artists. One of the most impressive aspects of this project was that the students actually approached liaison officers at the Japanese and Spanish embassies, who, after listening to their proposal, responded with what the students described as "cautious enthusiasm."

As regards the development of dramaturgical sensibility, my objective was to improve the quality of first conversations between directors and dramaturgs by encouraging the exchange of ideas and the development of a shared theater vocabulary. In addition, I was committed to placing student dramaturgs and directors in a purposefully nonhierarchical relationship, one not hindered by preconceived notions of dramaturg or director roles. It was of immense importance to me that this first collaborative venture be one of equal partnership, because out of this supposedly joint theater aesthetic would be born the play to be produced during the remaining ten weeks of the semester. For the dramaturgs, extended conversations with the directors about **something other than a play in production** established common ground necessary for the discussion of ideologies of performance and helped subvert the notion of the dramaturg as bookworm and academic drudge.

I remain convinced (and my colleague, Jackson Phippin, is in agreement) that had we not instituted the Ideal Theatre Project, the plays selected for production would have been far more traditional in nature. The three directors who worked with dramaturgs were clearly blasted out of conformity—inserting Shakespeare's mad scenes into an original play about Charles and Mary Lamb, attempting nontraditional fare such as Gertrude Stein's *Circle Play,* or combining seemingly incompatible texts, Miller's *Death Of A Salesman* meets Handke's *Offending the Audience.*

The Miller/Handke project was especially successful in that it placed two playtexts that require radically different performance methodologies in direct confrontation with one another. Selected scenes from *Death of A Salesman* were performed with Stanislavskian rigor under the gaze of Handke's "speakers," who, once a Miller scene was completed, would address the audience directly. Reciting selected Handke mantras ("You watched the past which by means of dialogue and monologue made believe it was contemporaneous. You let yourselves be captivated. You let yourselves become spellbound"[37]), they moved freely about the stage, pointing out the assumptions made by representational performance modes. The final shape of the piece grew out of improvisations in which the actor playing Biff, finding it increasingly difficult to resist the Handke text, abdicated his role, leaving Willy in mid-monologue to take his place within the Handke group. In turn, one of the female speakers, fascinated by Linda's speech over Willy's grave, entered into the Miller reality as a grieving daughter taking the place of the lost son. In every case, the rigor of performance style was never corrupted or satirized; text was repeated and juxtaposed, yet never lost its integrity in regard to the original work.

The two directors who worked without dramaturgs (the control group, as it were), continued down well-traveled paths, selecting Shaw's "In The Beginning" from *Back to Methuselah* and Pinter's *Out of Alaska*. Even in the earliest stages of the performance projects, it became clear that the presence of a dramaturg made a significant difference in the conception of the theatrical event. Perhaps two heads really are better than one or perhaps the dramaturgs preferred working on projects for which the preparation of a playtext was necessary. Regardless of the cause, the conversations generated by the initial project served as the backbone or, perhaps more accurately, a touchstone for creativity, allowing dramaturgs and directors to dream together for awhile before settling down to the task of making theater.

Dramaturg and Director: First Conversations

Ideally, there would be no such thing as "first" conversations. Instead, conversations about plays would be a natural, everyday occurrence between dramaturgs and directors, regardless of their level of experience. Discussion would begin in the form of tangential references made over the course of several months. Ideas would arise without either party knowing (or caring) how they got there; conversations would proceed without fixed agendas or territorial imperatives. The vocabulary—textual, visual, analytical—would be a shared one, and each collaborator would be eagerly influenced by the other.

My interest in first conversations was sparked when I began reading the journals of my dramaturgy students. Almost without exception, the student dramaturgs' unresolved issues could be traced back to their initial conversations with the student directors. Two collaborations, one judged a failure by the student dramaturg, the other admitting to "disappointment" with the final product, serve as examples of two common mistakes made by first-time collaborators: (1) failure to define terms, and (2) insufficient tracking of the narrative. What follows are some speculations about how the quality of those first conversations might be improved, whether they occur between beginning students or seasoned professionals.

First Student Scenario: A Post-Apocalyptic *Macbeth*

Both dramaturg and director used the word "realism" repeatedly in initial meetings. Unfortunately as rehearsal progressed, it became apparent that the word had no meaning, no context, no grounding in the visual or verbal text. To rephrase Tristan Tzara, *"Realisme ne signifie rien"* ("Reality means nothing"), especially in regard to producing Shakespeare. Since this realization came too late for them to rethink, redesign, or restage, their initial enthusiasm for the project **as well as** their interest in the collaboration dissipated and died. What becomes clear is that some words are too "loaded" to be of use unless introduced with a specific example in mind. Words such as "realism" and its qualifier cousins, "surrealism," "supra-realism," and "hyper-realism," demand careful contextualization, as do such terms as "deconstructed," "caricatured," "stylized," or "pushed."

Second Student Scenario: Maria Irene Fornes' *Mud*

Working on a text chosen by mutual agreement, dramaturg and director worked in close collaboration to create the world of the play. After they researched the geography, climate, and architecture of Appalachia, they devoted themselves to helping the actors visualize the room, the house, the countryside. Three weeks into rehearsal, the director and dramaturg discovered they were interested in telling different stories. Loving the play as they both had— coming to mutual agreements about casting, creating a successful visual milieu—they had assumed they were in complete agreement as to the focus of the narrative. No discussion ever arose concerning the journey to be taken by the characters or the audience. So busy were they defining the elements of production, they forgot their primary purpose; that whether the text be one of Mac Wellman's poetic allegories or Heiner Müller at his most obscure, there is a narrative to be discovered, a story to be told. The best piece of advice Leon Katz ever gave his first-year dramaturgy students was that they should sit down with the director and tell each other the story of the play. Such a simple-minded beginning, I remember thinking, could never yield serious artistic fruit. The more fool I. The more fool any of us who forget that we are first and foremost, regardless of the difficulties of the text, despite the abandonment of causality and the gradual decline of the linear play, storytellers.

Conversations with Directors[38]

Three professional directors responded to the question "What should a dramaturg bring to a first conversation?" For purposes of brevity, I present their responses in the form of a list:

- A strong point of view. "If they're not aggressive, I don't notice them." "I want someone to challenge me. I want a double-sided conversation."
- The ability to conjecture, to ask "what if?"
- A solid familiarity with the text.
- Expert skills in communication. "A great talker. A great listener." "Someone who knows how to develop ideas, how to make conversations jump faster, further."
- First impressions, ". . . especially images that strike them as unique or repetitive or gorgeous or weird."

Also informative was the directors' list of what a dramaturg should **not** bring to a first meeting, which included a dogged interpretation of the text, an interest in "winning," and extensive research.[39]

By far the most interesting suggestion came from a free-lance director who works primarily in regional theaters that maintain literary staffs of one or more dramaturgs who work on as many as six or as few as two productions each season. Although some of his experiences with these staff dramaturgs have been good ones, he has, on occasion, been saddled with a dramaturg who, because of scheduling problems, arrived extremely late in the prerehearsal process, one on the first day of rehearsal. "Unless the dramaturg is there from the beginning," he complains, "there can be no collaborative process. Instead of functioning as dramaturgs, they become note givers, which can be helpful, but is not dramaturgy. Given the lateness of their arrival on the creative scene, they by rights should be called "textual consultants" just as other specialists are designated "speech consultants" or "fight consultants."

Conversations with Dramaturgs

Three professional dramaturgs responded to the question: "What do you bring to a first conversation with a director you do not know?" Their responses are listed below.

- Arrive with ten important facts, two wildly opposing ideas about the play and **no** books (unless they're picture books).
- Be prepared to tell the story of the play having first traced the arc of the major character(s) and identified important images.
- Use production history to identify the clichés of interpretation and performance. "Strip away conventions and see what's left."
- Bring with you an exploration of the text from oblique, tangential, subjective angles, including secondary literature of the period, painting, sculpture, music, poetry, period (or not), colors, textures, and scents.
- Consider meeting on neutral, but fruitful ground. "Beginning work on a production of Edward Bond's *Narrow Road To The Deep North,* the director and I wandered through the Freer Gallery, the Smithsonian collection devoted to Asian art. There, among the painted screens and carved demons, we found a drawing of a wizened fisherman preparing to eat his lunch on the bank of a stream, and cried out in unison, "Basho!" (the narrator of Bond's play).
- If the director wants analysis, work through a thematic or action structure. Stay away from literary criticism. It's important for a dramaturg, but as homework only.

The value of dramaturgical study lies in its insistence that ideas be forged in the crucible of theatrical practice. Students must be encouraged to take risks, to question traditional assumptions about how the theatrical event should be configured, to eschew tepid theatrical thinking. Even as it teaches the discipline of dramaturgical practice, this exercise helps students clarify in their own minds **what it is a dramaturg might do.** For only by demanding that students ask better questions, pose better solutions, argue points of perception, and successfully avoid cliché, can we help them imagine the theater of the future, the theater they must and will create.

Why in the Hell Are We So Serious?
Keynote Address: Literary Managers and Dramaturgs of the Americas, Seattle, Washington, June 1992[40]
by **Arthur Ballet**

Arthur Ballet taught and directed plays for thirty very odd years at the University of Minnesota. For twenty of those years, he also served as the entire staff of the Office for Advanced Drama Research, reading as many as five unproduced new plays a day and circulating them to regional theaters for production. Along the way, he edited thirteen volumes of *Playwrights for Tomorrow,* served as an occasional dramaturg at the Guthrie Theater in Minneapolis (as well as briefly at the Ahmanson in Los Angeles), and for four years was program director for theater at the National Endowment for the Arts. Now a professor emeritus, Dr. Ballet continues to lecture in the United States and abroad about American playwrights. He also consults with theater companies and continues as an advisory editor for *New Theatre Quarterly.*

I thank you all—most sincerely—for inviting me to share my thoughts with you. I suspect I may abuse your hospitality and upset some of you, perhaps all of you. If so, I apologize in advance, but I also hope that I do not bore you. At least not too much.

My ramblings this evening must begin with a question: Why in the hell are we so serious? Dare I go on? So serious, so pompous, so angry, so pretentious, so portentous?

If theater isn't joyous, fun, for us, then how on earth can we expect it to be so for our audiences? Of course, I am indeed aware that our roots are supposedly in ritual, in gatherings, but I am willing to lay odds that there was some hanky-panky backstage at the theaters of Dionysus, and that even those monsters tossing youngsters into pits of fire were doing so with giggles and a sense of: "Hey, now, **that's** theatrical!"

At the same time, as I keep saying to anyone who will listen to me, our theatrical ancestors were charlatans, tumblers, medicine show impresarios, and con men who delighted, first, in entertaining and also in making a buck (often dishonestly) on the side. Our predecessors, in short, were fakers, pretenders, who must have enjoyed themselves as they fleeced the crowd.

Nowadays as I wander in the theater offices and backstage, I see and hear little joy, laughter. I look at program notes my colleagues (you) have prepared so laboriously, so intelligently, so earnestly, and I have to wonder who reads them and why? My observations would indicate that bored audiences rifle through programs to read the cast lists. The explanation of what the plot is about, and the "notes" . . . all this after they have inspected the ads. But remember, these are the people who have lost interest in the comings and the goings of the stage.

We are so intent on concept, on "meaning," and on being taken seriously as professionals and as artisans creating art that we forget that the whole art form is one of fakery and that we are deceivers (some gay and some not).

I urge these thoughts because I am concerned that our audiences are responding without joy, without excitement. Theater is becoming a classroom, and a dull one at that. As a teacher for thirty-five years of enormous introductory theater classes, I quickly learned one important thing from the students: keep 'em laughing and then punch home the critical tidbit. Laughter will lead to the moment of truth, if there is one.

Moving right along, I am saddened to find that playwrights by and large don't want us. At least they seem to reject us once we have recommended their plays to the artistic director. And I wonder why. Maybe the answer is that we have become scolding school teachers bent on correcting quizzes. I hate to say this, but I think we have become literary scholars rather than theatrical magicians; our senses and our defenses are becoming largely pedantic rather than truly dramatic. I would suggest that playwrights, of course, need dramaturgs, as do directors, but they need us as supportive resources, not as antagonists. They need to learn to trust us. And for them to trust us, we had damned well better have earned that trust by knowing **theater** and the gimmicks and trickery of theater, and perhaps we can stop worrying about meaning and about social and psychological guilts.

I have often puzzled, as I trod on through the years, about the fashionable play-of-the-year. You know, the play that every theater in the country clamors to "do" and to do NOW. After a plethora of productions of these trendy productions, the plays are quickly forgotten because, quite frankly, there isn't much in them to remember, to return to, to think about, to produce again. Oh. You want names? Sure: *That Championship Season, Driving Miss Daisy, Steel Magnolias* and *The Heidi Chronicles* for starters. I think they all will fall into the bin of lost plays in a year or so; some already have.

And then some conscientious literary managers will "find" one of these "lost" plays and plug it at a meeting about an upcoming season. I am talking now of the year 2050, let's say. They will forget that, by and large, plays are lost because they deserve to be forgotten. Oh not all of them, but many of them. Anyway, in 2050 I certainly won't be around for you to point out my miscalculations.

I was seriously admonished to deal in this speech with the future. I suppose this is because, as the oldest living American dramaturg, I have a lot of experience of the past. Good enough. Well, then, in the future, I think you should be urged to remind playwrights to be good **storytellers** or better still **storyshowers.** When most of us are asked what a play is about, we do after all still start with the **plot.** Sure, there are no new stories, but the old ones can have an infinite variety of new twists.

Further, I would urge you to consider finding in the plays the **actions** that entertain. Entertainment is a wide and varied commodity in theater, but I remind you (unnecessarily, I am sure) that, by and large, monologues, barren language, obvious ideas, and commonplace passions often as not are simply boring. Sure, the actor can make them alive for the moment, but the action, finally, is zilch. I believe that Nazimova, when pressed to perform on stage, brought an audience to tears reciting the Russian alphabet, but that doesn't make the Russian alphabet a play.

I urge you, too, to remember the audience. (Oh, I know I sound like the business office, but the truth is that when we plan, rehearse, and present our plays, too often we forget that to have theater we must have an action, actors to perform that action, a place that we accept as magical, and **an audience.**) Denigrating the audience, dismissing it as stupid, oafish, or provincial, I am afraid, will leave us (my old joke) playing with ourselves. The audience is where it is, and we *can* move it to new territory, but we need to move it gently, and we must move with it, or I fear our theaters will die, perhaps noble deaths, but deaths all the same.

I think that theater people, particularly in these times but perhaps always, need to **hustle** rather than ruminate, we need to be theatrical rather than pedantic, we need to tend the shop rather than try to resolve all ills in the world. And our shop is the stage, the house of illusions, the brothel of humankind.

My ramblings will continue, with your indulgence, a bit longer. I have some specific suggestions that I will outline as I did some five or six years ago.

A) LMDA needs to help theaters find competent readers of new plays, to set standards for what a literary manager or a dramaturg needs to bring to the job.

B) Yup, we have to start somewhere, and I think LMDA needs to begin by thinking through the notion of accrediting both theater dramaturgs and teachers of dramaturgy. Duchamp's "Whatever I spit is art" (or whatever he said— no one told me to be accurate) . . . will no longer suffice. I am frightened at what I hear some literary managers and dramaturgs and their teachers talking about. If I may (and try to stop me now) I would insist that all dramaturgy courses and degrees be grounded in **theater** rather than in literature.

C) I think LMDA must lead the way in finding some reliable means of getting rid of most of the scripts that clog our mails and our offices and our desks. The same tired manuscripts wander listlessly from theater to theater, and I fear that they only waste our time, our postage, and our patience. *The LMDA Script Exchange*[41] is a beginning, but it is only that. We need an exchange of reactions to scripts systems. Sure, I won't agree with you, but the worst of the plays will finally fall off the circuit, we would hope. I am not sure how to work it, but I think LMDA must devote its energy to this, or we will continue to plod through each and every script, and to little purpose. And yes, I feel guilty when I don't read the damned play . . . and even worse when I don't finish it. But I am old now, and I am willing to assume guilt. Anyway, should every script be read (competently or not) at every theater?

D) Some years ago I was advised not to try to write any kind of critique for the playwright whose work either I couldn't recommend or that we at the theater would not be considering for production. A dialogue (in writing) might be useful, but it is time consuming. So, in all the years that I have conscientiously read plays and written up notes for my own edification and failing memory, I never told a playwright what to do with his or her play, although at times I was tempted. (Read that as you may.) It is interesting that some writers flatteringly remember how helpful I was, although we didn't do the play; all I ever said was either "Let's see your next play, please" or "I wish I could find a theater to produce this play." On the other hand, once my theater was committed to at least a reading and maybe even a production of a play, I would then (and only then) **volunteer** (and let me stress the word "volunteer") to help if (and only if) the playwright wanted to know what I had to say. Sometimes they said yes, and sometimes they said no. More often than not they said yes and then didn't pay much attention to what I had said. That's fine. That's the game we play.

I think some words must be said about the National Endowment for the Arts (NEA), not in condemnation or in pleading for more money (which seems to be what *American Theatre* magazine does to excess) but rather to point out that to succeed, whether as a national funding agency (the NEA) or as theater, we need to clearly know what we are doing **and why.** In short, I see the NEA's apparent failure and perhaps demise as a matter of waffling, and I further see some of our theater's failures and perhaps demise as a matter of waffling as well, of trying to be all things to all people, of not knowing why we are doing plays (rather than delivering lectures or writing diatribes for example), of not taking a stand and sticking to it. Rather then than damning the NEA, I suggest that we look to our own houses.

Finally (at last) I hope that dramaturgs and literary managers, in their theaters and classrooms, might do some of the following:

- Encourage new writing where talent is perceived, where a voice is heard or even a "vision" is glimmered.
- Remember to preserve as best we can the traditions of theater. And I remind you that I think those traditions are filled with joy and excitement rather than condemning and drab.
- Keep constantly in touch with the past so that the wide, international heritage is not lost, including the constant search for plays that must be translated and brought to our audiences because they are theatrically exciting.
- Help inform the audience when the audience wants to be informed.
- Be ten years ahead of the artistic director in future seasons, so there is both rhyme and reason in each clump of seasons, rather than just whim.
- Keep an eye open for acting and directing talent as it grows in the company, and then seek plays to "stretch" those talents.

- Inform the company of what is going on in other theaters, in the world theater, in the world, if you will. Report on what other theaters, here and abroad, are doing and why this should matter to us or why we must avoid such pitfalls.

- Forget about being the intellectual gurus of the company and perhaps begin to assume the older, less respectable mantles of magician, charlatan, and (my own favorite) medicine show con man.

In other words, let's start having some fun back stage, in our offices, and on stage. Or, in still simpler terms: "Come off it!"

Break a leg or two along the way, and thank you very much.

Shaping Critical Spaces:
Issues in the Dramaturgy of Movement Performance
by **Heidi Gilpin**

HEIDI GILPIN is Assistant Professor in the Department of Dance at the University of California, Riverside. Since 1989 she has worked as a dramaturg for William Forsythe and the Frankfurt Ballet, and directed the Institute for New Dramaturgy in various locations in Eastern and Western Europe. She holds a Ph.D. in Comparative Literature from Harvard University. Gilpin lectures and publishes internationally on critical and cultural studies in performance, with an emphasis on issues of bodily practice and embodiment, literary, critical, and film theory, dramaturgy, new media technologies, contemporary European performance genres, and architecture. She is presently engaged in electronic media and internet projects, and is completing a book entitled *Traumatic Events: Toward a Poetics of Movement Performance.*

It also happens that, if you move along Marozia's compact walls, when you least expect it, you see a crack open and a different city appear. Then, an instant later, it has already vanished. *Perhaps everything lies in knowing what words to speak, what actions to perform, and in what order and rhythm; or else someone's gaze, answer, gesture is enough; it is enough for someone to do something for the sheer pleasure of doing it, and for his pleasure to become the pleasure of others: at that moment, all spaces change, all heights, distances; the city is transfigured, becomes crystalline, transparent as a dragonfly. But everything must happen as if by chance,* without attaching too much importance to it, without insisting that you are performing a decisive operation, remembering clearly that any moment the old Marozia will return and solder its ceiling of stone, cobwebs, and mold over all heads.

Italo Calvino, *Invisible Cities*[42]

MOVEMENT PERFORMANCE: ISLANDS IN AN UNCHARTED TERRITORY

How can we begin to think through the possibilities and process of dramaturgy for movement performance? How can we imagine ways to address the multidisciplinary issues inherent to dramaturgies for movement performance? Italo Calvino's invisible city of Marozia maps the site of this essay in several ways. First, it describes my experience of discovering any topic of inquiry, watching it vanish, and seeing it reappear in another guise, as if by chance. Calvino's question of what words to speak, what actions to perform, and in what order and rhythm, directs us to the heart of performing and witnessing motion in the simultaneous and various forms that are the focus of this brief exploration. The fundamental tenet of performance—especially the contemporary movement performance I will be exploring here—is that everything *does* lie in knowing what acts to perform in what order and rhythm. The expectation of a critic of such work is that everything lies in knowing what words to write—that one will have the ability to transport readers to a space that changes its surroundings, its heights, its distances; a space transfigured into transparency. A space that appears and disappears when you least expect it.

Yet the choreographers and directors of movement performance teach us that they never know what actions to perform, that there is so much uncertainty, and that uncertainty itself is the subject and focus of their work. The issues of disappearance, knowledge, transformation; captivating pleasure that transfigures and makes transparent; the notion of chance, the art of *sprezzatura,*[43] of effortlessness, lightness, that one would act gracefully and not call attention to the work behind the creation of the performance, attempting to maintain a state of dynamism in order to acknowledge stasis, and the memory and awareness of impending repetition: these are, in profound psychic and intellectual ways, the foundations of my work as a dramaturg. In order to keep Marozia from returning and soldering its ceiling of stone, cobwebs, and mold over all heads, then, let us hope that a gesture, as Calvino suggests, is enough.

It was gesture, the language of gesture, and its repetitions, that first mesmerized me as I watched a performance of Pina Bausch's company, the Tanztheater Wuppertal, in Wuppertal, Germany, many years ago. How could one scene of human interaction, without words, be repeated at least twenty-five times without any visible change in the gestural phrase performed, but produce an entire array of reactions, thoughts, and emotions in its spectator? How could psychological situations that seem so private take on a sense of collective experience? How could a director extract those particular experiences that seemed more collective than others, and then display them in settings alienated from their contextual narratives? Why were they so powerful?

Calvino's Marozia also resonates with my first experience of the work of choreographer William Forsythe and the Frankfurt Ballet: that was an overwhelming feeling and awareness of *sprezzatura,* of doing something for the sheer pleasure of doing it and intoxicating everyone who witnesses it to reconsider things in a different light (sometimes quite literally, and often with very little light on stage). It was also the experience of recognizing that if one attaches too much importance to anything, paralysis and stasis will set in. How to keep moving and thinking and producing, and how to decide how to move and think and produce: these were my questions of Forsythe. The "weak form" compositional strategies of Forsythe that initially so moved me years ago move me still; they have taught me how to enact such strategies myself, not only in work but in every aspect of life that performance imitates and challenges.

What these choreographers point to is what Calvino attempts to name also: that which is *not* audible or visible. It is this silence, this transparency, invisibility, endless repetition of disappearances, the failure of constancy and stasis to support our thoughts, our movements, our lives, that leads me to explore the realm of the performative, whether through Calvino's invisible cities, through architecture, or through philosophy. As Henri Bergson suggests, "there is no perception which is not prolonged into movement...."[44]

> The more you can let go of your control, and give it over to a kind of transparency in the body, a feeling of disappearance, the more you will be able to grasp differentiated form, and differentiated dynamics. You can move very very fast in this state, and it will not give the same impression, it won't give the impression of violence. You can also move with tremendous acceleration provided you know where you leave the movement—not where you put the movement, but where you leave it. You try to divest your body of movement, as opposed to thinking that you're producing movement. So it would not be like pushing forward into space and invading space—it would be like leaving your body in space.
>
> Dissolution, letting yourself evaporate. Movement is a factor of the fact that you are actually evaporating.
>
> William Forsythe[45]

It is fascinating that the process of dramaturgy, specifically for movement performance, has been largely overlooked by literary and theater critics: it seems to me crucial to explore critically the work of artists who are working within many disciplines at once in order to find and develop a contemporary language to express human experience. Perhaps this neglect is symptomatic of the sheer complexity of such work. The question of audience is a significant one for the dramaturgy of movement in performance, for there may be members of the audience familiar with dance or movement vocabularies, but they may not be familiar with philosophy or literary theory, for example. They may be unfamiliar with movement, but extremely well versed in film theory, cultural studies, architectural theory and history, or psychoanalytic theory. This situation is unique to movement performance. Unlike dramatic theater, where text is at the center of interpretational strategies for the audience, in movement performance productions the audience members are confronted with so many differing vocabularies (text, image, movement, sound) and disciplinary perspectives—none of which play a hierarchical central role—that they generally are not equally well versed in all of them.

It is therefore important to begin the process of how to think about the creation and interpretation of movement performance in light of the multidisciplinary, which is also evident in many other facets of contemporary cultural production. Ironically, one way to begin this process would be to consider our relation to textuality. Acts of reading have historically received a great deal of attention. Literary critics have focused on the question of how we read a literary text, film theorists have articulated how to go about reading the visual language of the cinema, and theater historians have observed the semiotic inflections of a dramatic text as it is staged, but few literary scholars have explored the question of how to begin to read the altogether more complex text of performance, particularly when movement is the protagonist.[46] How, if we are trained as readers of predominantly verbal texts, do we read or understand the "text" of the movement performance spectacle, a multilayered text composed of visual, temporal, auditory, technical, and physical languages? What tools can we use to understand this "text," when it is not simply a written work of dramatic literature portrayed in a theater, but a production involving such a large number of movement sequences that these sections take on the formal responsibility of the production? The act of reading we perform as members of an audience for movement performance spectacles on stage and on film requires our attention. It demands an acknowledgement and cognition of movement generally, and of moving bodies specifically.

Nonlinguistic elements have become a predominant force in contemporary performance work. Recent productions of classical dramatic texts, in the most extreme instance, no longer simply present the linguistic interactions of the characters as the central motivating device for the narrative. Instead, they may allow the weight of the narrative to be carried by the lighting or sound scores,[47] either by placing the locus of action in darkness,[48] or by rendering the words unintelligible through the layering of spoken and recorded texts.[49] This shifts the focus of our attention from the words spoken to the location of speech and to the notion of the visibility or invisibility of the speaker. Such productions often valorize physical movement by according it a significant role, allowing phrases of gesture or movement rather than words to become the essential bearers of meaning. When our attention is thus shifted from words to images, from speech to movement, from texts to bodies, and from speaker to moving performer, and when the result is made either inaudible or invisible, or both, we must begin to consider how such enactments of invisibility and absence urge us, perhaps, to reevaluate our training as readers, to reexamine our expectations of performance, of entertainment, of social, political, historical, psychic, and intellectual commentary, and to reconsider the importance of performance as an increasingly transformative mode of engaging the critical and spectre-filled issues of contemporary realities. Theater, in short, has developed sophisticated "performative languages" of light, sound, and movement that have come not only to prevail in contemporary performance productions, but also to take on more significance than the dramatic text itself. The concept of "the dramatic text" is cast aside or altered unrecognizably to the point where theater, as a concept, as psychic and physical architecture, as a building, even as a process, disappears. William Forsythe articulates this condition: "The theater institution has been disemboweled, and the architecture of the theater itself is politically disabling. It only lets theater re-present itself again as a denied screen concealing an orifice which has abandoned its contents."[50]

Contemporary movement performance, especially the work of a number of choreographers and directors who have worked primarily in Europe (William Forsythe, Pina Bausch, Jan Fabre, Maguy Marin, Tadeusz Kantor, Anne Teresa de Keersmaeker, Saburo Teshigawara, Reinhild Hoffmann, Johann Kresnik, and many others) offers previously unrecognized possibilities in its distinct manner of formally, conceptually, psychically, and physically manifesting the multidisciplinary. Its constant attention to other disciplines and other forms of expression make movement performance an inherently multidisciplinary genre. It is a large and necessary task for the dramaturgy of this genre to expose and explore how this multidisciplinary quality functions at the compositional level in the creation of these productions, as well as in the development of new discourses through which to interpret them. The attention accorded various texts, of literature, music, philosophy, architecture, and science, for example, is enacted as a search for the conditions of these "other" spaces, as an attempt to bring these "others" into the rehearsal studio, into the rehearsal process, and into the performance itself.

My experience with making and interpreting movement performance has enabled me to recognize it as an art form that exposes the impossible longing for performance to achieve permanence within any field of representation. Is the impossible desire for permanence in representation precisely what motivates movement performance to embody the multidisciplinary? Or is it our lack of training in the interpretation of the multidisciplinary that makes movement performance seem at once so alien and so compelling? The task of the dramaturg in this context is to confront the effervescent necessities of performing the multivalent and simultaneously make it resonate for audiences as a new form of perception. These productions have taught me to rethink the role of the body, of politics, and of theory within the spaces of performance on and off stage. The work of movement performance choreographers and directors has forced me to consider the processes and tactics of memory—for it is the vision of memory that remains when the performance vanishes.

The Dramaturgy Reader
by **Mark Lord**

Mark Lord is a graduate of Swarthmore College and the Yale School of Drama. Since 1987 he has directed the theater program at Bryn Mawr College. He is Artistic Director of Big House (plays & spectacles) in Philadelphia.

Once, perhaps, you loved to read.
From a shifting, swirling mass of markings, letters, then words, made
    themselves clear to you.
People read to you and you shaped the words, with your lips.
Words made pictures in your mind, and thoughts, and you were
    transported by them.
You read for pleasure because all reading was pleasurable to you and you
    became a different person because you were a *reader.*
Now, you are reading a textbook.
You read as quickly as you can.
Your lips do not move and you are proud of that; they remain closed,
    pursed, and you remain, at your desk. You are not transported;
    you are reading this textbook the way that they taught you: *for*
    comprehension.
These days, perhaps, you read a lot of textbooks.
And the joy of reading is harder to find for yourself now.
Perhaps it even feels as if the joy of reading has been taken from you.

Going to the theater is like that for me now, very often.

I was just at the theater, the other night, a major theater in a major Ameri-
    can city.
It was a city and a theater I was unfamiliar with and so the experience
    was charged with a sense of excitement for me.
I met the director before the play and he told me how excited he was
    about the work I was about to see, a jubilant work, he told me, about
    summer and love.
Taking my seat, I was pleased by the decor and the proportions of the
    room and by the expectant chatter of fellow members of the
    audience.

The lights went down. The lights came on again. And I was in hell. The
play was terrible. Worse than that: it was boring. I wanted to leave.
Lips pursed, limbs aching, I calculated the minutes 'til intermission.
I burned. I breathed. I counted breathing and admired the haircuts
around me and I ached and cursed.

I cursed myself for being there.
I cursed the director.
I cursed the city; I cursed summer and love.
I cursed the theater and wondered why.

Why was I so bored by the play I was supposed to be enchanted by?

I was bored because the play I saw was written and designed and performed to please me. That doesn't seem to make sense, but it's so.
Remember the time in your learning to read when you didn't need pictures anymore. When you didn't want help sounding out the words with
your lips. When you wanted to turn the page *yourself.* Your imagination
was insulted by the pictures in your book. You wanted to know the
shapes of your own lips. As a *reader,* you wanted to discover and to create for yourself. You did not want the simple revelation of being *shown.*
In particular, you raged against being shown what you already knew,
being taught what you had already learned.

And although, once, I could imagine no greater pleasure and went to the
theater all the time, I seldom feel jubilant there; now it often seems that
the pleasure has been taken away from me. This writing is for both of us:
for me, the unhappy theatergoer, and for you, the purse-lipped textbook
reader. I want us to think together about the theater that we know and
about the theater of our memories and of our dreams. I want to write for
us about the dramaturgy of joy, but I don't know yet what that is. Maybe
you will, after I tell you what I thought, that night, not long ago, while I
was bored at the theater:

When things are bad like that,
I close my eyes and I picture: Gertrude Stein
(with her assistance) at the theater.
A wide-eyed Baby (just sixteen), she watches with fawning eyes
Sarah Bernhardt chewing up the *Phaedra* scene, making
so concentrated a storm, thundering *en français*
(ununderstandable to Gertrude, rapt.) And

with Racine's phonemes washing over her
like (distant, still-imagined) Paris rain,
Miss Stein observed: the *oneness*
of what was seen and what was heard.
They came together for her in a delightful dance of one.
And she felt for the first time, *"the height in the air"* there,
a *presence* in that sound and image marriage, and her joy
was like the joy you felt at the first shapes of sense
that swam together from the shifting swirl

when you were learning to read. The theater is *here:*
in Gertrude Stein's moving landscapes.

Listen: it's important to think about this.
Dramaturgy starts here, *(it all does,*
it all) in these affections. You remember:
child games without rules
past what you make up as you go;
teams moving, in the distance, back and forth,
across fields, ... courts, ... diamonds; . . . . . trucks
in sites of construction or demolition,
Landscapes in motion.
From them, *with* them, I imagine Gertrude Stein
in the *ecstasy* of her *"very simple direct and moving pleasure,*
(. . .) a thing in itself and
it existed in and for itself,"
a perfection.

This, you are observing, is not textbook writing. You are so shrewd. But
perhaps you're puzzled by this departure from the norm. These words
don't march. They shuffle some, but then they leap or dive and connections tail behind them. Like flights of fancy. Maybe this is a glimmer, you
speculate, of the dramaturgy of joy. Let's hope so. Sitting there that night
in the dark theater, my mind raced just this way. Speculation (and even
hope) ran rampant as the devilish red taunting of the sign on the wall
advertising **EXIT** reminded me of

Bertolt Brecht, whom I read in my youth.
He spoke with such vigor (so Protestant,
so practical, so—middle class!) of a house on fire;
Leaving, he said, is the thing to be on your mind.
(No point in discussing the renovations now.)
This seemed to me so practical—and right—
and the world seemed so much like a house afire, that
in my youth I could (and sometimes can still
with eyes closed) feel the heat of that idea:
That the theater could be like a house afire
consuming itself was an idea that filled me with such awe
that I read all his psalms and sang his songs and, respected his
judgments.
His sense lit an ire in me that burns and burns and
never consumes itself quite. Even now, right now,
as I sit with lids screwed shut, imagining a time
(but now it's all gone by?).

It isn't. I remember:
passing for the first time from the windshield glint of parking cars
into the hushed canvas-dappled light of a circus bigtop. I recall
It was important *to be kept inside* there. And the circus did keep me,
it had that power over me. I learned:
the lesson of continence: of wanting to be contained.
(At the same time amazed by the incontinences of the elephants ...)
These observations were the beginning of my dramaturgical
education.

I learned later, in books and stages: first from *Three Sisters,* then *The
Maids;* from *Wild Ducks* and *Bald Sopranos* (live onstage); from wading
with Beckett, in his precise agony; and from falling (willing) into Shakespeare's deep, inviting world's-a-stage and other looking glasses-up-to-
nature; from the megaphone buzz of protest rallies; from the shrieking
rage of *The Clash* (best thing ever *on* Broadway); from the historical
echo of Hugo Ball's nonsensical intonations and the anguished *spiritual
purity* (oxymoronic even in his day) of his *Flight Out of Time;* and from
the unspeakable, unstageable stage directions of Peter Handke:
she moves
imperceptibly
under her dress.
Yes,

(I THINK) I LEARNED TWO THINGS:
1. To represent the world—in plays—is *hard.* The world is so elusive, so
full of movement, so deep, so shallow. And our impulse (to capture it)
often takes the *play* out. Almost always we miss what's subtle and most
true, in favor of something solid. (something easier to attain.)
A formula or a neatly packaged sentiment, like mine
(when I close my eyes
and think of Gertrude Stein).
And

2. In the theater, because so much of our staged reality (the words, gestures, entrances, and exits) is prearranged, we have the opportunity to
live beneath the surface a little deeper than lots of people ever have the
chance to go. We have the opportunity *to change ourselves.* (And we
share this with our audiences.)
Not by dressing up
not by becoming other people
but by living more carefully
in what Handke calls, *"the state of grace ... having time." (The Weight
    of the World)*
Time to focus on: bodies and minds and souls (if they exist)

all at once, all together, in time that's set aside
from *"the big blooming buzzing confusion."*   (Beckett, *Murphy*)

Those are the feelings I was chewing into thoughts when I decided to be
a dramaturg, when I was a young director looking for a way in the world.
I started making theater, being present in its writing, rehearsing, revising
and showing (day in day out) with this in mind: that the rhythms of this
activity (with its many tempos and perpetual grinding of ideas always
shifting the world beneath my feet, like in a construction site of the
spirit) would help me
to live as complete an experience as possible,
which is, I believe,
THE POINT.

All my assumptions expectations intuitions demands flow from here.

And my anger disappointment sense of loss start here as well.

When I open my eyes and look at the theater we are making, which generally is irrelevant to my concerns. THE POINT isn't touched on and the
place where dramaturgy begins—the play and wonder and love of
shapes in time and height in air isn't there—almost anywhere. We say so,
we who work in the theater, we say it is there—because we have to *(It's
our job now.)*—but for the most part we are
too busy for the state of grace,
too uncertain of the future to trust the present fully,
too in love with the surface to know,
that deeper is there, deeper still.

Oh, we complain; we make an excellent show of our complaining.
"Lamentation," Strindberg says, "is the universal language." *(A Dream
Play)* We amaze each other with the new bad news daily of funding lost,
tickets unsold, theaters folding, and the zealous right's threat to our free
expression (as if we *had anything* to express—and maybe we do, but
our complaining saves us the trouble of knowing). We gesture to excuses,
always careful to keep the blame away from ourselves. (Strindberg
again:) "What we are engaged in is keeping the dirt of life
at a distance."

It makes us feel *tough* to imagine ourselves in a *tough spot.* Our subsis-
tence existence is hard but convenient. We don't want to *implicate
ourselves* in the failure of our work. And it *is* convenient to be able to
forgive our friends' failures with frontier-land stories of the fight for survival in the cultural wilderness of North America.

When we are really brave (or bored, or lost) we flatter ourselves with the fantasy of our own demise. *This is it,* we imagine. *We are the last hurrah, the eleven o'clock number, the rest is silence. After us the savage gods.* With our heart-felt intentions dangling off our sleeves, we rehearse the gravity of the situation, and *pretend* that we can't picture a world without us, *imagine* that the world will miss us when we're gone, *pray* that our hypothetical departure might in some way wound someone or cause them a fraction of the sense of loss we feel when we close our eyes and realize:

Our work is not good enough.

Our work is not good enough because:
We're not even trying to do our best work. We're not honoring the wonder of the theater of our childhoods, the theater of our dreams. The theater of our time is an industry and the wonder it pursues is the wonder of its own survival.
We allow others to determine the rules for our creation,
We agree to a community standard of resources to make a performance that is inadequate.
We *so seldom* touch our world in any important respect. Our theater is not *vital* to our audiences.

Even worse (the worst, perhaps): *our work is not good enough because* enough administrators and so-called artists and consultants and foundation officers and corporate giving personnel are eking out a living as provisional members of the middle class that (perhaps) they have decided that *this* is *good enough.* Perhaps these individuals are so completely occupied by imagining their survival into next year, next week, tomorrow, that they haven't time to imagine theater that is better than what we make.

I imagine the perpetrators of that awful evening I spent, gathered in a conference room somewhere, going over the grisly statistics: audience aging; growing competition from television, movies, cybersex, pay-per-view—all capturing the imaginations of youth. *"We have a marketing problem,"* they decide. But we don't. If we have to market our art like Fruit Loops then our work is no closer to the center of our constituents' lives than Fruit Loops are. There are no marketing problems here, only products no one needs.

Our theater aspires to be what we will accept; it gives us what we'll take, not what we need. It doesn't challenge us to change ourselves; it doesn't *want* us to change. It loves us just the way we are.

Our work isn't good enough because, although we fantasize about *the end,* we know we'll never finish off the theater. Tourists will come to Manhattan whistling *New York, New York it's a wonderful town.* And we know that they'll settle for a T-shirt and a revival. We know that in the hinterlands, small communities will forever congregate in clean rooms to celebrate their civic pride and the inclusive exclusivity of their middle-American high society. And people, many of them young, who would be better served by doctors, will continue to aspire to be *stars* and will be encouraged to emote themselves into limpid pools of embarrassing amateurism in grimy basement studios. But we know that *there will always be theater,* ☺ and so we listen to these tales of apocalypse-soon with the glee of a child hearing a scary story while safe in bed, already tucked in . . .

It's not that we want things to be this bad. Most of us have something we can close our eyes and hearken to (as I close my eyes and picture Gertrude Stein) but as part of an *industry,* in our dealings with one another, and with funders and fund-raisers *etcetera,* we don't share those visions. We keep them to ourselves, like secret talismans of some potent art we wish we could make. Consequently, sadly, our visions as artists don't connect, don't touch each other any more than they touch us. We are separated from one another as we are separated from ourselves; we collaborators, *all together*
alone,
apart from ourselves,
alone.

Meantime the culprits are finishing their meeting with coffee and with *warm wishes* for a *better tomorrow* at the *Artistic Home,* and ignoring the conflagrated structure now "fully involved," (as the firemen say) burning down around them. They do not strain an inch to hear Bertolt Brecht's muffled cries. To hear them would mean no more coffee, would mean that some theaters would close (because they should) would mean that some careers would end and some patrons and philanthropists would be publicly embarrassed, ashamed to be recognized as the duped philistines they are. To hear Brecht would mean that we could begin to think about meaning something.
Because we would have to recognize
that we mean *nothing.*

You are thinking: *what does this mean for me? I am not part of this nothing. I am a reader and I am only reading.* And, of course, you are right. But: some of the people in the room, on the committee, well—in the meeting—drinking coffee on the periphery are readers too, and you might be one of them. They are close enough to be blistered by our little inferno; they are educated enough to understand the references now being made, but are not wise enough to read the signals through the flames as the handwriting on the wall, so to speak. They are dramaturgs, and they're just happy to be there.

Who are these people, who sit so still in a house afire, watching by flame-light their shadows dancing wild on the wall behind them? I want you to know, because it's a part of *your history:* how you, reader, came to be reading precisely *this,* which asks you *now* to picture peripheral figures in a conversation in a conference room in a house on fire. Picture me there, reader, because I am one of them. Picture *yourself* there as well.

STORYTIME: (A SELECTED HISTORY)
In different kinds of companies with different kinds of taste, over a period of several years, from the sixties through the early eighties, a gap was perceived between how intellectually engaging work was and how intellectually committed its makers (and the foundations that supported it and the training programs that fed it with young artists) wished it to be. Particularly in the hip poverty of young companies, the luster of *ideas* had an appeal.

Richard Gilman and Gordon Rogoff provided their reflections to the young Open Theater, helping Joe Chaikin connect what he was doing to what had been done before, the dramaturgs' ideas reaching out to the artists' creativity that was reaching out to them.

On the basis of a few isolated successes like this one, the theater invented a paradigm
(as it was inventing a paradigm for itself, or having one invented, to be applied in every instance, so that our "regional theaters" would not be so, well, "regional.") in which this relationship between dramaturg and theater was skewed and subsequently codified. Hammered out. Nailed down. Rather than the dramaturg's connection to specific creative artists, for example, the paradigm associated him (and eventually her) with an *institution,* adding to the marriage of true minds an impediment of some magnitude. In the paradigm's flow chart there was no difference discerned between a sustained, evolving collaboration between *individuals* and a *function* to be fulfilled on the *production,* as if the dance of ideas and creation was so easy that any two partners could do it. *In my own mind I imagine this as the difference between sex and fucking.*

The paradigm needed a sort of cerebral rescue squad to try to connect whatever was being done in the theater to the currents of thinking that were current, to demonstrate the thinking that was in the work if they could find it, to cover over its absence if they couldn't. And when the work that our mature regional theater made was generally devoid of intellectual content, it was crucial to have a staff member with the capacity to word-process up an essay for the program, best if littered with cryptic quotations from established literary sources, to provide the mask, the patina, of credibility to work that would be merely dull if the dramaturg could not provide the soft, fuzzy educational materials that would allow a cowed but baffled public, (willing yet unable to find our research in what it sees onstage) to pull the wool over its own sleepy eyes.

That we have dramaturgs in America at all is, I think, not even a token compensation for our theater's dearth of ideas; dramaturgs are hired because the place where the ideas should be is empty and nobody in control wants it to be their job to really fill that gap. We try to disguise the vapidity of our work with the *supplement* of one mind that is charged with giving voice to all the many languages of history and culture although we are neither capable of understanding those voices nor are we interested in listening too closely.

Our training programs, eager to dismantle their no longer fashionable programs in Theater History, began to graduate dramaturgs and our middle-aged theaters, already becoming comfortably bloated with middle-managers, hired them (or hired others) to perform what it considered the work of intellectuals: opening the mail, paging through and returning the annual landfill-full of hackneyed drivel exhausted by the Great American Play machine of the late '70s and early '80s; issuing the mumbo-jumbo of grant-writing that must flow to corporations and foundations to encourage the return flow of funds. Some of these dramaturgs were good enough at corresponding with writers and helping them to re-structure their writing into formulas the public could recognize that they were promoted from the mailroom—many of them to lucrative work in television.

Beyond these practicalities, the theater did not know what to do with this pack of semi-literates with the trappings of artists along with the professional obligation to remain objectively detached from the collaborative process (along with an unwillingness or inability to ever be truly *implicated* personally in their work). When there were at last enough of them to form a *complaint* of dramaturgs, they argued among themselves and with others about what they were allowed to do and precisely *why* they existed, what they should be allowed to do and with whom they should be allowed to speak.

That such petty discourse is routinely conducted with real zealousness is perhaps surprising to you, you idealist. But we were not educated to be mere mail room clerks and apologists for the mediocrity of the culture of our times. We were promised more than that, in exchange for all our dirty work; we were promised (at least in our own minds) that our work would have *dignity* and *meaning* and would be *respected.* Among ourselves we claimed to be (often without smiling) *THE CONSCIENCE OF THE THEATER.* It was clear to us, then, that the theater had no conscience without us. If we were to look carefully and honestly at the work we produce, we would admit (perhaps) that it has no conscience with us either.

(The theater became *Ubu,* big and dumb and needy, and we were a conscience like his: scrawny, kept in a suitcase, kept in the dark in case we were ever needed.)

It's almost time to open *your* eyes now, almost time for me to say: look at the theater around you, the theater that is being made now, in your time, and think hard about it.

Now we are in the fire room. Picture us there. Now we are asking the questions that make the others stare at their shoes. *Why isn't our work good enough?* What can the theater do that television, movies, and pop music cannot—and why aren't we doing it? Compared to the theater of other times and other cultures that you know about, how valuable does our theater seem to us? When you remember the joy of the world-through-child-eyes play, how *consuming* is *our* theater fun? Of all the possible theaters you can imagine, are ours the best?
IS THERE A REASON
FOR THE THEATER TO EXIST
IN AMERICA
NOW?

This is the discussion to be having and, in my opinion, this is a discussion for dramaturgs to *lead* because the issues the discussion will deal with are *dramaturgical* in nature. Yet dramaturgs don't have this discussion much. *Leading* it certainly doesn't figure into their job descriptions. Why?
Because (among our other failures) we have failed so completely to define dramaturgy.

LANGUAGE

As Wittgenstein instructs us, once we are able to understand how to use the terms of the language correctly, the errors of our short-sightedness and misapprehension will be cleared away and (perhaps) the path-way to clear thinking will be uncovered. *Then,* we will be able to take up the important *dramaturgical* problems currently threatening the theater.

We have mistakenly defined dramaturgy in relation to dramaturgs, wrongly assuming (perhaps) that a person is more real than an idea. Once *dramaturgy* is reduced to a list of duties performed by *dramaturgs,* we are in treacherous linguistic terrain. First, our definition is as useless as it is unassailable because it's a tautology. (Naturally, plumbing is what plumbers do, art is what artists do, and thermodynamics is what thermodynamicists do. But knowing this does not take us any closer to knowing what plumbing, art, and thermodynamics *are.*)

More important, this definition is unsatisfactory because the list of duties dramaturgs perform is only a list of what they've been *allowed* to do. By eliminating from consideration duties that dramaturgs perhaps *should* perform, we allow the term to be defined by the institution in which it has developed, which is to say that we allow it to be defined by the very theater that perceived (rightly) a shortcoming in its thinking faculties. Actually, our notion of dramaturgy has taken shape (as things do) in fits and starts through various blunders and coincidences of what office was free, what artistic director had an impulse to seem smarter, and how much and in which directions the myth of Lessing was bloated and distorted as it was whispered down the ivory tower lane.

What we have now are several quite different lists of functions based on work in many different kinds of companies pursuing different styles of theater and performance art. Clearly the lists don't match but at cocktail parties and family functions and in colleges and universities (where it would be embarrassing to say that we can't say what it is that we do) we have recourse to the metaphors we have invented for our work (play-doctor, midwife . . . you know the drill). All of these touch on some things that dramaturgs might do but none of them touches the center of what we mean when we speak of dramaturgy.

And even though we have found no comfortable place for *dramaturgs* in our theater, we do know what we mean when we speak of *dramaturgy* and we know its place. Just as we can prove (after G. E. Moore, Wittgenstein's pal) the existence of the exterior world by pointing to it, we can demonstrate the existence of dramaturgy through its work in the theater and the clarity with which we can speak of, say, "Pinter's dramaturgy."

We may (and do) have our petty academic squabbles over Pinter's dramaturgy, but we all understand what the playing field is.

Dramaturgy is the sort of intellectual *mise-en-scène*, the superstructure or the subconscious (depending on your intellectual heroes) of the idea-world of the theater event as expressed in its shapes and in its rhythms, and in its affinities with our world.

Its connection to the construction of the play and to the conceptualization and realization of a performance is so complete as to be virtually identical to them. Like Benjamin's concept of *ideology, this dramaturgy* is most easily visible after the fact, as a trace. (Pinter didn't start with "Pinter's dramaturgy" and write from there, of course; Pinter's dramaturgy accretes as he writes and won't be finished until he is.) Dramaturgy is, except in the most egregious instances (the formulas for TV sitcoms or "new" American plays) an unconscious thing. In truly remarkable circumstances, the dramaturgy of a work can be understood and articulated in the moments of its creation, but this is incredibly rare and requires a collaborative energy and commitment between artist and dramaturg (like that between a composer and lyricist) that surpasses anything that can be instructed.

*   *   *

"Every word uttered on the stage," Peter Handke tells us. "is dramaturgy."

This is generous, yet it doesn't go quite far enough. From the *word* plunked down out loud into the silence of the *empty space, dramaturgy* ripples outward (like water in dancing rings), to embrace, address, subsume, caress, the world around *every word uttered.* The *dramaturgy* allows the word to land on its intended mark; it determines what and if and how and why the word *means* and it knows where it comes from, the story of the word which explains its presence here.

More, the dramaturgy of a piece includes its connection to us, to the spectators, and the situation in which we meet the work: inside, outside, for free or for a million dollars, sitting on benches or in velvet chairs? By allowing the concept to ripple out we discover dramaturgy at the middle of it all and the dramaturg at the center of the process, interpreting the play's movement from word to event.

And this makes her (or him) responsible for calling out "fire!" in our (progressively less-crowded) theater. For example, here are four issues, none of them "uttered onstage," but each of them crucial evidence of stupid error lack of conversation no thinking in our theater could be so much better if these were addressed:

1. Since the invention of cinema (at least) our culture has been moving in the direction of processing information visually. Outside the avant-garde (part of which Bonnie Marranca has dubbed a "theater of images") we have made little movement in this direction. One reason that the youth of today has no interest in our work is that it is stultifyingly dull to look at; there is no movement, just a torrent of words. Our generation thinks and feels and expresses itself in pictures and unless the theater learns a vocabulary of images, our audience will continue to age, wither, and die (picture that).

Writing plays that are merely the records of spoken conversation is a dead art form. We need a new way to conceive of a performance coming to fruition.

2. Although we claim in our press releases and grant applications (and even demonstrate in some of our low-level hiring) to be embracing a multi-cultural agenda, we still teach our actors to talk in a ridiculous *Standard English,* robbing them of the dignity of who they are and making all of our productions sound just a little bit stilted, mannered, and phony.

3. Intermissions were invented for a theater that needed to change sets between acts and for an audience of bourgeois socialites who needed their talk time. The two-act play structure died with the subplot, the demise of which occurred when we could only afford to pay enough actors for one plot. Yet we continue this tradition of breaking the evening into two parts out of no need, only from our ignorance of our capacity to change (and to pamper our audiences and to pad our receipts by selling snacks).

4. Ancient Greek theaters were big enough to accommodate the entire community (because the theater functioned as a place for the entire community to gather). We make our theaters as big as we think we can sell tickets to fill, which is grotesque. Perhaps the most sacred aspect of the theatrical event is the community created in the act—and we let the market determine the dynamic of that community. The question to be asked: in the time of *our* theater, yours and mine, what should be the nature of this dynamic and what number of people will best support its creation?

Remember once more the theater in your mind
where you staged a procession of words

coming together from the primal sounds
you learned.
You prompted them with your lips
twisting them into realized forms, and the shapes wafted into
unfamilar totems of new ideas.
Before the tyranny of narrative
could lead your mind on ahead (for comprehension),
you made pictures, *vivid* just behind your eyes,
and heard sounds while you produced in your mind
the play of reading.
So lush, so thick, such a dazzling parade that the beginning was forgotten
by the time you got to the end, the prospect of the end so luscious you
fought yourself to put it off, and were delighted to lose. In your mind
then, every book was like a Gertrude Stein play, a landscape moving with
infinite *possibility.* You read your world then as an infinite number of
possibilities, shimmering above, behind, below, beside the present. All.
Possibilities.

A theater like that exists to be created, perhaps. If we all insisted on it.
It is, I hope you believe as I do, a possibility, one we should at least *enter-tain.* The possibility of such a theater is startling.

It would have to be created by the rules of the creation of theater rather
than the rules of economics. Its artists would take seriously its history
and would be at the very least conversant in its literature and in the
events of their time. The shortcomings of its public would be addressed
in its work and only the very best performers would be allowed to per-form for children so that the next generation of artists and audiences
alike should learn what the theater itself might re-discover: that a live
event, thoughtfully conceived and carefully presented, can bring people
to a sense of themselves and their relationships to the others in the audi-ence and in the world that is absolutely unique and, perhaps, transcen-dently valuable.

Members of the audience for this work might return several times to see
a single production because it would be dense enough and pleasant
enough that they would think of it, of being contained in the theater, as a
favorite way to spend time.

> *"We are the tail of Romanticism—*
> *but—oh, how prehensile!"*
> ANDRÉ BRETON

Dramaturging Education

by **Richard Pettengill**

RICHARD PETTENGILL has been Director of Arts in Education at Chicago's Goodman Theatre since 1988. He has served as dramaturg on such Goodman productions as *Black Snow,* directed by Michael Maggio; *Dancing at Lughnasa,* directed by Kyle Donnelly; *The Merchant of Venice,* directed by Peter Sellars; and *The Night of the Iguana* and *A Touch of the Poet,* both directed by Robert Falls.

From 1982 to 1986, he was dramaturg at Chicago's Court Theatre, where he also ran education programs and worked on more than twenty productions. He has freelanced at a number of Chicago theaters, and has published articles and interviews on rock, film, and theater. He has taught at the University of Chicago, Chicago Dramatists Workshop, Columbia College, Roosevelt University, and the University of Illinois at Chicago, and is currently Adjunct Professor of Dramaturgy at the Theatre School, DePaul University.

"Why was Richard II's throne suspended up in mid-air?" asks a student audience member after a high school matinee. I deflect the question back to the audience, and I'm off on one of the most fascinating aspects of my dramaturgical work.

"He wanted the crown so badly it was floating out of his reach."

"It's up closer to heaven, as in the divine right of kings."

"It represented that the throne was up for grabs."

"I thought it meant that the king had the weight of the throne on his head."

Watching young people discover the theater always reminds me of my own early theater experiences, all of which helped put me onto the path of dramaturgy. Looking back now, an early step in this direction was realizing something that at the time felt revelatory: that plays are meant to be performed. When my twelfth-grade class studied the text of *King Lear* and then saw Peter Brook's film, I remember brainstorming with classmates as to why Brook set the play in such a bleak landscape, and why he showed Goneril (or was it Regan) smashing her own head against a rock. Such questions excited me a lot more than studying the text as an end in itself. I didn't realize at the time that an essay by a Polish dramaturg, Jan Kott, had inspired the production.[51] Later on, during a year abroad in England, I decided I could make the same jump in my Shakespeare essays, and wrote about actual productions of the plays. I then flirted briefly with writing theater reviews during my senior year of college, but swore that off forever after hearing that an actor had been devastated by one of my reviews because I had neglected to mention his performance. I enjoyed writing about productions, but didn't see the point in making public judgements about people's work.

Then during graduate school at the University of Chicago, I began seeing shows at the Court, a new professional theater on campus devoted to the classics. Two aspects of their productions especially intrigued me. One was that the program booklets included lengthy, well-written essays about the playwright, the play, and the historical context, written by someone called the dramaturg. I began to arrive twenty or so minutes early (as did others, I noticed) to leave time to read up on Chekhov, Shaw, or Ibsen. These program notes really opened up the productions for me, and I saw for the first time a way in which scholarship could illuminate a live event for a general audience.

Court Theatre also had post-show discussions where you could actually sit around and discuss the show with the cast. This, you must realize, seemed positively thrilling to a graduate student accustomed to discussing plays as literature in windowless seminar rooms. Perhaps because my chirpy excitement came across at these sessions, or because someone put in a good word, I later received a call from the theater asking if I'd like to apply for the position of dramaturg.

> *"What's that?"*

> "Well, what we think you'd do is research plays, talk to directors, write program notes, give lectures, and lead discussions with the audience, and, oh yes, we want you to start a program for high school students."

It all sounded terrific, but when it came down to beginning work Monday morning, I had little clue as to where to begin. I was left pretty much to on-the-job training, and began to learn—sometimes the hard way—the differences between the worlds of academia and the theater. On my first production, Shaw's *You Never Can Tell,* I showed up at a prerehearsal meeting with the director and cast and assumed that the occasion was much like graduate seminars in which one is judged by one's bright, informed scholarly/critical observations. As the director began to talk about Shaw's characterization, I started jumping in with all the bright, informed comments I could muster. I noticed the director looking sidelong at me, but forged ahead anyway, assuming this must be what a dramaturg should do. Afterward, the stage manager approached me and said, with a level of tact for which I'll be forever grateful:

> *"Richard, do you have a theater background?"*

> "Well, I played Tybalt in junior high."

"Oh. Well, in general, in the theater, when the director is talking, you don't interrupt."

"I see. . . ."

So went that part of my initiation. It was actually a great relief to discover that at times just listening was going to be important in this new job. But I also had to unlearn other hard-won habits, such as speaking and writing for an academic audience in favor of attempting to communicate clearly with theater artists and audiences. A turning point was discovering the 1978 issue of Yale *Theater,* which was filled with interviews with the first generation of American dramaturgs. All of them had widely differing accounts of what they did in their various contexts, and I saw that I could forge my own definition in my own context. Four years later, I wrote about my Court years in Yale's second dramaturgy issue (*Theater,* summer/fall, 1986).

Here at the Goodman, I do one or two dramaturgy assignments a season. Although running education programs is my primary responsibility, the dramaturgy gigs give me a direct connection to the artistic life of the productions and of the theater itself; they keep my education work vital. Many of my counterparts in other theater education departments have expressed feelings of isolation from the artistic life of their theaters, but that's not a problem for me. Access to and involvement in the artistic life of a theater comes naturally when one is blessed by an enlightened administrative decision. It's key that at the Goodman, my assistant and I are members of the artistic staff rather than being off by ourselves or in the public relations, administration, or development departments.

When starting on a dramaturgy project, I like to immerse myself in a solitary way for a month or more in the text and background research before my initial meetings with the director, which, ideally, take place well before an approach to the production has been formulated. I begin by asking myself questions:

- What is keeping me from a full understanding of this play?
- Are there textual issues to be dealt with?
- What background do our artists and audiences need to know?

These questions form the basis for early discussions with the director, and having those discussions early on allows me to make a real contribution to the production. At first we just talk, and I hand over the fruits of my research verbally and on paper. As ideas evolve and become focused, and as an artistic direction for the production begins to emerge, my research in turn becomes more focused and underscores and stimulates the evolving point of view.

Sometimes my research can reinforce a director's artistic instinct on a play, as with *The Night of the Iguana,* directed by the Goodman's artistic director

Robert Falls. In our early discussions of the play, Bob said he viewed the play as a poem, and that he wanted to restore most of the poetic language spoken between Hannah Jelkes and the Reverend T. Lawrence Shannon in the second act, much of which had been cut on the road to the 1961 Broadway production. Going through Williams's essays, I found that Tennessee repeatedly wrote of *Iguana* as a dramatic poem, which served to corroborate a view Bob had already formed on his own. This fueled our sense that the production was going to reflect Williams's intention in a way that had not been previously explored.

The same kind of research and exchange takes place when I attend design meetings. I can feed the design process with ideas and images I've run across in my research, but it's also a big help to keep track of the visual ideas under consideration. I often use some of those images to spice up the subscriber newsletter in a way that visually reflects the production. My general rule on this is that I want to give the audience some of the same primary material that helped inspire the artistic team, so as to illuminate the distinctive wellsprings of this particular production. Rather than explaining a production's ideas, I want to set the audience up to discover them for themselves. In the *Iguana* newsletter, for example, those play-as-poem quotes took center stage.

I also try to avoid giving audiences statements of artistic intent such as director's notes; they run the risk of preempting an audience's true response by telling them in advance what to think. They might also rob the production of the chance to succeed on its own terms, for it may have evolved into something wonderful, but quite different from the original directorial statement. I made an exception to this rule for Peter Sellars' production of *The Merchant of Venice*. Because of the passionate political ideas behind his contemporary Venice Beach setting, I included an extensive interview with Peter that many found fascinating and useful. The production, however, turned out to be controversial more on an aesthetic than a political level, and the interview didn't really set audiences up for the experience. While walking to the parking garage one night after a preview, one subscriber pointed to her interview and said "I wanted to see *this* production!"

As rehearsal begins, I share as much information with the cast as possible. If the director wants, I'll provide the actors with packets of information tailored to anticipate each of their needs and interests. Often I make a presentation summarizing the research I believe might be useful in rehearsal. These early efforts help develop rapport with actors; they see what I've already done, and get ideas on what else I can do for them. For Kyle Donnelly's production of Brian Friel's *Dancing at Lughnasa,* for example, I spoke about pagan rituals, the Lughnasa festival, bilberries, and traditional Irish music and dance. I also try to find answers to questions that arise as the text is explored. At various points during *Lughnasa,* I was off finding pictures of 1930s Irish kitchens, or the sheet music for "Play to Me Gypsy." During *Iguana,* I was asked about women's Baptist colleges in Texas; for *Black Snow,* we needed Bulgakov's correspondence with Stalin.

I'm less present and more on-call after that first week, but as rehearsal evolves into run-throughs, I come back to give notes designed to help the director fine-tune the show. Being out for a while gives me a fresher perspective on the proceedings, and I can see the play more as an audience member might. Following each run-through, I type up my responses so the director can read them at leisure and not feel obligated to reply to me about each one. I want the director to feel free to take or leave my notes, though I admit it's satisfying when I can see that notes have been taken. Occasionally—and this is fun—I'll watch a director read my notes to the cast directly off my sheet. I figure this way of working puts me in the grand unthreatening tradition of dramaturgs putting good ideas on paper and having an impact, as when Jan Kott's essays inspired Peter Brook.

I continue giving notes as run-throughs give way to tech, final dress rehearsals, and previews, which is when I begin working with audiences. Previews fascinate me because there, artistic process and audience education intersect. Our preview discussions are geared less toward answering the audience's questions about the show than toward getting ours answered about how the show is working for the audience. Of course we end up doing both most of the time, and what we learn by drawing out the audience often aids us in fine-tuning the show. I include any useful audience comments in my notes to the director.

The post–opening night discussions are, for me, the culmination of my entire dramaturgical process. We invite the actors to join in, and these sessions are a chance to hear as many audience responses as possible. As with the subscriber publications, I try not to talk about the directorial point of view, at least not at first. What audiences most often want to know, especially on shows with a strong directorial take, is, "What did the director intend?" And the subtext of this question is usually, "Did I get it right?" I often know what the director intended, but I try to hold it back at first; people who are told the "truth" behind a production are less likely to trust their own responses, and the discussion can drag to a halt. Only after I've gotten four or five different and distinct points of view about the same production element—like the ones that begin this essay—am I willing to say "And here's what the director said." Wonderful things come out, especially with students. I find the student audiences in our free program for Chicago public high schools[52] to be the most candid, and discussions with them to be the most revealing. During previews, their teachers attend special seminars on each play and attend a performance. Then they have a month in which to prepare their students using the scripts, newsletters, study guides, and "Backstage at the Goodman" video documentaries that we supply. The students end up much better prepared than most adult audience members, having recently studied and discussed the play's text in depth in their classrooms, and I do my best to draw them out afterward.

In this excerpt from a student discussion after a matinee of *The Night of the Iguana,* the students ask about the German characters, a group of pro-Nazi tourists who frolic maliciously around Maxine's Mexican veranda. I tried here to give them a chance to articulate some of their responses, and then to contrast their views with those of the director.

Student: "I want to know, what was the whole point of the Germans?"

Dramaturg: "We actually talked about that question a lot in rehearsal, but first could you all let us hear your thoughts on the subject?"

Student: "I think they're comic relief."

Student: "They represent the historical time period of the play. In the study guide, it said that there really were Nazis in Mexico at the time."

Student: "They're oblivious to the angst going on around them."

Student: "The Germans remind the audience that there is a world war going on at this time, and that there's another reality besides the one on the verandah."

Student: "They're the only people who are really happy; they know what they want while everyone else is acting desperate."

Student: "They weren't real. They didn't feel anything."

Dramaturg: "It's interesting that many of you saw them as comic relief or as a reality check of what really was going on in the world, because a lot of productions of this play have omitted them. And when productions have included them, reviews often criticize Tennessee Williams for putting them in the play; they don't get why the Germans are there at all. But it's clear to us that all of you do get it; your responses are just what the director wanted. He wanted to make them big, present, not to hide them, and to totally contrast their behavior with that of the other characters.

The director believed the Germans were a crucial part of the play's texture, particularly in contrast to the sensuality of the Mexicans. And their self-centeredness and complete insensitivity to Hannah, Shannon, and Nonno (particularly knowing as we do what was to happen historically soon after the time of the play), provides the ultimate contrast to the play's core, which is what Hannah and Shannon offer each other. For this one night, these two souls each put the concerns of the other above their own."

Throughout the entire production process, I work with directors, designers and actors to share perspectives, provide information, and collaborate in the illumination of a dramatic text. Carefully chosen advance information is provided to audiences. Then as the production opens, I turn my attention to audience members and pursue an essentially similar goal. This direct contact with audiences provides me with a sense of closure and acknowledgement that other theater artists regularly receive through applause and reviews. Apart from our program notes, critics can't discern what dramaturgs do on productions, so our work doesn't get reviewed. But we do have the pleasure of reviewing our own work by exploring with audiences the rich and ongoing impact of the productions we work on and contribute to. In doing so we get to witness not only the work's ongoing impact, but also its ripening in the weeks that lead toward closing and strike. Along the way, we may even notice, in a way that no audience member or critic can, the fruits of our dramaturgical efforts in the performance onstage.

There is Clamor in the Air[53]
by **Michael Lupu**

Romanian born **MICHAEL LUPU** is Senior Dramaturg of the Guthrie Theater where, for the past sixteen (1981–1996) years, he has dramaturged numerous productions. He served as the Guthrie's outreach director between 1981 and 1984 and has since been actively involved in various educational programs for the theater. Mr. Lupu is the senior editor of the *Guthrie Study Guides*. He worked as dramaturg for the Bulandra Theater in Bucharest, the Midwest Play Labs Conference in Minneapolis and has been teaching classes at the Guthrie, the University of Minnesota, and other schools.

A compelling and sometimes quite "loud" case has been made, especially in the past decade, for legitimizing dramaturgy as a viable and vital profession in the American theater. Indeed, many concerted efforts have led to this recognition. The days when Robert Brustein had to debunk the prevailing perception that dramaturgy was a German "thing" or, as he sarcastically grinned, "an un-American activity," seem long gone. (Ed. note: See Brustein's selection in this volume.) But they are not forgotten! Their echo resounds with every renewed demand that dramaturgs emphatically assert their profession for the long-term benefits of the American theatrical world. And increasingly noticeable results have changed the way issues of dramaturgy are discussed.

Today the profession of dramaturgy has become relatively respectable, even fashionable, in both professional theaters and institutions of higher learning. We all have good reasons to be proud of and happy about this steady advance. A good number of nonprofit theater companies actually include paid dramaturgy positions (what better evidence of professionalism?) in their budget spreadsheets. Organizational charts now include dramaturg and literary manager as official titles no less important than other administrative positions. An increasing number of colleges and universities offer courses, programs, and degrees in dramaturgy. As a result, more and more people can claim they are dramaturgs because they have the papers and diplomas to prove it (much as I can prove to anyone who is doubtful, that I am an American because I have my naturalization papers and American passport). We often find the name of the dramaturg listed in the program credits, although many theatergoers continue to be puzzled by this title and wonder what it means. Literary Managers and Dramaturgs of the Americas (LMDA), too, has gained strength and influence, so that the collective voice of dramaturgy can be better heard across the Americas.

But when dramaturgs speak, does the theater listen? Or, in order to be heard, do dramaturgs need to move on within the system and ascend to higher and more prominent positions such as director, producer, associate artistic director, and, in some cases, artistic director? Given the sharply competitive environment in the generically named world of entertainment, today's practical realities bring into focus the struggle for survival of most theaters; this is a challenge to the dramaturg's lofty concerns for the highest standards of artistic quality. Institutional obligations and budgetary pressures often sidestep the "dream seasons" a dramaturg might aspire to see produced. That is why, perhaps, some dramaturgs seize proper career opportunities, move beyond their limited job description, and climb the ladder to reach the top of the chain of command. Yet, once arrived there, not all dreams come true, or at least not easily.

Under these circumstances dramaturgy still serves as a convenient stepping-stone for an upwardly mobile career in theatrical institutions across the country. During my years in America I have encountered many directors who first appeared "disguised" as dramaturgs. When I first met Douglas Wager in the mid-seventies he used to be part of the literary department at the Arena Stage in Washington, D.C., after having also worked in stage management. Two decades later he is primarily a director, in fact, the artistic director of the Arena Stage. Clearly his voice can be better heard now. Being artistic director at the Arena Stage may well enhance the influence and authority his dramaturgical persona exercises. Similarly, Oskar Eustis was a dramaturg with the Eureka Theatre in San Francisco while he participated in the theatrical project based on the murder trial of Dan White—a case that captured the attention of the nation in the late seventies. What was initially a dramaturgical idea turned out to be Emily Mann's successful docudrama, *Execution of Justice;* the play was produced all over the country, and Eustis himself directed it at some point. His voice is that of a director who integrates considerable dramaturgical work in productions staged at the Mark Taper Forum in Los Angeles or Trinity Repertory Company in Providence, Rhode Island, where he has assumed the position of artistic director in recent years. Such examples could be easily multiplied. Would any of these directors still call themselves dramaturgs? Or is it conceivable that a director, once recognized professionally and hired for directing jobs, no longer needs dramaturgical know-how? What, then, is the significance of a career path leading from dramaturgy to directing? Perhaps questions of this order are worth examining, although I am sure they would matter far less in an environment that does not pay as much attention as we do to institutional power structures, titles, and job descriptions.

Some producers also wear the dramaturg's garb. Madeline Puzo, who was for a number of years the Guthrie Theater's producing director/and has returned now to the Ahmanson Theatre in Los Angeles, is a good example. She once told me that her duties as a producer have paralleled in many ways (in more comprehensive and complex ways, I gather) those of the dramaturg. Her work binds literary, dramaturgical, and theatrical aspects: exploring the troves of myths and folktales for potential dramatic adaptations; germinating ideas for future stage projects; reading scripts commissioned by the theater and commenting on their merits and shortcomings; guiding the work of trans-

lators and adapters through workshops of their drafts; suggesting and selecting the best available creative talents suitable for a given project, including designers and performers who are capable of developing and shaping the scripts
we intend to produce. Why restrict such work to the exclusive domain of the
officially appointed dramaturg? A recent example that comes to mind was the
Marivaux project developed at the Guthrie under Madeline Puzo's supervision. This was a complex undertaking that had as its centerpiece *The Triumph
of Love,* to which scenes and characters were added from two short Marivaux
plays, *The Dispute* and *Slave Island,* thereby expanding the work thematically and theatrically. During the course of extensive consultations and exchanges of views, Madeline Puzo organized a creative team that included the
poet and translator Paul Schmidt (who wrote the English adaptation eventually performed on the Guthrie stage in the summer of 1993), the director Do-
minique Serrand, his dramaturgical adviser and collaborator Paul Walsh, as
well as my colleague Jim Lewis, at that time the Guthrie's dramaturg and literary manager. Ultimately, the director's stated dramaturgical intentions affected
every decision during the process of producing this work. This case is indica-
tive of the dramaturgical scope of a producer's work. Many dramaturgical
functions are needed to bring a theatrical project to its completion, and what
truly matters is that they are fulfilled, and not who is tackling them. Conversely, when a dramaturg initiates a project, for example, Anne Cattaneo's
idea of commissioning a group of American dramatists to adapt for the stage
their favorite Chekhovian stories, inevitably the producing aspects of the work
converge with the dramaturgical aspects. In truth, they overlap and cannot
easily be separated. (Ed. note: See Anne Cattaneo's account of this project in
section one of this volume.)

Consequently, I find it important to distinguish between the prevailing organizational practices set in place by various theaters that have dramaturgs on
staff and the essence of the creative and critical activity called *dramaturgy.*
Dramaturgy's vitality may be in jeopardy if its pervasive, open-ended, and flexible presence in a theater tends to become institutionalized and ends up stuck
in formulas. Dramaturgy can never exist as an autonomous sphere, and to
adopt a self-important posture seems detrimental to its very nature. Therefore, it is worth asking whether the benefits of an institutionalized profession-
alization could outweigh the liabilities of any self-aggrandizement of the
dramaturg's job. Ideally, we should hope to reap all the advantages available to
an organized profession, while always being guarded and at the ready to question prescriptive models and narrowly formulated norms and codes of dramaturgical practice.

Despite (or perhaps because of) all of the above, I stubbornly stick to my
conviction that dramaturgy is not, strictly speaking, a profession, just as to be
an ambassador is not a profession; not only career diplomats, but economists,
poets, lawyers, scientists, and other professionals get appointed as ambas-
sadors. They effectively carry out the assigned diplomatic duties. Similarly,

many theater professionals can function—and actually do function—in the very heart of what is called dramaturgy: playwrights, actors, producers, directors, critics, and others. A quick survey among us will probably reveal that our real professional identities (or at least secret aspirations) are tied to our common interest and competence in dramaturgy. Some of us are dramatists, translators, or adapters; others direct plays or perform in them; others consider themselves critics (with all due respect to Estragon's ultimate foe in Beckett's *Waiting for Godot*). Can theater exist without playwrights? Without actors? Without directors? Without designers? Without craftspeople? Without the "real" professions? Probably not. But it has proved to exist, even thrive, without dramaturgs and, as we know, it continues to do so.

Simply stated, dramaturgs—that is, individuals holding such a paid or unpaid position in a theatrical institution—are not necessarily indispensable. But dramaturgy—that is, a complex, creative, intellectual activity inherent within the universe of drama and theater—is indispensable. There is sufficient proof that bringing a play to life on stage can happen without the involvement of a dramaturg. For all practical purposes, though, the production will fail or will not happen at all if dramaturgy is blatantly ignored.

Some may find this point a matter of linguistic fastidiousness, or some sort of facile sophistry. In my opinion, it is essential to clarify the nature of the subject at hand, then try to approximate its territory. We ought to be aware that no single dramaturgical voice can be narrowly or exclusively identified within a single professionally specialized individual. Drama, and more comprehensively, theater, cannot exist without dramaturgy.

According to the *Oxford English Dictionary*, dramaturgy is defined as: (1) dramatic composition; dramatic art (a domain justifiably belonging to playwrights, which explains why in other languages—French, or my native Romanian, for instance, "dramaturg" actually means playwright); and (2) dramatic or theatrical acting. Now, we know that dictionaries always have to catch up with the changes that constantly occur in language. So perhaps a different definition may emerge in future editions of the *OED*. The complexity of the process, from composing a dramatic text to staging and performing it, entails many variables of unquestionable importance; yet among them dramaturgy remains a central constant. Throughout any theatrical process dramaturgy represents undoubtedly a function without which no play will truly come to fruition.

Then how should we go about defining the voice of the dramaturg? The best dramaturgs I know of are first and foremost the best playwrights. We can learn from them more than from any textbook or course in dramaturgy. They necessarily know better, not just because they are, obviously, creatively engaged firsthand in dramatic composition, but mainly because the best of them, miraculously, have perfect pitch, twenty-twenty vision, and an unerring dramaturgical voice. Perhaps, their voice cannot be as clear in their expert pronouncements about their own works. Rather, their dramaturgical voice reverberates in the rich resonance of their plays. Of course, these heightened abilities depend on the caliber of their talent. And none of us can do more than surmise the mystery of what we call talent, specifically, dramaturgical talent. We always need to notice it, acknowledge it, respect it, and admire it.

Take for instance my favorite dramaturg, Chekhov. He "knew better" why he called some of his plays comedies and insisted that they should be performed accordingly, in a comic vein. For Chekhov, the dramaturgical viewpoint that Stanislavsky brought to his plays was quite unpalatable. It was not just a question of taste that may have been left undisputed; for Chekhov, a dramaturgy of pauses, sighs, and sad longings was wrongheaded and deeply upsetting. His plays simultaneously laugh at and show compassion for the infinity of human foibles and crushed aspirations. His dramaturgy—all subtle hues and shades, a multilayered texture of ambiguities and ironies, laughter and tensions—captures the very pulse of everyday existence among pre-Revolutionary Russian middle and upper classes, particularly, the provincial intelligentsia. And Chekhov accomplishes that with a disconcerting transparency; he does not need conventional plot development. Stanislavsky found a different kind of dramaturgy in these plays and made his case for it when he produced them. Faced with dramaturgical and theatrical choices that were not his own, Chekhov complained bitterly and did not compromise. He stood by his dramaturgical guns without volunteering to make changes just to please the producer, the director, or the dramaturg on duty, as so many playwrights of lesser substance and stature might do today in order to see their work produced by a theatrical institution. In those days at the Moscow Art Theatre no one had the title of dramaturg, although in retrospect some theater historians have given this credit to Nemirovitch-Danchenko. The good doctor, with all of his lucidity and insightful ability to observe human follies, was both emotionally attached to and disengaged from the world he captured in his writing. That is why his plays lend themselves to multiple theatrical interpretations, as if continuously inviting new dramaturgy to grow out of a fertile soil that has never become parched.

Chekhov and other such giant "dramaturgs" as Euripides, Shakespeare, Molière, Goldoni, Büchner, Brecht (whether canonized or not in the academic world) make the strongest possible case for the importance of dramaturgy as a creative function. Their heritage provides a splendid testing ground for a diversity of dramaturgical explorations and interpretive angles or perspectives. It is known that an unprecedented dramaturgical impetus was brought about on the Continent, and especially in Germany, by the discovery of Shakespeare's plays in translation late in the eighteenth century. In our time, many outstanding playwrights, attracted by the chance to sharpen their understanding of dramaturgical structure and their own psychological insights, have undertaken English translations of Chekhov's plays. It is a great challenge to tackle Chekhov's simplicity and depth of expression and make them work in a different language while preserving the transparent quality of the dialogue.

In the same vein, major directors have approached Chekhov's plays with a specific dramaturgical interpretation of their own. Although Chekhov disagreed with his approach, Stanislavsky deserves credit for having conceived his directing and acting style on a dramaturgy steeped in detailed realistic character exploration—as fostered by the way he perceived the playwright's universe. *An Actor Prepares* is a compendium of how dramaturgical thinking and acting practices merged to create a far-reaching and influential school of stage performance.

The productions of Chekhov's plays at the Moscow Art Theatre constitute just the starting point, initiating the long production history of Chekhov's plays throughout our century. In recent decades, we can compare widely different dramaturgical and, consequently, directorial treatments of Chekhov's plays, such as: *Three Sisters* by Yuri Lubimov, G. Tovstonogov, Peter Stein, Liviu Ciulei, and Elizabeth LeCompte (she radically deconstructed the play and used the title *Brace Up!*); *The Cherry Orchard* by Giorgio Strehler, Andrei Serban, Peter Brook, and Lucian Pintilie; or, directly within my working experience at the Guthrie, *The Seagull* by Lucian Pintilie in 1983, and by Garland Wright in 1992.

It seems secondary if a dramaturg appeared on the credit list of these memorable theatrical productions. Truly of interest is the directors' anchoring of their stage work within a dramaturgical ground. It makes a great difference if one director (Lucian Pintilie) imagines *The Seagull* as a play that shows the dire consequences one suffers for entering the forbidden territory of art without the saving grace of genuine talent, while another director (Garland Wright) interprets the play as depicting a universe of unrestrained histrionic behavior on and off stage. No matter how contrasting their theatrical treatments, both plumbed the dramaturgical depths inherent in the play. In other words, directing any play entails a careful scrutiny of its plot structure, conflict, characters, and the identification of its inner voice and tone—in short, its dramaturgy. Only when a solid dramaturgical foundation lies underneath the interpretive approach can a compelling directorial case be made through the staging of a play.

If the director is not just the stage "traffic cop," dramaturgy is bound to be central to his or her preparation for the production as a whole. To limit the definition of dramaturgy to research and gathering of relevant background information is to leave out its true vitality and creativity. Dramaturgy functions as a sort of monitoring device meant to keep the process on course. Whether a barely audible yet persistent whisper or a vocally assertive and persuasive argument, dramaturgy does not emanate exclusively from one individual who qualifies as dramaturg. Rather, it forms the underpinning of all intuitive or deliberate choices, thoughts, debates, and nurtures the passionate search for artistic truth on stage.

The Compleat Dramaturg
by **Leon Katz**

LEON KATZ is currently Dramaturg Consultant at the Mark Taper Forum in Los Angeles, and Visiting Professor of Drama at the University of California Los Angeles. Until
1989, he was co-chairman of the Department of Dramaturgy and Dramatic Criticism at
Yale University, and he has also taught at Cornell, Stanford, Columbia, Vassar, Carnegie-
Mellon, Manhattanville, Barnard, San Francisco State University and the University of
Giessen in Germany. He is the author of several dozen original plays and adaptations
produced in the United States and abroad. A collection of his plays is published under
the title, *Midnight Plays.*

The compleat dramaturg, to be compleat, should have these skills:

1. A critical sensibility and the ability to write mature critical articles and
reviews addressed not merely to professionals and scholars but to reasonably
intelligent and generally aware readers and theatergoers.

2. A thorough knowledge, in depth, of the dramatic repertory based on a
wide range of reading in dramatic texts, scholarship and criticism in all periods and genres of drama, with special areas of expertise of his or her own.

3. The ability to do scholarly research, and also practical experience in tracking down scripts, options, copyright information, and publication and production histories of plays.

4. The ability to read and translate plays from, ideally, several but at a minimum one foreign language, and the even more valuable ability to adapt the
translated text into stageworthy dialogue in English.

5. The ability to read scripts intelligently, and to write resumes and appraisals
of them with professional competence.

6. The ability to cut scripts knowledgeably, with an understanding of how to
do so without destroying their logic or losing their essential dramatic and
theatrical values.

7. Experience in preparing Dramaturg's Protocols—a four-part pre-production
study of a play—together with a glossary of the text, for the information of the
Director and possibly of the rest of the company. The parts consist of (1) relevant historical, cultural, social or other pertinent background of the play,
(2) relevant biographical information concerning the playwright, (3) a critical
and descriptive production history of the play, and (4) a critical analysis and
breakdown of the play. The glossary consists of a script with facing notes explaining all unfamiliar or questionable terms and references in the play.

8. The ability to prepare useful background study guides for additional reading, to be available to anyone connected with the production of the play.

9. Experience and expertise in collaborating with directors and designers in planning a production concept or, if a specific "Concept" is not to be employed, an approach to the play and an articulation of its production goals.

10. Based on an intimate knowledge of a play, and on pre-production discussion with a director on this approach to the play, the expertise to contribute significantly to a play's casting and design.

11. Expertise in taking dramaturgical rehearsal notes (which can be of crucial value to a receptive director).

12. A thorough awareness of dramaturg's rehearsal decorum, knowing when and at what points in the rehearsal process notes are of value, what sort of notes are relevant at different stages of the rehearsal process, what sort of notes have constructive value and what sort have not.

13. Experience in working with a director during the rehearsal process, and knowing the do's and dont's—the decorum—governing conduct during consultation sessions.

14. In working with playwrights, the ability to break down a script, analyze its structural strengths and weaknesses, and make constructive suggestions for its revision (begins in training, continues for a lifetime).

15. Training and experience in appropriate writing styles and formats for program notes, informative articles, published interviews, and general publicity releases.

16. Experience in keeping notes for and writing up post-production records: production logs, season histories, post-production critical evaluations.

17. The experience of an apprenticeship in a particular theater, working within the framework of its particular procedures and policies, and gaining familiarity with its overall administrative and budgetary set-up.

18. Above all, developing an individual "idea of a theater" out of which she or he would, if this earth were heaven, map out seasons of repertory to advance that particular idea, and even though this earth is not heaven, developing the determination to work toward advancing such a theater, or orienting a theater toward that goal. And concomitantly, developing enough common sense to recognize that a theater will not normally adapt itself overnight to one's particular aesthetic orientation, but one must retain enough idealism to yearn and plan for that level of theater to exist, someday, somewhere.

SECTION NOTES

1. David H. Freedman, "Quantum Consciousness," *Discover* 15.6 (June, 1994): 94.

2. Jack Zipes, "Utopia as the Past Conserved: An Interview with Peter Stein and Dieter Stürm of the Schaubühne am Halleschen Ufer," *Theater* 9 1 (Fall 1977): 50-57.

3. Hélène Cixous, "The Last Painting or The Portrait of God," in *Coming to Writing and Other Essays,* (Cambridge: Harvard University Press, 1991) 114.

4. Stephen Jay Gould, "Full of Hot Air," *Natural History* (October 1989): 28.

5. Gould 30.

6. Gould 32.

7. Gould 34, 36, 38.

8. Charles Darwin, *The Origin of Species* (New York: Random House, 1993) 649.

9. See Barbara Furstenburg, "The Emergence of Drama in the Curriculum: A Study of Contrasting Images of the University Professor." *DAI* 29/12A, pp. 4299-4300-A. Yale granted the first MFA in Drama in 1931, and converted its Department of Drama into a separate graduate school, the School of Drama, in 1955.

10. See also Brustein's *Making Scenes: A Personal History of the Turbulent Years at Yale, 1966-1979* (New York: Limelight, 1984) 259-260. For a historical overview of the Yale Repertory Theatre, see my entry, "Yale Repertory Theatre," in *American Theatre Companies, 1931-1986,* ed. Weldon B. Durham (Westport, CT: Greenwood, 1989) 533-48.

11. Jonathan Marks, "Dramaturg's Guide: A Handbook for Student Dramaturgs at the Yale School of Drama and Yale Repertory Theatre" (Yale University, 1977). I would like to thank Susan Jonas for calling this document to my attention and providing me with a copy. I would also like to thank Jonathan Marks for reading and generously responding to this essay.

12. Brustein, *Making Scenes* 260.

13. Marks 3.

14. Marks's "Guide" describes all of these functions in detail.

15. Marks 11.

16. Leon Katz, "Dramaturg's Guide (Guidelines for Students Dramaturgs), Part Four" (Yale University, n.d.) 2.

17. Katz 10.

18. Mark Bly recalls that Joel Schechter, a 1977 DFA who taught at Yale from 1977 to 1991, played a major role in helping students translate destructive criticism into constructive dramaturgy. He encouraged them to pose questions in an honest but supportive manner rather than to write their reviews in advance of opening night. Interview with Mark Bly, November 23, 1994.

19. See Brustein article in this volume, p. 34.

20. Marks 10, 12. He is referrring to Richard Gilman, "The Necessity for Destructive Criticism," *Common and Uncommon Masks* (NY: Vintage, 1971) 12-22.

21. Marks 13.

22. See Katz, "The Compleat Dramaturg" in this volume, pp. 115-16.

23. Katz, "The Compleat Dramaturg."

24. Information about current Yale courses derives from two interviews with Mark Bly, May 8, 1994, and November 23, 1994. Also see Mark Bly's essay in this volume, and his "The Questioning Spirit and the Creative Process," *Theatre Symposium* 3

(1995): 12–17. I would like to thank Mark Bly for reading early versions of this essay and commenting on it.

25. Interview with Mark Bly, May 8, 1994.

26. H. Clay Harshbarger, *Some Highlights of the Department of Speech and Dramatic Arts* (Iowa City: University of Iowa, 1976).

27. For Brownstein's concept of the playwright/dramaturg, see his statement in "Dramaturgs in America: Eleven Statements," *Theater* 10.1 (1978): 18–19, *What Is Dramaturgy?* Bert Cardullo, ed. (New York: Peter Lang, 1995) 141–45. Brownstein left Iowa in 1979 to become head of the playwriting program at Yale under Dean Lloyd Richards.

28. Brownstein 18.

29. Brownstein 18.

30. Robert Hedley continued to head the Playwrights Workshop until 1990, when he left Iowa to become Chair of the Department of Theatre Arts at Temple University in Philadelphia.

31. For further discussion of the dynamics of this process, see my "Dramaturgy in Two Senses: Towards a Theory and Some Working Principles of New-Play Dramaturgy," in Cardullo 157–76.

32. James Magruder, resident dramaturg at Center Stage (Baltimore), in a telephone conversation with the author in May 1993.

33. This teaching model was developed during my years as Assistant Professor and Cochair of the playwriting program at The Catholic University of America in Washington, D.C. Conducted in tandem with a graduate directing class taught by Jackson Phippin (1993) and William Foeller (1994, 1996), class size was limited to between 6 and 10 students. Prerequisites included coursework in theater history, criticism, and dramatic literature.

34. Kathleen Dimmick, former dramaturg at The Mark Taper Forum (Los Angeles) and The American Conservatory Theater (San Francisco), in a telephone conversation with the author in May of 1993.

35. Founded by Anne Hamburger in 1986, En Garde Arts is a site-specific theater that uses New York City buildings, streets, parks, and piers as sites for original plays and performance pieces.

36. I suggest that they consult other theater manifestos, such as those written by Tristan Tzara, André Breton, Julian Beck and Judith Malina, or Charles Ludlam.

37. Peter Handke, *Offending the Audience,* from *Kaspar and Other Plays* (New York: Hill and Wang, 1969) 23.

38. Sources include my experiences as a production dramaturg in regional theaters and conversations with other professional directors and dramaturgs, including Mark Brokaw, Kathleen Dimmick, William Foeller, James Magruder, and Jackson Phippin, who willingly dredged up memories of best-case and worst-case scenarios, and were refreshingly frank when it came to discussing the agonies and ecstasies of collaborative work.

39. While the directors interviewed have notably different directing processes, interests, and tastes, it's worthwhile noting that they are united in their belief that their most adventurous work occurs when they work in collaboration with a dramaturg.

40. A version of this address appeared in *New Theatre Quarterly* 10 (1994): 24–27; Simon Trussler and Clive Barker, editors.

41. Ed. note: Under the direction of Lynn Thomson, LMDA publishes brief synopses of new plays and circulates them to members. For more information on LMDA and the services it offers see Victoria Abrash's piece in the appendix of this volume.
42. Italo Calvino, *Invisible Cities,* trans. William Weaver (New York/London: Harcourt Brace Jovanovich, 1974) 155, my emphasis. Original Italian edition: *Le città invisibili* (Torino: Giulio Einaudi editore, 1972).
43. The concept of *sprezzatura* merits further exploration in relation to the process of movement composition. Baldesar Castiglione, Italian diplomat and man of letters attached to the court of the Duke of Urbino in the sixteenth century, develops this notion within courtly life in provocative ways in the 1516 *Il libro del Cortegiano del Conte Baldesar Castiglione.* For Castiglione, *sprezzatura* is that seamless effortlessness with which complicated tasks can be completed, so that others are not aware of the difficulties involved in the performance of such tasks. A viewer should be overwhelmed by the grace and lightness of the performance (which in Castiglione's case usually concerned seduction and political/social interactions for personal gain) and by the finesse of the performer, and thereby be taken by or convinced of the gesture (whether physical, emotional, or mental) without noticing the hard work and effort that contributed to its success. This could be seen as a paradigm for movement performance generally, especially for such genres as classical ballet, where the signs of success include the same ever-smiling lightness and effortlessness as affects that conceal the sweaty hard labor taking place. Cf. *The Book of the Courtier,* trans. Charles S. Singleton (New York/London/Toronto/Sydney: Anchor Books/Doubleday, 1959).
44. Henri Bergson, *Matter and Memory,* trans. N. M. Paul and W.S. Palmer (New York: Zone Books, 1991) 94.
45. In Heidi Gilpin, *Eidos : Telos* (Frankfurt: Ballett Frankfurt, January, 1995) 33.
46. Recent attempts to address the body in motion and the spaces of the body from multidisciplinary perspectives include, among others: *Zone 6: Incorporations,* ed. Jonathan Crary and Sanford Kwinter (New York: Urzone, 1992); *Sexuality and Space,* ed. Beatriz Colomina (Princeton: Princeton Architectural Press, 1992); and Barbara Maria Stafford's *Body Criticism: Imaging the Unseen in Enlightenment Art and Medicine* (Cambridge, MA: The MIT Press, 1991).
47. Cf. for example, Robert Wilson's production of Shakespeare's *King Lear,* which premiered at the Bockenheimer Depot of the Schauspiel Frankfurt 26 May 1990. (*König Lear,* with Marianne Hoppe playing Lear. Production, Direction, and Set Design: Robert Wilson. Dramaturgy and Collaboration: Ellen Hammer. Costumes: Yoshio Yabara. Lighting: Heinrich Brunke and Robert Wilson. Music: Hans Peter Kuhn. Movement: Suzushi Hanayagi.) One of the more contemporary examples of this phenomenon, among many others, is Wilson's production of Gertrude Stein's play (produced as the musical Stein intended it to be): *Dr. Faustus Lights the Lights* (premiere April 1992 at the Hebbel Theater, Berlin, with a world tour of performances in Frankfurt, New York, Houston, and elsewhere May–November 1992), with lighting by Wilson and the sound score and musical numbers by composer and sound artist Hans Peter Kuhn, a collaborator of Wilson since 1979. Cf. Theater am Turm, Frankfurt, Programbook for *Dr. Faustus Lights the Lights,* 31 May 1992; and John Rockwell, "The Chirps in 'Dr. Faustus,' and the Artist Behind Them," *The New York Times* 5 July 1992, p. 3.

48. There are many examples of this, although one of the more interesting for our purposes here is a movement performance production that does not take as its source a dramatic text per se, but rather, the moving body as text. Cf. William Forsythe's evening length production *Limb's Theorem* (premiere Frankfurt, 17 March 1990. Choreography: William Forsythe. Music: Thom Willems. Dramaturgy: Heidi Gilpin. Set Design: Michael Simon. Costumes: Férial Simon. Lighting: William Forsythe and Michael Simon).

49. Some of the productions of the former East German dramatist Heiner Müller employ such strategies, as in, for example, his *Quartett* (premiere West Berlin, 1982), as directed by Robert Wilson in collaboration with Müller, and performed at the American Repertory Theater in Cambridge, Massachusetts, with previews 5–9 February 1988, and the premiere 10 February 1988. According to ART records, Wilson was the sole director of this production; Müller, however, was present in Cambridge during the rehearsals and contributed to them. (Direction and Set Design: Robert Wilson. Assistant Director: Jane Perry. Lighting: Howell Binkley and Robert Wilson. Translation: Carl Weber. Music composition and adaptation: Martin Pearlman. Sound Design: Stephen D. Santomenna. Costumes: Frida Parmegianni.) Müller's own productions of his *Hamletmachine* (premiere Brussels, 1978) and *Germania Tod in Berlin* (premiere Munich, 1978) are also relevant here. Müller discusses his approach to theatermaking in a number of the texts in his *Germania* (edited by Sylvère Lotringer, translated and annotated by Bernard and Caroline Schütze. Semiotext(e) Foreign Agents Series (New York: Semiotext(e), 1990)). Samuel Beckett however, is clearly an agent of suggestion and inspiration for much of the performance material to which I am alluding here: his early work with the technologies of reproduction, to be found in *Krapp's Last Tape* and other plays, proposes the necessity for productions which call into question the unity of the speaking voice, and the simultaneous presence of multiple voices. In addition to Beckett's plays, cf. *The Theatrical Notebooks of Samuel Beckett*, general editor, James Knowlson. (Vol. II: *Endgame*.) Vol. III: *Krapp's Last Tape*. With a revised text, edited by James Knowlson (New York: Grove Press, 1993). Cf. also a discussion of Beckett's position vis à vis contemporary performance aesthetics in Mel Gussow's "Wipes Dream Away With Hand," *The New York Times Book Review*, March 7, 1993, p. 10.

50. This is one of the topics addressed in "Emissions: A Discussion with William Forsythe and Heidi Gilpin," *Critical Space* No. 10 (1993): 151–159, which documents a particular moment in the trajectory of the creative process in Frankfurt, and attempts to make accessible for viewers and readers the kinds of questions and issues at stake for Forsythe both in performance and in the choreographic process.

51. Kott's essay, *"King Lear* or *Endgame"* is included in his volume *Shakespeare Our Contemporary* (New York: W.W. Norton and Company, 1964). Also included there is his essay "Titania and the Ass's Head," which reportedly influenced Brook's famous 1970 production of *A Midsummer Night's Dream* at the Royal Shakespeare Company.

52. For more information on this program, the Student Subscription Series, see "Education and Community Programs at the Goodman Theatre, 1996" in section three of this volume.

53. This essay is a revised excerpt from a piece by the same title published in *Theatre Symposium* 3 (1995): 37–45. Published by Southeastern Theatre Conference and the University of Alabama Press; Paul C. Castagno, editor.

SECTION 3

MODELS OF COLLABORATION

The emergence of the dramaturg in American theater, this new person at the rehearsal table, has occasioned a good deal of discussion about how we work together when we make theater. Geoffrey Proehl looks at ways in which dramaturgs have written about their place in the process over the past thirty years. He identifies metaphors they have employed to describe their work and considers the implication of those metaphors for theatermaking. As coeditor of this volume, he links these images to articles throughout the book in order to help the reader navigate the volume.

Tori Haring-Smith continues this discussion with a consideration of the roles we assume, particularly in director/dramaturg relationships. Her piece is part of a general reconsideration of the production models that American theater absorbs from both the culture around us and historical precedent.

Allen Kuharski interviewed Joseph Chaikin and artists with whom he worked in order to trace the changing nature of Chaikin's collaborations with playwrights and dramaturgs from The Open Theater (1963–73) to The Winter Project (1977–83) and the "Night Voices" radio series with a particular emphasis on post–Open Theater developments. Kuharski traces in microcosm the emergence of the dramaturg in this ensemble and in doing so, reflects how the idea of a dramaturg worked its way into the daily life of American theater over the course of these years. More importantly, this article explores issues of collaboration and creativity in the creation of performances that do not begin with established texts. This piece should be read in concert with Mira Rafalowicz's excellent "poem" on both her work with Chaikin and the collaborative process in general.

Royston Coppenger (dramaturg) and Travis Preston (director) comprise a team remarkable in American theater for the closeness and the duration of their collaborations. In this collection of short pieces by each of them on a variety of topics, they reflect on their work together, particularly as it relates to their view of the rehearsal process: they argue for an approach that defies rigid categorization with respect to process and aesthetics.

Gregory Gunter has worked with numerous contemporary directors including Tina Landau and Anne Bogart. In his article, he describes one of the most important ways in which dramaturgs collaborate with directors, actors, and designers: not through words but with images, pictures, colors, and shapes. Another important area of collaboration is between playwrights and dramaturgs or literary managers. The panel discussion, "How to Talk to a Playwright," features dramaturgs and playwrights candidly exploring ways in which these relationships can go wrong as well as ways in which they can succeed, addressing issues of culture, gender, and terminology. Additional reflections on how playwrights and dramaturgs work together are found in many of the selections in section five, "Developing New Works."

Educational initiatives around the production of plays comprise a major area of collaborative dramaturgical activity in American theater: in this instance between dramaturgs and their communities. Allen Kennedy examines some of the most exciting and innovative of these programs at theaters such as the Guthrie Theater in Minneapolis, the Huntington Theatre in Boston, and People's Light and Theater Company in Malvern, Pennsylvania. Some of the programs and activities he describes are long-lived, others come and go with the individuals who develop them. His article is not so much a history of this work as it is a source of ideas for those who would create their own programs. Kennedy's piece is followed by Richard Pettengill's summary of the kinds of initiatives that the Goodman Theater in Chicago offers its community. It provides a detailed look into collaborative possibilities this single theater has discovered.

Finally, at the heart of our collaborations is the language we use to describe our work together on a play. This section concludes with two selections that explore this language from different perspectives. Lee Devin's neo-Aristotelian approach to play analysis provides one model that readers may wish to apply to scripts on which they are working: it develops a vocabulary that directors and dramaturgs might use to clarify the parts of plays and how those parts work together. Readers may or may not agree with the categories Devin suggests (mention Aristotle and expect an argument), but beneath these categories lies an even more important concern of Devin's: that collaborators search with some rigor for a language that will describe their undertakings and allow them to more effectively communicate with one another about playscripts and in rehearsals. This piece should also be compared with pieces in "Developing New Works," particularly those by Weeks and Katz (both wary of the abuse of pre-existent models derived from Aristotle and the well-made play) and Sanford, who, like Devin, finds Aristotle useful in his daily work.

Overall, the relationship between dramaturgy and contemporary critical theory has not been a smooth one: in part because of American theater's trenchant anti-intellectualism and determined pragmatism; in part also because of the theory's tendency toward bloodless jargon. John Lutterbie encounters head-on the tension between theory and practice so often experienced in American theater. He makes a strong case for pulling down the barricades and for dramaturgy as a place in which more overt theoretical reflection can serve to enrich and deepen practice. In doing so, he introduces the reader to several theoretical positions and makes suggestions for further reading. The current maze of theoretical languages can be daunting; Lutterbie offers an initial map of the terrain. The distance from Proehl to Lutterbie may seem long (and this section does encompass a variety of interests and concerns around collaboration), but both pieces argue for the ability to step back from what we do and gain some perspective on the metaphors and languages that condition our work. Ideally, that stepping back will in the long run make our coming together more productive.

Of course, many other selections in this book deal with collaborative models. Jim Niesen in section four ("New Contexts") discusses ensemble-based theatermaking, as does Finque and Frisch/Weems in section five ("Developing New Work"). Mazer in "New Contexts" further explores the role of critical theory in collaborative dialogues and Power, also in "New Contexts," deals with how an ensemble communicates with a community that it hopes to represent faithfully on stage. In these and other ways, models of collaboration present themselves throughout this volume, for without a collaborative ethos the dramaturg has no existence in the production process.

The Images Before Us:
Metaphors for the Role of the Dramaturg in American Theatre
by **Geoffrey S. Proehl**

GEOFFREY PROEHL teaches, dramaturgs, and directs at the University of Puget Sound in Tacoma, Washington. Prior to joining the faculty there, he chaired the graduate studies program in theater arts at Villanova University, where he taught dramaturgy and supervised the work of student dramaturgs on university and professional productions. He holds an MFA in directing from Wayne State University and a PhD in directing and dramatic criticism from Stanford University. He has authored articles for *The Journal of Dramatic Theory and Criticism* (on Eugene O'Neill and Michel Foucault) and the *Encyclopedia of English Studies and the Language Arts* (on dramaturgy and theatricality), as well as the book *Coming Home Again: American Family Drama and the Figure of the Prodigal* (Fairleigh Dickinson University Press, 1996). Research grants and the support of colleagues from Villanova University and the University of Puget Sound have made work on this project possible.

Dramaturgy can refer to an attribute, a role, or a function. As **attribute** we use the word to describe the dramaturgy of a particular playwright or play, as in the dramaturgy of Richard Wagner or Bertolt Brecht or Caryl Churchill. In this sense, dramaturgy roughly equals dramatic structure or the conventions unique to a playscript, playwright, or performance. Dramaturgy as a **role** describes that person whose name appears on a program opposite the title "Dramaturg." Within university and regional theaters, the presence of this title on programs is increasingly common. It has appeared in film credits and an episode of the television sitcom "Empty Nest" even featured a character who had this job title, a sure sign that dramaturgy as a role is making inroads into popular consciousness.[1] As **function,** dramaturgy refers to a set of activities necessary to the theatermaking process, often centering on the work of selecting and preparing playscripts for production, activities that various individuals—producers, directors, designers, actors—if not someone specifically called a dramaturg, must perform. Dramaturgs and those who teach dramaturgy will often point out that even though a dramaturg is not at work on a particular show, someone is still performing these dramaturgical functions.[2] Those who make this point underscore the importance of dramaturgy as a concept without insisting on the nomenclature of the person performing the job. This use of the term asks for some rethinking of assumptions about how theater works, suggesting that plays are made not just by playwriting, directing, designing, and acting (even if the same person does all four tasks) but also by something called "dramaturging." An awkward noun becomes an even more awkward verb.

A conversation has been going on in American theater for the past thirty years or so about the potential for dramaturgy as a role or function in theater-making, about whether this word should be used as more than a term to denote dramatic structure. That conversation has taken place in and around university and regional theaters in discussions between directors, actors, designers, playwrights, and other theater-makers; at conferences in panels and presentations; in course work and curriculum plans at universities; in grants for funding proposals; in documents for tenuring dramaturgy professors; in professional organizations such as the Theatre Communications Group (TCG), Literary Managers and Dramaturgs of the Americas (LMDA), and the Association for Theatre in Higher Education (ATHE); and most publicly in numerous periodicals and books, particularly two ground-breaking issues of Yale *Theater* (edited by Joel Schechter and Mark Bly) devoted to the role of the dramaturg in American and European theater.[3] Like most subjects in contemporary American life, it even has its own e-mail distribution list.[4] The conversation is large and rather wonderfully messy: sometimes extremely eloquent; sometimes fairly prosaic. What is perhaps most remarkable about all this talk of dramaturgy is that it continues to circle around a question that will not go away: "What is a dramaturg?"

It is, of course, easy to be cynical about this extended process of self-definition. Dramaturgs themselves have tired of continually explaining to themselves and others just what it is they do or *want* to do. For some dramaturgs, this initial stage of self-definition, thankfully, now seems to be coming to an end, at least within the circle of theater professionals with whom they work on a daily basis: role and function are established. I recently talked with a prospective undergraduate at the university where I teach. When I mentioned "the word," expecting to need to supply a brief definition, she surprised me by saying she already knew about this word. More often than not, however, it is still easier to avoid the questions, to say, "I direct or act or design or teach theater history," than to begin another definition that will be met with another set of vague, slightly confused, moderately supportive nods.

The extant body of self-defining literature on dramaturgy is remarkable for its patience, persistence, and its seriousness. It demonstrates a consistent willingness to think and rethink its own modes of operation, to question even the validity of its own existence.[5] In particular, I am intrigued by metaphors for the role of the dramaturg that emerge from these conversations: "the dramaturg as. . . ." What interests me is the way in which dramaturgs both position themselves and are positioned by others, along with the effects that this positioning has on their work and self-image. More importantly, listening in on this dramaturgy talk offers a chance to reflect not only on how we construct the role of the dramaturg but also on the process of theatermaking itself in the last quarter of twentieth-century America. This conversation implicitly and explicitly invites us to reconsider the role of self (or aspects of the self), other, and textuality (from playscript to history to theory, and so forth) in the making of a performance: indeed this invitation is perhaps one of dramaturgy's most significant contributions to theater in North America. This essay then is not primarily about how-to-be-a-dramaturg or what-is-a-dramaturg, but about what we can learn from the conversation that has circulated around these topics.[6]

> I sit behind him, usually to the left, and I try to see things as he sees them.[7]

These words come from Laurence Shyer's book, *Robert Wilson and His Collaborators,* from a section titled "Writers, Dramaturgs, and Texts." In particular, they are the words of Maita di Niscemi describing her work with director Robert Wilson. I choose them to structure this inquiry because, for better or for worse, they capture an image of the dramaturg (as **role**) in American theater: sitting, behind, to the left, trying to see as the director "sees." On one side, there is the proscenium stage, filled with a light that illuminates and silhouettes Wilson's performers; on the other, Wilson himself, making the stage picture, controlling that light with the help of his designers and technicians. The dramaturg is, in a sense, on neither side, neither in the light nor in control of it.[8] She or he is in the dark or semidark (not necessarily an undesirable place to be—some people are comfortable in the light, others are not), perhaps taking notes, ideally located to whisper a word or two in the director's ear, ready to respond to questions or problems. The dramaturg is behind and off to one side, not in the director's line of sight but still a function of it, on the left side (as metaphor would have it), on the side of the brain that science now suggests is responsible not for visual images but for words and sequentiality.[9] Ear and eye: the dramaturg has access to the director's ear and tries to see through his or her eyes.

TAKING THE QUOTE APART, PART I: "I TRY TO SEE" (READING, WATCHING, CONSCIOUSNESS)

Dramaturgs see. They use their eyes intensively. They spend many hours reading and watching. One dramaturgy conference used a fingerprint as its logo (dramaturgs leave their invisible mark on the work they touch). I would use one big eye. One result of the discourse on dramaturgy, particularly as role or function, has been to draw attention to the role of sight and its related functions (watching and reading) when we make a play. Because seeing foregrounds awareness, we might think of the dramaturg as an **image of almost pure consciousness;** in terms of reading, as a **historical, critical, literary, and philosophical consciousness;** in terms of the rehearsal process, as that **watchdog** charged with protecting the interests of the director, the play-

wright, the artistic director, the community, the theater, or some other entity—
on guard as the **critic-in-residence** or the **conscience of the theater,** or
the **audience's surrogate,** as their eyes. All of these various notions of dramaturgy as consciousness (for this, after all, is what the eye most connotes)
find frequent expression in writings on dramaturgy and the dramaturg. (I will
provide endnotes throughout this piece to point the reader to articles in this
volume and elsewhere that support and further develop these metaphors.)

Participants in this conversation on dramaturgy generally expect dramaturgs and literary managers to exhaust their eyes as the **designated readers** of a theater or a production. They must read the dramatic literature, new
and old, of many different countries, and in the original languages if possible,
so they can help plan the theater's season. We also expect them, especially in
their role as literary managers, to be aware of the best new writers and to
bring their plays to the attention of the theaters for whom they work.[10] In
terms of secondary sources, articles on dramaturgy pile up lists of potential
fields of inquiry: "performance theory, theater history, . . . textual and acting
criticism,"[11] "historical research," "the sociopolitical background of a classic,"[12]
"background material about the author, the subject matter of the play, and its
social or political implications,"[13] and so forth. As in the Yale dramaturgy training program, dramaturgs prepare elaborate dramaturgical protocols for the
plays on which they collaborate, bringing the light of intensive reading to
bear on questions surrounding the world of the play, the author's world, and a
play's production history.[14] They sort through critical, contextual, and imaginatively related literature in search of what Judith Milhous and Robert Hume
call "producible interpretation": the insight gained from reading that can live
and flourish onstage.[15] We expect dramaturgs as readers to so have the pulse
of the library that they will be able to find answers to questions posed by actors, directors, designers, and audience members. In an early article on the
profession, William Ellwood sums up this position when he positions the dramaturg as "a meaningful link between the practicing professional theater" and
that citadel of discursive thought, "the university."[16]

The dramaturg as designated reader or even as **a sort of Talmudic
scholar** surfaces in one way or another again and again in literature on the
subject. Thus, the discourse on dramaturgy encourages theater to think about
the role of the written. It draws attention to the variety of secondary sources
noted above, provoking discussion about the role that these written materials
might play in rehearsal and performance. Of course, directors, actors, and designers used these materials prior to the advent of dramaturgs, but the role of
the dramaturg has brought persistent attention to the place of these materials
within the process. If the dramaturg can show the usefulness of secondary
sources to the performance, she or he has a place.

Shyer tell us that di Niscemi's work with Wilson on *Death Destruction and
Detroit* began in 1978 when he (a fabled nonreader) showed her a picture of

Rudolph Hess and asked, "Do you know who this is?" Her response was, "I know absolutely who it is."[17] That response, a miniature version of a transaction that regularly occurs between directors and dramaturgs, meant she had a role within the production process. She would read (her acquaintance with Hess was not personal, but discursive); he would make images. As Gregory Gunter demonstrates elsewhere in this volume, dramaturgs may also be the **miners of images** and indeed some of the best work performed by dramaturgs occurs when they bring dozens of pictures to rehearsals, but the image of the dramaturg as the **word-person** persists and indeed the ability to unleash the potential energy of written materials is a fundamental source of his or her appeal.

Closely related, the dramaturg as **keeper of the text** draws attention to the role of primary sources and in particular to the making of the playscript: to finding, compiling and establishing the text; translating, adapting, and editing it; analyzing it; glossing it; revising it; even recording its final shape. Discussions of this aspect of the dramaturg's work draw us into an ongoing consideration of the possible relationships between script and performance. Cary Mazer effectively explores possible approaches to this question in this volume, as have others elsewhere.

Marvin Carlson, for example, finds that the possible relations between script and performance are those of **illustration, translation, fulfillment,** and **supplement.** The notion of production as **illustration** gives primacy to the text and denigrates the particular staging: the individual performance is of no more lasting significance than the pictures found spread throughout a Dickens novel; it is the text that endures, that is real. For someone who conceives the production as a **translation** of the playscript, the text still maintains primacy as the original language of the drama, but the performance becomes a parallel, if secondary, version of it. Production perceived as **fulfillment** underscores the incompleteness of the playscript: without a performance the text is unrealized. The text is no more than a residue or trace of an earlier performance; in the making of a production, it is only one element among many. There may be no initial script at all or it may change for one performance to the next.[18] Any specific production now has primacy over the script. The final category, **supplement,** which Carlson borrows from French philosopher Jacques Derrida, seeks to balance these competing claims: neither script nor performance is primary; both demonstrate that neither is ever complete; they add to and subtract from one another simultaneously, just as a supplementary dictionary entry adds to the original entry at the same time as it reminds the reader of its own incompleteness: one supplement suggests the next and so on.[19] Whether we accept Carlson's schema or Mazer's or others developed here and elsewhere on the relationship between a preexistent script and a specific production, dramaturgy highlights these issues: if dramaturgs are **keepers of the text** then they will have to determine just what it is they are keeping and to what end they possess it.

TAKING THE QUOTE APART, PART II: "I TRY TO SEE AS HE SEES" (WAYS OF DEALING WITH CONSCIOUSNESS)

The most problematic words in this quotation are the next three: "as he sees." Whom or what will the dramaturg's eyes serve? It is at this point that dramaturgy runs most directly into questions of self and other: the self, to the extent that dramaturgy comes to stand for the role that consciousness and reflection play in an individual's creative processes; others, to the extent that dramaturgy asks a creative team what they will do with this person who reads and watches and thinks, what his or her relationship will be with the director, designer, actor, and audience member. For example, with respect to both playwrights and directors, the dramaturgical conversation often keys on the word "vision." Good dramaturgs, so the conversation almost always goes, will be able to intuit the playwright's or the director's vision and serve it (dramaturg as **servant**). Less often are they expected to have their own visions of the play: they will see as "he sees"; they will be other-directed.

Related to this is the image of the hapless intellectual and first-time dramaturg who blurts out a comment at the wrong moment in the rehearsal.[20] Descriptions of the dramaturg's work focus relentlessly on the need to learn rehearsal decorum: how to give notes; the need to identify strengths before dealing with problems; the importance of framing comments as questions not criticisms; how, in general, to forward the vision and not block it.[21] All this advice about giving advice is fine and certainly necessary. Knowing when to speak, and how, is critical in all collaborations. New dramaturgs, who may not have extensive experience in how actors and directors usually work, need to learn the conventions of the rehearsal hall. But those conventions are, of course, not universal or value free, and part of this advice is clearly about dramaturgs learning who the boss is and how to talk to her or him.[22] But what most interests me here is the way the presence of the dramaturg foregrounds this question: *When a play is being made, how will its makers deal with an activated and energized consciousness?* Put another way, how do actors, directors, and designers deal with those eyes that sit behind and to the left and watch the rehearsal before it is a final performance? Those eyes actually belong to them as well. The dramaturg embodies the presence of consciousness, embodies the critical eye that every theatermaker possesses and with which every theatermaker must come to terms.

Theories of creativity—whether articulated informally by teachers and practitioners or in handbooks such as those on acting and directing—consistently call into question conscious, as opposed to intuitive, approaches. Tyrone Guthrie summarizes an intuition felt by many artists: "The sought idea is nearly always, in my opinion, the beta-plus idea. The alpha-plus idea arrives from literally God knows where."[23] The dance between those elements of the self that we perceive as conscious and unconscious is delicate enough that the insertion of a particularly heightened consciousness (that is, the dramaturg's eyes) threatens to upset the entire process. The discourse on dramaturgy persistently attempts to negotiate a right relationship with this pair of eyes and the rehearsal process.

One response is to emphasize the strength and independence of consciousness itself. The dramaturg as **critic-in-residence** and as **conscience of the theater** are familiar terms in writings on dramaturgy, periodically in and out of vogue. The notion of **critic-in-residence** receives valorization from the mythos of Lessing as founding father of dramaturgy, although as Joel Schechter points out, the Hamburg National Theater may have hoped more for a publicist than a critic.[24] The dramaturg as conscience has been a pervasive enough concept so that in the 1986 issue of *Theater* devoted to interviews with dramaturgs, Mark Bly asked several participants if they saw themselves in this light. Critics and consciences both have strong visual components and imply a degree of independence from authority. They see, presumably, not as "he sees" but with their own eyes. They watch what actors, playwrights, and directors do, and may, by the power of their watching, change behaviors. Closely related and also related to metaphors of sight is the image of dramaturgs as those who see beyond what the German dramaturg Dieter Stürm calls *Scheinwissen,* or illusionary knowledge.[25] Stürm sees dramaturgs as **destroyers:**

> My work as dramaturg, especially in such projects as the *Antiquity Project,* could always be considered essentially destructive. For me, the manner of work with the actors does not involve so much the accumulation of knowledge, the illumination of things, or their analysis, but it precedes these tasks and continues along with them. I call it the destruction of illusionary knowledge (*Scheinwissen*).[26]

The artist's fear, of course, is that this ferocious consciousness will not only destroy "illusionary knowledge," but also the work of art itself for theater is, after all, just this: illusionary knowledge, knowledge brought to life by the power of illusion. The dramaturg as the **smart kid in class** (critic or skeptic) or as the **good kid in class** (conscience) suggest strategies for coping with consciousness. One response is to play dumb. In the Shyer piece, di Niscemi proudly proclaims, "I'm not an intellectual and Bob's not an intellectual."[27] Whether or not we agree with this proposition (it sounds like the proud declaration of a middle-class couple from Iowa), the assertion is familiar in both America and in American theater. Dramaturgs must continually work to demonstrate that they are not that dreadful other: the academic, the theoretician, the desiccated scholar, even that "critic-in-residence" (that is, the person who thinks and reads and writes, but who supposedly never dreams or sees or feels). Like smart children who often believe they must hide their intelligence in order to be buddies with the most popular kids in class, or, to change metaphors, wives who believe they must never appear smarter than their husbands, dramaturgs often believe they must establish their credentials by distancing themselves from those negative others (who may be, in a sense, within), involving a degree of self-renunciation or even self-hatred.[28]

Oskar Eustis, a well-known dramaturg and director, spoke to this issue in a Yale *Theater* interview:

> My biggest fear is that somehow dramaturgy and dramaturgs will see themselves and be seen within the theatres as part of an intellectual and academic tradition rather than as part of a living cultural tradition. . . . If you separate out the dramaturg as the sole intellectual voice, you're creating a kind of separation between the ideal function and the emotional function or the artistic function, and I think that is inappropriate and it's wrong. It's what I'm trying to resist.[29]

Although Eustis's language is appealing, here again is the juxtaposition of intellect and academia with life, living, and emotion. Many intellectuals and academics would affirm that they *are* part of a "living cultural tradition," despite Eustis's assignment of them to death. Who can argue with the urge towards a holistic vision, towards an eye that has a heart, towards an end to simplistic distinctions between sense and sensibility, but Eustis's position all too easily slips into an all too familiar American anti-intellectualism.

The dramaturg as good kid can also be a problem: she/he is always spoiling everybody's fun, like some Victorian school marm. When Mark Bly queried dramaturgs about this, Martin Esslin was unafraid to embrace the concept: "The dramaturg is the conscience of the theater in two ways: he's the artistic conscience of the theater, and he's the social conscience of the theatre."[30] Others were more uncomfortable with the idea. Just as many contemporary dramaturgs reject the designation of intellectual-in-residence with its connotations of academicism and pedantry, so others refused to take on the role of conscience with its vaguely ministerial resonances. Arthur Ballet's response was particularly strong: "It's a phrase I have never used, thank God. I think what this means to the people who use this stupid phrase is that they believe that they have been entrusted with the faith."[31] The discomfort felt with these models is particularly American: in the mythos of the Wild West the teacher and preacher were regularly feminized and thereby marginalized. The weakening of these two positions also owes something to a cultural climate of uncertainty regarding intellectual and moral absolutes of any sort. Arthur Ballet's remark is also more than a little ironic. As one of America's most tireless and distinguished dramaturgs, he devoted many years of his life to the development of American playwrights—an act of faith and of conscience, if ever there was one.

Another way of dealing with this situation appears in the relationship developed between critics and dramaturgs at the National Playwrights Conference at the O'Neill Theater Center. In 1967, critics and playwrights clashed, leading the conference to search for ways to establish a "symbiotic relationship between critic and playwright."[32] In 1969, a Critics Institute was literally moved "off the grounds," while dramaturgs were brought in and assigned to "specific plays . . . asked to read them, attend rehearsals, and performances, and preside (with the director, playwright and artistic director) at a general Conference discussion held the morning after the second performance."[33] Eventually, these dramaturgs would serve as guest lecturers at the Critics Institute, and Critics Fellows would be brought back into the process by being assigned to dramaturgs with whom they then worked on specific projects. One sort of critical consciousness is distanced, while another is embraced and co-opted by the playwright and theater, although with more success than the Hamburg theater had with Lessing. The O'Neill record, inadequately summarized here, reveals an ongoing and significant attempt to work out the role of the critic/dramaturg within the production process. This change is partially brought about through new nomenclature: with the dramaturg as the "critic-in-residence," but without the negative connotations that the word *critic* often carries in theatrical settings.[34] This model is of the dramaturg as *partner and friend.*[35] Elsewhere, Joel Schechter describes this transformation as from critic to *ally.*[36]

The dramaturgy as **watchdog** deals with this critical eye by giving it a clearly defined task. This metaphor places the dramaturg in a position of being on the lookout for threats of one sort or another and can take conflicting forms. Peter Hay writes that the "dramaturg represents the author's interests in a production,"[37] and, as noted above, an article of faith in many conversations is that the dramaturg will protect the playwright's vision. In this instance, trying to see "as he sees" means just that: the dramaturg aligns his/her vision with the playwright's and works to advance it. Hay also suggests that the dramaturg might serve the director in a similar manner, making "sure that the interpretation which he and the director had agreed on in the relative tranquility prior to production, is adhered to, deepened and sharpened."[38] These two demands are not necessarily irreconcilable, since the dramaturg could first represent the author's interests in working with the director and then protect the director's interpretation during the course of the rehearsal. At some point, however, the author's interests might well conflict with the director's interpretation. Artistic directors who expect dramaturgs to protect the theater's interests further complicate the situation, as their concern might not be for the author's interests or the director's concept, but the impact of the production on the community or its financial success.

Another metaphor is the dramaturg as **fixer,** suggesting dramaturgs fix broken plays by using their skills as writers, translators, adaptors, and editors. A 1970 article from *Modern Drama* refers to German dramaturgs undertaking the "partial or total rewriting of plays," in this instance Shakespeare's *Measure for Measure.*[39] Barbara Field of the Guthrie Theater sets forth a more modest agenda for cutting and editing that includes "unobtrusive rewriting" of particularly archaic passages in Shakespeare.[40] This function extends to new work—often to the dismay of playwrights. Joel Schechter describes the dramaturg as discussing "cuts, rewrites, and reordering of scenes with the author," and notes a similarity to the Broadway **play doctor,** although the latter is presumably more concerned with commercial than artistic considerations.[41] The dramaturg as watchdog needs a threat, while the dramaturg as fixer or play doctor needs a text to be broken or ill. Without threat or brokenness, these models have no reason to exist.[42]

In an insightful essay in this volume, Jayme Koszyn, by way of William Arrowsmith, Greek mythology, and Friedrich Nietzsche, suggests another set of metaphors for the relationship between dramaturgs and their collaborators. In *The Birth of Tragedy,* Nietzsche distinguishes between two forces in the creation of tragic drama: the Apollonian and the Dionysian. The Dionysian is primary, standing for rapture and music; intoxication and inspiration; the irrational and the loss of self. The counter-force, the Apollonian, is to some extent an accommodation, but a vitally important one. It stands for cognition, the clarity of the dream, plasticity, the perception of form, lucidity, individuation and light. With respect to this useful paradigm, Koszyn notes that dramaturgs most often seem to perceive themselves as **apostles of Apollo** to the extent that they stand back from the work and help others see its form: the Dionysic writer creates; the Apollonian dramaturg shapes. This is at times a necessary relationship, but one with a potential for damage, when, for example, a middle-class Apollo reshapes supposedly incoherent plays into conventional marketable forms.[43] This Apollonian metaphor for dramaturgs may also inform their decision to attend only a select number of rehearsals in order to avoid losing critical distance by being too caught up in the chaos of creativity.

Di Niscemi prides herself on bringing "greater unity" to the "visual and aural content" of Robert Wilson's work.[44] She has encouraged Wilson to bring together the aural and visual tracks of his pieces, "has contributed to his growing awareness of history and literature and to the opening of his work to the discursive possibilities of language and narrative."[45] Here, she is the dramaturg as **lion tamer,** one who limits the imaginative and emotional range of the director or playwright, perhaps for their own good. Few dramaturgs would embrace this image, but the dramaturg as a conservative, even bureaucratic figure is far from unrecognizable.[46] The dramaturg as lion tamer is not far from the dramaturg as **middle manager,** an institutional figure with relatively little power, who relies on the institution for sustenance, whose allegiance is to the institution not the art form or the artist. His or her agenda is to maintain a healthy subscribership.[47]

Of course, the dramaturg as **hell-raiser,** as **anti-institutional figure** counters this move. As Koszyn suggests, this romantic figure, this dramaturg as **Dionysus,** refusing to play the role of Apollo, creates chaos not order; refuses to answer all the questions; surrenders that treasured objectivity and perhaps even joins the actor onstage.[48] The Dionysian dramaturg becomes **a kind of walking Verfremdungseffekt,** making strange what has become overly familiar, and enabling us as theatermakers and audience members to see again a world to which we have become all too accustomed.

The extreme version of trying to see "as he sees" is the dramaturg as **co-dependent,** to borrow an over-used term from the recovery movement. Here consciousness does not have a discreet function that clarifies its role within the creative process: to be on guard, to fix, to clarify, to challenge. As a member of a dysfunctional family system, the co-dependent dramaturg, (director as husband; dramaturg as wife or child) focuses entirely and obsessively, to the point of self-abnegation, on serving the needs of others within the production process, facilitating and enabling in a manner that might seem saint-like (the dramaturg as **saint**), but is in reality unhealthy. Di Niscemi describes having to calm "Bob down" on occasion.[49] She prides herself on being able "to gauge" her director's "needs and act quickly on them."[50] Shyer says of di Niscemi: "She is only too willing to drop everything at a moment's notice and run to the library or jump on a plane should 'the master' call with an urgent request."[51] Clearly, dramaturgs do not prescribe co-dependency as an operating mode, but in a theater structured around the power of the director, where the dramaturg is too often an entry level position, the potential for this sort of negative domestic arrangement certainly exists. Other relational metaphors that rely on domestic or romantic imagery, though not necessarily as negative in connotation, are still loaded: for example, the dramaturg as **midwife** assisting at the birth of a new work of art or the dramaturg as **lover, spouse** or **soul mate.**[52]

TAKING THE QUOTE APART, PART III: "I SIT BEHIND HIM, USUALLY TO THE LEFT . . . (FINDING A PLACE)

Finally, di Niscemi's words also call attention to the question of position, particularly that of between-ness. The position between the director and a world beyond the darkened interior space places the dramaturg on the threshold of the door into and out of the theater itself. The Latin word for threshold is **limen.** Dramaturgs are (at least potentially) creatures of the limen, individuals who function in spaces most notable for their placement between one stable locale and another—places outside the routines of daily life that invite alternative forms of behavior. The work of anthropologist Victor Turner suggests the significance of the dramaturg's liminal status.[53] Turner describes activities at the threshold or on the margins as crucial to our understanding of how a society functions and recognizes this position is charged with potential for transformation and innovation.

In writings about dramaturgy, metaphors of in-between-ness or mediation occur again and again. According to Peter Hay, the dramaturg serves as "the interpreter of the author's ways to the director and vice-versa."[54] This approach shifts the metaphor from dramaturg as watchdog to dramaturg as **diplomat** or **mediator.** One commentator, for example, refers to the dramaturg as the liaison "between the actors and literature."[55] Here the position is not between two people but between a body of texts and those who use them to make theatrical performances, including actors, directors, designers, theater staffs, as well as the community at large. Martin Esslin, in describing the role of European dramaturgs, notes that they must plan their theaters' seasons so that members of the community will have over the course of time the opportunity of "seeing the main works of Shakespeare, the German classics, Ibsen, Chekhov, Molière, Shaw, supplemented by some classical Greek or Spanish plays."[56] The dramaturg as literary manager also moves back and forth between a fluid body of new plays (including adaptations and translations) and a theater's future plans. Dramaturgs may be seen to stand at the threshold of theaters, taking in hand the plays that writers leave at the door, suggesting the dramaturg then as **gatekeeper,** a role between potential scripts and their performances that no doubt contributes to the animosity of playwrights toward dramaturgs.

In other instances, dramaturgs find themselves between performances and audiences. They speak to audiences in pre- or postshow sessions and moderate discussions among audience members, actors, directors, playwrights and scholars. They frame audience responses to productions by way of program materials or study guides. These written materials might contain information on the rehearsal process, "explanatory and background material, essays on the author and the subject matter of the play, material about previous productions," presented verbally and visually.[57] These mediating activities do not require that the dramaturg predigest the theatrical event for audiences, but they do underscore the dramaturg's role in shaping the performance experience prior to, during, and after the fact.[58] Like their collaborators, dramaturgs find themselves between the inception of a theatrical project and its eventual performances. Within this process, they often function in roles most notable for their liminal characteristics. As translators or adaptors, they work in a space between the language of the original text and the language of the potential audience. Working with the director and ensemble in a process of adaptation, they stand between older versions of the play and the new one that will be made, making choices from the old in the creation of the new. Perhaps beginning with no text at all, they help create a performance from a topic or image, in the process finding themselves between various scenarios for what the performance might be. Dramaturgs often also stand on the threshold between the library and the theater. They read carefully, productively, and intensively with an awareness— informed by their own aesthetic and that of their collaborators—of the kinds of materials that will serve a potential production. Dramaturgs need not, however, limit themselves to reading. They might stand between the theater and anything outside its walls: specialists (formal and informal), special collections, music, visual materials, museums, lived experience in whatever form it takes.[59] The dramaturg moves not so much between the director and the stage, but between the director and those places beyond this theatrical space: the library, a pile of new scripts, a conference with a playwright, a word processor for writing program notes or study guides, any one or any place that might offer insight into the world of the play. Indeed, part of the dramaturg's power is this mobility, the ability to leave the rehearsal hall (in the middle of rehearsals if desired) and go somewhere else. Of course, this same ability to come and go without immediately affecting the progress of rehearsals, also signals a potential dispensibility: if dramaturgs do not have to be there for the show to go on, then strictly speaking they do not have to be there at all.

Between theatermakers, between literature and repertoire, between spectators and performances, between discursivity and theatricality—between-ness and the dramaturg are synonymous. Little wonder then that dramaturgs have spent so much time and energy trying to explain to others who they are and what they do. To some extent they are nowhere and defined by who they are not: not one or the other; not playwright or director; not audience member or performer; neither pure discursivity nor absolute theatricality, but somewhere on the edge, somewhere at the margins.

Of course, theater itself lives in a state of between-ness—between absence and presence, illusion and "reality," imagination and experience, spontaneity and control. Actors, directors, and playwrights can also claim for themselves this medial position. The state of being between may not make dramaturgs unique within the theater so much as paradigmatic and may signal that they have indeed found their place. Nonetheless, in a land of borders they are alienated. In some ways, they are a particularly postmodern phenomenon—one that signals an acceptance of marginality as a place of choice, one that in turn might question the entire logic of positionality, of insides and outsides, of centers and peripheries, so that finally marginality itself would mean something different to us.[60]

Though strongly tempted to valorize this final place or non place with respect to some of the other metaphors just described, I resist this, in part because valorization makes a resting place out of a dynamic position. Furthermore, in-between-ness is not without its own potential problems. It encourages non-commitment or a fear of risk-taking; can reify myths of neutrality or sublime objectivity, or even reduce complex situations into simplistic bipolar structures when more, not less, complexity is needed. In short, in-between might make a fine place to visit but a lousy home. In sum, then, I advocate an enjoyment of a variety of these and other models and a delight in a certain lack of definition. For the conversation around this attribute/role/function we call "dramaturgy" invites us to think and rethink the role of consciousness in the rehearsal hall and to think and rethink how together we make this thing we call theater.

The Dramaturg as Androgyne:
Thoughts on the Nature of Dramaturgical Collaboration
by **Tori Haring-Smith**

TORI HARING-SMITH is the dramaturg at Trinity Repertory Company in Providence, Rhode Island, and an Associate Professor at Brown University. She has directed for several years throughout the Northeast. In New York, she assisted Joseph Chaikin with *Night Sky* (produced by The Women's Project) and directed *The Country Wife* at the Jean Cocteau Repertory. Most recently she directed *An American Cocktail* (world premiere) at Trinity, *The Swan* at Alias Stage, and *Tales of the Lost Formicans* at Brown University. Her translations of *The Seagull* and *The Miser* premiered at Trinity, and Olympia Dukakis directed her *Seagull* at Arizona Theatre Company in 1994. Also in 1994, she served as the American dramaturg for the Third International Conference of Women Playwrights in Adelaide, Australia. She coordinates the Jane Chambers Playwriting Award for the Women and Theatre Program, and has published several books and articles on writing, teaching, and theater including *From Farce to Metadrama: A Stage History of The Taming of the Shrew, 1594-1983* (Greenwood), *Writing Together* (HarperCollins), and *Monologues for Women, by Women* (Heinemann). Her translation of Eduardo de Filippo's *Napoli Milionaria,* which premiered at the Jean Cocteau Repertory, was published by Dramatic Publishing in 1996.

I want to focus not on WHAT a dramaturg does but on HOW she does it. How do dramaturgs work in collaboration with directors to influence a production? How can they be effective, active collaborators without becoming a distraction—the extra cook who spoils the soup? We usually think of collaborators as equals; in fact, collaboration is often cited as an organizational alternative to hierarchy. But this is not an accurate picture of the dramaturg's role—the dramaturg is not the director's equal. Like the designers and the actors, she must answer ultimately to the director. Her work must support and further his. She can shape his work, but he retains the ultimate authority. How, then, can dramaturgs be effective and influential while remaining subordinate in the artistic hierarchy that is the production team?

Because she is usually working within the stylistic and conceptual choices made by the director, the dramaturg needs to learn to see as the director sees. She needs to form a kind of "mind meld" or empathic connection with the director in order to be able to determine what kind of research the director may need, to contextualize the production in program notes and educational materials, and to talk to the director using his language. To see through the director's eyes, I have found that I need to sit in rehearsals as much as possible in order to understand the director's intentions—to learn his interpretation of the play, his taste in theatrical styles, and the shorthand language that he uses with the actors and designers. Once she has learned to see the play through the director's eyes, a dramaturg can offer all kinds of positive and negative feedback without seeming to "fight" the director. In other words, she can work from her base of knowledge and experience to influence the production in a constructive, noncompetitive manner.

This kind of collaborative mind meld has been defined by several psychologists as a "feminine" way of thinking. In their book, *Women's Ways of Knowing,* Mary Belenky, Blythe Clinchy, Nancy Goldberger, and Jill Tarule describe this feminine or "connected" knowing as "the deliberate, imaginative extension of one's understanding into positions that initially feel wrong or remote."[61] They say that "connected knowers develop procedures for gaining access to other people's knowledge. At the heart of these procedures is the capacity for empathy. Since knowledge comes from experience, the only way they can hope to understand another person's ideas is to try to share the experience that has led the person to form the ideas. . . . Connected knowers do not measure other people's words by some impersonal standard. Their purpose is not to judge but to understand."[62]

The importance of connected thinking came home to me when I was working with Clinton Turner Davis on a production of *The Good Times are Killing Me,* for which I was serving as musical director as well as dramaturg. Davis avoided staging the final song through most of the rehearsal process, and we were fast approaching previews. Needless to say, the actors were concerned. I urged him to try something—anything—and then we could work on it. Finally, putting on my musical director's hat, I said that if he wanted me to, I would suggest a staging for the final moment, since it involved a song. After Edna's final speech, she and Bonna would be left center stage, looking straight out. The black characters would emerge on one side of the stage, and the white characters on the other, the two groups separated by as wide a gulf as possible. Then, as they sang, "Uncloudy Day," a young black boy and a white girl would emerge on a higher level upstage and begin to play a clapping game together. Gradually, the characters would turn and notice the children playing together innocently, as the lights pulled into a spot on the children and then faded out with the music.

This staging captured the end of the play as I saw it, emphasizing the gulf between the races, a gulf that only young, presocialized children could cross. Davis didn't like it, but finally we had a specific scene to talk about, and so he was able to articulate what he wanted from the end of the play—the battle against racism was fought first and foremost by individuals, not groups. Once I could see the play as he saw it, I could suggest several different ways to stage the ending, which he could accept, reject, or modify. By talking through these ideas with me, Davis was able to clarify what he wanted, and he staged the scene before the day was out. Once I knew what the director wanted from the play, I could be an effective collaborator. Without that knowledge, my vision competed with his, instead of supporting it.

Some dramaturgs are reluctant to talk about the need to empathize with the director, to subordinate their vision to his, believing this weakens their position, makes them seem mere toadies doing the master's bidding. I never feel, however, that I sacrifice my vision just because I learn to adopt the director's vision at will. I do not lose my perspective or my ability to judge the play from outside—I just learn to turn that ability on and off. I shift back and forth, seeing the play through my own eyes and then through the eyes of the director, like playing those perception games where one looks at a black and white pattern and first sees two faces, then a vase, then two faces. Both images are present, even though you can only see one at a time.

In fact, the use of connected knowing to create a mind meld with the director allows the dramaturg to influence the production in powerful ways. In her book, *Caring,* Nel Noddings explains that seeing the world through the eyes of another—what she calls "engrossment"—is crucial to changing people's minds. She offers the example of a math teacher trying to convince an uninterested student that the subject is useful and exciting. Simply asserting, from the teacher's "outside, informed perspective," that math is enjoyable will probably not convince the student. Even dazzling him by performing the joy of math probably won't change his mind. Instead, the teacher should try to see the problem through the student's eyes, asking "What would it feel like to hate math? Why might I hate it?" Only if she can stand in the student's shoes does the teacher have the opportunity to change the student's mind. She must understand his point of view and empathize with him in order to bridge the gap between his vision and hers.[63] So, too, the dramaturg who hopes to lead the director to see his production in a new light must understand the director's position and begin from there in order to convince him. For example, instead of commenting that the lights in the first act of *The Seagull* are just too dark, a dramaturg who knows that the director is interested in faithfully reproducing the Russian setting of the play might remind that director that summer evenings in Russia are very light.

Some people may find this use of "connected knowing" manipulative. I would argue that any attempt at persuasion is by definition manipulative; it attempts to influence an outcome. Dramaturgs are supposed to be influential. Using my special knowledge of a director's intentions to talk to him about his production seems no more manipulative than providing feedback in terms of hypothetical spectators' responses or by presenting the director with admittedly selective research materials. Since I am not imposing my point of view upon his, I do not try to alter a director's intentions, but to provide feedback on how they "read." Using my special knowledge of a director's intentions to shape the way I discuss his production is like deciding to adopt a particular professional jargon when talking to, say, a deconstructionist. The choice of a common language simply indicates that both parties are capable of sharing a worldview.

Some dramaturgs believe that empathy is a less sophisticated way of thinking than distanced critique. But such an assessment is grounded in an incomplete theory of intellectual and moral development. As Carol Gilligan demonstrates, the common assumption that achieving critical distance is more sophisticated than establishing empathy or understanding is founded on the developmental theories of Piaget and Kohlberg, both of whom did their research primarily on males and built their theories on Freud's gendered theory of maturation.[64] Like Piaget and Kohlberg, Freud described the process of maturation from the male perspective—as a gradual separation from the mother. One aspect of this separation is the ability to distance oneself from an argument and critique it from the outside. Looking at social and intellectual development from the female perspective, however, yields a different assessment of empathy. For the female, as Gilligan and others have shown, maturation involves increasing levels of identification (with the mother) and empathy.[65] Because gendered behavior is a product of both biology and enculturation, of course, not all females follow this "feminine" model of maturation, any more than all "males" necessarily follow the "masculine" model of Freud, Piaget, and Kohlberg. But Gilligan did find that as girls matured, they relied increasingly upon empathy in making moral decisions, whereas boys relied increasingly upon abstract moral principles. Perhaps, then, we should see distanced critique and the mind meld of empathy as complementary, equally valid modes of analysis.

Developing this "feminine" mode of thinking is not the only way in which dramaturgs can collaborate effectively. In fact, we need to develop the "masculine," distanced stance as well. I often need to step out of the director's perspective to discover how an uninitiated spectator or critic might see the play. In a production of *Measure for Measure,* the director, Brian McEleney, had set the show in a modern urban underworld that was rapidly careening out of control. The show began with a panorama of the city at night. As the citizens bought drugs, had sex in corners, and drooled over pornographic dancers, the duke made his way to the center of town, carrying his suitcase. Ringing a bell, he managed to attract everyone's attention, and announced his plans to leave and put Angelo in charge. The citizens were unhappy with the choice of such a strict ruler but were aware of the need to remain in Angelo's good graces, so they applauded him loudly. When the duke announced that Escalus, a more popular man, would be Angelo's deputy, the people were confused. Escalus was the logical choice for duke-pro-tem. Why was he being demoted? They applauded less enthusiastically for him because they were confused. These responses made perfect sense to those of us who knew the story behind why the crowd was applauding more enthusiastically for the conservative Angelo than for Escalus. It seemed to me, however, that the uninitiated spectator would probably assume that the citizens preferred Angelo over Escalus and were glad to have him rule. At times like this, a dramaturg needs to cultivate naivete rather than empathy, ignoring the director's intentions in order to provide helpful feedback.

In most discussions of dramaturgy, this "outside" perspective is stressed. The dramaturg is likened to "a play doctor" or "the conscience of the theater" or an "in-house critic."[66] Belenky, Clinchy, Goldberger, and Tarule call this kind of thinking "separated knowing," which they describe as the kind of thinking most often encouraged in schools, one that applies principles, standards, and "impersonal reason" to answer questions: "presented with a proposition [or, for our purposes, a production], separate knowers immediately look for something wrong—a loophole, a factual error, a logical contradiction, the omission of contrary evidence."[67] The dramaturg becomes a separate knower when she arrives to "critique" a run. Notepad in hand, she looks at the play either as an uninitiated spectator or a skeptical critic, searching for problems. What is confusing? What is boring? What is old hat? The notes that result from asking these questions can prepare a director for the kind of response that a newspaper reviewer might have. One "male" standard-bearer foreshadows the response of another.

These two modes of thought—separated and connected knowing—are actually complementary. The "feminine" ability to empathize with a director gives dramaturgs the flexibility to work with many different kinds of directors—conventional, postmodern, visual, literary—while the "masculine" ability to distance oneself, to stand outside of a production and resist understanding, gives dramaturgs a distinct vantage point from which to help directors improve their work. Martin Esslin summed up this balance, saying, "The best dramaturg must be schizophrenic: with the left side of his brain he knows the play better than anybody else; with the right side of his brain, he is a completely naive spectator who has never heard the play before."[68]

This view of collaboration also bears on the dramaturg's relationship to a playwright; all writers need to bounce ideas off of someone who fully understands their intentions and their script, as well as knowing how uninitiated eyes see their work. When dramaturgs collaborate with writers, they work from a consistently subordinate place within a definite hierarchy, just as they do with directors. It is always the playwright's script, just as it is always the director's production.

A good production dramaturg is a consummate collaborator. In the space of a few hours, she may talk to the playwright about script changes, deliver program copy to the graphics department, give the artistic director a two-minute report on the progress of the production, research the copyright on a piece of music, approve a list of panelists for an after-show discussion, answer an actor's question about the meaning of a line, and discuss the staging of the play with the director over lunch. The dramaturg is at the center of the communication web that emanates from any production and influences the final work in countless ways.

It is clear that the dramaturg helps shape a production through the kinds of questions and comments she gives the director, and in some cases the playwright, during rehearsal. Just as the costume designer helps determine the style of the production by showing the director particular sketches or pictures to suggest how a character might look, so a dramaturg influences the production through the kind of research she provides the director. I worked, for example, on a fairly traditional production of *Come Back, Little Sheba,* in which the director was most interested in the issue of alcoholism in the male characters. I was able to complement that interest by bringing in materials on the pressures young girls felt to marry young in the fifties. The more the director and the actors learned, the more that interest was reflected in production choices. For example, the female college student in the play was initially played as a child who "falls" passively into an early marriage. But after the director read the research I provided, he reshaped the character into a young woman who understands the mandate to marry and actively seeks out potential husbands.

The dramaturg also has the opportunity to shape the audience's perception of the show through the program materials or lobby displays that contextualize the production. For *Come Back, Little Sheba,* for example, my dramaturg's notes focused on a phenomenon called "housewife's syndrome." This malaise affected women who had worked in the factories during World War II and then were asked to return to the relatively isolated and circumscribed life of a suburban housewife when the men returned from overseas and reclaimed their jobs. Those in the audience who read the program notes saw the production informed by this material. Similarly, constructing a lobby display of famous rich men from Howard Hughes to Scrooge McDuck moved Trinity Rep's production of *The Miser* out of the seventeenth century and into the present.

When I work on classic texts, I often describe my work as "text designing." I consider the nips and tucks that I take in Shakespeare to be no less important than the nips and tucks that the costumer makes. When I suggest to a director that a given scene or speech could be trimmed or revised, I am suggesting a means of shaping the story of the play. Sometimes the director rejects my textual emendations, but then he usually works harder to make the text work where I suggested that it could be cut.

Despite their many duties and the extent of their influence, most dramaturgs remain relatively invisible—a hidden but powerful force like the epigramatic "good woman" who stands hidden behind every "good man." The director and the actors may see the dramaturg in the rehearsal hall, but the public usually does not realize the extent of her influence upon a production, in part because many theaters do not routinely list her with the other artistic staff on the program title page. Similarly, most theater reviews regularly list the director, designers, principal actors, and the stage manager for a production at the top of a review, but they do not list the dramaturg.

I have heard it said that the majority of production dramaturgs are women because men would never agree to do so much work for such little compensation. They would never allow themselves to be invisible. Why are women drawn to this dramaturgical role? There are several possible explanations. It is notoriously difficult for women to get hired as directors. (In fact, that is why I have consistently referred to dramaturgs as "she" and directors as "he" in this essay.) For some women, work as a dramaturg is probably as close as they can hope to get to professional directing. While many women feel that their visions are notably absent in the American theater, dominated as it is by male directors, playwrights, and artistic directors, the role of the dramaturg allows them to bring their voices into the production through research, program notes, and their very presence in the rehearsal hall.

Unfortunately, for some theaters, having a woman dramaturg "solves" the problem of how to get women on the artistic team. This past year, I have worked on two plays (both written by women) in which I was the only female member of the artistic production team. In short, the role of dramaturg satisfies many women's need to have a prominent voice in the development of a production, without forcing the theaters to invest much in them.

On a less cynical note, I would like to think that so many production dramaturgs are female because women make better androgynes than men do, being better trained to combine the empathic and distanced points of view that define a dramaturg's outlook. Men are rarely asked to learn or perform "feminine" modes of thinking and are ridiculed when they act or dress "like women." But when women act or dress "like men," they are usually praised. Women are trained to be androgynous, to go from selling a new ad campaign or arguing a legal case to soothing a child's bruised knee or a boss's bruised ego in a matter of seconds. For them, the role of dramaturg offers considerable influence—even if that influence is rarely visible.

All too often, our society upholds individual achievement at the expense of undervaluing the work of collaborators. We praise the work of writers like William Wordsworth and Henry James, but fail to note the contribution that their families (and especially their sisters) made to their work. We seem to assume that an artist's greatness is diminished when his work is acknowledged to be a collaborative product.[69] The dramaturg's role is an active objection to the notion that all great art is the product of a single individual's activity. The growing presence of dramaturgs is one of many signals that our individualistic culture may soon come to recognize creativity as a social activity. When that transformation occurs, dramaturgs will be more readily recognized. To help foster this epistemological revolution, however, American dramaturgs, both male and female, need to fight for more visibility now. This is our chance to define our role before someone defines it for us.

Joseph Chaikin and the Presence of the Dramaturg

by **Allen Kuharski**

ALLEN KUHARSKI teaches directing and theater history in the Theatre Studies Program at Swarthmore College. He has directed Joseph Chaikin in performances in Poland and the United States. He works as Associate Editor for *Periphery: A Journal of Polish Affairs* and as Performance Review Editor for *Theatre Journal.* His translations include Eugène Ionesco's *Rhinoceros* (with George Moskos) and Witold Gombrowicz's *History* (with Dariusz Bukowski). His articles have appeared in *Theatre Journal, New Theatre Quarterly,* Yale *Theater, Themes In Drama, Periphery, 2B, The San Francisco Review of Books, Dialog,* and *The Theatre In Poland.* He is preparing a book on Polish playwright Witold Gombrowicz. The research for this article included personal interviews with Chaikin, Jean-Claude van Itallie, Susan Yankowitz, Mira Rafalowicz, and Rick Harris.[70]

Joseph Chaikin (b. 1935) has been a fixture in the American alternative theater since his early work as an actor with Judith Malina and Julian Beck in the Living Theater in New York City in the early 1960s. Best known as the founder and leader of The Open Theater (New York City, 1963–73) and as the author of *The Presence of the Actor* (1972), Chaikin has earned an international reputation as a director, actor, playwright, and theorist. Attracting far less attention, however, has been Chaikin's collaboration with dramaturgs such as Mira Rafalowicz and Bill Hart in the late work of The Open Theater and the subsequent New York City productions of The Winter Project (1977–83) and the "Night Voices" radio series (1982–83)—work that has continued in a number of more recent projects, as well. As much as with the "presence" of actors, Chaikin's theatrical projects through the years have been concerned with questions of the presence and absence of playwrights, dramaturgs, and even play texts. Chaikin's ongoing work with Rafalowicz and Hart has developed into a distinct movement within the practice of contemporary American dramaturgy. It is both clarifying and inevitable to trace this "school" of experimental dramaturgy through the career of Chaikin, who has consistently worked to guarantee a creative space for its practice. My focus here will be on the role of the dramaturg in the collaborative work of The Winter Project and the "Night Voices" radio series—work that Chaikin calls the most artistically demanding of his career to date—and its significance as a response to the discoveries and crises of The Open Theater before it.

Chaikin's experimental work with actors in The Open Theater was combined with a questioning of the role of the playwright and the play text in relation to the actor. This questioning produced unprecedented working relationships and theatrical results among both the actors and the playwrights involved. The Open Theater's work with playwrights in turn set the stage for the arrival of a new kind of dramaturg, one suited to the group's mission of ensemble developmental work. The presence and absence of playwrights and dramaturgs in The Open Theater was dynamic, varied, and fluid—and defined the group's artistic mission over time no less than its innovative acting techniques. The factors that contributed to Chaikin's controversial decision to disband The Open Theater in 1973 included chronic and unresolved tensions around the role of playwrights and dramaturgs in the ensemble's work. In spite of these tensions, the group's work was artistically fruitful, and is credited with laying the foundation for a new school of American playwriting in the work of Jean-Claude van Itallie, Megan Terry, Susan Yankowitz, and Sam Shepard. For Chaikin, however, the end of The Open Theater marked the start of a period of heightened investment in his collaboration with dramaturgs in the development of new work.

In the later work of The Open Theater and its successors The Winter Project and "Night Voices," the ensembles under Chaikin's direction worked consistently without either a preexisting script or a collaborating playwright. According to playwright Jean-Claude van Itallie, Chaikin's most consistent artistic collaborator since the early 1960s, the director has a "love–hate" relationship to words, an ambivalence clearly reflected in his investigations with both playwrights and dramaturgs. According to van Itallie, Chaikin from the beginning of their work together desired to be free of any received theatrical or dramatic form. The result for The Open Theater and The Winter Project was that both ensembles adopted an openly critical stance in regard to "classical" American realistic playwriting, particularly of the Clifford Odets school, and gave highest priority to the development and performance of original work. This work, moreover, was consistently presentational in style, always pursuing a heightened theatricalism distinct from the realism sought in method acting studios. This impulse on Chaikin's part echoes Antonin Artaud's earlier call for a theater liberated from the service of past "masterpieces."[71] The eventual "absence" of either a ready script or a resident playwright eventually created the opportunity for the ensemble dramaturg to assume a radically heightened collaborative and creative role.

In their embrace of a collective ensemble structure and commitment to the collaborative creation of original work, The Open Theater and The Winter Project paralleled similar efforts by a wide variety of theater companies in the 1960s and 1970s. Like the Living Theater, such companies were influenced to varying degrees by pacifist, anarchist, Marxist, and feminist political theory—and were often organized as collectives. Some companies, such as The San Francisco Mime Troupe, worked consistently with a playwright in the creation of new work. In others, acting ensembles created original work without a designated playwright. Examples included the Royal Shakespeare Company's production *US* (1966, directed by Peter Brook), the Polish Laboratory Theater's *Apocalypsis cum figuris* (1969, directed by Jerzy Grotowski), and Le Théâtre du Soleil's *1789* and *1793* (1970–72, directed by Ariane Mnouchkine). Although Brook, Grotowski, and Mnouchkine's companies all created major projects through the process of collective ensemble work without a playwright, none of these artists has made the sustained commitment to the process that Chaikin has since the late work of The Open Theater. Rough parallels to the dramaturgical work of Rafalowicz and Hart can be found, however, in Ludwik Flaszen of Grotowski's Polish Laboratory Theater and the later work of Norman Frisch and Marianne Weems with The Wooster Group in New York City. (Ed. note: See the Frisch/Weems account of this work in section 5 of this volume.)

The role that the dramaturg assumed in The Winter Project and "Night Voices" was an inevitable response to the challenging and ultimately paradoxical position of playwrights in The Open Theater. In the classical theater that Artaud critiqued, the play text is present and the playwright absent, with the dramaturg often functioning as proxy for the absent author. At its most evolved, as in the case of a critic/dramaturg such as Jan Kott, the role of the dramaturg in such situations is as a full collaborator with the director and company in the search for the most meaningful and relevant contemporary stage interpretation of the play. In contrast, The Open Theater evolved from an improvisation-based acting workshop, a process that eventually was extended to include the participation of playwrights. In Chaikin's later words, his interest in this process was in "working from the person to the part rather than the part to the person."[72] In a precise reversal of the practice of classical repertory theaters, The Open Theater's point of departure was generally the absence of a ready playscript and in its stead placed a premium on the active presence of the playwright. By producing primarily new work in collaboration with such resident playwrights, The Open Theater paradoxically created its own variation on the historic practice of the original "classical" theaters of Aeschylus, Shakespeare, or Molière, whose "companies" consistently created original works with the playwright fully present in the working and performing life of the group. In this regard, the Open Theater under Chaikin's leadership also addressed one of the great unresolved problems of Stanislavsky's Moscow Art Theater, that being the extension of the ensemble work of actors and directors to include playwrights.

Van Itallie's *Interview* (1965–66), the first part of *America Hurrah,* was the first of the playwright's works to be based on an Open Theater improvisational exercise. The development of the text involved the playwright attending an improvisational workshop by Chaikin and the actors. On the basis of these improvisations, van Itallie drafted a script that sought to capture the essential effect of the improvisation without actually transcribing the actors' words, which in turn was then revised in consultation with the director. In van Itallie's words, his function was to create a "honeycomb" outside of rehearsal that could contain the actors' improvisational "honey." The collaborative process in *Interview* became the prototype for van Itallie's later work with The Open Theater on *The Serpent* (1968), which marked a watershed in the group's developmental work and established its international reputation. Significantly, van Itallie's long-term collaboration with the ensemble for *The Serpent* only began after three months of improvisational work by the group without either a playwright or a dramaturg present. Megan Terry also often employed improvisational exercises developed by The Open Theater, though her work on *Viet Rock* and other early plays often took place in workshops she led outside the group. Susan Yankowitz's later collaboration with The Open Theater on *Terminal* (1969) picked up the working model first used by van Itallie in *The Serpent*.[73]

One result of the working process with playwrights that evolved within The Open Theater was the innovative structure of pieces such as *The Serpent*. Entirely lacking in linear dramatic narrative, *The Serpent* was instead structured as a theatrical montage, jumping from a scene of a contemporary autopsy to a reenactment of the assassinations of John and Robert Kennedy and Martin Luther King, to the stories of Adam and Eve and of Cain and Abel from the Bible. The segments that make up the piece represent the fruit of various sessions by the group around the themes initially introduced by Chaikin, and whose relationship one to the other can often only be explained by the logic of poetic association or theatrical juxtaposition, rather than that of narrative cause and effect. In narrative time, in fact, the piece moves from the modern to the earliest possible point in mythic history and then forward again. Variations on the collage structure that first appeared in *The Serpent* would become the norm of new work by both The Open Theater and The Winter Project thereafter, with Chaikin typically relying on the playwright or dramaturg to find the final arrangement of the segments within each piece.

The playwrights working with The Open Theater had to share intuitively in the director and the company's agendas for the project while still in development, find or generate appropriate materials for those agendas, and yet be ready to defer to the director's judgement as to the final form of the piece as a whole. The paradox that eventually emerged in The Open Theater's work with playwrights, however, was the simultaneous desire to include and nurture young playwrights within a new kind of collaborative theatrical model alongside the gradual diminishment of the role of these same playwrights in the group's working process. In van Itallie's words, "the writers who have worked with Joe have not felt valued." Susan Yankowitz, a bit less categorically, has stated:

> My name does not appear on ads, and often, not in reviews. It is irritating and amusing to be the author of an "authorless" piece. I'm trying to find in myself the proper balance between detachment and the need for recognition. I don't want to succumb to the demands of my ego for that

transcient, slightly contemptible gratification. But then again, why
should recognition be denied in the service of some illusion that The
Open Theater, without its writers, is a totally self-sufficient artistic unit?
For certainly, it is not.[74]

The moment of truth for Yankowitz during her work on *Terminal* on this
score was in a confrontation with Roberta Sklar, the project's codirector, and
the actors over the company's desire to depart at times in performance from
the lines earlier set by the playwright. Yankowitz categorically refused to allow
such changes in her absence, and eventually won Chaikin's support on the
point. According to Chaikin himself, by the time he decided to dissolve
The Open Theater in 1973, the level of such conflict (by no means limited to
the playwrights involved) had become a major motivating factor in his action.
Van Itallie and Yankowitz shared a concern that the fruits of their collaboration with The Open Theater be in a form that could be published and made
available for performance by other groups. This raised issues of copywriting,
performance and publication royalties, and such, of unique complexity because of the collective nature of the group's work. Chaikin's later collaborations with dramaturgs, in contrast, consistently produced works in forms that
proved problematical for both publication and subsequent production by
other companies.[75]

The early and middle work of The Open Theater included no designated
dramaturg distinct from the playwright. The "talking circle" of the group included from early on critics such as Gordon Rogoff and Richard Gilman, and
for *The Serpent* in particular various academics and intellectuals (including
Susan Sontag, Joseph Campbell, and Paul Goodman) were invited to give lectures or lead discussions with the ensemble on topics relevent to the group's
explorations. Such guests and friends of the group apparently functioned as
ad hoc dramaturgs in this early phase.

Roberta Sklar, who shared directing credit with Chaikin on *Terminal,* has
been described by both Susan Yankowitz and Chaikin as working on a day-to-
day basis more as ensemble dramaturg than as a director. As such, Sklar functioned as a critical sounding board in relation to Chaikin and the acting
ensemble in their work, and less as an initiator of their improvisational explorations. According to Yankowitz, the playwright met outside the rehearsals
only with Chaikin, though in the rehearsals both Chaikin and Sklar gave notes
to actors.

Sklar again shared directing credit with Chaikin on *The Mutation Show*
(1971–73),[76] which credited no playwright or dramaturg, but rather two successive "writers-in-residence" (W. E. R. La Farge and John Stoltenberg)—neither
of whom worked with the project through its first public performances.
Sklar's ill-defined function perhaps symbolized the transitional nature of the
project, which marked the full eclipse of the playwright in The Open Theater's development. If one ignores Sklar's de facto function as dramaturg,

The Mutation Show appears to have been defined by a triple absence: of play text, playwright, and dramaturg. Describing the play at the time, Mel Gussow wrote:

> As the title indicates, the structure is that of a show, in the sense of a circus or vaudeville—a freak show, conducted by a ringmaster (Shami Chaikin). With fanfare, she introduces the characters: the Bird Lady, the Man Who Smiles, the Man Who Hits Himself, the Petrified Man. They march out as if on a midway, each with humorous, idiosyncratic gestures—repeated as a refrain later in the play. . . . Characters established, the acts begin. . . . The basic image is a Kaspar Hauser–like boy in a box, a person isolated from civilization, then suddenly plunged— without preparation, words, or comprehension—into civilization. This is not simply a play about Kaspar Hauser, but a consideration of all mutations—the violent changes that man experiences between birth and death.[77]

The critical response to the piece generally affirmed the ensemble's efforts to create in the absence of a playwright. Gussow described the work as having "no wasted time or energy; everything is precise and concise, including the use of words," and went on to describe the production as "perhaps the group's finest achievement to date."[78] In 1971, *The Mutation Show* won first prize in the Belgrade International Theater Festival (BITEF) and in 1972 was given an Obie Award for "Best Theater Piece." According to Eileen Blumenthal in her account of the development of *The Mutation Show,* however, the experiment of having neither playwright nor dramaturg revealed the problems of having no foil or balance for Chaikin's powerful personal presence in the ensemble and also resulted in an unusually long period of indecision about the piece's final form.[79] The apparent untenability of Sklar's position as codirector/dramaturg presumably explains her departure from the company after *The Mutation Show.*

It was in The Open Theater's last production, *Nightwalk* (1973),[80] that Mira Rafalowicz became the group's first credited dramaturg. In the development of the piece, Rafalowicz assumed a central collaborative role in shaping the piece to essentially the same degree that playwrights such as van Itallie or Yankowitz had earlier. Among Rafalowicz's functions was to collect and induce writing from various sources, including "contributing writers" and the actors themselves. As always, some material for the piece was generated through improvisational sessions led by Chaikin, in response to which Rafalowicz would take notes (in contrast to van Itallie, who often relied on a tape recorder) and later draft a text that would then be brought back to the director for further work. According to Chaikin, Rafalowicz's greatest strength was in coaching and responding to improvisational work rather than providing ideas for the improvisations themselves. According to Rafalowicz, her goal was to reach a point of synchronicity within the ensemble where ideas for work were coming from every possible source within the company—an ultimately collective process within which Chaikin functioned as the "trigger." For the contributing writers (playwrights) involved with the process after the hiatus of *The Mutation Show,* the new arrangement was disorienting. In Blumenthal's words:

> Since none of *Nightwalk's* several authors was central to the shaping of the piece, they found themselves working with little sense of the complete play. Sam Shepard, sending in material from London, wrote to Chaikin at one point that he was "vague about the real direction of the piece," and that his "main stumbling block" was "how to find a space for myself for adjusting to a way of collaboration."[81]

Unlike any of the writers involved, Rafalowicz had a hand in shaping every section in the final form of *Nightwalk,* assuming the kind of key role that van Itallie and Yankowitz had in earlier projects. In spite of the distance of the playwrights from the new collaborative process led by Rafalowicz, at least one major critic (Arthur Sainer) nevertheless considered the contributions of Megan Terry, van Itallie, and Shepard as "some of their best work."[82] Jack Kroll described the final form of *Nightwalk* as

> ...a nocturnal fantasia in which a panoramic sampling of *Homo Americanus* is observed by two birds.... As the birds (male and female) take off on their midnight ramble, they encounter a succession of types who, as refracted through the eyes of the birds and those of the audience, are more often than not a brilliantly conceived mixture of human and animal traits.... On carts—the kind of carts that roll through the streets of the garment district—the humanoids come wheeling through in tableaus of representative madness. One group, wearing aviator caps and goggles, is writing an "indictment" of an absent defendent—perhaps God himself. Other characters intone pop songs or catatonically act out the trap of self-consciousness.... The climactic point is a mad dinner party at which the characters talk in a bestial parody of human speech that is meant to convey the futility and bad faith of most communication.[83]

Though *Nightwalk* proved to be the last production of The Open Theater, it provided the prototype for Rafalowicz's future collaborations with Chaikin.

During the hiatus between *Nightwalk* and the establishment of The Winter Project in 1978, Rafalowicz wrote her one published statement on her work as a developmental dramaturg with Chaikin. Written in free verse, Rafalowicz's lucid and pithy "poem" (whose complete text is reprinted following this article) opens with a concise definition of her role as dramaturg as "an internal critic, an intimate participant, an outspoken audience member, a collaborator, an extra eye...."[84] She goes on to define four distinct stages in the collective developmental process, describing both the excitement of its discoveries and the rigor and detachment required in the ultimate selecting of the material generated. Roughly summarized, these four stages consist of: 1) locating a common agenda for the group's explorations, a period of mutual questioning and dialogue in search of a shared theatrical vocabulary; 2) the exploration and shaping of the chosen materials, together with a setting of limits on the group's explorations; 3) finding and committing to the piece's final shape, in part through the consultation with "outside eyes" invited to respond critically to the group's work; 4) fine tuning the piece's form in actual performance, combined with the care and feeding of its vitality and honesty through repeated performances.[85] Rafalowicz's "poem" can be taken as the dramaturgical credo of The Winter Project workshops that commenced a few months after its publication.

The role of the dramaturg in The Winter Project and "Night Voices" clearly evolved from the experiences of the The Open Theater in creating *The Mutation Show* and *Nightwalk*. While the experience of *The Mutation Show* apparently convinced Chaikin of the need for some sort of dramaturgical presence in future projects, *Nightwalk* marked the end of the involvement of playwrights as such. Blumenthal has dubbed this type of exploration as "playwriting without a playwright,"[86] or what could be described as the move from ensemble-with-playwright(s) to ensemble-as-playwright. The day-to-day working of the Chaikin-Rafalowicz collaboration in The Winter Project closely followed the model established earlier in *Nightwalk,* with the dramaturg in this case taking particular responsibility for finding the initial shape for the performance text from the various found and created materials, and thereafter consulting with the director on the piece's final form. In a significant departure from his practice with The Open Theater, Chaikin himself began to write material for the productions of The Winter Project, particularly *Trespassing* (1982). Rafalowicz's goal for both the developmental explorations and the final performance was, in her words, "a gorgeous collage," and she emphasizes that for both The Open Theater and The Winter Project their "Platonic model" for theatrical work was always drawn from other art forms (music, painting, sculpture, film) and never from other theater. In the late stages of their working process, the work of Rafalowicz and Hart could be roughly compared to that of a film editor.

In The Winter Project and "Night Voices," the dramaturg emerged as a full creative participant in the work of the ensemble in ways that playwrights such as van Itallie and Yankowitz had previously in The Open Theater. As dramaturgs, Rafalowicz and Hart now functioned no less centrally and actively than Chaikin as director, the resident designers, or any of the actors involved. Yet no one (including the dramaturgs themselves) would describe Rafalowicz or Hart as playwrights. A new and quite distinct creative function had been discovered and refined. In the opinions of van Itallie and Yankowitz, The

Winter Project productions suffered as a result of the absence of a playwright per se, and indeed a detailed comparison of the performance texts of The Open Theater and The Winter Project might prove enlightening on this score. Unfortunately, the general lack of published play texts or recordings of the performances of The Winter Project make such a project difficult. Steven Gomer's 1983 documentary film *Joseph Chaikin: Going On,* is one significant exception on this score, containing filmed fragments of both the rehearsals and performances of several of The Winter Project productions.[87]

Beginning with *Re-Arrangements* in 1979, The Winter Project produced a total of five works-in-progress performed at the La MaMa Experimental Theater Club in New York.[88] Financial difficulties plagued The Winter Project from start to finish, limiting developmental rehearsal time as well as the number of performances given. In contrast to the much longer developmental time devoted to Open Theater pieces such as *The Serpent,* The Winter Project productions typically involved only three months of group rehearsal work, though this was usually preceded by at least six months of prerehearsal preparation by the participants. In spite of the significance both Chaikin and Rafalowicz have retroactively attached to the work, neither has left a significant written account of their collaboration in this period apart from Rafalowicz's statement discussed above.

Like the earlier work of The Open Theater, The Winter Project workshops depended heavily on Chaikin's gift for creating improvisational exercises for the generation of potential performance text. Used throughout the developmental work of The Winter Project were exercises designed to help verbally create and define character. In one used in each of the versions of *Tourists and Refugees,* a character was partially defined through a verbal improvisation in which the actor had to speak the character's inner wishes. In another, the members of the ensemble sat in a circle around a single actor and each wrote a monologue for the one in the middle. Once a character had been defined through this or other means, a series of improvised "questionings" of the character often followed, with members of the ensemble improvising the roles of various appropriate interlocuters. An actor playing a character would also typically be asked to provide a litany of statements beginning with "I know...." Eileen Blumenthal has elaborated on these processes:

> A person being questioned would try to make present a past or current emotional state, while staying within the interview format.... Chaikin would heighten this duality by having the actor's voice remain totally in the reality of the workshop while the body inhabited the condition being described: this variation came, in part, out of Chaikin's demonstration of locating extreme conditions somatically. But usually the interview testimonies, like the stories, were allowed to employ a full theatrical vocabulary of words, sounds, and gestures.... Question-and-answer exchanges became a way of exploring inner states. A character in mourning, in physical pain, in love, in retreat from feelings, in a world

of the dead, in a place of extreme physical desires, might be asked "What thoughts are a comfort to you?" "Do you think you're more sensitive than most people?" "What do you think the next moment will be like?"[89]

According to Rafalowicz, scenes based on such exercises found their way into virtually every Winter Project production. Gordon Rogoff has described the results of this type of work in the performance of *Re-Arrangements* in the following words:

> Set in the form of a series of interviews with the actors (called simply "The woman with red hair," "The woman with gray hair," etc.). . . . the work begins with a growling *agitato* accompaniment on a double bass, suggesting that the hour or so ahead of us will be grimly fraught with tension and hysteria. Instead, the agitation is followed immediately by the sound of laughter. Ronnie Gilbert is sitting behind the center drop-curtain . . . which is raised by the first two interviewers, dressed in the hats and gloves of vaudeville comedians. Gilbert's laughter is warm, enveloping, convulsive, halted only for a moment as she tries to remember the answer to the question, "Is there any joke that makes you laugh every time?" Through her laughter, she tells a joke about Mr. and Mrs. Beethoven (which is already a joke, since Beethoven was never one half of a couple), a wonderful performance and a joke that are squarely in the tradition of music-hall entertainment—both of them hard acts to follow. The set-up is clear: here will be perturbations and disturbances, but nothing too charged, nothing too dangerous. . . . When actors are in rehearsal, talk and analysis yield much less information than their attempts to visualize something in action. In *Re-Arrangements,* those attempts are the story.[90]

Rafalowicz describes the dramaturgical structures arrived at in The Winter Project productions as consistently originating in the articulation of such questions—and more the question than its anticipated answer.

The work of Rafalowicz and Hart in this period partly involved the collection of found texts (poems, songs, and such) that could become the raw material of developmental work, and might or might not end up as part of the actual performance. Rafalowicz reports that for The Winter Project, for example, poets such as Grace Paley and Allen Ginsberg were at times invited to attend and contribute pieces to the workshops as part of the developmental work of a piece, though this was not always reflected in the final version performed. This was but one example of what Rafalowicz describes as the "creative waste" required by the process, such "waste" thereafter being subjected to Chaikin's widely acknowledged talent as a rigorous editor of performance text. An early example of this aspect of Chaikin's work was a diary entry written by a schizophrenic girl brought by actress Joyce Aaron to The Open Theater during its work on *Terminal.* Originally eight pages in length, in the final performance version it became a stylized, telegraphic monologue ("The Responsible One") of but a tiny fraction of the original text.

The nature of Rafalowicz and Hart's contributions as dramaturgs was inseparable from the collective nature of the endeavor and the ultimately nonnarrative, nonlinear nature of the performance texts developed in The Open Theater, The Winter Project, and the "Night Voices" series. Unlike van Itallie and Yankowitz in their work with The Open Theater, Rafalowicz has consistently argued that texts such as *Nightwalk* or those created by The Winter Project not be published—and if published, not made available for production elsewhere. The text of *Re-Arrangements* that Rafalowicz did prepare for publication in *Performing Arts Journal,* was preceded by the following note:

> Since the piece *Re-Arrangements,* as performed, was a series of moments woven together in a harmony between images, words, music, colors, lights, costumes and environment, we feel that a "complete" document would be impossible/misleading; e.g., there is continuous music from overture to the end. So we extracted some pictures and texts that may give the reader some impressions of the piece.
>
> NOTE ABOUT THE TEXT:
>
> Unless specifically stated otherwise, material and text for each character or embodiment of experience was contributed by the actor playing the character; e.g., character of the Reserved Person was brought in by Paul Zimet, except for the parts that are specifically marked as taken from material by Sam Shepard, etc.[91]

To heighten her point about the problematical nature of the authorship and publication of the text, Rafalowicz extensively footnoted the passages from the "found texts" used, including ones by Shepard, van Itallie, Chaikin, and the actors involved. In Rafalowicz's words, she wanted through the published text to show how the performance was in fact largely a collage of quotations. An occasional recycling of performance texts from one Winter Project production to another became a feature of the dramaturgy of this period, explained by Rafalowicz as a device again inspired more by the practices of visual artists than playwrights. For example, *Re-Arrangements* "quotes" passages from Chaikin's previous collaboration outside The Winter Project with playwright Sam Shepard on *Tongues* (1978), and passages first created in *Re-Arrangements* were in turn incorporated in Chaikin and Shepard's subsequent project *Savage/Love* (1979). In this practice, The Winter Project paralleled the roughly contemporaneous work of Tadeusz Kantor in Poland (a director much admired by Chaikin), whose theatrical work was even more consciously based on the techniques of dadaist, futurist, and surrealist collage.[92]

The Winter Project's mission of developing the ensemble-as-playwright, with Rafalowicz as dramaturg, inspired serious—if divided—critical discussion. In spite of short scheduled runs, The Winter Project productions were all widely reviewed by the New York press, and in the cases of *Tourists and Refugees No. 2* and *Lies and Secrets* also toured abroad. The variety of structural forms and strategies employed by The Winter Project over time was emphasized in Michael Feingold's 1982 review of *Trespassing:*

> Chaikin has brought along with him many stylistic devices, trophies of his explorations: a fragmentation of scenes, sometimes cutting them down to single sharp images; a heightening of speech to the level of music; a reduction of the banally naturalistic moments to their Absurdist minimum; a juxtaposition of everyday gesture with a violent, stylized, but nonballetic, equivalent. These devices are engaged in a dialectic with the realistic situation (a woman is dying) and the detailed verbalization of the feelings it calls up (crystallized in the woman's soliloquies). . . . The two elements challenge and interrupt each other, rub up against each other, sometimes merging and sometimes fiercely juxtaposed.[93]

Gordon Rogoff, a fellow-traveller with Chaikin from the earliest days of The Open Theater, praised *Re-Arrangements* (1979) as a whole, but was critical of its text:

> The actors are compelled to supply too much of the text, and while their facility and intelligence are never in question, their phrasing rarely matches the subtle immediacy of their acting, nor should it be expected to do so. Like the denial of the eye, the denial of the shaping word and governing shape are losses that the piece need not have suffered. The pleasures in Chaikin's theater derive from the evidence within each moment that nothing will happen that is entirely predictable. The cost, however, is high: in a theater of barely written moments there can be no sustained intensity.[94]

Erika Munk responded appreciatively to the text of *Tourists and Refugees* in 1980, writing:

> The staging's physical means are simple. The script is patched from found texts, interviews, and what sounds like company improvisation; performed by five actors and three musicians. The meanings, however, aren't all simple, though no single moment is obscure. As in a collage, each fragment amplifies and clarifies the other scenes and images.[95]

In her 1983 review of *Lies and Secrets* (The Winter Project's last production), however, Munk complained about the piece's use of "recycled" material and described the text as :

> Bits and pieces, some clever, some banal, some moving; but nothing holds them together. The moments never pile up, the scenes never increase each others' meaning.[96]

When *Lies and Secrets* toured to London later that year under the title of *Trio,* two separate reviewers in the London *Times* commented on the piece's musical logic and structure. In one, Irving Wardle wrote:

> ...this collaborative piece tackles its theme through linked quotations, staging and music.... Its subtext is that the world is full of suffering and danger, and that there is probably nothing the theater can do about it. However, here is some evidence of how we cheat and threaten each other, presented as honestly and openly as the circumstances of public performance permit.... I could not detect the promised ABA form, but a structured contrast does develop between the deceptions and secrets of private life, and those of history, religion, and global politics.[97]

In spite of the critics' obvious awareness of The Winter Project's mission to create original performance texts without a playwright, the nature and significance of Rafalowicz's presence as dramaturg throughout was also consistently overlooked. This was the case even among critics who were intimately familiar with the group's history, artistic priorities, and inner workings such as Gordon Rogoff, Richard Gilman, and Eileen Blumenthal. Out of the sampling of twenty reviews of The Winter Project productions collected for this article, for example, only one referred to the dramaturg by name or her function in the creation of the piece. Rafalowicz has expressed frustration that both the popular press and the few academic studies of the work of The Winter Project (including Blumenthal's) have created a false impression of the ensemble's work as "auteur theater" with Chaikin as the single defining presence—this in spite of the director's own efforts to emphasize the significance and mutuality of his collaboration with dramaturgs such as Rafalowicz and Hart. Rafalowicz's frustrations on this score begin to echo Susan Yankowitz's quoted earlier.

On the basis of the early projects of The Winter Project, public radio producer Rick Harris proposed the idea of an experimental radio series using a similar process, which eventually led to the production of the four-part "Night Voices" series in 1982–83. By virtue of being recorded for radio, "Night Voices" is in fact the best preserved example of Chaikin's developmental work with dramaturgs and yet ironically remains the most obscure of his various projects—again in spite of the artistic significance he and his collaborators have attached to it. The series has not left the usual traces of a theatrical production such as reviews, production photos, or a published script, nor has it been discussed in the critical studies of Chaikin's work to date. For "Night Voices," dramaturg Bill Hart wrote monologues for each half-hour episode as well as connective material between sections. Hart's material was then combined with that written or collected by the actors in the group (Ronnie Gilbert, Roger Babb, Tina Shepard, and Chaikin) over several months in advance of the actual recording sessions in response to the initial ideas and themes provided by Chaikin. Recorded improvisations by the actors were also used. The final editing of the material was a collective effort by Chaikin, Hart, producer Rick Harris, and audio technician Miles Smith—with Chaikin, in Harris's words, assuming a stance of "nondirective directiveness," but holding final veto power over any choice. The theme of the series was announced by its subtitle "Writings and Improvisations About the Time Between Wake and Sleep." The four episodes carried the titles "Insomnia," "Intimacy," "Mysteries," and "Pattern." Significantly, no complete performance text in written form ever existed for "Night Voices" either for use by those involved with the production or for later publication. The broadcast recording is the only form the final performance "text" has ever existed in as a whole.[98] Thus it was arguably in "Night Voices" that the presence of the play text *per se* reached its nadir in Chaikin's experimental work to date.

Both Harris and Chaikin have emphasized the essential similarity of the working process of Hart and Rafalowicz, with the significant exception of Hart's actual authorship of the monologues and other materials mentioned above. Hart has described his work on the series in the following words:

> The process was really analogous to other theater pieces, but in this case we started with a theme rather than a story. We were really interested in the creation of a world, focusing on the twilight period between waking and sleeping. . . . My role was never all that clearly defined—the whole process was more instinctual, and the piece evolved through a dialogue between dramaturg and director, rather than just the dramaturg bringing in material and then leaving. We were interested in creating collages illuminating a particular theme, so it was a journey through the topic through a lot of debating and negotiating with each other. Like making a movie, only aural. And I guess my major part was in the sequencing of the piece, making suggestions about order, the breakdown of the different parts. . . . We were most concerned with how to hold attention and create a mood that was revealing, haunting, beautiful. The different parts sort of came together around those ideas. "Night Voices" had a sort of freedom that I liked, with the ensemble contributing stories from their own experiences—such as the story about waking up and finding your father dead, or the thing about sleeping in a bed where somebody no longer slept.[99]

The production time frame for the series' four half-hour segments was a total of six months, and more than fourteen hours of recorded source material were generated before the editing process began. Chaikin has characterized Hart's dramaturgical style as more realistic than Rafalowicz's, describing her work as more "poetic and political" in spirit. The use of such realistic material from the experiences of the ensemble members applied in "Night Voices" reemerged in Hart's more recent collaboration with Chaikin on a long-term developmental workshop in New York using disabled actors, which began in 1994. Still untitled, Hart has emphasized the particular need in this "disabilities project" to base the ensemble's explorations in the actors' own experiences, in part due to the variety of disabilities represented in the group.

The diminishment of the role of playwrights in favor of dramaturgs coincided with a broadening of the nonverbal theatrical explorations in The Winter Project and "Night Voices." The work of composers and musicians as well as designers assumed a new importance in this phase of developmental work—as emphasized in the note to *Re-Arrangements* quoted above. This aspect of the work by The Winter Project and "Night Voices" ensembles can be seen both as a formal refinement of the work of The Open Theater and as an elaboration of the collective and collaborative mission of the earlier group. Whatever the qualitative judgement of their textual *products,* The Winter Project and "Night Voices" remained intimately connected to the questions of *process* first posed by The Open Theater.

To focus on Chaikin in framing the discussion of dramaturgs such as Rafalowicz and Hart admittedly risks further reinforcing the image of The Open Theater, The Winter Project, and "Night Voices" as tacitly "auteur" theatrical projects. Yet to underplay the director's role as catalyst and collaborative partner in the process of these ensembles' work would be no less a distortion than the neglect of Rafalowicz and Hart in the existing literature on the subject. For whatever reasons, few other theaters have taken up the challenges and rewards of the working process of The Winter Project and "Night Voices." As a result, the history of such dramaturgical work still remains largely that of the situations where Chaikin has insisted a space be made for it. Though not a dramaturg himself, Chaikin has opened—and guarded—the door for a new kind of dramaturg to enter the American theater. The question now no less than when Mira Rafalowicz first accepted Chaikin's invitation to join The Open Theater is who will cross the threshold.

Dramaturg in Collaboration with Joseph Chaikin

by **Mira Rafalowicz**

MIRA RAFALOWICZ, dramaturg, born and bred in Amsterdam, the Netherlands, studied Yiddish and English literature at the Hebrew University in Jerusalem and pursued further Yiddish studies at Columbia University and Hunter College. Rafalowicz started working as a dramaturg in New York with Joseph Chaikin and The Open Theater on *Nightwalk,* the last piece of that group. She continued working with Joseph Chaikin in The Winter Project, where in collaboration with actors, musicians, writers, and designers the following pieces were developed: *Re-Arrangements, Tourists and Refugees, Trespassing, Lies and Secrets* (renamed and reworked as *Trio*). Recently (1995) the group regrouped with additional artists to create *The Firmament.* Other collaborations with Joseph Chaikin include *The Dybbuk* (for the Public Theatre, New York, translated from Yiddish into English, adapted together), and another version of the same play for the Habima Theater, Tel Aviv (version translated into Hebrew by Yehuda Amichai). She collaborated on yet another version of the same play in Dutch with Judith Herzberg and a straight translation for the Royal Shakespeare Company (1992). She also worked with Joseph Chaikin in Jerusalem on a collaborative piece with Jewish and Palestinian Israelis. In Amsterdam Mira Rafalowicz works with Toneelgroep Amsterdam and director Gerardjan Rijnders. Montage productions include *Bakeliet, Titus geen Shakespeare, Ballet, Count Your Blessings, Anne Frank the Exhibition,* and (with director Leonard Frank) a new play by Judith Herzberg, *Rijgdraad.* She is the Artistic Director of a five-yearly international Yiddish festival in Amsterdam. The following article originally appeared in the 10.1, 1978, issue of *Theater,* published by the Yale School of Drama; Joel Schechter, editor.

> people ask me what I do in the theatre,
> this is a selection from my list of answers:
> an internal critic
> an intimate participant
> an outspoken audience member
> a collaborator
> an extra eye
> I work in dialogue with the director and the writer(s),
>   if there are any
> I help asking questions and finding doubts.
> the questions are essential, answers and solutions
> are part of the end of a process. we don't always find them.
> I give my opinion about just about everything.
> People either listen to my advice, my opinions,
> or they don't.

I talk endlessly with the director, with writer(s),
with some actors who find me useful.
I talk after working hours.
what wonderful work for someone who likes to talk a lot.
usually, hopefully I am part of the process from
beginning till end—from the earlier stages of thinking
till the last day of performance.

In the traditional theater dramaturgs read and select
plays, choose the repertoire of an existing company,
sometimes translate plays, write program notes,
give historical backgrounds and literary explanations
of plays and write theoretical articles about the theater.

I have done several of those things too.
I have translated plays (from English and French
into Dutch, from Yiddish into English), I have
adapted plays with different friends/directors,
I have written program notes.

But I have mainly worked in theater and with people
who believe in and thrive on collaboration and
dialogue, a theater in which functions merge and
overlap in the earlier stages of work.

Ideally in the first and basic
stage of the work, there is a meeting of minds,
an openness to each other's concerns and ways of thinking,
a merging of ideas.
In the kind of collaborative work
I'm trying to describe, a context of thinking—
working is established, a fruitful ground from
which ideas sprout.

collaboration is not to be confused with equal input
or democratic procedure.
In reality some people's input is more inspired and
inspiring.

As a dramaturg I try to give the process of working
shape, which might be described in these stages:

the different stages of work — the changing questions.

stage 1.:
we define the area of exploration.
we try to find the questions we will concern ourselves with
and open them up.

questions:
what has value for us to attempt to express,
personally, theatrically, socially, politically?
what are we attempting to explore and express with
this work?

we don't try to find solutions, answers,
but we promote a dialogue, a consciousness about
these questions.

at this stage the different labeled functions
in the work merge and overlap. actors, director,
writer(s), invited guests, dramaturg—all
contribute according to their own ability and skill.
the dramaturg contributes to the texture of thought.

together with the questions, we start to establish
a vocabulary, a code, a common work-history.
a cross-current work is going on between writers,
actors, director, dramaturg, through improvisation,
devising of exercises and through dialogue.

stage 2.:
we develop and shape material.

the questions become more focused:
what is transmitted, what is evoked?
what can be repeated?

everything is still fluid in this stage of the work.
everything still seems to be possible, but it isn't.
this stage is about necessary limitation, about finding
a focus, a direction. There are no longer
unlimited possibilities.

some ideas sound wonderful, but when they are brought up
and tried out, nothing happens.
does the idea stink?

maybe the writer is not inventive enough
or do the limitations of the actors/creators stop
the idea from growing?
some ideas just dry up, we have to give them up.

some ideas create a wonderful initial excitement,
but the improvisation could never be repeated
and nobody can find the impulse again.
the idea has to be dropped.

some ideas are wonderful and exciting, the work
coming out of them is wonderful and exciting,
but it all turns out to belong to a different piece.
It's hard to give those up.

Some ideas find their life in some other working circumstances.
In this stage some of the different functions
re-emerge.
the actor, whether or not s/he is working on material
s/he has created, needs feedback.
the differentiation between those who act
and have to repeat the chosen action and those who shape the
        material
becomes clearer.

in this stage we start eliminating, choosing, cutting.
trying out sequences, finding a beginning structure.
in this stage too, we ask the actors to tell the story
of the unformed piece.
very often the story is not formed yet, so it has to be invented on
the spot, improvised, and we learn from those stories,
about what is alive, what is important, what we miss.

stage 3.:
in this stage the piece is starting to emerge,
it is finding its shape.

at this stage we can still change things, cut scenes
and speeches, change the sequence, add a scene here
and there, but we are losing control, power.

by this time none of us participant onlookers
are "objective," we have to recognize the limitation
of our perceptions. We are too involved.

our questions change. we cannot ask those questions
among ourselves any longer, we need "real" outsiders
and ask them questions.

at this stage we invite friends, friendly outsiders,
our first, still safe, audiences.
safe, because we are also vulnerable. the wrong thing
said to any of us at the wrong time can close possibilities.
we now ask:
what does the piece actually express?
what do you, audience, outsiders, perceive or understand?
is anything transmitted of what we thought, wanted, planned, tried
to express?

at this stage we, the non-actors, director, writer, dramaturg have to make a
difficult re-adjustment.
we have to re-create distance, to re-see, re-examine
we have to listen to outsiders' comments, judgments,
criticism
we have to figure out what is really there or not there,
rather than wish it were there. we have to give up
ideas that don't work, even if we still have some
hope that they might work.

but we also have to evaluate other people's comments,
pick out the perceptions that are valuable to the
intentions of the work, screen them, use them carefully.
and especially: we have to try to stay open.

ex.:
when I first translated the *Dybbuk,* we discovered
that a word in Yiddish has many different
possibilities of translation. sometimes more than one
word covers one word in the original language, sometimes
it is hard to know which way of saying something is better.
so I made a multiple choice translation, giving
the actors a chance to feel out different ways of saying
something. giving us a chance to listen. But also
indicating to the actor that s/he has a right to think.

stage 4.:
the performance has found its independent life.
at this stage we have to find even more distance,
painful separation.

we have to find out what this creation has become.
this is the end of a process, a time for re-evaluation.

in this late stage, details can be changed,
small changes can be made.

the questions now become questions about
repetition, about how to keep a piece alive,
about maintaining or deepening intentions.
this is the point at which we have to
let go, accept the limitations of the work done,
appreciate and stimulate the actors in what
remains interesting and strong. we have to
become a supportive eye and give the piece over
to the actors.

we non-actors in the theater (shapers, developers,
critics, reviewers, dramaturgs) should be conscious of tired eyes,
        of the
limitations of our perceptions. Only
with that consciousness can we constantly re-open
ourselves to experience anew. At least we should try.

as a dramaturg I am limited in whom I can work with.
I can help make something better, clearer, only
when the basic working relationship is one of
mutual respect. Not uniformity of thinking and
feeling (there is no creative dialogue possible
in uniformity, total agreement), but a basis of
sympathy. Ideally with everyone involved in the process.
So I can really only work with friends. When I run
out of friends to work with in the theater, I
will do something else.

The Way We Work

by Travis Preston and Royston Coppenger

TRAVIS PRESTON is a director of theater, opera, and film. His theater work in the United States includes the world premiere of *Democracy in America* at the Yale Repertory Theater; the theatrical premiere of Brecht's *Berlin Requiem* at the American Repertory Theater; the American premiere of Buero-Vallejo's *The Sleep of Reason* at Center Stage; the world premiere of Ted Tally's *Terra Nova;* and, in 1995, the American premiere of *Roberto Zucco* by Bernard-Marie Koltès. In collaboration with The Private Theater, Travis Preston and Royston Coppenger created *The Last American in Paris*. This work was mounted at the Center for the Performing Arts in Purchase, New York and is currently being prepared for a European tour. He has been Resident Director at the American Repertory Theater, an Associate Artist at Center Stage and the Yale Repertory Theatre, and is the recipient of a directing fellowship from the NEA. In New York he has directed *Hamlet, The Maids, The Ghost Sonata, Woyzeck,* and *Apocrypha*. Travis Preston and Royston Coppenger were also commissioned by the City of New York to create *Paradise Bound: Part II,* an "Oratorio for Boom Box and Chorus" presented at Summerfare in Central Park. He has directed extensively abroad: *Prometheus Bound* (Poland), *Alexander* (Norway), *The Seagull* (England), *Macbeth* (Denmark), and *The Balcony* (Hong Kong). Mr. Preston's opera work includes productions of *Don Pasquale, Falstaff, Don Giovanni,* and *Saul and the Witch of Endor.* In 1996, he will direct a production of Alban Berg's *Lulu* in celebration of Copenhagen's selection as the Cultural Capital of Europe. His feature film, *Astonished,* has been shown throughout the world, including festivals in Montreal, Paris, Berlin, Munich, Florence, and Hong Kong.

ROYSTON COPPENGER has worked with Travis Preston since 1983. Their collaborations include: *Hamlet, The Ghost Sonata, The December Project,* and *Apocrypha* in New York City; *Don Juan: A Meditation* at the Mark Taper Forum; *Twelfth Night* at the Indiana Repertory Theatre; and *A Doll's House, Litte Eyolf,* and *Ghosts* at the American Ibsen Theatre in Pittsburgh, where Mr. Coppenger served as Resident Dramaturg. Mr. Coppenger and Mr. Preston are coauthors of *Paradise Bound Part II,* an oratorio for chorus and portable radios based on the Bernard Goetz confession, which was produced by the City of New York in 1987, and *The Last American in Paris/Le Dernier Americain à Paris,* an award-winning original theater piece produced by The Project Theatre in Ann Arbor and subsequently by the Private Theater in New York. Most recently, they collaborated on the English-language premiere of Bernard-Marie Koltès' *Roberto Zucco,* which Mr. Coppenger also translated, in New York City. For this production they were both honored with OOBR awards (*Off-Off-Broadway Review*) for translation and direction. Mr. Coppenger's other translations of Koltès include *Key West* and *In the Loneliness of the Cottonfields.* For his translations of Koltès' Mr. Coppenger received two National Theatre Translation Fund commissioning grants. His critical writing has appeared in Yale *Theater* magazine and *Actes du Théâtre.* Mr. Coppenger has taught courses in theater, film, and popular culture at Carnegie-Mellon and Harvard Universities, and New York University. He is currently Assistant Professor of Drama at Hofstra University.

TRAVIS PRESTON—THE CONCEPT

One might say that my attitude toward making theater is anticonceptual. The directorial "concept," as it is conventionally understood and used in the contemporary theater, is a device to facilitate communication between artistic collaborators and between the production and its audience. It is a method of reduction whereby an expansive work is made smaller, and the investigation and collaboration among artists conducted within its confines are similarly reduced. Viewed as a natural outgrowth of interpretation, the concept is thought of as the seat of directorial power and authority. In it resides a means to assert point of view and should thereby lead to a more individual and personal work of theater, but it actually has the paradoxical effect of creating a more generic artistic production. As elements are brought within the confines of the conceptual framework, idiosyncrasy and personal response are muted. I believe the source of its popularity lies in another quarter altogether.

The concept has grown in importance because it makes the practice of theater more efficient, hence more economical. It combines the efficiency of commercial production with the intellectual aspirations of resident theater. It lends the patina of artistic legitimacy to assembly-line institutional production. Its supposed virtues of providing aesthetic unity and making the "message" of the production clear reduce the theater to mere information processing, a task the theater is poorly equipped to perform. The concept actually strips the theater of its complexity and attendant mystery.

The process I seek is far more chaotic and, indeed, is designed to disrupt and complicate the normal and accepted channels of communication. I am interested in the gaps in communication and in impulses that are not immediately verifiable by any objective standard. My goal is a process that is ever expanding. I conceive of it as rather like the "Big Bang" theory of contemporary physics: fragments hurtling to unknown distances from an explosive center. This center is the clash between the artistic team and the play we will produce. There is no effort to subsume the play within our understanding of it; in some fundamental way the play is seen as autonomous. So, too, are the collaborators. The vital anarchy of interaction between the play and the individual artists is central. They will not help to create an engaging piece of theater if they tailor their ideas to what they believe is my "concept" of the play. What is required is unbridled passionate engagement with the text and one another.

ROYSTON COPPENGER—THE CONCEPT

Dramaturgs in America frequently belabor themselves with the question of whether or not their audiences will understand their work. Somehow the audience's ability to grasp an intellectual formulation has been raised to unnaturally high value, taking precedence over more ephemeral types of understanding, be they visceral, emotional, or aesthetic. In response to the anxiety of communication, we have developed a packaging tool called the concept, usually a declarative statement that is transmitted entire to the audience by the end of the play. It often takes the form of an object lesson or a gross generalization about the theme of the play. I don't believe that anything worth saying in this life can be articulated in one of the brief statements that comprise a production concept. Even if it could, the theater is at best an inefficient vehicle for sending messages; a telegram is much more direct and economical. The "statement" Shakespeare was trying to make with *Hamlet* took several thousand lines of iambic pentameter; our statement, the production of *Hamlet,* took upwards of three hours, twenty actors and months of creative effort. Theater is responsible to its audience to provide an experience, of which intellectual stimulation is only one part. Statements of concept take place in past tense. The concept has to be agreed upon by the production committee before rehearsals begin. Yet theater must exist in the present tense. I cannot demand that my ideas in rehearsal fit into a conceptual boundary established before the rehearsals started. The dramaturg, armed with a predetermined concept, enters rehearsal like a soldier going onto the field of battle. The concept becomes the dramaturg's unshakable certainty in the face of the chaotic and everchanging development of a theater piece. To make exciting theater we have to be uncertain. The more determined the dramaturg is to hold on to the concept, the more passive he or she becomes in the face of the production. How can last month's idea be stronger than the excitement of discovery?

Travis and I engage in exhaustive study of plays we work on. We're both well read, the products of classical educations. My personal interests run toward the study of history and culture, and toward severe structural analyses influenced by the science of semiotics. We try to attain a comprehensive understanding of the play before we go into rehearsals. But this understanding is extremely fragile. It can be blown apart in the first readthrough in the rehearsal space, by an actor with an unexpected impulse or an unusual inflection. The play, which is ephemeral and abstract, has changed shape and meaning in the face of the artists gathered to execute this specific production. This process of transformation will continue long past opening night. An idea is an idea, and a play is a play. A concept is, well, a concept. It is an abstract formulation. A production is a real thing. As Marx pointed out in *Das Kapital,* money is an abstraction. Bread is not.

ROYSTON COPPENGER—OBJECTIVITY

When I was being trained as a dramaturg, I was taught to attend rehearsals only sporadically, no more than three or four times a week. I was told this practice would help me maintain my "objectivity." Assuming for a moment that it is possible to remain objective about a work of art that carries your name in the program, the question still remains: what do we gain from being objective? Theater is by nature a subjective art form. The artists in rehearsal must bring their dreams and imaginations to bear upon the play, which has no form until it is given life through the act of rehearsal. Objective dramaturgs are sometimes described as in-house critics. Most theater people regard critics with fear and loathing. Is this really how we want to describe ourselves?

The more a dramaturg strives to be objective, the more he or she takes on the passive role of a spectator. The spectator-dramaturg, who can only respond to last week's conversation or last month's production meeting, will always be unsatisfied: deprived of yesterday's discovery and last night's conversation in the bar, the dramaturg has no way of bringing his or her impulses to bear upon today's need, today's crisis. Is it any wonder that so many directors, embroiled in the here and now of rehearsal, don't want to listen? If the dramaturg keeps safely away from rehearsals, nothing can assault the integrity of the predetermined concept. Being absent from the process means that the dramaturg doesn't have to share in the possible failure of the production. But the objective dramaturg also relinquishes any claim to the production's success. If dramaturgy is to have any relevance in the theater, the dramaturg must become a creative artist, sharing the danger that actors and directors face every day.

TRAVIS PRESTON—SOME BASIC ASSUMPTIONS OF OUR WORK TOGETHER

A basic tenet of our work together is that we reject the notion that a production can be definitive. In dramaturgy this is associated with the obsessive desire to be comprehensive. Compulsive devotion to research and analysis creates the illusion of objectivity. The notion of definitive production seduces one into thinking that an objective criterion of judgment exists and is desirable. We view this goal as both unattainable and undesirable as an artistic aspiration.

Another assumption of our work is an inherent faith in the validity of impulse. The impulse is the nexus of instinct, intelligence, learning, and identity. Its essence may be only vaguely understood by the artist, and its objectives almost entirely unknown. It does not aspire to a global encompassing of the play but rather tends to illumine a mere instant or minuscule fragment—or is not related to the play at all but emanates from some inspiration or powerful association emerging from an obscure point of origin. Royston and I have never quarreled over some point of interpretation. I do not consider this a reflection of a remarkable consonance of taste but the result of a collaboration that recognizes a multiplicity of impulses. We support the free generation of myriad impulses from all artistic collaborators.

Another premise underlying our work together is that the theater event is the most important thing—more important than the play it is based on. The play as a literary entity is a work of art waiting to be realized. My reading experience of the play as literature and my experience of the play as a theater event are fundamentally different aesthetic realms. Finally, one thing that fuels our artistic relationship is the belief in collective creation, that labor on a play, project, or idea can be so focused and intense that individual identity disappears in the struggle with the material. This is a faith that reveals discomfort with the division and hierarchy of labor inherent in the very notion of dramaturgs, directors, designers, and such, and asserts that ideas cannot be possessed.

TRAVIS PRESTON—ANARCHY

The nature of the process is reflected in the final production. More and more our theater is mirroring the corporate structures from which it arises. Ways of working that are consistent with corporate values inevitably emerge; while those that are contradictory to smooth institutional functioning are suppressed. It is only natural for institutions that thrive on stability, efficiency, and consistent operating procedure to reject that which is anarchic, abrasive, or chaotic. The "not-for-profit corporation" is a telling oxymoron. The corporation, the very structure of which is designed to generate profit, may be the form of organization least conducive to creating exciting theater. There is no doubt in my mind that a general transformation in the quality of theater production will not occur until innovations develop in producing structures.

Anarchy is synonymous with vitality and creativity. Creativity is unstable. Royston contributes to this instability. I do not ask him to be less of himself by restraining his impulses within some abstract reduction of the play, nor do I believe he should do this within his own interpretive frame. I want more of his energy and investment than that. I expect it to cost him more, and I anticipate that some of it will be extremely personal. The quality and level of such engagement can radically disrupt the smooth working order of any process. Royston's participation serves to destabilize my process—to create greater anarchy, not less.

This seems to be the opposite of most processes employing a dramaturg. Their functions, whether intentional or not, appear to bring greater order and stability into the rehearsal process. The unconscious objective is to minimize the possibility of failure. The production histories, the protocols, the surveys of criticism all seem to be ordering tasks that serve an almost ritual function. (This ritual function is complete if one considers the prospect—altogether a possibility—that no one actually reads these amassed documents.) It is a form of academic protection, talismans to ward off the evil spirits of doubt, anarchy, and uncertainty.

ROYSTON COPPENGER—VULNERABILITY

Our work is based on the idea that the entire creative team, director, actors, designer, and dramaturg, must be vulnerable in the presence of the play. We must allow ourselves to be continually refreshed and excited by the play as it comes to life. Because of my background, my impulses will be different from those of the other team members. I can be quite erudite in my reading. But the play may be smarter than I am. I may not be able to make logical sense of it all. I may have to rely on dreams, whims, and half-baked ideas. Sometimes my unconscious mind is telling me something that my conscious mind can't yet comprehend. I can't go forward by editing my impulses before I've seen them tried out on stage. Sometimes ideas that sound stupid, insupportable, prove themselves in a moment.

An idea proves itself when it makes a moment work on stage, if it makes sense of a scene that made no sense before. But ideas can't be validated simply on the basis of their relationship to one another. It is necessary for dramaturgs to be sensitive to the needs of the time and place; we also have to keep our personal agendas in mind. When Travis and I did *Hamlet* we labored for weeks over Ophelia's funeral. Somehow the scene never worked. We couldn't manage to convey the weight of Ophelia's death at that point in the play.

During the early weeks of rehearsal, my grandmother died. One night I had a vivid and strangely comforting dream in which my grandmother stood, invisible to all but me, watching as the family went through her possessions after the funeral. The next day I told Travis about this dream. He suggested that Ophelia should watch her own funeral, unseen to all the other characters. It worked, because of the specific emotional resonance of the image as it interacted with the play. But we cannot, within an orderly intellectual framework, explain why.

If my intellect were to prevent me from recognizing a strong impulse when it came up, then my intellect would be the enemy. Dramaturgy can't limit itself only to what can be explained. I'm a smart human being, dramaturgs generally are smart human beings. We don't have to be our own intellectual watchdogs, or anybody else's.

ROYSTON COPPENGER—INSTITUTIONS

Perhaps dramaturgy has no place as an institutional function. American institutional theater is set up according to the time-honored industrial practice of division of labor. Every person in a theater institution must justify their existence, and therefore their salary, by fulfilling a clearly defined role and producing a discrete and irreplaceable body of work. This organizational philosophy is appropriate in the production of shoes, automobiles, and cruise missiles; it may not be so appropriate for the creation of exciting theater.

In every project we've done, the time has come when it was impossible, with a few exceptions, to distinguish which member of the team had what idea, and how the ideas evolved. I can't tell you for example who first suggested that Mrs. Linde in *A Doll House* should be a Christ figure, or that Pastor Manders should have his eyes ripped out on stage. Once the energy of collaboration had taken over, we all relinquished our claims to conceptual territory. As a result, it is often impossible to demonstrate the cost-effectiveness of dramaturgy to the production. Dramaturgy becomes an integral part of the gestalt of the production.

For the institutional dramaturg, conceptual territory and labor divisions take on inordinate importance. To jump-start the profession, a number of functions have been proposed as integral to the theater's operation; all are best executed by the trained dramaturg. These include play reading, audience outreach and education, research, and the all-important program notes. By fulfilling these functions successfully, the dramaturg proves his or her worth to the organization, as long as the organization accepts that these jobs need to be done. And so, many theaters have now hired dramaturgs or their better-established *Dopplegängers,* literary managers. That title contains the curious dilemma many dramaturgs face in professional theater, conflating as it does the postindustrial title "manager" with the ancient and ill-defined concept of "literature." How does one manage a work of literature?

In some theaters a sneaking suspicion may linger that the dramaturg is not really doing much that needs doing. Dramaturgs often complain that their suggestions for seasons are not taken seriously enough. We all know that in the real world, theaters choose their seasons based on reports from the business office, combined with the whim of the artistic director and the tastes of the directors who work there. We may talk wistfully about the German system, in which dramaturgs not only choose seasons and hire directors, but get their homes cleaned by upstart business managers, but in reality the American system has some rough virtues of its own. There is at least the chance in American theater, that a director will be hired to stage a play that he or she really wants to work on. There is at least a chance that American regional theaters will bear the stamp of the artistic director's personality.

To continually justify themselves, institutional dramaturgs wind up performing a jumble of administrative activities, a far cry from the passion for theater that drove them into the academy in the first place. The institutional dramaturg yearns for the day when he or she can be in rehearsals, close to the creative energy that is absent in their offices. Yet for every minute the dramaturg spends in rehearsal, there's a minute where, on paper, the business office can't see any work being done. The balance sheet shows only time lost and output diminished.

Paradoxically, theaters don't even get the benefit from engaging these in-house *litterateurs.* Overwhelmed by the demands of serving seven to ten productions a year, they have little time or patience to read the scripts that come in, so most employ readers, underpaid or nonpaid college students who have none of the training or sensibility that might allow them to pick out something truly wonderful and strange. Dramaturgs continue to search for the formula that will allow them creative input in the theater, while missing the point: the theater has bought them off and sees no further responsibility to entertain them.

I have chosen to work as a freelance dramaturg because my interest lies in what happens on stage. I do not want to be responsible to the institution for making sure the high school kids have something intelligible to read about the play, or that unsolicited scripts are read and rejected according to a reasonable schedule. What I enjoy about being a dramaturg is the discovery, the collaboration, the problem solving. In ten years of professional work I have been integral to the creation of numerous exciting productions. I have felt myself grow as an artist, and I have had a lot of fun.

ROYSTON COPPENGER—RESEARCH

The word implies the hunt for something hidden, important information that has somehow been misplaced. To look again. But what are we really looking for? Classically, dramaturgical research breaks down into three categories: historical research, critical research, and production histories.

Historical research can help answer logistical questions within the play. (What, for example, is Horatio talking about with the 'companies of children' speech?) By looking at the period surrounding the play's writing, one can also get clues to unlocking the significance of events within the play. Through imaginative application of historical information, we can understand better what was important to the playwright. But in researching history and culture it's important to look beyond the surface, to analyze information as it's collected. A book on social etiquette might tell me that Molière's audience indulged in extravagant codes of dress and behavior; an economic history of the seventeenth century might tell me that the lower aristocracy Molière wrote about faced financial ruin brought on in part by the collapse of the feudal agricultural system; a book about Louis XIV might tell me that Louis developed a system of patronage so extreme that court largesse was frequently the only means for well-bred paupers to survive; another book might tell me that syphilis and frequent smallpox epidemics had left so many Frenchmen with scarred faces that heavy makeup and masks became fashionable. All this research becomes dramatically viable if it reveals the impulse beneath the appearances in Molière's plays. It doesn't matter if the characters in *Don Juan* look, walk, and talk like seventeenth-century Frenchmen. It matters how they feel and how we understand their story.

An assumption of critical research is that plays contain a finite amount of truth, which we are seeking to unearth, and which then will provide the final word on Allmer's character or Hamlet's indecision. Of course postmodern schools of critical thought have come along to challenge these assumptions, but overall the field of dramatic criticism remains concerned with the search for definitive readings that are intended to silence any further debate.

I prefer to think of critical research as a foundation of a dramaturg's training, in the same way that pianists learn scales and professional ballet dancers continue to take classes. The study of criticism can open one's imagination to the breadth of opinion about a given play and can sharpen one's thinking by presenting conflicting interpretations that must be accepted or rejected. But for the purposes of production it is vital to treat the play primarily as a catalyst for one's own imagination and a vehicle for personal expression. The critical reading we have done will always be there, feeding who we are in the moment we encounter a play. But it cannot, in and of itself, provide answers for the difficult and exciting problem of realizing a play on stage, with a specific group of collaborators, at a particular time. For this we must turn to our own resources; these resources may include, but cannot be limited to, years of specialized study.

Production histories operate on the related assumption that a finite number of good ideas exists. The production team, it is assumed, is so impoverished of resources that they'll need to know how Richard Mansfield handled the second Ghost scene. The production history assumes that plays exist in a vacuum divorced from our own time and society, and that an idea that worked in 1927 will work again now in the same way. Travis and I have always worked on the assumption that great plays will elicit from us great discoveries; we steal a lot from ourselves, our actors, our times, and our history. We've never felt the need to go out and conscientiously steal from someone else.

TRAVIS PRESTON—THE ROLE OF THE DRAMATURG

It seems to me that discussions concerning the "role" of the dramaturg often reflect an institutional problem rather than artistic need. The position of dramaturg in the institution reads like a job description. There is no role or set of functions that Royston consistently fulfills in our projects. What he should do varies enormously according to the project, my needs, and, above all, his predilection. This is not to say, for example, that Royston might not research a play; he often does. His reasons for doing so, however, are entirely in response to his own artistic needs and interests. Neither does he have an analytical function, though he might provide analysis. Royston is defined in the production process by the very fact of his presence. I do not think of him as a dramaturg. I think of him as Royston.

Over a period of a few years I watched the work between Ludwig Flaszen and Jerzy Grotowski.[100] It was absolutely impossible to determine any definable role that Flaszen played in Lab productions, but the quality of engagement was quite vigorous. In the end, I don't think Flaszen either confirmed or denied any of Grotowski's impulses, but he was present. And his presence was defining and significant. Flaszen was someone in whose presence Grotowski could work, and, perhaps, needed to work. They inspired one another in indefinable ways. That exists between Royston and me.

ROYSTON COPPENGER—UNDERSTANDING

Dramaturgs frequently mention the problem of helping audiences understand what we are trying to show them in the theater. Program notes, after-play discussions and clearly articulated concepts are a few of the dramaturgical techniques developed to educate our audience enough to be able to enjoy what they are seeing. Yet for the past generation or so, Americans have been deserting the theater in droves, turning instead for entertainment to chaotic and inherently complex media such as television, action movies and video games, or to live entertainments such as monster-truck rallies, sporting events, and pop music extravaganzas. In response to this crisis of dwindling audiences, many theaters have consciously "dumbed down" their seasons or spent more and more time trying to explain their work to an audience that is perceived as having debased and unsophisticated tastes.

It has been our experience that so-called unsophisticated audiences, if given the chance, are perfectly able to enjoy the theater as long as the theater is challenging enough for them. In 1984 we mounted a production of *Little Eyolf* at the American Ibsen Theatre in Pittsburgh. The production was extremely complicated, emotionally and aesthetically. That summer, the theater had been trying to find ways to fill the audience and generate word-of-mouth publicity about our work. Our managing director discovered a support organization in town that arranged picnics and outings for unemployed steelworkers. We gave them free tickets and papered many houses with these workers and their families, many of whom had rarely entered a theater. Every night they were in the audience, I would lead a postshow discussion with the audience and the actors, because we feared the production, which was austere and expressionistic, might need some explaining. But I found to my surprise that this uninitiated audience experienced the play most directly. They spoke about the characters, about the story, about the relationships that grew so complex over the course of nearly three hours. One night a woman spoke of when her young son had been killed in an accident, and how the play reminded her of the agony she and her husband had been through. Not one of those people had any problem with the dozens of oriental rugs that covered the stage, of the twenty-by-forty-foot Norwegian flag we raised at the end of the play, or with the entrance of the Rat-Wife, or with the ambiguous ending. They knew, I suspect, that life hits most of us like a speeding train, with little explanation. I think they appreciated a piece of theater that reflected what they knew and didn't try to simplify it. At the end of the summer, when the manager of the steelworkers' support group asked his clients what they'd enjoyed most in the past year and what they wanted more of, a large majority of them responded that their favorite excursion had been to see *Little Eyolf.* As I remember, we even won out over a Pittsburgh Pirates game.

It's been our experience that when we're true to our fantasies, audiences respond. Dramaturgs often talk about "educating" audiences, so they'll enjoy being dished up the cold remains of the West's intellectual banquet. I propose, instead, that we let ourselves be true to what we enjoy, and invite the audience to share in our pleasures. Collaboration offers the chance for theater to embrace a multiplicity of perspectives, serving as a vehicle for expressing the overwhelming reality of life today. What happens if they don't understand it? Indeed, what happens if they don't like it? Our theater today attracts less than 5 percent of the American public. Can we do any worse by letting go of our allegiance to a principle that does not seem to be working?

Exploration Through Imagery:
Gregory Gunter Talks about Working with Anne Bogart

by **Gregory Gunter**

GREGORY GUNTER has worked as dramaturg and imagist with Michael Greif on Tony Kushner's *Slavs!* and Diana Son's *Boy* at the La Jolla Playhouse (LPJ) and a workshop of Jonathan Larson's *Rent* at the New York Theatre Workshop (NYTW); with Tina Landau on Jose Rivera's *Cloud Tectonics* (LJP), Charles L. Mee's *Orestes* (American Repertory Theatre, EnGarde Arts), *Stonewall* (EnGarde Arts), and others; with Anne Bogart on *The Medium* at the Saratoga International Theatre Institute (SITI), NYTW, *Small Lives/Big Dreams* (SITI), and others; with Joseph Chaikin, Sam Shepard, and Robert Woodruff in workshops; with Chuck Mee, as collaborator on *The Bacchae, Philoctetes, Agamemnon* (Actors Gang), and *Trojan Women: A Love Story.* He is the former Literary Manager/Dramaturg of New York Theatre Workshop and currently Literary Manager/Associate Dramaturg of La Jolla Playhouse. The following article is excerpted from *Anne Bogart Viewpoints,* edited by Michael Bigelow Dixon and Joel A. Smith (Smith and Kraus, 1995).[101]

I've been fortunate to work as dramaturg and imagist with Anne on a number of projects. We met while I was dramaturging Tina Landau's production of Charles L. Mee Jr.'s *Orestes* at the American Repertory Theatre Institute. Tina had asked me to find some images for the play, so I spent about four days scouring the recesses of the Harvard libraries for books of photographs that related to it. I literally covered a thirty-five-foot section of wall with a collage of pictures using an occupational therapy technique I learned during my unfortunate incarceration in a loony bin in Texas. As an actor and playwright I'd used images to storyboard a play, a technique I also incorporated into the mural.

This visual interpretation of the text, if you will, told the story of the House of Atreus at various points throughout history. Scenes from the girlhood of Clytemnestra and Helen of Troy were juxtaposed with broken Greek statues representing the death of Agamemnon. I also attempted to find a lighter side to some of the tragic family members. For instance "Menelaus' hairy backside" was enlarged from a picture of a wealthy older man in a very small and unflattering bathing suit. The idea, then, was to create a past, present, and future for each of the characters, with each relationship and each major action explored through images. The photocopied images were used for educational purposes only and were to be displayed only in rehearsal to protect against copyright infringement. They provided the actors access into the characters in a way that hadn't before seemed possible.

Anne, having seen this visual imagery project, asked to use it in Japan. So I gathered all of the images and compiled them in a book in the same style as the mural. Her own production of *Orestes* would inaugurate her new theater company, the Saratoga International Theatre Institute, which she formed with Tadashi Suzuki. Her production would be radically different from Tina's but could still use the "historical material" provided by my research. Actors in Toga, Japan, were invited to look at the book at the beginning of rehearsal and were encouraged to peruse it throughout. Anne had the actors re-create certain poses of the real-life characters in the photographs as a way of entering a "state" on the stage. Ellen Lauren, who was acting in Suzuki's *Bacchae* at the time, told me the actors treated it as a bible for the production and that the images allowed them to discover a world they could not find in the mountains of Toga. Soon after, Anne asked me to work on another play she was developing based on the life and writings of Marshall McLuhan.

At a meeting regarding this new play, Anne gave me a list of things she knew and didn't know about the piece. The "Things I know" list for *The Medium* included the following (although this is from my recollection and not an actual list):

- The play is about Marshall McLuhan;
- McLuhan is one of the characters in the play;
- All of the others characters are dead or part of his memory;
- The play takes place during the moment of his stroke.

From this, I compiled a list of images to locate. Regarding the first point, "The play is about Marshall McLuhan," I asked myself some of the same questions that Anne asked: "Who is McLuhan?" "What does he look like?" "What was his home life like?" I then found images of McLuhan, his family, his workplaces, his hometown. The second point only made the need for physical images of McLuhan stronger. And though Tom Nellis, who was playing McLuhan, created his own unique character, the images at least provided the company with some of the physical states of the man. The third point, "All of the other characters are dead . . ." led me to images of death and memory, and images of people who appear "dead" even though they're walking, interacting, and so on. Some of these images were of people who'd suffered strokes. It's important for Anne, I've found, to follow every impulse—that's part of what keep her work so vital and alive. I never knew until she or her company of actors really delved into the material what would strike them. Following intuition and my growing knowledge of Anne's needs as a director, I found images that enabled them to get a handle on a scene or a character.

The "Things I don't know" list was more complex, because I knew she'd discover those points of confusion while working with the actors. This list included:

- Is Marshall McLuhan the only one who's had a stroke?
- What physical manifestations of stroke do the other characters have?

- Are the other characters dead all the time?
- What is the world of the other characters when they're not in "television land"?

From this list I began to get ideas about what Anne was searching for. The first question was hard for me to work with, so I moved on to the next and found examples of physical manifestations of strokes. I went to the Aphasia Institute, interviewed a doctor there and found information on stroke victims, such as what specifically happens to them during the stroke and after. I searched for other avenues that might lead me to answers for the cast. I called stroke networks for material and dropped by the American Heart Association for pamphlets.

The third question, "Are all the other characters dead all the time?" was answered by the fourth. They, like McLuhan, were hurled into this technoworld of pop philosophy primarily through McLuhan's exploration of television. They became characters. Because Anne never watched television as a child and had no references for the sitcoms, westerns, and detective stories she wanted to use to tell the story, I found images of "television land" for her. And finally, for the question "When they're not in television land, where are they?" I looked at the blank screen of my own television and imagination. I found images of broken sets, blank sets, blurry screens, and "snow." The actors constructed from these images the place of the characters in between scenes.

As imagist, I usually riff on an idea until it's completely spent. So images of memory—a hard thing to find, let me tell you—could be classic Americana, "the good old days," a 1960s issue of *McCall's*, or such obvious images as a picture of a man who appears to be thinking juxtaposed with an image of a young woman holding her finger to her chin as if perplexed. I use my imagination to find connections and dichotomies where perhaps they didn't exist before. I try to ask myself what I would need as an actor or what would excite me about this research. Anne uses the work to stimulate her actors to stretch their imagination beyond literal exploration. She asks a lot of her actors. She asks them to create a wholly different physical life for the play than the one most of them are comfortable using as a way to heighten reality, sometimes to an exhausting point. The images, then, are a springboard for her company members to begin from. They move beyond it quickly, because each actor brings with herself or himself a great wealth of imagination and experience. But there will always be one image to refer back to, one body position to recreate to achieve a state of being unlike any other, and that's rewarding.

When I dramaturg for Anne Bogart I try to think of myself as a member of the ensemble. I know that she considers every idea from every person in the room, from actor to production assistant as part of the whole process of discovery. When I am working on a visual imagery project, somewhere miles away from where the actual rehearsal will occur (which is usually the case), I first immerse myself in the play. Then, much as Anne does before a production, I ask myself hundreds of questions. I think about each character's past, present, and future; each relationship, no matter how trivial, is represented and explored in my work—particularly as imagist for the play. I know that Anne's sense of heightened reality (pardon that boorish term) produces connections where a director with a more realistic style might find none. Through Anne's techniques of questioning each moment, of collaborating with each participant, and of exploring the life of the play, my work is going to have an impact on the style of the piece, or the movement of the actors, or the life of the play.

How to Talk to a Playwright

From an edited transcript of a panel discussion with ERIC OVERMYER (playwright), JOHN GLORE (Literary Manager, South Coast Repertory Theatre), SANDY SHINNER (Associate Artistic Director, Victory Gardens Theatre), PHILIP KAN GOTANDA (playwright), STEVE CARTER (playwright), and CONSTANCE CONGDON (playwright and dramaturg): Literary Managers and Dramaturgs of the Americas Annual Conference, DePaul University, Chicago, June 1990. The editors wish to thank these individuals for permitting us to publish their comments here.

Eric Overmyer: This panel asks, "How to Talk to a Playwright," and my initial gut reaction is don't. I don't believe that dramaturgs should talk to playwrights in the best of all possible worlds, meaning production. I believe that the dramaturg should talk to the director, and the director should talk to the playwright. I think it's a better way of working. If you can't avoid talking to the playwright and you're in development hell, there are some things to bear in mind, at least I would want you to, if you were my dramaturg. Question your assumptions. I think the main assumptions that exist in the American developmental phase of theater are that a play needs fixing and someone besides the writer is able to do that. Question that.

Question your received ideas about what a play should be. Ponder whether what you perceive to be flaws to be fixed aren't, in fact, just characteristics that make the play. (There is no such thing as a perfect play except for *Uncle Vanya.*) A lot of what happens when developing a play is that those things get fixed. Those peculiarities, those oddities, those problems, get written out, and the play becomes better crafted and much less interesting.

Also, if you could keep in mind that getting notes is existentially annoying to a writer. A dramatic writer, a screenwriter, a playwriter spends a lot of his or her career getting notes telling you how to do what you do from people who *don't* do what you do and *can't* do what you do. That is, even with the best of intentions and in the most congenial tone of voice, existentially annoying.

The last thing is, if you can possibly discern what the intentions are and help the playwright realize those intentions, **that** is how the play needs to be developed or fixed, not with notes "as if I had written this play." It would be this other play. But it's **not** that other play, it's **this** play. And if you can help the playwright realize this play, that is what you should try to do. That's all I have to say.

John Glore: I've known Eric for about fifteen years now, back to college days, and we've kept up a correspondence and met in various cities around the country over the years and I've been a big fan of his work. I didn't get the opportunity to work on one of his plays until about a year and a half ago when my theater did *In Perpetuity Throughout the Universe.* For some reason, despite the past history, I never felt comfortable talking to Eric about his play, and now I know why. The question put to us is, "How do you talk to a playwright?" and like any good dramaturg I'll start by critiquing the question. It's fraught with potholes. The question implies that there is a methodology that can be codified and then communicated to other people. I don't know if I believe that's true. I know that when I work as a dramaturg, it's a liquid process and it's at least 50 percent instinct, so it's difficult for me to stop and say, "Okay, what do I really do when I talk to a playwright? What is the rule of thumb that's implicit in the way I work with a playwright?" That's one caveat.

Another thing is that as soon as you start talking about a methodology, you also imply that you can talk to one playwright pretty much the way that you talk to another playwright, and I definitely don't believe that's true. I wouldn't talk to Eric Overmyer the way I would talk to Connie Congdon.

The question we should ask is "How do you talk to Eric Overmyer?" which you don't—obviously. And "How do you talk to a Connie Congdon?" The question has to be answered in each particular instance.

The third thing is obvious: you don't talk **to** a playwright. You talk **with** a playwright, or you don't have a conversation at all. So, with those caveats in mind, I will try to answer the question put to us.

First of all, you shouldn't talk with a playwright until you've prepared yourself to do so. The way that you prepare yourself is by learning as much as you can about the play, immersing yourself in it trying to know it as well as the playwright. If you haven't done that, you have no business talking with the playwright about his play.

You don't talk with a playwright about his or her play until you've earned the right to do so, and I think the only way you earn the right to do that is by making a commitment to the writer, whether that's a personal commitment, or one-on-one commitment, or an institutional commitment. The latter is the best, because it means your institution has said, "We want to work with you on this play with the hope that we'll want to produce it."

As a correlate to that, I make it a personal policy never to give feedback to writers along with a letter of rejection. When I return a play to a playwright with the bad news that South Coast Rep does not want to work on his or her play, I never give feedback, although many writers specifically ask for it. I don't think that I have the right to. I've only read it once, because in most cases I only need to read a play once to know whether or not my theater will want to work on it . I can't really know a play well enough to offer feedback after one reading. Secondly, there's a big difference, a spiritual difference, between talking about a play when you know that the playwright will get something out of it with a production, and when a play will ultimately go back in the envelope. I get a little nervous thinking about this feedback service now developing, whereby dramaturgs will get paid to offer critiques to writers who request them; I'm not sure there's enough of a commitment there to give dramaturgs the right to tell playwrights how they might improve their plays.[102]

It seems obvious that a dramaturg listens to the playwright before talking to the playwright. You go into the conversation assuming the playwright knows what he or she is talking about. There is no room for arrogance among dramaturgs. God knows there's enough arrogance and ego in the theater as it is, so dramaturgs have to be the least arrogant and most self-abasing. Maybe that's concomitant with having one of the most over-arching views of the process.

While there's no room for arrogance, there is room for ignorance. Ntozake Shange complained yesterday about a dramaturg with whom she had worked, who did not know something that he or she should have known regarding a particular project. My response is this: As a dramaturg, I don't claim to know everything—even after I've done all the research that I can about a particular world. I have the right to be wrong. However, I must have the humility to recognize when I've been wrong.

When you, as a dramaturg, begin talking to a playwright tell what you love about the play. That establishes common ground and expresses your personal commitment to the project. A dramaturg should strenuously avoid working on a play that he or she doesn't love or can't come to love quickly, because if you don't have that commitment to the project, you have no business trying to exert an influence on it.

You need to establish a better understanding of that writer's vision. To do so you must be willing to admit that you don't fully understand the vision, and that that might be **your** failing rather than the **play's**. You also must be willing to accept that your understanding or interpretation of the play may be wrong. Know when it's time to stand back and listen hard to what the playwright has to say, both on the page and orally—even if you like your version of what the play has to say better than the playwright's.

In trying to help a writer make a play better you should be inquisitive, rather than inquisitorial. You should ask questions, express confusion, and identify what you think has led to your confusion. Above all, don't prescribe. Do what you can to help a writer remain in touch with his or her original vision—the originating spark—to the extent that you are able to identify it. I've worked with writers who get so muddled in the process that they almost lose touch with that vision, and it never hurts to say, "Well, I remember early on you said such and such. Does this jibe with that?" Maybe it doesn't, and maybe it shouldn't, but at least you raised the question.

When I was studying in a professional training program to do this job, it was popular to describe the dramaturg's role as that of surrogate or in-house critic. It's much more healthy to think of ourselves as surrogate audience members. A critic sets himself or herself up as someone whose opinion counts more than others', and whose opinion is broadcast to thousands of readers. The typical audience member is not in that position; the typical audience member has only his or her own reaction. Although a good dramaturg, an intelligent dramaturg, an informed dramaturg, can't possibly anticipate a typical audience member—there's no such thing—he or she **can** be an audience member for the playwright, before the real audience shows up.

The last, and maybe the most important thing I have to say, is that I don't think you talk to a playwright unless your voice is needed. We all have to accept that some writers sometimes don't need us, because they're ahead of us. I have found that the quality and lasting value of a play seems to decrease in direct proportion to the amount of work I put into it. The plays and the playwrights who have excited me the most over the years were those who required the least of me. They were those rare writers who commanded my utmost respect because I knew they could show me new ways to think and take me to new places. So I have taken the leap of faith and followed them; I didn't try to lead them.

It's a sad, cynical thing to say, but as a dramaturg of new plays, I spend most of my energy working in service of plays that we could describe as good, as promising, but if we are really honest, we are talking about the vast mediocrity we all deal with on a day-to-day basis. That can be a depressing thought; it certainly was when it occurred to me this morning.

On the other hand, I cheered up a little at the idea that just because a play is merely good, doesn't mean it isn't worth being seen and heard. Furthermore, by serving an entire body of work, dramaturgs are helping to create and maintain an environment whereby truly brilliant works can flourish and rise above the rest and amaze us all. So I think of myself as an environmentalist in that sense—the environment of the drama. And I guess that I'm content to do that for a while.

Sandy Shinner: I work on a project only when I believe that even if nothing ever changed in the script during rehearsal I would still be interested in working on that project with that particular person. That's one of my personal rules.

I'm certainly willing as a dramaturg to support and help in whatever capacity the playwright wants me to serve. I disagree with Eric a bit, because sometimes I've been able to help playwrights most when the playwright has been able to talk to me as the dramaturg and I have been able to bring that information to the director. I have been able to serve as a person in the middle when the playwright was hysterical—and rightly so in certain matters—and it might have been catastrophic to confront the director, who was hysterical over other matters at that particular moment. As somebody whose ego is not particularly involved, I could be the mediator. I could translate what the playwright had to say into terms that the director could work with at that particular moment.

I agree about asking questions, not assuming you know the answers. Some good questions are: "I think that this is what I am getting from the piece. Is that the intent? Am I missing something?"

I'll switch hats and talk about literary management issues. At Victory Gardens we have a sincere commitment to working on new material, especially with Chicago playwrights. I've begun to believe recently that in our enthusiasm, we have probably been misleading some playwrights. We sometimes forget that words of encouragement, given perhaps randomly through a form letter or even a personal note, if they are the only contact the playwright has with the theater, could be misleading. We're in the process of elongating our form letters to tell playwrights exactly what's going on. We are, in fact, only interested in a particular kind of play. It's come to my attention recently that playwrights who have not had a lot of production experience immediately assume that when they submit plays, they're submitting them for production consideration. However, we don't necessarily look at it like that, because we already have a core of writers we have chosen to support. It's difficult for someone who is not already in that core or in Chicago to get in. I think we have been remiss in not making that information clear. If we say we are going to read a play within four to six months and we hold it longer, some playwrights believe we're expressing interest. Their hopes are raised, but in fact we may just have not gotten to it. So I would encourage you to be very clear, even blunt. It's neither supportive nor encouraging to be vague and to mislead writers. Playwrights hang on any words from the theater, so you must make sure that your words are incredibly well chosen.

I did a quick lunch-hour survey and asked a few playwrights about their responses to dramaturgs. Here are some examples of what playwrights said were the worst things that dramaturgs had ever said to them. They may make some of you smile, and some cringe, but they all have a point.

"You've taken all the vitality out of it in this draft."

"We can't afford to wait until we've seen it for you to change it."

"Do you think that you could make it better?"

"If you don't change it, we can't do the play."

"I love the play, but . . . " is the big one, the big but—and so I leave you with these things to think about.

Philip Kan Gotanda: I decided to address the idea that there are cultural vantage points in terms of material. I write about the world of Asian America, and at times specifically Japanese America. For me, that is a whole, consistent world. Take for example the word "sushi" or "sashime,"—raw fish. For a lot of people it means the Eagles, Jackson Browne, the seventies, being hip in L.A. eating raw fish. It is more Americanized in the latter part of the eighties, and in the nineties it's "food of the enemy." Now for me, when someone says "sushi" or "raw fish," it means being about seven years old and growing up in Stockton. My father returns from the Delta, he's got this big striped bass. He throws it into the sink; he scales it; he cuts it up. We sit around the dinner table. My mother has made this pot of rice, which she stirred and cleaned in a particular way that is not Japanese, but Japanese-American. It's American-grown Japanese rice. We sit down and eat this big raw fish, and it's great. For me, that's what "sushi" is, and that's what it will always be. In other words, there is a consistent whole world in which I live, and it's called Japanese-America. It's been around for hundreds of years, and I write from that vantage point. It has smells, textures, its own little nuances, its language.

Years ago, I was sitting in a Louis Valdez play, *Zoot Suit.* I was watching this play and thinking, "I understand theater." But there was something going on, and it was more than just not getting the words like "ese," and Edward Olmos was sitting up there talking about being a "vato." There was something happening in there, with regards to the large Chicano and Latino audience. They were seeing a different play than I was. Something was happening between the material and the Chicano audience that I was not getting. I would get moments where I could kind of lean into it for a moment, as if there was this huge bubble that I could dip into and catch a bit of its breath. And it was a wonderful ride. But I was not always getting it. A lot of the black plays that I go see, I sit there and I enjoy them, thinking "I get this play. This is a brilliant play. I'm a person of color, I'm politically correct. . . ." But in fact, I know Asian-America, I know Japanese-America. And I run with friends who are Chicanos, who are African-Americans. But that does not mean that I get the play in toto, or that I am experiencing it the same way an African-American audience experiences it. Certainly for Asian-Americans, Chicanos, African-Americans, there is a whole lineage of history that involves politics at this time, what happens in South Africa, what happens in Bensonhurst, what happens between the Koreans and African-Americans in New York right now—the interracial tensions. That is to say that there are cultural vantage points. We talk about "multiculturalism," the new buzzword; we all say we like that idea and we accept the term intellectually, but the next step, in terms of bringing it back to the dramaturg and the playwright, is to ask what that means? There is multiculturalism as an abstract term, and multiculturalism as we live it.

I have a play. The dramaturg sits down with me. I would like, in terms of being able to talk to the dramaturg, for him or her to understand the idea of cultural vantage points, so that he or she can lean into my world and see the play through **my** eyes. That is the beginning; at least we're in the same ballpark. Because even structural choices, even matters we consider purely technical or aesthetic are tied in with this world view.

I was just up at a writers' colony in Canada. A writer came up to me and said, after listening to a play, "You know, I don't get it in terms of my own writing. I come from a different cultural vantage point; I am a Native

Canadian. Because of that I don't think in the linear fashion of the playwright; my dramaturgy is different." There is a dramaturgy/aesthetic related to culture.

Early on in my career I was working on *The Wash*. We were sitting around a large table critiquing it. They were making a lot of comments, and they were bright people. I was listening and taking all the notes, but something was amiss. I went home and thought about it. One of the criticisms was that in one scene two characters were not direct enough. "Philip, you're beating around the bush a little bit," one person said. At the time I thought, "Well, sure. I guess I should rewrite it. They *are* just dancing around each other." I thought for bit and realized what was wrong. In a Japanese-American family, people do **not** address each other directly. They, in fact, dance around everything. They, in fact, talk indirectly. That is an example of an aesthetic world that exists, and unless you are on the inside looking out, you're not critiquing it in the appropriate fashion. So I would like to ask you to enter into the dance with me, so that we lean in together and look at that world view. Look on the play that way, and by the time it reaches the stage, the audience members have a better chance to get a sense of what that world view is from the perspective of the playwright and the play.

Steve Carter: I have been a fortunate playwright. In the instances I have had a dramaturg assigned to the play, I have brought a little more celebrity to the project than the dramaturg. That usually means that he or she is too afraid to say anything. I don't always like it that way, because I like people with spunk—but not too much spunk.

I write from a West-Indian-American background. One time I was assigned a dramaturg at a West Coast theater, and this dramaturg, like myself, had never been to the Caribbean. Unlike me, he did not come from Caribbean-American background, but he proceeded to tell me what Caribbean-Americans are like—how they talk; and how they act; how they dance. It was at this point I said, "I think I know a little bit more about this than you do." He said, "Not so." That really ended it. For once I really just listened, because I figured, "There really is never any sense in arguing with a complete asshole. If these people are going to tell me how my folks sing and dance, and whatnot, I am going to listen to them and just ignore everything they say."

I have had two artistic directors from two different states call me up to talk about commissioning me to write a play. Both of them asked me the same question: "We'd really like to commission you to write a work for our theater. Can you write as well as August Wilson?" I'm sixty years old. I just hang up the phone.

I would like to be talked to as I talk to playwrights when I serve as a dramaturg. One of the first things I'd like to get rid of, when talking to playwrights as a dramaturg, is the word "dramaturg." They like to be talked to in English, so I get rid of that word right away.

Connie Congdon: To those of you who studied dramaturgy in academic institutions and heard about the dramaturg being the conscience and the mind of the theater: I think it's absolute bullshit and you should just, like, call up your teachers and tell them to stop using those terms, because they give the impression that everyone else is a drooling idiot and has no conscience.

I'm a nonhyphenated American, unless you put Wonder Bread in front of it. I wrote a play several years ago in which a young girl was a major character. She's about fifteen to sixteen years old. I was working on it with a woman who said, "You know, this play never explodes, Connie. It doesn't really have an arc. Could the guy grab a knife or something?" This is a woman for whom I have tremendous respect, and it's a comment that comes out of desperation, because in desperation we always go back to our stereotypes. Later, I'm driving and thinking, "So, all right, fine. Make the girl a boy, and then she could grab the knife." All of a sudden bells went off in my head and I thought, "I have a well-made play! That's it, I change the gender! I'll make the girl a boy." And that led to a revelatory moment about sensibility.

When we start writing they tell us, "Write what you know." Whether that's an emotional territory or something literal, like a story that happened to you. I delved into what I knew, and what I found again and again was that, when it came to the so-called "big, dramatic moment," when I tried to imagine it in a real way, I didn't do any of those things; because I'm a girl, I'm probably not going to be grabbing knives. It's possible I could, but when I think about really horrible moments in my life, it's been much more like glass-shattering far away than violence happening right there in the living room or the kitchen or in outer space.

Maybe I'm a little touchy because people have often said, "Nothing happens in your plays, Connie." I would hate to say that there is a female sensibility, because I can think of four male writers who have the same sensibility. And who wants to put herself into a category? But the sensibility idea is even beyond culture; it goes down to the microscopic—to the individual—and it affects form as well as content.

There's a lot of prejudice. I am tremendously sensitive when I hear terms like "arc" and "through-line." They make me flinch; they piss me off. So I don't know how you talk about a play. I have my own language that I make up in the moment. I say things I believe, and try to avoid buzzwords, because they underlie what I think a lot of playwrights think: that dramaturgs are these literal, academic people who have some idea of what is right and what is wrong, what a play should be; and who will put an A, B, or C on their scripts and turn them back to them. Anything you can do to dispel that prejudice is good to do.

Audience: My question's for Phil in response to your story about *The Wash* and the particular point about the characters not being confrontational. Did you not think that the question itself might have been valuable in terms of provoking the thought process that afforded you the chance to come to that realization?

Gotanda: Yes, that idea is fine, but it would have helped me at that point in time when the group was already aware of that particular model of family units, so that we could have jumped ahead to other questions, and dealt with other issues, because the play did need work. I get furious when I have to take time away from my play to go talk to someone about why I wrote this, what is supposed to be in it, what it means. Let's go watch the actor do it, and **then** we can talk about it.

I don't get a chance to spend enough time with actors and directors. I don't want to talk **about** the play. I don't want to answer questions. I want to **see** it. I want to **hear** it. **Then** I might take time out to go answer some questions. But the adventure and the commitment is to **do** it. These conferences we have to have with the dramaturg are time I have to spend away from rehearsal and these questions are for somebody else to do after I have gotten to see exactly what it is I wrote.

Audience: What do you think of the play development process in this country?

Overmyer: Let me amplify my remarks just a little. I said I prefer the dramaturg to talk to the director. It's not that I don't think there's a place for the dramaturg in theater; I very much do. But I think it's helpful for the director to sort through notes. I worked at a theater where you got notes from about twelve different people. That's not helpful. It's helpful for the director to sort out production notes from text notes. Also, it is my experience that dramaturgs are weak on the practicalities of theater. I would encourage you all to get your hands dirty a bit. The more you know what actors and directors and designers do, the better your work is going to be—with both the playwright and the director.

Audience: One person in the process of literary management can get ignored—the literary agent. I would very much like not to have to personally write a critique of every play I've returned, but I get lots of phone calls from agents saying, "I deserve to know why this play was returned to me. You had a success with one of my client's plays. I think my clients deserve better." I find that's one of my greatest personal agonies. How many scripts do you get a week?

Glore: I don't know how many I get a week, but about a thousand a year. So that averages to about twenty a week. How do you keep up with that load? Well, first of all, I have a partner, Jerry Patch. And until a couple of years ago, he and I dealt with all of the scripts; we were getting fewer then. We now have a small staff of script readers who help us.

Audience: I don't like the Hollywood system, but there's one thing they do very well. When you submit to a studio or executive of development, you hear quickly, especially if you are a writer who is known; it's an offense if it takes longer than two weekends to get back to you. In theater, there's often a four- to six-month lag. One way to keep writers in the theater is to, when a writer with a track record submits a script, read it within a week and respond immediately. That's a relationship. You don't have to talk directly. You can say through the agent, "We're passing. These are the reasons why." And if you want to keep that relationship going with that author, you'd better be able to give enough reasons. The theater is about developing long-term relationships with writers. We want a body of work from our writers, not a one-shot thing. So we need to look at how the literary offices are being run, particularly at the individual relationships between agent-managers, artistic directors, and writers.

Audience: We're focusing so much on what the dramaturg does during production or during development that we've lost sight of one of the most important things that a dramaturg does, and that is to get the play produced in the first place—whether that's lobbying the artistic director or sending the play to a theater or a number of theaters that might produce the play. That is what I spend a lot of my time doing, because Berkeley Rep does not produce much new work. So when I find a promising script, I hustle it all over the country. A lot of literary managers do exactly that.

Audience: You know, I'd love to have the time to send scripts that I get to other people, but I work for an organization. My responsibility is to find the best plays for that organization. We get five thousand script a year, and I demand of my staff that every script is read.

Audience: Does anybody think that too many people are being encouraged to write plays? I mean, they're writing plays in prisons. They write plays in the third grade. They write plays because "It's therapeutic." Maybe it is. But, as dramaturgs, do we really have to deal with all those plays?

Audience: I don't see anything wrong with it unless it leads to murder.

Moderator: On that note, shall we call it a session?

APPLAUSE, LAUGHTER

Professional Theater and Education:
Contexts for Dramaturgy
by **Allen Kennedy**

Allen Kennedy has acted in Broadway, stock, and regional theater productions, in feature films; on daytime and serial television; and has directed in New York, regional, and stock venues. As Literary Associate with Broadway producers McCann and Nugent; he created a new adaptation of Edgar Wallace's *On the Spot* for Jill Eikenberry and Michael Tucker. At Classic Stage Company (CSC), where he served as consulting dramaturg and coordinator of the education program, he dramaturged Carey Perloff's production of Strindberg's *Creditors* in a new translation by Paul Walsh, and his theater criticism appears from time to time in the *Village Voice*. Allen currently chairs the Theater Department at the Dalton School in New York City, and serves as Treasurer of the Literary Managers and Dramaturgs of the Americas (LMDA).

Although philosophy, substance, and strategy are contentious issues in our volatile political environment, there's general agreement that improved public education holds the key to the nation's survival. The truly bipartisan federal education initiative "Goals 2000, Educate America"[103] states that *"the congress finds that the arts are essential to educational reform.... [They] will transform teaching and learning in America."*[104] Across the country both the government and educational establishments increasingly look to the arts for innovative strategies to improve the overall performance of the nation's schools. Partnerships between artistic and educational institutions are envisioned as engines of social change and cultural enrichment. Professional theaters, called on by the government and their communities to help revitalize public education even as funding dwindles and the need for greater earned income becomes more critical, will increasingly require knowledgeable artists committed to educational outreach. This work demands abilities and interests that most dramaturgs already possess and others will find useful to acquire. Communication skills, scholarship, and interest in community and audience relations often place them at the center of their theater's education programs. Because they participate early in a project's development, dramaturgs are uniquely prepared to make vivid, process-based connections between audience and artist, and their proximity to the original artistic intent lends a unique authenticity to their work with students.

This brief look at a vast and rapidly changing field—the role of institutional dramaturgs and dramaturgy in efforts to manifest the enormous educational value of theater art—is neither comprehensive nor a survey. I refer only in passing to the realm of "children's" or "educational theater," which has powerfully influenced many initiatives discussed here.[105] My purpose is to offer the emerging dramaturg a sense of the rich artistic, ideological, and institutional contexts for educational work they may encounter, with a representative sampling of exemplary models to be emulated, experimented with, and improved upon. Programs are developing so quickly that these descriptions will be not be accurate for long. It's a field of moving targets where theaters of all sizes continually experiment, borrow, refine, and test, working to ensure that the power of theater art can have maximum impact where it's needed most—on tomorrow's audience.

EXPOSURE: THE CORNERSTONE

At the core of most traditional education programs is the presumption that exposing students to quality professional theater has unique, powerful pedagogical value, especially when supported by strong classroom preparation and follow-through. Since the resident professional theater movement began in the early nineteen-fifties, most educational initiatives have been built around getting students into theaters to see productions. The nation's oldest and most influential resident theaters have longstanding, highly evolved "exposure-based" educational approaches with numerous variations and well-documented efficacy. The goals of most such programs include the desire to impart theater literacy: a basic awareness of the conventions, etiquette, and potential rewards of theatergoing. Most also seek to use issues in the plays to connect both with local school curricula and with personal concerns in students' lives.

When I came to New York City's Classic Stage Company[106] as consulting dramaturg and education coordinator in 1991, an exposure program called City Stages had long been in place, and my work there as production dramaturg dovetailed nicely with the supplementary work in education. The program at that time was typical of the traditional exposure approach, illustrating a common form of involvement by a dramaturg in a professional theater education program. Each mainstage production had student matinees scheduled for three weekday mornings during its run, and through the years the theater had cultivated a pool of high school teachers who regularly brought their classes to fill the special student performances. City Stages helped the theater fulfill its community outreach mission and attracted welcome funding to support administrative and production costs.

Teachers were usually given study guides well in advance of their class's theater trip, to help prepare the students for the experience. Typically photocopied desktop publications, study guides are a mainstay of exposure programs, and creating them is often the dramaturg's responsibility. They generally give background on history, period, playwright, play, some introduction to the production strategy/scenic metaphor, and notes from the director.

Their purpose often goes beyond giving teacher and students information, for the best study guides suggest through pictures, exercises, and games, an active, participatory way into the world of the play.

On performance mornings before the show, someone, often the dramaturg, gave a brief introductory address including some discussion of etiquette in the theater. After the show there was "Q-and-A" with the actors and artistic staff. The dramaturg's best opportunity to get up on stage before an audience is frequently as moderator of pre- and postshow discussions, which vary widely in content and duration, and often feature panels of artists or relevant guests. Students are delighted to talk to the actors, who in turn welcome the energy and relevance of provocative youthful discourse. Any theater with an established exposure program has files bursting with student and teacher responses providing strong anecdotal evidence that exposing children to professional theater is an efficacious educational enterprise.

INVOLVEMENT: ENHANCING EXPOSURE

In recent years many new approaches have emerged designed to involve children in the creation of theater pieces, sometimes quite independent of exposure to mainstage programming. Proliferation of these involvement-based models is driven in part by the creativity of the individuals charged with education at theaters (including many dramaturgs) and in part by requirements that education professionals document "student outcomes" as proof of return on funders' investments. At the same time, funders seem less interested in subsidizing study guides, school-bus rentals, student tickets to mainstage shows and the administrative and production costs associated with most exposure programs. By merging exposure with involvement, many theaters are forging connections across cultural boundaries, developing new audiences, and exploring the theater's full potential as a civilizing, problem-solving, bridge-building enterprise. Among funders, theaters, and educators, interest is growing in projects for which mainstage productions, though often integral to the program's fabric, are not necessarily the culminating event.

Children now increasingly share the spotlight with the show. These newer initiatives focus first on the child, then on the art. They place artists in schools and children on stages, foregrounding hands-on experience, especially with many forms of play-making: improvisation, sound and movement, playwriting exercises, interview techniques, and oral histories. They're less about exposure to professional theater than getting kids to participate in theater, to make plays and thereby create meaning, which then may help them gain access to the subject matter and circumstances of mainstage programming. Increasingly, in order to improve student self-expression, problem-solving skills, and engagement in their overall school experience, many programs are developing involvement-based theater techniques to increase student "ownership" of the art.

THREE EXEMPLARY PROGRAMS: THE GUTHRIE, THE GOODMAN, AND THE HUNTINGTON

The Guthrie Theater of Minneapolis's educational department offers more than twenty different programs including the MAX Conference (Maximizing the Arts eXperience). At the center of the Guthrie's effort is what may be the country's largest exposure program—a student ticket policy that enables between fifty thousand and sixty thousand students within a five-hundred–mile radius to attend mainstage productions as part of the general audience at up to a 50 percent discount. School trips to the Guthrie have been a staple of cultural enrichment in Minnesota for many years, and the theater has directed substantial energies and resources to make it inexpensive and convenient for classroom teachers to bring classes to see plays and choose from a menu of related exposure-based supplements, including backstage tours, multimedia presentations, as well as pre- and postshow discussions. Glossy, substantial study guides are distributed to every student at no charge, and the theater actively cultivates relationships with teachers to keep them coming back. For the schools' convenience, most classes attend weekday matinees as part of the general population, and there are nearly always some students in every audience at the Guthrie—evidence of the efficacy of this exceptional exposure-based program.

The Guthrie's MAX Conference represents an exemplary blending of involvement and exposure with cross-generational team dramaturgy at its center. The annual conference brings Guthrie dramaturgs and education staff together with teachers, students, and their families from Minnesota high schools for three one-day meetings during the summer, culminating in fall visits to the Guthrie for mainstage shows with discussions following. According to dramaturg Michael Lupu, "the overall shape of the program emanates each year from the dramaturgy department," and themes change completely while format varies somewhat from year to year. For the seventh annual rendition in 1994, titled "The Theatrical Metaphor: Meaning on Stage," then artistic director Garland Wright explained: "We seek ways, with you, to show that metaphor can be as deep a means of understanding as literalness. *Hamlet* is a useless invention, even if it is by Shakespeare, if he is only the Prince of Denmark and not a metaphorical embodiment of every question that every youth has asked on the road to maturity."[107]

For the 1994 MAX Conference, "Metaphor and Meaning," high school teachers from across the state who served as team captains, led by Guthrie artistic staff, gathered in Minneapolis for an in-depth exploration of theatrical metaphors: how they construct and convey meaning; how to teach metaphor to secondary level students; how metaphor might relate to mainstage productions of *As You Like It* or Kleist's *The Broken Jug*. Back in their far-flung communities the captains met informally throughout the summer with their teams of about ten students and parents to develop theatrical metaphors for one of the plays. Participants read the scripts, prepared a production concept, and one team with several German-speaking participants even prepared an original translation of Kleist's play. One-day preconferences at regional centers across the state then gathered teams to share their proposals in a more intimate setting a few weeks before formal presentation during the conference in August at the Guthrie. Finally in the autumn, all teams saw the production of the play they'd been working on, compared their scenic metaphor/production scheme with the professionals at the Guthrie, then discussed the process and product together after the show.

Although ultimately based on exposure to mainstage programming, the MAX Conference demands high-level involvement in sophisticated dramaturgical preparation. And it is precisely this kind of "constructivist"[108] project that educators believe is most valuable for today's students. Taking a text and generating a scenic metaphor to support the expression of a specific point of view to a particular audience requires the type of high-level thinking skills that help students to *make meaning,* rather than merely retain and repeat information. The MAX Conference models a hybrid—exposure based, but with a strong humanities involvement component—in which dramaturgs can play important roles at all levels, from initial planning to moderating conferences and vetting team proposals.

If the Guthrie's education program is distinguished by its enormous size and scope, another of the great Midwestern resident theaters, The Goodman in Chicago, offers an almost purely exposure-based program that focuses intensively on a comparatively small group of mostly inner-city students. The "Student Subscription Series" serves widely as a model for emerging programs elsewhere. Its key distinguishing feature is that participating students become **subscribers** to the mainstage season at no charge; they come back four times in a school year and many develop a personal relationship with the theater, both as institution and as art. Chicago funders support the Student Subscription Series at increasing levels, including the video documentaries that Richard Pettengill, Goodman dramaturg and director of art-in-education, produces as a teaching enhancement for each show.

Pettengill is emphatic in his conviction that exposure to the Goodman's high-quality productions coupled with strong preshow preparation and culminating postshow discussion is a pedagogical end in itself. His article elsewhere in this volume gives ample evidence that exposure based need not mean passive. These students actively engage in extensive preparation under the tutelage of dedicated classroom teachers who must compete to bring them into the program. The Goodman's study guides are models of involvement, provocative games, and exercises interspersed with effectively presented production research. "By the time they've seen the first two productions," says Vernon E. Mims, teacher of world literature at Chicago's Lane Tech, speaking of his junior English class, "they don't want to see the video until after the performance. We read the script and do work from the study guide, but they don't want to take away from the live experience by looking at the tape."[109] This exercise of critical discrimination turning down the chance to watch television in school to preserve the integrity of an upcoming artistic experience, would appear to spring from an engaged and theater-literate audience with a proprietary sense of the art they enjoy.

The education staff at the Huntington Theater Company in Boston,[110] along with Huntington dramaturg Jayme Koszyn and an advisory board of teachers created to help improve service to the strapped Massachusetts public school system developed two programs blending involvement and exposure. The Drama as Discovery Institute (DAD) is directed toward disadvantaged and at-risk students, and the Young Critics Institute is an enrichment program for high-achieving and college-bound students. Both are humanities-based programs[111] and use exposure to many aspects of the Huntington's artistic milieu to provoke student involvement in educational exploration.

In the DAD program, groups of fifteen to twenty students from some of Boston's tougher neighborhoods gather weekly for what Koszyn calls "structured group dramaturgy." The small group size is reminiscent of private school or college classes, and the program places high expectations on children from whom little is often expected. Ten-week sessions are structured around an upcoming mainstage production. Field trips and guest artist visits are interspersed with demanding student research assignments on topics pertinent to the production. **Exposure** to open rehearsals generates **involvement** in the artistic process. A visit to the Boston Public Library is linked directly to research for the play. With teaching loads of 130–150 students, most high school English teachers assign few papers (they take so long to grade), but children in the DAD program complete frequent writing assignments including two-page "reaction papers" that are responses to issues raised during research. Periodically groups spend a session "webbing" or brainstorming to crystallize connections between historical, political, psychological, philosophical, societal, and artistic issues. The DAD program exemplifies constructivist thinking in education by using the entertainment value of theater art to entice children to make their own "webs" linking history, myth, literature, and sociology to their lives, much the way production dramaturgs bring research to support productions and help forge connections across disciplines for the collaborating artists.

The Young Critics Program seeks to exercise and polish similar high-level thinking skills and hone critical expression in students with relatively strong academic records. Under close supervision, the young critics immerse themselves in a wide-ranging critical investigations of plays not exclusively at the host theater. Groups of about ten students meet weekly for eight weeks to conduct dramaturgical research into period, playwright, and related literary streams of influence. Small groups function like graduate seminars: reading and writing assignments are at a level appropriate for students who work side by side with scholars and guest critics, attending plays at other Boston theaters, discussing and comparing each other's work and opinions.

Both DAD and Young Critics focus on the Huntington's mainstage programming, and they demand active processing of materials from many related fields as well as interaction with the productions, artists, and dramaturgy as a discipline. Although the curricula and pedagogy have an academic feel, the students are away from school and in a functioning artistic environment, which frees them from habitual in-school attitudes and allows them to regard their work with the theater not as academic assignments, but as "real world" obligations. This high level of engagement enables them to respond as mature individuals to the rich environments—rehearsals, libraries, theater shops and classrooms—they encounter.

NEW INITIATIVES: TESTING STRATEGIES

Playwriting exercises, improvisation, theater games, and role-playing in the classroom have long been staples of "educational theater" and "creative dramatics" programs because they socialize children, stimulate personal involvement with literature, and provide opportunities for self-expression. Professional theaters are increasingly exploring these techniques both in school and at the theaters to support established exposure programs and to connect with a broad range of student populations, sometimes quite independent of mainstage programming. The creativity of many new initiatives is impressive. Here are a handful of strategies representative of developments in the field.

The Teamworks pilot project at American Place Theater (APT), initiated in 1993, brings theater artists into special-needs classrooms to explore the usefulness of theater games, improv, and role-playing in teaching the high school social studies curriculum. The social and communications skills of these students are so rudimentary that the teaching artists must begin their semester-long residency with basic theater exercises just to open kids up. Name games such as "shake-shake-shake-freeze" and "space sculpture"[112] help to provide a basic vocabulary. Affirmation games[113] then help the diffident and shy take the risks necessary for later improvisation and role-playing. In close consultation with the classroom teacher, the Teamworks artists devise theater exercises to help teach specific lessons. For example, they animate the federalist structure of our government by assigning students to "play" the executive, legislative, and judicial branches as each in turn consider a law abolishing school lunches. Issues are chosen in which the children are most likely to have some stake—the invasion of Haiti, emancipation of the slaves, and immigration policy are matters of which even children reading at third and fourth grade levels have some knowledge and often a point of view. Each exercise culminates in a simple writing assignment, an important and often difficult step for many.

Teamwork's charge is to get the children, through theater, to apprehend their subject holistically, rather than by linear units of information.

The One-on-One and Playmaking programs are initiatives of The 52nd Street Project in New York City that feature close, intensely personal relationships between artists and children, developed under the leadership of Willie Reale. In One-on-One, an adult professional theater artist and a child from a poor neighborhood who has been referred by a community center are paired one-on-one and packed off for a week to a country retreat where they collaborate on the creation of a play that the two will perform together. The adult professional tailors the work to each child's particular qualities, and after a week of rehearsal back in the city, artist and child perform their piece in a program of ten other one-on-one collaborations at an Off-Broadway theater on loan for the event. The Playmaking program brings together a maximum of ten children for an eight-week playwriting class based on a curriculum developed by David Judah Sklar. In this active, participatory workshop the children learn the fundamental grammar of dramatic writing: conflict, character, and action. Each student writer is then assigned two professional actors and a professional director, and on a weekend retreat at a borrowed country house, the young people write a ten-minute play, which the director then stages for a culminating Off-Broadway presentation. The 52nd Street Project's reputation for high-quality work has attracted prominent artists to Reale's roster of two hundred teaching artists, including playwrights Charles Fuller, Wendy Wasserstein, Jose Rivera, and Craig Lucas. With a student to teacher ratio ranging from one to one to an extraordinary one to three, the resulting work is the project's most effective promotion. "The big exposure programs efficaciously enrich the lives of many," says Reale. "But we're about turning around the lives of individuals one at a time. . . . We've never had a potential funder who actually came to see our work, fail to offer support."[114]

The World Theater Project is an in-school initiative focusing heavily on pre- and postshow artist–student involvement developed by New York City's Theater for a New Audience (TFANA). TFANA, an important institutional contributor to the artistic life of the city's public schools, continually experiments with new approaches to help students absorb the richness of the company's contemporary approach to classic programming, especially Shakespeare, and express their reactions, often through original dramatic writing. A cadre of guest artists teamed with classroom teachers uses improvisation and games with fourth through twelfth grade classes to give them an understanding of the world of the play and the circumstances its characters confront before they see the show. After the trip to TFANA the artists enable their classes to experience the process from the inside by coaching students in performing scenes from the play they saw at the theater. Some high schools are able to accommodate a more intensive playwriting approach offered by TFANA.

A pilot program that started in the early '90's and featured prominent artists such as Elizabeth Swados, Willie Holtzman, and Eduardo Machado,[115] has evolved into New Voices, a project that puts artists in schools one day a week for eight to sixteen weeks to lead high school classes in dramaturgical analysis of the structure, metaphor, style, and issues of a mainstage play. The teaching artists help each child to write a play drawing on the raw material supplied by the classic text and TFANA's production. As the student plays begin to take shape, a team of five company actors visits each class to rehearse, polish, and revise the student work through collaborative dramaturgy led by the guest artist in partnership with the teacher. The revised work is then performed by the same actors at an assembly for each school. Finally, in a strongly affirming marathon presentation, the army of student playwrights (six hundred in 1994) see their work in staged readings at an Off-Broadway theater.

TFANA education director Margaret Salvante offers a fine example of an innovation to the program derived from exploratory work of the acting company and contributing directly to the goals in the classroom:

> We all agreed that the students had enormous difficulty listening at times, making it hard for them to follow the complexities of Shakespearean action and language, especially during soliloquies. We were fortunate to have the Royal Shakespeare Company's Cicely Berry for a residency to work with our acting company, and the teaching artists who were observing her workshop seized on one of her exercises and adapted it to their own classroom use to help teach listening.[116]

In the exercise, as a professional actor reads a monologue aloud a student must stay in continuous motion. But each time the text takes a different direction, the student must also change direction. The structure of the piece is thereby illustrated with action cued by the student's attention—instantaneous dramaturgy based on listening. Markedly increased attentiveness among children trained in this technique has convinced TFANA's teaching artists that they've made a breakthrough.

The exposure program at Manhattan Theater Club (MTC) features intensive preshow preparation that similarly culminates with students writing plays. Teachers are also partnered with teaching artists in the MTC approach, but before classes come to the theater the students participate in an eight-session unit of study that includes four artist-led workshops and at least four lessons taught by the classroom teacher. This in-school, involvement-based preparation resembles an active dramaturgy in practice; writing, researching, examining a play's structure and contexts, and exploring the relationship of text to audience—in this case themselves. The main innovation is the extensive participation of teaching artists, especially actors, as facilitators and performers of students' dramatic writing **before** classes see the plays. "Teachers preparing students to see *The Piano Lesson* might ask the kids to write about a dispute over a family heirloom," says MTC Education Director David Shookhoff. "Then in a week or two a professional actor comes in and performs the students' scenes, really bringing them to life. You can feel the self-esteem travel through the room like a shock wave—'Hey, I'm a writer.'"[117]

Becca Manery, former education director at Chicago's Court Theater suggests, "The most significant thing I could do to improve our program would be to put an actor in every classroom."[118] Shookhoff clearly agrees, pointing out that "Every school trip to the theater, even to MTC, isn't necessarily going to be a epiphany for every student, but bringing a professional actor into a schoolroom is pretty likely to make the day memorable."[119] By permanently assigning teaching artists to particular schools, Shookhoff hopes to integrate the program into the community and bring continuity and duration to the student–artist relationship.

Living History, an initiative of The Intiman Theatre in Seattle, also uses teams of actors in the schools, but here week-long team residencies begin with an assembly in each school that presents professional performances of four to five scenes from world drama taken from the Intiman's repertory. These scenes, carefully chosen to relate to the school's curriculum in history, social studies, and English, become the focus of the next four days' work, where actors in costume interact with students in their classrooms. Dramaturg Robert Menna plays an important role in developing, training and rehearsing the actor teams for the real work of this exemplary initiative established by education director and former dramaturg Daniel Renner. Three main exercises rely on costumed professional guest teams improvising in character to get students involved in making artistic and ethical choices that express their own ideas and opinions. "Hot Seat Improvisation" has a talk show or town meeting format with two actors playing characters in conflict from the historical time, place, and circumstances of a scene performed in the earlier assembly. The third actor serves as an activist moderator, provoking the students to question the "panelists" about their period, culture, and personal views of the conflict depicted in the scene. "Debate," in contrast, takes themes from the plays' period settings and places them in difficult contemporary contexts. Each student must choose and defend a position on an ethical dilemma: a scene from *Antigone* becomes a heated debate about justice, revenge, and the law in an urban neighborhood. *Waiting for Godot* leads students to examine teenage suicide, its ramifications, and an individual's free will. "Synthesis/Analysis" resembles MTC and TFANA's playwriting initiatives: by analyzing the structure, style, and components of the professionally performed scenes, students must employ critical thinking and reasoning skills that enable them to separate and recombine a play's dramatic elements, actually synthesizing new work (and making artists of themselves in the process).

Like Teamworks, Living History seeks to provide "a fresh way of exploring the humanities in high school classrooms through the energy and expertise of multiracial, professional actor/teachers. Theatrical techniques are used to link historical events to current political and social issues."[120] Throughout, students are confronted with ethical and critical choices without the teaching

artists imposing their view of right and wrong; the guest players instead facilitate the children's own analysis of the consequences of a proposed position
or course of action. Though the program builds on themes and historical contexts derived from shows that have been produced on Intiman's mainstage,
students needn't travel to the theater for exposure—the theater brings work
to them. Living History seeks to empower young people to analyze situations,
take a stand on issues, and act in accordance with their own beliefs.

OUTREACH AND ART: INTEGRATING THE MISSION

Theater companies often express a commitment to community outreach and
education as part of their fundamental mission, continually working to tailor
their efforts to the particular needs of the communities they serve. Certain
theaters and individuals have had particular success integrating their artistic
and educational missions. As recently as 1992, The People's Light and Theater
Company (PLTC) of Malvern, Pennsylvania, called its education work "outreach" as theaters commonly do, but under the leadership of Artistic Director
Abigail Adams an uncommon commitment to education has prompted the
company to drop the term. "If the work is truly central to the mission it's not
'outreach,' it's *the work*,"[121] explains Adams. "There isn't a separate wing
called 'education' here. It's at the core of what we do." Since its founding in
1974, when their premiere production toured Pennsylvania prisons, People's
Light has demonstrated an unusual commitment to what most theaters call
outreach. No fewer than twelve thousand children each year see the PLTC Elementary School Tour. Started in 1976, it's the oldest and largest primary school
arts outreach program in the state. A remarkable forty-five thousand children
annually are served by PLTC programs—truly extraordinary figures for a theater with seating for fewer than four hundred. PLTC's many education programs are now collectively called Project Discovery, and they're inseparable
from the artistic life of the company.

The elevation of education to equal status with mainstage programming
isn't the only uncommon aspect of People's Light. It's one of a handful of theaters that maintains a resident company; roughly thirty artists, including Equity actors, playwrights, designers, literary staff, and directors are under
seasonal contract. Eight to ten of this group, called "Stone Soup," have broad
backgrounds—in law, education, dance, psychology, and business—in addition
to strong theater training. This education cadre participates in mainstage
shows and is engaged in company life at the same level of responsibility and
artistry as the rest of the company, but at least half of their time Stone Soup's
members are working with young people in PLTC's many programs. The
name, "Stone Soup," which suggests making something nourishing out of next
to nothing, is emblematic of the group's resourcefulness and commitment to
nurturing creativity. Their collective will and wisdom helps provide direction

and staffing for the many faces of Project Discovery. Members of Stone Soup are compensated on the same scale as other company artists, another important indication of the theater's priorities.

The shifting developments in the programs that come under Project Discovery's capacious umbrella make straightforward categorization difficult, but nearly every model discussed elsewhere in this piece is represented at PLTC in some form, including two large exposure programs, an intensive theatrical summer day camp called Summerstage, and an Elementary School Tour. The Elementary School Tour reaches forty schools with sixty performances and its own preparatory guide for teachers. Adams and members of Stone Soup develop each year's show by going into schools and interacting with students—improvising on a central theme—which Adams then crafts into a scripted play. The actors then tour the finished work to the schools, incorporating about twenty kids from each host school into the performance, costumes and all. Having different children take roles alongside the professionals at each school helps give "ownership" of the work to that community. Two other initiatives in particular, the New Voices Ensemble and the High School Residency Program, stand out as innovative examples of interdisciplinary involvement.

In 1989 the theater made an exceptionally long-term educational commitment. Determined to expand the demographic base of the company beyond its upper-middle-class suburban milieu, PLTC went forward with a plan to work with a small group of sixth-graders from the city of Chester, Pennsylvania, for six years, until they graduated from high school. Chester is one of the three most depressed cities in the United States. Its population is about 95 percent African-American, the entire school system is "at risk," and it has little in common with neighboring Chester County, which sports an abundance of lovely horse farms and gracious Main Line residences, as well as The People's Light and Theater Company. The New Voices Ensemble, as these children came to be called, is at the center of Adams's program. After six years' immersion in the culture of People's Light, these young people have emerged as accomplished theater artists. They've trained and taught, created and toured original work, performed in mainstage productions, and now most are off to college—not a likely option for many when they started the program. And now a second group from Chester, built around siblings and neighbors of the first group, are starting a new six-year cycle.

The New Voices children are well versed in a wide range of theater training techniques—improvisation, scene study, Alexander technique, voice, and movement work. Those I met were serving as teaching assistants in the Summerstage day camp program. Adams's work with New Voices is based on teaching them how to function as theater artists, so they're accustomed to working side-by-side with adult professional actors as peers. "There's no attempt," she says, "to address social circumstances through subject matter. We get together and do plays." These children talk easily of the company's process-oriented ideological roots in Jasper Deeter's legendary Hedgerow Theater,[122] where the resident company is actively involved in program selection.[123] And they can function as dramaturgs when called upon. Each child was asked to examine the plot and structure of *Romeo and Juliet* and develop a two-minute version, which they subsequently performed for picnicking summer audiences as a preshow diversion. I had the pleasure of witnessing several of these highly individual, entertaining and sophisticated condensations, which used contemporary language, character, and situation to provide a way in to the rich poetry and complex architecture of the classic tragedy. At PLTC, everyone does dramaturgy.

Like most of the Project Discovery programs, PLTC's High School Residency is continually in development. At an early stage, Stone Soup was spending one week in residence at each school, leading improvisations on a mainstage text as an enhancement to the company's exposure program. Spurred by the success of their long-term commitment to New Voices in Chester, Stone Soup undertook an extended year-long residency at The Center for Arts and Technology in Phoenixville, Pennsylvania.[124] With the guidance of director David Bradley a total of 150 students (of whom 30 were performers) devised, built, rehearsed, and performed *Roadshow,* an original play with music based on the automobile as a metaphor for freedom. Using the auto-body shop to create props, and the cosmetology students to design makeup were among the more obvious ways the project sought to involve the school's vocational training to support the work. The school's administration is solidly behind the program, and People's Light has received substantial support from the National Endowment for the Arts (NEA) to continue and expand the program, with the aim of creating a theater arts class as one of the school's occupational programs.[125] Bradley explains his belief in the program:

> I'm not looking for documentation that this program raises grades or keeps truants in school. There's real danger in making grandiose claims for our work, promoting it as some kind of panacea. But I do believe deeply in the theater as a medium for learning, and we *can* prove that we teach essential life skills—problem solving, consistency, collaboration, and group responsibility to quality—that these kids will find essential in the workplace, and these are not small accomplishments.[126]

At the end of a long day as counsellors in the Summerstage day camp and before curtain for a free evening performance of *Romeo and Juliet,* a group of six New Voices children talk readily about how they've changed and watched each other change since the sullen, rebellious, sometimes destructive early days when they behaved as might be expected of youngsters who knew life only in a setting as squalid as any in the nation. They speculate about where they'd be without People's Light and Abbey Adams. "Probably dead," says one.

These are normal teenagers—shy, outrageous, rambunctious—but they know important things many adults never learn. They have some control over their lives and can influence the lives of others. They can moderate their reactions when frustration strikes, and sacrifice or modify their own agendas for the good of the group. They know these things, and what's more they know they know them, because they've had to learn them in order to make theater art.

GROWTH OF A FIELD

The programs cited above are representative of developments throughout the professional theater community, and the field continues to experiment and grow. Dramaturgs and education program leaders who share a strongly collaborative view of theater have made particular contributions through their eagerness to share new developments and participate in artistic cross-pollination, where an idea takes root in one theater, is refined at another, then copied by a third. Stephen Welch is among the first individuals to hold the title of director of education at any professional theater in the United States. He began in 1983 at Washington D. C.'s The Shakespeare Company (then The Folger) in box office, subscriptions, and group sales. At that time the theater had no contacts with the District's arts-impoverished public schools, but from his position in group sales he began to build relationships with teachers and schools. When Michael Kahn became artistic director, Welch was given full support, and by 1995 their education budget exceeded one half million dollars. As a pioneering theater administrator and educator, Welch reached out to colleagues across the country working in relative isolation and formalized a network among many of those most active in the field.[127] Theater Communications Group (TCG), the national service organization for professional non-profit resident theaters, has sponsored a series of teleconferences among that same group to facilitate ongoing relationships and stimulate shared projects and replication of promising ideas.[128]

Classic Stage Company (CSC)'s educational program, now called Classic Adventures, has developed markedly since my brief tenure, under the direct influence of some of these models. Because she saw the mainstage productions of the company as the greatest asset of CSC, managing director Patricia Taylor knew that exposure to that work must continue at the center of the theater's educational effort. Taylor saw that children were not to be found in general audiences, they came only to student matinees, rarely choosing the theater as an entertainment or cultural option. By offering and aggressively marketing[129] a student ticket policy admitting any high school student on a "pay-what-you-can" basis and any college student for ten dollars, overall student attendance at CSC rose from 8 percent to 20 percent in one year, a striking figure by any measure, with more than half attending regular evening performances.

A site visit to Chicago's Goodman Theater on a TCG observership convinced Taylor of the cumulative benefits to students and teachers who repeatedly attend and develop a relationship with the theater, and she adapted the student subscription concept to CSC's use. Twelve classroom teachers who'd participated regularly in the past formed a "teacher core group," which began taking part in teacher seminars and meeting before preview performances over dinner as the theater's guests. Their students became season subscribers to CSC with all attendant benefits and privileges for a "recommended" price of five dollars per show or fifteen dollars for the three-show season, though the pay-what-you-can policy made it possible for many to come for less. Adults attending with adolescents were admitted for a recommended price of ten dollars.

Placing artists in classrooms may be the ideal involvement-based enhancement to an exposure program, but their salaries and administrative overhead put such efforts beyond the reach of many smaller companies. To increase student involvement, CSC's education director, Holly Wolf, borrowed an idea from New York City's Second Stage, where earlier she'd held the same position, and suggested that a "Teen Advisory Group" of twenty-five high school students meet each Friday at the theater to attend rehearsals, discuss themes relevant to upcoming productions, and prepare to introduce the play to their peers at "Teach-Ins" held at the theater for subscribing schools. Having witnessed the powerful positive effect of incorporating young people into the daily life of People's Light and Theater Company, Taylor readily agreed and set about making CSC a place where high-school-age students and their particular energies are welcomed, valued, and encouraged. In a risky initiative that may be unique to CSC, the 1994–95 Teen Advisory Group developed exercises and partially usurped the dramaturg's role by creating the study guide that was distributed to all Classic Adventures attendees as a companion piece to the theater's more formal dramaturgical insert. In the following season, a similar study guide, also generated by the Teen Advisory Group, would merge with the dramaturg's materials to create a new program insert for all general audiences as well.

Theaters and their dramaturgs have much to offer the communities they serve, but the converse is less well understood: working with young people is astonishingly seductive. It shares with parenting certain rewards and frustrations that can transform an obligatory assignment to "theater in education" from a prosaic trudge up the career path into a calling.

Education and Community Programs at the Goodman Theatre, 1996

by **Richard Pettengill**

This outline of education and community programs at one major regional theater is intended to provide only an example of such programs, and readers should be aware that theaters all over North America and Europe have similar programs in place. Dramaturgs often participate in such programs, and dramaturgical training and internships can be a good background for work in this field.

1. The **Student Subscription Series** serves students and teachers in Chicago public high schools with an in-depth, season-long educational supplement to the existing high school curriculum. Each year approximately fourteen hundred students and fifty teachers from thirty-five schools receive:

a) a *free* **four-play subscription** to Mainstage productions

b) **copies of play scripts** for each student and teacher

c) specially designed **student guides and teacher guides**

d) **Teacher seminars,** where artists from each production discuss the play and the production with teachers and strategize on ways to prepare students for the performance

e) **post-performance discussions** with cast members

f) **"Backstage at the Goodman" educational video documentaries** featuring interviews with directors, designers, and cast members, combined with performance footage. These are designed to illuminate particular aspects of each production, and serve as archival documents. Titles include: *Landscape of the Body, A Flea in Her Ear, Romeo and Juliet, The Piano Lesson, The Rover, The Misanthrope, The Meeting, The Winter's Tale, Joe Turner's Come and Gone, A Midsummer Night's Dream, The Visit, Miss Evers' Boys, Twelfth Night, The Good Person of Setzuan, The Skin of Our Teeth, Two Trains Running, Black Snow, Richard II, The Night of the Iguana, I Am A Man, The Merchant of Venice, Seven Guitars, Three Sisters, Journey to the West, All's Well That Ends Well, Black Star Line, Arcadia, A Touch of the Poet,* and *Randy Newman's Faust.*

The Goodman Arts in Education office also maintains copies of study guides for the above titles, as well as guides for selected Mainstage productions prior to 1988, and selected Studio productions.

g) **classroom visits by cast members**

h) a **parents program,** that provides free Goodman tickets to parents of participating students

2. Studio Student Matinee Series: This program targets schools and classes in terms of their interest in specific issues and topics presented in each Studio play. The program also offers

   a) teacher seminars in an intimate setting

   b) study guides, scripts, and **post-show discussions**

3. "Onstage at Goodman" Lectures: These lectures, held at the Chicago Public Library Cultural Center, provide audiences with background historical information on each Mainstage production.

4. Post-Performance Discussions: These Wednesday and Thursday evening sessions provide an informal forum for audience members to discuss issues raised by each play. Discussions are led by Goodman artistic staff, and actors participate in post–opening night discussions.

5. Special Events: These events, held at various community sites, illuminate aspects of each Mainstage production, and stimulate community interest in the Goodman Theatre. A recent example: August Wilson spoke about his play *Seven Guitars* at the DuSable Museum of African American History, followed by a reception with live blues by Son Seals and his band.

6. Chicago Arts Collaborative for Teachers (CACT): A three-week summer arts workshop for teachers with extensive school-year follow-up, CACT began in 1993 at the Goodman Theatre. A collaboration between the Goodman, the Art Institute of Chicago, the Chicago Symphony Orchestra, the Dance Center of Columbia College, and Urban Gateways: the Center for Arts in Education, the program's fiscal agent is Whirlwind Performance Co. The program proceeds in two phases:

   a) The first phase is **a three-week workshop** for Chicago area K–12 teachers in all four art forms (music, theater, dance, visual arts), designed to train teachers to utilize the arts in all facets of their teaching.

   b) The second phase is **a follow-up program** during the school year that includes artist visits to schools, funded field trips, teacher reunions, and a teacher stipend for arts related needs.

7. Neighborhood Arts Partnerships: Corporate retailer Marshall Field's/Dayton Hudson initiated this program in 1993, preliminarily offering planning grants for partnerships made up of arts organizations, neighborhood organizations, and Chicago schools to create curricular arts programming in city schools. After the planning year, partnerships submitted applications for major funding with which to implement those programs. The Goodman is involved in two such partnerships:

   a) South Side Arts Partnership. The "anchor" on this project is the Hyde Park Art Center, and participants include the Goodman, The Smart Museum of Art, the Chicago Children's Choir, dancer Maggie Kast, the Ray School, and the Murray Language Academy. The Goodman's involvement includes working with Ray and Murray teachers on The *Christmas*

Carol Project, in which students study Dickens's story and other ghost stories, along with the Victorian period, the Industrial Revolution, child labor, and so on. Some classes each year study the Goodman stage adaptation, partake in field trips to the Goodman to see the production, take backstage tours, and meet with artists from the production in their classrooms. The program is geared sequentially to different grade levels.

b) West Town Arts Partnership. The coanchors are the Sherwood Conservatory of Music and the Northwestern University Settlement. Participants include the Goodman, the Chicago Symphony Orchestra, the James Otis School, the Elizabeth Peabody School, Wells Community Academy (also participants in the Student Subscription Series), the Community TV Network, the Mordine Dance Company, the Marwen Foundation, and Partners in Mime, Inc. The Goodman's involvement has included sending bilingual actors to Wells Academy to do scenes from *Romeo and Juliet,* and providing an acting coach and set design for a Wells student production of *West Side Story.* The Goodman brought this production to the Goodman Studio Theatre for two performances in June 1995.

8. The Committee on Communities: The Committee on Communities is a board composed of individuals from all three of the Goodman's boards (the Board of Trustees, the Women's Board, and the Discovery Board), all of whom share a commitment to increasing the Goodman's presence in Chicago's various communities. The committee has helped to raise funds for the following programs:

a) Goodman/Chicago Housing Authority (CHA) Youth Drama Workshop. The Goodman/CHA Youth Drama Workshop, a seven-week program, began in the summer of 1995 with teens from the CHA's Dearborn Homes. The workshop was taught by a program director and two program instructors with extensive, proven experience teaching such workshops. The first weeks were devoted to script work on *Two Tales of Anansi,* an original adaptation of two African folktales. Then the group as a whole began to design, rehearse, and perform their play for an invited audience on the final day of the workshop. The program also included field trips to the Goodman and other theaters in Chicago, both during the summer and throughout the school year. Students saw plays professionally performed, had backstage tours, and met with theater artists representing all areas of theatrical art. All students who successfully completed the workshop received a stipend.

b) Goodman Internship Program. The internship program is designed to offer a challenging, professional experience for qualified college seniors, graduate students, and young professionals committed to careers in the professional theater. Interns work as staff members in a department, exploring every facet of work in a producing theater. Internships are available in artistic adminstration (casting, arts in education, dramaturgy, and literary management), arts business management, development, stage management, and production. When funding allows, stipends are currently offered for internships in arts in education and stage management.

9. Community Engagement Program: In 1995–96, the Goodman Theatre received funding from the Joyce Foundation to explore new ways to engage people from communities throughout Chicago who would not ordinarily attend the Goodman Theatre. The proposal called for two new advisory councils, the Student Alumni Advisory Council (consisting of "alumni" of the Student Subscription Series), and the Community Advisory Council (consisting of a broad cross-section of community leaders from around the city) to advise the Arts in Education department in new ways to bring in new audiences, and to suggest strategies for implementation. A pilot program was launched in the summer of 1996, with the intention of expanding and refining those efforts in the seasons to come.

Conceiving the Forms
Play Analysis for Production Dramaturgy
by **Lee Devin**

LEE DEVIN holds a PhD from Indiana University. He has taught at the University of Virginia, Vassar, and, since 1970, at Swarthmore College, where he is Director of The Theater. He's also Dramaturg at the People's Light and Theatre Company. He has worked extensively in the professional theater, both academic and commercial. He has won writing prizes for both stage and radio. His acting versions of *Oedipus, Summerfolk,* and *A Doll House* have been produced at theaters and schools; operas on his librettos played at the Minnesota Opera and the Guelph Spring Festival. Equity roles he's played include Malvolio in *Twelfth Night,* Mitch in *A Streetcar Named Desire,* Piet in *Lesson from Aloes,* and Nat in *Ah! Wilderness.* As a visiting artist or consultant he's been in residence at Columbia University, the Folger Library, Ball State University, the music theater program of the Banff School of the Arts, University of California San Diego, Bucknell University, and the Minnesota Opera.

What are the parts to this thing? How do they go together? These questions are only part of my obligation to the late Bernard Beckerman. I have similar debts to Hubert Heffner, Herbert Muller, Kenneth Telford, Theodore Shank, and Susanne Langer. These questions address materials and arrangements of materials. They focus our attention on form, leaving aside discourse, rhetoric, and subject matter. They are at the heart of that part of play-making we call dramaturgy. The form of a play, whether it's a script to be read and discussed, a rehearsal to be watched and analyzed, or a performance to be developed over time, is a conceit we make when we imagine the play's parts and create the many patterns their arrangement will support. I suggest "conceit" because "conception" and "concept" have such loaded meanings in theater practice. A director reads a play and decides what it will be like when produced. The director is said to have a "concept" according to which he or she will guide (dictate) design, casting, and rehearsals. My notion of a "conceit" puts no such prior limitations on production.

Skillful artists are so good at making plays that resist analysis that we dramaturgs probably never will find complete agreement on all our labels and categories. And yet, in order to make good theater, we need a vocabulary that will allow precise and helpful discussion among the members of a production team. In the early stages of production, these conceits come from reading the script. Later, actors in rehearsal are their main material. Let "conceiving" label the processes of imagining a conceit that is a play's form in its current phase of development. These processes operate on the play script, the rehearsals and the performances (if the run is long enough to support development).

The form of the play is a constantly changing conceit we construct in imagination. This construction begins with repetition.

> **PROMETHEUS:** I gave to them the mother of the arts, hard-working
> memory.
>
> *Prometheus Bound,* Aeschylus[130]

When a movement, object, place, activity, sound, word, image, idea, or action repeats in a play, the past and present, or other disparate elements, come together. Meter and rhyme are simple examples of how form is made of repetition: a poet makes an iambic pentameter couplet by repeating sounds in a prescribed way. In Ibsen's *A Doll House,* the sound of the front door encloses the play between Nora's first entrance and her final exit. Two events may be connected by mention of a third in each of them, as when Shakespeare uses repeated references to Hamlet Senior's death to unify widely diverging moments of *Hamlet.* Repeated materials may be closely related to the play's action (lamps, light, and Blanche's obsession with her age in *A Streetcar Named Desire*) or almost arbitrary (Stanley throws meat at Stella, pork chops on the floor, and celebrates his child's birth with a po'boy sandwich, also in *Streetcar*).

Writers, directors, designers, and actors repeat various materials as they make the play. We can see these repetitions best if we conceive the developing play as an organization of parts; I suggest three categories of useful parts.

A play has finite parts, with identifiable boundaries. There are lots of them, some—words, lines, speeches, scenes, and acts—are made by the writer. Others are made during work on the production. Nowadays it's unfashionable to have three intermissions; a dramaturg invents a Part I that includes all of act one and some of act two, a Part II that includes the rest of act two and all of acts three and four. Actors may divide a scene into beats: each beat continues a particular action or motive. The lighting designer may divide the same scene into slightly different beats in order to guide the movement of the design.

The language of the well-made play gives us a list of parts that are helpful in conceiving a script's form by observing its repetitions.

Exposition: the background we need to understand the coming action.
Point of Attack: the moment that starts the play's action.
Rising Action: a sequence of increasingly exciting scenes; the protagonist's
      fortunes rise and fall.
Complication: a scene or beat in which the action takes a turn, usually toward
      defeat for the hero, victory for the villain.
Crisis: the turning point or most significant moment in a scene.
Climax: the turning point or most significant moment in the play's action.
Denouement: the action ends and a new status quo is revealed.

These are old-fashioned terms, but handy as a way to step back from a play's narrative flow, its persuasive emotional demands, and look at the materials the writer uses. Although some contemporary plays do not use narrative as an underlying structure, most plays do, and these parts can help a dramaturg discover significant patterns of repetition in a script or in the flow of rehearsal. What's on stage for the Exposition? Where else in the play do similar materials appear? What's on stage for the Denouement? What materials from the Exposition are important in the Denouement? What materials are similar? How did the writer move from one to another? In the first moments of *Oedipus Rex,* for instance, Oedipus addresses the suppliant crowd as "My children," and asks how he can help them. At plays' end, his own blood children appear, and he addresses them as "My children" while he apologizes and pleads with them to forgive him. For the producers of an *Oedipus Rex,* this observation may be helpful. It won't establish a discursive meaning for the play: it won't tell us what Sophocles thought about children, because in this play "children" isn't a theme or part of a "meaning." "Children" is material Sophocles arranges to plot a story into a play.

The smallest and most important of these finite parts doesn't appear in the script: the gesture. A gesture is a single movement or noise that has limits. You can't find it in the script because an actor must perform it. You can infer some gestures from the script, but only a few of the many that will make the finished play. Moreover, each gesture, because a human being performs it and current conditions influence it, will be unique; not always noticeably different from last time, but different nevertheless. A gesture might be a combination of many observable movements that make up lighting a pipe (Nat in *Ah! Wilderness*), or it might be a single cry (Cassandra in *Agamemnon*).

Gestures in a play differ from activity in ordinary life. Recognizing this fact is essential to an understanding of rehearsal and performance. A person moves or performs a task in life so as to accomplish something; a character makes a gesture in a play so as to be perceived, aiming for affect, not effect. Actors make a stage fight out of a collection of gestures designed to be experienced by spectators as if it were a fight; they don't use actions designed to injure or intimidate one of the fighters. Gestures are real, but not ordinary. The tears that stream down the actor's face are real, and they are the symptom of a state of mind, just as in ordinary life. But they were created on a cue, for the purpose of playing. Ordinary tears are made for other purposes entirely.

For particular plays the dramaturg may simply declare parts or classes of parts. Consider a production of *Misalliance.* Shaw called this play a "conversation," by which he meant audiences to understand that talking was the major action of any play.[131]

Shaw's characters (or Shakespeare's, or Chekhov's, or anyone's, for that matter) use spoken language to learn the news, suffer its effects, deliberate on alternative courses of action, and decide. In *Misalliance,* all characters make a journey: they get some kind of upsetting news, they suffer the effects of that news, and each comes to some kind of decision as a result. Tarleton, for instance, accustomed to philandering, gets a shocking (if sympathetic) refusal from Lena. For once his true emotional self engages in relationship with a woman; instead of making love to her, he cries. This leads him to a rudimentary sympathy with his daughter, and he makes the choice to help her marry the man she wants. Shaw's arrangement of the play's many different insights, sufferings, and choices is complicated and compelling. Before each moment can be seen as working in éach of several different journeys, the dramaturg must artificially explode the script by isolating moments in each journey as if they were separate parts. By extracting the separate stages (getting the news; suffering its effects; deliberating; deciding what to do) in each character's journey, the dramaturg can think about them, see how they resemble each other, observe what materials they're made of, and so on; one at a time the separate stories staged in the play can take shape; and finally the many stories can be reconstituted in a conceit that is both articulate (so the artists can fine-tune their creation) and seamless (so the audience can enjoy the production's complex illusion of life).

The second useful category of parts contains those that have identifiable boundaries but have no meaningful reality without reference to the others in their sequence. I call these three sequences the relational parts.

The first of these is Beginning, Middle, and End. Incidents in the play's Beginning have no antecedents in the plot. The Beginning uses materials drawn from audience experience, to which it gives form; the material for the Middle dictates the Beginning's form. Incidents in the Middle of a play have the Beginning as antecedents and the End as consequences. The Middle is made out of the beginning, which it forms, and is the material of the End, which is its form. A play's final incident, or End, has the rest of the play for antecedents and has no consequences. The End is made of materials drawn from the Middle; nothing further is made out of it.

I've borrowed these terms and the tautological quality of these definitions from Aristotle as a means of emphasizing the self-referential quality of plays that accounts for their unity and contributes to the difficulty of analyzing them.[132] Each part of a play relates to every other part. In the case of the sequences, the parts can only be known by their relationship with the others. That is, if there's no Middle, there can be no Beginning or End; the End can't exist without its Beginning and Middle. Identifying the Beginning incidents of a play doesn't tell you anything about its discursive meaning, its place in history, or the biography of its author. Understanding its Beginning, Middle, and End does tell you about the play's structure and materials.

If a play's first incidents have no antecedents in the plot, how do spectators make sense of them? Henri Poincaré suggests that we perceive space by using our sense of our own bodies as a kinesthetic template, a category of perception. That personal measure is the basic unit with which we construct the spatial world around us, measure it, and fix our position within it.[133] Spectators do something similar when a play starts. Embarking on the experience of a play, they locate themselves in its action by using their own history, constructing a virtual action out of their own physical and mental experience. The first actions of a play, then, will be notably similar to the ordinary life of the spectators, or to their experience of seeing plays. Such plays as *Henry V* or *Our Town* direct an audience's attention to details of performance, as well as to the antecedents of the story.

To illustrate, let's imagine a short passage from Ibsen's *A Doll House,* Nora's entrance in act one. We'll use a few questions to point at some of the materials of this play's Beginning and how they repeat in the Middle and End:

The curtain opens. What do we show? Should the housekeeper Helene pass through on a domestic errand? Something to do with a lamp, say? If she did, she would move a couple of the several doors. Because doors and lamps are major materials of the play, it might be well to introduce them right away. What sounds do we make? The first noticeable sound (if we don't bring Helene on) will be the opening and closing of the front door downstairs. How big a noise is that? We make the choice in relation to the other times this door opens and closes, especially, of course, the last time. We might even want to think about developing the sound throughout the play so that, although the first few times it is recognizably and simply like a "real" door, by the last time it is enhanced beyond verisimilitude (The *Fool for Love A Doll House*). We might not want to do that. We will, however, want to look at doors through the Middle and at the End of this play.

Mind you, *A Doll House* isn't "about" doors any more than *Oedipus Rex* is about children. Doors are part of the play's material. A spectator may well think about being shut in and shut out, about prisons and escape, but while we're making the play, we concentrate on the form these doors help us conceive. The repetitions and similarities out of which a playwright and director make sequences are, during the process of making the play, quite independent of the processes of ordinary life, or the meanings and personal significances the play will have for the audience that sees it.

The Middle of a play begins when an incident has its antecedent in the play itself, and not exclusively in the prior experience of a spectator. In *Hamlet,* Francisco, Bernardo, and Horatio exhibit fear; spectators can interpret these gestures with reference to experience in ordinary life. When the cause of this fear turns out to be a ghost, for which most of us have no ordinary experience, the ghost relates, not to our ghost experiences, but to the fearful gestures of the play's characters. The play, which began in ordinary experience, has moved to nonordinary or poetic experience.

There's no smooth line in the script where this happens; one incident with antecedents in the play's Beginning might be followed by another with no such antecedents. Again, from *Hamlet,* the tension in the court scene between Claudius and Hamlet may not immediately exhibit its cause, but there's no mistaking what it is. We all know it from our own lives. It's a Beginning incident that happens after a Middle incident (the Ghost's appearance to Horatio, Bernardo, and Francisco). Gradually the play's own events support whatever happens; the credibility of an incident will rely on poetic considerations, not on considerations of ordinary life.

The End of a play may not be the end of its characters' story. In Ibsen's *Ghosts,* the play's End leaves a question: What will Mrs. Alving do? Look back to the Middle: it's full of incidents that connect Oswald to his dead father. Those incidents, in turn, are made of materials from the Beginning: Mrs. Alving's history (staged as her action of telling Pastor Manders how what he believes is untrue) of her husband's long decline into death. She tells Manders how thoroughly she regrets having nursed the Captain so faithfully. In the play's Middle, Ibsen carefully and particularly connects Oswald with his dead father: his looks, the pipe, the flirtation with Regina, and so on. As a result, no matter what we might imagine Mrs. Alving doing after the curtain falls, this plot can't contain her nursing Oswald and remain unified.

None of this, of course, has much to do with ordinary life or probabilities: it's simply a technical look at Ibsen's plotting. Maintaining a separation between life and poetry is especially important when we consider the next set of relational parts: Likelihood and Necessity. Let Likelihood be our label for the potential of an incident as the antecedent of future incidents. That is, any moment in a playscript or rehearsal contains material that will be repeated or varied in certain other moments to come. In the economy of a play, this may be the merest repetition ("People don't do such things," from *Hedda Gabler*) to fairly elaborate conventions of story telling and play plotting.

Let Necessity be our label for the similarity of an incident to its antecedents in the plot. This is the key to the credibility a play's events have for an audience. Most of us watching *Hedda Gabler* have no basis on which to form a judgment about the psychological truth of her suicide. The suicide's credibility doesn't depend on our experience, however; it depends on the poetic connection between a startling action and its antecedents in the plot. These antecedents are, for the most part, simple repetitions of key materials out of which the startling incident is made. In the case of Hedda's suicide, the most notable materials are: General Gabler's pistols and Hedda's uses of them (She shoots at Judge Brack and gives one to Lovborg, urging him to kill himself "beautifully."); General Gabler's portrait, a constant reminder to Hedda of her reduced circumstances; the piano; Aunt Julie's hat and Hedda's hurtful pretense that it belongs to "the servant"; the repeated remark, "People don't do such things"; and Hedda's many statements about death and suicide.

Fear, Pity, and Catharsis make up the final sequence of relational parts. These are the affective significance of each event. They are labels, each of which can apply to any part of the play. Any incident, beat, or gesture can be conceived as having each kind of affective significance. That is, any gesture of the play has the potential to excite audience emotions. The words we use,

Fear and Pity, have an irresistible connection with feelings we all experience in ordinary life. They lead us almost inevitably to the subject of audience reactions, away from the structure of the play. In fact, these terms may seem too limited by their ordinary meanings. Fear and Pity make sense in a tragic plot, but can be confusing with respect to comedy, unless we think of Fear as any affective potential an incident has. A later gesture will connect to that gesture and that potential may be enhanced or developed. A third gesture in the series will reconfigure the relation between the first two. Think of the sequence 2, 4. The first "incident," 2, has certain potentials—3, 4, and so on. When the second "incident" appears, it creates a relationship with the first and reduces the number of potentials. The sequence might be arranged to create the relationship "counting by twos." Then, when a third "incident" occurs, it might be a surprising 8. This changes the original relationship from "counting by twos" to "multiplying by two." Or, the third "incident" might be 16, still another relationship.

Early in the play, we recognize potentials by comparing the dramatic actions to similar actions in ordinary life. When the potential is realized, our expectations are met or surprised and we form an opinion about the connection between the antecedent and its consequences. In a tragedy or melodrama, this opinion often is that the misfortune was undeserved. (Hence Aristotle's term, Pity.) In a comedy or farce, we might opine that the misfortune is thoroughly deserved. Our tears on the one hand and our laughter on the other are the affective expression of these opinions.

Oedipus Rex opens with a scene in which characters are afraid. The affective significance of the Suppliants' description of the plague is double: looking forward to possible events in future, it is Fear (Only misfortune can come from this plague.); looking backward to events of the story that happen before the plot begins, it is Pity. (No action of the Suppliants is connected to this misfortune; we say it is undeserved.) Creon changes the affective significance of these materials when he reports the Oracle's statement. His report resolves the Fear potential and the Pity opinion of the plague. He declares the situation an opportunity. His report has its own potential for future events, for success or failure. The play's action moves forward. This change to a new significance as a result of new information or action is what we can call Catharsis. Catharsis is a constant process in the play, as incident follows incident and each one changes the significance of its antecedents.

At the end of *Oedipus Rex* Sophocles plots a Catharsis for the entire action. As Oedipus moves closer and closer to achieving his aim, the plot contains several moments when actions which apparently led one way suddenly lead another. Finally, Oedipus discovers his own guilt by asking a question designed to prove his innocence. Sophocles plots a clear connection between the horrific events and their antecedents in the actions of Oedipus. He's guilty. He rushes into the palace. When he returns, he has discovered his dead wife and blinded himself in expiation of his terrible deeds. His misfortune is now complete, but it's clear from the plot that the misfortune is undeserved: no act of his was designed by him to accomplish what happened. The Fear potential of the play's events has resolved to a potential for Pity. At this point, Sophocles makes the grand Catharsis, in a single great line. In strophe two of the Exodos, the Chorus asks Oedipus why he blinded himself: "What god was it drove you to rake black night across your eyes?" And he replies: "Apollo, dear children, the god was Apollo . . . but the blinding hand was my own." By taking responsibility, Oedipus completely alters the significance of all that has gone before; his actions now appear "deserved," but in a new and tragic pattern that includes desperate misfortune for individuals even as it affirms a coherent, if difficult, life. The resolution of the poetic structure metaphorically creates this affirmation at the most fundamental level of the art work.

When conceiving the form of the particular production of *Oedipus Rex* that we're planning and rehearsing, we don't require a single opinion about what that significance actually is. In fact, each of us (and each spectator) will probably have a slightly different opinion. To me it means that life is hard, to you that life is unfair, to someone else that you can't win. For the Chorus it might mean that life isn't over 'til it's over. There may be as many of these significances as there are people to assign them. The fact of the change is what's dramaturgically important.

Aristotle proposed a list of six purely imaginary parts. His method, decried by many as too literary, is the best way I know of to think about the poetic complexity of a script and the sensual overload of a rehearsal or performance. It's possible to pore over a script until you understand it, but there's no way to take a play home to study. Aristotle's handy idea is this: any element of a play—every gesture, sound, word, activity, or action—can be considered as displaying or being any of the six parts he proposed. He called them parts; they're more like qualities, but with a little practice the idea of parts makes sense. He imagined the parts as fitting together in a double relationship of material to form, form to material. Each part relates to the others as follows: starting with Spectacle, each part is material used to make the next part. Starting with Plot, each is the form used to organize the material of the adjacent part.

Spectacle. The most fundamental quality of plays, Spectacle includes everything you see in the production, including other spectators and the theater itself. Spectacle is much more than the setting. The most important part of Spectacle is the human presence and behavior of the live actor. Spectacle is the material of music, as movement is required to produce sound. That is, in order to make sounds that an audience understands as the play's words, the actors must move in certain ways. Too often we think of what the spectator sees only as the set design.

Music. Everything heard in a production, planned or accidental, including the audience coughing and the sirens outside, is part of the material the audience uses to create the finished play. Music and Spectacle together make the most basic difference between drama and other kinds of poetry. The most important dramatic Music is the human voice. Music forms Spectacle, insofar as actors make movements to produce sound. Music (sound) is the material out of which the play's words are made: consider them, not as writing, but as talking; made of sounds, not letters.

Spectacle and Music don't exist, of course, until actors create them. Some aspects of them can be inferred from the script; but the important things, the psychic force of the actor and the infinite emotional range of his or her voice, are sensuous qualities, not to be known by reading a script. Playwrights have little control over this aspect of production; this drives them crazy.

Diction.   The words. The most important aspect of Diction in drama is that an actor speaks the words in public performance; they are heard, not read. Diction is the material thoughts are made of, and is the limiting form for much of the play's Music and Spectacle.

Thought.   The poet organizes words into the major actions of drama: suffering, deliberation, and choice or decision. Characters use language to get what they want. Thought forms the Diction in this sense: to become thoughts, words must be organized; unorganized they may have individual meanings but collectively they'll be gibberish. The idea of language as dramatic action isn't always easy to grasp. Sometimes a writer will stage the physical action of a story, as in "The Murder of Gonzago." More often the poet stages the suffering: "O, what a rogue and peasant slave am I!"; the deliberation: "I have heard, that guilty creatures, sitting at a play. . . ."; the choice: "I'll have these players here play something like the murder of my father. . . ."; and the aftermath: "Give me some light, away!" Claudius "suffers" the effects of Hamlet's scheme by saying, "Give me some light, away!"

At this point, for this vocabulary to be useful, we have to agree that theater is a mimetic art. It imitates human action, and the main action it imitates is the use of language to accomplish purposes. Dramatic language doesn't describe, it doesn't tell us about a character: dramatic language is what the character does. When a character asks a question, that language doesn't "mean" that the character is asking a question. That language is the question and the act of questioning. Likewise, but not quite so easy to see, when a character speaks of its suffering, it isn't telling about that suffering; rather, that speaking is the action, to suffer.

Think about Aeschylus' *Prometheus Bound* as a way to understand this. Some guys bring another guy on stage and nail him to a rock. They leave. Prometheus is alone. He talks. His words describe his predicament and its causes. Visitors come. They ask him why he's in this fix. He tells them. As he tells them, he also defies Zeus, the god he disobeyed and who is punishing him. Zeus sends him a messenger who tells him to knock it off. He refuses, and finally Zeus explodes the whole mountainside, including Prometheus. I don't think we have to be jaded media freaks to regard that as pretty thin stuff for a tragedy. And I don't think the Greeks would have felt differently. Remember, they saw *Prometheus Bound* after a night of celebration that included a lot of notably lively behavior, especially in the areas of alcohol and sex.

Now, what if Zeus decided to punish Prometheus this way: nail him to a rock and make him tell everyone why he's being punished; get him physically with the nails (and by having the eagle come and tear his liver out), but also get him psychically by making him tell the crime over and over again until he understands his mistake.

This changes the play from a storytelling session to an action of defiant suffering. Prometheus suffers as dramatic characters do most things, by using language. He uses his suffering, and his refusal to knuckle under, to defy his punisher, to reproach and embarrass him. The actor now has a vivid and compelling action to play. To tell about what happened to me isn't a particularly dramatic action; to suffer the wrath of Zeus, and to turn my suffering into a challenge: that has possibilities. The audience experiences that vivid and compelling action as it happens, instead of merely listening to a story about how it happened once upon a time.

The modern drama has added something that Aristotle didn't imagine: some of the Diction and Thought in a modern play is created by the actor, not the playwright, and is not spoken aloud. The famous observation is attributed to Stanislavski: "The audience come to hear the subtext; they can read the text at home." This subtext is an aspect of Diction and Thought that has no existence before rehearsal. It never gets written down, except maybe in an actor's notebook. Sometimes it will be spoken aloud, as a rehearsal technique. The audience will never know it, except by inference.

Character. I've found it best to use this word to mean differentiation among the agents of the play, and to avoid using it to refer to personality or predictibility of behavior, or eccentricity, as I might in everyday life. Character is the material of Plot, the form of Thought, Diction, Music, and Spectacle. The most important aspect of Character is moral choice resulting from deliberation. Agents in a dramatic action are most thoroughly differentiated by their choices of what's right and what's wrong. In dramaturgy, it's essential to remember that, in spite of the persuasive presence of the actor, characters are works of art, not human beings; they are subject to rules different from the rules of ordinary life. Further, no thing called a Character is referred to by the script. Character, as a part of a play, doesn't exist without performance.

Plot. The arrangement of all the elements of a play. Plot is form to Character and is its own form or purpose. The aesthetic principle on which artists make plot choices is the organic unity of the Plot itself, its own particular beauty. Plotting is the major poetic skill for playwrights.

Plot often refers to the sequence of events in a play's story. This makes for difficulty in rehearsal and analytical discussion among artists. There must be a distinction between story—a chronological sequence—and Plot—a dramatic sequence. To conceive a play's narrative/dramatic form, compare the chronology of the story with the Plot of the play. Where in the story is the play's Point of Attack? Early, as in Shakespeare's plots? Late, as in Sophocles or Ibsen? The poet's choices about the Point of Attack lead directly to other choices about which events of the story will be represented by enactment and which by narration, and which will be left to inference.

There's no denying that it's often difficult to use these imaginary parts creatively. It can be awkward and frustrating to treat a play as if it had no discursive meaning. This is a tricky part of dramaturgy. Often we start a production with a desire to share something with an audience. That's fine, even important. But artists must respect the developing form of the work they are making as well as the integrity of the spectators for whom they make it. To impose preconceived notions on a developing art work will stunt or inhibit its growth; to insist on particular "meanings" for an audience will deny them the use of their own experiences and imagination as they respond to the play's actions and conceive its form. The one is merely bad art; the other is bad rhetoric and coercive politics. I pray you avoid them.

Play analysis creates categories with which to perceive the complexity of an object or process that won't reveal its construction otherwise. Without a sense of that construction, the artists making a play production from a play script have no way to conceive the forms their work takes as it develops to final fruition.

Theory and the Practice of Dramaturgy

by John H. Lutterbie

JOHN H. LUTTERBIE is an Associate Professor at the State University of New York at Stony Brook, where he is Chair of the Theatre Arts Department. Lutterbie has published essays in *Upstaging Big Daddy: Directing as if Race and Gender Mattered* (University of Michigan Press), *Theatre Journal, The Journal of Dramatic Theory and Criticism, Theatre Topics* and *The Journal of Psychiatry and the Humanities.* The University of Michigan Press is publishing his book, *Hearing Voices: Modern Drama and the Problem of Subjectivity.*

Theory has a bad reputation in the theater. Practitioners cringe at the mere mention of the word, perceiving theory as the antithesis of practice, as an obstacle to the visceral and emotionally charged communication between actors, as interfering in the psychological relationship that inevitably and necessarily develops between the actor and the director. Theory is associated with pedantry, with a deadly theater that is dogmatic from its inception and polemic in its manifestations. And there are instances where a dependence on theoretical constructs has resulted in boring and obscure performances; but on the other hand there are as many, if not more, productions that are just as deadly created by those who condemn theory out of hand. Furthermore, to say that theory leads to bad theater is disingenuous, because it ignores the many outstanding productions where theory is seamlessly integrated into the fabric of performances that are scintillating and aesthetically transcendent.

To lay the blame for antitheoretical sentiments at the feet of the theater practitioners is equally inappropriate, however. Theorists have a lot to answer for as well. The language in which they couch their theories often seems unnecessarily obscure and, because most theorists are writing out of different disciplines, the usefulness of their constructs to the practice of theater is not always evident. Inaccessibility gives an aura of aloofness that breeds contempt, exacerbating the imagined distance between theory and practice.

I say imagined distance because the attitudes of pro- and antitheorists appear to ignore the necessary relationship between theory and practice: there is no theory without practice; there is no practice without theory. To make sense of this seeming paradox requires a definition of theory. Theory, according to the *Oxford English Dictionary,* comes from the Greek root *thea* meaning "looking at, viewing, contemplation, speculation." This act of contemplation has as its end the defining of a "scheme or system of ideas or statements held as an explanation or account of a group of facts or phenomena."

Theory provides a statement of principles or methods on which the practice, in this instance, of theater is based; it is a type of knowledge. For example, in order to revitalize the theater Constantin Stansilavski contemplated the art of the actor and developed a statement of principles that outlines a theory of actions based on the belief that in the theater, like life, we act because we wish to achieve certain objectives. Students are regularly taught to analyze texts by breaking them into beats and determining the character's objective at a particular moment. However, they are taught this concept as a practice rather than a theory. The actual breaking down into smaller units of action *is* a practice and provides a specific knowledge about the play. But it is not possible without another kind of knowledge, that provided by theory, in this case the principles underlying the hypothesis that acting is improved by performing small, containable actions relevant to a set of specific circumstances. Theory is derived from practice; and practice is based on theory.

For Patrice Pavis this shifting of perspectives is the exercise of two different types of knowledge.

> Thus it is not really possible to erase the boundary between the two discourses, quite simply because creation and reflection are two different modes of knowledge, which may coincide in a single individual, but not in the same discourse, or *only at different moments of the same discourse.*[134]

The act of theorizing is integral to the practice of theater. Theory and practice simply define "different moments of the same discourse."

I do not wish to argue that because theory is inevitable in the practice of theater we all need to become theoreticians—that is, more than we already are. There are sufficient numbers of virulently antitheoretical practitioners willing to denounce any such demand. Rather I hope to show that theory is a valuable tool for the dramaturg, and that consciousness of theoretical foundations—the ability to define grounds and shift perspectives—can improve the quality of our practice as dramaturgs.

First, however, I must insist that this is not an attempt to introduce a rarefied or elitist vocabulary to the practice of theater; quite the opposite. Jargon, the use of language as sound bytes without reference to rigorous thought and the practical experiences from which they arise, has, with good reason, been condemned. One word that has become virtually synonymous with jargon is *deconstruction,* which I will discuss later. The term, loosed from its philosophical moorings, has become merely a means of justifying old practices in a new context. What often passes for deconstruction in the theater is simply a rationalization for doing violence to a text because a director has the desire to be avant-garde or to present what she or he perceives as being daring and new. However, when used with integrity, a deconstructive reading of a text can be challenging and provocative, resulting in marvelous theatrical events, such as JoAnne Akalaitis's production of *'Tis a Pity She's a Whore.* Utilized selectively, judiciously, and with common understanding, such terminology can improve communication, provide insights into texts, and increase efficiency in rehearsal. It is when a systematic shorthand of overspecialized terms supplants clear and reciprocal communication, that theory, by becoming a privileged syntax, becomes a negative force.

Actually, the danger is not that a specialized language will be introduced to the rehearsal space, but that *another* set of terms will unnecessarily complicate a process that is already laden with its own jargon. Terms such as *upstage, beat,* and *objective* are elements of a discipline-specific language that makes sense only when placed in the context of theater production. Alien concepts such as deconstruction, paradigmatic shifts, and postmodern, when applied to the theater become the bane of practitioners unfamiliar with the disciplines from which these concepts are derived. The tendency, all too often, is to recoil from strange terminology, as if fearing contamination, rather than to inquire how the ideas associated with these terms might enrich theatrical production.

FRAMING

Part of the difficulty with theory, as we have seen in these few paragraphs, is that it varies in scope from the specific and everyday to the general and abstract. Returning to our earlier definitions, theory involves three steps: perceiving, reflecting, and speculating. A couple of examples might help. When preparing to produce a play, we immerse ourselves in the script, think about how the different elements of the text interact with each other, and develop a concept about what the play means. Or, when casting, we compare the actors auditioning with the demands of the play, and choose those who will give us the best performance. These decisions, as anyone who has attempted to make them knows, are never as simple as they seem. Part of the difficulty is the element of subjectivity always involved in any activity; and, as any director can attest who has struggled for the right language to help an actor overcome an obstacle, the personal complicates the practical. It is similarly true of subjectivity and the application of theory. It is to this problem that we must turn our attention.

Anne Cattaneo, dramaturg at Lincoln Center, has developed a project for training dramaturgs in which the students are asked to adapt Georg Büchner's *Woyzeck* from the perspective of different dramatic forms. For instance, they are asked to look at the play as if it were a neoclassic tragedy or written in the romantic style. When various points of view are applied, the text changes in shape, creating profoundly varied theatrical effects. What is at issue in the exercises is not the license to reconceptualize texts, but an implicit understanding that the perspective used to read a play will inevitably affect what the play means to an audience.

Thomas Postlewait provides us with a similar example in his discussion of how historians define periods or ages when writing histories of the theater.

His argument is that the way in which time is divided and the names given to each division affects how we look at and understand a particular period. For instance, to call a certain moment in English history the Age of Shakespeare privileges the life and work of a particular playwright/actor/poet and renders insignificant in comparison the writings of Christopher Marlowe, Ben Jonson, John Webster, and many other fine playwrights. An alternative approach to period is to divide the age into the Elizabethan and Jacobean Ages. But this creates a different kind of distortion by ignoring the fact that a majority of theater practitioners at this time, including Shakespeare, wrote during the reigns of both monarchs. To distinguish between Elizabethan and Jacobean playwrights does violence to their writings and our understanding of them. Similarly, either classification devalues the significance of theater architecture, the structure of acting companies, audience demographics, styles of acting, and theater as a cultural force—all of which are important to understanding the theater of any age.

The point of view brought to play analysis or research encourages us to revel in certain qualities of a play while rendering others uninteresting by comparison. This operation marks our attitude toward the subject matter. The literary theorist Kenneth Burke, who has analyzed this phenomenon, claims that the approach we use in analyzing a script creates a frame or a filter that limits the possible meanings the text can have. He calls this frame a "terministic screen."

> Not only does the nature of our terms affect the nature of our observations, in the sense that the terms direct the attention to one field rather than another. Also, *many of the "observations" are but implications of the particular terminology in terms of which the observations are made.* In brief, most that we take as observations about "reality" may be but the spinning out of possibilities implicit in our particular choice of terms.[135]

The words we choose to describe our theatrical activities—psychological realism, tragedy, the absurd, deconstruction, or whatever—will determine the kind of production we create. Furthermore, what we select as evidence to support an interpretation will mean something different depending on which screen or filter we use. For instance the witches in *Macbeth* might be said to represent an externalization of Macbeth's ambition to be king if we look at the main character's aspirations to the crown as a tragic flaw; or, from a psychoanalytic point of view, the crones might be seen to figure the force of the irrational when unconscious desires are not sufficiently checked by the superego. Both interpretations are acceptable, but would result in significantly different performances of the characters.

However, the idea of terministic screens in Burke is more complicated. Decisions made when interpreting a play tend to be conscious choices based on other evidence in the text and the aesthetics of the production team. But, for Burke, the factors used in determining how to produce a play are not merely a question of choice. They are determined—in the last analysis—by the languages we speak. "The human animal, as we know it, *emerges into personality* by first mastering whatever tribal speech happens to be its particular symbolic environment."[136] Language, Burke argues, defines a way of thinking and, therefore, predisposes us to look at the world from a particular perspective. The old adage that Greek and German are the languages of philosophy, French the language of criticism, and English of business, suggests that the structure of language affects the way in which we perceive the world. For example, the fact that we call a theatrical event a "production" implies a certain attitude to artistic creation, as does the term "show." The emphasis on *displaying a product* positions theatrical activity in an economic frame that emphasizes the consumption of material goods. The fact that the experience of theater is ultimately immaterial—in the sense that there is no remaining object, only a memory of the experience—may indicate why theater is so undervalued in this culture. The point, however, is that how we think about theater is determined by the terms we use to frame our explorations. To alter this perspective we need to employ a different terminology. This is why some theater practitioners choose to think of the theater as an ongoing process rather than the creation of a product.

THE DRAMATURG, THEORY, AND THE TEXT

The ability to change terministic screens, to shift to new frames of reference—one of the values of complex language systems—is central to defining the dramaturgical function. The dramaturg must be able to move from one perspective to another as the situation demands, constructing lines of communication that facilitate production planning. To use a French term, the dramaturg must be a *bricoleur*, someone who builds using the various materials at hand. The concept of *bricolage* was made popular by the structural anthropologist, Claude Lévi-Strauss, who found that approaching another culture from a single theoretical position was dangerous. The results of such investigations tended to validate the theory rather than offer useful insights into the society. Indeed, he found the data gathered by anthropologists to be self-selecting, providing the conclusions needed to support the hypothesis framing the study. A better and, he believed, more reliable approach to the examination of culture is to uncover the evidence of structural relations in the society, and only then devise a model to explain the phenomena. The method, however, has several problems: Who is to determine what is or is not evidence? Are the structures that appear between pieces of evidence actually there, or are they supplied by the anthropologist? And what kinds of distortion occur in the effort to get the pieces to fit?

In other words, what Lévi-Strauss fails to understand is that no objective way exists to collect data in the study of culture. The investigator always brings a personal frame to every investigation and any study will be limited by that perspective. What we can do—and it is at this point that the concept of the *bricoleur* becomes useful—is increase the number of frames we use in our research. The relationship between such a concept and the field of dramaturgy is clear. Rather than seeking out one answer, the dramaturg—becoming a *bricoleur*—remains flexible, uncovering a number of solutions and opening the possibility of information coming together in new and exciting ways.

Discovering viable new plays and fresh interpretations of established texts is a primary responsibility of the literary manager and dramaturg. If, however, dramaturgs are schooled only in traditional approaches to texts, that is, based on models of the well-made play and theories of realistic acting, they will be ill-equipped to engage innovative writing on its own terms or read established plays from perspectives other than that of psychological realism.

Similarly, the growing awareness that American culture consists of diverse races, ethnicities, genders and sexualities and that care must be taken in choosing images to depict these populations, requires that theaters take responsibility for the representations that appear on their stage. Dramaturgs, while not the conscience of the theater, must be able to recognize images that are prejudicial, even though they may appear innocent. This is not a call for political correctness—the issues are considerably more complex—but a need to be keenly aware that our choices, made with the best intention, can do harm. The dramaturg can make the director and playwright aware of areas of contention and initiate a discussion about the relative merit and potential meanings of specific choices, whether in staging options or in season planning.[137]

To adequately fulfill this function and to develop a vocabulary for engaging new writing, the dramaturg needs tools for analyzing images and the ability, in the process of analysis, to shift perspectives. Fortunately there are numerous analytical frames available to the dramaturg. Unfortunately, because they come from critical studies they often carry names and are written in ways that are most often not "user friendly." Such theories as postmodernism, deconstruction, materialism, feminism, queer studies, postcolonial discourse, and cultural studies are potentially useful theoretical models, if the dramaturg takes the time to understand how they can be used in the creation of theater.

Postmodernism is known for its skepticism and belief in the relativity of values and for its focus on issues of representation, particularly the question of whether or not we can identify the "real." Jean Baudrillard, for instance, holds that reality has been replaced by simulacra, or copies. Responding to the media's ability to construct realities that are more seductive and interesting than everyday existence, postmodernists believe we are creating a world in which it is impossible to differentiate between a media world and day-to-day experience. Instead, the reality of an image is defined by its context and not necessarily by what we perceive as the real world.

Therefore, in place of a traditional emphasis on interpretation, postmodern performances juxtapose a number of contradictory ideas, each of which is viable independently, but when placed next to the others is insufficient to support a single statement of meaning. It is somewhat like looking at an M. C. Escher drawing in which the background and foreground continually trade places. The main difference is that a synthesis takes place when viewing an Escher work and meaning presents itself, however tenuous and difficult to hold onto. Postmodern performance does not even give that solace to the viewer, insisting on the absolute relativity of content. This theory locates meaning, as Peggy Phelan argues in *Unmarked,* in the process of reception rather than in the art object itself. An understanding of a postmodern performance is most likely to occur after having left the theater, and then will usually revolve around questions of form rather than content. The return to the everyday experience on the streets outside of the space of performance provides a framework for engaging the material, if for no other reason than that it is the very incoherence of life that provides the material for postmodern theater.

Deconstruction preceded postmodernism. Whereas postmodernism locates reality on the surface of images, deconstruction seeks to reveal structures of meaning that exist beneath the surface. Deconstruction, as in the writings of Jacques Derrida,[138] focuses on moments when logic and language fail and tropes, or figures of speech, are used to disguise gaps in the logic of the argument. Exploring the tropes in a text, deconstructors find that by unveiling and exploring these gaps, new meanings surface that often contradict the manifest meanings of the text. In the theater, deconstruction is a means of investigating plays in order to reveal unintended and contradictory contents in a text. For instance, a deconstruction of *The Tempest* might focus on Prospero's inhuman treatment of Ariel and Caliban, presenting the magician as an imperialist who may or may not desire an erotic relationship with one or both of the spirits. While sounding preposterous and overly analytical, such a production, in the right hands, could result in an exciting and extremely unsettling performance. Unfortunately, some practitioners use the term *deconstruction* to justify a superficial approach to staging, what has become known as a "concept production." In such performances the rigorous act of analysis exercised in deconstruction is replaced by a facile relocation of the story in another milieu, in order to make a traditional reading of the text appear fresh. These often simplistic approaches cause many critics and practitioners to dismiss deconstruction, without exploring its power as a form of critique.

Deconstruction holds that there is nothing but the text, and to investigate a play is to unravel the various discourses that appear within its weave, but without reference to an objective external reality. This privileging of discourse is opposed by materialists, who believe in the existence of material relations of power and the need to analyze the hierarchies and inequities in structures of repression. Of central interest are the ways in which systems of oppression are reproduced in cultures without the direct exercise of state power.

The theater theorist most clearly identified with materialist critiques is Bertolt Brecht, who developed an approach to theater and acting that sought to make his audiences aware of inequities in the exercise of power and to encourage them to change the world. This overtly political approach to theater is seldom embraced because it is perceived as being polemical and didactic, and because most American theater practitioners do not believe that the theater is the place for politics. On the one hand, such perceptions ignore the highly entertaining forms of political theater, such as that of Dario Fo and John McGrath, who combine the best in entertainment with political commitment; on the other, they assume that there is such a thing as nonpolitical theater. Political theorists argue that all representational forms are ideological and promote one system of values or another, thereby encouraging a particular set of relations among people. While all theater is political, a political theater acknowledges this fact and explores ideology, its effect on people, and the means by which it is reproduced.

The desire to generate change is also the basis of feminism, which seeks to secure basic human rights for women and to increase awareness of the violent physical and psychological effects of media images and patriarchal discourses on differences between men and women. This results in two approaches to theater. One challenges the representations of women in mainstream theater, particularly in plays by men. These forms of theater focus on a critique of patriarchal structures and seek to create political solidarity among women in order to resist forms that repress women. The other seeks to create performance opportunities for and encourage writing by women as a means of engaging and validating their experiences. A primary focus of feminism is locating strategies for eluding the oppressive patterns of patriarchal discourse and finding ways of representing themselves that do not reproduce negative images of women. Efforts to surmount these conflicts have led to a division among feminists. One group seeks ways of writing that express what is unique to the experience of women. They are identified with what French feminist theorists Hélène Cixous and Luce Irigaray call *écriture feminine,* a way of writing that renders visible those aspects of a woman's life that are rendered invisible by patriarchal discourse. The other, materialist feminists, seek ways of subverting the structures of oppression that disenfranchise them and keep them from being recognized as people with rights.

A similar division exists in the relatively new form of theoretical thought called queer theory. It seeks strategies for defining and resisting homophobic responses to nonheterosexual life-styles. One line of inquiry examines homosexual writers and another identifies "queer" thematics and aesthetics in literature traditionally perceived as heterosexual. In the theater, the first approach manifests itself in writing that validates gay and lesbian life-styles through sensitive portrayals of same-sex love—Tony Kushner's *Angels in America* is one example—while the identification of "homosexual" themes in "heterosexual" writing can be seen in Split Britches' production of *Little Women: The Tragedy,* which looks at forms of lesbian desire in the life and writing of Louisa May Alcott. A third mode of exploration is exemplified by Tim Miller, whose *My Queer Body,* a more radical and sexually explicit performance, seeks to empower gay men to celebrate their sexuality. Queer theory supplies the dramaturg with a frame for examining issues of homosexuality and homophobia in the theater.

Strategies for fighting other forms of discrimination can be located in postcolonial discourse, initiated by Edward Said's book *Orientalism.* This theory investigates how countries exoticize inhabitants of countries they colonize, disseminating images of populations that mark them as decidedly "other," that is, as simultaneously exotic and inferior. The need to control the sexuality and "irrationality" of the other becomes a justification for imposing forms of order that deny indigenous populations basic human rights. As with other theories discussed here, the critique of representations is complemented by a search for ways of resisting discourses that limit people's opportunity to express their own identity. Theaters dedicated to multicultural performance are an obvious place where such strategies are explored; but the dramaturg in any theater can benefit from the ability to analyze and evaluate representations of different cultures for ideological content. Images selected with the best of intentions can often replicate racial and cultural stereotypes.

There are, of course, other theoretical frames than those discussed here. I am well aware that the psychoanalytic discourses of Freud and Lacan, the formalist and semiotic methodologies, the newly formed cultural studies programs, theories on the practice of everyday life have not found expression here. It was always my intention to present only a sampling of the different kinds of frames available to the dramaturg in approaching the interpretation of a play, or in the conceptualizing of a production. The list, at first, seems daunting. But with selective reading one can gain insight into these theories and begin to determine how they are useful in the practice of theater.

THEORY AND THE SPACE OF REHEARSAL

The one place in which many theater practitioners fear the introduction of theory is the rehearsal studio. Here, it is generally believed, the intellectual must accede place of privilege to the psychophysical explorations of the performers. Generally, I would agree that *excess* of thought can diminish the energy of performance, stealing vitality and emotional intensity from the acting. But this loss also tends to reflect either poor training or an inability to translate ideas into the words of action, and not, as many would have us believe, an insidious quality inherent in rational thought that, as we suppose of Hamlet, reduces us to inaction. Used as a spur to experimentation and investigation in the rehearsal space, theory can ignite the imagination. Herbert Blau's work with the KRAKEN company is an example of how theory—in this case, pushing the limits of thought—can become the basis of theater explorations;[139] or from a very different perspective, Jerzy Grotowski's investigations into culturally encoded resistances to expression, and the emotional and physical suppleness needed for the actor's body to communicate the complexity and intensity of human emotion.[140] Significantly, and with few exceptions, the most influential and heralded performances of the past thirty years were developed by artists who were investigating theater from a specific theoretical position, whether it be an approach to acting or a means of interpreting text—although most often one goes hand-in-hand with the other.

When theory does become an obstacle it is frequently because insufficient time is available for exploration or because theories have not been fully assimilated, especially when taken from literary or critical studies. It is dangerous to assume, as sometimes happens, that abstract concepts can be easily translated into terms appropriate to performing bodies. Moreover, it should not be surprising that the practitioners most influential in articulating theories of theater and performance are those handsomely subsidized over an extended period of time. The limitations placed on creativity by commerce, such as the standard three week rehearsal period, make an integration of theory into practice virtually impossible—unless the director's concept is sufficiently precise before rehearsals begin. However it is not my intent here to convince practitioners to become theorists. Those who have had a positive exposure to theory will realize the value of such research and will seek productive ways of incorporating theory into their practice.

Instead, as I noted at the beginning of this essay, I am interested in identifying the role theory *already plays* in the practice of theater, because we cannot improve the processes of theater without first investigating the assumptions underlying the practices that currently exist. As soon as we begin to ponder alternative ways of making theater, or even understanding how rehearsals are presently structured, theory comes into play. Dramaturgs, at least those who wish to have a place in rehearsal, need to identify the hierarchies and organization of the rehearsal process: that is, the relations that exist between the various members of the company and the modes of communication used. This is not a new function for the dramaturg, but an inevitable consequence of engaging in rehearsals. The value of theory is that it makes conscious an activity that all too often remains subconscious, allowing us to be better prepared to respond to the needs of the director and actors, to be of use should there be a break in the lines of communication.

In any organization there is going to be a hierarchy that defines relations of power and authority. Traditionally the director appears at the apex of a pyramid as the person responsible for interpreting the text, defining a concept, organizing the company and helping the actors embody the concept through rehearsals. There are, of course, institutional structures, such as length of rehearsal time and associated personnel (stage managers, designers, assistant directors and dramaturgs), that constrain the freedom of the director and place her in an existing system of power relations. However, as anyone who has been involved in the rehearsal process knows, interpretation and conceptualization are considerably more collaborative than the traditional model suggests. Actor's influence interpretation through the negotiations that occur as they prepare for performance; and a good director is sensitive to the needs of the performers. Similarly, the designers in the exercise of their creativity and with their authority as professionals interpret the visual concept, adjusting however marginally the contours that define the shape of the production.

The dramaturg needs to understand the structures of power and modes of communication within the company. For instance, every actor develops a personal approach to evolving a character, and there are going to be certain images or word choices that serve as keys to unlocking the performance for them. A dramaturg who has conceptualized how a particular performer works will be able to help the actor and the director should an obstacle arise. But dramaturgs are going to be effective only if they have a model for the lines of communication and authority. In certain circumstances it may be best to discuss the issue directly with the performer, whereas in others such a choice might cause more problems than it solves. A way of communicating needs to be chosen that harmonizes with the rehearsal process.

Relatively little has been written about the relationship between the different members of the production company, particularly the actor and director. This is undoubtedly because so much of the relationship occurs in the "trenches" of rehearsal and is, therefore, difficult to formalize; and because the relationship is so variable, depending on personalities and subjective ways of working. Nevertheless, it is possible to devise paradigms for defining such relationships that are not rigid, but that are attendant to the fluctuating intensities of intersubjective relations.[141] By paying attention to the flows of intensity between the different players in the process, the dramaturg can define and utilize modes of communication that allow for effective and constructive intervention in the rehearsal process. It is possible to depend on intuition and not articulate a theory. However, it is equally possible that, with the best of intentions, depending on intuition can be disruptive, increasing rather than decreasing tension.

By becoming familiar with different approaches to directing and acting, by observing how practitioners operate in the rehearsal space and reflecting on the similarities and differences between various approaches, we can develop theoretical models that improve our understanding of how the collaborative process operates and allow for ways of working that will make the dramaturg an even more useful force in practice.

SELECTED BIBLIOGRAPHY

Burke, Kenneth. "Terministic Screens." *Language as Symbolic Actions: Essays on Life, Literature, and Method.* Berkeley: University of California Press, 1966.

Pavis, Patrice. *Theatre at the Crossroads of Culture.* Trans. Loren Kruger. New York: Routledge, 1992.

General Introduction to Critical Theory

Rabkin, Gerald. "Waiting for Foucault: New Theatre Theory." *Performing Arts Journal,* 14.3 (1992): 90–101.
Reinelt, Janelle G. and Joseph R. Roach, eds. *Critical Theory and Performance.* Ann Arbor: University of Michigan Press, 1992.

Postmodernism

Baudrillard, Jean. *Simulations.* Trans. Paul Foss, Paul Patton and Philip Beitchman. New York: Semiotext(e), 1983.
Blau, Herbert. *To All Appearance: Ideology and Performance.* New York: Routledge, 1992.
Foster, Hal, ed. *The Anti-Aesthetic: Essays on Postmodern Culture.* Port Townsend, Washington: Bay Press, 1983.
Kroker, Arthur and David Cook. *The Postmodern Scene: Excremental Culture and Hyper-Aesthetics.* New York: St. Martin's Press, 1986.
Lyotard, Jean-Francois. *The Postmodern Condition.* Trans. Geoff Bennington and Brian Massumi. Minneapolis: University of Minnesota Press, 1984.

Deconstruction

Derrida, Jacques. *The Ear of the Other.* Trans. Avital Ronell and Peggy Kamuf. Ed. Christie MacDonald. Lincoln: University of Nebraska Press, 1985.
___. *Writing and Difference.* Trans. Alan Bass. Chicago: University of Chicago Press, 1978.
Norris, Christopher. *Deconstruction: Theory and Practice.* London: Methuen, 1982.

Materialism

Althusser, Louis. *Lenin and Philosophy.* Trans. Bren Brewster. New York: Monthly Review Press, 1971.
Balibar, Etienne and Immanuel Wallerstein. *Race, Nation, Class: Ambiguous Identities.* London: Verso Press, 1991.
Benjamin, Walter. *Illuminations.* Trans. Harry Zohn. Ed. Hannah Arendt. New York: Schocken Books, 1979.
Eagleton, Terry. *Criticism and Ideology.* London: Verso Press, 1976
Williams, Raymond. *Problems in Materialism and Culture.* London: Verso Press, 1980.

Feminism

Burke, Carolyn, Naomi Schor and Margaret Whitford. *Engaging with Irigaray: Feminist Philosophy and Modern European Thought.* New York: Columbia University Press, 1994.
Case, Sue-Ellen, ed. *Performing Feminisms: Feminist Critical Theory and Theatre.* Baltimore: The Johns Hopkins University Press, 1990.

de Lauretis, Teresa. *Technologies of Gender: Essays on Theory, Film and Fiction.* Bloomington: Indiana University Press, 1987.
Phelan, Peggy. *Unmarked: The Politics of Performance.* New York: Routledge, 1993.

Queer Theory

Butler, Judith. *Bodies that Matter: On the Discursive Limits of Sex.* New York: Routledge, 1993.
___. *Gender Trouble: Feminism and the Subversion of Identity.* New York: Routledge, 1990.
Case, Sue-Ellen. "Performing Lesbian in the Space of Technology: Part I and II." *Theatre Journal.* 47.1 and 3 (1995): 1–18, 329–343.
Clum, John M. *Acting Gay: Male Homosexuality in Modern Drama.* New York: Columbia University Press, 1992.
Savaran, David. *Communists, Cowboys, and Queers: The Politics of Masculinity in the Work of Arthur Miller and Tennessee Williams.* Minneapolis: University of Minnesota Press, 1992.

Post-Colonial

Said, Edward. *Orientalism.* New York: Vintage Books, 1979.
Chaudhuri, Una. *Staging Place: The Geography of Modern Drama.* Ann Arbor: University of Michigan Press, 1995.
Gainor, J. Ellen. *Imperialism and Theatre.* New York: Routledge, 1995.

SECTION NOTES

1. For other instances of dramaturgy's inroads in popular culture, see "Dramaturgy: A Compendium of Quotes" in the appendix.
2. Michael Lupu at the Guthrie Theatre first suggested to me this way of thinking about dramaturgy; see his piece in this volume.
3. For representative examples of the conversation on dramaturgy, see Brustein's and Ballet's pieces originally delivered at meetings of TCG and LMDA, the panel discussion of Molière's *The Misanthrope*, "How to Talk To a Playwright," Borreca's discussion of the development of dramaturgy programs at Yale and the University of Iowa, and Abrash's account of LMDA, all in this volume; the bibliography in the appendix cites the Yale *Theater* issues, along with most of the other literature written on dramaturgy in American theater. See also Bert Cardullo, ed. *What Is Dramaturgy?* (New York: Peter Lang, 1995).
4. For information on the LMDA University Caucus e-mail list, contact the author: gproehl@ups.edu.
5. For a writing on dramaturgy that questions its existence as a profession see Carol Rosen, "The Ghost Lights of Our Theaters: The Fate of Comtemporary American Dramaturgs," in Cardullo 177–93.
6. The literature on dramaturgy is, of course, not as homogenous as I make it here, but for the purposes of this piece I treat it as a single discourse, looking for recurrent metaphors in this body of advice.
7. Laurence Shyer, *Robert Wilson and His Collaborators* (New York: Theatre Communications Group, 1989) 108.

8. Shyer describes di Niscemi's role as Wilson's "chief researcher, advisor and co-author," as one who encourages and oversees "the gradual enrichment" of Wilson's works with "biographical and literary material" (93). Although Shyer does not use the word *dramaturg* to describe di Niscemi's role, her placement in the book and her activities as described by Shyer clearly make her a potential model for the role.

9. Of course, dramaturgs are not always word-centered (see Gregory Gunter's piece in this section), but writings on dramaturgy frequently foreground language-based activities: play reading, translation, historical and critical research, the writing of program notes, and so forth.

10. See, for example, Martin Esslin both in this volume and as cited in the bibliography on the dramaturg's obligation to both old plays and new ones; see Arthur Ballet, also in this volume and as cited in the bibliography, as one who devoted himself to a lifetime of reading new plays.

11. Joel Schechter, "Enter Dramaturgs," *Theater* 10.1 (1978): 5.

12. Joel Schechter, "American Dramaturgs," *The Drama Review* 20.2 (1976): 89.

13. Martin Esslin, "The Role of the Dramaturg in European Theater," *Theater* 10.1 (1978): 49.

14. On dramaturgical protocols, see, for example, Leon Katz, "The Compleat Dramaturg" in section two of this volume; Borreca's discussion of Katz and the Yale program also in section two; for a strong negative response to aspects of this practice see Kushner in section five of this volume.

15. Judith Milhous and Robert D. Hume, "The Concept of Producible Interpretation," *Producible Interpretation: Eight English Plays, 1675–1707* (Carbondale: Southern Illinois University Press, 1985) 3–34.

16. William R. Ellwood, "Preliminary Thoughts on the German Dramaturg," *Modern Drama* 13.3 (1970): 257.

17. Shyer 95.

18. See also Lee Devin in this volume on the relationship between playscript and performance.

19. Marvin Carlson, "Theatrical Performance: Illustration, Translation, Fulfillment, or Supplement?" *Theatre Journal* 37 (1985): 5–11.

20. See Richard Pettengill's good-natured account of such a moment in this volume.

21. On rehearsal decorum see Katz in section two of this volume as a representative example; see also Haring-Smith in this section and Borreca in section two.

22. In opposition to this employee/boss model see Esslin and Preston/Coppenger in this volume: Esslin almost reverses the positions; Preston and Coppenger emphasize parity.

23. Tyrone Guthrie, "The Audience of One," *Directors on Directing: A Source Book of the Modern Theatre*, ed. Toby Cole and Helen Krich Chincy (New York: Bobbs-Merrill, 1963) 252; for a more recent example, see Keith Johnstone's *Impro: Improvisation and the Theatre* (New York: Theatre Arts Books, 1979).

24. See Schechter on the history of dramaturgy in this volume.

25. Jack Zipes, "Utopia as the Past Conserved: An Interview with Peter Stein and Dieter Stürm of the Schaubühne am Halleschen Ufer," *Theater* 9.1 (Fall 1977): 50–57; on dramaturgy and the questioning spirit see also Mark Bly in this volume.

26. Zipes 52.

27. Shyer 109.

28. For other writings on dramaturgy that use a marriage metaphor see Jan Selman, "Workshopping Plays," *Canadian Theatre Review* 50 (Spring 1987): 15–23 and John Lahr, "Green Room: I Lost It at the Theatre," *Plays and Players* 20.4 (1973): 12–13. Selman's focus, however, is directed more towards ways of thinking about playwright/director relationships than dramaturgs and directors (i.e., "There are many more 'unmatched' playwrights and directors across the country than 'happily married' ones.") The metaphor, only briefly developed, has a predominately positive tone and functions without specific reference to who is the wife and who the husband. Lahr focuses on the literary adviser/dramaturg and, in this instance, the image takes on gendered, negative connotations: "When a critic becomes a part of an institutional theatre, he loses his intellectual virginity. . . . The term 'Literary Adviser' elevates the critic from a chippie walking the theatrical beat to the status of favourite wife." Lila Wolff-Wilkinson in an article on teaming student dramaturgs with faculty directors ("Comments on Process: 'Production Dramaturgy as the Core of the Liberal Arts Theatre Program,'" *Theatre Topics* 3.1 (1993): 1–6) does not use the marriage metaphor, but her description resonates with a kind of post-World War II domesticity: the relationship requires "mutual trust"; it will require a certain vulnerability on the director's part, but will relieve a degree of "directorial loneliness"; the dramaturg will need to learn to keep "quiet during rehearsals" and give "tactful, constructive notes."

29. Oskar Eustis, "Dramaturgy at the Eureka: An Interview with Oskar Eustis," *Theater* 17.3 (1986): 12.

30. Bly interviewing Esslin in *Theater* 17.3 (1986): 19–24.

31. Bly interviewing Ballet in the same issue of *Theater* 32; see also Ballet and Constance Congdon ("How to Talk to a Playwright") in this volume.

32. George White, "The O'Neill Experience: a Practical Experiment in Helping New Writers," *Theatre Quarterly* 4.15 (1974): 34.

33. White 36.

34. For a similar transformation from adversary to ally, see Brustein's discussion of Michael Feingold and the genesis of the Yale dramaturgy program in this volume.

35. See Martin Esslin in this volume on a related concern: that dramaturgs should not become so comfortable with their collaborators that criticism is blunted.

36. Joel Schechter, "American Dramaturgs," *The Drama Review* 20.2 (1976): 90.

37. Peter Hay, "Dramaturgy: Requiem for an Unborn Profession," *Canadian Theatre Review* 8 (1975): 44.

38. Hay 44; see also Tori Haring-Smith's perceptive discussion of the director/dramaturg relationship in the following essay in this volume.

39. Antony Price, "The Freedom of the German Repertoire," *Modern Drama* 13.3 (1970): 243.

40. Barbara Field in "Dramaturgs in America: Eleven Statements," *Theater* 10.1 (1978): 20.

41. Schechter, "American Dramaturgs" 88; emphasis added.

42. On the dramaturg as **fixer of plays,** see Eric Overmyer ("How to Talk to a Playwright") in this volume.

43. On the process of revising plays to meet preconceived patterns see Leon Katz and Steve Weeks in section four of this volume.

44. Shyer 109.

45. Shyer 92.

46. See Jan Kott's humorous piece "The Dramaturg," *New Theatre Quarterly* 6.21 (1990): 3–4.
47. On the dramaturg's complicity with status quo theater see Mark Lord's essay in this volume.
48. See in this volume Frisch/Weems and the Wooster Group as a model for dramaturgs who move back and forth between Apollonian and Dionysian functions.
49. Shyer 108.
50. Shyer 108.
51. Shyer 93.
52. For more on gender roles and dramaturgy see Tori Haring-Smith in this volume.
53. Victor Turner, "Liminal to Liminoid, in Play, Flow, and Ritual: An Essay in Comparative Symbology," *From Ritual to Theatre: The Human Seriousness of Play* (New York: Performing Arts Journal, 1982) 20–60.
54. Hay 44; elsewhere in this volume, Cary Mazer refers to the dramaturg as translator.
55. Price 243.
56. Esslin 49.
57. Esslin 49.
58. For more on these educational roles, see Pettengill (sections two and three) and Kennedy (section three) in this volume.
59. For an example of the range of opportunities available to the dramaturg in these journeys between the play in rehearsal and the world-at-large, see Harriet Power in this volume.
60. For a further discussion of dramaturg as liaison see David R. Gowen, "The Role of the Professional Dramaturg in Contemporary North American Theatre" master's thesis, University of Calgary, 1993, 87–91.
61. Mary Belenky, Blythe Clinchy, Nancy Goldberger, and Jill Tarule, *Women's Ways of Knowing* (New York: Basic Books, 1986) 121.
62. Belenky et al. 113, 116. Peter Elbow calls this kind of thinking "methodological belief," which he describes as a conscious, systematic, and disciplined attempt to "see as someone else sees." See Peter Elbow, "Methodological Doubting and Believing: Contraries in Inquiry," in *Embracing Contraries* (New York: Oxford, 1986) 289.
63. Nel Noddings, *Caring* (Berkeley: University of California Press, 1984) 15–16.
64. Carol Gilligan, *In a Different Voice: Psychological Theory and Women's Development* (Cambridge: Harvard University Press, 1982). See also Sigmund Freud, *Three Essays of the Theory of Sexuality* (New York: Basic Books, 1962) and *The Question of Lay Analysis* (New York: Norton, 1950); Lawrence Kohlberg, *The Psychology of Moral Development* (New York: Harper and Row, 1984); and Jean Piaget, *The Moral Development of the Child* (New York: The Free Press, 1965).
65. For example, see also Nancy Chodorow, *The Reproduction of Mothering* (Berkeley: University of California Press, 1978); Carole Klein, *Mothers and Sons* (Boston: Houghton Mifflin, 1984); Nona Lyons, "Two Perspectives on Self, Relationships, and Morality," *Harvard Educational Review* 53 (1983): 125–145; and Jean Baker Miller, *Toward a New Psychology of Women* (Boston: Beacon Press, 1976).
66. See the interviews with American dramaturgs in *Theatre* 17.3 (1986), especially the introduction by Mark Bly ("American Production Dramaturgs"). Charles

Marowitz also uses the term "in-house critic" in his discussion of British theater in *Directing the Action* (New York: Applause, 1986).

67. Belenky et al. 104. Peter Elbow calls this kind of reasoning "methodological doubt," which he defines as the "systematic, disciplined, and conscious attempt to criticize everything no matter how compelling it might seem." (See Elbow 257.) This is the kind of thinking that educational researchers such as William Perry rate as the most highly developed. His *Forms of Intellectual and Ethical Development in the College Years,* an extended study of male students at Harvard, has done much to shape college curricula so that they favor separated knowing at the expense of connected knowing. See William Perry, *Forms of Intellectual and Ethical Development in the College Years* (New York: Holt, Rinehart, and Winston, 1970).

68. "Dramaturgy at the Magic and the O'Neill: An Interview with Martin Esslin," *Theater* 17.3 (1986): 21.

69. See Alfie Kohn, *No Contest* (Boston: Houghton Mifflin, 1986), and Andrea Lunsford and Lisa Ede, *Singular Texts/Plural Authors* (Carbondale: Southern Illinois University Press, 1990).

70. The research for this article included personal interviews with Chaikin, Jean-Claude van Itallie, Susan Yankowitz, Mira Rafalowicz, and Rick Harris in July and August, 1994. Except where indicated otherwise, all citations of their statements are based on these interviews. For comprehensive bibliographic references on all aspects of Chaikin's work, see Alex Guildzen and Dimitris Karageorgiou, *Joseph Chaikin: A Bio-Bibliography* (Westport, Conn.: Greenwood Press, 1992). The author gratefully acknowledges the Swarthmore College Research Fund for its support in the preparation of this article.

71. Antonin Artaud, "No More Masterpieces," *The Theater and Its Double,* trans. Mary Caroline Richards (New York: Grove Press, 1958).

72. Joseph Chaikin, quoted in Eileen Blumenthal, "Open Wide: Chaikin's Adventures," rev. of *Re-Arrangements,* by The Winter Project, *The Village Voice* 7–13 March 1979: 61.

73. Sam Shepard's working relationship with The Open Theater was seemingly distant and marginal, his participation mainly being as a regular observer of the group's work, with his one credited contribution being a monologue in *Nightwalk* that he mailed to the company from London. Nevertheless, early Shepard works written outside The Open Theater such as *Cowboys #2* (1967) often carry the earmarks of improvisationally based playwriting such as *Interview.*

74. Quoted in Eileen Blumenthal, *Joseph Chaikin: Exploring the Boundaries of Theater* (Cambridge: Cambridge University Press, 1984) 148.

75. In practice, van Itallie's plays developed with The Open Theater have enjoyed significant production independent of the group, while Yankowitz's *Terminal* has not. The unconventional form of the performance texts created in the late projects of The Open Theater, such as *Terminal,* is certainly part of the problem, as can be seen from reading the published texts, which are available in the collection *Three Works by The Open Theater,* ed. Karen Malpede (New York: Drama Book Specialists/Publishers, 1974). Though included in this collection, the texts of *The Mutation Show* and *Nightwalk* were not made available for production by other companies, and the accurate crediting of work on the texts clearly demanded complex and scrupulous acknowledgements in published

form. Confronted with similar issues in the publication of the texts for their productions *1789* and *1793,* Ariane Mnouchkine's company simply listed "Le Théâtre du Soleil" as the playwright in print.

76. The acting ensemble for *The Mutation Show* consisted of Ray Barry, Shami Chaikin, Tom Lillard, Jo Ann Schidman, Tina Shepard, Paul Zimet.
77. Mel Gussow, "Open Theater Presents a Splendid Mutation Show," rev. of *The Mutation Show,* by The Open Theater, *New York Times* 29 March 1973: 40L.
78. Gussow 40L.
79. Blumenthal 149–150.
80. The acting ensemble for *Nightwalk* consisted of Ray Barry, Shami Chaikin, Ralph Lee, Tom Lillard, Ellen Maddow, Jo Ann Schidman, Tina Shepard, Paul Zimet.
81. Blumenthal 145.
82. Arthur Sainer, "A Walk Among Outer Humans," rev. of *Nightwalk, The Village Voice* 13 September 1973: 66.
83. Jack Kroll, "Night Birds," rev. of *Nightwalk, Newsweek* 24 September 1973: 127.
84. Mira Rafalowicz, untitled, Yale *Theater* 10.3 (1978): 27.
85. Rafalowicz 27–29.
86. Blumenthal 148.
87. *Joseph Chaikin: Going On.* A film by Steven Gomer, 1983. Distributed by Films for the Humanities, Princeton, N.J.
88. The performance dates and acting ensembles for The Winter Project productions are as follows:
    Re-Arrangements: March 9–25, 1979. Performers: Joyce Aaron, Ronnie Gilbert, Will Patton, Mark Samuels, Tina Shepard, Paul Zimet;
    Tourists and Refugees: July 9–August 3, 1980. Performers: Ronnie Gilbert, Will Patton, Atsumi Sakato, Tina Shepard, Paul Zimet;
    Tourists and Refugees No. 2: April 29–May 24, 1991; later performed in a revised version in July at the International Theater Festival in Caracas, Venezuela. Performers: Ray Barry, Ronnie Gilbert, Robbie McCauley, Tina Shepard, Will Patton, Paul Zimet;
    Trespassing: Feb. 23–March 21, 1982. Performers: Roger Babb, Cristobal Carambo, Gloria Foster, Ronnie Gilbert, Tina Shepard, Paul Zimet;
    Lies and Secrets/Trio: March 9–23, 1983; May 1983 tour to London. Performers: Roger Babb, Ronnie Gilbert, Harry Mann.
89. Blumenthal 81–82.
90. Gordon Rogoff, "Questioning Love," rev. of *Re-Arrangements,* by The Winter Project, *The Village Voice* 19 March 1979: 85.
91. Joseph Chaikin/Mira Rafalowicz *Re-Arrangements, Performing Arts Journal* 4.3 (1980): 147.
92. To a much greater extent than The Open Theater, The Winter Project was influenced by the consistent collaboration of designers with the ensemble, particularly set designer Jun Maeda of La MaMa, whose impact on the group's work was, according to both Rafalowicz and actress Ronnie Gilbert, as profound as any member of the group. Mary Brecht designed costumes for all five of The Winter Project productions, and Beverly Emmons designed lights for all but *Trespassing.*
93. Michael Feingold, "Chaikin's New Path," rev. of *Trespassing,* by The Winter Project, *The Village Voice* 9 March 1982: 83–84.

94. Rogoff 85.

95. Erika Munk, "Exiles," rev. of *Tourists and Refugees*, by The Winter Project, *The Village Voice* 16–22 July 1980: 75.

96. Erika Munk, "New Clothes," rev. of *Lies and Secrets*, by The Winter Project, *The Village Voice* 29 March 1983: 86.

97. Irving Wardle, "Trio," rev. of *Trio*, by The Winter Project, *Times* (London) 19 May 1983: 15. See also Anthony Masters, "Chamber Music in Action," rev. of *Trio*, *Times* (London) 19 May 1983: 15.

98. Audio tapes of the original "Nightvoices" series, while not commercially distributed, can be obtained by writing the author, care of Swarthmore College, 500 College Avenue, Swarthmore, PA 19081.

99. Bill Hart, unpublished interview by Midori Ferris. December 16, 1993.

100. Jerzy Grotowski is an international leader of the experimental theater who became famous in the 1960s as the director of the Polish Laboratory Theatre. Ludwig Flaszen was his dramaturg during this period.

101. Michael Bigelow Dixon and Joel A. Smith, eds., *Anne Bogart Viewpoints*, (Newbury, Vt.: Smith and Kraus, 1995).

102. Ed. note: To the best of our knowledge, the feedback service John Glore mentions was discussed but not put into existence.

103. Developed by the Bush administration and passed during Clinton's presidency, this bill is a benchmark of government support for arts education.

104. From the bill "Goals 2000."

105. There are many examples of influential programs in these categories, especially those based on the "Theater in Education" and "Drama in Education" curricula that every child in the United Kingdom encounters in the course of public primary and secondary education. Suzan Zeder discusses several of the most important of these approaches elsewhere in this volume and testifies eloquently to their effectiveness.

106. A small but important Off-Broadway theater whose mission is to reinvigorate the classics with new translations and approaches.

107. From the artistic director's letter to participating teachers in the 1994 MAX Conference.

108. Constructivist education theory posits that children learn to think best in learning environments where they must analyze and manipulate objects, language, and data in order to solve problems, thereby "making meaning." This approach is in part a reaction to pedagogies that emphasize acquisition of knowledge by learning facts, theories, or procedures by rote.

109. Interview conducted during site visit to The Goodman, 4/24/94.

110. About fifteen thousand students annually come to see plays at Boston's Huntington Theater Company through its exposure program, a series of student matinees that provide curriculum guides for teachers as well as study guides for students and in-school workshops.

111. Funding is largely from the National Endowment for the Humanities (NEH).

112. These are just what they sound like—games that require each child to say their names aloud, which most can do, in association with some other factor, a color, flavor, or favorite something. "Shake . . . freeze" gets blood flowing, bodies involved, and generates funny poses, giving everyone a chance to star. "Sculpture" asks them to perceive the negative space they create while moving as malleable and palpable, triggering imaginary visualizations useful in later exercises.

113. One child leaves the room and another must say three positive things about the absent person who then returns and must guess who gave the description.
114. Interview with Willie Reale, 2/1/96.
115. In all, fifteen playwrights work with twenty New York City high schools. Each makes about seventeen visits to their assigned school over several months.
116. Telephone interview with Margaret Salvante, 7/23/95.
117. From an interview with David Shookhoff conducted at Classic Stage Company, 5/18/94.
118. Interview with Becca Manery at the Court Theater in Chicago, 5/14/94.
119. Manery interview.
120. From an Intiman fact sheet describing Living History.
121. On-site interview with Abigail Adams at People's Light and Theatre Company, Malvern, Pennsylvania, 7/9/94.
122. Deeter was founder and guiding spirit of The Hedgerow Theater, a highly respected artists' collective during the 1920s and '30s in Moylan, Pennsylvania, just south of Philadelphia. The company lived together, shared housekeeping and cooking chores, and was renowned for its highly disciplined work ethic and fine ensemble playing.
123. Projects, once selected, undergo a process called "phased development," which is nothing more than what all theater artists deeply desire—extended rehearsal and development time, often spanning years from first rehearsal to mainstage production.
124. The Pickering Campus is a comprehensive public vocational high school.
125. This grant, one of seven awarded nationally in 1994, is part of the NEA's "Arts Plus Initiative" awards designed to support partnerships between arts organizations and schools that move toward including the arts as a basic element of public school prekindergarten through twelfth-grade curricula.
126. Interview with David Bradley at PLTC, 7/9/94.
127. In 1993, Welch conceived, organized, and hosted the first Resident Theater Education Director's Conference in order to gather a group of colleagues representative of the field yet small enough to make personal connections and "share the joy and frustration inherent in this work." Welch has published a forty-five-page conference report on that gathering that strongly influenced this effort. Reports on subsequent annual conferences, held again at The Shakespeare Theater in spring of 1994, 1995, and 1996 (available on request from the theater's education office), will doubtless add significantly to knowledge of the field.
128. TCG sponsors "observerships" enabling theater artists and administrators to visit and observe other programs in all areas, including education.
129. The operator of six New York MacDonald's Hamburger Restaurant franchises was so impressed by CSC's innovative classics programming that he printed special placemats and table tents promoting the "pay what you can" policy.
130. *Prometheus Bound,* Aeschylus, in *Three Greek Plays,* trans. Edith Hamilton (New York: Norton, 1937) line 460.
131. "Mr. G. B. Shaw's Ban on Applause," in *Bernard Shaw, Collected Plays with their Prefaces,* editorial supervisor Dan H. Laurance (New York: Dodd, Mead & Company, 1972) 4:262.
132. My favorite translation of *Poetics* is *Aristotle's Poetics: Translation and Analysis,* by Kenneth Telford (South Bend: Gateway, 1961). I am obviously and gratefully in his debt.

133. Henri Poincaré, "Science and Method," quoted in *Feeling and Form, Susanne Langer,* (New York: Charles Scribner's Sons, 1953) 91.
134. Patrice Pavis, *Theatre at the Crossroads of Culture.* trans. Loren Kruger (New York: Routledge, 1992) 88–90. Emphasis added.
135. Kenneth Burke, "Terministic Screens," *Language as Symbolic Actions: Essays on Life, Literature, and Method* (Berkeley: University of California Press, 1966) 46.
136. Burke 53.
137. I do not wish to imply that a literary manager or dramaturg should become a censor, or that they should attempt to determine the political agenda for the theater. These issues need to be decided by the producing organization. Nevertheless, it is up to the dramaturg—but not the dramaturg alone—to address ethical and moral questions within the ideological context of the institution. It is naive to assume that such questions are irrelevant to a theater producing in these times.
138. See Jacques Derrida, *Of Grammatology,* trans. Gayatri Chakravorty Spivak (Baltimore: The Johns Hopkins University Press, 1974) and Chistopher Norris, *Deconstruction: Theory and Practics* (London: Methuen, 1982).
139. See Herbert Blau, *Take Up the Bodies: Theater at the Vanishing Point* (Urbana: University of Illinois Press, 1982).
140. See Jerzy Grotowski, *Towards a Poor Theatre* (New York: Simon and Schuster, 1968).
141. See Jessica Benjamin, *The Bonds of Love: Psychoanalysis, Feminism and the Problem of Domination* (New York: Pantheon Books, 1988); Ellen Donkin and Sue Clement, ed., *Upstaging Big Daddy: Directing as if Race and Gender Mattered* (Ann Arbor: University of Michigan Press, 1992); and John H. Lutterbie, *Hearing Voices: Modern Drama and the Problem of Subjectivity* (Ann Arbor: University of Michigan Press, 1997).

SECTION 4

NEW CONTEXTS

Susan Jonas begins this section with a discussion of strategies for the radical re-contextualization of canonical texts. Drawing examples from specific projects she has undertaken, Jonas argues for ensemble dramaturgy and suggests specific strategies for opening up texts that may seem closed to us.

Carl Weber brings to the second piece in this section many years of experience in academic and professional theater from his association with Bertolt Brecht and the Berliner Ensemble to his more recent work as a translator of the plays of Heiner Müller. He examines the state of translation in American theater including some of the reasons for the relative dearth of translated work on American stages. He also provides an overview of issues that those who would like to translate for the stage will want to consider.

These two articles on adaptation and translation launch an examination of various approaches for making new performances ("new contexts") out of old plays, plays with a history, whether that history spans centuries, as in Jayme Koszyn's work with Euripidean drama at the Huntington Theatre in Boston or just a few years as in Harriet Power's production of Caryl Churchill's *Mad Forest* at Philadelphia's Venture Theatre. Throughout this section individuals recount their work on specific projects in the areas of production dramaturgy, translation, and adaptation. The reader will find here an array of approaches, often in the form of case studies, to a variety of plays from different times, countries, and cultures.

In discussing her work with Greek tragedy, Jayme Koszyn illuminates fundamental assumptions about what dramaturgs should do when they work on a play, as well as some problems those assumptions can create within the rehearsal process, especially if left unexamined. She advocates a dramaturgy that is at least as Dionysian in spirit and methods as it is Apollonian.

In "Textual Collidings," Jim Niesen draws upon his work as member and director of Irondale Ensemble Project to describe that company's reworking of Shakespeare's *As You Like It*. Irondale does not identify a single person as the dramaturg in their work, but instead disperses the dramaturgical function among the entire company in their search for new approaches to old texts.

Cary M. Mazer's case study highlights the role that new theoretical insights can play in rehearsal and production. Mazer brings a theater historian's perspective to the work of the dramaturg. He describes four basic methods by which directors and dramaturgs might approach playscripts from other periods than our own, offering specific examples from his own work on *The Duchess of Malfi* at the University of Pennsylvania. Mazer puts into practice the kind of work John Lutterbie recommends in his article in section three, "Theory and the Practice of Dramaturgy." Mazer's distinction between universalizing tendencies and approaches grounded in various forms of historical awareness also should be read alongside Steve Weeks' historical contextualization of how-to books on playwriting in section five.

Robert Falls, Richard Pettengill, and Walter Bilderback discuss their work on Molière's *The Misanthrope* at both the Goodman Theater and La Jolla Playhouse. What emerges are the kinds of energies that undergird the decision to mount a particular play from the past and the processes of translation and adaptation that a production team goes through in trying to communicate those energies to a contemporary audience.

In a similar manner, James Magruder's case study takes us on his journey as translator of Marivaux's *Le Triomphe de l'amour* (*Triumph of Love*) from his first work with this text while a student at Yale to its premiere at Baltimore Center Stage. What emerges is his love for both the play and the translator's art. Magruder's detailed case study complements Carl Weber's overview of issues in translation.

Elizabeth C. Ramírez addresses issues of multiculturalism, translation, and adaptation in her case study of a production that turned Beaumarchais' *Marriage of Figaro* into *One Crazy Day* for the Arizona Theatre Company. The author describes her work with director David Ira Goldstein and translator Roger Downey in moving the world of the play from its original European setting to a nineteenth-century Mexican region that is present-day Arizona. She describes the care required to create a culture on stage that will reach out to a theater's whole community.

Laurence Maslon also explores issues of community and the re-staging of a play but from yet another perspective: musical theater at a major regional theater in the nation's capital. Still, many of the principles are the same: thorough research, careful consideration of the original work and its audience, an equally careful consideration of our own historical moment and the audience that shares it. Maslon believes that musical theater requires the same dramaturgical care that we give to new plays and works by playwrights such as those discussed throughout this section. He demonstrates this care in his description of his work on these projects.

Finally, Harriet Power concludes this section with her account of the dramaturgical preparations she and her ensemble undertook for a production of Churchill's *Mad Forest: A Play from Romania.* Worthy of note, in particular, are the ways in which the entire ensemble participated in this process and the use of resources that went well beyond a trip to the library. This production of *Mad Forest* was chosen as a best production of the year in Philadelphia. Without doubt, the depth of preparation evidenced in this article was a key to this show's artistic and critical success.

Also applicable to the themes explored by these articles are a number of other pieces found in different sections of this volume. Anne Cattaneo in section one deals with the dramaturg's role in working with both classics and contemporary plays; also particularly relevant to the field of production dramaturgy are pieces by Mira Rafalowicz, Royston Coppenger, Travis Preston, and Gregory Gunter, all in section three, "Models of Collaboration."

Aiming the Canon at Now:
Strategies for Adaptation
by **Susan Jonas**

SUSAN JONAS has worked as a director, dramaturg, adapter, translator, and administrator with The Acting Company, The Circle Repertory Theater, the Yale Repertory Theatre, the Lincoln Center Institute, The Irondale Ensemble, The Ensemble Studio Theatre, and the Classic Stage Company. She has taught on the faculties of Princeton University, SUNY–Stony Brook, Connecticut College, Cooper Union, and University of New Hampshire. She is the cofounder and Artistic Director of The Knickerbocker Studio. Recently her adaptation, with Helen Graves, *The Importance of Being Wilde,* was presented at the Manhattan Theatre Club, and her adaptations and translations of Marivaux have been produced regionally. She is cofounder of the University Caucus of Literary Managers and Dramaturgs of the Americas (LMDA), an officer of the Dramaturgy Forum of the Association for Theatre in Higher Education (ATHE), and editor of *The LMDA Source Book: Resources on the Teaching of Dramaturgy.* She received her BA from Princeton University, her MFA and DFA from the Yale School of Drama.

My work as a director is inseparable from my training as a dramaturg and my curiosity about social context. I cut my teeth on the canon, predominantly authored by the currently vilified dead white male. The "classics" fueled my desire to be an artist. Like many, I've felt deeply acknowledged and befriended by Camus, Shakespeare, Dostoyevski, Flaubert, Homer, Williams, and (Preston) Sturges. Like many, I've also sometimes felt disparaged, disfigured, and overlooked by the very authors I love. As a feminist dramaturg-director, adapter, and teacher, I've had to weigh the damage against the ecstasies. This conflict is especially germane to the medium in which the currency is the live presence of the actor—the theater. There the reader's imagination cannot as easily compensate for the particularized presentation of gender, race, and sexual preference. So then, how do we produce the classics for our contemporary audience?

A production conveys a vision of humanity that may be sensitive, empowering, and progressive—or not. Considering the risk of reinforcing deleterious doctrine, we might first ask, "**Why** do the classics?" Any canon intrinsically preserves itself by admitting only what will pose no real threat to its own ideology. But theorists such as Susan Lanser believe that feminist productions can, "expose the universal as masculine, the natural as cultural, the textual as political."[1] Theatermakers can employ the canon to **reveal** its own biases about gender, as well as race, sexual preference, and other issues and sensitivities. Dramaturgy can not only elucidate but question authority in these matters. It is at the heart of my process, as I search for ways to address issues surrounding exclusion of what the dinosaur mainstream regards as "other," and I regard as "us." I rewrite plays to give voice to those silenced because of gender, race, or sexual preference, because I am making plays for my friends, so they can participate as collaborators and audience members. So they and I can dream through them, I reenvision plays, argue with them, infiltrate them.

The canon is as unavoidable and frustrating as is the English language. Both may be enlarged and amended, but remain as necessary as the designated pole to an explorer. Furthermore, to avoid the canon is to leave it as is; by wrestling with it, we can reshape it. (Oscar Wilde said our one responsibility to history is to rewrite it.) In fact, the more conversant with the canon are we theater-makers, educators, students, and audiences, the greater the possibility of engaging in profound dialectics with our source material. Using reactive or subversive adaptation strategies, such as: re-contextualization, interpolation, interruption, transposition, simultaneity, reversing gender and sexual preference, we can create production texts that are dramaturgical dialogues with source material. In brief, by using the canon as a point of reference or a point of departure, we can consider where we came from, where we are now, and how we got here. I do not rewrite plays to obscure history, but to observe and criticize it. In that, I am with Santayana and Brecht; either we learn from history or we are destined to repeat it.

The classics provoke paradoxical feelings, from reverence to repudiation, and this friction is gold. Often I direct the classics to dramatize **relationships** to plays. Rather than pretend an absence of distance between the world of the play and our world, my productions are **about** that difference. This requires a willingness to allow the audience to be uncomfortable, angry, even appalled by difference, rather than normalizing to gloss over it.

My focus here is on the methods of adaptation toward such ends. The processes described suggest creative uses of dramaturgy in the development of performance texts based on the classics. They also suggest ways in which the making of theater can be the centerpiece of the university education, rather than on its periphery. None of these tactics are new, and many overlap, but delineating them may provide a useful resource of playful models and points of departure for other adapters. The basic strategies have been deduced—as is most theater theory—in retrospect. Using examples from three university productions I directed, as well as from the work of others, I offer some sense of how research can provide a "way in" to a play, as well as ways around it. Extending like a spine of inquiry throughout the research and rehearsal process is the question:"**Why** is this considered a classic? What of it is timeless and universal? What is not?"

STRATEGIES FOR ADAPTATION

Though it is cliché to insist that the credit for a production be shared by all participants, I must emphasize that the work described was developed in ensemble.

PROCESS

I select a play based on my desire to investigate a quandary, then invite others to investigate their relationships to the realm of concern. Then we construct a performance text based on ensemble dramaturgy. As director, I see my role as a facilitator, organizer, mentor, editor, and most significantly, as the maker of milieu, responsible for creating an environment in which each participant is excited to explore the issues personally and politically.

I moved toward ensemble performance text development for several reasons. First, the inherited power-structure model can be demeaning to actors and dull as paint for the director. She can become a "father figure," dominating through some accepted notion that her vision has priority, manipulating collaborators so that they produce a preconceived effect without realizing they have been manipulated. Second, having become adept at puppeteer psychology, I grew tired of the predictability and isolation it engendered. Third, I am deeply suspicious of power, especially my own. I feared I was playing into a real character weakness—my appetite for control. Wanting to grow beyond that, I purposefully constructed situations to avoid absolute authority over the text and event. I invite actors to share the dramaturgy, the adaptation, and often the directing.

Toward that end, I also try to work with a codirector who is expert in something about which I know little. I worked with a mask and movement specialist to adapt *The Odyssey* and with a choreographer on *The Front Page*. And I invited related experts into the rehearsal discussions (much as Gordon Rogoff and Richard Gilman worked with the Open Theater, and Joseph Campbell with Martha Graham). Among instances of "live" versus "page" research, a newspaper journalist with a forty-year career talked with *The Front Page* ensemble about the day-to-day life and evolution of his profession. I invited the director of the campus multicultural program to discuss racial sensitivity. Further, each student collaborator was assigned to present in rehearsal independent research on a self-designated topic, putting actors in roles of all sizes on equal footing as dramaturgs.

The seeds of this approach were sown while touring with The Acting Company. The troupe spent half a year moving from one impersonal motel in an unfamiliar town to another. As welcome as steady work may be, the rigors of touring are surprisingly depersonalizing. Director Jennifer McCray and I initiated group dramaturgy on our production of my adaptation of the children's classic *The Phantom Tollbooth,* exploring linguistics; magic in various cultures; the history and psychology of fairy tales; Jungian archetypes; gender stereotypes; and the works of Joseph Campbell. The actors quickly overcame their initial reluctance and found themselves swept up by the play of ideas. Certainly this enriched the adaptation and the production, but more importantly, it made the process exponentially meaningful. Now we seized every opportunity we could find in the production process to think, introspect, discuss, muse, and learn. The result was greater ownership and valuing of both process and product. I took with me from those years a deep conviction that the group process of dramaturgy has value in and of itself because it elevates the enterprise of the theater for all its participants.

The great boon of directing in the setting of a university is that—at least in theory—it credits education for its own sake and values process over product, so that, at its best, the making of a production becomes an opportunity to maximize interdisciplinary learning. What more compatible paradigms are there than education and theater, both of which honor the integrity of both the parts and the whole? What better way to integrate disciplines and perspective into a practical collaborative education? In many of the productions I've directed at universities and theaters, myriad extra-theater subjects—history, psychology, sociology, philosophy, politics, economics—found their way into our theatrical process, demonstrating dramaturgy as an excellent model for interdisciplinary education, especially when undertaken by a group. But not only was the production the filter or terminus for all of this research, it acted as the pinched center of an hourglass; all manner of information funneled to the center and then out again. The production was discussed in history, psychology, sociology, religion, and politics classrooms, as well as in Introduction to Theater and other arts programs. This adaptation model might be seen as a university of ideas that ripples out from the participants to the classroom, throughout the campus, and beyond to the community.

With *The Front Page,* the ensemble did a great deal of "standard" period research, then incorporated it subtly, as in the Edward Hopper-esque scenic design, and overtly, as with the interruptions of musical numbers. For *Odyssey,* the ensemble researched different theater techniques, from the Open Theater to the making of *Nicholas Nickleby,* then applied the research to sections from the book. The most comprehensive process was with *Tit for Tat.*

My long-standing desire to do *Measure for Measure* was exacerbated by a national climate hostile to freedom of expression in areas from art to sexuality. Shakespeare's play warns that the inevitable result of repression is hypocrisy or violence. I was intent on investigating this theme comprehensively, using a breadth of history as my resource as well as making the comedy thrive on its own terms. Indeed, if the impulse behind comedy is procreation, as Northrop Frye among others suggests, then comedy is as irrepressible and life-giving as it insists sex to be.

At the end of the summer preceding the production of *Tit for Tat (Measure for Measure),* I put aside the volumes of criticism and production histories that I had been reading. Though I usually share such research with my collaborators, I wanted to focus our development time on creating relationships with the play. My team of actors, dramaturgs, designers, and assistant directors set to work developing interpolations and substitutions based on their research. Books on religious fanaticism; articles on medical "cures" for homosexuality; personal accounts of persecution for religion and sexual preference;

videotapes of Golden Era movie stars, drag queens, and slapstick comedy; footage of campaign efforts by political candidates; interviews and biographies of champions of the Right; sermons from Luther to Pat Robertson; pictures of chastity belts; cassettes of music styles from Gregorian chants to country; speeches about the NEA; direct mail appeals from Left and Right—a deluge of materials changed hands daily, provoking a level of conversation rarely enjoyed in the Green Room.

The research created an environment in which the play's themes and issues were insistently current, and generated production text, interpolations, and staging. All of the material came from documentation, which was taken seriously in its own time. Although we did much cutting and pasting, the quotes were direct, whether from scientists specializing in "deviant" psychology or George Bush. Sometimes we melded characters, letting Hitler borrow a line from Goebbels. Our research had no boundaries. Everything fed the resource from which we created a sampler of historic and current doctrines of discrimination, repression, and censorship as shown in detailed examples in the ensuing sections.

My interest in doing the production lay not only in my vision of the performance, but also in having the opportunity to discuss the personal, local, and national sensitivities (and lack thereof) to issues of inclusion and censorship. In fact, the most satisfying aspect of the enterprise was reading a quote in an interview in one of the local papers with one of the actors. He was an athlete who admitted that he had unthinkingly held certain attitudes towards homosexuals, and that through the process of developing the production, he had found that he now socialized unselfconsciously with "out" gays and lesbians, which he would not have done before. Both the process and the product were civilizing.

CHANNELING

An element of the performance script is developed in "fidelity" to the play text. (This may seem like a repudiation of the critical impulse, which insists intentionality is unknowable, but it's really just a leap of faith.) I begin by taking the play personally (as with Flaubert's "Madame Bovary . . . C'est moi!") How is the play the author, the author the character, and the character and author I? Call this **channeling.** I share Odysseus' wanderlust, weariness, and longing for home. I internalize Hildy's struggle to reconcile his work as a newspaper journalist with his desire for the comfort of a personal life in *The Front Page.* I identify with the playwrights' ambivalence about journalistic ambulance chasing, the thrill of the chase and censure of its sensationalism and inhumanity. In *Measure for Measure,* I hear my own dumbfounded rage brilliantly and humorously articulated by Shakespeare's insistence that puritanical attempts to legislate sexuality are destined to wreak havoc and ultimately fail.

TRANSPOSITION

With transposition, a form of re-contextualization, elements are translated into comparable or familiar terms. Describing translation, Peter Arnott offers, "It means evoking the mood of the society for which the play was originally composed together with the attitudes and preconceptions that the author could assume in his audience, and presenting them to another audience in another time and culture in ways that it can understand."[2] In an analogous way, transposition can yield moving equivalents, as with Lee Breuer's evocative transposition of *Oedipus at Colonus* from ancient Greece to gospel in *The Gospel at Colonus.* Transposition can suggest new relationships, as did Bob Fall's *The Misanthrope,* which drew parallels between the neoclassical French class system and our Hollywood star system. (See Richard Pettengill's article on *The Misanthrope* in this volume.) Transposition can also imply evolution or a continuum, as in *Tit for Tat* when Angelo's opening monologue is supplanted by Dan Quayle's speech. In *Odyssey,* Circe might have been Marilyn Monroe—a worn substitution, but as a more generalized cinematic femme fatale, the implication became the persistence of the seductress stereotype itself.

Long popular, transposition verges on overuse, especially with Shakespeare. Too often it involves an obvious, wholesale resetting—*All's Well that End's Well* dressed Edwardian. Clever associations can also become tired quickly—witness the current prevalence of inner-city *Romeo and Juliets,* and O.J. Simpson *Othellos.* The perils of transposition are that it can remain merely cosmetic, provide an easy one-to-one correspondence, or a static equation. Moreover, it hardly seems worth the effort if it normalizes the play's otherness. After all, one of the greatest appeals of the theater is that it takes us on journeys, stretching experience and imagination. If we don't guard against the impulse to, as Gershon Shaked puts it, "translate differences to our own world of experience, . . . bring distant near, make the past present, and the incomprehensible understood,"[3] our journey may not venture past the backyard. On the other hand, extreme distance renders the original experience incomprehensible. What's a dramaturg to do? Shaked's wise counsel: "Understanding of the past, as of another culture, is a constant process . . . permitting communication . . . but . . . creating . . . misunderstanding is productive. . . . [Although] we can approach one another, some distance must remain."[4] Patrice Pavis, also on translation, advocates "effecting a compromise . . . by producing a translation that would be a 'conductor' between the two cultures and . . . cope with proximity as well as distance."[5] At its best, transposition, like translation, can bridge cultures.

RE-CONTEXTUALIZATION, INTERPOLATION, INTERRUPTION

Elements of the production text derive from the desire to contextually situate or resituate the play. My purpose in rendering "period" is not to invite the audience to lose itself in another place and time, but to regard the past as an artifact that must be processed to yield comparison and contrast, by putting it in a new context. Material found in other media—music, dance, film, historical data, custom—not only illuminates the play by supporting its intentions, but also by revealing paradoxes. I dramatize relationships to the play by staging the research, background, the context, and the juxtapositions. With *Miss Julie,* for example, I might interpolate excerpts from a treatise by Strindberg on the evils of female emancipation, or from a Scandinavian or American etiquette book by his contemporaries.

When asked to do a classic comedy, I swiftly chose *The Front Page,* too often rendered as a witty depoliticized romp. It is in fact a bitter satire that exposes a heartless appetite for catastrophe; a romanticization of professionalism where ends justify means; matter-of-fact bigotry and misogyny. Usually the journalists' racist remarks are excised, and the deprecation of female characters made incidental. Having become familiar with the lives and works of the playwrights, I knew that Ben Hecht and Charles MacArthur were neither racists nor misogynists. Though not central to the plot, criticism is implied by their frank observation of such attitudes. Hecht and MacArthur's sophisticated dramaturgy precludes easy relationships to characters, allows paradox, and makes the audience work. Our ethos has changed. Schooled by television and the oversimplification of drama, we expect the author's finger to point unwaveringly to "the bad guys." My audience might perceive characters' racist and sexist sentiments as those of the authors. Worse, and more likely, my particular audience might **not** be offended by such views, or worst still, share them.

In order to prevent this, I sought to re-contextualize the play. To effect critical distance rather than inclusion, the alienating device I exploited most was the interpolation of musical numbers. I began harmlessly enough, creating a safe, historicized haven of stereotype. Chorus cuties in revealing, spangly costumes moved in "cheesecake" hieroglyphics: lips pursed, bottoms out, hands up, mincing and squealing in celebration of Lucky Lindbergh and happily-ever-after heterosexual love. At first these extravagant period Busby Berkeley–esque numbers came at logical breaks in the action, like old-fashioned entre-actes. As the play progressed, however, the interpolations interrupted at awkward moments, disrupting scenes and moments of identification—like little mental slaps in the face. The irreconcilability of the extravaganza's racial and sexual stereotypes to the grim bigotry of the play became increasingly uncomfortable, breaking the spell of identification long enough to alienate the audience into a thinking state. The nature of the choreography became more abstract and violent. Hildy's fantasy about domestic bliss is cut short by a desexualized Apache dance of domestic violence, in chilling contrast to a megaphonic, vibrato 1920s rendition of "My Blue Heaven." Over much departmental protest, I had kept the script intact, preserving every utterance of "nigger." So that the audience would not become acclimated to the casual racism, I heightened it through a variety of means (the most obvious way would have been to cast black actors, but there were none) culminating in a flashy finale, a minstrel number performed in period-accurate blackface (illegal in New Hampshire)—equal parts Jolson and Genet.

Pulling the background into the foreground enhanced the relationship between the main plot and subsidiary concerns with gender and race. Compatible with the spirit of the play, the invented context of the 1930s musical review emphasized social criticism in the original, which might otherwise have been misperceived or overlooked. The play text remained relatively intact, but the re-contextualization altered the way in which we processed it, by dramatizing the relationship between the play and its period, and the distance between that period and our time.

Oddly enough, performing a play "intact" can also be a form of re-contextualization. If the audience for whom the play was originally intended differs substantially from the contemporary audience, then, as timeless and universal as advertising may claim the play to be, it will nonetheless be **received** differently. We might try to adapt the play so that it has an effect similar to that of the original audience, or we may **invite** a different response. For example, contemporary use of melodrama without alteration can produce an intentionally comic effect, as with the National Theatre's production of *The Voysey Inheritance*.

Re-contextualization can emphasize how changed are the sensibilities of the audience by acknowledging ideas and events to which the original audience was not privy. The performance of one of Marivaux's refined inquiries into the metaphysics of the human heart by the noble inmates in the Bastille might invite nostalgia for the lost leisure art of "delicacy," like hanging a scrap of lace on the guillotine, or it might put the luxuries of the privileged in perspective with the peasant's need for bread to survive. Viewing these complacently aristocratic plays in light of the French Revolution, which occurred a mere few decades after these plays premiered, also gives a hard edge to Marivaux's dramaturgy of "the surprise of love," with its obstacles of self-deception and pride. Re-contextualization can create an equation that productively frustrates the play's impulse by placing it in tension or irony.

What impressed me most about the way Ingmar Bergman re-contextualized *Hamlet,* was the bold certainty with which Bergman preyed upon the audience's expectations and reverence for *Hamlet* (the play and the character). While watching the play in Scandinavian, the Brooklyn Academy of Music audience automatically mouthed the lines in English. Hamlet made his entrance, a sulky, narcissistic poseur, wearing a long black duster and movie star glasses ("I vant to be alone . . ."). He sulked center stage and delivered a lengthy melodramatic sigh, the personified parody of the Melancholic Dane. The "hero" was dead before his death. During the final scene, with the palace interior filled with the requisite corpses, Horatio gave tribute to the "sweet Prince." Suddenly, tearing through the back set wall from some place external to the play, crashed several futuristic militia men with technoweapons. In stomped Fortinbras, who surveyed the corpses, gave Hamlet's a bit of a kick, and summarily ordered the execution of Horatio. Then he summoned the paparazzi and delivered his paean to he who "would have proved most royal" for the benefit of the cameras and reporters. (I stole this for Angelo, who delivered his speech, "We must not make a scarecrow of the law . . ." for the benefit of reporters.) This brutal cynicism shows a humanity so devolved that tragic heroism and transcendence are no longer possible: The tragedy was the death of the **idea** of Hamlet—the death of tragedy itself. We mourned our lost myth. Such masterful manipulation depended on deep knowledge of the play and the audience. Of course we cannot often depend on this level of literacy, but effective re-contextualization always depends on deep dramaturgical knowledge of the play, as well as of the audience's expectations and level of familiarity.

It also depends on an accurate sense of the context of current events. Our production of *Tit for Tat* opened a few weeks before the 1992 presidential election, and in the midst of vigorous national condemnation of the National Endowment for the Arts (NEA) in the name of "decency," and proselytizing about "family values" predicated on the assumption that only white Christian heterosexuals could subscribe. On the local level, Durham, New Hampshire, had just enjoyed a rash of gay-bashings, called to my personal attention when one of my students came to me covered with bruises and cuts, apologizing for having missed class.

As I began to describe, I exploited re-contextualization with *Tit for Tat* by pulling up the divisions of time. We transposed the play to "Amerka," conjuring fantasy and proximity with a scenic design reminiscent of Orwell, ancient Greece, even "Star Trek." The costuming was a strong element of the *mise en scène,* with a hodgepodge of visual reference, blending Hollywood and history, as if the cast had raided the closets of Mussolini, Francis of Assisi, Mae West, Fragonard, Barbara Bush, Tammy Faye Baker, and a few sex shops on Times Square. This was a world in which the three-piece suit or hair shirt was as fetishist as leather and cross-dressing. We created a world in which all time was concurrent—then, now, always. In this world, Shakespeare's characters could stand beside Goebbels and Anita Bryant.

As a result of our ensemble work, we created layers of re-contextualization, using interruptions and interpolations. The presence of ushers in military apparel—somewhere between Brownshirts and Boy Scouts, set the tone even before the audience entered the theater. Once in, they were scrutinized by conspicuously inconspicuous "spies" patrolling the aisles. To give the reader some sense of the audience's experience, I'll describe the show's opening:

House lights dim.

We hear a woman's officious but soothing voice over the loudspeaker: *"Citizens, welcome to the University of New Hampshire Theatre and Dance Department presentation of* Tit for Tat. *Please take your seats and remain alert during the announcements to follow. Smoking in the audi-*

torium and lobby is strictly probibited, as is the taking of photographs. Violators will be dealt with severely."

We hear Jerry Lee Lewis singing, "Somewhere Over the Rainbow," as the curtain rises on Claudio and the very pregnant Juliet, dressed pastoral Elizabethan, embracing and reciting flirtatiously Shakespeare's *Sonnet 17: "Who would believe my verse in time to come . . . If I could write the beauty of your eyes . . . and number all your graces . . . But were some child of yours alive at that time, You should live twice, in it and in my rime."* The couple is disrupted by an oncoming crowd, dressed eclectically from all periods, which clusters in all manner of couples.

Angelo, in Lutheran ascetic garb, carries a soapbox, which he sets and mounts, then delivers Dan Quayle's speech: *"We are in a war between traditional values and a cultural elite that mocks families, religion, and patriotism. They seem to think that the family is an arbitrary arrangement of people who decide to live under the same roof . . . that parents need not be married or even of the opposite sexes. . . . Let us be clear— we defend the rights of all Americans. We are for compassion and tolerance. We are after all, commanded to love our neighbor. But we do not believe that being compassionate and tolerant means abandoning our standards of right and wrong, good or bad. . . ."*

Among the onlookers is The Queen, wearing tall black boots and long black gloves, black shorts and a vest, a boa, and long cigarette holder—reminiscent of Marlene Dietrich. She studies Angelo and the crowd; some are rapt, and some self-consciously adjust their behavior to conform to Angelo/Quayle's prescriptions.

Angelo intones his closing line: *"My friends, no matter how rough the road may be, we can, and we will, never, never surrender to what is RIGHT!"*

The crowd's laughter erupts as he slinks away humiliated.

A reprise of "Somewhere Over the Rainbow."

At intervals between the scenes, the loudspeaker voice makes announcements directly to the audience, as if exploiting a public gathering to disseminate propaganda (*1984*). Perhaps the announcements relate to the new laws mandated by Angelo. Our version of those laws and proclamations were based on scientific and legal premises taken seriously in their time. For instance:

"Citizens, your attention please. The CIA is currently experimenting with the following time-honored cures for homosexuality and other sexually

deviant behavior: aversion therapy, shock therapy, castration, enhanced fecal elimination, ingesting pulverized lamb embryos, LSD, estrogen, testosterone, Kellogg's breakfast cereals, radiation therapy, lobotomy, ice baths, saltpeter, cod liver oil, the love of a good woman, and strangulation."

and:

"Citizens, your attention please. Proclamation #502 bans works of all identified as Undesirables and Un-Americans. Prohibited works must be destroyed. Violators will be prosecuted to the fullest extent of the law."

Other loudspeaker interpolations listed artists, writers, scientists and politicians who were or would have been designated "Undesirables" due to their sexual preferences. The list began during one announcement (*"Socrates, Oscar Wilde, Michelangelo, Horatio Alger ..."*), and continued during a second (*"Leonardo Da Vinci, Liberace, Rock Hudson, Shakespeare ..."*) and a third, by which time the loudspeaker voice was wearying, and even she expressed surprise at some (*"Henry David Thoreau, James I, Eleanor Roosevelt ... **Eleanor Roosevelt?"***)

During intermission, the militia wandered through the crowd, ostentatiously taking notes and directing audience members back to their seats dictatorially. When the audience was seated for the second act, some soldiers pulled protesting members from their seats and took them by force from the theater. (Shills, of course.)

Another series of interpolations built upon Claudio's incarceration. When Lucio meets the bound Claudio being dragged off to prison, he asks for what crime? (*"Murder? Theft? Buggery?"*)[6] Claudio explains it is for getting Juliet with child when not legally married to her. Before exiting, Claudio is isolated in a spot to muse *Sonnet 29:"When in disgrace with fortune and men's eyes, I all alone beweep my outcast state ... Haply I think on thee, and then ... I scorn to change my place with kings."* A spot flashes dimly on Juliet. Later prostitutes are herded into the upstage barbed-wire prison pen. Some are dressed in streetwalker apparel and some in exotica such as a see-through Puritan costume. Later still, while Billie Holiday sings a yearning version of "They're Writing Songs of Love, But Not For Me," a group of apparently gay men are herded into the pen, accompanied by epithets of *"Fag!"* A few scenes later, during Madonna's "Like a Virgin," a group of extraordinarily pregnant women are herded roughly into the cell by a blond specimen of male Aryan perfection dressed like a Nazi youth, whose *"Sieg Heil"* is perfunctorily returned by the tender-hearted Provost. Later, we interpolated a scene set to Presley's "Any Way You Want Me," of Angelo coming to meet Isabella, who is actually the disguised Mariana, his spurned fiancee. She approaches him with tenderness. He responds in kind at first, then turns her face away from him, and takes "her" from behind by force. (That's all he knows.) The scene ends in silence. The Aryan Boy Scout then hauls a screaming pregnant woman from the pen to her execution.

As I often do, I interpolated music between scenes to heighten irony and create some distance. For me, songs are like Brechtian signs, only funny. And I think in "standards." For instance, when the novice Isabella finds herself attracted to the kindly Monk, Chet Baker sings tauntingly, "It Could Happen to You," and act 1 ends with a jazzy rendition of "Something's Gotta Give."

Interpolations can also deepen matters. I interpolated Shakespeare's love sonnets as letters and monologues between and about the lovers, Claudio and Juliet. I wanted to keep the potency and purity of their feelings for each other in the front of the audience's minds, to constantly remind one and all of the wrongheadedness and violence of Angelo's convictions, and the Puritanical cruelty of Isabella. She comes to visit Claudio in prison and advises him, *"The sense of death is most in apprehension."* Claudio musters, *"Thanks, dear Isabel,"* but moments later his stoicism dissolves as he confronts his fear: *"... but to die, and to go we know not where ... 'tis too horrible ..."* and begs, *"Sweet sister, let me live."* Short on sympathy, she responds, *"O, you beast ... faithless coward ... wretch ..."* and *"Die, perish! ... fie, fie, fie!"* Exhausted, hopeless, and ashamed, Claudio weeps, giving *Sonnet 66: "Tired ... for restful death I cry ... Save that, to die, I leave my love alone."*

RESURRECTION

Michael Frayn rewrote the youthful and inferior *Platanov* as if he were the mature Chekhov; the result was *Wild Honey.* I sometimes try to imagine the un-dead playwright taking up his script from centuries before and drafting it anew, incorporating material from the intervening years. (It's impossible not to view *The Merchant of Venice* through the filter of the Holocaust, or a play about the Holocaust through the filter of Bosnia.) I borrow the great "What if" from Stanislavsky's acting training, and muse, "What if Shakespeare wrote from a contemporary vantage point? What if I put the balance of history at his disposal? Might Angelo have been advised by Jesse Helms and Hitler? Might Hildy have been gay or female?"

SIMULTANEITY

Creating a simultaneity of scenes, scripted and unscripted, can bring a similar perspective into the staging and can restore marginalized voices. When Odysseus is having his affairs, do we see Penelope simultaneously? Is she weaving in patient ignorance, or is she hurt or enraged? Where exhausted ideology has prescribed absence, we can give presence.

Using interpolations of Shakespeare's sonnets, I created a simultaneity for Claudio and Juliet. Although they disappear from the action for long periods of time and are kept separate for the duration until the last scene, I wanted to keep their true love in constant view of the audience, emphasized in contrast to lust and accusations of promiscuity, and to keep their stakes high. Often, when one was speaking, the other could be seen watching.

RIFFING

In *Tit for Tat* I enlarged upon authorial intentions, as if the play were the melody and I were jazz-riffing on the theme, with all of history as the music at my disposal. In this, I have been greatly influenced by The Irondale Ensemble's textual collidings, particularly one that riffed thematically on the outlaw motifs in *As You Like It,* so that Rosalind, Pretty Boy Floyd, and Herbert Hoover seemed equally at home in the Forest of Arden. (See the Niesen article in this volume.)

ARGUMENT

Some measure of the production text also derives from the desire to argue with the playwright. Irondale's *As You Like It* ended with Pretty Boy Floyd's exhortation to Rosalind to profit from her consciousness-raising and lead a Marxist revolution, rather than return to court. Many adapters have argued with plays by rewriting the endings, among them Charles Marowitz and Ingmar Bergman. (Sequels, too, have asked, "What happened to Nora after she slammed that door?") Like revisionist folklorists, who question the "happily-ever-after" of fairy tales, Gay Gibson Cima recommends "writing beyond the end of romance plots,"[7] which suggest marriage and procreation as sacrosanct resolution.

I, too, like to take on the playwright. Because there's no point arguing with someone for whom you have no respect, I try to render the author's views but heighten them to display their insidiousness, or give counterargument in dramatic terms. One way to accomplish this is by creating a reaction not inherent in the text. A character's sexist or racist comment can be criticized if the remark is "heard" by an onstage character of the insulted gender or race.

CROSS-GENDER CASTING

As a reader, I had always identified with Odysseus, whose resources were endlessly taxed in his effort to get home. I did not identify with Penelope, who waited. The necessity of casting real gendered bodies disrupted this identification. Being mandated a cast of six women and two men seemed at first a practical joke that would make my task impossible, but it became, as it always does, the very way into the play. I had considered casting one of the women as Odysseus. Cross-gender casting draws attention to gender construction and allows performers and audience members to cross-dream. ("Madame Bovary . . . C'est moi!" takes you only so far.) In part because *Odyssey* would tour areas where the viewers would not have read and might never read the source, I elected to cast one of the males as Odysseus. He was to be the touchstone, a traditional guide into a nontraditional world exploring gender construction. I cast a woman as the boy Telemachus and drew attention to the question, "What is it to become a man?" I emphasized imitative behavior that was not only martial—of necessity—but also increasingly insensitive to women. As Telemachus adolesces, he behaves according to his received definition of manhood, addressing his nanny rudely and dismissing his mother from the room. This behavior contrasts to Odysseus' respectful treatment of Penelope in the final scenes. The balance of the cast was female, and they played everything from the sailors to the Sirens, from animals in the forest to the elements. Here the cross-gender casting emphasized transformation and objectified gender (and species). Still, I was unable to dream through Odysseus; I was left at home to wait for him.

As with Telemachus, cross-gender casting almost inevitably examines the social construction of gender roles. This can be accomplished through exaggeration, just as productions have self-consciously exaggerated beyond credulity the stereotype of the Jew in *The Merchant of Venice* such that the characterization becomes self-critical. Over-playing gender construction can objectify and expose the ludicrousness of the sexual stereotype; a "bimbo" is revealed by her behavior and not her gender when portrayed by a masculine male. The same might apply to playing Blanche Dubois cast cross-gender.

Angelo's spurned lover Mariana was played persuasively as a woman by a man. Here the relationship between self-abnegation and gender was observed and criticized more subtly.

GENDER-REVERSAL

Reversing the gender of a character can provide a distinct stylized critical layer, or it can be inlaid naturalistically. In the case of *The Front Page,* where I changed Hildy from a male to a female, played by a woman, the examination of social or gender masks actually served to heighten the author's intention. The character's dilemma, professional ambition versus longing for a personal life, has become an issue more pertinent to the contemporary working woman. Also, for her the stakes were higher; the biological clock implies greater urgency. And the choice between her dominating boss Walter and her submissive (or at least passive–aggressive) fiancee, now called "Paul," implied a more intense conflict between worker and wife. (I toyed with the idea of retaining the gender of Hildy's lover, but decided that a lesbian lover would posit a choice between the closet and out, rather than suggesting a struggle for self-definition within a maze of mutually-exclusive received constructions of gender, relating to the work-place, *polis,* and the hearth, *oikos.*) We emphasized, to comic effect, Hildy's switching from playing a socially prescribed feminine role with Paul, and playing (and winning) by the "man's-world" rules of the newsroom. As the plot exerted escalating pressures on the character, she became increasingly unable to keep up with the required pace of change. This confusion characterized the original, but here was more pointedly comic and more profoundly costly. In locker-room mentality, the "boys" overlooked Hildy's sex by way of complimenting her. But when they made a sexist remark, they and she remembered, and the script got a tense edge it did not have before. Choosing between career, in which Hildy's gender was not equalized but denied, and marriage, which asserted her gender but suppressed her aspirations, placed her between a rock and a hard place.

Hildy was played as a woman in *His Girl Friday,* with Ben Hecht's enthusiastic approval, and a love interest between Hildy and Walter was added. In my adaptation, for a variety of reasons, I wanted to avoid this romance. Reducing the story to a romantic triangle would make the play too easy. Hildy would be choosing between two men, rather than negotiating with larger issues of self-definition, thereby trivializing the larger implications.

But something kept bothering me about the last scene. The actor playing the blustery Walter finally whined in frustration, "C'mon, can't I kiss her?" My favorite words in directing vocabulary are, "Try it;" it was right on. Walter's nature was to try any means at his disposal to achieve his end. Hildy could identify herself through her profession at the cost of sexual assertion, or through marriage at the cost of her self-sufficiency. The dynamic between the two had to threaten to become sexual, otherwise it would have been untrue to the characters, and would have meant a weak exit for Hildy. Walter had to try his last sleazy card; Hildy had to satisfy her curiosity. The kiss was about power and sex, and Hildy enjoyed it. She wasn't denying her sexual attraction, nor was she its pawn. She strode purposefully off stage without looking back, walking away from Walter, and from her determination to compete at a game which was not of her own making, and which claimed too high a price. We didn't know what she was going to do, and neither did she. (She and the play had rushed past Paul too quickly to learn who he was.) We assume that, for better or worse, Hildy will find out after the final curtain.

Walter was left onstage jarred by the kiss and by her departure. Had he been a different man, she might have stayed a colleague and perhaps a lover, equal to him in both. He picked up the phone and told the police to detain her on the pretext that she stole his watch. Other film and theater versions suggest Svengali wins. This version knew that Hildy would laugh it off and continue on her self-determined path. At the end of the play she was on the beginning of her journey of self-definition, and, like the women **and** men in the audience, would have to negotiate with and beyond social gender construction, breaking the rules and making new ones. The ending remained inconclusive, but weighed more heavily the likelihood of Hildy's self-actualization, an outcome I feel sure the resurrected Hecht and MacArthur would have condoned.

GENDER ABSTRACTION

I recently dramaturged a production of *Danton's Death,* in which the three female principals were played by one woman. The actress playing the parts approached me, complaining that this directorial concept reduced the characters to some depersonalized abstraction of women. I heartily agreed, but had no success persuading the director. It would be an interesting strategy to similarly abstract male characters, demonstrating the categorization of men by women. Of course the effect of this would be short-lived, and the abnegation of men is only slightly preferable. It might, however, persuade some that this tactic, indulged in by too many directors and playwrights, is disfiguring.

REVERSAL OF SEXUAL PREFERENCE

Of course the theater has far from held the mirror up to nature in terms of gender, race, and sexual preference. If you are a woman and neither an ingenue or femme fatale; an African-American or Latino and not a domestic; or a gay or lesbian person not dying from AIDS, then the models and loci through which to dream are few and far between in contemporary theater, and scarcely apparent in classic theater. I've tried to people such landscapes with the inhabitants of the world in which we live. For that reason I have also re-imagined Shakespeare's liberal humanism to embrace explicitly gay and lesbian couples. For instance, in *Tit for Tat,* the Duke became The Queen and her interest in Isabella remained romantic. Friar Thomas the Duke's confidante merged with the nun Francisca, who became The Queen's lover and Isabella's supervisor. Of course we had to track the implications through the script, and sometimes we were treated with delicious unforeseen ironies, as when Lucio slandered the disguised Queen, insisting he knows her personally and can vouch that she is a "strumpet" and "drunk," adding 'she has some feeling of the sport," accompanied by a lewd parodistic gesture of intercourse. The Queen/Monk replied, "She is not inclined that way." Lucio insisted that he had "inside" knowledge, and the Queen/Monk insisted "'Tis not possible." Her lesbianism added a layer of comedy to Lucio's ignorant bragging. Pathos also insinuated itself. When The Queen confided her plans (". . . see what our seemers be . . .") to her lover, the nun Francesca, whose now-open habit revealed some elaborate lingerie, the monarch's *"Believe not that the dribbling dart of love/Can pierce a complete bosom . . ."* had a sharp edge for

Francesca, who was clearly in love. The scene ended with an impending embrace, interrupted by a blackout and loudspeaker announcement:

> *"Citizens, your attention please. The newly established Clinic for the Investigation of Aberration, hence referred to as the CIA, has determined leading causes of homosexuality and other deviant behavior. The following are therefore prohibited under proclamation #468: disco music, smoking marijuana, masturbation, female teachers, and uncut meat."*

Mistress Overdone, played in drag by a large, masculine man, became a transvestite, wearing a sequin gown, boa, and blonde wig *à la* Mae West. Her pimp Pompey was played by a diminutive female in the loud plaid suit, bow tie, bowler, and moustache of the English vaudeville. Side by side they reinforced each other's unexpected size. They played their parts "straight," and made for a touching duo. When Mistress Overdone was hauled into prison, shortly after the gay men had been herded off, she, or he, appeared stripped down to a G-string, wig net, and running make-up, holding his blonde wig piteously, and protesting in a deep voice.

Claudio and Juliet remained heterosexual male and female. I had toyed with making them a gay couple, but when Dan Quayle attacked the television newswoman character "Murphy Brown" and single motherhood, while advocating "family values," Juliet's pregnancy took on an irresistibly current slant.

SHUFFLING GENDER AND PREFERENCE

The strategy and dramaturgical principle was to so shuffle sexual identities that after a while the audience could not keep track of who was "what," and stopped caring. They were compelled to experience and judge the characters on their merits, rather than on preconceived ideas.

MASKING AND UNMASKING

Like the use of metaphoric masks, actual masks can provide critical distance from stereotype. For *Odyssey,* a series of fabulous encounters with gender stereotypes, we used masks designed by my codirector, Jackie Davis, also a brilliant mask artist, inviting the audience to wonder what was beneath them. We explored the distance between the mask and the "real" character beneath, sometimes filling the space with our fanciful speculation and attribution of motives.

Penelope "played" the stoic patient wife when it suited her with the suitors, but dropped her pale, pretty inscrutable mask when she was with her son (until he began to disrespect her) or a maidservant, revealing the real and less pretty anguish of a deeply intelligent person, keeping cool in a lethal situation. When she chose to raise and lower the mask became a critical leitmotif. The moving denouement came with her painfully slow revelation when finally convinced her husband was restored. It was the person and not the mask she presented to her equal, but only after he had unmasked himself. Naked face to naked face, their acknowledging mutual gaze was an intimate satisfaction to the suspense engendered by masking.

For Circe we created layers of masks; she took one off to reveal another and then another, from femme fatale to witch to helpless girly-girl to human being. It was a virtue on the part of Odysseus that he could see through the masks of stereotype to the person underneath, conferring dignity upon Circe and earning her help.

EMPOWERING THE OPPRESSED

The attribution of strong motives to weak behavior is a challenging but profitable method of adaptation. "Channeling" the characters, we ask, "Why would I behave that way?" The three subsidiary female characters in *The Front Page* had an enormous effect on the male space.

The journalists flirted aggressively with Jenny, the cleaning lady, played as a woman of low intelligence, who was at first delighted by the attention, but later, as the treatment became more coercive, found it increasingly unpleasant. She was unable to confront her tormentors without risking the loss of her job. The men only dared to press the issue with a woman of such meager resources. Hildy would brook none of this. The social context and practical motivation emphasized class and strengthened the cleaner's motivation to exceed stereotype.

The actor playing the prostitute Molly Malloy projected exceptional intelligence, determination, and moral courage—without a trace of the helpless desperation and romanticization usually given her. She stepped out of the window to save the criminal, Earl, not as an hysteric but as Joan of Arc.

Mrs. Schlosser, the neglected wife, who comes to the newsroom in search of her errant husband, was brutally ignored as the men closed ranks to protect their mate by trying to make her the butt of the ancient wife joke. Undeterred, she confronted them one by one, forcing each to acknowledge her before each one turned away in shame. Her rage heralded some decline in sexist disparagement. In both cases, their weak "feminine" behavior was adapted to a position of strength.

ADMITTING THE VICTIM

Sometimes "as-is" depiction of stereotype, uncomfortable as it can be, provides frank observation. The strategy then can be to embrace the archetype with empathy. The actress playing Calypso in *Odyssey*, a brilliant student and committed feminist, resisted the character at every turn. We used improvisation to reach the pain underneath the resistance. It was agonizing to watch her strip away self-reliance and dignity, become absolutely vulnerable, with self-worth utterly dependent on the reciprocation of a man's love. This is not a gender-specific place, but historically it has been feminized; I do not wish it on my female children. The resulting performance was one of a pathetic character who begged the rejection of Odysseus and the audience. Compassionate understanding of stereotype does not preclude critical viewing. It felt brave and difficult to admit the Calypso in ourselves (as it was with Mariana in *Tit for Tat*), to acknowledge that self-abnegation and servile love win neither respect nor affection, and to allow the audience to share in discomfort.

Similarly, it was difficult for me to stage the reconciliation scene between Penelope and Odysseus. They climbed into their special bed and exchanged stories about their decade of separation; she recounted her adventures with her suitors while he enumerated his extramarital sexual encounters—some happy ending. Excising this would have been cheap and untrue to the characters; they would be frank with each other. We could have allowed the audience to feel alienated by the implied blissful resolution, painting Penelope as contented hearer. Instead, I allowed Penelope to hear as I would have, creating a tension between the happy ending experienced by Odysseus and the unvoiced but apparent pain of his wife.[8]

CONCLUSION, SORT OF . . .

In lieu of a conclusion, I'd like to end this brief catalogue with another excerpt from the narrated production script of *Tit for Tat,* in the hope of giving the reader a sense of the audience's experience. For, in the end, that is what the strategizing, analysis, and research must serve.

> Enter the "zannis": George and Barbara Bush, Jim and Tammy Faye Baker, Jerry Falwell, Dan and Marilyn Quayle, Pat Robertson, Anita Bryant, and Hitler, all in colorized, but clownishly accurate apparel. The "Laugh-In" style intercut monologues, all verbatim quotes,[9] are performed as persuasive imitations:

> **HITLER:**

> Art must be cleansed from all manifestations of our rotting world . . .

> **DAN:**

> Like so many Americans, family comes first . . .

FALWELL:

The NEA funded blasphemous art of Jesus and Lazarus in a homosexual embrace . . .

DAN:

When family values are undermined, the country . . . er . . . suffers!

FALWELL:

. . . kissing . . .

HITLER:

There must be no art for art's sake. Art must be popular . . .

FALWELL:

I must ask you to make an emergency gift of $5 to battle the NEA disgrace . . .

HITLER:

Politics, too, is art . . .

FALWELL:

I don't think Jesus of Nazareth was a sissy at all . . .

JIM:

I confessed my sins.

FALWELL:

I think he was a he-man baked by the Eastern sun, and I think his body was all wrapped in muscles from hard work.

TAMMY:

GOD!

FALWELL:

In my age we laughed at queers and fairies.

TAMMY:

I gotta talk to you.

JIM:

It was an isolated incident!

TAMMY:

It's about the guinea pig. You see, we tried dogs and they wet on the carpet, and our cats ran away . . . so I asked you what would be just right, and I thought I heard you say, "A guinea piiig. . . ."

DAN:

In these difficult times . . . America needs the very best. P-O-T-A-T-O-MMM
(Marilyn slaps her hand over Dan's mouth without even looking at him.)

The crowd and principals join the zanni behind police barricades to await The Queen, then fall to their knees upon her entrance. She soon leaves on an errand. The "Monk" returns and is unwittingly unmasked by Lucio. She greets Isabella, *"Your father is now your Queen—not changing heart with habit."* Isabella is doubly amazed. Angelo is exposed, rejoined with his wronged fiancee Mariana, and condemned to death—*"measure for measure."* Isabella begs mercy for him. The Queen lovingly wipes the tears from Isabella's cheeks. The revived Claudio embraces his sister, and they are joined by Juliet and the baby. The Queen proposes to Isabella, *"Give me your hand and say you will be mine."* Long pause. The novice slowly removes her veil and takes The Queen's hand. As a finishing touch, The Queen compels Lucio to marry Kate Keep-down, who rushes on in a garish wedding dress, shouting *"OH! O,O,O,O . . . ";* he pleads for death. The cast turns to the audience, and The Queen leads *Sonnet 116,* with each cast member speaking a line or phrase, following seamlessly as if one voice:

> *"Let me not to the marriage of true minds*
> *Admit impediments; love is not love*
> *Which alters when it alteration finds . . .*

It is the star to every wand'ring bark,
Whose worth's unknown, although his height be taken . . .
Love alters not with his brief hours and weeks,
But bears it out even to the edge of Doom. . . . "

Over the loudspeaker we hear a man's sonorous voice—perhaps Shakespeare's—and the cast looks up: *"If this be error and upon me proved/I never writ, nor no one ever loved."* (We changed "no man" to "no one.") The actors turn to each other as the stage transforms into a Roseland ballroom, with a glittering mirror ball and Dionne Warwick singing "It's Very Clear, Our Love Is Here to Stay." Isabella takes The Queen's proffered hand and they lead couples and triples of all types into a waltz, celebrating diversity and romance.

The curtain falls, then rises. The actors take their curtain call to the dreamy strains of Judy Garland's "Somewhere Over the Rainbow." A blonde debutante, dressed as Miss New Hampshire in red, white, and blue spangles, enters upstage to fanfare and gestures Vanna White–style to a large sign of lights. It says the New Hampshire slogan, "LIVE FREE OR DIE!" Then it flashes "VOTE!"

Foreign Drama in Translation:
Some Reflections on Otherness, Xenophobia, the Translator's Task, and the Problems They Present
by **Carl Weber**

Carl Weber was an assistant director to Bertolt Brecht, an actor, and a dramaturg at the Berliner Ensemble from 1952–56, and then a director, actor, and dramaturg with the company until 1961. In 1966, after being a resident director and dramaturg with theaters in West Germany, while also directing in the United States and Scandinavia, he joined the faculty of New York University School of the Arts, at which he chaired the directing department, 1971–83. He has directed in New York at Lincoln Center, the Brooklyn Academy of Music, American Place Theater, Off- and Off-Off Broadway as well as at regional theaters such as Washington's Arena Stage, Yale Repertory Theatre, and Princeton's McCarter. Since 1984, he has served as the Professor of Directing and Dramaturgy at Stanford University. He has published numerous essays in *The Brecht Yearbook, The Cambridge Companion to Brecht, Performing Arts Journal, The Drama Review, Theater Journal, Theater Heute,* and other books and journals. He edited and translated three volumes of Heiner Müller's writings and an anthology *Drama Contemporary: Germany.* At present he is preparing a fourth volume of Müller's works.

When we compare the repertoire of theaters in the United States with that of their counterparts in countries of a comparable theater culture, one feature immediately catches the attention: the relatively small number of plays in translation performed in the United States versus the numerous productions of translated foreign drama in other countries. Translations constitute, at best, 25 percent of the American repertoire. In the German-language theater, for one, more than 50 percent of the plays presented each season are in translation, and the repertoire spans theater history, from the Greeks to contemporary authors such as Ayckbourn, Boal, Bond, Dorfman, Fo, Fugard, Havel, Koltes, Kushner, Mamet, Mishima, Mrozek, Petrushevskaya, Pinter, and so forth. If a new play attracts attention anywhere in the world it will, as a rule, be produced in translation by an Austrian, German, or Swiss theater the following season.[10] Elsewhere in Europe we discover a similar situation, from Lisbon to Moscow and points farther east. A Russian translator recently told me that five productions of plays by Tennessee Williams had competed on Moscow stages during the same season—even before the implosion of the Soviet system eliminated any cold-war restrictions of the repertoire. Could we imagine anything like that happening with the plays of Chekhov and Gorki in New York or Chicago? With all due respect to the achievement of American playwrights in the twentieth century, it can hardly be claimed that their work is in every respect superior to that of their foreign colleagues writing from the fifth century B.C.to the present. What, then, is it that has made the American theater so comparatively inhospitable to the drama of other cultures, past or present?

The question has always been a vexing one, and though most American theater artists would vehemently deny that they are xenophobes, they often seem to shy away from presenting plays that are not firmly rooted in the Anglo-American tradition. This phenomenon is the more amazing because they live in the most ethnically "mixed" nation on earth, and one that continues to assimilate immigrants from every culture of the globe. Even if today's multicultural climate has encouraged Americans to re-discover their "roots" and cultivate their ethnic heritages, the number of plays representing those "root" cultures has not increased noticeably on the country's professional stages. American theater culture appears to have internalized a deeply imbued xenophobic attitude, a discomfort with plays in translation that is quite evident but rarely admitted. A number of reasons may have contributed to such an attitude during past history. The manifest desire of the young Union to turn its back to Europe and its Old-World corruption and decadence could well be one of them. There also is the increasing dominance of English as the global language of economy, technology, and popular culture that has pushed most other languages into a somewhat inferior status and probably also diminished the respect for their literatures, if on a rather subconscious level.

The theater's reluctance to embrace the "other" may quite simply be due to the fear of alienating its paying audience, given its assumption that Americans are averse to the unfamiliar and don't appreciate narratives and characters with which they cannot immediately identify. European audiences are usually curious about foreign cultures. Eager to explore the unfamiliar, they are intrigued by "otherness." This fascination with the "exotic" may be traced back to the time of the crusades; it grew steadily since the Renaissance, in step with the rise of colonialism and the growth of a world market. The enormous success of literary narratives that described far away countries and their strange populations is proof of this European fascination. Take the Elizabethan and Jacobean theater, for instance: it used translated or adapted material of foreign origin in abundance, functioning quite like a telescope that offered its audience a view of other peoples' cultures and mores, even as the lens would grossly distort the objects presented.

The American audience, in contrast, appears to have always preferred a look inward at themselves, adopting what amounts to a cultural Monroe Doctrine. As a result, only a few major American writers and poets became interested in translating and/or adapting plays from foreign languages. There were, of course, noteworthy exceptions. Ezra Pound and Thornton Wilder come to mind or, in more recent years, Arthur Miller, Paul Schmidt. David Mamet, Eric Overmyer, Richard Nelson and Tony Kushner. But they are the exceptions. If we look at German literature, for example, we will find that, beginning with Schiller, the best poets and dramatists maintained a tradition of translating or adapting plays from the non-German repertoire. There were, for instance, the poets Schlegel and Tieck who, with several collaborators, translated all of Shakespeare in the early nineteenth century and thus made the Bard the most performed playwright in the German language. Georg Büchner translated Victor Hugo, Grillparzer adapted Calderon. In our century, Brecht and his collectives of collaborators, as well as Heiner Müller, Peter Hacks, Peter Handke and other successful playwrights, have done translations and adaptations. Highly talented writers often devote themselves nearly exclusively to the art of translating. A look at the British theater shows us that names like Howard Brenton, Christopher Hampton, Tom Stoppard, or Timberlake Wertenbaker appear on the playbills of translated or adapted foreign plays.

The theater culture, which supported these writers and is conducive to the performance of translated plays, depends on the subsidized theater system that is shared by all of the European countries, at latest since World War II. The American theater has never enjoyed any support by the body politic that is even remotely comparable to the subsidies granted to the Central and Eastern European or Scandinavian theaters. As long as producing an unfamiliar foreign play is regarded as a somewhat hazardous enterprise, many a theater would rather present the tried and true instead of risking an unpredictable reaction of audiences as well as critics and the resultant low box office sales. American professional theater practice rarely encourages authors to spend time and energy on translation, since the prospect of adequate remuneration is slim.

The academic theater departments with their multitude of stages all over the country present each year a considerable number of new and classic plays from the international repertoire, and many translators are subsidized in kind by their teaching salaries. Nevertheless, the academic repertoire is still dominated by plays from the Anglo-American tradition. "Departments [don't] want to do anything that might alienate audiences, university officials, or funding sources."[11]

It is not the economic aspect alone, however, that accounts for the modest number of translations produced. There also appears to be an "ideological" reason, a result of the prevailing philosophy of acting and actor training in the United States. Assumptions about the actor's art are widely accepted that do not encourage curiosity about foreign cultures and their performance traditions. Improvisation, that is using the actor's personal mode of expression, is recommended as one of the most effective ways of exploring character and plot. Some acting coaches instruct their students that "the text is your enemy," many admonish them that their "stage character" should elicit the spectators' empathy. The still-dominant tenet of "psychological realism" demands a performance that is "real" and "believable" and brings the character as close to the audience's own perceptions as possible. Many of these approaches and techniques have their merit, of course, and should be part of any acting training, but they tend to ignore other paradigms of acting and favor a dramatic literature that is easily accessible and close to home. Poetic language, texts employing a physical performance mode, and many other so-called "nonrealistic" techniques required by the international repertoire, cannot be mastered by actors with such limited training. The prevailing education and practice of actors privileges the performance of American plays on American topics or, at best, of such foreign plays that articulate the experience of specific segments of the American audience. Actors trained in psychological realism and improvisation are useful to television and film, but less for the demands of the wide variety of literary styles we find in foreign drama, classic or contemporary.

Such a repertoire is also hardly supported by an audience that grew up with a daily dose of television—the barrage of rapidly changing images, stereotyped narratives, and a temporal format that rarely exceeds half an hour while constantly being interrupted by commercials. Viewing television has greatly diminished the audience's capacity to appreciate the comparatively slow progress and length of stage plays, the attention demanded by the narratives and complex metaphoric language of classic as well as contemporary texts. With actors trained in a naturalistic acting style, and spectators who acquired their viewing habits in front of a television set, we need not wonder that many directors and dramaturgs in the professional theater have lost the confidence to explore a foreign repertoire that may overtax their actors' training as much as their audience's perception. The problem appears to be less acute in the academic theater. Yet, even in this rather sheltered realm, audiences are often reluctant to attend plays whose title or author are unfamiliar—a fact that cannot but influence faculty and students' choices of plays.

The American theater's preoccupation with a dramatic literature that is uniquely "American" is demonstrated by the multitude of foundations, earmarked endowment funds, awards, and playwriting contests devoted to the promotion of "new American" plays. The few institutions that actively support the translation of foreign drama can be counted on the fingers of one hand. Published translations are consequently in their majority the work of academic scholars who specialize in the original text's language and literature. There is certainly good reason to be grateful for their efforts; without them many foreign playwrights would never have come to any attention outside of foreign language departments.

But a solid scholarly translation is not necessarily a good text for the stage, and many a translation has created the unfortunate impression that the respective play is not particularly stageworthy. Furthermore, such texts usually premier at a college or university theater, and when a theatrically weak script may meet an equally weak production team, the result will hardly do justice to a play's true potential. On the other hand, the academic theater frequently does foreign authors a great service, as the examples of Brecht, Büchner, Frisch, Havel, and Mrozek, for instance, have shown. These writers received their first American production on a college or university stage and consequently were picked up by the professional theater. Still, few of the many translated plays premiered on university stages have achieved a permanent place in the repertoire of the professional theater.

The position of non-English drama in the American theater is indeed a precarious one. What strategies might be pursued, then, to improve this sorry state of affairs? Or is there actually neither need nor reason to promote work from other cultures in the American theater? The argument has been made that any theater should address itself foremost, if not exclusively, to issues that are of urgent concern to the community and audience for which it performs. True enough, this has always been one of the theater's most important missions. But there also is the theater's power of opening new perspectives, new insights and vistas of the world at large, that raise an audience's view above and beyond the parochial realm of their quotidian life. The audience ought to have occasion of seeing the riches foreign cultures have to offer, so that the "other" will be better understood and, in all its otherness, be appreciated for its affinity with the audience's own experience, shedding a new light on the concerns the spectators are struggling with in their lives.

There are many good reasons to broaden the repertoire of the American theater, and the burden of such an enterprise rests first of all with dramaturgs and writers who would be interested in doing translations and adaptations for the stage. Their task is quite different from the one translators of nondramatic literature have to master. Of course, like any translation of literature, translated drama should try for poetic qualities that come close to those of the original—an ideal rarely attainable to perfection, alas. It is also evident that the meaning—that elusive essence—of the foreign text needs to be captured as precisely as possible while being made fully comprehensible in the new language's own logic. The way drama translations differ from those of other literary forms is determined by their intended use: play texts are to be spoken, and not merely spoken but acted. They only come to life when performed by actors for an audience.

There are several conditions the translation of a dramatic text needs to meet, beyond the quality of language and the clear communication of meaning. The most obvious one is that the construction of sentences has to comfortably "fit" the actors' mouth, their instrument of speech. Tongue-breaking syntax, phonetically cumbersome words, and whatever else may obstruct the fluent articulation of a spoken line simply won't do—except, of course, when such obstacles of speech have a dramaturgic function in the play's texture—as, for instance, when a stage character's utterance is meant to confuse his or her antagonist by using convoluted or obfuscating language. Another requirement is that the spoken text should have a "flow," a rhythm and tonality that correspond to the original's rhythms and sounds as closely as may be achieved within the various innate patterns of the English language. It is, for instance, of importance how a line in the source text scans, and how closely the translation can approximate the original line's number of words and metric pattern.

It is absolutely crucial that the meaning of each spoken line be grasped by the audience in the flash of a second and by ear only, however fast and eccentrically the actors may deliver their text. A line that is not properly understood will immediately disrupt the spectators' attention. The moment they spend on puzzling over what has just been said will take their mind away from the play's unfolding narrative. They will lose some of the context and may not again fully engage their attention in the performance. The clear verbal expression of everything a line is supposed to communicate, in all its associative layers, is also of the essence. Appropriate idiomatic terms and turns of speech in English have to be found, wordings that provide an equivalent to the original's layered meaning but may sometimes veer far away from a literally correct rendering of the source text. The more complex the meaning to be conveyed the more immediately graspable the translation must be. Striving for instant intelligibility may entail using irregular grammar, slang, contemporary advertising slogans, popular idioms, and comparable catch phrases.

What should be strictly curbed, however, is the penchant to use the colloquial and vernacular for their own sake. As much as the text's meaning ought to be instantly grasped, there is no gain in stripping it completely of its foreign flavor. As much as the translation should try to make the "other" understood, it should not reduce that otherness to the point where it disappears. Part of the audience's enjoyment of a foreign play is the discovery of all that they may have in common with the play's world while still clearly recognizing it as a foreign world. A thought of Brecht applies here, that distancing the familiar—by way of showing its counterpart in a foreign culture—will defamiliarize and problematize it, so it will be opened to new insights and intervention. The audience should not merely believe, "These stage characters and their conflicts, that's us!" but rather conclude, "These characters have to cope with life's vicissitudes as we do, but they do it in their own, quite different way and that raises questions about our ways to cope!" The audience should be enabled to identify with the play's characters and at the same time clearly perceive their otherness. It is the translator who facilitates or impedes such a response. Only later in the process will the actors, the director, and the designers assume much of that responsibility when they create the complex system of visual, verbal, and other signifiers that constitute a performance.

Rehearsals will quickly demonstrate if the translator has accomplished one of the more difficult tasks in transposing a play from one culture or language to the other. As soon as the actors begin to delineate their stage characters, move by move and line by line, it will become evident if the translation supports or inhibits the creation of an appropriate "gestus," to employ Brecht's term for the totality of all the physical and vocal markers that define a character's "persona" on stage, at a given moment as well as for the entire play. As long as the translated text does not offer the speech pattern, rhythms, inflections, and tonality that facilitate the desirable character gestus, the actors won't be able to "make it work." They either may protest or simply improvise and rephrase the text according to personal preference, for better or for worse. The translator needs to pay close attention to the gestic content of every single line in the source text and try to approximate it as closely as the new language will permit. Brecht, when preparing the English text for the American production of *Galileo* in 1947, worked more than a year with the actor Charles Laughton who was to play the lead. Brecht read to Laughton a literal rendering of each line's meaning in English, and then Laughton paraphrased and enacted numerous versions of the line, moving and acting out physical details while Brecht watched. Only when the playwright was satisfied with the actor's gestus in delivery of the line, did he inscribe that version into the English text. This was, of course, an enormously time-consuming process that included repeated revisions of text that had before been accepted as "final."

Working this way with actors in rehearsal is of great advantage, yet the time limits imposed by prevailing production schedules rarely allow for it. Nonetheless, the translator should be present during rehearsal, ready to rewrite lines whenever the desired acting gestus cannot be achieved. Either the director or the actors may point this out, although the translator also ought to be able to spot the problem. It's clearly better for the translator to participate actively in the rehearsal process than to allow a practice during which the actors at random change lines that do not work for them. Whenever the translator cannot attend rehearsal, a dramaturg should take on the task or, better still, share it with the director. Dramaturgs should be trained as translators and adaptors, as all translators need experience as working dramaturgs.

It is during this part of the process that director, dramaturg, and translator would conduct a continuous exchange of thoughts and suggestions, closely collaborating toward what will become the conclusive text for the performance. I am stressing "for the performance" because, in a perfect world, a translation would be adapted for each new production of the text. Another cast of actors will bring a different set of personalities to the play, and the new actors' personal gestus won't articulate with the text in the same manner as that of their predecessors in previous productions, nor is the new target audience of similar composition. Such a practice of recurrent rewriting may raise issues of authorship and textual integrity but, as mentioned earlier, a play does not live on the printed page. A translation will succeed artistically as well as communicate effectively only if the acted lines and their appropriate gestus will be instantly comprehended. Any translation offers merely one among the numerous potential readings of the source text and thus will always invite reinterpretation.

These considerations all point out that a translation for the stage cannot be considered a definitive text. It remains open to intervention because it serves as an outline rather than a precise prescription. T. S. Eliot said that any translation of poetry or drama should be made anew every ten years. Even within the short span of a decade, language—that living organism of communication—will change, grow some new limbs while others wither. Aged translations rarely speak with their former clarity and effect to audiences of later decades. It is, of course, practically unheard of that plays are newly translated every ten years. As a rule theaters must make do with translations that are considerably older than merely a decade.

If a new translation cannot be commissioned for reasons of finance, schedules, and so forth, director and dramaturg should carefully sift through the available translations and select the most desirable one. Often a thorough revision of the text may be needed, ideally in collaboration with the original translator. It may well be that a translation from a time close to, or of, the source text's period, if sensibly revised, will be more useful than a later translation that is marked by the translator's ideology of another historical moment, as any translation is prone to be. For a production of Molière's *The Miser*, which I directed at Lincoln Center's Beaumont Theater in 1969, I looked with the dramaturg, the late Susan Bloch, at all versions available. We decided on a text from the early eighteenth century because it came closer to the original's gestus than any of the later translations. The old British authors clearly understood the sensibility of Molière's age, which for them was as recent as the 1930s for us. During rehearsal, a certain amount of rephrasing and updating the language had to be done, of course. The final performance text was fully comprehensible for our contemporary audience, yet it retained a distinct period flavor that supported a corresponding gestus of the actors that, being a far cry from the still frequently employed convention of precious behavior and silly flourishes, came rather close to the acting mode that would be seen in Ariane Mnouchkine's 1976 film *Molière*.

It goes without saying that any translation cannot but reflect the translator's ideological stance, even when a conscious effort had been made to avoid this. Internalized ideology will have guided choices such as the specific phraseology and the shaping of the characters' verbal gestus, leading to the inevitable, if unintended, spin the new text will add to the source's pattern of meaning. If this holds true for the script with which a production starts, it certainly applies to the final text of performance after the collaborative interpretations of the director, the actors, and the designers have all been folded into the production and are watched by an audience of which every single member will respond according to his or her individual ideological stance. As the French translator Francois Regnault pointed out, "The translation presupposes first of all the subordination of the *mise en scène* to the text, so that—at the moment of the *mise en scène*—the text in turn is subordinated to theater."[12]

Of course, any play in performance has passed through several interpretative screens, be the spoken text by the original author or by a translator. Nonetheless, translation is perhaps the most stringent of these ideological filters; it will pass only what the translator's mind will agree to. We might conclude then that we always should think in terms of adaptation instead of translation, and that all translating for the stage ought to be scrutinized for its ideological bias.

After all has been written, staged, and performed, even when a translation tried hard to correctly render the source text's meaning and successfully created an effective gestus and a language that could be spoken "trippingly on the tongue," there will always remain the unbridged cultural gap between the original and the translated text. Each culture breeds language under the conditions of history with its never-ceasing shifts and changes, and each culture's language and theater are created by a different history. There never can be a total alignment with or unconditional understanding of the "other." What might and should be achieved is the discovery of all things that do align with the spectators' own culture, and thus will create respect for the other's values. This task appears more important than ever in a moment of history when peoples and cultures are becoming increasingly fractured, alienated, and deeply hostile to each other. The American theater ought to join the fight against this pernicious trend of our historical moment. Toward this end, the American theater should do more than it has done in the past to attract and actively support adaptors and translators who provide stageworthy versions of foreign drama. .

An additional problem that needs help: translated plays first of all must appear in print to come to the attention of stage directors, dramaturgs, managers of theaters and, of course, a general readership interested in dramatic literature. If the American theater has been less than enthusiastic in its efforts of promulgating foreign drama, American publishing appears even more negligent. With the exception of a few houses, such as PAJ Publications, Grove Press, Johns Hopkins, and other university presses, Farrar Straus & Giroux, plus a few more, American publishers apparently see little advantage in publishing plays in translation. If at least some of the numerous institutions committed to the support of playwriting would also offer financial assistance to translations, they might encourage publishers to put foreign drama into print. They might then expect some form of subsidy complementing the comparatively modest sales. Not only should university drama departments present more foreign plays, but the various language departments should strongly encourage the study of drama, providing thus another incentive to publish translations. At present, many a good translation has never become widely available to interested theaters and has been staged only once or twice, if at all. Some of the leading regional companies might feasibly commission and premiere a new adaptation or translation in collaboration with a publisher—a small desktop operation, for instance—who would then put the book on the market.

It would be desirable to create two versions of a text, one as performed, the other one intended for reading and academic studies, and make both versions available in print for scholars and general readers as well as the theater community, respectively. Few publishers, however, would consider two editions of the same work. The published version usually must arrive at a compromise, presenting the literal meaning of the source text as closely as possible while rendering it in a way that is actable and true to gestus. As with any compromise, sacrifices must be made on both sides to achieve a reasonable balance. In my opinion, a translation should rather privilege a text's performance value instead of the absolutely accurate elaboration of the original's intricacies. The latter may be taken care of by annotation and introductory remarks. A play needs to first capture and then engage the audience's or reader's attention, and this requisite should guide all of the translator's choices. For instance, it is often preferable to devise a new title if a literal translation of the original one would sound obscure or confusing to the American reader or spectator. The new title should clearly convey the gist of the source's topic. When I translated Heiner Müller's early text *Der Lohndrücker,* I chose for the English title *The Scab,* which offers Americans an immediate clue to the play's topic and its protagonist's predicament.[13]

Operating in a field that is both of the theater and of academe, which touch as much as they are separate, the adaptor or translator can hardly avoid displeasing either the theater practitioner or the scholar. On the other hand, negotiating their divergent and often contentious concerns presents an invigorating challenge.

Having discussed some of the problems the translator's craft must contend with in our contemporary culture, I would like to close by freely paraphrasing a remark Brecht once made about the classics' relevance in his own historical moment: A translated play is of true merit only if it can speak lucidly to a contemporary audience and articulate with its experience and the actual reality the audience is living in. Neither the pedantically pure text nor one that recklessly panders to the audience will suffice. Brecht also held that the theater's "task is to entertain the children of the scientific age, and to do so with sensuousness and humor."[14]

This advice applies to translated drama and the act of translating, too. Raymond Chandler, whom Brecht much admired, insisted, "A writer who hates the actual writing, who gets no joy out of the creation of magic by words, to me is simply not a writer at all."[15] Translators who are not excited by playing with language, do not enjoy exploring a foreign text into every nook and cranny of its multiple meanings, take no pleasure in the rehearsal process by which script becomes performance text, better should pursue some other endeavor. Translating, like acting, designing and directing, must be a true delight to its practitioners or it won't well serve the theater.

The Dramaturg and the Irrational

by Jayme Koszyn

JAYME KOSZYN has been the Literary Associate for the Huntington Theatre Company since 1988, where she has functioned as production dramaturg, adviser, and program annotator for more than thirty productions. As a Boston-based director, Ms. Koszyn has staged the city's premieres of *Sight Unseen* by Donald Margulies, *This Way to the Gas, Ladies and Gentlemen* by Tadeusz Borowski and Barbara Blatner, *Medea* by Georg Benda (with conductor Christopher Hogwood), and her play *The Paradise,* which had its premiere at the Huntington in 1995. She teaches directing, script analysis, and theater history on the faculties of Boston University and Boston College. Ms. Koszyn is a graduate of Princeton University.

Literature is for our immediate happiness and for the awakening of more literature; and the life of it lies in the very seed and kernel of the grain. Footnotes and critical information attack the creative instinct. The spirit is daunted, if tongue-tied by them. Many a lad has known less about Shakespeare after a college course on Shakespeare than he did when the only phrase he knew was "Aroint thee, witch,"—and he didn't know where that came from. Now he can write the etymology of the words on an examination paper; the witch herself has vanished. Information is an enemy to poetry. If the old Greeks had known as much about Achilles as we do, the **Iliad** *would never have been written....* [16]

Dramaturgs may balk at this quotation from John Jay Chapman, so possessive are we of our function as the "etymologists" of a given play. We begin our research and relentless analysis with the noble intention of bridging the gap between our world and that of the play, with its mysteries—its very life blood—all too often becoming the casualties. How can dramaturgs resist the desire to answer the unanswerable? How can we, while maintaining that information may be an enemy to poetry, reverse the charm and prevent the witch from vanishing?

Nietzsche writes in *The Birth of Tragedy* about Apollo and Dionysus, the two "art-sponsoring" deities whose "two creative tendencies developed alongside one another, usually in fierce opposition, each by its taunts forcing the other to more energetic production . . . until at last . . . the pair accepted the yoke of marriage and, in this condition, begot Attic tragedy, which exhibits the salient features of both parents." [17] If there are two spheres of expression—Apollo and Dionysus—the dramaturg has dwelled in the former. By calling themselves "script doctors," researchers, the "conscience of the theater," dramaturgs have overdeveloped their Apollonian muscles, often relegating themselves to the mere realm of the intellectual and the rational.

To distinguish between the Apollonian and Dionysian spheres within the rehearsal process may be helpful. To operate in the Apollonian mode is to cast oneself in the role of light shedder and answerer by charting the cause-and-effect relations within the play's structure, action, and characters. It is to emphasize recognizable forms, trace signposts along an often linear path, grasp what is tangible, intellectual, and knowable. Apollonian dramaturgs have an appetite for control, and if they do not know exactly what the play is about and where it is headed, they will tend to have a vivid, prescriptive map in their heads of its landscape.

To be Dionysian is to relinquish control. It is to hurl oneself heartlong into strangeness. It is to give in to fate, to chance. Even though Nietzsche defines Apollo as the dream guide, the Dionysian state is also a dream state—not the Freudian dream state, with its recognizable iconography, but of dreams that defy interpretation. The dramaturg as Juliet of the Spirits. It is to jettison all of the best-laid plans for rehearsal. To be Dionysian is to be anarchic, chaotic. It is to avoid answers, as answers are anathema to that which we cannot know and therefore need art to articulate. Uncannily, the Dionysian dramaturg intuits that within the chaos a deeper order can emerge, an organizing principle that gloriously transcends standard notions of structure, whether it be the structure of a play or rehearsal process. Above all, to be Dionysian is to succumb to the body through dance, the soul through music.

I first learned to "trust Dionysus" while serving as dramaturg for Euripides' *Iphigenia in Aulis and Tauris,*[18] which was presented during the Huntington Theatre Company's 1991 season. Initially, I approached the process with a Stanislavski-through-Clurman rationale, because this mode of working seemed best suited to this production, which was rooted in family drama. By finding psychologically grounded motivations for the actors, we hoped that their feeling of alienation from this difficult text might dissolve. At the time, this approach seemed to bridge the gap between the ancient world and the actors, many of whom had never performed in a Greek tragedy before. The common language among this diverse group was the language of Stanislavski, that of "beats and objectives"—the standard realistic/psychological lexicon. Although I knew that this manner of unraveling *Iphigenia* might be inappropriate for the choral sequences, which stand outside time, place, and mind, it was at least a way into the maze. Little did I know at this time that something wondrous was at the maze's center, a mysterious monster that was in grave danger of being domesticated.

Director Tazewell Thompson and I outlined what I now perceive as external goals: to provide the actors with a thorough background of the Greek myths and Homeric allusion; to discover a truthful acting style without muting the operative charge of the Euripidean aria and choral ode; and to find a strategy for reducing the seemingly insuperable differences between our audiences and the play's original spectators who attended the theater with shared references and expectations. These objectives were knitted together by the notion that *Iphigenia*'s secrets could be revealed through the idea of the family drama. We were applying our traditions and methodology to an alien world.

Within the winding gyre that is the director–dramaturg relationship, in which the inner and outer strands are sometimes indistinguishable, it is often difficult to pinpoint the true distinctions between the functions of each. The dramaturg must be in the service of the director's vision of the play, to perceive it through the same lens, yet at the same time question the very nature of the seeing. (Ed. note: For further discussion of this issue see, among others, Haring-Smith, Preston/Coppenger and Mazer in this volume.) While experimenting with ways to help directors find the best means for communicating onstage the story they are trying to tell, including research and consulting on *mise en scène,* the dramaturg often floats on the edge of paradox, supporting while questioning and defying. It is the dialectical function of one who must, ultimately, defer to the image of the play that the director upholds. And at times, as was the case with my work on *Iphigenia,* this paradox is most clearly unwound during the course of rehearsal, when all of the creative participants distinguish from amongst the babel of voices one pure melody—the "style" of the play and its production.

In order to find personal, realistic analogs for the actors, with the family drama as the crossover genre, I developed a list of questions that I hoped would be planks of the bridge we were building between then and now. All were part of what I have come to call the "Magic If" of dramaturgy, a simple key to opening up even the most inaccessible plays: What are the questions that the play asks, and how can we ask the same questions of ourselves? For *Iphigenia,* those questions included: What is sacrifice? What is a community of women, and how do its members behave? When have I reconnected with a loved one? When have I chosen career over family? What is my experience with broken bonds? With betrayal? When have I grappled with the conflict between loyalty to myself and loyalty to the greater good? Each of these questions had the potential to open up a channel between the director and the text, the actor and the character, the then and the now.

Although this form of bridging eventually did bring us closer to the issues of the play, they were ultimately facile and reductive. I was still wrestling the glorious minotaur into its mundane form—naturalizing the Greek world rather than firing our own with its grandeur. I found that I had to learn to "think Greek" in order to find connections between that universe and this one; to communicate these to the director and cast, I had to dream on that universe. My guide came in the form of classicist Herb Golder, a Boston University professor who was willing to share his knowledge of the classical world with me—knowledge that embraced insoluble mysteries. Under his influence, supported by recommended readings, the search for the Greek world's etymology began to lose primacy in favor of its deeper secrets.

Dr. Golder and I started with the question of whether Greek tragedy is ever successfully received by a modern audience. He cited Lee Breuer's *Gospel at*

Colonus[19] as most closely achieving the ideal relationship between a classical text and contemporary audiences, because gospel music embodies an indigenous American art with a spiritual base. The modern audience that attended the *Gospel* was unified, like the Greek audience, by a collective context. Fifth-century theater spectators shared an urge—if unconscious—for self-knowledge, an urge reflected in the plays themselves. "Know thyself" is the great impulse for the tragic heroes, even if knowing oneself means learning that one has killed father and married mother. Could one connection between audiences then and now be that deep within the collective heart of modern theatergoers is also the desire to know themselves through the lessons of the stage?

The great irony in presenting the research for a classical text is that mystery is embedded in the very information provided. Answers carry the embryos of new, larger questions. Even the plays' stories themselves are interpretive layer upon interpretive layer of the Homeric myths. Yet the character of Iphigenia does not even appear in Homer, and Euripides fashions her from legend to align with the *zeitgeist* of his era. Even within Euripides, his character experiences a sea change: the Iphigenia of *Aulis* is simultaneously Daddy's girl and a Joan of Arc of the Greek world, while in *Tauris* she is a reluctant murderess with bad dreams. I armed myself with the background of the myths, thorough knowledge of other translations, and an instinct backed by research into what made the Iphigenia plays specifically Euripidean. However, indispensable as this research was, not one patch of this dramaturgical safety net could break the free-fall of an actor willing to hurl himself into the void of the unanswerable. Or, in more direct terms, I quickly learned that the meaning of the text could not be derived from ready answers about the play. Even if I could engage the director, cast, and designers in a year-long study of at least ten classical texts with heavy emphasis on Euripides, books such as E. R. Dodds' *The Greeks and The Irrational*[20] and C. M. Bowra's *The Greek Experience*,[21] Hellenic art, and what musicologists have conjectured to be the period's music, we could never in two thousand years bring the Greek world to us. Hubris or no hubris.

This is when chaos—call it the Dionysian principle—came to rescue us. Although basic research was essential (actors had to know what they meant when they referred to each of the Achaian fleets by name, or the lineage of Achilles), vast stretches of text were completely terrifying to us because they defied simple cause-and-effect relativity. Most of these passages revealed an attitude toward human behavior that no one wanted to embrace (they lie to their wives when the going gets rough, they kill their daughters, they murder their mothers), or language swollen with the gory burden of alien genealogies.

I could not grant a year of study to the company; I could only make small inroads by creating a cursory understanding of the allusions to Greek myths. But I could certainly spark a healthy awareness of those frightening, impossible passages, and encourage the necessity for disorder. I could also help name the thing that we were all afraid of—the possibility that we might not solve the mysteries, and that, simply, we might have to be cowed in the face of them.

My own informed ignorance charged me with the task of being selective about what materials I could present to the actors that would ignite, not douse, the creative spirit: inspiration takes no time at all. After a three-day rehearsal mini-course about general issues surrounding the text, with supplementary packets incorporating explanations of the play's allusions to Greek myths, I spread around the rehearsal hall a kind of dramaturgical mulch: images—some having nothing to do with Greek life, but of people in extreme situations, fathers and daughters, religious temples and icons, and war—poetry, other plays, and literary treatments of the Atreaid. I sat back, shut up, and appealed to chaos.

Gradually, the mulch yielded. The actor playing Orestes, David Patrick Kelley, created his own parallel universe from research. Orestes' fate as pariah drives him through the play; as punishment for the crime of matricide, the very earth has aborted him, belched him from her belly. After learning about this and other "facts" about his character, Kelley sequestered himself from the cast during rehearsals. He appeared at an early read-through of *Tauris* with a bandage on his hand; only later did we learn that he was not really hurt, but had gleaned from the materials that the Furies had the capability of wielding such bodily trauma that Orestes most probably broke bones often, and sustained other forms of injury during his journey to Tauris. He wore the bandage during the performance. During the first staging rehearsal for the play, Kelley climbed onto "shore," pulled out a small leather satchel, and drew from it bright red petals, which he spread over the altar. "My character does this in the play *Orestes*," said Kelley by way of explanation. The improvisation was retained as the staging for the opening sequence of *Tauris*.

In addition to the prerehearsal research that Kelley and other actors had done on their own, and my own materials (which were planned with all the logic of Chapman's "etymology"), it became necessary to encourage company members to contribute to the image, text, and music compost that grew daily. These materials were not geared to educate any of us in any logical way, but would eventually contribute to the actors' gradual linking of the ancient world of the play to current times. From picture postcards of contemporary Greece to audiotapes of music used during chorus warm-ups, from newspaper clippings incorporating themes related to *Iphigenia* to playful articles of clothing that, when worn by the chorus in rehearsal, helped them to become one in physical life—all were freely associative contributions by the actors. Used in tandem with the actors' packets and in the spirit of experimentation—as complement to literal information about the play's background—our compost inspired characterizations and helped to unify the company. Each member felt an intrinsic part of creating an improvisational approach to the play. This approach, one I had never used before but have since employed in other rehearsal periods, transformed us all into dramaturgs—not merely of the word, but of the play's spirit, music and dream-images.

Initially, however, we began work on the choral sequences methodically, even realistically. We mapped out the objectives of the chorus members— Why are they telling this story? Who are they talking to? Why tell this story now?—in much the same way one would approach a scene with a linear logic. But we learned rapidly to trust the music, movement, and rhythms of the odes much more than post-Freudian motivation. Some of the words were sung, others underscored with music; the language of Dionysus was also made manifest in dance and movement.

Trusting the mysterious within the text led to my insistence on retaining some of the more cryptic, obscure choral passages that had initially been cut; I wanted to preserve the poetry—even when it muted the dramatic through-line—because of an instinct for the necessity of allowing the audience to let those poetic images fold into the irrational sides of their natures. And because the performers, by letting go of the more traditional methods of approaching character, were becoming more committed to these ambiguous sections, the audience would also feel more connected to them. Both the psychological and the irrational merged to create the choral sequences, and I became indebted to encouraging the interplay between both, not one in the service of the other.

An event controlled by the fates, and therefore completely undetermined by the careful planning of rehearsal, also enriched this interplay—in spite of its somewhat tragic nature. An eighty-seven-year-old actor was having great difficulty learning lines and remembering blocking. With tremendous sadness and, as in all such situations, uncertainty about whether the decision was the right one, the actor was unable to complete the rehearsal process. The loss stirred up feelings about cycles of life—here was an actor at the end of a long career—that reverberated throughout the cast and crew. For the first time in the course of rehearsal, we felt as a community the nature of sacrifice for the good of the whole, which was what the act entailed—and what *Aulis* is ultimately about. Because everything that occurs in rehearsal, including relationships, conflicts, and changes, is blended into the whorls of feeling and instinct that make up a production, the fate of this actor marked a turning point in our work. By emphasizing the importance of this "sacrifice" to the director, I mined what I have since viewed as part of the dramaturg's function: to be ever-sensitive to relationships as they develop within the rehearsal process, and how they affect the storytelling; to be aware of the "play within the play" that unfolds in rehearsal, and how that awareness can serve to create an inspired rehearsal atmosphere.

By trusting the irrational side of the work on these ancient plays, we unconsciously allowed the god of fertile disorder to slip into the rehearsal hall When Nietzsche writes of Apollo and Dionysus' marriage, he could not have foreseen that in the American theater in the late twentieth century that union is experiencing tremendous difficulties, with the dramaturg as the possible midwife of its divorce, and Apollo inheriting the partnership's spoils.

As members of this profession, some of us have been trained to develop the Apollonian sides of our natures, and by extension to emphasize and draw out the knowable, the linear, and the tangible on the productions on which we collaborate; some of us have developed amnesia about the potency of chaos, music, the body, and nonliterary impulses as natural partner/antagonist to the Apollonian, rational function. Even in the *Bacchae,* whose author Nietzsche calls the most "non-Dionysiac" of playwrights because of his intellectual sympathies with Socrates and rational discourse, Dionysus triumphs over all, drowning the other impulses. Are we dramaturgs doomed to be the Pentheuses of American theater? If that is or has been our fate, no wonder many artists run away from us.

What I learned from this experience, however I learned it, has informed and transformed the way that I approach all plays. I no longer attempt to answer the play's questions initially, but float the play's mysteries. I dream on the plays and free associate more during readings. I employ images, music, and movement as well as literary and historical research—all of which are answers that carry the embryos of newer, larger questions. By approaching rehearsal this way, I took from the Greek way of thinking a model for the irrational. I used my imagination.

There is power inherent in "I don't know yet." If dramaturgs are seen as providers of answers, then they must not even utter the phrase. How can we search for answers through the rehearsal process if we claim to know them already? The great paradox of the creative artist is to seek answers while acknowledging the impossibility of finding them, and to revel in that impossibility.

Since *Iphigenia,* I strive to teach the course and to keep the witch, an acolyte of Dionysus' temple, boisterous and clamoring. I try to remember that in his later years the philosopher woke to a floating voice in a dream telling him to "Practice music, Socrates! Practice music!"

Textual Collidings:
Group Dramaturgy and the Irondale Ensemble Project
by **Jim Niesen**

JIM NIESEN is a cofounder of the Irondale Ensemble Project and has served as its Artistic Director since the company's inception in 1983. In that time he has directed more than twenty shows for the company including five works by Bertolt Brecht: *Good Woman of Setzuan, Galileo, Threepenny Opera, St. Joan of the Stockyards,* and the American premiere of *Conversations in Exile.* He conceived the scenarios and directed Irondale's radical reinterpretations of such classics as *Uncle Vanya, Peer Gynt, As You Like It, The Inspector General, Ubu Roi,* and *Peter Pan.* Prior to founding Irondale he performed and directed at regional theaters including the Long Wharf Theatre (New Haven), GeVa Theatre (Rochester, New York), Horse Cave Theatre (Kentucky); and the Center for Music, Drama, and Art in Lake Placid, New York. His articles have been published in *Gestus, the Magazine of Brechtian Studies* and *Theater Three.*

From 1986 to 1989 the Irondale Ensemble created a series of what we eventually came to call "textual collidings," deconstructions of classic plays against which we bounced off completely original story lines of our own making. The new plots were capable of standing on their own, independent of the plays that inspired their creation; but, when intercut into the preexisting text, they commented on or paralleled key elements of the original play. Sometimes the new plots would actually replace sections of the source text in an attempt to convey to our audiences the visceral sensation of a dramatic moment in the original text without referring to actual information or story points from it. Above all, these collidings were never straightforward relocations (a textually accurate production of *The Merchant of Venice* set in pre-fascist Italy, for example); they were instead new plays, incorororating completely new worlds and characters.

Typically, scenes from the new story alternated with selected ones from the original, chosen to bring out a strongly conceptualized view of the play. At a given point, the disparate worlds of both stories began to merge into a third "warped" reality in which, somehow, all the various plots and characters came to exist in the same time and place. The new material was always developed collectively and improvisationally, coming very much out of the actors' own sensibilities, sense of truth, politics, and individual voices. Invariably, we would early on isolate a quality or theme in the original text. This would be something that we believed to be vital to our interpretation but difficult sometimes for audiences to accept as being an integral theme of the original play. Often we believed the baggage that accompanied the play's stature as a classic prevented audiences from taking a fresh look or reevaluating it under a fresh light.

Of these "collidings" my personal favorite remains *Outside the Law* (1989), our reworking of Shakespeare's *As You Like It*. In many ways this was also the most unique piece in the series in that the original material was created not so much to illuminate the original play but to argue with it. I'd been disturbed for some time by what I took to be the moral stance of the play. I was troubled by the fact that after creating such a dark and menacing world in the opening scenes (a virtual police state ruled by the despotic Frederick), and presenting Rosalind and Orlando as potentially powerful charismatic revolutionaries, Shakespeare was content to allow his young heroes to fritter away their time and powers playing love games in the forest. I was appalled by the *deus ex machina* device employed at the end to set the world back on its proper course. The shift in tone from part 1 (the court scenes) to part 2 (the forest) seemed too abrupt. The threat posed at the beginning was too dark, too real to write off the conversion of the evil Duke simply as a convention of an "it's after all a comedy, of course this could happen" world. It reminded me too much of what has happened with too many liberal voices in this country, beginning with the Reagan/Bush years when often the strongest words of protest progressives seemed able to muster were "this too shall pass."

At the same time, though, I found myself drawn to other key elements in the play. Rosalind is without question one of the best written characters in all the Shakespeare comedies. Her scenes in the forest are sharp, witty, and direct, devoid of many of the period references and puns that often render Elizabethan humor inaccessible to modern audiences. I sensed this humor and the straightforwardness of much of the play's language would make a good match with the Irondale actors.

We began work by examining the text for all references to death, violence, and banishment, three words that had repeatedly come up during group discussions. We then isolated the specific scenes in which these references appeared, using them as the basic building blocks for a series of games we call "extensions." In these exercises a scene was continued improvisationally past the moment at which the actual dialogue of the scene stops. The aim was to heighten to a more intense level the climactic moment by allowing the action to continue to progress. Much of this work inevitably centered on the scenes taking place at the court of Duke Frederick in the play's opening acts. The "extensions" increased our understanding of the depth of the evil lurking at the play's heart. They also provided us with raw material that we would later incorporate into the finished piece—the establishment of Oliver as a CIA-like operative of Duke Frederick, an interrogation of Rosalind by the Duke's henchmen, and a somewhat deviant affection shown by Frederick towards his daughter Celia.

At this point in the process, though, we still had no clear ideas as to the nature and specifics of the second company-created story that would "argue" with what we took to be the moral indifference of *As You Like It*. From our work on earlier pieces, certain precepts for creating material had emerged.

First of these was: Don't look for all the answers too soon. Fight the temptation to "think" things up. All the good ideas arise organically in their own time. A corollary to this might be: Fight the temptation to put the bits and pieces of material that are created into an overriding structure too quickly. Trust the day-to-day working process, and answers will reveal themselves. In this particular case, a chance listening to Arlo Guthrie's recording of his father's depression-era song "The Ballad of Pretty Boy Floyd" provided us with the material necessary for our "argument" story. To the victims of the Oklahoma dust bowl, Charley (Pretty Boy) Floyd was something of a modern Robin Hood, robbing money from foreclosing banks and using the loot to help poor farmers make their mortgage payments. According to the Guthrie song, Floyd was driven to his life of crime after killing a surly deputy sheriff. The sheriff had been "using vulgar words of language" in front of Floyd's wife. Like many of his contemporary outlaws, Floyd was eventually tracked down and shot by J. Edgar Hoover's FBI, but not before he had become a legendary figure, said to have often left a thousand dollar bill under his dinner plate to poor families who had offered him a meal and a night's shelter. Floyd's direct approach to dealing with the forces of oppression and injustice made him the ideal expression of the qualities we believed to be lacking in Rosalind and Orlando. Now we could face our next developmental problem—the search for an initial contact point between the two stories.

I think it's important to note the difference between solutions that come from happenstance and those that emerge from the collective unconscious. The former do occasionally occur but are truly the product of serendipity and cannot be relied on as a viable part of the working process. The latter, which are much more in keeping with our creative methodology, depend more on identifying and living with the dilemma or artistic problem, and then staying available to possible solutions that are being worked out on the unconscious "back burner" of the mind, what some people call "right brain" thinking. In this way of working the actors and director become fishermen waiting for the appropriate idea to get caught in the net. Equal parts patience and heightened vigilance are necessary for success. At a certain point in the process, as the group's energy gets more and more in sync with the project, the air can become thick with possibilities; the trick is making sure that you are concentrated enough to be available to the one you need as it darts past you. In our case, the end to the search for the contact point came from one of our theater's educational programs.

As a part of our outreach mission, Irondale conducts extensive workshop programs within the New York City public high schools. These classes are taught individually and in teams by members of the company, as a way for us to stay more in touch with the larger world beyond the theater, and as a means of exploring the uses of theater beyond the traditional actor–audience relationship. During the time we had been working on *Outside the Law,* our company's choreographer was using our theater games and techniques with her

English class in the attempt to get students to arrive at an imagistic and sensorial, as well as an intellectual, understanding of Hawthorne's *The Scarlet Letter.* She wanted them to be able to see that a piece of literature could be absorbed on many levels. With her students, she had been exploring the use of the forest as a visceral, central metaphor—the forest as a strange, mythical place inhabited by all sorts of beings and creatures, in which sometimes wonderful, sometimes horrible events had the potential to occur. At the same time as she was teaching this workshop, I was researching other significant productions of *As You Like It* over the past few years and came upon an article written about Peter Stein's version performed in Berlin. Stein's environmental production took place in an enormous hangar-like structure that had been converted for the occasion into a giant indoor forest. Stein discussed in his notes for the program what a powerful image he believed this was for West Berliners, who had little access to woods and open country in the divided Germany of that time. Stein peopled his setting with a variety of forest-based literary figures (Robin Hood and the Merry Men, the White Rabbit from Alice in Wonderland), who were glimpsed from time to time between scenes but never actually interacted with the play's characters or became part of the central story line in any way. They served to heighten the magic and wonderment implicit in Stein's forest image.

The Hawthorne workshop and the Stein production inspired in us the notion of a universal forest, able to contain many worlds and always larger than the stories contained within it. The universal forest was the place where characters went to seek refuge and have adventures. Rosalind fled to Arden, Floyd in the ballad "took to the trees and timbers of the Canadian River shore," but for our purposes it would all be the same place. Initially, the forest took on the particular characteristics and atmospheres as demanded by the alternating needs of the two stories. Rosalind's forest featured some of the physical details of medieval France. Floyd's reflected an Oklahoma of the 1930s. Rosalind's forest was seen peopled by Shakespearean rustics, Floyd's inhabited by poor Midwestern farmers; but, as the various characters from the two plots inevitably met up in the woods, their forest worlds began to merge as well. Silvius, for instance, soon found himself working at a gas station and not long after recruited as a member of the Floyd gang.

Soon we were feeding elements of the merged forest world back into the court scenes as well. Duke Frederick, still speaking much of his original text, was transformed into J. Edgar Hoover, Oliver into his aide Oliver North, and Touchstone into the pop journalist Tom Wolfe. The inclusions of such characters who, in reality, belonged to neither of the play's two dominant worlds, is a device we have often used. These figures must have an iconic identification that provides an instant, imagistic shock of recognition for an audience. They can only appear in the story when the color they bring to it is so precise and telling that their removal would create an irreparable tear in the fabric of the piece once they have been introduced. They are a carefully chosen "spice" that, when used correctly, keeps matters from becoming too predictable while also serving as a reminder that the play is taking place in a world that does not allow itself to be defined in conventional terms.

We continued developing additional new material through a series of collaborative sessions involving the entire company. The actors would be split into groups of four or five, and I would offer them suggestion for possible scenes. (What would Floyd be doing if he were alive today?) Scenarios for these short scenes were developed in forty-five minutes to an hour by each group. They were then improvisationally staged. Promising scenes were further developed and adjusted through the same kind of group work. The first scenario, based on the "if Floyd were alive today" premise, produced a confrontation between him and a group of New Age health faddists. The scene was altogether too whimsical and lightweight for our purposes. I set up a second improvisation, "What kind of a guerilla action might he initiate if he were alive today?" This produced another comic scene in which the Floyd gang kidnapped the Reagans en route home after leaving the White House. The gang's attempt to hold them for ransom was shown to be totally frustrated by the ex-President's inability to comprehend that he had been taken prisoner. A running gag in the scene had him constantly berating Nancy for hiring such incompetent servants. This was, perhaps, the funniest improvisation ever created by the company; but it, too, proved unusable as material for the final piece. The scene was rooted in the almost gentle humor of a Johnny Carson sketch. The Reagans as depicted were too easy a target to serve as the specific rather iconographic figures needed to sharpen the politics of the piece. More fruitful was the response to "What would Celia be like if she had been raised by J. Edgar Hoover?" This scene did much to clarify the specifics of the relationship between the two characters and was later shaped into a usable sequence in which Hoover presented Celia to a live television audience as a virginal model for the nation's youth. At the same time he was subtly fondling her in a less than fatherly manner. Throughout this phase of the work we placed much more emphasis on making the improvisations come to life on their own terms rather than concerning ourselves with how they might fit together in the final piece. At this point in the development, I believe it is one of my chief duties as the director to keep interesting and even entertaining elements in rehearsals on a daily basis. The kind of material we are trying to generate cannot come out of a "grinding it out" mentality. I try to look for even the smallest moments that offer possibility and build on the impulses behind them. A shared understanding of the nature of the piece, its aesthetic, and its theme is being developed in this phase, and the contributions of each member of the group must be carefully weighed, nurtured, and brought together.

To flesh out the events of the Floyd plot, we employed a game we have also used on many occasions called "Docudrama." A team of five or six actors is given a brief outline or description of an historic occurrence and two hours to create a dramatic structure in the style of a typical made-for-television dramatization of a true life story. The sheer inanity of the form's conventions usually proves a liberating device and gives the actors permission to play fast and loose with what could potentially be a stultifying historical pageant. For the Floyd docudrama we went back to the Woody Guthrie ballad for our source document. This resulted in a twenty-minute mini-play that we then broke down into a series of individual episodic scenes and added to the "pot" of ingredients from which the finished performance would eventually be brewed.

We also used the Guthrie ballad to create a satire of a period newsreel in the style of "The March of Time." The actors worked out a series of comic tableaus with an outside voice-over narration, parodying the manner in which the exploits of the Floyd gang might have been shown to a 1930s movie audience. The newsreel exercise was an example of a case in which we drew upon individual talents and interests of company members. Several of our actors possessed sophisticated understanding of theater and film history and performance styles. Their knowledge and enthusiasm for these subjects were resources that provided a depth of insight we could not have reached starting from scratch under the time constraints of even our three-month rehearsal period. This demonstrates another "rule" of our creative process: Learn what the group knows and is good at and try to find ways to use this.

At the same time that we were creating scene material, our choreographer and music director were each moving ahead, working independently with the actors, creating work based on their own individual responses to *As You Like It*. Without knowing where or how the material would eventually be used, our choreographer created a duet for Celia and Rosalind, a steamy tango to be performed by the entire ensemble, and a mock Astaire and Rogers number for Rosalind and Orlando. Our music director spent weeks meticulously teaching the group a massive Latin choral ode. All of this material would be used without change in the final performance.

For years it seemed that whenever we rented a performance space, there was always a pole or supporting column somewhere in the middle of the stage. Rather than being hampered by its presence our scene designer always managed to employ it as a strength, imaginatively incorporating it into the overall design. The pole became a catalyst, opening up new possibilities rather than posing rigid limitations. Music and dance elements often served as functions in the collidings, becoming keystones interspersed throughout the piece—lighthouses pointing us firmly and clearly along our journey.

Our rehearsal periods for the "collidings" typically lasted ten to twelve weeks. The first eight were spent in the rehearsal studio, followed by a move into the actual performance space. At this point our designer began his active participation evolving the set around the actors (sometimes even as we rehearsed) as the various scenes and dances came together. One day he brought in a photograph from the library's picture collection. It showed a weather-beaten two-story frame building from the 1930s. Rows of old tires were nailed to its front. "What do you think?" he asked. The tires became the dominant visual image of the design. A waterfall of old tires was constructed that ran from ceiling to floor along one side of the playing area. This was balanced by a tree of gleaming hubcaps on the other side of the stage. The mundane materials contrasted beautifully with the sculptural elegance of the overall design and caught the perfect balance between the dustbowl and Arden.

Three weeks before our first performance, we began assembling the various individual pieces into a finished performance score. Each day I would bring into rehearsal a proposed running order of improvisationally developed scenes, dances, Shakespearean text scenes, and songs. The actors would be thrust into daily run-throughs of continually changing versions of the show, at the end of which they would informally offer their comments and reactions. At this point, though, I, as the director, would have the final say in shaping the material and the ultimate responsibility for shaping the collective contributions of the company into a unified whole.

Through a combination of intuition and a technically grounded understanding of dramatic structure, we evolved the final shape of the piece. We began it by cutting back and forth in alternating scenes from the two major story lines, looking for events that would emphasize parallels between the two stories: Floyd seen losing his job, followed by Orlando being driven from his estate; Floyd's killing of the deputy, followed by Orlando's defeat of Charles the wrestler; Floyd's flight to the woods, intercut with Rosalind's banishment. Once all the characters were in the forest, the two plots came together producing longer, more developed scenes. Out of this, additional characters came into being as the story started taking off in new and unexpected directions. A young George Bush, complete with Yale baseball cap, was added as a protégé of Hoover. This helped forge a link between the menacing world of Hoover's FBI fiefdom and the police state aspects of today's CIA, which an older Bush would someday direct. It also became apparent that a character substitution of some sort was needed for the exiled Duke Senior, Frederick's good older brother, who seemed to be getting lost in what was now the world of the play. That very week the *New York Times* reviewed a new book on the life of Lord Baden-Powell, founder of the Boy Scouts. The name resonated with a certain too hardy, simplistic optimism and a life credo as out of touch with modern realities as Duke Senior is with the Machiavellian workings of his brother's court. In addition Baden-Powell conjured up strong images of colonial power and the white man's burden, both of which could easily be associated with Duke Senior and his followers, who have come to live the rustic life among the simple people. At the last moment, Oprah Winfrey, played by a white actress wearing no makeup, was added in the role of Hoover's public relations director, for no other reason than it felt organically right. The musical key and melody of the performance were becoming increasingly clear to us. It was now easy to see when a new element was in or out of tune with the rest of the composition.

Near the end of *Outside the Law,* Pretty Boy Floyd was shot down in cold blood by the young George Bush, bent on fulfilling his own political ambitions. Bush killed off Floyd, the human embodiment of idealism in his era, much in the same way that the Bush administration and the forces of the far right he attempted to use to his purposes have attempted to kill off idealism and progressive sensibilities in the soul of the country in our own time. But, in keeping with the production's Marxist interpretation of history, Hoover received word almost immediately that Floyd had just robbed another bank in Oklahoma. The ghost of the fallen outlaw then appeared to Hoover and informed him that "What you fail to understand, Mr. Director, is that you cut a tree back to make it grow stronger. So, if you manage to kill Pretty Boy Floyd—AND EVERY TIME THAT YOU KILL HIM—you just convince more people that he's got to live."

We were now a week away from opening. Floyd, through his course of action, had presented Rosalind (and by extension Shakespeare) with his moral argument; but we still lacked a resolution to the piece. For some time I had been considering a production of Brecht's *The Visions of Simone Machard* with the company, primarily because of the stirring scenes between Simone and the character of the Angel.

Simone is a retelling of the Joan of Arc story, set in France as it is being run over by the Nazis in 1940. It struck me that Arden, too, was located in France, albeit a mythical one of Shakespeare's imagination. I re-read the Simone/Angel scenes. A quote from one of them offered the perfect solution to our problem. The ghost of Floyd would appear one more time in the play. In the midst of the wedding scene from *As You Like It,* Pretty Boy appeared on a promontory overlooking the clearing where the wedding was taking place. He interrupted the ceremony, and he and Rosalind spoke the following lines from *Simone*:

FLOYD (THE ANGEL):

Don't let them take you away. Hold out. Don't go back to your family. Not yet. Stay. The enemy may burst in from one moment to the next.

ROSALIND (SIMONE):

How can I fight? The enemy has already won.

FLOYD:

Is the night wind still blowing?

ROSALIND:

Yes.

FLOYD:

Is there a tree in the yard?

ROSALIND:

Yes, a poplar.

FLOYD:

Do its leaves rustle when the wind blows?

ROSALIND:

Yes.

FLOYD:

Then we must fight, even if the enemy has already won.

In the final days before opening, the performance score was at last set. The piece was finished; or, at least, we were showing our audiences as much about it as we knew at this particular moment. We had a story that kept our audience engaged and alienated in a Brechtian fashion, and that argued against complacency, both in our acceptance of Shakespeare and in our attitude towards the times in which we live.

Rebottling:
Dramaturgs, Scholars, Old Plays, and Modern Directors
by Cary M. Mazer

CARY M. MAZER is Associate Professor of English and Chair of the Theatre Arts Program (which offers an undergraduate liberal arts major) at the University of Pennsylvania. He is author of *Shakespeare Refashioned: Elizabethan Plays on Edwardian Stages*[22] and articles on Shakespeare in performance, Victorian and Edwardian drama and theater, and performance pedagogy. He has worked as a guest dramaturg at People's Light and Theatre Company in Malvern, Pennsylvania. At the University of Pennsylvania and elsewhere he has directed students in productions of Shakespeare's *Pericles, As You Like It,* and *Richard II, Not I* and *Rockaby* by Beckett, *The Devil's Disciple* by Shaw, *Electra* by Euripides, *The Duchess of Malfi* by Webster, *Miss Julie* by Strindberg, and *Playing with Peter,* based on Barrie's *Peter Pan.* He is theater critic for the Philadelphia *City Paper.*

Just before the semester began, a few weeks before auditions, I met over coffee in a local restaurant with my assistant director and my dramaturg to talk about a play. The play was John Webster's tragedy, *The Duchess of Malfi,* which I was about to direct for the undergraduate liberal arts Theater Arts program at the University of Pennsylvania, where I teach. The assistant director was a junior theater arts major who was being groomed for a directing thesis project of his own in his senior year. The dramaturg was a doctoral student advisee in the English department, specializing in Early Modern British drama and theater, with considerable interest in performance issues and stage-centered analysis of dramatic literature, but with little experience in actual theater production.

We talked about the play—a grisly Jacobean revenge play in which the title character, a young widow, defies her powerful brothers (Duke Ferdinand and the Cardinal) and secretly marries her steward, by whom she has three children. The Duchess is spied upon by a member of her household who is secretly Ferdinand's agent; and, after her marriage is discovered, she is pursued, imprisoned, tormented, and murdered.

I laid out for the assistant director and the dramaturg my basic approach to the play—or rather, the unanswered questions I had about the structure, issues, and emotional action of the script, that would serve as our point of entry with the actors into the life of the script in performance: questions about women's control over their households, their private lives, and their bodies; about men's desire, and fear, of watching; about doubling, mirroring, and twinning (Ferdinand and the Duchess, we learn late in the play, are twins); about the difficulty of interpreting omens, and the parallel deceptiveness of theatrical signs; and about the ambiguous frontier between life and death, particularly as they are represented in the theater.

The assistant director—a first-rate student of dramatic literature, theater history, and script analysis, as well as a competent actor and an able young director—had just read the script for the first time, and offered his sense of the characters, and in particular of the pivotal character of Ferdinand. Of the Duchess's two brothers, Ferdinand is more obsessed with his sister's remarriage; and, after her murder, he loses first his sanity and finally his life. The characters, the assistant director suggested, were all on a "quest for their identity."

The dramaturg jumped in. There was, she explained, no such thing as identity, in the modern sense of psychological interiority or individual subjectivity, at the time that the play was written. Unlike the assistant director, the dramaturg already knew the play well, having studied it in a wide variety of courses with several members of the English department, virtually all of whom are practitioners of the "New Historicism," a school of scholarship that aims to situate literary production in the cultural issues of the larger society. Power, sexuality, the family, the physical body, and notions of the self, this school of thought argues, are all provisional, subject to the definitions constructed by each culture and society in each particular time and place. At times of social crisis, at times when paradigms are shifting, cultural products (such as plays performed in public playhouses) manifest a society's "fault lines," the points at which accepted definitions no longer hold, when understandings of the world and of the self are adrift, just as colliding tectonic plates generate volcanoes and uplift mountain ranges.

The cultural definition that, New Historists argue, changed most dramatically during the Early Modern period is that of subjectivity—how individuals understand the boundaries between their selves and the world around them. Today we regard our selves as discrete entities: our physical bodies are the containers of a defining psychology, a private interior essence that, we believe, gives us our true identity; we alone are privy to our interior consciousness, and we posit the existence of an even more private subconscious existence, that shapes and is in turn shaped by our "interiority," the part of us that only we can see. But, the dramaturg pointed out, this sense of a private, interior, defining self was at best only emerging at the time that Webster was writing his play. The action of *The Duchess of Malfi,* she explained, dramatizes the shift from the deferential society of primogeniture, patronage, and power, where marriage is dictated by hereditary property and one's sense of self is generated by social position, to a society in which a private space can begin to be imagined, in which marriage and sexual desire can conceivably be based on affection and domesticity. The play, she argued, citing Catherine Belsey's seminal study, *The Subject of Tragedy: Identity and Difference in*

Renaissance Drama, manifests the troublesome and terrifying shift from a "premodern" to a "modern" sense of "bourgeois subjectivity," a possibility that is imagined (if not fully realized) by some characters in the play, and is violently suppressed by the others.[23]

Ferdinand, the avatar of the older deferential order, cannot be on a quest for identity, the dramaturg argued, because he doesn't know what an identity—in our modern sense of the word—is; he cannot lose his sense of self when he goes mad in the latter half of the play, because he doesn't have a "self" to lose—at least not one that we would recognize, and call by that name, today.

Here, in the disagreement between the assistant director and the dramaturg, was a seemingly irreconcilable conflict between two differing interpretive sensibilities and two differing approaches to dramatic literature and performance. More significantly, I now see that the disagreement is emblematic of the conflicts and dualities at the heart of the dramaturgical process, particularly as it is applied to the staging of plays from earlier bodies of dramatic literature and earlier eras of theatrical activity.

When mounting a production from a playscript from an earlier period, the dramaturg often assists the director by researching the conditions of the play's original performance, along with the social, cultural, and material values that inform the "world" of the characters in the play. The director then uses this material to help the actors create a sense of reality in which they can build their characters, and to create a world (through a wide range of theatrical signs, and a wide choice of historical periods) on the stage to make the characters, their values, and their behavior comprehensible to the audience.

But the philosophical conflict between my assistant director and my dramaturg suggested something else altogether: that the distance between the historical playscript and the contemporary theater perhaps could not be bridged merely by understanding Jacobean stage conditions, by dressing the actors in the right ruffs and doublets (or finding nice contemporary equivalents for the class and power of each character as manifest in dress), or even by a wider understanding of Jacobean property laws, with a few appropriate quotations and illustrations included in the program notes. What was really at stake were the radical differences in two cultures: differences that affect questions of character and action, the basic building blocks of the theater event; differences that ultimately affect how actors build character and how audiences understand it.

To tell the story of the play—indeed, to decide what story could even be told—required us to acknowledge, if not to bridge, the differences between the two cultures. And to do so we needed to articulate what the dramaturg does in such a process: how the dramaturg mediates between old playscripts and the modern theater pieces that can be built from them, and how the dramaturg mediates between the world of scholarship and the world of theatrical practice.

OLD WINE, NEW BOTTLES; OLD SCRIPTS, MODERN DIRECTORS

Why should a theater company produce an old play at all? Why draw upon a library of "classics," some well known to theatergoers, and others known only to antiquarians and students of dramatic history?

Let's put aside questions of cultural status—the notion that regional not-for-profit theaters, summer Shakespeare festivals, or university theater departments, should do plays from certain historical periods in order to validate their status as cultural institutions. Let's put aside as well the all-too-frequent cases where directors are hired by theater companies to direct plays that have already been selected by others and have already been advertised in the subscription brochure, to which the director has little intellectual or artistic commitment beyond the paycheck. And let's put aside cases (such as, say, The Wooster Group's *LSD: Just the High Points*) where a canonical script (in this case, Arthur Miller's *The Crucible*) is appropriated as a "text" to be deconstructed, or as material to be used as part of a larger theatrical collage.

Aside from these special cases, modern theaters and modern directors choose to produce plays from previous decades, centuries, and millennia for the same reason that they produce new plays: because they believe they can build contemporary theater pieces from playscripts that can be moving, meaningful, and entertaining. Directors read a script and imagine the performance that can be built from it. Or, to quote what directors usually say when they "discover" old plays that interest them (or when they finally read the plays their dramaturgs have long tried to bring to their attention), they find that the plays "speak to them"; and they imagine that they can create a performance that can, in turn, make the plays "speak" to audiences.

Some directors describe their role conservatively: the play "speaks for itself," and the director's job is to help the play say what it has to say. (Such directors, however, would be wise to remember Peter Brook's warning in *The Empty Space:* "If you just let a play speak, it may not make a sound. If what you want is for the play to be heard, then you must conjure sound from it."[24] At the other extreme are directors who willfully choose to make the play "say" something distinctly different from what they perceive the play is saying; the text, to use the familiar play on words, is a pretext for the director to make his or her own statement, and the director owes no allegiance to the perceived intention of the author.

Despite one director's invocation of the playwright's intentions and the other director's rejection of these intentions, these positions are not in fact all that far apart: directors who believe that they are only fulfilling the playwright's original intentions simply have an inordinate confidence in their own ability to identify what that intention is. And the theater pieces that these directors build from the old scripts at hand do not necessarily bear any greater resemblance to a playwright's intentions than the theater pieces built by more interpretively aggressive directors who willfully ignore or bypass these intentions. One doesn't need to invoke the "intentional fallacy" or to proclaim the "death of the author" (as literary theorists did in the 1970s) to conclude that a playwright's intentions are almost certainly unknowable; and in any event, the playwright's intentions do not necessarily dictate the nature of the theater piece that the director may wish to create from a preexisting playscript.

It is more useful to describe the director's work with old scripts in another way: modern directors and their collaborators create performances out of the theatrical raw materials at their disposal, materials that include (but are not limited to) the playscript. They wish to tell a story; and they wish to find a theatrical means of telling this story, according to the particular material conditions in which they are working. The story they choose to tell might be the one that they perceive to be in the script; and so these directors will conceive of their role as that of agent or deputy of the playwright, and will conceive of their activity in staging the play as realizing the author's intentions. Or the story they choose to tell might be distinct from the story that they perceive to be in the script; these directors will conceive of their roles as that of independent creative artists, and will conceive of their activity in staging the play as work that deliberately disregards or overrides the author's intentions. For example, in his introduction to his adaptation of Marivaux's *The Game of Love and Chance,* director Neil Bartlett writes, "our Silvia was considerably older than our Dorant. We weren't interested in making a show about the confusions of an *ingénue;* we wanted to make a show about just how much someone who has very good reasons to be single has to lose when they fall in love with someone in every way unsuitable."[25] Here, the translator-adaptor-director is acknowledging the story he wishes to tell with the script, and is confessing his willingness to transform the text to accommodate this story.

The key here, then, is not whether or not the director conceives of his or her role as creative or re-creative, as primary or secondary, as originative or interpretive. The more important issue, for our purposes, is how the director conceives of the relationship between the original script and the contemporary performance built from it—how the director reads a preexisting script from an earlier period with an eye toward creating a contemporary theater event from it. We read plays, Bernard Beckerman has remarked, wearing spectacles—the spectacles of our times, our values, and our aesthetic assumptions.[26] The way a director reads a script theatrically, with an eye toward creating a modern theater piece, depends upon the spectacles he or she is wearing—upon the director's several levels of theatrical and historical awareness.

And the director's method of reading—the director's understanding of the play as a living work and as an historical artifact—will also affect the role that the dramaturg assumes, and the work that the dramaturg does, in the theatrical process. The role of the dramaturg, in the staging of old plays, is to help the director and the other theater artists working to build a theatrical event to tell the story they have chosen to tell, using the raw material of the existing historical script, along with the other raw materials (of the cast and company) available to them. What story the director wishes to tell, and how that story is to be told theatrically, depends upon how the director reads.

DIRECTORS AS READERS, DRAMATURGS AS TRANSLATORS

I wish to propose four simplified and admittedly schematic ways that a director reads an old script with an eye toward building a modern theater piece from it. Each version suggests a different role that the dramaturg might assume in the theatrical process. The first is, on the surface of it, the least controversial and arguably the most common. The other three represent different responses to the first approach.

1. Universalizing Directors; the Dramaturg as Bulldozer.

The first way that a director might read a script—the way that a director might define the nature of theatermaking and theatergoing—can best be described as "universalizing." According to this way of thinking, there exist universal truths to human psychology, emotions and behavior, and there are universal principles of art. Because there are these universal and eternal truths to human behavior, and because the theater event is constructed from the materials of human behavior, the great plays of the past can be seen as repositories of universal human behavior, and theater as an art form as a medium for enacting and reenacting, in contemporary performance, the universal truths found in these great plays. Not every male has, say, killed his father and married his mother (nor, with apologies to Freud, does every male even want to). But the experience of having done so strikes a human chord that crosses all cultural and temporal boundaries; and so we can restage Sophocles' *Oedipus,* and it can still speak to us across the twenty-four hundred years since the play was written. We are able to read the great plays of the past because we can relate to the human experiences dramatized therein; and we continue to stage these plays because the dramatists, with their extraordinary sense of the dramatic, their ability to portray character and action, and their transcendently brilliant theatrical language, have created scripts that can still be made to speak to audiences, despite their unfamiliar cultural signals (about class and power, for example), despite their antiquated theatrical conventions (such as Greek choral odes and English Renaissance boy actors), and despite problems of translation from foreign or antiquated languages (such as ancient Greek or early-modern English).

When assisting directors who believe that drama and theater are repositories of universal and eternal experiences, the dramaturg's task is to help the director to unlock these experiences from the script, and to make it possible for audiences to have the fullest experience of the events and emotions of the script. The dramaturg will assist the director in removing or naturalizing the barriers of theatrical convention and language that may stand in the way of the audience experiencing the events as something identical to what they could conceivably experience in their own lives.

The barriers of period and place must also be removed. If the director decides to keep the action of the play in its original setting, then the specific material conditions of daily life, the particularities of social and political institutions, the peculiarities of that time's dynamics of class and gender, must be made familiar, or at least comprehensible. Or a director may, with the dramaturg's assistance, choose a new time and place, either historical or contemporary, in which to set the action of the play, with a new set of social codes that provide an analogous and more comprehensible frame for the play's characters and actions. At all events, the specifics of time and place are the frame for the event, the temporal "ground" to the universal "figure," and not the thing itself.

2. Historicizing Directors; the Dramaturg as Barricade Builder.

Not everyone shares this view of human experience, or of the theater's ability to communicate a universal experience contained embryonically in the playscript. Bertolt Brecht, the playwright, director, and theatrical polemicist, would reject all of these assumptions, arguing instead that human character, human behavior, and, most significantly, human action are all shaped by social conditions and are therefore not universal across time and space. According to Brecht, to think that behavior is universal is to surrender to the inevitability of social structures and centers of power as though they were eternal, God-given, and unchangeable. Theater, Brecht argues, is capable of demonstrating the opposite: by showing the mechanisms by which a particular society operates, the theater can demonstrate that these power structures could have been overthrown; by forcing audiences to recognize the provisional nature of the social and material conditions of their own world, people are empowered to make choices that can actively change their lives and the world in which they live.

When assisting directors who share Brecht's view of social structures and human behavior, the role of the dramaturg will be very different indeed. Even if the director does not choose to employ Brecht's favorite devices to defamiliarize the theater event, and thus to defamiliarize the mechanisms of society being represented in the theater event, the director will want to make the audience aware of the particular, rather than the universal, features of the world in which the play's characters operate. The dramaturg, who had helped the universalizing director make the world of the play comprehensible by making it seem familiar, will here help the director make the world of the play comprehensible by making it unfamiliar, by stripping away the glossy surfaces, revealing the mechanisms at work beneath. For the universalizing director, the play's setting was a context; for the Brechtian director, the play's setting—the social and political mechanisms of the world that shape the sensibilities of the characters and affect the endless series of decisions they are obliged to make—is the subject itself. The dramaturg will therefore want to help the director, the actors, and ultimately the audience, see the differences between their world and the world of the play. A director and dramaturg working on Brecht's *Life of Galileo,* for example, will want to make explicit the political and economic forces in each of the play's various locales; Venice as a commercial republic, where scientific research in universities is supported so long as it is profitable; Florence as a principality, where science is subject to aristocratic patronage; Rome as a papal city, where research that challenges religious authority can be proscribed; and the *campagna,* where landowners allow no new ideas that might inspire the peasants to challenge their economic hegemony. Knowledge may indeed be subject to power in our world as it is in Galileo's; but only by using the performance to demonstrate how knowledge is subject to power in his world can we understand how it works within the specific structures of ours.

3. Theater-Historicizing Directors; the Dramaturg as Translator.

Although Brecht's vision is compelling, there are other grounds for rejecting a universalizing view of human behavior and society, and these can be found in the lessons taught by theater history. Just as, Brechtians would argue, there are no universals in human emotions and behavior, theater historians would argue that there are not necessarily universal ways that the theater communicates emotions and behavior to its audience. The study of theater history is based on the assumption that aesthetics and theatrical conventions are not universal at all, but are specific to any particular time and place: artists create theater, cultures value theater, people go to theater, and audiences experience theater, all in different ways, for different reasons, and according to different social and aesthetic codes, in any given time and place. For example, the differences in acting between any two periods, a sophisticated theater historian would argue, is not the difference between styles of enunciation or delivery or posture, but—as theater historian Joseph Roach has shown—of radically different understandings of what an emotion is, how an emotion is experienced by the body, how that emotion is manifest in gesture and expression, and consequently how a spectator, viewing these outward gestures and expressions, accepts the actor's emotions as real and their expression as natural.[27] And Alan C. Dessen has demonstrated how the visual and spatial conventions of the Elizabethan stage represent a language of signification that is distinctly different from post-nineteenth-century aesthetics of mimetic realism.[28]

Everything about the theater event is specific to its time and place: not just how the theater event communicates, but why the audience seeks to experience what the event has to communicate, in this particular medium and social occasion. And these historical conditions and aesthetics of the play's original performance are encoded within, and inseparable from, the theatrical script.

A universalizing director will view some of the more antiquated conventions of the playscripts as minor impediments that stand in the way of modern audiences being able to relate to the emotions and actions of the characters in the play. To a theater-historically sensitive director, however, these conventions are integral to the script, and are inextricably interwoven with the represented action and behavior. The dramaturg working with such a director should not try to persuade the director to reproduce the staging aesthetics of the theater for which the plays were originally written; these can no more be recaptured than can the original occasion for the theater event or the social practices of theatergoing. Instead, the dramaturg is a translator, translating the play from one aesthetic system into another, just as a verbal translator translates speech from one language into another. When verbal translators translate a phrase from one language into another, they do not translate the words, but rather translate what the speaker is trying to say, finding new words in the new language that relate as closely as possible to the thought being expressed as the original thought did to its original language. So, too, the dramaturg helps the director find a theatrical form for the theater event that relates to its modern audience analogously to the way the original event related to the audiences of the playscript's original performance. For example, the physical relationship between actor and audience in the original theater might not be reproducible in a modern playhouse; but an analogous relationship can be established between actor and audience, within the auditory and visual dynamics of contemporary architecture. In *The Gospel at Colonus,* Lee Breuer and Bob Telson, adapting *Oedipus at Colonus* by Sophocles, replicated not the architecture but the occasion of the original performance and the original audience's celebration of the sanctification of the city of Athens by reframing the play as a contemporary gospel service, and defining the modern theater audience as congregants. The relationship between the emotions of the dramatic character and the passion of the actor, between the actor's emotional instrument and the physical and visual manifestation of those emotions, may similarly be translated from one vocabulary and grammar and syntax into another. Even if the director chooses to tell a different story with the playscript than the story told in the original theater event when the playscript was new, the dramaturg, equipped with the history of the theater, can show the director how the new story can best be told. For the tale and the way it is told are intrinsically connected through the particular aesthetics of the particular theater, and the particular audience to whom the tale is told.

4. Cultural-Historicizing Directors; the Dramaturg as Brickmaker.

These three ways that a director might read the script—universalizing, political historicizing, and theater-historicizing—differ in the ways they define the relationship between the script and the performance. A politically historiciz-ing director will disagree with a universalizing director about the relation of the social and material world of the script to the ways that individuals behave within it, and may therefore disagree about the way the world of the play and the behavior of the characters are to be presented to the audience in the con-temporary theater. And the theatrically historicizing director may disagree with both the universalizing director and the politically historicizing director about the relation of the events and behavior presented by the script to the aesthetic codes of theatrical communication encoded within that script, and may therefore disagree about the means that must be found in contemporary performance to create a theater event from the script that can communicate effectively to today's audiences. But the three approaches nevertheless share an understanding of the basic building blocks from which a play is built: char-acter and action. People—for whatever universal or historically specific reasons—want things, respond to stimuli, and act on their desires; and these actions—by whatever universal or historically specific theatrical means—can be represented by actors before live audiences in theaters.

But there is another way of reading a script historically that, as my collabora-tors and I discovered with *The Duchess of Malfi,* proved even more trouble-some. For even if we are right to assume that the theater is always built from character and actions, can we assume that character and action always mean the same thing? What if the very notion of character and its constitution are rad-ically different from one culture to the next? Even if drama is composed of ac-tions that characters generate based on their desires, can we be sure about the ways in which these desires stem from the psychological constitution of the in-dividual? What if a culture's ways of defining psychology, individuality, motiva-tion, behavior, biography, personality, and subjectivity are so radically different that it affects not only how people understand one another, but how they un-derstand their own selves? What becomes of the scripts that are built (as all scripts arguably are) from character and action, when the definition of character and the relation of character to action is so radically different from our own? How can we begin to read those scripts? And how in the world can we build a theater event from those building blocks when our understanding—as readers, as theatermakers, and as theatergoers—is so radically different?

And, finally, what is the role of the dramaturg—whether as facilitator, trans-lator, researcher, historian, or advocate—in helping the director and the other collaborators build a theater event from these building blocks, blocks that no longer seem as rectilinear, as sturdy, or as structurally sound as they once did?

DIRECTORS AND SCHOLARS

These were precisely the questions raised that day by the disagreement be-tween my student assistant director and my student dramaturg discussing

The Duchess of Malfi. The assistant director had argued that the actions of the play, and the psychological constitution of the characters from which these actions sprang, were the same as our own, that they were therefore knowable and recapturable, and that an effective and comprehensible theater piece could therefore be created from these materials. The dramaturg argued—whether she knew it or not—that the actions of the play sprang from such a radically different set of definitions of personality and subjectivity that the play and its characters simply might not be understandable to modern audiences at all, and could perhaps only be communicated through the medium of the scholarly article.

I was, of course, staging a play and not scholarly article. And here lay the challenge facing the twin enterprises of theatermaking and scholarship: do directors and scholars have anything useful to say to one another? Does contemporary scholarship have anything useful to contribute to the theater process? And, if so, how can the contributions of scholarship be framed in ways useful to directors and performers in the service of the task at hand: creating theater pieces? Judith Milhous and Robert D. Hume's useful term for this is "a producible interpretation."[29] The problems of communication between scholarship and theatrical practice are considerable, even among the small number of scholars and theater practitioners genuinely interested in one another's work. The scholar and the director are engaged in exercises that define the relation of the script to the performance in different ways. For the scholar—at least for those even minimally interested in performance—the performance realizes the script. For the theater practitioner, the script enables the performance.[30] These approaches might sound compatible, but there is a crucial difference. For the scholar, the playscript contains within it, in embryonic form, the potential of the theater event; for the theater practitioner, the script is merely one small, if important, part of the raw material from which the theater event is crafted, a means by which the director can tell a story.[31]

Because of this difference in sensibility about the relation of script to performance, the director and the scholar will seek different things from one another. Directors look to scholars for validation of the stories they have chosen to tell in the performance they are building from the playscript: they seek out articles and books that interpret the dramatic text in order to confirm that, yes, that particular story can indeed be found in the script, and that the director is therefore justified in using the script to tell that story in contemporary performance. (For this reason, ironically, directors will turn more often to scholars who do not write with a performance sensibility, who are more interested in explicating what a text means than in exploring how the script works in performance.) Conversely, scholars interested in performance will look to contemporary performance to validate the performance potential they believe they have discovered in the script. Performances that "realize" the text in the ways they believe the text asks to be realized are good; performances that tell a story different from those imagined by the scholar are deemed to be wrong.

It is up to the dramaturg to overcome this natural antipathy between scholars and directors. And it is up to the dramaturg to provide material from scholarship that neither dictates to the director the story that must be told in performance, nor merely restates the story that the director has already decided to tell.

THE DUCHESS OF MALFI

Scholarship had already proven useful in our process of conceiving our production of *The Duchess of Malfi*. For example, my dramaturg brought to my attention an article (by Andrea Henderson, written, coincidentally, when she was a graduate student in English at the University of Pennsylvania) that laid out the issues of theatricality and the ambiguities of theatrical signs that we already knew we wanted to explore in performance.[32] This article confirmed matters about the story we had already chosen to tell: that the characters' inability to interpret divine and supernatural signs (the nosebleed, the echo) corresponds to their inability to interpret the signs of each other's private behavior (Bosola trying to confirm that the Duchess is pregnant), or to trust the theatrical displays they create for one another (the wax replicas of Antonio and his eldest child, presented to the Duchess as though they were corpses; and the courtiers mistaking the Cardinal's real cries of distress as the distress he had told them he was going to feign).[33]

Catherine Belsey's much-debated (and subsequently much-qualified) study of shifting dramatic representations of character and "subjectivity" in seventeenth-century England, *The Subject of Tragedy*, proved to be a different matter altogether. This scholarship neither confirmed the story we had already decided to tell, nor compellingly suggested a story that we might tell instead. Rather, the whole question of subjectivity raised several questions about the basic building blocks of the theater piece that we were constructing and made us doubt whether a theater piece could be constructed at all from this old dramatic material.

At first, Belsey was useful in helping us to articulate some aspects of character and action that we thought we understood. She, and we, saw the Duchess as an emergent voice of volition, articulated within the bourgeois domestic sphere of the family and the household, and exercised by her in her choice of a husband.[34] Belsey was also useful in helping us see the severe limitations of the Duchess's emergent inchoate sense of individuality. The domestic sphere offers little protection from the patriarchal forces that repress the Duchess's choice; indeed, the Duchess's claim to a private, domestic space virtually invites the patriarchal forces to suppress it.[35] The Duchess's own definitions of subjectivity and individuality are still provisional and ill-defined: she has no name other than her title; in her ordeal in prison (significantly, her own household), Belsey observes, the Duchess "is claiming a political place not a personal identity" when she asks Bosola, her tormentor, "Am I not thy Duchess?"[36] And so, in our production, the Duchess's subsequent statement "I am Duchess of Malfi still" became not a defiant assertion, but a troubled question, grasping at the few remaining definitions of a self, definitions that could never be verified within the patriarchal world in which she was imprisoned. Like the character Hamlet, created ten years earlier, the Duchess offers the possibility of a recognizably modern sense of subjectivity that the play finally cannot sustain or confirm; as Belsey writes about Hamlet, "The play, which has begun to define an interiority as the origin of meaning and action, a human subject as agent, cannot produce closure in terms of an analysis which in 1601 does not yet fully exist."[37]

The Duchess's crisis, as Belsey and as we were defining it, was the result of the inroads she had begun to make into a recognizably modern sense of subjectivity. The character's tragic downfall, and even her final confusions about her self, could therefore, we believed, be intellectually and emotionally grasped by the actor, and could be played by the actor using modern emotionally-based histrionic techniques. Modern actors often conceive of the emotional lives of their characters over the course of the play as a "journey." As a dramatic character, the Duchess stands, historically, at the threshold of a definition of character that would be capable of undergoing such a journey; and so, an actor could play the Duchess's plight as a journey, and the audience could understand it.

We ran into much greater problems, though, in understanding Ferdinand, the Duchess's twin brother and persecutor. His story, above all others, epitomized scholarly issues about the premodern absence of bourgeois subjectivity. And therefore we had reason to doubt that we could ever tell his story using the building blocks of the theater as we knew it. As the dramaturg had pointed out to the assistant director, you can't be on a quest for self if you don't know what a self is.

In his obsessions about preventing his sister from remarrying, and in his rabid response to the news that she has done so against his wishes, Ferdinand is sexually possessive to a brutal and irrational degree. Actors playing the role normally try to account for Ferdinand's obsessions by seeking character flaws and biographical determinants for the character's behavior: if Ferdinand is repelled by his sister's sexuality, and if (as we discover only after the Duchess is dead) his sister is his twin, then Ferdinand, they speculate, is perhaps repelled by her sexuality because he fears his own. But why? Perhaps Ferdinand is a narcissist confronted by his own image in the mirror image of his twin; he loves himself and sees in her an image of the object of his desire; but because she is his sister that desire is seen as incestuous, and therefore taboo. Or perhaps Ferdinand is a closet homosexual, and because the Duchess is his twin, he sees in her desire for Antonio a horrifying image of his own desire for men.

But we couldn't assume that character, biography, personality, and psychology operate in these "modern" ways. In particular, we could not take for granted the fundamental equation of modern psychotherapy and modern psychological acting: that you are what your earlier experiences (particularly the traumatic ones) have made you. Audiences tacitly employ this same assumption: they account for a character's behavior by drawing conclusions about the character's identity. We didn't want the audience to draw any assumptions about an identity we felt that Ferdinand didn't have. But we feared that we wouldn't have any choice in the matter: using our modern acting methods and our modern theatrical means, we feared that we might not be able to tell the story at all in the premodern characterological terms that the dramaturg was suggesting; and yet we had no other means, aside from actors playing characters in action, to tell our story. One simply cannot turn a theatrical performance into an enormous, three-hour, live, scholarly footnote.

Our goal, then, was to redefine the nature of the character's emotional journey, to establish a "map" for the character's deepest desires and greatest fears, that was both consistent with the issues of premodern subjectivity at the center of the conflicts and actions in the play, and at the same time comprehensible to both the actor and to the audience. And to make all this comprehensible to both the actor and the audience, we needed to find emotional actions (in the modern method-acting sense) that the actor could play. Actions, as we normally think of them, are based on needs or desires; and needs and desires are in turn based on identity and biography. These definitions of identity and biography, though, are alien to the ways that dramatic character is conceived in Webster's 1612 script. Could we identify playable actions that were divorced from identity, or at least not dependent upon the existence of a stable, subjective, interiorized identity?

Our solution was to find premodern ways of describing Ferdinand's desires, and modern ways of describing his fears: what if Ferdinand's problem were not his secret desires—the signs of a stable, modern, interiorized, subjectivity—but the stability of the definitions themselves? In this scheme, Ferdinand's desires are based on what he could confidently know about his premodern social and emblematic "identity," defined according to his social position and political power; and his fears are based on the challenges to these definitions posed by his sister's new paradigms of identity. Ferdinand's sexual jealousy of his twin sister is not based on narcissism or incest. Rather, he looks to his twin, not as an object of desire, but as a mirror of his own definitions of self, as a measure of his own, safe, familiar, hierarchical, nonsubjective boundaries. For the Duchess, sexual activity, sexual choice, and control over her domestic sphere, are ways of asserting a new basis for her identity. Consequently for Ferdinand, unable or unwilling to make this leap into subjectivity, the Duchess's sexual activity is a threat to the definitions that he uses to confirm his own existence.

When Ferdinand first learns of his sister's secret marriage, he says, intemperately, to his brother the Cardinal:

> I could kill her now,
> In you, or in myself, for I do think
> It is some sin in us, Heaven doth revenge
> By her. (32.5.63–6)[38]

On the face of it, this is a statement about sin and polluted blood. But in our schema, the speech serves as an agonized and confused expression of dissolving boundaries and shifting definitions. The Duchess's violation of traditional boundaries threatens to violate the boundaries of Ferdinand's sense of his own identity. Unsure of the boundaries, he can no longer precisely determine where his "self" ends and his twin sister's begins. He can therefore kill her by killing the essence of her that he finds in himself; he can punish her by killing himself. In performance, the actor drew his dagger on that line and placed it at his own throat.

Ferdinand's stumbling traversal of the play can hardly be called a journey. Rather, the events of the play threaten Ferdinand's sense of self—however he defines this, even in premodern, pre-subjective terms—and he acts, with varying degrees of success and at great cost, in a vain attempt to preserve his definitions and boundaries.

Little of this was explicitly discussed with the actor in rehearsal; but we made this sense of Ferdinand's traversal a regular part of the actor's work. We created exercises, improvisations, and scene work for the actor, which served to translate this description of Ferdinand's crisis of self into playable actions. For example, through mirror and shadow exercises, the actor learned to view his scene partner as a mirror of his self rather than as an object of forbidden desire.[39] At all cost, the actor was encouraged to respond to stimuli, to act upon needs and desires, and to fear the things that terrified him—all playable actions—without inventing a biography, identifying a childhood trauma, or psychopathologizing Ferdinand's character. Actions, playable by a modern actor and recognizable to a modern audience, were devised that could dramatically tell a story about a crisis in the character's premodern, pre-subjective definitions of identity. And so a modern theater piece was built from a 380-year-old script that neither ignored the script's unplayable definitions of character and action, nor surrendered to its unplayability by turning it all into a footnote.[40]

THE DRAMATURG AS LENS GRINDER

There are, no doubt, other ways of "reading" this 1612 script, and other stories that modern directors may choose to tell in the theater pieces they create from this script. And the role of the dramaturg in our particular rehearsal process was never clearly articulated, in part because of my own role as teacher and director, and my experiences elsewhere as a dramaturg and as a theater historian. But the production nevertheless helped us to articulate what, in principle, the role of the dramaturg might be, as a reader of old plays and of new and difficult scholarship: the dramaturg not only helps the director tell a modern story, but helps the director determine what story is there to be told; and, most significantly, the dramaturg helps the director and all of the other collaborators in the theater process find the theatrical means to tell this story in today's theater, using the theatrical building blocks of today, in order to communicate with today's audiences.[41]

Production Dramaturgy Of A Classic:
Molière's The Misanthrope *at La Jolla Playhouse and the Goodman Theatre*

Throughout this section the reader will find case studies in which individuals recount their work on specific projects in production dramaturgy, translation, and adaptation. These studies take the reader into the specific processes that dramaturgs go through when they work on a project, and complement other contributions more reflective or theoretical in nature. Case studies allow the reader to look over the shoulder of practitioners as they make theater. This case study comes from a panel discussion among director **ROBERT FALLS** and dramaturgs **RICHARD PETTENGILL** and **WALTER BILDERBACK** on a production of Molière's *The Misanthrope* for both the La Jolla Playhouse and the Goodman Theatre. The production took place in the summer and fall of 1989, and the panel took place at the annual conference of Literary Managers and Dramaturgs of the Americas in June 1990 at DePaul University in Chicago.

Falls: The production of Molière's *The Misanthrope* that we had the great privilege to work on happened very, very quickly, and most of what happened following the decision to do it was more accidental than some sort of model of dramaturgy. I must say, though, that it was one of the most extraordinary productions I've ever been involved with, an unusually pleasurable one that I learned a great deal from.

It began in February of 1989. I received a phone call from Des McAnuff, artistic director of the La Jolla Playhouse. He asked if I would consider doing something in the final slot on the La Jolla mainstage. I said I was interested, because we actually had been planning to do another production to open the season at the Goodman, but it had just fallen through. So why not talk about the possibility of a collaboration between the two theaters, whereby that production—whatever it might be—would go into rehearsal in July in La Jolla, play during the month of August in La Jolla, and then move directly to Chicago to continue playing at the Goodman Theatre? It was kind of that wonderful, simple concept of "let's make this happen." It turned out to be much more difficult in terms of the actual working it out, but it began with that simple desire to collaborate. Des asked if I had any ideas. His words were something like, "Bob, I'd like you to do anything you want as long as it's a small cast, one-set comedy with some bite. I'd like it to have some guts to it, a comedy." I asked what he thought of Molière. He said, "Great! What do you think of *The Misanthrope*?" and I said, "No! No, no, no! Not *The Misanthrope*!"

I hung up the phone and I wondered why I was so terrified of *The Misanthrope*. I realized that it had long been a work that terrified me. It's a play that I have seen a lot. Most productions I have not been impressed with. I frankly think it's one of the greatest plays ever written, and now having worked on it my feelings are more than confirmed In about ten seconds, I realized I was scared of the work because I have a strong personal affinity with the character Alceste, in all of his foolishness and horribleness, and that I share a certain vision and worldview with him. I also realized that I had recently been cultivating that worldview in a deeply personal way with my girlfriend, who had suddenly left the house after eight years to become a Hollywood star. In the past year and a half, I had gone back and forth numerous times to Los Angeles, and suddenly found myself immersed in a complex emotional relationship with Los Angeles and a woman who was now finding stardom and who loved Los Angeles. Then I thought of a friend of mine, an actor who was ending a relationship with a famous Hollywood star.

Suddenly, in the course of the minute and a half that these thoughts were running through my head, I got it. I really understood that *The Misanthrope* is about two passionate, foolish, brutal people on a journey through darkness against a Hollywood backdrop. I saw the whole production instantly, emotionally. I wasn't at all connected to the comic or satiric elements. The production came to me in a highly personal way that I didn't understand, but I did know that I was really scared of the whole idea. I remained scared of this relationship for months and months of work on this play—the heart of that bleak relationship between Alceste and Celimene. I went back to the play that night and reread it; indeed, the Hollywood framework was my own highly personal entree into this classical work.

When I realized what I wanted to do with *The Misanthrope,* the next question was what translation to use. I knew only Richard Wilbur's magnificent version, which I'm sure all of you here are familiar with. My first instinct was to invite a playwright to work with me on a new adaptation/translation. The names that came to mind were playwrights who could in some way grapple with the Alexandrine verse scheme. I thought of John Guare, Eric Overmyer, Mac Wellman—all writers that we know have wonderful verbal imaginations.

The designs were due in about a month. That's how quickly we were moving. I called Des back and said I'd do it. We decided to go with Richard Wilbur. But when Des called Dick Wilbur's agent, we got a flat "no"— Mr. Wilbur refused to have his translation of *The Misanthrope* done in any other period than the one Molière wrote it in. I tried to point out that in Chicago alone, I'd recently seen two modern-dress productions, set in both the 1920s and the 1930s.

Pettengill: Bob didn't realize it at the time, but I was all ready for this project because I had just dramaturged both of the productions he mentioned. The first one was at the Court Theatre in 1984, directed by Munson Hicks. He set it in the 1920s Paris of Scott and Zelda, Nancy Cunard, and Josephine

Baker. Celimene wore a flapper dress, and set designer Michael Merritt packed her salon with African art. John Mahoney played a hilarious, simpering Oronte. Munson didn't worry about there being no direct analogy in his setting for the power of Louis XIV over the characters' lives. He said in his director's note that "change and whim were so prevalent in Louis' court: his whims dictated what everybody was wearing and doing and thinking. In the Paris of the '20s it was almost change for change's sake."

The production just last year at The Theatre School of DePaul University, directed by David William, was set in the 1930s in the British milieu of the Duchess of Windsor. Here Alceste was a relentlessly howling creature in a black turtleneck, banging his head against the conspicuous excess of the times. William wrote at the time that: "In the society led by the Prince of Wales (later Duke of Windsor) that frequented the town and country houses of Europe of the 1930s, many of the conditions of Molière's world are present: wealthy, frivolous people meeting to gossip and flirt; the hypocrisy, the intrigue; the laughter, and the hatred—it is all there."

Interestingly enough, both of these productions did use the Wilbur translation.

Falls: Apparently, these producers had never informed Mr. Wilbur of their intention to update the play or, I assume, they wouldn't have been granted the rights. We were refused the rights. Des and I were prepared to go to Mr. Wilbur's house to petition him to let us do this play. I was not going to change one word of his text and had no desire to do anything unfaithful to it. It would be uncut, unchanged. I simply wanted to explore this parallel contemporary universe of Hollywood in a completely modern production using Mr. Wilbur's text. He did not want to meet with us. There was just a flat "no."

Well, quite by accident, this turned out to be the best thing that ever happened. That afternoon I was thinking about what I would do. There were some alternatives. Tony Harrison had done a modern-dress production in 1972 at the National Theatre in London; it was set in 1966, DeGaulle's Paris, with a political background. Des loved the Harrison version, but the more I read it the less I liked it. Its rhythms are unbelievably English, and it didn't solve my problem because it had nothing to do with the world of Hollywood. Then I read in the *London Theatre Review* about a new adaptation by Neil Bartlett for Red Shift, a small touring company in Great Britain, which got wonderful reviews at the Edinburgh Fringe. It was a Thatcher-bashing modern-dress production of English yuppies, set in the contemporary media world of London. It sounded really cheeky, way too cheeky for my conservative take on this, but I thought it could be inspirational just to get a copy.

In the meantime, I was starting to design and cast the show in terms of the Harrison version. We hadn't gotten the rights from Mr. Harrison yet. We talked to him about adapting it to a Hollywood setting. He said, "No, I don't think that's a good idea. I think it ought to be set in Washington, D.C., at a party of society people with their hands in power."

Pettengill: We finally got hold of Neil Bartlett's version, which we loved, although it was extremely British, filled with unmistakably British sayings and references to that 1980s London media world. It didn't work for us as is, so we called Bartlett and said, "What do you think? Do you mind if we work with this? We really want to set it in Hollywood." He said, "Fine. Why don't you let me take a look at it. I don't speak American. But I'll give it a go." So he went through it and made some good initial changes. Then, kindly and generously, in a collaborative spirit that is completely characteristic of him, said, "I trust you. Go ahead, do whatever you like to the script. It's yours to work with." This was an incredible boon for us at that point.

Falls: Neil Bartlett is actor-oriented and really believes that 'a work is a work is a work." He understands that whoever has to deal with a work has to take it into their own hands, and that it's an ongoing, evolutionary process. Bartlett is a remarkable actor, director, translator. He comes from the London fringe and works from a gay aesthetic. He had been commissioned to do this version of *The Misanthrope,* and I thought it was brilliant. It retained—unlike Wilbur's iambic pentameter—Molière's twelve-syllable hexameter Alexandrine rhyme scheme, and from what I could understand from my readings of some literal versions of the play, it was completely faithful to the spirit of Molière. He also added some contemporary jokes to the text.

I should also tell you that it was given with this project that each theater had a dramaturg. These gentlemen have never met until this afternoon. This dramaturgy took place by fax machine and over the phone between two different cities and in two different phases.

Pettengill: The minute Bob came into my office and said, "I'm doing *The Misanthrope,*" I handed him a pile of research. Because of the other two productions, I had all the Molière background research ready to go. And it was a good thing, too, because the dramaturgy on this project had less to do with going to the library and finding scholarly essays than getting right into the text. As soon as we got the go-ahead from Bartlett, it was a matter of Bob and me sitting down for six hours at a time until we were absolutely burned out and unable to say or think another thought—just going through the script and saying "This is a little much, what shall we do with it?" Then I'd say "I'll look at that" or Bob would say "I'll look at that." We'd both go off and write some things, and then reconvene. Today I brought along a copy of the final version, and here are a few examples of the changes we made in Neil's script. Early on in Neil's original version, Philinte challenges Alceste with:

. . . So you'd walk up to old Emilie
And tell her straight that it's not really on to be
Wearing low cut frocks and that much rouge anymore?

That sounded a bit British, so we came up with:

> . . . So you'd walk up to old Emilie
> And then inform her that it's not that hip to be
> Wearing those hip-hugging jeans at age sixty-four?

You can tell this process was great fun. A little later, when Neil has
Alceste railing:

> In public he's "seerusly smart," "brill-yunt," "aux fait."
> In private, we wouldn't sell him the time of day.

that wasn't going to play in L.A., so we wrote:

> In public, he's "totally hot," "blows me away."
> In private, we wouldn't sell him the time of day.

In every case we went back to the original French, and came up with a literal
translation of the original. Then we did our best to remain true, if not always to the precise literal truth of Molière's lines, then to the spirit of
them. Another interesting example, which happened during rehearsals,
was Celimene's line about having a headache.

Falls: That was actually the single most interesting line and the only controversial line in the play. The line in Neil's first version was "Only leave me
alone; You give me a headache." We went back to the French with the help
of Mary Coleman, a directing intern in La Jolla who was also fluent in
French, and she translated the line as "You're breaking my head." In rehearsal, the original line just didn't work in the moment. We were playing
an intensely passionate production, and the British coolness of "Only leave
me alone" at the height of an extraordinary fight scene just didn't work.
The actress, Kim Cattrall, couldn't make it work. She was screaming the
line. She was really in Alceste's face. So we confronted the translation.
What happened spontaneously in the room is that Kim said:

> Just leave me alone. Go away. Stop fucking with my head.

It was perfect both rhythmically and emotionally for the pitch that the
scene was being played at, although it became quite controversial because
of the profanity. It really stood out from the rest of the text. We tried it in
performance on and off and ultimately decided to stay with it because it
was absolutely right. It was absolutely shocking. Ultimately, the call

dramaturgically was that it was accurate to the French. It was as faithful a rendering of "You're breaking my head" as we could possibly get. This was actually just one of hundreds upon hundreds of changes made in the text, both in rehearsal and earlier with Richard in Chicago.

Pettengill: You could say that I was the prerehearsal textual dramaturg on the initial changes in the script. We entered it into our computer and did a desktop publishing job on it so that the students in our high school program could have a booklet copy they'd want to keep.[42] Then I got in touch by fax and phone with Walter Bilderback, who took over on the La Jolla end. I should just mention that while this was the most stimulating, exciting project I've ever worked on, it was also one of the most frustrating—to be involved in such an incredibly high pressure, high speed, high-creativity prerehearsal process and then, all of a sudden, nothing. I was stuck in Chicago, nothing happening. I took a week's vacation in August only to find out when I got back that Bob had called, saying, "Send Richard out here, I need him." By the time I returned, it was too late; I almost died. Walter had picked up the ball in La Jolla, but I'm sure that he, too, was frustrated not to have seen the initial stages.

Bilderback: In exactly an inverse way, I had the same experience that Richard had. It came on real fast. Every week or so I would get half a script or another version of a whole script by express courier, or a scene would suddenly come spitting out of the fax machine. As I would read it over, my basic purpose was to watch out for gratuitous Hollywood-bashing, or to see if there was anything that I had picked up from being a hundred miles away from Hollywood that would be noticeable to an audience that was basically San Diego and Los Angeles.

Anyway, I would jot a few notes down and mail them back, but it was frustrating initially because I saw all of this work going on and my fear was that I was going to be a bureaucratic fifth wheel when it got to rehearsal. Whenever you work with a director for the first time, you can often spend the entire rehearsal period just trying to figure out a common language. The first time Bob and I really got a long chance to talk about it was when we were doing the L.A. casting. It was interesting because once we actually got into rehearsal, I felt very much a part of the process. The production table in the rehearsal room was more crowded than this table because we had Bob, an assistant director, me, an assistant dramaturg (a student from the University of California at San Diego), and stage management. Then there was a whole wall of people watching all of this going on.[43] The first thing I was responsible for was throwing in some sort of background information to the actors that would connect Louis XIV to present day Hollywood. The *New York Times* and *Los Angeles Times* had been most cooperative. The weekend before we went into rehearsal, they each published cover articles on Mike Ovitz, who heads the Creative Artists Agency, the most powerful agent in all of Hollywood.[44]

Falls: The production bashed California no more than Molière was bashing Paris or French society. What we were trying to do was be as truthful and as honest to our time as Molière was to his. The Ovitz articles were all the more interesting because of the element of fear that exists in Hollywood about offending a man as powerful as Mike Ovitz. In *The Misanthrope,* the only real action is a group of people at leisure waiting at a party for the "Sun King" to hand favor to them. In Molière's text, it's all about "him"; it's about "the man." In our production, they were all in a major deal with the same studio, and they were all waiting for someone who had the power over their lives to make something happen.

You would think that one of the major problems for a 1989 *Misanthrope* is the character of Oronte, who appears and reads a poem. One episode in the play revolves around a dispute over Oronte's poem, which Alceste rightly thinks is a piece of shit. Oronte fancies himself a poet. In rehearsal, the first question that came up was "Who reads poetry anymore? What about Oronte as a screenwriter reading his first draft of a screenplay?" But I didn't want to change the text. The game was not just to write a new play about Hollywood. It was the tension between Molière's original and our production. My theory was that, yes, Oronte is a screenwriter, a director, but he's also a poet. I mean, he fancies himself a poet. Screenwriting is just what he does for the bucks; his real art is in his poetry. Lo and behold, on the the second day of rehearsal in the *Los Angeles Times* was an enormous article about a place in L. A. called Cafe Largo where all of the Hollywood stars go to read their own poetry. The current hottest thing is for Justine Bateman or Rob Lowe to get up and spill their souls with their original poetry, and the club is filled with all of these Hollywood stars. Dennis Hopper comes down and he's like "the King" doing his poetry. There it was. We didn't worry about whether the audience knew about Cafe Largo or not, but we wanted to be true to it. So a specific line went into the script: When Alceste says he thinks the poem's a piece of shit, Oronte says "They loved it down at Cafe Largo."

We also had the good fortune of having Kim Cattrall, who is a movie star, playing the role, so we had an unusual entree into accuracy about that world.

Bilderback: Most of what I was doing was in that intangible realm of rehearsal dramaturgy, watching what was going on, trying to address questions that came up in the moment, occasionally throwing Bob notes on things I saw. This was La Jolla Playhouse's "dark season," so—unlike usually—I kept being asked, "Is it funny? Is it funny?" And I kept saying "It's very good." And Bob and I kept asking each other "Is this supposed to be funny?" because it was just so dark.

Falls: We did not for a moment, with the exception of one scene—the Oronte–Alceste scene, which is just a pure classic comic Molière scene—actually think it was very funny. And at the same time that we were rehearsing, Des McAnuff was rehearsing a play about mass murder across the hallway, and we would hear peals of laughter coming out of that room. They would just roar and laugh and his actors were in the best mood all the time. And we were miserable. You never saw such tears, fights, bruising, scar tissue—real physical and emotional scar tissue—from the exploration of this text. The only other quick dramaturgical footnote to this, which is kind of funny, is that Mary Coleman discovered a fairly common French text that many of you might know, by Jacques Guicharnaud. He wrote a book on Molière, focusing, I believe, on *Tartuffe, Don Juan,* and *The Misanthrope.*[45] The way Mary put it was, "I found this wonderful essay. I think you're going to like it. I'm translating it for you. I think you'll find it useful." In auditions, she presented me with about ten pages of the single best essay I have ever read on Molière or *The Misanthrope.* It was absolutely true to my vision of the work and was so brilliant in its criticism and its guidance that I couldn't wait for Mary to finish. Mary spent the next two months translating this article and it turned out to be a ninety-page, line-by-line analysis of the text. It was my road map I found it so important that I demanded that Mary stay up all night to translate act 2, scene 3 because I was going into rehearsal with it the next day. That's how tight we were translating this article.

So we've talked a lot. Do people have any questions?

Q: *Can you talk about the set?*

FALLS: George Tsypin, the Soviet-born set designer who collaborates a lot with Peter Sellars and JoAnne Akalaitis, designed a brilliant set that was very much a part of the play. It was modeled, in a loose way, after Madonna's house. Another touchstone for our production was Madonna's relationship to Warren Beatty. Our Alceste had a great deal of Mr. Beatty, and our Celimene had more than a touch of Madonna as this object of his desire. And *Vogue* at the time of our production did a spread on her house in the Hollywood Hills, which is actually more tasteful than the one we created onstage. The play was set on the precipice of the Hollywood Hills. It was literally a dangerous set; you could fall into the pit. We wanted it absolutely dangerous as if to spite all of the bullshit these people are going through with "what does it matter if the earthquake comes." It was a large force of God that could rip them all apart, so it had a sense of danger at all times. It was also a very small acting space and it was very vertical. We parked an actual sports car, a red Austin Healy, up above in a carport.

I should mention that Madonna's house is dominated by two things: she collects eighteenth-century Italian furniture and exercise equipment. Also shoes. It was a brutally white set. It's hard to describe, but it did feature a brilliant metaphor (which was completely the designer's idea) in the center of the set. There was, of course, beautiful and delicate Louis XIV furniture, and at the center of the set was what looked like a sculptural art object. It was twenty-four feet high, and at a certain point it turned to reveal itself as an exercise machine. But when you see it in operation, it's a guillotine. As the machine is going up and down, you see it has a blade—it was a guillotine, this enormous terrifying black image of fascistic Southern California devotion to exercise and egocentric workout. So the final image was of Celimene working out all alone, abandoned in her house to the sounds of Madonna's "Express Yourself," while the blade of the guillotine went up and down.

Love Has Entered My Vocabulary:
A Cautionary Tale
by **James Magruder**

JAMES MAGRUDER is in his fifth season as Resident Dramaturg of Baltimore's Center Stage, where he has worked on plays by Shakespeare, Molière, Ibsen, Goldoni, Chekhov, and George Walker. *Three French Comedies,* a book of his translations of Lesage, Labiche, and Marivaux, was published by Yale University Press in 1996. He holds degrees in French literature from Cornell and Yale and a doctorate from the Yale School of Drama, and when he can, he contributes to *American Theatre* magazine.

THE PAGE

The dramaturg as translator? One more dart in the quiver for the dramaturg perpetually besieging the American theater for work. Translating may not be as useful an institutional skill as being able to work the room at a corporate fundraiser, but any dramaturg who, in addition to the other twenty or so requisite talents and attitudes, carries within himself or herself a secret list of a dozen amazing, unclaimed masterpieces (if not outright translations of a couple of them) is that much more likely to get hired by a theater. That, I assume, is the reasoning behind the translation requirement for a Yale School of Drama MFA in dramaturgy and dramatic criticism. Every candidate must have translated a full-length play, classic or contemporary, in order to graduate. This tends to discourage monolingual applicants to the program and that is, I think, sound practice for the profession. Students who have not immersed themselves in the language, literature, thinking, idiosyncracies, and civilization of at least one foreign culture should find another function in the theater. For what is the dramaturg but the Repository of all Culture, Votary to the Flame of Dramatic Tradition, etc., etc.?

I wasn't thinking of these lofty wherefores during my Thanksgiving break from Yale in 1986. I recall being unable to enjoy New Hampshire that weekend, because act 1 of my translation was due in class the following Tuesday, and I resented it, and I hadn't even started. I *had* picked the play. Gitta Honegger, my translation professor, knowing my background, had cued me to Marivaux's *Le Triomphe de l'amour.* This utterly obscure play by its only slightly less obscure playwright had enjoyed a noteworthy rediscovery the previous year in a German production at the Schaubühne. (Marivaux is not obscure to the Europeans.) Unlike several of Marivaux's better known plays such as *The Game of Love and Chance* or *False Confessions, Le Triomphe de l'amour* had, at that date, never been translated into English.

I didn't know the play, but I knew Marivaux and his place in the French canon. Prior to my years in drama school, I had served time in a doctoral program in French literature at Yale. Literature departments are traditionally hostile to theater and drama; at Yale French in 1983, literary deconstruction held implacable sway, and because theater—that most bourgeois of art forms—resists advanced theory, my interest in eighteenth-century dramatic literature could find no high-powered chaperone. Before defecting to Yale dramaturgy, I did study Marivaux in a doctrinally unfashionable course: Literature of the Regency (1715–23), and wrote a poorly received paper on one of his philosophic journals. What I recalled of Marivaux, as I bent over a makeshift desk near Moultonboro, New Hampshire, a photocopy of *Triomphe* and three heavy dictionaries at my side, was that Voltaire hated him and that his writing was considered precious, feminine, and not to everyone's taste.

Well, as my writing and I have chronically been accused of possessing these same three qualities, Marivaux and I appeared to be a perfect fit. By translating *The Triumph of Love,* I envisioned myself blowing the dust off his rococo style, making him live for an American audience, and not incidentally, fleeing New Haven with an MFA. Someday I might even earn royalties for my pains (another reason why dramaturgs should translate).

That was almost ten years ago. At this writing, all of the above has happened, only slower. Today, after completing countless drafts and personally participating (or intervening) in three different productions of the translation, at Center Stage in Baltimore, the Classic Stage Company in New York, and at the La Jolla Playhouse in La Jolla, California, I feel qualified to assert that *The Triumph of Love* is a reclaimed masterpiece, but a play that nevertheless had to wait for the twentieth century to appreciate its merits. The dramaturg who can translate is especially equipped to reclaim plays like this, ideally combining a sensitivity to linguistic and cultural nuance with an innate, hard-won knowledge of what works onstage and what doesn't.

Marivaux is considered one of those untranslatable playwrights, like Kleist and Racine, a writer too contextually and linguistically rooted to an alien culture with alien thematic preoccupations to make stage sense. Following Molière by fifty years, Marivaux was after something quite different in his work. A private man in that hysterically public and most theatrical of centuries, he once wrote "I have spied in the human heart all the different niches where Love can hide when it is afraid to show itself, and each one of my comedies has for its object to make Love come from out of its niche." In a century of awakened sensibility and delicacy and artifice, Marivaux's enduring dramatic revolution is to make self-reflection both the substance and the sole obstacle in his theater. Pride, vanity, ego, self-consciousness, and self-delusion stand in the way of the young lovers, as opposed to the traditional comic roadblocks like irascible parents, jealous rivals, penury, or low birth. A Marivaux play limns the delicious, agonizing, protracted process of falling in love; in a sense he is dramatizing the celebrated *Carte du Tendre* or *Map of Tenderness.*

Appearing first in Madame de Scudéry's romanesque novel *Clélie* and one of the wackiest documents in the history of French literature, the *Carte du Tendre* is a *précieuse* visualization of all the highways and byways on the bumpy road to Love, marked by places like The Lake of Indifference, The Cliffs of Pride, and The Town of Sincerity. As dramaturg Catherine Sheehy aptly puts it, Marivaux's dramaturgical benchmark was "the examination and exposition of an objective correlative of the emotional state of his characters. That's a fancy way of saying Marivaux seemed to have the answers not only to the musical question, 'Why do fools fall in love?' but 'How?' as well."

And, to do so, Marivaux invented the psychological language of love which bears his name—*le marivaudage*—for the *commedia dell'arte* characters he inherited, refining them and the French comic tradition in the process. It is a language of emotional half-steps, fidgets, and tics, neurotic projections and hesitations. The scenes between his young lovers tread a fine line between the highly profound and the dangerously adolescent. One of the great eighteenth-century estheticians of emotional foreplay, Marivaux (along with Richardson and Rousseau) must share responsibility for the discovery and articulation of such deathless sentiments as "I love you, but I'm not *in* love with you." When too faithfully translated, *le marivaudage* is painfully stilted and about as amusing as *Parsifal*. Too loosely or colloquially translated, and the young lovers wind up sounding neurotically coy, like Inge without the sex.

Le Triomphe de l'amour was not a success in its 1732 premiere, and it fell into obscurity for nearly two hundred years. Given the prevailing twin peaks of French neoclassical doctrine—*bienséance* (seemliness or decorum) and *vraisemblance* (verisimilitude), it's not difficult to see why. The plot: The philosopher Hermocrate and his maiden sister Léontine have taken to the woods to escape a frivolous, unreasoning, lovestruck society. They have raised Agis, a royal foundling, to scorn love and the sexual act that incarnates it. Princess Léonide has glimpsed Agis reading in a forest and fallen in love with him. He also happens to be the rightful heir to the throne upon which she sits. Her aim is to win his love at any cost and restore him to power.

Unlike most Marivaux heroines, Léonide is in love before the play begins and is well beyond being derailed by its exquisite divagations. She knows how to manipulate love and its powers to her advantage; her stratagem is the quicksilver improvisation of four separate identities to spring the prince from his garden retreat. In the first two acts she seduces the three hermits in dazzling turns. Disguised as Lord Phocion, a comely young scholar seeking wisdom from philosophic mentors, she appeals to the long-dormant vanity of the aging Léontine. Hermocrate, with his advanced powers of reason, discovers "Phocion's" true gender immediately, but, instead of revealing her true identity to him, the Princess invents another female guise on the spot, that of Aspasie, a Portia-like casuist who trusses up the philosopher with his own logic. And after the defenseless Agis has two itchy, homoerotic encounters with young Lord Phocion, she reveals a second Aspasie to him, an utter gamine who, ostensibly seeking his protection, exploits his sexual naiveté nonetheless. Is the real Léonide any one of these assumed masks? Or is she the haughty princess who threatens to put Harlequin and Dimas, her rustic henchmen, in jail for their greed?

As act 3 begins, all three lovers expect to marry their beloved. The ancient laws of comedy cannot provide a triple wedding for four people, but Marivaux unties his plot with scant regard for awakened sensibilities. After revealing her ruse, the princess tells Hermocrate and Léontine that they deserve to be humiliated, and she walks out with her prince. She restores the throne to its rightful owner without bloodshed; the servants have been paid; but the jilted siblings are destroyed by the revelation that they are prey to human emotion just like everyone else.

Love is delightful and love is cruel, leaving victors and victims in its wake. Marivaux honors both extremes in his play. Princess Léonide is clearly a dangerous force, the brainiest and most diabolical female in Marivaux's theater. In terms of *vraisemblance,* contemporary critics found her swaggering demeanor more in keeping with a romanesque adventuress than the Spartan princess she is. Reveling in her role playing, she is thrilled to debase the hapless philosopher and his bluestocking sister. Her cross-dressing and the resulting androgynous erotics in her scenes with a confused prince were a telling violation of *bienséance.* A patent flair for dishonesty made her a woman too problematically powerful for eighteenth-century theatrical convention, yet make her a fascinating twentieth-century heroine.

As I mentioned, it didn't initially matter to me that Marivaux was untranslatable or possibly unworthy of translation, because act 1 was due on Tuesday. I don't mean to sound too flip; I took the task seriously. I wrote the first two drafts of the play over a period of three months, and I do recall several early— and fateful—tactical decisions. First, this was in no way going to be an academic (read: fusty and unstageworthy) translation, so I decided not to be overly respectful of Marivaux. I decided if I were to work him onto the twentieth-century stage, he and I would have to meet each other halfway, and to do so, we would have to agree that we were *both* comic writers preoccupied with effects of language and style. In other words, we were a great match. This pact accomplished, I was able to move forward with the guiding principle of *entertaining myself.* If I found it funny, others might. I embraced flourish and euphony. I went for the laughs.

Second, I decided (or quickly learned by following my instinct) that the best way for me to approximate the tortuous verbal agitations of these characters *and* portray the four distinct identities of the princess *as well as* her effects upon the philosophers and the prince was to translate their multifarious, wobbly emotional states as aggressive shifts in diction. And when the text didn't suggest them, I would invent them. As a writer and critic, what personally fascinates me, what keeps me entertained as I survey the world I live in, is the raucous mixture of high and low culture, of refined and vulgar impulses, that informs our daily actions and utterances. I am irresistibly drawn to patois of every persuasion. Language is a weapon in Marivaux, because Love makes the characters say dangerous things; they express themselves and their dawning emotions in languages and utterances that betray their class, age, sex, station, education, and spiritual extremis—my job would be to heighten the nuances as they happened. The sexual tension would be maintained, stoked, betrayed by the gaps between what they said and what they felt. In other words, my solution for *le marivaudage* would be exuberant diction shifts, and with twice the number of words as French, the English language would be of enormous help.

My third tactical decision related to the characters. Marivaux wrote for a specific troupe of *commedia dell'arte* actors. Some of the parts in *The Triumph of Love,* particularly the clown roles, are less well written than others; they must have relied upon specific comic personae to flesh them out. In order to keep myself entertained and "translate" them for a modern audience, I found that it helped to work from a popular image for several of the characters. For example, the sidekick Hermidas as written is rather colorless. She is burdened with conversational tags ("Go on.""Yes, that is so.""How interesting.") that have more to do with neoclassical conceptions of the confidante than they do with more modern ideas of genuinely consecutive dialogue. The first scene, loaded down as it is with extended exposition is especially difficult to keep lively. Yet, once I visualized Hermidas as a combination of Ethel Mertz and Bette Midler, possessed of many fresh and skeptical and earthy tones, Hermidas became easy to hear, and therefore translate. In a sense, I didn't translate her lines so much as I adapted her language into a combative relationship of rim-shot salvos with her mistress. Similarly, I was having trouble with how Lady Léontine should sound until I recalled the bell tones of the perpetually aggrieved Margaret Dumont, Groucho's romantic foil of a certain age. I certainly wasn't writing Marx Brothers dialogue for them, but I did find it liberating to structure the Phocion/Léontine interchanges as a series of comic deflations visited upon a dowager by a slightly off-color bounder. (Léontine ultimately turned away from her Marx Brothers antecedents in rehearsal, but I am getting ahead of myself.)

Then there was Dimas, the gardener. He speaks a garbled peasant dialect in the original; that is the source of Dimas's humor for a French audience. How does one render that in American English? A faithful syntactical mangle of his speech would only turn him into an idiot, negating his agrarian cunning, which stands in relief to Hermocrate's cold-hearted sophistry. Dimas could conceivably bear a regional American accent—Southern or Brooklyn or the Bronx—but those choices are too cheap and insulting, even for me, and would limit the choices an actor could make in the role. Finally, taking a cue from Marivaux, who occasionally has Dimas express himself botanically, I decided that Dimas would draw his metaphors exclusively, if not ceaselessly, from horticulture and its practices. Critics or academicians might carp that such firm-handed decisions about character from a translator might warp Marivaux's intentions or unnecessarily dictate an actor's choices. My answer is that some measure of contextual adaptation of the *commedia* spirit was necessary. We may no longer reference the dramatic confidante, but we do certainly apprehend why Lucy needs Ethel to succeed.

DEFENSE AND ILLUSTRATION

Some concrete textual examples of what I was up to:

Hermidas: Tiens, d'une bagatelle: Madame a vu Agis dans la forêt, et n'a pu le voir sans lui donner son coeur.
Harlequin: Cela est extrêmement honnête!
Hermidas: Or, Madame qui est riche, qui ne dépend que d'elle, et qui l'épouserait volontiers, voudrait essayer de le rendre sensible.
Harlequin: Encore plus honnête!
Hermidas: Madame ne saurait le rendre sensible qu'en liant quelque conversation avec lui, qu'en demeurant même quelque temps dans la maison où il est.
Harlequin: Pour avoir toutes ses commodités.
Hermidas: Et cela ne se pourrait pas, si elle se presentait habillée suivant son sexe. . . .

Hermidas: A bagatelle. My mistress saw Agis in the forest. One look and she couldn't help but rend her heart to him.
Phocion: Render.
Hermidas: Same difference.
Harlequin: Touching.
Hermidas: My mistress, who is rich, independent, and eligible, would like to make him sensitive to her feelings.
Harlequin: Very touching.
Hermidas: As far as we know, the only way to tenderize him is to engage him in conversation and sleep in his—(**Phocion** coughs delicately)—house.
Harlequin: You mean share in all his comforts.
Hermidas: I like that you're bright. Now my lady can't do that walking around here in her own sex. . . .

In this exchange, Harlequin, who has immediately discovered that Phocion and Hermidas are women, threatens to reveal their ruse, so Hermidas, who knows how to manage the lower orders, steps in. Unencumbered by refined egos, Marivaux's wise servants fall briskly in love and push their poky masters along with their sexual alacrity. Because both Harlequin and Dimas later claim to have the hots for Hermidas on very little textual encouragement from her, I wanted to set up some chemistry between them from the outset—"touching" for *honnête* and "sleep in his house," which is more pushed than a literal translation like "staying some time in the house where he is." (Hermidas of course is about to say "sleep in his bed" until the princess reroutes her sentence.)

Marivaux writes that Hermidas' mistress would "willingly marry him" (*l'épouserait volontiers*); I changed that to "eligible" so as to give Hermidas room to use this description of her mistress as a self-description as well. It's one of several come-ons to Harlequin in this section, the most obvious being "I like that you're bright." Most essential to the philosophical spirit of the translation is the quibble of "rend" or "render" her heart. This invention lends weight to their class difference, shows who's boss, and demonstrates that the princess is *very* precise about language. Neither choice is particularly faithful for *donner son coeur,* but Hermidas' retort *same difference* alerts the audience to the idea that Love can tear one apart in this world, and that the princess intends to be ruthless with her foes.

Hermocrate: Ce n'est pas sans raison que j'ai voulu vous parler en secret; j'ai des soupçons dont l'éclaircissement ne demande point d'éclat; et c'est à vous à qui je l'épargne.
Phocion: Quels sont donc ces soupçons?
Hermocrate: Vous ne vous appelez point Phocion.
Phocion: (à part) Il se ressouvient de la forêt.
Hermocrate: Celui dont vous prenez le nom, est actuellement à Athènes, je l'apprends par une lettre de Mermécides.
Phocion: Ce peut être quelqu'un qui se nomme comme moi.
Hermocrate: Ce n'est pas là tout: c'est que ce nom supposé est la moindre erreur où vous voulez nous jeter.

Hermocrate: I have some suspicions which crave enlightenment.
Phocion: What are these suspicions?
Hermocrate: First, you are not called Phocion.
Phocion: I'm not.
Hermocrate: The man whose name you assume is currently in Athens, or so a letter from Mermicide informs me.
Phocion: Phocion is a common name.
Hermocrate: An alias is the least of your falsehoods.
Phocion: (aside) He remembers the forest.

In their first meeting, Hermocrate proves more terrifying to the princess than she anticipated from her chance encounter in the forest. To give this initial exchange more dramatic force, I condensed Hermocrate's longer French line, which shows more of his hand into the simpler, more pointed "I have some suspicions which crave enlightenment." The more powerful a person is, the less he or she has to say in order to exercise that power. Love will later make Hermocrate garrulous, but for now he is as forbidding as a Mafia don.

Similarly, "An alias is the least of your falsehoods," is harsher than the original text—it's meant to sting and forces her aside about the forest, which I have delayed for two reasons. I thought it heightened suspense to stall her realization that he's seen beneath her disguise, and I thought it was more dramatic to watch her remain a "man" and attempt to brazen it out with "I'm not," and "Phocion is a common name"—terse, ballsy statements to match his.

Dimas: Je m'embarrasse bian de voute gorge, ha ha! des femmes qui baillont de l'argent en darrière un jardinier, maugré qu'il les treuve dans son jardrin, il n'y a morgué point de gorge qui tianne, faut punir ça.

Dimas: What do I care? That's choice—women pulling stumps behind the gardener's back, and I found them. I'll prune 'em all.

Dimas is speaking the language he knows best. I think that "What do I care?" better suits the moment and his relationship to Harlequin than a more literal repetition such as "I could care less about your throat," because Dimas is looking ahead to the next thing: money. In the French, he mentions his *jardin* and the insult of women trying to put one over on him, so I chose the somewhat suggestive metaphor of pulling stumps, and while retaining the idea of throat-cutting in the last phrase here, I changed it to "I'll prune 'em all"—an image at once horticultural and castratory.

Agis: (d'un ton embarrassé) Sur ce pied-là, ne vous exposez pas à revoir la Princesse; car je suis toujours le même.
Phocion: Vous m'aimez donc encore?
Agis: Toujours, Madame, d'autant plus qu'il n'y a rien à craindre; puisqu'il ne s'agit entre nous que d'amitié, qui est le seul penchant que je puisse inspirer, et le seul aussi, sans doute, dont vous soyez capable.
Phocion et Agis (en même temps): Ah!
Phocion: Seigneur, personne n'est plus digne que vous de la qualité d'ami: celle d'amant ne vous convient que trop; mais ce n'est pas à moi à vous le dire.
Agis: Je voudrais bien ne le devenir jamais.
Phocion: Laissons donc là l'amour: il est même dangereux d'en parler.

Agis: (confused) Don't ever go near that evil princess again! (pause) I still feel as I did.
Phocion: You still like me then?
Agis: And forever, my lady. Even more now . . . since there's nothing to fear. Since we feel so . . . friendly, right: right? So like . . . that's all we . . . no doubt . . . and . . .
Phocion & Agis: (sighing) Ahhhh!
Phocion: My lord, as a friend you are overwhelmingly worthy. (dreamy) As a

lover, you are only too qualified. (catching herself) I say that as a friend.

Agis: I hope never to become a lover.

Phocion: (crushed) No? (catching herself) Let's set love aside. It's dangerous even to speak of it.

These beats have turned out to be among the most difficult to perform in the play. Phocion has just revealed to Agis that she is a woman, one Aspasie who has fled the land of her birth, because the Princess Léonide has ordered her to marry an unappealing cousin. Agis is torn between feelings of horror to be near a woman, nascent jealousy over this imaginary cousin, and an intense rush of libido. Phocion, for her part, has to mediate her arousal and her calculation at the same time. The scene combines the sexual moodiness of *Splendor in the Grass* with the ingenuousness of the soda fountain scene between Emily and George in *Our Town,* and it cannot be camped. I added "evil" to "princess" in Agis's line to reinforce his doctrinal misogyny and the danger Léonide is in, should she be discovered. Marivaux breaks up Agis's syntax somewhat in his "Toujours, Madame, d'autant plus . . ." speech; I have chosen to make him sound completely adolescent: stammering and pausing, yet the ellipses in the speech give the actor many things to play. In the translation, he repeats the word "lover" ("I hope never to become a lover.") to keep the word in the air, play up the tension between *lover* and *friend,* and provoke Leontine's invented response ("No?").

Hermidas: Hermocrate n'a point paru; mais sa soeur vous cherche, et a demandé au jardinier où vous étiez: elle a l'air un peu triste, apparemment que le philosophe ne se rend pas.

Phocion: Oh! il a beau faire, il deviendra docile, ou tout l'art de mon sexe n'y pourra rien.

Arlequin: Et le seigneur Agis promet-il quelque chose; son coeur se mitonne-t-il un peu?

Phocion: Encore une ou deux conversations, et je l'emporte.

Hermidas: Hermocrate never turned up, but his sister is looking for you. She was asking Dimas where you'd gone to. She looks sad—evidently old stoneface won't budge.

Phocion: He resists in vain! I'll sculpt him to my pleasure, or all the art of my sex is worthless.

Harlequin: And does Lord Agis promise anything? Has his heart simmered enough?

Phocion: Two more interviews and he'll be cooked clean through.

Here, immediately after Agis exits, Léonide checks in with her three henchmen, and turns a complete about-face from the giddy Aspasie. In Marivaux, Hermidas says, "The philosopher won't give in." In keeping with my teased-up conception for the role, Hermidas says, "Old stoneface won't budge." This intensification of image continues with the use of "sculpt." In the original Hermocrate's conversion is stated passively—"he will become docile" (*Il deviendra docile*); ever interested in keeping the princess fierce, I changed her line to the active "I'll sculpt him to my pleasure, or all the art of my sex is worthless." The related image sequence of stone/sculpt/art, not in the original text, nevertheless mimics a technique of *marivaudage*: one word thrown out by a character is picked up by the second, emended or elaborated upon, and thrown back for furthur elaboration, and so on. In this little sequence, Harlequin drops the art idea and switches to cooking: "Has his heart simmered (*mitonner*) enough?" Phocion's reply: "Two more interviews and he'll be cooked clean through," turned out to be the one line that every actress to date has balked at. The original, more faithfully rendered, might read "Still one or two conversations, and I will carry it off." Perhaps I was being unnecessarily perverse when I intensified her response to Harlequin's culinary sally, but I was and am interested in keeping her in control and drunk on her newfound power to seduce. This rapid change in diction from her dewy moments with Agis makes the audience gasp, but I think it's in keeping with her quicksilver identity, and why not have her remain ahead of the audience? Truthfully, Marivaux's original line is not particularly sympathetic to begin with.

Phocion: . . . Je suis chez vous; vous m'y avez souffert; vous savez que je vous aime; me voilà pénétré de la passion la plus tendre; vous me l'avez inspirée, et je partirais! Eh! Léontine, demandez-moi ma vie, déchirez mon coeur, ils sont tous deux à vous; mais ne me demandez point des choses impossibles.
Léontine: Quelle vivacité de mouvements! Non, Phocion, jamais je ne sentis tant la nécessité de votre départ; et je ne m'en mêle plus. Juste ciel! Que deviendrait mon coeur avec l'impétuosité du vôtre?. . . .

Phocion: I am here with you; you know that I love you; you see me penetrated by the most tender passion, *you* inspired it, and *I* should leave? Oh, Léontine, ask me for my life, tear my heart to bits—my life, my heart, yours, they're yours, yours, yours! Don't ask the impossible.
Léontine: (aside) What . . . vivid . . . fluctuations! (aloud, grandly) No, Phocion. Never have I felt more the necessitous obligation of your imminent departure.
Phocion: Translation please?
Léontine: You must go. (pause) I wash my hands of this affair. O just heavens! Joined to the impetuousness of your heart, what would I become? . . .

This is from Phocion's second encounter with Léontine, when the older woman has refortified herself (she thinks) against her assailant. Fresh from her triumph with Agis, the princess takes her Casanova persona even further;

in this section, like a gigolo frustrated with a truculent charge about to give him his walking papers, he blames Léontine for the way he feels and becomes less delicate as he goes. The repetition of the words "life" and "heart" (not in Marivaux) and the series of thrusting "yours, yours, yours," is the discourse of a man who wants what he wants when he wants it. Léontine, for her part, after allowing herself a moment of private delight ("What vivid fluctuations!") draws herself up and tries to conceal her mounting sexual panic within her formerly adamantine identity. "Never have I felt more . . . " may sound like a bad literal translation of the French, but I deliberately made her sentence more convoluted than necessary—adding the word "necessitous" to "obligation" as a clear redundancy, and "imminent" to "departure." Of course, this diction is so high that Phocion has to have it translated both for herself and for the audience. A tongue-in-cheek reminder of my process, "Translation please?" forces Léontine to say what she means and cleanly demonstrates Marivaux's prevailing interest in showing at what cross-purposes his characters' hearts and minds are working throughout act 2. Mediating the two pulses is the movement of all his plays; Hermocrate and Léontine ultimately deserve to be punished for neglecting their hearts at the expense of their minds. ("Translation please?" also gets a healthy laugh, and I am never above that impulse.)

Léontine: Ah! vous voilà, mon frère; je vous demande à tout le monde.

Léontine: There you are. I've been asking after you everywhere. No one can sit still today.

"No one can sit still today," is another invented line designed to acknowledge the formal artificiality of the play, an artificial sequence of entrances and exits (a hallmark of classical dramaturgy) quite at odds with the real emotions that threaten to blow up the rigid, ordered world that Hermocrate and Léontine have spent their lives constructing. "Today" is a tip of the hat to the neoclassical unity of time. The princess—*Love*—has set them all in motion, and until this moment near the end of act 2, everyone has been hurtling in and out of the garden convulsed by their secret feelings. Here at the end of act 2, Hermocrate and his sister are about to have a painful conversation that provides the tonal balance to the increasingly farcical shenanigans wrought by Léonide's multiple disguises. Earlier, Léontine has cried out "Love has entered my vocabulary," and now they both have to deal with the consequences. At this point, the siblings have surrendered their hearts, one to Phocion, the other to Aspasie, and they are left to wonder out loud whether perhaps quitting society was an error. Hurled into passion's chasm in their twilight years, gradually awakening to the force of love, they are like children groping for speech. When each tells the other, abashed, that they are not too old for romance and are even *attractive,* Marivaux achieves an unsentimental, Chekhovian pathos. If the rest of the play has been translated as a mad dash for Agis before the troops come in, I was careful to let this scene, the emotional heart of the play, the only time in fact in the play when there *is* time to sit still, breathe. I broke up their speeches slightly and allowed them to be even more tentative and halting with their declarations of loneliness.

THE STAGE

I got a good grade on the translation and graduated in May of 1988. I had no cause to recall *The Triumph of Love* for a year until Michael Mayer, then a brand-new director, contacted me to say that he had a Valentine's Day reading slot open at New York Theater Workshop (NYTW) and did I have anything appropriate? I reluctantly parted with *Triumph,* thinking that despite my writerly antics, the text probably wasn't worth staging and the translation was probably too arch.

On February 13, 1990, a week before I left to work at the La Jolla Playhouse, 227 years after the death of its author, *The Triumph of Love* had its first hearing in the New World. I won't soon forget the first question out of the mouth of the actor playing Hermocrate: "Is this a comedy?" Well he might ask. I also recall the late, star arrival of Ruth Warrick (of *Citizen Kane* and *All My Children* fame): the other actors wore sweats and Evian and backpacks; Ruth, resplendent in a red wool suit trimmed with black fur cuffs and collar, was a spectacularly glamorous and touching Léontine. Hardest to forget was Marcia Gay Harden's nearly cold take on the princess: a combination of Katherine Hepburn, Elizabeth Bergner, Rita Hayworth, and Lucille Ball, manipulative as all hell but sexy and funny and vulnerable and warm. Her performance led me to believe that the play was a one-woman *tour de force.*

Nothing in my professional life had ever gone so well. But the artistic director of NYTW was not there to catch the magic, so no offer was forthcoming. I left for the West Coast. A dramaturg friend, making pennies by reading scripts for the late, lamented Los Angeles Theater Center (LATC), convinced their literary department to have a workshop reading of *Triumph* in September of 1991, which meant there would be three full days of rehearsal and time to refine the text. I suggested Lisa Peterson, a trusted friend and collaborator, as director. Lisa, who has one of the best dramaturgical minds I know, and I had several phone calls before the reading. I remember doing a lot of rewrites for her, only becoming alarmed at her interest in cutting out a lot of the verbiage (aka *le marivaudage*), which she believed impeded the action. As best I could, I said that those speeches were what made Marivaux Marivaux. Pause. "You should still think about trimming them." I didn't, but I added enough new jokes to placate her.

As for the reading, same song, different verse—they laughed, they loved, they cried. What an amazing play. What a great role for an actress. What a difficult ending. The artistic director offered me a contract—two weeks before his theater permanently closed its doors. No time for tears—I was already on my way to Baltimore. Irene Lewis, who had just assumed interim leadership of Center Stage, had invited me to dramaturg her productions of *Pericles* and *The Misanthrope* while I finished my doctoral dissertation for Yale. As an act of welcome to me, she held an impromptu reading of *Triumph* the week I arrived. We all laughed ourselves sick. After three readings, I was now the translator of America's most amazing classic comic secret, but three days into our working relationship, I wasn't about to spoil my chances with my new boss by insisting she produce my work.

A year and a half later, however, while picking the 1993-94 Center Stage season, Irene gave in to *The Triumph of Love;* even better, she would direct. Did I mention that, in addition to being an amazing play, *Triumph* requires one set and only seven actors? In the world of the classics, that's a cheapie. But enough about me. Rehearsals began on September 7, 1993. Without really stopping to consider it, I had created a translation that was so particularized in its language, so all over the map linguistically, it basically guaranteed postmodern design and staging. In preproduction, directors and designers quickly discovered, mostly to their relief, that pannier skirts, Watteau imagery, and a traditional *commedia* baton for Harlequin would never square with lines like "I think I've blown it with him" or "No, my lady, finish him off."

The actors were less relieved at the discovery. How could Hermocrate say to Phocion: "The blackest soul, the most vulgar lovers, the maddest knaves and damsels, never feel the agitations that pierce my breast" only to say, five beats later "just don't blubber now"? The princess was alarmed by the marathon she was to run and was certain the audience would throw fruit at her for being so evil to the older philosophers. Harlequin thought he had to get a laugh on every line because of his name. Agis was worried the character was so naive and slow that he appeared mentally retarded. Irene seemed certain—all the way through the second preview—that the theatrical rococo would sail right over Catholic, boiled-potato Baltimore. I was kept out of rehearsal, but daily textual questions were served up to me by the stage manager. I found myself looking at the French for the first time in years, quite a sobering experience. I dickered with the text; first to go were the Margaret Dumont–inspired fat jokes at Léontine's expense. I stole a French tirade from Racine and gave it to the princess to say to humiliate Harlequin when he spills her secret to Dimas. Chief on the list was the injunction—*"Please* soften 'Two more interviews and he'll be cooked clean through.'"

In the end, Irene, the designers, and the cast created a gorgeous production that fully honored all the pain and the comedy and the passion in the play. I was less surprised at the positive reception to the work than Irene was, because I knew it was a good play and knew from four previous collaborations with Irene as her dramaturg that she is immensely gifted at getting more out of a play than one ever expects. Her production was a revelation—Marivaux hadn't written a good play; he had written a *great* play. I learned an awful lot from that first production and put my discoveries to good use in the subsequent productions in New York and La Jolla. Some discoveries were more obvious than others. It is not a one-woman show. The play is essentially a romantic fairy tale, and the audience will forgive Léonide everything, and I mean *everything,* "cooked clean through" and all, if it believes that she would give her life up for Agis. Act 1 is a setup for the rest of the play; no matter what the actors do with my jokes, audiences will laugh only at Harlequin in act 1, because they're listening closely to the princess's schemes. The language just lays there if the actors don't invest the consonants with an almost operatic relish. Finally, and most important, the actress playing Léonide has to enjoy her liberation, hide her transitions, and stay on the offensive. All of the actresses who have played her have initially resisted the bravura, self-dramatizing side to the character. "You *love* yourself in this!" was the most frequent note I gave in run-throughs and previews in Baltimore, New York, and La Jolla.

I'll finish with an anecdote. One night in Baltimore, late in act 1, an older gentleman in the audience, realizing in a flash that the princess was intending to make emotional hash of Hermocrate, cried out "She's a deceiver!" He had been there, and he felt compelled to warn Hermocrate. And so had everyone else in the house who laughed at his spontaneous advice. Audiences respond to *The Triumph of Love* not because they have been trained to appreciate classic theater, but because *everyone* has travelled the Bumpy Road to Love. Everyone has done time at the Lake of Indifference. Everyone remembers that first Agis, or when they were Agis, or when they were duped by a Phocion, or when they were Phocion, obsessively pursuing someone hammer and tongs, consequences be damned.

I see that I keep returning to the audience. Dramaturgs aren't necessarily trained or predisposed to put the audience first. (If we attempted to honor their wishes first, there would be far too many productions of *The Diary of Anne Frank* and no productions of *Woyzeck.*) Generally, we're around to protect the intentions of the playwright, living or dead. Then our allegiance is to the director and the collaborative process in rehearsal. Consequently, it's easy to feel superior to the audience and discount its reaction when something isn't working onstage—*they* don't get it, *they're* not smart enough, what do *they* know? I discovered that the dramaturg who translates cannot afford the luxury of that pose—I wanted *Triumph* to connect, the jokes to land, the patrons to care. A dramaturg with foreign languages is ultimately ideal for the task of translation, idealistic enough to ferret out unclaimed masterpieces and practical enough to draw upon hard-earned stage sense and make them matter again.

Multicultural Approaches in Dramaturgy:
A Case Study
by Elizabeth C. Ramírez

ELIZABETH C. RAMÍREZ, Regional VP, LMDA; former Fellow in Dramaturgy, American Repertory Theatre; reader, NEA Playwriting competitions; and founder and former director, Chicano Theatre Program, California State University, Sacramento; received her doctorate at The University of Texas. She has taught at Harvard University, University of Texas, and University of Arizona, and published *Footlights Across the Border: A History of Spanish-language Professional Theatre* and numerous articles and reviews on Chicana/Chicano/Latina/Latino theater. She has served as dramaturg for Anne Bogart, Andrei Serban, David Wheeler, Ed Call, and Gary Gisselman, and most recently Jim Edmundson for the Oregon Shakespeare Festival's production of *Blood Wedding*. Currently the Director of Ethnic Studies and Assistant Professor in Theatre Arts at the University of Oregon, her professional affiliation is with the Arizona Theatre Company.

"America cannot be a melting pot anymore. That's an image from a phase of our life that belongs to the history books, a time when, by dissolving one culture into another, we thought to create the signature of our land: e pluribus unum—out of the many, one. . . . The highest attribute of nature is its diversity. It has taken billions of years to evolve its manifoldness. And so, one day the highest accomplishment of manmade civilization, following nature, will be precisely that—its diversity."[46]
ZELDA FICHANDLER, IN A SPECIAL ISSUE OF *American Theatre* DEVOTED ENTIRELY TO "RETHINKING MULTICULTURALISM" IN AMERICA.

The premiere of *One Crazy Day or The Marriage of Figaro* in October 1992 opened the twenty-sixth season of the Arizona Theatre Company (ATC) under the direction of its new artistic director, David Ira Goldstein. Roger Downey's translation and adaptation of Pierre Caron de Beaumarchais' (1732–1799) *La folle journee, ou, le mariage de figaro* (1783), known in English as *The Marriage of Figaro*,[47] was commissioned and premiered by the Arizona Theatre Company. I served as the dramaturg for the production.

This case study will examine one production that provides examples of cross-cultural explorations on the American stage. In this case study, race and ethnicity are at the heart of the performance, and the approach serves to educate the audience about the Chicana/Chicano experience.[43] This project also suggests one of many ways to address issues and ideas that revolve around multiculturalism and diversity in the wider spectrum of negotiating performing culture.

David Goldstein had been wanting to direct *The Marriage of Figaro* for a long time, but he had been searching for just the right context. Goldstein noted that he wanted to open his first full season as the new artistic director with evident attention to the Chicana/Chicano cultural tradition in the Southwest that surrounded the two theaters that his company served. The Alice Holsclaw Theatre at the Temple of Music and Art in Tucson and the Herberger Theater Center in Phoenix would offer a bill of fare that would witness the fruits of a rich cultural heritage that had been virtually untapped by regional stages. Intent on drawing from the talents of renown artists who could originate challenging and innovative work, Goldstein wanted "something that was ours, something that we created." [49] On one of his many trips as a guest director of ATC, Goldstein had heard a Mariachi band perform, and the seed was planted for his idea of a new project that would examine adopting a Southwestern context for the classic comedy.

Although set in Spain, Beaumarchais' classic contemporary comedy of manners pointedly criticized his own French society, where the nobility during the 1774–1793 reign of Louis XVI had become exorbitant despite Louis' attempts to curb its privileges, much to the dismay of the middle and lower classes who were burdened with taxation but allowed few civil rights. [50] To the traditional "laughing" comedy, typified by Goldsmith and Sheridan in England, Beaumarchais added an unprecedented edge of political and sociological satire. His character, Figaro, who first appeared in the playwright's earlier *The Barber of Seville* (1775), is the extreme logical outcome of the evolution of the Arlecchino (Harlequin) character from the *commedia dell'arte* tradition.

Like the original character, Figaro lives by his wits, but this servant also suggests the potency and menace of the coming French Revolution. The plot of *The Marriage of Figaro* borrows from Roman comedy, but suggests consequences more dangerous to the status quo. Count Almaviva has made Figaro the majordomo of his castle in return for services rendered in the earlier play. The night before his marriage to Suzanne, the countess' chambermaid, Figaro discovers that the count intends to invoke an old feudal privilege, "droit de seigneur," by claiming the new bride himself on the first night. [51] A battle of wits between the powerful nobleman and the resourceful former barber ensues, provoking fast-paced complications and mix-ups. Figaro's antics in trying to thwart the scheming amorous advances of his boss toward his bride-to-be provide a complex plot that culminates in the duping of the count: he ends up making love to his own wife, mistaking her for Suzanne. By the end of the piece, Figaro has evolved from the count's accomplice to his adversary, and levied explicit criticism against rank and privilege.

Although Beaumarchais had set his play in an imaginary chateau in an imaginary Spain to avoid trouble with the French censor, Goldstein wanted to transpose the setting for different aims, to connect the play's themes more directly with his own surrounding community. Issues and ideas about family, honor, trust, the power of women's voices, and the values of the insight of the common person in a structured society were all important aspects of life to consider in this reinterpretation. Roger Downey, a long-time friend and collaborator of Goldstein, was commissioned to adapt the play. He would transform the setting into nineteenth-century Sonora, Mexico, the Mexican region that is present-day Arizona. I was invited to join the production team to help accomplish this transformation of the text.

My work as dramaturg began in July 1992. My initial involvement on this project was working primarily with the translator on the adaptation. I was to provide expertise in Spanish-language performance studies to aid in experimenting with Spanish/English narrative, textual analysis, and production participation. I also provided information, research and background materials, and insight to the total production concept both for the director and the translator/adaptor. The preliminary intent was to work with the translator/adaptor to establish the setting and themes that promised to connect the indigenous Arizonian heritage to a broader contemporary community.

Downey believed that the period of Mexican rule in the Southwest provided an appropriate setting for a plot that revolved around an aristocrat's power over his underlings, including both servants and family members. Downey noted that although Mexico in the 1830s was nominally a republic, a few miles outside of Mexico City and Guadalajara, a great landowner like Beaumarchais' Almaviva would still have absolute power over his tenants and servants: "For us, a setting for the play in preannexation Arizona about the time of the Alamo seemed to offer the perfect balance between historical reality and a certain *Mark of Zorro* touch appropriate to comedy." [52]

From the project's inception, Goldstein had intended to integrate the Chicana/Chicano experience as fully as possible in all aspects of the production. While the director and the translator/adaptor brought notably Western European, that is, Euroamerican Anglo voices (along with those of collaborators, resident set designer Greg Lucas, and costume designer David Kay Mickelsen, a long-time designer for ATC), significant Latina/Latino voices were evident. Striving for accuracy, the company invited Gema Sandoval as choreographer, Nicholas Reveles as composer, along with a local group of Mariachi musicians, and cast numerous Latina/Latino actors.

Choreographer Gema Sandoval, founder and artistic director of Danza Floricanto/USA, has been involved with Mexican folk dance for more than twenty years, and is a recognized activist in Latina/Latino affairs in Southern California. Her use of regional Mexican dances in *One Crazy Day* expressed the culture of the contemporary Chicana/Chicano experience and its traditional heritage. The dances, which included traditional costumes and music, were integrated throughout the production, climaxing in the wedding celebration of Figaro and Susanna.

Nicholas Reveles brought indigenous music to the production, with songs and Mariachi music provided by live musicians and on tape, creating the south-of-the-border flavor with a unique blend of Spanish, Latino, and Mexican music. His original compositions included wandering Mariachis with show-stopping fanfares from the trumpet player. This kind of music was already well known to the Latina/Latino audiences, and even non-Latinos had some familiarity with it, thanks to the popularity of recordings by Linda Ronstadt, a local native, as well as those of other artists.

My cultural background is both Spanish (descending from the original Canary Islanders from Spain who settled in San Antonio, Texas), Mexican, and indigenous Mexican Indian. Both of my parents are second-generation Mexican Americans, both born in the United States. I was born and reared in Texas. My continuing research in American Spanish-language performance history and cultural studies keeps me informed of the many Southwestern resources available to authenticate my various projects that deal with reconnecting the Latina/Latino experience with U.S. audiences. My experience with new plays and adaptations of translations stems from my earlier work as founder and director of the Chicano Theatre Program at California State University, Sacramento. Later projects include adding Italian into the English translation of Carlo Gozzi's *The Serpent Woman* when I worked with Andrei Serban, and Spanish into the English translation of Calderón de la Barca's *Life is a Dream* when I worked with Anne Bogart.[53] Also, I had previously served as dramaturg on several projects at ATC, and my expertise in theater research was evident.[54]

Downey sought my input on milieu, characterizations, the historical *hacienda*—a large estate or farm—setting, along with my suggestions for Spanish terms that could be interspersed and used in substitutions. However, although culture could be apparent through the use of visual as well as aural aspects of the production, Downey viewed the use of language as the integral part of performing the Latina/Latino culture on this Southwestern stage. Thus, we established primary categories to help illustrate this representation of culture, through visual representation, character development, and language.

In the case of visual representation, my research included discovering maps to define location—sites where class distinctions were an integral part of life—and identifying characteristic emblems of the desert Southwest.[55] The results of my research on locale helped the designer to immediately immerse the audience into the world of the Southwest. Using a frontispiece curtain, an antiqued and weather-worn map drawn on parchment-colored fabric indicated the "Hacienda Aguas Frescas," a sprawling ranch. The map key at one corner noted in Spanish that this was indeed the "map of the province of His Excellency Alonso Solano Cesareo Ibarra," who would soon be revealed as the Marquez d'Almaviva himself. Immediately, the audience was immersed in the Old Southwest, in a "hierarchical world where a single exalted man runs a province and, likewise, where a wealthy hacendero runs his own terrain unchallenged."[56]

The set included a crepe-paper *piñata* of a sun and a moon with a wisely smiling face. The picturesque hacienda was complete with red tile roofs, arches and pillars. The painted backdrop of the vividly blue sky of Arizona included mountains that seemed akin to those surrounding Tucson itself.

To build authenticity, the director and translator/adaptor asked me to investigate the hacienda system of class structure and particular details about the entire establishment. I found documents that detailed certain buildings and enabled me to verify how they were used so that the designer could best situate the central plaza, the chapel, and specific rooms such as bedrooms, a *sala* or living room, dining room, and kitchen to determine entrances, exits, and acting areas. For instance, we not only needed to establish the bedroom, but also the kitchen in order to plan the servants' entrances and exits. By identifying the use of stables and garden areas, we could also add other business for the actors. For example, the direction of the stables would allow Querubin a place to chase after Frasquita for a romp in the hayloft, and the garden areas provided Antonio room to clip away at the flowers that bountifully adorned the plantation in order to listen in and meddle into the activities of the household instead of minding his own business. A convenient hedge would allow Figaro and Susanna a private moment or the count an advantageous hiding place for his indiscretions.

Because we had determined that this enterprise was set up for profit from planting and ranching, we tried to situate the fields, the water wells, and other such required locales. Much of my research revolved around identifying the animals typically found on haciendas, and determining the ranching patterns and systems of work and profitability, including growing cotton and other crops, and principle commodities for this region. This research led to determining that the enterprise involved raising sheep, goats to a lesser extent, with the larger business focused on cattle and horses.

By establishing the play's timeframe as 1820 to 1847, the resources could be more easily localized. The sociology of this place had to coincide with the demands of the original text. If the Southwestern hacienda system was replacing the French society found in the original play, then what rules could still apply, substituting Spanish aristocracy for the French nobility? My knowledge of Texan cultures made it clear that drawing from chronicles and resources in the rich multicultural history of Texas would provide us with the most informed research.

Vital resources for this information included materials available only in Spanish and found in the Special Collection of the Latin American Benson Library at The University of Texas at Austin. Handling these materials requires on-site research and careful use of the fragile pages. I had previously used these materials on a National Endowment for the Humanities Travel to Collections grant and had done earlier work in this library and so gained special permission to copy some of the illustrations as well as examine them closely for detail about color and line.

The *Viaje pintoresco y arquelógico por la República Mexicana: 1829-1834*[57] provided many illustrations of place, color, and structure.Close examination also offered information about foliage, building materials, and climate and surroundings. For example, extant materials indicated the type of cacti and flowers bountiful in this extremely arid climate, and thereby provided important clues about available dyes and typical dress for the period. I found that clay was plentiful, and dirt was cool enough to warrant bare feet and people wanting to lie close to the ground for respite from the harsh sun.

I found that varying types of fountains not only illustrated water sources but also indicated the type of work in which servants engaged throughout the day, toting great *jarros* or clay jars of water to quench thirst or to wash off hallways from dust that the winds would spread throughout the evening.[58] While these resources provided information about the hacienda structure along with the rules of the lords and peasants in that community, they also peripherally told us of other matters within the scope of this nineteenth-century world, such as furniture types and styles, typical work tools, and methods of cooking, cleaning, travel and communication with neighbors and visitors and so on.

Two weeks of tedious scrutiny and selective photocopying of these delicate materials yielded more than two hundred illustrations and copies of relevant articles and information. Turn-around time was vital, so I would forward the materials to the director in overnight mail, and Goldstein, in turn, would direct the materials as he saw fit, either to the translator/adaptor or the designers or to everyone.

Most of the worthwhile material was available only in Spanish, but I was not on hand to translate for the designers or the director. I knew of some important resources in English that could aid the team in further research of their own. The library collection reading room had been restrictive in terms of what could be copied; hence, some of the more widely used texts that included richly colorful illustrations became crucial. The most useful were the well-known *A Treasury of Mexican Folkways* by Frances Toor[59] and *Life in Mexico* by Frances Calderón de la Barca.[60]

While I was documenting reliable facts about the setting, David Kay Mickelsen began to make inquiries about appropriate dress. Mickelsen knew of several important resources he had to use, but he was in Minneapolis and could not get his hands on them at the time. On the other hand, I had them immediately at my disposal at The University of Texas libraries. In most cases, the research tools required to answer the costume designer's questions also aided greatly in informing the total project, especially in terms of the story and setting. The most valuable text was Claudio Linati's *Trajes civiles, militares y religiosos de México,*[61] available in its original first edition, published in Brussels in 1828, as well as the later 1978 Mexican edition. Although the 1828 edition could neither be photocopied nor taken out of the library, the later edition, available for library use only, could be photocopied in the Fine Arts Library at Texas. Hence, while the copied illustration could show practice, the important use of vivid color had to be described to the designers and others in great detail.

Corroborating color required researching available dyes for the region during the time under scrutiny. Teresa Castillo Yturbide's *La Tejedora de Vida*[62] helped provide understanding of the use of color, texture, and available fabrics. José R. Benitez's *El traje y el adorno en México, 1500-1910*[63] included further detail about both dress and adornment throughout the region. In English, Chloe Sayer's *Costumes of Mexico*[64] provided detailed descriptions and color illustrations of the fabrics and was even more helpful in delineating costume history, including weaving, embroidery, and distinct male and female dress. Without the Spanish-language resources, information verifying the setting and dress would have been scant and difficult to corroborate indeed.

The information I was discovering was getting dangerously close to reinforcing stereotypes of Mexico and Mexican customs, therefore reliable resources were crucial. Gonzalo Obregón's *El México de Guadalupe Victoria (1824-1829)* provided valuable corroborative materials that distinguished fact from merely stereotypical buffoonery. I had to provide careful documentation so that we could always rely on the research to accurately reinforce the basic method of selection for the concept we had defined.

The translator/adaptor had asked me to confirm the accuracy of the setting to the point where he could firmly establish the hacienda as an authentic and appropriate place for Figaro's comic mayhem to occur. My research yielded reliable materials to support his choice. Here Figaro appears as the manager of the hacienda. Still, as Goldstein explained: "There's a sense of authenticity, but this is not a history lesson. It's a celebration. We wanted to have fun with anachronisms, and to achieve a sense of fantasy and fun, with great life and color." Although the comic anachronisms were most apparent in the eccentric mother and old Bartholomew, the use of traditional colorful *piñata* effects of crepe paper on papier-mâché and brightly colored flowers and ribbons everywhere further enhanced that mood of gaiety. And what better means of creating that sense of comic irony and enjoyment where intrigue and ribaldry occur than the setting of the "Hacienda Aguas Frescas, in the old Southwest," that is, a great land of "Fresh Waters" that Downey ironically named in contrast to the setting's quite notable parched desert lands?

Various character types were created to situate the event in the old Southwest. Bartholomew T. Bankhead, described as an American lawyer in the cast list, striding in as a wily shyster with a Texan twang, replaced the original Bartholo, "a doctor from Seville." Count Almaviva, the "Governor of Andalusia" in the original now became the Marquez de Almaviva, the "Governor of the hacienda," and his wife, the countess, was now named Rosina instead of Rosine. Figaro's betrothed, Suzanne, was now Susanna, and Marceline, the housekeeper, became Marcelina, a schoolmistress, who in some ways illustrated the New Woman who had made her way in the world through her own shrewd means and acumen. In the case of Antonio's daughter, Fanchette, changing her name to Frasquita did more than create a Mexican name equivalent; the stimulating play on words evokes a *frasco* or jar that could be shaken, ready for a romp and mischief, and always filled with interesting tidbits of gossip and intrigue. Using Spanish terms for the characters brought attention to place and ethnicity, as with the old Spanish priest, Father Anselmo, who was often referred to simply as "Padre," and the peasant crowd that often appeared as the field-workers, referred to here as *campesinas* or *campesinos,* or others within the household, all evidently coming directly from the countryside. It was my task to verify the use of appropriate names and to suggest possibilities.

Although Downey provided a basic story filled with comic routines and humor, realizing the connection to race and ethnicity was often left up to the actors. It would be up to the actors to improvise comic routines to establish their particular characters within the revised context. The director expected me to make suggestions and urged me to encourage improvisation among the Latina/Latino actors toward that end. The resources I suggested to draw from in creating characters were the great Mexican comic actor, Cantinflas, and many notable servant types that they could easily view on the local Spanish-language television station and listen to on the local Spanish-language radio stations that often featured comic routines. "Simplemente María" was one example of a long-running melodramatic soap opera series that provided easily recognizable types. On the other hand, the typical Three Stooges and Marx Brothers routines available on video were also important because they showed universal comic routines and were applicable to all ethnicities. One of the major obstacles to developing believable and appropriate comic character types was the danger of supporting standard stereotyping rather than truthful, recognizable figures. With severe warnings about the dangers of stereotyping found in such films as *Viva Zapata, The Alamo* with John Wayne, or "Zorro" reruns, I suggested that any of these films could be informative in defining contrasting Texans and Mexicans in a similar period and setting. In our production, the central roles, those of the Count and Countess Almaviva, were being played by non-Spanish-speaking Euroamerican actors requiring Mexican characterization. In these parts, for example, the more serious *The Alamo,* could illustrate ways of extending farcical elements and exaggeration for their roles as well as show typical business, such as the use of a fan, shawl, or bowing in style. Bartholomew, also played by a Euroamerican, was already playing a recognizable Anglo type trying to fit into the Mexican community, so in his case he could benefit from *Viva Zapata* and "Zorro," but the director would always remind all of the actors about the dangers of negative stereotyping that I consciously saw as a potential detriment for the community that would view these figures.

The earlier photocopied materials I had sent the director were now also useful to the actors, whom I also supplied with photos, drawings, articles about typical "business," and information appropriate for their parts, including standard customs that distinguish characters by class and job responsibilities on the vast hacienda. The materials suggested business of several sorts: making the sign of the cross, for the mother and some servants who sought to ward off evil or the devil, using a sombrero for effect, typical ways of carrying baskets of flowers or fruit, or holding large *jarros* of water or ale; the many uses of the *serape,* that broad cloak or shawl that could provide comic routines of hiding and sudden revelations; and countless ways of bowing to or approaching the aristocracy appropriate to the period. Otherwise typical business—women using fans, servants sweeping off dusty floors or answering doors, and men taking off their hats—soon became useful for tools illustrating race and ethnicity for the varying assortment of individuals on this large property.

Improvisation for developing character types emerged out of the rehearsal process, as Downey had intended from the onset. For example, Downey provided skeletal exchanges between Figaro and his master in which Figaro could supply business and language, drawing from the materials, printed articles, and books I had supplied. Also, I had discussions about business typical to each. Susanna had to be distinct from the countess, but the countess also had to feign the part of Susanna. Appropriate business for each established the differences that persuaded disguise and provided comedy.

Perhaps the most valuable effort the director had made in order to target the Latino subject and audience was his decision to use Latina/Latino actors and to bring new names and new faces to the regional stage. Coming from as far away as New York, many actors were auditioned in Los Angeles or Seattle, and local actors were also hired. Al Rodrigo as Figaro, Leticia Vásquez as Susanna, and Alma Martínez as Marcelina brought the use of language, regionalisms, and direct experience to the production and often corroborated choices we had made. Roberto García as Pedrillo, a stablehand, Roberto Guajardo as Antonio the gardener, and Norma Medina as the *campesina* also helped to inform the overall concept. I evaluated the performance as a whole and commented on the effectiveness of choices.

While visual representation and character development had been basic elements in creating cultural representation, the most essential work of this project was to use language to reveal the integral place of Chicanas/Chicanos in the Southwestern experience. Although his background in Spanish included having lived in Peru as a boy and attending Spanish-speaking schools, Roger Downey was after the unique Chicano flavor that could particularize 1830s Arizona while it was still part of Mexico. Language was at the very root of that experience.

The translator/adaptor sought to explore the use of Spanish and Spanglish—a unique blending of English and Spanish typically used by Chicanos in the Southwest. Downey expected this code-switching style (switching from one language to the other, often within the same sentence) from the first, and asked me to encourage the actors to use this method and suggest possibilities for them. My task was to serve as the overall listener, evaluating how added terms supported the text. For example, in telling Susanna how he would like to speak to his boss, Figaro might say: "Oh, *no que no,* how I'd love to take you on, *mano a mano* . . . but that's not how to handle a man, *un hombre* who owns every bush, burro, and coyote from here to the horizon."[65] Throughout the text, recognizable Spanish words and improvised asides were used to transpose the earlier version of the play, including: *amo* or *jefe* or *Patrón* for "boss" or "master"; *amor* or *querida* for "darling"; *mi señora* for "my Lady"; *fiesta* instead of "party"; *Padre* for addressing the priest; endearments of *mujer* for "woman" and *viejo* for "old man"; and the proper titles of *don* and *doña* for the count and countess.

The notable hierarchy that would establish the chain of command on the hacienda could be determined by who used the titles and in what order. Although the count was the person in the highest rank, Figaro as his manager could also be addressed by others as a landlord or "patrón" to indicate his status and that of his future bride in contrast to others beneath him. This hierarchy allowed a greater use of recognizable Spanish terms to link the Mexican culture to the story.

The greatest test of authenticity was in how these Spanish terms sounded. The director made every attempt to have everyone, except for Bartholomew, speak Spanish proficiently and with the appropriate accent. I served as the dialect coach and gave notes about pronunciation. The actor playing Figaro, for example, was Puerto Rican and would sometimes use a rhythmic pattern different from a Southwestern Chicano. If I was unavailable, I would assign Spanish-speakers to make corrections.

Overall, the project proved successful, a success attested to not only by critics and the regular theater subscribers in the area, but also by the more critical eyes of the Chicanas/Chicanos whose background and heritage were being examined. Still, we had to face a thorny issue with regard to authentication. Although David Kay Mickelsen's costumes complemented the set through their magical brilliant colors and textures, it was difficult to prove to the audiences that our depictions of figures and settings, which were associated with stereotype, were in fact accurate. Despite having once believed that the stereotyped Mexican, sitting cross-legged on the street with a serape over his shoulders, *guaraches* for shoes, and a huge straw hat, or the señorita with embroidered cotton fabric blouse filled with decorated flowers and birds of all colors were inflammatory and derogatory, my research had confirmed such regional dress for this hot climate. Because the program included no space for notes, we could not rely on it as a forum for discussion about this matter. Yet we did have the ongoing series "By Design," with a lecture-seminar format, and that was the logical place to present and explain our extensive process to authenticate this much-neglected Chicana/Chicano heritage of the Arizona community. With support from the Arizona Humanities Council, ATC had already made "By Design" a part of their season's program. In this case, discourse between scholars, artists, and audience included authorities speaking about the Chicano experience in relation to the history of the Arizona territory, and this exchange served as a useful tool in explaining our intent and extensive preparation to arrive at our goal.

Latina/Latino theater in the United States is highly diversified in artistic expression and cultural heritage. Latinas and Latinos represent the fastest growing underrepresented group in the United States, and there is little reason to believe that growth will cease. This population includes 18.7 million Mexican Americans, Cubans, Puerto Ricans, Dominicans, Central and South Americans in the fifty states and more than 3.3 million Puerto Ricans living in Puerto Rico.[66] With all of its diversity, Hispanic expression, stemming from as far back as when the Conquistadores provided the first dramatic performance on American soil, continues to make a significant, vital contribution to the theater of the United States.[67]

The Arizona Theatre Company's attempt to address multiculturalism and diversity can shed light on practical means to understand other cultures within the dominant community. For several years now, there has been concern and anxiety about multiculturalism and diversity in the United States. In evaluating social policies related to multicultural development, we have witnessed little success. Individuals along the entire political and economic spectrum seem to be growing impatient, a matter made especially crucial because of changing U.S. demographics. If we do not find workable solutions to the multicultural issue "a fragmented, highly factionalized society" will result.[68] The changing demographic mix in the United States requires changing ideology and practice.

Instead of turning the issues into "political action, protest and street theater," demanding "equal rights and cultural recognition" for all, with each group competing, "demanding its own share of media attention, admiration, awards and foundation funding, as Robert Brustein fears,[69] we must find the positive value of these issues. I would argue for an "intercultural" approach, or perhaps a broader cross-cultural exploration. Clearly, omitting or ignoring the contributions that people of color have made to the multicultural richness of theatrical history is not the answer.[70]

With a Song in My Art:
Dramaturgy and the American Musical Theater
by Laurence Maslon

LAURENCE MASLON is currently a faculty member of the graduate acting program at New York University's Tisch School of the Arts. For seven years, he worked at Washington D.C.'s Arena Stage, where he served as Associate Artistic Director. At Arena, he directed the world premiere of Janusz Glowacki's *Antigone in New York* as well as several other plays and adapted works by Luigi Pirandello, August Strindberg, Manfred Karge, and Charles Dickens. He has written extensively on American comedy in the 1930s and is a graduate of Brown and Stanford Universities.

It seems to be a generally accepted commonplace among the critical community that when we go in search of profound or ineffable truth about a given topic, we march straight to the front steps of the temple of serious drama. If we wanted apposite examples of, for instance, how American society sees itself in this century, we would turn to Odets, Miller, Mamet, and probably Tony Kushner. In general, we apotheosize serious drama, and with exceptions of, say, some of Shakespeare and Molière, we only allow comedy in the temple through the unlocked back door. Musical theater, then, is left to scratch at the window, unless it can eventually scramble up the drainpipe and break in on the second story.

Anyone working as a practitioner in the current realm of resident or not-for-profit theater in this country can see that perpetuating such a critical stance is at best shortsighted and at worst, dangerous. As resident theaters become more resourceful at production—and more sensitive to their audiences' tastes—more revivals and original pieces of musical theater will be produced on their stages. As the Gershwins more frequently join Ibsen and Tennessee Williams on the season schedule, there will be a greater need for dramaturgs to create a methodology for dealing with these musical texts. My experience as a dramaturg on three particular musical projects at Washington D.C.'s Arena Stage has given me insight on how to change and adapt one's dramaturgical skills to accommodate musical comedy: not at all.

Since the early 1980s, Arena Stage has almost every season produced a musical as one selection in its eight-play subscription series and, with few exceptions, the musicals have been directed by Arena's artistic director, Douglas C. Wager. Guided by Wager, the Arena has taken the position that musicals are dramatic texts of substance as well as amusement and should be accorded the same dramaturgical support as any text by Ibsen or Williams. The three musical revivals I will discuss are not only of historical importance within the field, but also display relevant qualities of American social and cultural history: *On*

The Town (1944), with book and lyrics by Betty Comden and Adolph Green and score by Leonard Bernstein; *Of Thee I Sing* (1931), with book by George S. Kaufman and Morrie Ryskind, score by George and Ira Gershwin; and a concert version of *I'd Rather Be Right* (1937), book by Kaufman and Moss Hart, score by Richard Rodgers and Lorenz Hart.

My approach to these shows followed the same methodology I use with nonmusical or "serious" drama. Beginning with the securing of the rights to the shows (no mean feat when dealing with highly commercial and revivable properties), the process included acquiring all pertinent previous drafts, deciding on a definitive text, researching the production history, and providing general background research on the context of the show's setting. Although these musicals were licensed by major companies such as the Rodgers and Hammerstein Theatre Library, the texts they supplied were by no means definitive. Musicals, more so than many straight dramas, are subject to constant and often expedient revision prior to their first productions due to the vagaries that beset the creative teams: changes in personnel, tailoring script material for a performer, and so on. Therefore, a published text, which may have been prepared to appear before opening night, will differ greatly from the licensed text as the result of last-minute alterations. We were lucky enough to retrieve the first drafts of all three shows from the Library of Congress' music division. In some cases, original material from these drafts was incorporated into our performance text. More importantly, these drafts provided a creative road map of the creators' original intentions.

The addition of music and, subsequently, dance to text is not merely a matter of going from one genre to another; the dramaturg must consider the nature of the music, how it is integrated into the text, and the way it informs the text. This requires the dramaturg to work closely with the musical director as well as the director and to take into consideration the songs themselves, as well as the way the music will be presented. In all three cases, the Arena revivals sought not to reproduce the Broadway versions, but to reconceive the original material. As with a "classic" text: we considered the staging resources available to the creative team and asked, What is the intention behind reviving the piece? What does it have to say to a contemporary audience? How can the dramaturg support the director's concept of the show?

The 1989 revival of *On The Town* was an excellent demonstration of how to apply this methodology of musical dramaturgy. The 1944 Broadway debut of this unabashedly effusive musical comedy made history because of its spectacular integration of music and dance and launched the careers of Leonard Bernstein, Betty Comden, Adolph Green, and choreographer Jerome Robbins—all in their twenties and, subsequently, all major contributors to the form. The premise of *On The Town* (plot may be too strong a word) concerns three sailors on a twenty-four-hour leave in "New York, New York, that helluva town."[71] Each finds a paramour for the day, and together the three couples have a whirlwind adventure, taking them all over Manhattan, to Coney Island, and finally, inevitably, back to the Navy Yard in Brooklyn just in time for the three sailors to ship out once more.

It requires little rationalization to revive this musical. The score is quite brilliant, and the effusiveness of the show would soften the hardest heart. Although the 1949 MGM film version, starring Gene Kelly and Frank Sinatra, is well known and well regarded, the show had no major professional productions, aside from a brief 1971 Broadway revival. I asked the company that held the rights, Tams-Witmark, if it was too extravagant to revive with its twenty-six orchestra parts. "No," replied the representative. "It's just dated." But it was precisely that "dated" quality—which director Wager, who went to college during Vietnam, saw as the innocence of an earlier generation who had markedly less ambivalence and anxiety about war—that made the material worth reviving. "I was very drawn into the spirit of the time," he explained. "My own experience with wartime, obviously, is coming of age in the sixties. My own perception of a national attitude toward the military (and national unity) is much different. . . . My guess was that if we could get that original spirit to travel through time to 1989, we could experience [the musical] in a meaningful way."[72]

Wager's perceptive comment is somewhat subversive, for although *On The Town* was first performed deep into World War II, there is hardly a mention of it in the final text. Typical of the show's anodyne approach to the contemporary global catastrophe, the three sailors never mention either the origination or the destination of their waiting battleship. In an early version, two of the sailors pledge their friendship to the third because he saved them in the South Pacific. In the final draft, he pulls them "out of the drink." No one speaks of the war because, of course, in 1944, no one had to. In an interview, Comden expounded on how the show was more than a valentine to New York City:

> And there was a tremendous emotional base for the story line. The fact there was a war on was working for us all the time; the fact that these boys had just twenty-four hours beginning with their coming off the ship and ending with their saying good-bye and getting on the ship going who knew where. The song "Some Other Time" [in which the couples express their hopes to meet again] . . . is full of emotion. In wartime it had a tremendously poignant feeling.[73]

To confirm Comden's point, one need only watch the 1949 Hollywood film, which is set in peacetime; "Some Other Time" was entirely deleted and the "tremendous emotional base" is gone.

So, Wager's approach demanded a curious battle plan for the dramaturg: restore the subtext of the 1944 production—the unspoken anxiety over the war—and the *super* text—the consciousness of the war. We turned first to a copy of the first draft, registered at the Library of Congress' manuscript division, written by Comden and Green before they submitted the play to its eventual original director, George Abbott. This draft's few references to the war were mostly in the form of gentle jokes; for example, a sailor reads the electronic display in Times Square of news headlines concerning the evacuation of Dunkirk letter by letter. Ultimately, after a meeting with Comden and Green in New York, Wager, choreographer Marcia Milgrom Dodge. and I decided it would be less clumsy to go with the licensed text.

We had to look elsewhere to emphasize the wartime atmosphere of the show. One enormously helpful aspect of the show was the variety of Bernstein's score—an eclectic compendium of jazz, swing, blues, rhumba, and popular song, which functioned as a kind of symphonic juke box of the period. In collaboration with musical director William Huckaby, Wager decided to hire a full orchestra of nineteen for the show, giving full priority to the integrity of Bernstein's music. This was a sizable commitment for a resident theater such as Arena, as it meant eschewing the more financially feasible options of a reduced orchestration or taped music, but it greatly enhanced the theatrical vitality of the show.

Research on the time period was copious and easy to obtain. Books such as Studs Terkel's oral history *The Good War* and Richard R. Lingeman's *Don't You Know There's a War On?* provided many accessible accounts of the homefront.[74] Of course, several movies from the forties gave a tremendous amount of detail and suggestions of period behavior. Two Hollywood films, *A Guy Named Joe* (1944) and *The Clock* (1945) provided glimpses of wartime service and romance that complemented the mood of the musical. A recent documentary, *Hollywood Goes to War,* showed how various aspects of the confrontation were dealt with in both the world of Hollywood and the real world. Most useful was *Why We Fight,* Frank Capra's series of documentaries made for the Office of War Information, which recounted the story of our entrance into the war with a wonderful sense of the spirit and commitment behind our decision to fight.[75] Other visual material, such as Alfred Eisenstaedt's famous photos for *Life* magazine of departing sailors and their gals were wonderful embodiments of the "emotional base" to which Comden referred. Practically everyone in the cast and on the staff had relatives who had been in World War II, and anecdotes flowed freely. The cumulative effect of all this research was to evoke, for a cast that barely remembered Vietnam, a time when an entire nation bravely subordinated its fear and anxiety about warfare to the principles of freedom and democracy.

Such research was good for making the cast comfortable with the attitudes and behavior of Americans during the Second World War, but a fair amount of the responsibility for transporting the audience back to 1944 fell on the shoulders of set and costume designer Zack Brown. Working in Arena's full-square eight-hundred-seat space, Brown had to create a different kind of environment from the traditional proscenium demands, such as front-cloth crossovers, that are written into the show. Brown placed architectural elements of 1940s

Manhattan, such as the Empire State and Chrysler Buildings in each of the space's four "voms," or entrances to the stage. (When I told him that, however beautiful, his recreation of the Empire State Building wasn't accurate because it had no TV antennae in 1944, it was met with the kind of reaction that dramaturgs deserve from time to time. The antennae might not have *been* true, but it certainly *seemed* true, and it stayed put.) To make the wartime context more explicit, next to each of these was a billboard with posters that could only exist in 1944:"Man the Guns:Join the Navy," "Buy War Bonds." These were in permanent view and, along with the inclusion of a few more on-leave soldiers and sailors in the chorus than called for by the script, they were a constant reminder of the time and place.

Research for these design elements, as well as for costumes and properties, was particularly easy in Washington, D.C. The National Archives photographic division has extensive records of American military uniforms and period clothing, as well as an encyclopedic collection of full-color period war-effort posters, four of which were reproduced on the set. The Library of Congress, which houses a marvelous compilation of photos taken as part of the Works Progress Administration, was also extremely useful. A trip to Manhattan to the photographic collection of the New York Historical Society provided accurate details of period architecture, including the exact neon signs in Times Square during the spring of 1944 as well as the Empire State Building (without its current TV antennae).

The research culled from these collections served two other purposes. Wager had the idea of redecorating Arena's lobby with artifacts from the period. This became a dramaturgical assignment, and soon the lobby was festooned with recruitment and war bond posters, photographic blow-ups of Eisenstaedt's sailors and other news photos, front pages of New York newspapers, and an ongoing loop of the "Hollywood Goes to War" video. In addition, the copiously illustrated program for the show aped the form of a 1944 guidebook to New York City with statistics designed to give a sense of context and distance (subways cost a nickel, a poll taken in 1944 revealed that 90 percent of all New Yorkers considered themselves happy, and so on). Audience members who had lived through those times were reintroduced to old memories, and audience members who hadn't could smile at a world so gently alien to their own.

One personal recollection of the war made a strong impact on the production itself. My father, who had served in the army in 1944, mentioned that during the course of the fighting every Broadway show and movie presentation opened with the playing of "The Star-Spangled Banner." Was this something we could use? Wager thought so, as did Comden and Green, so each performance at Arena began by flying in a fifteen-foot-wide American flag—with 48 stars, of course. The oldest member of the cast stepped forward and asked the audience to support "our valiant men and women fighting overseas and join us in the singing of our national anthem." Then the orchestra struck up a rousing rendition of the anthem and, invariably, the audience stood up. Some younger audience members giggled or murmured, "Play ball" at the anthem's end, but the gravity of the older audience members' memories pervaded the theater, and the mood of the production was quickly established. Every review mentioned this opening, and Edwin Wilson, critiquing the show in the *Wall Street Journal,* understood Wager's vision of the show. Wilson found "the custom symptomatic of the combined patriotism and innocence that pervaded the U.S. at the time." He went on to write:

> The current *On The Town* operates on two levels. The first is a charming if lightweight musical from another era. The second is the inevitable comparison audiences will make between today and yesterday, and it is here that the innocence and apparent simplicity of the wartime U.S. become evident.[76]

That juxtaposition between the past and the present occurred again with a vengeance on a later Arena musical project. *Of Thee I Sing* was, by one objective definition at least, the first Broadway musical to be taken seriously. In 1932, the Pulitzer Prize committee for the first time awarded the prize for drama to a musical, honoring librettists George S. Kaufman and Morrie Ryskind and lyricist Ira Gershwin the prize for drama (although, ironically, overlooking George Gershwin's musical contribution).[77] With the possible exception of *Show Boat, Of Thee I Sing* was the first American musical to merit such recognition. The plot and the score were integrated with charm and sophistication, and the show was the first attempt to take on the presidency in a satirical vein. It traced the rise of candidate John P. Wintergreen and his new First Lady Mary from his election through the first year of his administration.

Written two years into the Depression, the show is a response by four witty, sardonic writers to twelve years of compromises, ineptness, ward-heelers, and hacks in the federal government, and it insistently pokes sharp fun at American politics and archetypes. Wintergreen, a somewhat empty-headed opportunist, is packaged to run on a ticket supporting "Love" in its most general application, which his handlers figure is a sure thing, because no one in America cares about the issues. A beauty pageant is cooked up so that Wintergreen can make good on his party platform by marrying the winner. Instead, he jilts the winning Southern bombshell for Mary Turner, a savvy secretary whose prowess at baking corn muffins is irresistable to him. He is elected, nonetheless, but the spurned woman attracts media attention and the public condemns Wintergreen's lack of romantic resolve. Impeachment proceedings begin, but are thankfully interrupted by the announcement of Mary's pregnancy and the ultimate arrival of twins. One of the more memorable characters in the play is Alexander Throttlebottom, a vice-president so dim and inconsequential that he is barred entry to his own nomination and subsequent inauguration ceremonies. The plot precis alone demonstrates not only the scope and zaniness of the musical's political satire, but its enduring applicability. The caustic libretto is supported by a score from the Gershwins that is jazzy, accessible, stately, and hilariously pompous—the closest Americans had got to Gilbert and Sullivan.

Having already directed two musicals written by Kaufman in the 1920s for the Marx Brothers at Arena, Wager was anxious to see how Kaufman's other satiric musical comedies fared.[78] Certainly a musical comedy with *Of Thee I Sing*'s pedigree and subject matter would appeal to a Washington audience, but from the early 1980s on, when Wager became interested in the material, Arena could not find a slot nor muster enough enthusiasm for the show. And although it may seem absurd to lay this particular calumny at his feet, the fault was largely that of Ronald Reagan. Reagan was certainly a ripe figure for political satire, but the difference between his administration at its height, with its genial laissez-faire and bellicose optimism, and the chintzy, cynical corruption mocked in *Of Thee I Sing* was vast enough to scuttle a revival. A revival of the musical would work best in an election year, and the eighties never really provided the right contrast to the Republican administration.

The year 1992 changed all that. The result of twelve previous years of Republican administrations exactly paralleled the world of 1932. People were annoyed with the economy, change was in the air, we had a young presidential candidate with a jilted Southern beauty in his past and a savvy wife with considerable baking prowess, and, blessedly, in the opposing camp, we had a vice-president apparently as dim as his musical counterpart. With *Of Thee I Sing* as the 1992–93 season opener, Washington would have the actual election running simultaneously with the fictional one. (Three other revivals of the show ran concurrently across the country.)

At Arena, our dramaturgical battle plan was almost the obverse of our strategy with *On The Town*. There, the poignancy was created by showing how much things had changed; here, the humor was created by showing how little things had changed. Wager and his musical director, William Huckaby, made an initial key decision. Instead of using a full orchestra for this large show, they chose to use only two grand pianos for accompaniment. This not only saved a good deal of money, but also put the focus of the production on the words and hence the satire, subtly reminding audiences of topical humorists such as Tom Lehrer and Mark Russell and the kind of hit-and-run political satire beloved by Washington audiences.

Again, our first task was to go to the text. Although it was enormously tempting to change the text or update it (as Frank Rich ultimately suggested in his *New York Times* review of our production), that would have been an enterprise fraught with disaster. Kaufman and Ira Gershwin tried this when they revived the show on Broadway in 1952, but the post-Truman climate was even less appropriate and relevant to this material than the Reagan years, and the revival quickly folded. It was far more exciting for us to produce a sixty-year-old show relatively intact and for the show to seem newly minted to a

1992 audience. This would create an amusing historical distance for the audience and add to their enjoyment. Fortunately, the first draft, found in the Library of Congress, was quite similar to the final product. (*Of Thee I Sing* had undergone almost no last-minute revisions or renovations.) There was also some slight divergence between the 1932 Alfred Knopf text, which went to press before the opening, and the licensed version from Music Theater International.

However, it would be wrong to suggest that we presented an unalloyed version of the 1931 text. For a variety of reasons, some changes and substitutions proved necessary. We made cuts for length in both text and music, especially in the second act, when Ira Gershwin's penchant for Gilbertian reprises got the better of him. We substituted obscure names or events alluded to in the text with better known ones; for example, a "knock-out performance by Richard Mansfield" became one by John Barrymore. We also changed obscure jokes as well as ones offensive to contemporary sensibilities, but we were eager to capitalize on any discarded jokes that might be more pertinent in 1992. In the musical's second scene, the handlers are discussing the possible party platform. The first draft contained this morsel:

FULTON:

We need something that everybody is interested in, and that doesn't matter a good God damn.

WINTERGREEN:

How about golf?

LIPPMAN:

Too important.

WINTERGREEN:

My God, Fulton, you ought to know. You sell twenty million papers a day. What's the one thing that people are more interested in than anything else?

FULTON:

Adultery.

WINTERGREEN:

That's it! What a campaign! I'll tour every state in the Union!

At the height of the Bush–Clinton campaign, this made for an amusing—and bipartisan—addition to the show. Ira Gershwin's lyric revisions for the ill-fated 1952 production were occasionally drafted into the show, including this apposite gem. Wintergreen's inaugural address

> I have definite ideas about the Philippines
> And the herring situation up in Bismarck.
> I have notions on the salaries of movie queens
> And the men who sign their signature with this mark.

became

> I have definite ideas about the deficit.
> I have plans about our tonnage on the ocean.
> But before I grow statistical, I'll preface it
> With a statement growing out of sheer emotion.

One significant change had more to do with the wheel of history than to the appeal of a good laugh. Prior to 1936, all presidential inaugurations were held on March 4. The text and lyrics made several references to this, so we "backdated" them to January 20, in order to avoid confusing the audience (What *is* true isn't always what *seems* true). Unfortunately, this got us into a bit of a mess in the last scene, when White House staffers conjecture about whether the date of the expectant Wintergreens' conception preceded their wedding date, which was inauguration day—but, by changing around the various months involved, it all got sorted out.

Throughout the rehearsal period, we had considerable research material at hand, drawn again from the Library of Congress and National Archive photographic collections, which provided excellent visuals of the 1928 and 1932 presidential elections for both the cast and design team. (Of course, Zack Brown, the set designer also passed most of the musical's settings on the way to work every morning.) Philippe Mora's clever 1975 documentary *Brother, Can You Spare a Dime?*[79] was particularly helpful in depicting for the cast the Depression-era conditions that led to Roosevelt's election in 1932. Wager and Brown kept things looking period and fairly accurate, with some tips of the hat to contemporary sensibilities. The published text called for a slide show (or "lantern" show, as it is called) that bridges two scenes by describing Wintergreen's election to the presidency, district by district and state by state. The pace of a slide show would never do for an audience conditioned to CNN, so we reformatted the sequence as a newsreel. This meant storyboarding the sixty-six separate events in the original text, matching it with period film clips, and transferring it to video with a newly recorded voice-over. Some jokes had to be reconstituted, but new ones appeared in their place. A printed concession speech in the original became a film clip of Herbert Hoover from 1930, overdubbed to have him concede the election to Wintergreen. One bit of recent nostalgia was too good (and too wicked) to leave out. Instead of a photo of a freckled teenager appearing with the voice-over "Candidate John P. Wintergreen at age twelve," the audience was treated to the ubiquitous grainy black and white film clip of young Bill Clinton shaking hands with President Kennedy.

We scarcely needed a lobby exhibit for this show. The audience could read about the vagaries of elective democracy in each morning's paper, but the program provided a little extra humor and resonance. One of the few elected high officials who ever attended Arena Stage was Walter F. Mondale, and, as he had been both a presidential candidate and a vice-president, he was an ideal choice to write the program article we commissioned with funding we received from the National Endowment for the Humanities (NEH). Mr. Mondale sportingly contributed a witty and timely "few helpful hints for any new president—whether his name is Wintergreen or Clinton." The essay, which the NEH feared was too partisan, concluded by recommending "Finally, Mr. President, obey the law, have a good time (you'll find the perks aren't bad) and, above all, be kind to your vice-president. Like Wintergreen in *Of Thee I Sing,* you never know when the vice-president might show up to help fulfill you the duties of your office."

This reminded the audience of the truth underlying the comedy, as did a bit of participatory democracy that occurred every night. A slip of paper included in the program allowed each audience member to vote for Bush, Clinton, or Perot. The straw poll was tallied during intermission, and then Gary Beach, the actor playing Wintergreen, read the results at the curtain call (he often slipped in a vote or two for Wintergreen—obviously his stay in Washington was not in vain). The results invariably paralleled those of the D.C. metropolitan area with Clinton maintaining a vast lead. These shenanigans continued until the evening of November 3, when Clinton won both on stage and off, and overnight the festivities and follies moved from Arena Stage across town to Pennsylvania Avenue. *Of Thee I Sing* had a little more gas in it for the next couple of weeks, but the Washington audience was more excited by the prospect of a new real-life administration. In this case what *was* true quickly superceded what *seemed* true.

The nominal distinction between politics and theater in Washington was blurred beyond immediate recognition with our next project, the only musical collaboration between the teams of Kaufman and Hart, and Rodgers and Hart, the 1937 musical, *I'd Rather Be Right.* The show, a spoof of Franklin D. Roosevelt and his New Deal policies, had never been revived by a professional company and was preserved in most people's memories only by an excerpt performed by James Cagney as George M. Cohan—as FDR—in the 1942 film *Yankee Doodle Dandy.* Very much in the tradition of *Of Thee I Sing,* this was the first show to put a living president onstage front and center and to make him the target of its humor. It was also a show that would have specific appeal for a Washington audience and support Arena's mission of reviving rarely produced American treasures.

However, the musical had some unique built-in problems. *Of Thee I Sing* had the advantage of being entirely fictional and, hence, metaphorical. *I'd Rather Be Right* specifically depicted an historical figure and his times, and had more in common with the Living Newspaper productions for the Federal Theater Project, which it also manages to satirize. The basic storyline involves a young couple who want to get married, but can't afford to unless President Roosevelt balances the budget. This proves difficult as Congress and the Supreme Court create nothing but gridlock and opposition. This gives the show, shall we say, an enduring charm, but, without a progressive president in office, the text and the context didn't match up.

In 1993, however, Arena planned a benefit performance for the theater intending to involve both actors and key federal office holders. This provided the perfect opportunity to produce *I'd Rather Be Right,* in a concert version that combined professional actors with professional politicians who impersonated their counterparts from the Roosevelt administration. The timing seemed perfect. Washington was again in the grip of budget-balancing fever (the first-act closer was a song entitled, seriously, "We're Going to Balance the Budget"), and again we had a Democratic president whose programs for social change were under constant siege.

A concert version that presented the highlights of the material as a staged reading with music may have been the best way to present the material, for, interesting though it was, it might well be too obscure to attract an audience consistently for several months, even in a theater with a subscriber base. Despite the fact that the show would not be fully produced, a text must still be prepared, and the audience needed a context that would throw them head-first into the world of the New Deal. As both director and dramaturg, I followed the same battle plan as *Of Thee I Sing:* find the original drafts, keep the jokes honest, and show how little things had changed. Clearly the audience for the benefit would be more interested in the humor of the book than the songs (and my options for singing senators were extremely limited), so I cut the two-act musical to a ninety-minute one-act excursion, keeping the most tuneful or amusing songs (including, of course, the ever-hopeful "We're Going to Balance the Budget"), streamlined the jokes, and dispensed with the more esoteric references to the thirties. It all required a certain amount of improvisation; in a few cases, cut songs left gaping holes and new lines had to be created for transitions.

We were extremely fortunate to cast two actors who brought contextual associations along with their talents. Edward Herrmann agreed to play FDR, which was doubly felicitous because not only was he a former Arena company member, but is also the actor most associated with Roosevelt, thanks to his performance on the acclaimed television miniseries "Eleanor and Franklin." Kitty Carlisle Hart, widow of the book's coauthor Moss Hart, played FDR's mother, the imperious Sara Delano Roosevelt. We were able to cast sixteen elected or appointed officials in the supporting parts, although not without a fair amount of negotiation. After Sandra Day O'Connor agreed to portray the chief justice of the Supreme Court, she found out that judges were not allowed to participate in fundraisers, so that eliminated a score of possibilities. Robert Bork was proposed, over considerable opposition from some of Arena's staff, but he, too, eventually declined saying that playing the chief justice who was out to get Roosevelt was "too ironic, even for my taste." A noted Constitutional lawyer, John Barnum, eventually got the part. Two of the more successful casting solutions were Secretary of Health and Human Services Donna Shalala playing Secretary of Labor Frances Perkins the first woman ever appointed to the cabinet (Shalala even bought a little red 1940s hat to pay homage to her idol), and Senator Alan Simpson, playing Alf Landon, FDR's Republican challenger in 1936, who was reduced (in the musical) to serving as Mrs. Roosevelt's butler. In a particularly partisan and amusing moment, Simpson's Landon reminded Roosevelt that, as a Republican, he had managed to balance *his* budget.

An introduction to the evening by Anne Kaufman Schneider, the playwright's daughter, helped make the evening extremely easy to follow, even for those whose knowledge of the New Deal was not fresh. The real-life politicians gave the evening identity and import and, because as professional politicians they're supposed to be competent at their jobs, they also made the foolish political characters they played onstage seem more hilarious (and foolish) than if they had been played by "mere" actors. Moreover, amusing as the evening was, it was very much in keeping with Kaufman and Hart's original design: that Roosevelt, in his sympathy for the young couple who wish to marry, trots out all his friends and foes in the Capitol in order to get them to balance the budget. The idea of trotting out real politicians—politicians who, ostensibly, really *could* balance a federal budget—provided for a production that worked on two levels. And because the elected officials were playing characters *other* than themselves, but very much *like* themselves, it preserved the integrity of the musical and made for a more interesting evening than if, say, they had played themselves in a contemporary rewrite of *I'd Rather Be Right*. If politics is theater, as Kaufman and Hart implied, then the concert version provided a dramaturgical verfication of that truth—as well as its inverse.

These three musicals have much in common that makes them highly idiosyncratic; they happen to be three texts that deal with slices of Americana from several previous generations, often satirical in intent, but certainly attempting to capture the world in which they were written inside a gloriously entertaining jewel box. The way in which Arena Stage presented these texts will not be to everyone's taste, and the descriptions of these productions are in no way meant to be prescriptions, but the methodology may be of use to any directorial and dramaturgical team determined to revive American musical theater texts.

A classic or undiscovered musical text may well yield insights about the world in which we live (or the world in which we lived), sometimes better than a contemporary play. In July of 1994, *Fiddler on the Roof* was revived in London, and every critic was moved by the musical's depiction of a pogrom to make reference to ethnic cleansing in Serbia. Musical theater may be high-minded or frivolous, but, along with jazz, it is one of America's great indigenous art forms, constantly following the beat of our nation's frantic and fascinating rhythm.

Re-imagining the Other:
A Multiracial Production of Mad Forest
by **Harriet Power**

HARRIET POWER is former Resident Dramaturg and current Artistic Director of Venture Theatre, a freelance professional director, and an Assistant Professor of theater at Villanova University, where she teaches graduate dramaturgy and acting. She has dramaturged and directed many productions around the United States, including premieres at Bay Area Playwrights Festival, West Coast Playwrights, the Iowa Playwrights Festival, and Philadelphia area theaters. Recent directing credits include *Measure for Measure, Scapin, Marvin's Room, The Gigli Concert, Reckless,* and *Inspecting Carol* (codirected with Mary B. Robinson). The *Philadelphia Inquirer* named her Best Director of the 1993–94 season for her production of *Mad Forest.* She is current chair of the University Caucus within LMDA (Literary Managers and Dramaturgs of the Americas).

In 1992, Venture and Temple Theaters decided to coproduce one play per season in order to build on our shared interest in diversity. Venture Theatre was founded in 1987 by H. German Wilson and Betty P. Lindley to produce socially engaged works that explore our contemporary cultural differences. Temple University produces culturally diverse theater that showcases the work of its students, and includes in its professional training program in acting a final-year "bridge" during which master of fine arts candidates work with professional theaters.

After Venture and Temple's first coproduction (of Athol Fugard's *A Lesson from Aloes*), we sought a work that would again illuminate issues of culture and difference, but might further challenge us with a larger cast and a more complex structure and style. Caryl Churchill's *Mad Forest: A Play from Romania* became an intriguing consideration. Internationally recognized as one of the most innovative contemporary playwrights, Churchill and British director Mark Wing-Davey visited Romania twice in 1990, shortly after the December 1989 revolution that overthrew dictator Nicolae Ceausescu, to gather material for a play. They were joined on the second visit by the designers and acting students who eventually staged *Mad Forest's* premiere.[80] From the many encounters between these British theater artists and a diversity of Romanians, Churchill created *Mad Forest,* a three-act play with more than forty characters. Focused on two families of different class, its thirty-four scenes (some realistic, others fantastic; some brief and one an extended polyphony of eyewitness accounts of the revolution) together create a compelling portrait of Romanian life. The elements of Churchill's dramaturgy that theater artists have come to expect—highly economic language, actors playing multiple roles across class and gender, nonlinear structure, overlapping dialogue—figure centrally in *Mad Forest.* Churchill's theatrical style, coupled with *Mad Forest's*

Romanian setting and subject and challenging themes, seemed ideal for Venture and Temple's next endeavor. Because a multiracial cast is a given of Temple/Venture co-productions, our staging of *Mad Forest* would be nontraditional. Unlike *Aloes,* where a diversity of actors is organic to the text, a mixed cast for *Mad Forest* would be a choice. We asked ourselves, as we do about choices for any production, how multiracial casting might shape the audience's process of making meaning of the stage event, especially in light of the play's unfamiliar form and content. We also questioned why many regional theaters around the United States, despite professed commitments to cultural pluralism, had produced *Mad Forest* without actors of color in their casts. What does it mean, we asked, to represent the "other" with a diversity of performers, to push the boundaries of photographic accuracy?

In considering the effects of mixed casting for *Mad Forest,* we looked to Churchill's title for insight, since the term *mad forest* is a metaphor for the challenges of confronting the unfamiliar. It refers to the old, dense forest (later razed to make way for Bucharest, Romania's capital city) that was impenetrable to the foreigners who did not know its paths. Furious at being forced to take the long way around, they called it the "mad forest." In so titling her play, Churchill manages to echo the frustration of those early outsiders attempting to penetrate alien territory while acknowledging her own "tourist" status and the confusions of those who stage and watch *Mad Forest.* Romania's culture and history are not easily traversed; *Mad Forest* is not an easy play. Churchill's very title implies the difficulty of "translating" events that few Romanians, let alone foreigners, can fathom.

Production dramaturg Clay Goss, whose primary artistic identity is that of playwright, was outspokenly enthusiastic about the use of black and white actors for our production. Citing Churchill's groundbreaking use of nontraditional casting, he contended that Churchill would approve: "Case in point: *Cloud Nine.* We're talking cross-racial, cross-gender, cross-generational casting here."[81] This unprecedented use of actors for *Cloud Nine,* of course, served specific thematic purposes, unlike our multiracial cast for *Mad Forest.* But in a larger sense, the very act of creating plays for an ensemble of actors who must play across class, race, age, and gender embodies one of Churchill's central political agendas: to give actors and audience a living experience of the arbitrariness of, and possibilities for movement across, such categories.[82] In *Mad Forest,* for example, an actor first portrays a member of the laboring class, and subsequently plays a *Securitate* (secret police) officer, one of the most privileged members of pre-revolutionary Romanian society. The audience, in experiencing such oppositions within a single performer, can understand viscerally how class and privilege, more than individual personality or race, direct a character's action.

Clay, our dramaturg, gave our multiracial casting a name—a "re-imagining" of the mad forest—and a context: for him, the play anticipates the pulse of the twenty-first century. Re-imagining the Romanian revolution with black and white actors, he suggested, though not photographically accurate, could create a more resonant stage event that invited American audiences to associate political unrest from other places and times with the Romanian struggle. Clay's feeling that *Mad Forest* forecasts the turbulence of the coming century derives from his certainty that rapid social and political change, which have transformed once-familiar neighborhoods or countries into "mad forests," will continue. His idea that known territory (whether a city block or a nation) can become unfamiliar turf, suddenly impenetrable or terrifying, invited the rest of us to connect the play to personal experiences of community and global turmoil.

On the first day of rehearsal, a diverse group gathered: the ensemble, essentially biracial, consisted of three African-American actors, eight white;[83] the artistic staff ranged from African American (Clay and German) and Anglo American (Temple's director of theater Joe Leonardo, scenic and lighting designers Daniel Boyland and Curtis Senie, and myself) to Norwegian (costume designer Lailah Kjoersvik Swanson); also present were our African-American stage manager and white assistant stage manager. Our key point of commonality was that none of us knew anything about Romania. We felt like tourists, armed with dictionaries, maps, curiosity, and trepidation, taking tentative first steps into an unknown country.

The process of research in preparation for *Mad Forest* yielded much more than we anticipated. Our ignorance was a healthy leveling factor that created a democratic working method: we all felt compelled to immerse ourselves in Romania and share responsibility for research. The dramaturg is often seen as the person who does production research and encapsulates it for the cast. We rejected that prototype. In fact, our mutual ignorance of the subject, our mutual passion to locate and exchange information, and our mutual exhilaration in the face of our discoveries was a powerful creator of ensemble. Such strong incentives to research an unfamiliar culture create a model for group dramaturgy that empowers performers and enhances the entire production process.

As is typical of other-oriented productions, we investigated Romanian history and culture through pictures, newspapers, diaries, poetry, short stories, and music. We spent almost the entire first four days of rehearsal (and hours outside of rehearsal) reading and discussing Romania's political and social milieu, looking at photographs and art, listening to Romanian songs and speech. Most of Churchill's scenes, though written in English, were initially so foreign that we would have felt like imposters had we attempted to rehearse them immediately. Each member of the production had to become a dramaturg in the attempt to imagine and embody Romanian life.

Our single most valuable research tool was *Moments of Revolution,* a photojournalistic account of the 1989–90 upheavals in Romania, Czechoslovakia, East Germany, and other Eastern European countries.[84] Thirty-three color photographs of the Romanian revolution and its aftermath supplied scores of answers to actor, designer, and director questions concerning the playtext: the attire and attitudes of children, adults, and the elderly; the appearance of public squares, including the vast "People's Palace"; the look of church interiors; the color and shape of the candles held to honor the dead; the *Securitate* uniforms and paraphernalia; the carnations stuck in the barrels of the defecting army's guns (a fascinating visual echo of Vietnam-era protests); the victory salutes; the Romanian flag with the Communist emblem ripped from its center; the soldiers cleaning the blood-soaked streets; the interior of the hospitals and makeshift morgues. Two images, in particular, inspired the scenic designer—a smiling portrait of dictator Ceausescu, and a young rebel soldier watching Ceausescu's execution on the dictator's own office television. For the actors, viewing the tears, joy, terror, and determination on hundreds of faces of those who were there amplified Churchill's often terse text.

Among the many written sources, Andrei Codrescu's *The Hole in the Flag* was most informative.[85] Codrescu, a Romanian, fled the country at age nineteen to become a prominent author, educator, and public radio commentator in the United States. He visited Romania, after a twenty-five-year exile, shortly after the revolution and recorded his unique Romanian/American view of Romania's postrevolutionary freedom, chaos, hope, and cynicism. We experienced *The Hole in the Flag* as a prose version of *Mad Forest;* uncannily, almost all of Churchill's impressions were echoed by Codrescu (who was unaware of her play at the time of his visit and subsequent writing). *New York Times* accounts of the Romanian revolution and subsequent unrest and disillusionment provided additional essential background.

Although our reading and pictorial research were extensive, it became clear that talking to Romanians was crucial. The most telling details of culture are subtextual and dynamic, and are best learned through personal interaction. The world and American premieres of *Mad Forest* set precedents for such field research: Churchill, Wing-Davey, and their ensemble believed they had to go to Romania before they could create the play; subsequently, Wing-Davey took his American cast to Queens, New York, to meet with Romanian expatriates. Venture Theatre public relations director Delores Brown made the initial contacts that led to our own twelve-hour field trip to Queens. Although our hosts and guides, dissident filmmaker Ian Onchoiu and his wife Sue Fallon,[86] had plans to take us to several Romanian sites, we could not tear ourselves from their apartment for the first three hours, so numerous were our questions about language, politics, rituals, and music. How did the Onchoius manage to flee Romania? How are passports procured? How do class and ethnic distinctions manifest themselves in Romanian society? Along with the larger philosophical and historical queries were ordinary, day-to-day basics: How do young Romanians socialize? Where do they meet for drinks or food, and what is served? Does American music play in restaurants? How frequently did Romanian homes lose electric power? How much do Romanians smoke? How prevalent among the general populace is bribery, fear of the *Securitate,* ethnic prejudice? What are the protocols and traditions of a wedding reception? Their answers were infinitely more detailed and evocative than the best of our printed sources. After leaving the Onchoius' apartment, we met and talked with other Romanians ranging from wine merchants and government bureaucrats to Romanian Orthodox priest Reverend Father Casian S. Fetea. It was revelatory to speak with two distinctly different types of Romanians: dissidents such as Mr. Onchoiu who left the country, and party members who still work for the current Ion Iliescu government. We enjoyed tasting the Romanian cheese, bread, and wine that figure centrally in certain scenes of *Mad Forest,* and watching how Romanians toast each other. Father Casian performed a complete wedding ceremony in his church, with the traditional nuptial crowns and candles, using two of our actors as bride and groom. To our surprise, a Romanian observer conjectured that Father Casian's choosing African-American actors to stage the wedding could have had serious consequences had he performed such a demonstration in Romania.

Our most dramatic confrontation with "otherness" did not come until late in the day. An encounter with United Nations General Consul Dr. Gheorghe Dumitru suggested that valuable dramaturgy often emerges out of spontaneous, sometimes awkward outbursts—what Deavere Smith calls "the break from the pattern."[87] Midway through dinner at an Israeli-Romanian restaurant, Dr. Dumitru arrived with his three-man entourage. They chose to sit at a separate table, which perplexed us; soon Mr. Onchoiu indicated that as director I was expected to join them there. Introductions seemed stiff and formal—a contrast to the warmth we had experienced all day. As I sat amongst them, deeply conscious of being the only non-Romanian and the only female, Dr. Dumitru asked coldly, "How dare you think **you** can capture the Romanian soul? We are a Latin people. We are not a Slavic people. We are not a Turkish people. We are not an **African** people [emphasis his]. We are **Latin**!"

Here was a moment where the stakes involved in otherness were thrown into focus, a moment that epitomizes where those of us involved in culturally pluralistic theater find ourselves now: HOW DARE WE? How dare we approach each other? Do we have the right to approach each other? And what are our special responsibilities when that approach includes **performing** the other?

I was frightened, uncertain. "Dr. Dumitru," I said, "as I learn more and more about the complexity of your culture, I know we will fail. We will not be able to capture fully the Romanian soul. It is not possible in our short period of research and rehearsal. But you have been in this country two years now—long enough to have experienced, probably, the sad fact that many Americans don't even know where Romania is, or tend to lump it vaguely with 'all those other Eastern European countries in upheaval.' I have to believe that giving a group of theater artists a reason to become passionately interested in your country, its history and traditions, and in turn communicating that passionate interest to our audiences, will be some compensation for our failure to do your culture full justice."

Dr. Dumitru's fear, so honestly spoken, allowed me to hear what we always seek in the theater—his subtext. His seeming concern about African-American actors gave way to a larger fear. "This play presents caricatures of Romanians. What are you going to do about that?" I asked him if he had read the play. "No," he answered. "But I heard about it, and read the reviews [Mark Wing-Davey's 1992 revival at the Manhattan Theatre Club]."

I told him that I had not seen the New York productions and could not comment on charges of stereotyping. I did, however, explain that our actors, dramaturg, and designers shared with me a determination to create specific, nuanced characters rather than caricatures, and invited him to attend our production and tell us whether we had succeeded in our portrayals.

"I would like to come to a rehearsal," was Dr. Dumitru's response.

I said that he would be welcome any time, and asked why he preferred to attend a rehearsal over a performance.

"Oh, I will be at your opening, but—(and here he hesitated) I like to see the process of things." I sensed that Dr. Dumitru, uneasy about our depiction of his culture, wanted to be able to advise and perhaps control our interpretations.[88] But surely his input might prove helpful. While rehearsals are often jealously guarded, opening them to outsiders can expand our conception and practice of dramaturgy. In plays such as *Mad Forest,* the members of the focal culture may be outsiders to the rehearsal process, but they are insiders to the world of the play and are therefore important dramaturgical allies. The fact that Dr. Dumitru did not join us until opening night suggests that by the end of our evening together he did not feel the need to investigate our work. But our choice to include many Romanians in the rehearsal process was to prove invaluable.

To conclude our dinner and field trip, the cast gathered to sing "Wake Up Romania," the anthem banned under Ceausescu, for Dr. Dumitru and his companions and for our generous hosts, Mr. Onchoiu and his family. ("Wake Up Romania" must be sung during *Mad Forest,* but we had learned it early for the occasion of our field trip.) All were obviously moved to witness a group of others singing in Romanian the most significant verses in Romania's history. And their response to our singing—tears, embraces, champagne, and standing ovations—was deeply moving to us.

Anna Deavere Smith, whose other-oriented work demands a willingness to reenact people distinctly different from herself, has asked, "Who has the right to speak for whom?"[89] Dr. Dumitru's "How dare you" in effect raised the same question, and our field research suggested an answer. The trip to Queens, particularly Dr. Dumitru's articulation of his suspicions, his willingness to listen, and his ultimate gift of trust, together constituted, in retrospect, a journey from tourism to friendship. As with tourists, some of our explorations were safe, pleasant: handshakes, nibbles of cheese and salami from the Romanian deli, toasts, tours. Passion, stakes, vulnerability, whether derived from the ardor of Mr. Onchoiu's tales of his escape from Romania or the initial fears of Dr. Dumitru, became preconditions of friendship—that state of empathy and "seeing" that allows the humanity of both "others" to connect. A tourist cannot hope to speak for, much less as, the strangers who are encountered. A friend sometimes can. Beyond the wealth of specific insights provided by the field trip, our experience of moving into friendship created, especially for the actors, the belief that we were no longer complete outsiders; that we might be able to think, feel, and behave as Romanians.

It is ironic that *Mad Forest,* which is such a powerful response to Romanian experience, came through the eyes of a foreign artist. In a 1992 interview, Romanian-born director Andrei Serban called *Mad Forest* "the only active piece of writing about what happened during the revolution and right after. It's almost like a photograph of ourselves. . . . There's great material for drama, but no Romanian is writing about it."[90] Had Churchill and Wing-Davey not believed and acted on their "right" to approach the many citizens with whom they conversed, watched, ate, and traveled, an important work that has moved and challenged audiences from Bucharest to London and across the United States would never have come into being. Crucial to the success of their encounter was the heightened awareness of their own otherness, the highly sensitive and respectful listening that resulted, and the understanding that reality in times of upheaval is relative rather than absolute. Wing-Davey acknowledges this directly: "We may tell some truth, but there isn't the Truth."[91]

The discomfiture that triggered Dr. Dumitru's "How dare you?" derives partly from the reflexive belief that an outside perspective is implicitly inaccurate, inappropriate, or unworthy. Churchill's ability to capture the complexities of Romanian experience, and our many contacts with Romanians themselves, encouraged us. Our desire to keep growing beyond "tourism" made dramaturgy an ongoing, inseparable aspect of rehearsal.

Many Philadelphia-based Romanians came to our rehearsals, and were surprised and pleased at the diversity of actors who would be portraying them. "The only black people in Romania," one woman explained, "are the African students who come to Bucharest to study. There is much ethnic hatred in Romania; many people associate only with their own 'tribe.'" The unselfconscious ease with which our Romanian advisers cited the pluralism within our own ensemble fed the friendships developing among the group of Romanians and Americans, with race and prejudice (too often taboo subjects in America) readily emerging as topics of exploration.

Our Romanian visitors became key dramaturgical partners in the area of language. In *Mad Forest,* actors must speak and sing Romanian. Besides the "Wake Up Romania" anthem, the ensemble must recite in Romanian a poem praising Elena Ceausescu, the hated wife of dictator Nicolae. Churchill also includes titles for each scene, spoken first in halting phrase-book Romanian, then English, then fluent Romanian. Actors must also learn to speak Romanian-accented English for the middle act, composed of the actual recollections of eleven ordinary citizens of Bucharest who witnessed the revolution. The Romanians who visited us in rehearsal were wonderfully tickled to hear us speak their language, and the unplanned reactions during their visits again proved most illuminating.

One of our first Romanian consultants, a man of twenty-two named Edouard who had fled the country with his family as a seventeen-year-old, was infectiously funny—a wisecracking rebel who chuckled even as he described remembered deprivations or terrors. Practically midstory, we asked if he could help us sing "Wake Up Romania." The instant he saw the Romanian lyrics, he burst into tears and was unable to speak for some time. Though we had all read about the importance of this anthem, banned under Ceausescu, directly experiencing Eduourd's reaction was revelatory.

During load-in, our language coach, Clarisse Dumitrescu, stopped by to listen to the accents and saw the set for the first time, a prominent element of which was a large banner of Ceausescu. Clarisse had entered the theater engaged in banter with one of the actors, but upon seeing the image of Ceausescu, she was transfixed, the color draining from her face. When she was finally able to speak, she said, "I haven't seen **him** (Romanians called Ceausescu and his wife He and She, almost never by name) for so long. I just feel so—angry. Enraged!" Again, though we had read dozens of accounts of Ceausescu's cruelty and the Romanians' hatred of him, the power of Clarisse's outburst was singular. In witnessing such spontaneous responses, actors are infused with an empathy that gives facts a human context. They gain a visceral grasp of character subtexts such as those that caused so many Romanians, after seeing a performance, to ask, "How did you know? You captured us. . . . You understand us. . . . How?" We didn't anticipate the bonds that developed between our Romanian advisers and ourselves. One family invited our entire group to their home, cooked a five-course traditional dinner, and shared photos, artifacts, prayers, and songs from the country they had fled. Most Romanians expressed amazement that Americans could be so interested in their country, and told us that they tended to keep silent about their roots, because most Americans seemed indifferent to Romanian culture and history. Not only did our questions spur them to remember things forgotten, or rekindle pride in their heritage; they became freer to ask us questions about their new country, a place they often find confusing and contradictory. They wanted to explore potential differences in perspective among our various cast and crew members, and were eager to compare the prejudice toward Hungarians in Romania with the history of African Americans and others of color in the United States.

The involvement of so many people across race and culture in the creation of *Mad Forest* resulted in the most diverse audience in Venture Theatre's history. I must admit that throughout the opening-night performance, I was terrified beyond the usual director's jitters. What would our production say to the Romanian dissidents who had fled their country, to those such as Dr. Dumitru still in the employ of Iliescu, to our mixed American audiences?

To the credit of Caryl Churchill, our wonderful team of artists, and the spirit of inquiry and excitement this project generated, the production seemed to speak powerfully across audiences. Dr. Dumitru, who attended the opening with a twelve-member entourage, stood during curtain call and asked permission to present the cast with a huge formal floral arrangement. Mounting the stage, he shook each actor's hand and kissed both cheeks of each actor in the Romanian style—a tribute to the power of theater to bring diverse peoples together. At the reception, Dr. Dumitru smilingly recalled his initial fears about our production, and amidst accolades, commented that although conditions in Romania today are better than in 1990 when Churchill completed *Mad Forest,* the play indeed "told a truth that is painful but that we must remember." The many Romanians who attended *Mad Forest*'s month-long run, including Cultural Consular Ioana Ieronim of the Romanian Embassy in Washington, D.C., expressed surprise and gratitude that we could tell their story so accurately. Most commented that seeing themselves enacted by non-Romanians was especially meaningful.[92]

Both Venture and Temple Theaters, because of their ties to black and white communities, bring people together in the theater who are not usually together. Beyond the common experience of appreciation for *Mad Forest* was the value of particular experience. For example, when Churchill's sole Hungarian character, Ianos, is rebuffed by his girlfriend's grandparents (they react to his handshake as poison), many African-American audience members at various performances reacted with a collective groan. In the moment of such a response, the pain of ethnic hatred is brought home. The unspoken dialogue a play constantly creates between actors and audience, and between audience members, is given an extra charge when viewers respond audibly.

Our audiences' experience of the casting, which we learned through post-performance conversation and written feedback, tended to follow a similar pattern. When viewers familiar with Venture and Temple Theaters attend a production, they expect to see a multicultural cast. To our Romanian guests and American audiences new to Temple and Venture, the mixture of races onstage was initially noticeable, even jolting. As the play progressed, and Churchill's key device of each performer enacting a range of characters accumulated, viewers tended to background race and foreground characters and events. Moreover, a kind of "seeing double" occurs, in which race can suddenly zoom into awareness. For example, many audience members, black and white, reported moments (such as the Ianos handshake) when the multiracial casting prompted personal associations between our country's racial conflicts and Romania's ethnic tensions—particularly during the eyewitness accounts of the revolution, and the final scene of the play, in which a fight breaks out at a wedding reception and all the characters start talking at once. One of our earliest production concepts—that this postrevolutionary cacophony of voices and viewpoints would be powerfully (if painfully) underscored by a diversity of actors onstage—was widely experienced by our audiences. Such audience feedback affirmed that mixed casting made our production more powerful and immediate.

> The central political task of the final years of this century . . . is the creation of a new model of coexistence among the various cultures, peoples, races and religious spheres within a single interconnected civilization.
>   Vaclav Havel[93]

One paradigm our *Mad Forest* experience suggests is that what persists as today's "risks" or exceptions becomes tomorrow's standard practice. It is now hard to contemplate an American production of *Mad Forest* with an all-white cast. Feedback from audiences and colleagues attested to the richer imagery and ideas that derived from watching a diversity of actors enact Romanian characters.[94] Moreover, photographically naturalistic casting would have deprived actors of color of the challenges and rewards of working on *Mad Forest.* And finally, the inclusion of a diversity of actors in the cast had the ripple effect of attracting a greater diversity of audience members.

The experience of hearing one's story told by others—of which our diverse cast of Americans telling a Romanian story is but one example—seems under certain circumstances to generate special insight. When we enact stories beyond our own, when we can truthfully embody an "other," an interest beyond self-interest is implied. Anna Deavere Smith speaks to this with particular eloquence:

> The boundaries of ethnicity . . . have been the only conceivable response to . . . a mainstream that denied the possibility of the development of identity. On the other hand the price we pay is that few of us can really look at the story of race in its complexity and its scope. If we were able to move more frequently beyond these boundaries, we would develop multifaceted identities and we would develop a more complex language . . . [which] our race dialogue desperately needs.[95]

What of the dramaturg's responsibilities when otherness figures so centrally in the playtext and the production team? In collaborating with actors, designers, directors, and those "outsiders" whose culture defines the world of the play, the dramaturg must help create situations that allow face-to-face contact and foster vulnerability, intimacy, and respect. Research becomes proactive: field trips are dramaturgy; going to dinner is dramaturgy; encouraging friendship is dramaturgy. The stereotype of the dramaturg as someone who lives in the library and works with books is naive and outmoded; the most effective dramaturgy often happens outside the library.

The right to "re-imagine the other" can and should extend beyond specific productions to theater institutions, whether professional or educational. As dramaturgs, we can use our centrally involved roles to stimulate ongoing dialogue and choices in and around otherness, with audiences as well as colleagues. We can advocate for diversity in as many projects and settings as possible; we can encourage working methods that value difference, mutual learning, friendship, and the sharing of power. Finally, as dramaturgs, we can reflect upon and record the ways that multicultural commitments and choices shape our theaters and positively influence the communities we seek to serve.

At Venture Theatre, we look forward to the day when multiculturalism is a defunct term: when our mission's emphasis on diversity has become so integral to theater practice that we must reframe it. Otherness, however, is likely to remain a vital, challenging, potentially rich realm of discourse and struggle.

SECTION NOTES

1. Susan Lanser as quoted in "Strategies for Subverting the Canon" by Gay Gibson Cima in *Upstaging Big Daddy: Directing Theater As If Gender and Race Matter,* ed. Ellen Donkin and Susan Clement (Ann Arbor: University of Michigan Press, 1993) 93.

2. Peter D. Arnott, *Introduction to the French Theatre* (Totowa, N. J.: Rowman and Littlefield, 1977) 157.

3. Gershon Shaked, "The play: gateway to cultural dialogue," trans. Jeffrey Green in *The Play Out of Context: Transferring Plays from Culture to Culture,* ed. Hanna Scolnicov and Peter Holland (Cambridge: Cambridge University Press, 1989) 13.

4. Shaked 13.

5. Patrice Pavis, "Problems of translation for the stage: interculturalism and post-modern theater," trans. Loren Kruger in *The Play Out of Context* 38.

6. The original lines: "What, is't murder?" "No." "Lechery?" "Call it so."

7. Cima 99.

8. Recently I saw the superlative Footsbarn production of *The Odyssey* at the Avignon theater festival. I awaited their resolution with great anticipation. Penelope bathed Odysseus' feet with an almost impersonal ritual respect, while he, infinitely exhausted, began his story. After a moment into the telling, they simply looked at each other—really looked at each other—simply, deeply, and wordlessly. Then the play ended. That profound moment of recognition, one of the type that sustains a lifetime of memory and artistic aspiration, dwarfed all other considerations of gender and social context.

9. The quotes were excerpted verbatim from the speakers to whom they were attributed with one exception. Some quotes from Goebbels were attributed to Hitler.

10. Compare, for instance, production schedules published by the journals *American Theatre* and *Theater Heute* in their October 1994 issues, respectively. In *American Theatre,* 277 theaters announced for the 1994/95 season 473 productions. Three hundred forty-six from the English language repertoire, 204 American plays, and 160 plays of English, Irish, or South African origin in translation, 109 plays were announced, 14 from the German. In *Theater Heute,* 148 theaters in

Germany, Austria, and Switzerland announced for October 1994 alone 266 open-
ings; 130 from the German language repertoire, 136 were of plays in translation,
36 of them American plays. Although these numbers don't allow for a completely
correct statistical comparison, they speak for themselves.

See also Michael Evans' pertinent comment in "How the Other Half Writes,"
American Theatre January 1995: 7.

11. See Bonnie Marranca's instructive essay "Theatre and the University at the End of
the Twentieth Century," *Performing Arts Journal* 17.2-3 (1995): 60.
12. Francois Regnault, "Postface a Peer Gynt," *Theatre National Populaire* (1981): 72.
Quote translated by Loren Kruger.
13. "Scab" is not the accurate equivalent of the German as I pointed out in an introductory note that explained the more obscure meanings of the German text. Recently, Loren Kruger, in "Stories from the Production Line," *Theatre Journal* 46.4
(1994): 501, proposed as a preferable choice *The Wagebuster.* I agree with her
that the term would capture more precisely the original's complex meaning but
still believe the catchy *Scab* serves well for an American audience unfamiliar with
the socioeconomic structures of the former German Democratic Republic.
14. Bertolt Brecht, "A Short Organum for the Theatre," *Brecht on Theatre*, ed. John
Willett (New York: Hill & Wang, 1964) 204.
15. From a letter by Raymond Chandler, as quoted in James Wolcott, "Raymond Chandler's Smoking Gun," *The New Yorker* 25 September 1995: 104.
16. John David Chapman, *Lucian, Plato, and Greek Morals* (Boston: Atlantic Monthly
Press, 1920) 92.
17. Friedrich Nietzsche, *The Birth of Tragedy,* trans. Francis Golffing (New York: Doubleday, 1956) 19.
18. *Iphigenia* was a merging of two plays by Euripides, *Iphigenia in Aulis* and *Iphigenia at Tauris,* presented as Parts I and II respectively on the same evening.
19. *The Gospel at Colonus* had its premiere at the Brooklyn Academy of Music
in 1983.
20. E. R. Dodds, *The Greeks and The Irrational* (Berkeley: University of California
Press, 1951). This book is essential reading for the preparation of any classical
Greek play. I am indebted to *The Greeks and the Irrational* as a source of inspiration and the title of this article.
21. C. M. Bowra, *The Greek Experience* (New York: New American Library, 1957).
22. Cary M. Mazer, *Shakespeare Refashioned: Elizabethan Plays on Edwardian
Stages* (Ann Arbor: UMI Research Press, 1981).
23. Catherine Belsey, *The Subject of Tragedy: Identity and Difference in Renaissance Drama* (London: Routledge, 1985).
24. Peter Brook, *The Empty Space* (New York: Atheneum, 1978) 38.
25. Pierre Marivaux, *The Game of Love and Chance,* trans. and adapted by Neil
Bartlett (Bath, England: Absolute Press, 1992) 6-7.
26. Bernard Beckerman, *The Dynamics of Drama* (New York: Knopf, 1970) 3.
27. Joseph R. Roach, *The Player's Passion: Studies in the Science of Acting* (Newark:
University of Delaware Press, 1985).
28. See Alan C. Dessen, *Elizabethan Drama and the Viewer's Eye* (Chapel Hill: University of North Carolina Press, 1977), and Elizabethan Stage *Conventions and
Modern Interpreters* (Cambridge: Cambridge University Press, 1984).
29. See *Producible Interpretation: Eight English Plays, 1675-1707* (Carbondale:
Southern Illinois University Press, 1985).

30. I am indebted to Lee Devin (in conversation) for this phrase.
31. Marvin Carlson catalogues different ways of describing the relation of script to performance in "Theatrical Performance: Illustration, Translation, Fulfillment, or Supplement?" *Theatre Journal* 37 (1985): 5-11. Although he rejects the first three terms of the article title, his preferred term—supplement—still gives excessive priority to the text over the performance built from it.
32. Andrea Henderson, "Death on the Stage, Death of the Stage: The Antitheatricality of *The Duchess of Malfi*," *Theatre Journal* 42 (1990): 194-207
33. In our staging of the play, we exploited these ambiguities through the conventionality of our mode of theatrical presentation: for example, the wax replicas were represented by the same actors who played the characters whose corpses the wax replicas were designed to resemble. For a scholarly review of the production, see Jean Peterson's review and "Space, Signs, and Voyeurism in *The Duchess of Malfi*: An Interview with Cary M. Mazer," *Shakespeare Bulletin* 12.2 (Spring 1994): 28-30.
34. The senior theater arts major playing the Duchess later wrote, in her honors thesis about playing the role, that, not feeling any real romantic on-stage chemistry with the actor playing Antonio, the Duchess's secret husband, she played the courtship scene as an act of willfulness and defiance and not of desire.
35. As Belsey observes, "Domestic relations are defined as affective rather than political in a discourse which works to suppress recognition of the power relations which structure the family, and by this means liberalism opens a gap for the accommodation of an uncontested, because unidentified, patriarchy" (199).
36. Belsey 39.
37. Belsey 42.
38. I quote from the New Mermaid edition, ed. Elizabeth M. Brennan (New York: W. W. Norton, 1983).
39. In performance, much of Ferdinand's confrontation with the Duchess in 3.2, when he discovers his sister talking to her unseen husband while she combs her hair, was played as though Ferdinand and the Duchess were looking at one another and at themselves in a full-length mirror, the same invisible mirror in which the Duchess, in an image we introduced earlier in the play, contemplates her pregnant body.
40. It is crucially important that good scholarly ideas be translated into playable actions, and not just interpretive or stylistic glosses. Recently, in a major regional theater near Philadelphia, a scholar who had written an excellent book on the comic structure of Shakespearean tragedy was a dramaturg for a production of Romeo and Juliet. The director wisely tried to put the dramaturg's scholarly ideas into practice. But rather than having the actors act on their desires as though they were in a comedy by placing extraordinary importance on their smallest desires, turning trivial impediments into monumental comic complications, and turning their own behavior into mechanistic obsessiveness—thereby generating a comic structure in the play's overall action—the director dressed Capulet in a brightly colored shirt and suspenders and introduced bits of comic stage business.
41. I am indebted to my many collaborators on *The Duchess of Malfi*, particularly Sarah Werner, David Hafken, Emily Hellström, and Jeffrey Coon.
42. The Americanized text then appeared, with a few cuts restored by Bartlett, in the July/August 1990 issue of *American Theatre*. The original English version was

published in *Berenice* by Racine; *Le Misanthrope, The School for Wives* by Molière; trans. and adapted by Neil Bartlett (Bath, England: Absolute Classics, Absolute Press, 1990).

43. One of the onlookers was Jim Carmody, a faculty member at University of California at San Diego, who subsequently published an essay on the production, "Alceste in Hollywood: A Semiotic Reading of *The Misanthrope*," *Critical Theory and Performance,* ed. Janelle G. Reinelt and Joseph R. Roach (Ann Arbor: University of Michigan Press, 1992): 117–28.

44. Michael Ovitz became, in 1995, president of The Walt Disney Co. after its merger with Capital Cities/ABC. *Entertainment Weekly*'s yearly listing of the 101 "Most Powerful People in Entertainment" listed Ovitz at number eight for 1995. Everyone ahead of him on the list had also been involved in a major merger within the past two years, with the number one place going to Ovitz' partner/employer, Michael Eisner, the CEO of Walt Disney. In 1989, when *The Misanthrope* was taking place, Ovitz was a much shadowier presence. The New York and Los Angeles articles were the first stories devoted to Ovitz in any daily paper, and his clout was reflected even there. The *New York Times* article reported that many Hollywood insiders refused to speak about Ovitz even off the record, fearing possible retribution. In his personal research in Los Angeles, Robert Falls reported that friends would often refuse to discuss Ovitz in public places, fearful that anything they would say could get back to Ovitz himself.

45. Jacques Guicharnaud, *Molière; une aventure théâtrale: Tartuffe, Dom Juan, Le Misanthrope* (Paris: Gallimard, 1963).

46. Zelda Fichandler, "Our Town in Our Times," *American Theatre* October 1991: 143.

47. There are two available English translations of *The Marriage of Figaro*: Jacques Barzun, *Beaumarchais's Figaro's Marriage* (New York: Farrar, Straus and Cudahy, 1961) and John Wood, *The Marriage of Figaro* (Baltimore: Penguin Books, 1964). Downey found the extant translations static and heavily literal, lacking the theatricality that could bring this play to life on the stage for a contemporary audience. He took the Gallimard edition of the French, considered the best example of the French text and, line by line, he studied the French before reworking the text into English. In this way he was able to retain the original rhythm, for as Downey points out, "In theater, the original rhythm is far more important than the literalness of a line. If you don't understand how it was said, you will misinterpret the meaning." See Kyle Lawson, "ATC returns *Figaro* to its roots—sort of," *Phoenix Gazette* 29 October 1992. The play was thus changed considerably, moving it from eighteenth-century Spain to nineteenth-century Sonora, and eliminating superfluous characters and updating the dialogue. In Downey's view, "It's an adaptation," for while "eighty percent of Beaumarchais' plot is there, only 20 percent of his dialogue remains." See Richard Nilsen, "'One Crazy Day' dawns in new form," *Arizona Republic* 30 October 1992.

48. Although U.S. Latinas/Latinos are the fastest growing population group in the United States today, Chicanas/Chicanos constitute the largest particular ethnic group in the Southwest. Some important sociological and political histories about this presence have emerged in recent years and have brought about a better understanding of Chicanas'/Chicanos' contributions to American and world history. See, for example, Rodolfo Acuña, *Occupied America: A History of Chicanos,*

3rd ed. (New York: HarperCollins, 1988); and Ronald Takaki, *A Different Mirror: A History of Multicultural America* (Boston: Little, Brown and Company, 1993) 311-339. The term *Latina/Latino* will be used to designate the larger U.S. population of women and men descended from Spanish-speaking groups. The term *Chicana/Chicano* will be used for women and men of Mexican descent residing within the United States for any length of time. Although the term has certain ideological and political meanings connected to the "Chicano Movement," this researcher supports the view that this term is generally accepted as appropriate for this particular underrepresented group in the United States. Because of the issue of gender in Spanish words, the slash will be used for inclusion of women and men as appropriate.

49. M. Scott Skinner, "One Crazy Play: Adaptation of Beaumarchais' *Figaro* Raises Curtain on the New ATC Season," *Arizona Daily Star* 2 October 1992.

50. Oscar G. Brockett, *History of the Theatre,* 7th ed. (Boston: Allyn and Bacon, 1995) 278.

51. Theodore Shank, *500 Plays* (New York: Drama Book Publishers, 1988).

52. Program Notes 36.

53. Andrei Serban, director, *The Serpent Woman* by Carlo Gozzi; and Anne Bogart, director, *Life is a Dream,* American Repertory Theatre, Cambridge, Massachusetts, 1988–89 season.

54. See for example Elizabeth C. Ramírez, *Footlights Across the Border: A History of Spanish-language Professional Theatre in Texas, 1875-1935* (New York: Peter Lang, 1990) 1-194; "Combination Companies on the American Stage: Organization & Practice in Texas," *Theatre History Studies* (1989): 77-91; "Compañía Juan B. Padilla," in *American Theatre Companies: 1888-1930,* ed. Weldon Durham (Westport, Conn.: Greenwood Press, 1986) 353-358; and "A History of Mexican American Professional Theatre in Texas Prior to 1900," *Theatre Survey* 24 (1983): 99-116.

55. The Special Collection of Maps at The University of Texas is extensive, and includes many originals and copies of original maps of Mexico showing the border land areas of early America.

56. Margaret Regan, *Tucson Weekly* 14 October 1992.

57. Don Carlos Nebel, *Viaje pintoresco y arquelógico por la República Mexicana 1829-1834* (Mexico, 5 May 1849) translated from the French, *Voyage pittoresque et archeologique dans la partie la plus interessante du Mexique* (Paris, 1836).

58. Gonzalo Obregón, *El México de Guadalupe Victoria (1824-1829)* (Mexico: Empresa Editorial Cuauhtemoc, 1974).

59. Frances Toor, *A Treasury of Mexican Folkways* (New York: Crown, 1976).

60. Frances Calderón de la Barca, *Life in Mexico* (London: Dent and Sons, 1970).

61. Claudio Linati, *Trajes civiles, militares y religiosos de México* (Brussels, 1828, and Mexico: Editorial Innovación, 1978).

62. Teresa Castillo Yturbide, *La Tejedora de Vida* (Mexico: La Banca Publishers, 1989).

63. José R. Benitez, *El traje y el adorno en México, 1500-1910* (Guadalajara: Imprenta Universitaria, 1946).

64. Chloe Sayer, *Costumes of Mexico* (Austin: University of Texas Press, 1990).

65. Downey 9.

66. Joanne Pottlitzer, *Hispanic Theater in the United States and Puerto Rico* (New York: Ford Foundation, 1988) 1.

67. Elizabeth C. Ramírez, *Footlights Across the Border: A History of Spanish-language Professional Theatre in Texas, 1873-1935* (New York: Peter Lang, 1990).
68. Open hearing on the subject of "Diversity and Multicultural Concerns: Their Impact on the Preparation of Theatre Professionals," in "Notes and Sample Issues" presented by the National Association of Schools of Theatre (NAST) for discussion by the Task Force on Multicultural Concerns at the 1991 Annual Meeting and Retreat, Tucson, Arizona.
69. Robert Brustein, "A House Divided," *American Theatre* October 1991: 45.
70. Citing Guillermo Gómez-Peña's work as "among the most powerful examples of intercultural performance," Richard Schechner argues for an "intercultural" approach, which he describes as the following: "Where multiculturalism falters, where fusion does not occur, interculturalism happens. Just as mountains rise where continents collide, and deep ocean basins form where they pull apart, so new arts, behaviors, and human interactions are negotiated at the interfaces and faults connecting and separating cultures." See Richard Schechner, "An Intercultural Primer," *American Theatre* October 1991: 30, 135.
71. The show was inspired by the earlier ballet *Fancy Free,* also created by Robbins and Bernstein.
72. Anthony Chase, "Comden and Green: A Hell of a Team," *TheaterWeek* 26 June 1989: 22-27.
73. Symposium, "*On the Town,*" *The Dramatists Guild Quarterly* (Fall 1986): 3-15.
74. Studs Terkel, *"The Good War": An Oral History of World War Two* (New York: Pantheon Books, 1984) and Richard R. Lingeman, *Don't You Know There's a War On? The American Home Front, 1941-45* (New York: Putman, 1970).
75. *A Guy Named Joe.* Dir. Victor Fleming. MGM, 1944; *The Clock.* Dir. Vincente Minnelli. MGM, 1945; *Hollywood Goes to War.* HBO/Brentwood Home Video; *Why We Fight,* Dir. Frank Capra. US War Office, 1942-45.
76. Edwin Wilson, "Remembering the Way We Were," *Wall Street Journal* 14 June 1989: 16.
77. The same collaborators had worked together four years previously on an antiwar satire called *Strike Up the Band,* which, in its original form, closed quickly out of town in Philadelphia (prompting Kaufman's oft-cited remark that "Satire is what closes on Saturday night").
78. Wager's original idea in the early eighties was to pair *Of Thee I Sing* with its 1933 sequel, *Let 'Em Eat Cake,* which brought Wintergreen and Co. into a civil insurrection, and conflate the two shows into a single evening. This proved to be an infelicitous idea for several reasons: the Gershwin estate would not permit conflation of the material; the sequel is not nearly as good as its predecessor; and, finally, the Brooklyn Academy of Music eventually did its own concert version of both scores in 1987 with narration replacing the book (apparently the Gershwins were not conflatable, but Kaufman was).
79. *Brother, Can You Spare a Dime?* Dir. Philippe Mora. VPS/Goodtimes, 1975.
80. *Mad Forest* premiered at the Central School of Speech and Drama, London, on June 13, 1990; the production played at the National Theatre of Bucharest, Romania, on September 17, 1990. (Romanian audiences heard the English performance via headsets).
81. Clay Goss, *Mad Forest* program notes (Philadelphia: Temple University Office of Publications) 6.

82. Anna Deavere Smith talks of "creating artists who can move freely between the confines of ethnicity, gender, politics, and social class"—a strategy that describes Churchill's work as well as her own. In Michael P. Scassera, "A Jury of One," *TheatreWeek* 28 March 1994: 19.

83. Venture and Temple are both committed to expanding the diversity of their actors and staff, and were hoping for a greater "mix" of actors. One of our white actors is American born of Argentine parents, but we were unable to cast Asian or other Latino actors; not only are there few in Philadelphia, but our production budget precluded New York City casting.

84. David and Peter Turnley (photographs), and Mort Rosenblum (text), *Moments of Revolution: Eastern Europe* (New York: Stewart, Tabori & Chang, 1990).

85. Andrei Codrescu, *The Hole in the Flag* (New York: W. Morrow 1991).

86. Because our research suggested that ethnic prejudice characterizes a significant portion of the Romanian population, I chose to mention to Mr. Onchoiu and Ms. Fallon, before our visit, that we were staging *Mad Forest* with a mixed cast. Their response: "You are risk-takers. Good for you."

87. Deavere Smith, *Fires in the Mirror* (New York: Anchor, 1993) xxxix.

88. *Mad Forest* openly criticizes both Ceausescu's regime and that of Ion Iliescu, the "liberator" whose behaviors are little different from the tyrant he unseated (and who remains president of Romania today). As U.N. General Consul, Dr. Dumitru ultimately works for Iliescu; his concerns about *Mad Forest*'s projection of his country are understandable.

89. Deavere Smith xxviii.

90. Andrei Serban, interview by James Leverett, *Performing Arts* (Berkeley Repertory Theatre's playbill) November 1992: P-1.

91. Gerard Raymond, "Return to *Mad Forest*," *TheatreWeek* 26 October 1992: 23.

92. Venture Theatre premiered Richard Kalinosky's *A Beast on the Moon* in March 1995 (just prior to its premiere at Actors Theatre of Louisville's Humana Festival); our Armenian audiences were similarly moved at seeing themselves so well portrayed by Latina and Anglo-American actors.

93. Vaclav Havel, Independence Day address (Philadelphia: 4 July 1994).

94. In a subsequent *Philadelphia Inquirer* article on nontraditional casting, Clifford Ridley, discussing Nicholas Hytner's revival of *Carousel* and our *Mad Forest,* described the naturalness of experiencing a plurality of performers on the contemporary stage, and the excitement of those moments when an actor's racial or ethnic identity deepens the viewer's associations and understanding.

95. Deavere Smith, *Twilight: Los Angeles, 1992* (New York: Anchor, 1994) 25.

SECTION 5

DEVELOPING NEW WORKS

Scott Cummings begins this section on dramaturgy and developing new works with a look at the history of new play development in the United States and at some of the forms it has taken in recent years, noticing benefits, pitfalls, and paradoxes, along the way.

Many readers will almost instinctively want to read this book in search of a simple formula for dramaturgy, as a "how-to-do-it" book on dramaturgy. To some extent this anthology does participate in that tradition, even as it warms readers of simple formulations. It makes sense, therefore, to look at the how-to tradition itself, as Steve Weeks does in his examination of books on how to write a play. In doing so, Weeks asks readers to examine the historical presuppositions that inform their idea of what makes a good play. Even more specifically, he challenges dramaturgs who work with new playwrights to recognize that what they or others might consider to be universal characteristics of a good play are actually functions of historical circumstances, in this instance, a still persistent late nineteenth-century tradition of advice that drew on Aristotle and the well-made play for its formulations.

The ideal companion piece to Weeks's essay is Leon Katz's insightful critique of much that passes for new play development. Weeks's article explores the historical foundations of what Katz denounces. Readers might also compare both selections to Mazer's discussion in section four of universal versus historicizing approaches to playscripts and Bly's consideration in section two of the desire to codify the work of the dramaturg. Readers might also contrast Weeks and Katz studies with Sanford and Devin's advocacy of Aristotelian categories as dramaturgical tools. Finally, Weeks's essay with its emphasis on the pioneering work of George Pierce Baker at Harvard and later Yale complements articles by Marks, Brustein, Brockett, Borreca, and Bly in earlier sections. Together these writers sketch a history of theater at Yale and other schools that underscores ways in which the university has shaped American theater in the twentieth century.

The next set of pieces comes from dramaturgs, literary managers, and artistic directors at nonprofit theaters engaged in developing new works. Paul Selig (playwright) interviews Morgan Jenness (New York Shakespeare Festival/Public Theater). One of the most highly respected dramaturgs in the field of new play development, Jenness discusses the journey that brought her into the field and shares insights gained through many years' experience working with writers. In particular, she explores the dance between the search for a structure to guide one's work as a dramaturg or playwright and the refusal of any one structural solution.

Michael Bigelow Dixon introduces the work of Actors Theatre of Louisville, a theater that has, with the National Playwrights Conference at the O'Neill Center in Waterford, Connecticut, been a leader in producing new plays for the American theater. His key word is "dialogue," and he discusses how that word informs the work of the Actors Theater.

Mame Hunt (Magic Theatre) and Susan Mason (California State University, Los Angeles) explore the role of the literary manager, dramaturg, and artistic director in working with new works and in shaping the aesthetic/ideological function of a specific theater. Hunt is one of a growing number of artistic directors with a primary background in dramaturgy and literary management.

Tim Sanford, another literary manager who is now an artistic director, describes his work at Playwrights Horizons. Sanford argues for the relevance of contemporary theoretical studies and Aristotle to his day-to-day practice. Readers might compare his use of Aristotle with Devin's in section three and Weeks's concern about the misuses of Aristotle in this section. Like Mazer (section four) and Lutterbie (section three), Sanford is convinced that theoretical approaches developed in literary studies and other branches of the humanities are worth the effort they take to master.

Paul Castagno draws upon his experience as a playwright a teacher of playwriting, and a dramaturg to discuss how young dramaturgs might first begin their work with new playwrights. The collaboration between dramaturg and playwright is fragile and vulnerable to many and various false steps. Castagno examines some fruitful places from which to begin this delicate process.

Playwright Suzan Zeder explores emerging models for developing plays for young audiences and the role that dramaturgy is playing in these programs. She argues strongly against facile distinctions between adult and "children's" theater, urging the importance of careful dramaturgical work regardless of the intended audience.

Susan Finque asks dramaturgs to reconsider presuppositions about gender and sexuality that they invariably bring to their work. Her account of a group of young actors collaborating with a director and playwright on an ensemble-generated piece (*Contents Under Pressure*) stands in the tradition that Chaikin and The Wooster Group represent. Finque, Kuharski, Rafalowicz, Jonas, Niesen, and Frisch/Weems (see below) together offer a variety of ideas and methods for a dramaturgy grounded in the idea of empowering the ensemble.

Tony Kushner stands for a new generation of playwrights who have come of age in a time of theater when dramaturgs and dramaturgy were a more regular part of the process. In an interview with Susan Jonas, he discusses his work as it relates to these relatively new members of the production team. In doing so, Kushner argues for a dramaturgical approach that has a strong ideological and political foundation, as opposed to the more or less indiscriminate gathering of research materials.

Finally, Norman Frisch and Marianne Weems offer a detailed account of the role of dramaturgy and the dramaturg in The Wooster Group (New York), one of the most important experimental theaters in the United States today. Their accounts of the journeys that brought them to the Group and of the development of pieces such as *LSD (...Just the High Points)* and *Frank Dell's the Temptation of St. Antony* offer valuable insights into the role dramaturgs might play in an Ensemble that radically questions conventional ideas of textuality, rehearsal, and performance.]

Garden or Ghetto?

The Paradoxy of New Play Development

by Scott T. Cummings

SCOTT T. CUMMINGS is a dramaturg, critic, and teacher based in the Boston area. For three years, he was the Resident Dramaturg at City Theatre in Pittsburgh and, prior to that, he served as a production dramaturg at Baltimore's Center Stage and the Yale Repertory Theatre. He has written criticism for *American Theatre, Theater,* and the *Boston Globe, Boston Phoenix,* and *Pittsburgh Post-Gazette,* and published in scholarly journals. He is the author of a forthcoming book on the theater work of Maria Irene Fornes. With his essay, he wishes to acknowledge with gratitude his permanent indebtedness to the wisdom and inspiration of Leon Katz.

How does a playwright find a producer for a new play? How does a producer find a new play worth producing? In contemporary American theater practice, these questions lay at the heart of the phenomenon known as "new play development." In its broadest sense, new play development refers to what might be called the larval stage in the life of a play, the period that begins the day a playwright first gives somebody a new script to read and ends on the night of the play's professional premiere.

Strictly speaking, all that is required to "develop" a new play is to produce it—invest the time, money, and resources necessary to give it the fullest possible life on the stage. However, not every play springs from the playwright's mind full-born and ready for the stage. Theater is risky business, financially speaking, and economic realities often demand that a new play be tested and improved under laboratory conditions before a full production seems feasible.

This is particularly true for playwrights whose mettle is unproved, but even proven dramatists are obliged to try out new material in workshops or showcases before a producer will expose it to the commercial and critical pressures of the marketplace. An established playwright can rely on a network of professional relationships to provide much of the support necessary to complete a play. But how does an aspiring playwright get along? How does he or she find a community of fellow artists, a place to work with them on a continuing basis, and the material support to make it possible? Ultimately, the process is idiosyncratic and somewhat haphazard, but new play development, as it has been practiced in the United States during the past forty years, represents a loosely coordinated effort to facilitate, to codify, and, in a sense, to democratize the discovery and support of promising, new playwrights.

A BRIEF HISTORICAL OVERVIEW

What we call new play development today has its roots in the effort of a handful of theater professionals earlier in this century to transform American theater into an art form and to give it a distinctly American voice. George Pierce

Baker (1866–1935) initiated formal instruction in playwriting at Harvard and then moved to Yale in 1925. Under the leadership of George Cram Cook, the Provincetown Players (1915–1923) dedicated itself to the small-scale production of new plays by playwrights whose work was not yet commercially viable (notably Eugene O'Neill). In the 1930s, the Group Theatre promoted a socially conscious, contemporary theater by performing the work of Clifford Odets and other activist playwrights. These and other pioneers sought to overcome the commercial restraints of Broadway and to create a serious American drama.

Nevertheless, in the first half of the twentieth century, Broadway so dominated "legitimate" theater, musical and nonmusical alike, that without the imprimatur of a Broadway production, a new play was not perceived to exist. New play development was largely a matter of hasty overnight rewrites in hotel rooms in Boston, Philadelphia, and other try-out towns. Sometimes a "script doctor" would be called in to punch up a script with fresh dialogue or a new scene before a play's make-or-break debut on the Great White Way. After World War Two, Broadway's monopoly on legitimacy began to dissolve for various reasons, two of which have particular bearing on new play development as it stands today.

First came the revival of Off-Broadway theater in the 1950s and the Off-Off-Broadway movement of the 1960s. Inspired by Julian Beck and Judith Malina's Living Theatre, a loose-knit community of artists gathered in New York's Greenwich Village to create theater experimental in approach and free of commercial constraints. An "anything goes/anything is possible" attitude led to vest-pocket theaters springing up in churches, cafés, and lofts all across lower Manhattan. New plays (often one-acts) expressing the ethos and imagination of the nascent sixties counterculture were produced in great numbers and always on a shoestring budget.

If Off-Off-Broadway's fecund atmosphere created few masterpieces, it nevertheless nurtured dozens of playwrights, including Sam Shepard, Lanford Wilson, Maria Irene Fornes, and Megan Terry. Their carefree disregard for established conventions opened up a vast new territory for theatrical exploration and highlighted the poverty of the legitimate theater. The need for more creative playwrights and more of them became palpable.

The second coincident phenomenon that challenged the Broadway hegemony was the accelerated growth and federalization of the resident theater movement in the 1960s. A concerted effort was made to support and stabilize theaters around the country with the highest artistic aspirations. Monies from the Ford Foundation, administered by W. McNeil Lowry, head of the Ford Foundation's arts and humanities programs, helped catalyze the effort; the Theatre Communications Group, a national service organization formed in 1960, supervised it; and it was facilitated by the establishment in 1965 of the National Endowment for the Arts..

Classics tended to dominate the regional repertoires at this time. However in 1968, the Arena Stage of Washington, D.C. moved their production of Howard Sackler's *The Great White Hope* (the story of black boxing champion

Jack Johnson) to Broadway, where it enjoyed a long commercial run. New plays became more and more attractive. Aware of the excitement being generated by Off-Off-Broadway and by such concurrent developments as Arthur Ballet's Office of Advanced Drama Research in Minneapolis and George White's Eugene O'Neill Theater Center in Connecticut, the regional theaters joined in the search for the next Great American Playwright.

During the next three decades, the genesis and source of new plays squarely shifted out of the commercial theater world in New York and into the not-for-profit theater communities of Chicago, Minneapolis, Seattle, Los Angeles, San Francisco, and other cities. The evolution of Tony Kushner's *Angels In America* or any of the plays of August Wilson demonstrates this paradigm shift. The two evening-length parts of *Angels In America* were shepherded through the early stages of development by Oskar Eustis at the Eureka Theatre Company in San Francisco and the Mark Taper Forum in Los Angeles. Only after premieres there and a critically acclaimed production at the Royal National Theatre in London did New York producers get in a bidding war over the rights to produce the play on Broadway. In the late 1980s, August Wilson's association with director Lloyd Richards afforded his plays an enviable development track that started with a workshop at the National Playwrights Conference and led to a premiere at the Yale Repertory Theatre, before taking the play "into" New York.

A new play of national interest used to make itself known in New York and then move out into the "provinces." Nowadays it gathers momentum in one region or another and then moves to New York—or avoids it altogether lest a critical failure there doom it to oblivion. The decentralization of American playwriting has been accomplished through a variety of means and methods under the umbrella term "new play development." Various mechanisms and programs were devised to discover new plays and playwrights and to foster their work, wherever they might be. These include:

- new play festivals (such as the Actors Theatre of Louisville's Humana Festival of New American Plays), which showcase a half dozen or more new works at one time;
- smaller professional theaters devoted exclusively or predominantly to producing new work;
- the advent of the literary manager as a theater's administrative staff member charged with reading and evaluating solicited and unsolicited manuscripts submitted for production consideration;
- the formation of local playwrights' organizations (such as New Dramatists in New York or the Playwrights' Center in Minneapolis) to provide support and developmental services;
- summertime workshops (such as the Eugene O'Neill Theater Center's National Playwrights Conference) where a new play can be read and

rehearsed under laboratory conditions and the playwright can try out on-the-spot revisions or collect information for possible rewrites;

- the publication of new play anthologies, theater magazines that include a new play in every issue, handbooks and how-to guides for aspiring playwrights, and newsletters that list and describe new plays awaiting further development;
- the establishment of numerous contests, prizes, awards, commissions, grants, and fellowships for playwrights that provide monetary support and production opportunities;
- most emblematic of all, the staged reading.

A NARROWER VIEW

All of these services and programs fall under the general rubric of new play development and all seek to promote the work and welfare of playwrights. However, there is a more specific sense of new play development, one that refers particularly to active work by theater professionals on a script toward a speculative full production. This work often culminates in some manner of approximate production. These forms and levels of new play development have at least one thing in common: they incorporate theater's interactive and collaborative processes into the completion of a script. They recognize that a play is presented by a group (actors) to a group (spectators) and that its ultimate success or merit depends on the interest these two parties take in it. So, before the writing of the play stops, its rehearsal and tentative performance begins. From here on we will focus on new play development in this more particular, hands-on sense.

Developmental work on a new script divides into four categories:

The informal reading.   Scripts are distributed, roles are assigned, and the play is read out loud, often by friends and associates in a relaxed and informal setting such as a living room or a lounge. Preparation is kept to a minimum: the readers may not even receive the play in advance. The playwright has a chance to hear how the play sounds and to get feedback from sympathetic colleagues.

The concert reading.   The play is read out loud in a rehearsal room, recital hall, or studio theater set up to differentiate readers and listeners. The performers sit or stand in a row facing the audience and holding their scripts, although they may direct their attention to the character with whom they are speaking. Physical movement and interaction are kept to a minimum. Stage directions are read aloud as text. Rehearsal time, usually limited to a few hours, is devoted to making the story, the characters, and their relationships clear through vocal and emotional expression. Lines may be cut, added, or changed up to the last minute.

The staged reading.   Without fully memorizing their lines and putting down their scripts, the actors concentrate more and more on character development and the dynamics of performance. A director devises a groundplan and simple blocking patterns that allow the actors to interact and suggest how the play might look if fully staged. Crucial props, costume elements, and set pieces may be introduced. The reading of stage directions is kept to a minimum in an effort to maintain the flow of dramatic events. Rehearsals last for a few days or as long as a week, allowing for significant revisions along the way and even the addition of new speeches or scenes.

The workshop production.   With costumes, props, and set pieces mostly pulled from stock and a week or two to rehearse, the play is mounted as fully as possible. The budget is kept to a minimum, and if the play demands elaborate and expensive special effects, inventive ways must be found to approximate them. The script may be finished at the start or rewrites may continue during rehearsals, but as actors get "off book," blocking and technical cues are set, and opening night approaches, the addition of new material becomes increasingly problematic.

These four types of presentation need to be seen more as bands along a continuous spectrum than as distinct categories with conventional boundaries. Positions on the spectrum can be read by the relative presence or absence of the script as a material object. In the informal reading, the script rests casually in the reader's lap or on a table, somehow awkward or alien, still belonging more to the playwright across the room than the actor turning the pages. In the concert reading, the script occupies a formal and intermediate position between reader and listeners, held up and out at arm's length or on a music stand perhaps, as if the actors were channeling the spoken dialogue back through the keyhole of its pages. In the staged reading, the script becomes an ungainly extension of the actor's hand, held at the side during familiar exchanges of dialogue, consulted freely during longer speeches, tucked under the arm when two hands are needed, used as a gestural prop, or set down on the stage somewhere when not needed. New audiences for staged readings often marvel that the script becomes invisible in the actor's hands; it starts out as a conspicuous appendage, but soon they hardly notice it. In the workshop production, governed as it is by the conventions of a full performance, the script disappears altogether. On rare occasions when new material has been inserted at the last minute, the actors may carry a few pages or a new scene.

Following a reading or a workshop, the playwright usually receives all manner of feedback, variously formal and informal: an audience discussion in the theater immediately afterwards; friendly banter over wine and cheese at a public reception in the theater's lobby; more heated private discussion between friends and collaborators late at night at a bar; a morning-after conference with the artistic director, dramaturg, and director; an exchange of letters or telephone calls once the dust has settled; and so on. After months or even years of wondering how a script will play, the playwright is bombarded with comments, quibbles, suggestions, and opinions. As gratifying as it is to be recognized and treated as a Playwright, the novice can be overwhelmed and even paralyzed by the volume and variety of responses, which often seem to cancel each other out. The practiced playwright learns whose opinions to trust and what types of feedback are valuable, letting the rest fall away like so much verbal chaff. And, reciprocally, those trusted colleagues learn the limit of their influence and the most effective angle of approach for their comments.

Central to the strategy of new play development is establishing a working environment that nurtures the talent and serves the artistry of the emerging playwright. An atmosphere of freedom and safety is sought. The playwright and the new play are in some way shielded from conditions and forces inimical to the creative process, chief among them the fear of taking risks and the expectation that the play be "finished." Various conventions of new play development ask that final critical judgment be suspended or conditional. The audience is usually private in some sense, limited to members of a theater's staff or specially invited colleagues, guests, board members, patrons, or subscribers. When the public is invited, admission is free or a fraction of a full ticket price, and the presentation is often preceded by a curtain speech or a program note reminding the audience that this is a "work in progress." Actors carry "script-in-hand" not simply out of necessity but as an explicit signal that the play is young and needs time to grow. Even when the work is more fully produced, as at new play festivals, the "coming out" atmosphere conditions audience response and makes the public more forgiving of the ungainly, the unusual, and even the ineffective.

In order to achieve the optimum working conditions, some developmental organizations, such as the National Playwrights Conference, take what might be called the "Walden Pond approach." They offer seclusion and protection from the compromises and exigencies of the workaday theater world in the form of a summertime retreat to a bucolic setting: Eugene O'Neill's country home on Long Island Sound; Robert Redford's ranch in the mountains of Utah, a small town in rural Indiana once home to a nineteenth-century utopian community; a settlement in the Shenandoah Valley; the cloistered lawns of a college campus abandoned by students for the summer. The work that goes on is often intense and demanding, but the general atmosphere is something like a summer camp for theater professionals (many of whom are happy for a respite from "the city"). The pastoral impulse behind these reclusive new play colonies symbolizes the idealism of new play development. The farther we get from the madding crowd, the thinking goes, the closer we get to a fertile creative environment. The lower the financial stakes, the higher the chance of an artistic breakthrough.

In these situations, the playwright's most useful feedback usually comes during the rehearsal period, when director, dramaturg, actors, and, in rare instances, designers grapple with the play in its confessedly amorphous condition. This process mirrors an all-out rehearsal-and-production situation. Before sitting down with the actors, the director and the dramaturg confer with the playwright, identifying areas of concern and sorting out immediate goals versus long-term goals. Rehearsals usually begin "around the table," with the actors reading through the play aloud, pausing along the way to ask basic questions (about pronunciation of names and words, for example, or time sequences from scene to scene), waiting until the end to raise more general concerns. The actor looks for the various cues and clues, some textual, some inferential, from which to fashion a preliminary understanding of the character. In turn, the playwright listens to discern if all (or enough) of the evidence is there for the actor to "get it."

The director supervises the process and mediates between actor and playwright, determining what types of communication between them will be most useful. For example, the playwright is often called upon to describe the genesis of the script or even to explain what he or she is trying to say. A playwright may be asked to read the play aloud to the cast so that they might glean something of the "voice" of the play in his or her own voice. Reciprocally, actors will offer visceral responses to the script and press the playwright for every available detail about a character's nature and identity. In some cases, once the character is familiar, the actor may be asked to improvise a scene alluded to but not included in the script, as a way of further exploring the character or perhaps even laying the groundwork for an additional scene.

This feeling-out, get-acquainted period proceeds on the basis of professional courtesy, mutual respect, and a presumptive commitment from all parties to the collaborative process. If the rehearsal period allows and the playwright wishes, rewrites and new material may be incorporated into the evolving script. As rehearsals and conferences continue and working relationships are formed, things get trickier as each party to the process forms opinions about the ability of others to get the job done. Sometimes, in the interest of the best possible presentation, compensatory adjustments are made through the acting, directing, or writing. This runs the risk of being a quick fix or a patch-up job that leaves the actual script no better than it was at the start. The process requires the vigilance of everyone involved to get into the script what must be there and eliminate what is superfluous. Playwrights must learn how to leave room for the creative contributions of their collaborators and, in turn, those collaborators need to be cautious about resolving desirable contradictions or mysteries in the play.

THE PARADOXY OF NEW PLAY DEVELOPMENT

The various stages and strategies of new play development constitute a delicate process, and if problems arise along the way, they stem as much from its paradoxical nature as from the personalities or talents of the participants. The play and the playwright benefit when serendipity reigns over potentially troubling factors and built-in contradictions:

Paradox #1. The actors, director, dramaturg, producer, and playwright are all assumed to be sufficiently in command of their respective disciplines to put into a script and to get out of it all that is needed to meet professional standards of excellence. Yet, paradoxically, the particular script at hand is assumed to be somehow insufficient or incomplete; otherwise, it would be ready to go into production and not require "development."

Paradox #2. The process simultaneously authorizes and infantilizes the playwright. That is, the commitment to serve the playwright empowers him or her to define how the process will be conducted (within reasonable limits); yet, the process defines the work and, by extension, the playwright as (professionally) immature and in need of care, maybe even coddling. The rhetoric of new play development repeats the word "nurture" like a mantra.

Paradox #3. The process is simultaneously radical and conservative. That is, the play is chosen for development because it in some way breaks new ground. It expresses something new and different. It points the way to the future. Yet, the actor, director, and dramaturg are present expressly to bring their professional concerns to bear on a nascent script in order to bring it toward their conventional practice. As willing as they are to follow the script's lead, their work is to some degree normative (especially when the playwright is regarded as a novice who needs to learn how the industry really works).

Paradox #4. Nobody involved in new play development, including and especially the playwright, is there for purely idealistic and artistic reasons. Financial remuneration is minimal. Making new contacts, showcasing one's talent, and other forms of career advancement motivate participants as much as the charitable and creative desire to promote and produce theater art. The two often go hand in hand, but the process is vulnerable to bad-faith participation. It only takes one or two people with hidden agendas to poison the atmosphere and undermine a particular project.

Paradox #5. The process is both a stepping stone and a dead end. Theater as an art form is already a marginalized fraction of American culture. New play development takes place in a margin of the margin. For some playwrights, it provides a sanctuary in which to grow as an artist, to find partners who share a vision of theater, and to move into the profession. For others, it becomes an artistic and professional ghetto where they whittle away at one script or another under the supervision of a committee of creative know-it-alls. Over time, the dream of a career or even a fully mounted production becomes an unsustainable illusion.

By no means do these paradoxes invalidate the process. To the contrary, they constitute a set of impulses, assumptions, values, and goals that might be called the paradoxy of new play development. New play development attracts and benefits those who share a commitment to playwriting and a belief in the collaborative process. These people enjoy working in the unresolved dialectic between practical realities and aesthetic ideals. The work asks for a curious double consciousness on the part of the participants, who from hour to hour must assert or yield professional prerogatives as they share back and forth their creative power and influence. Even with consummate trust, sincere participation, and equal talent levels across the board, confusions arise, misunderstandings occur, and the process gets bogged down. Nevertheless, to assist in the birth and delivery of a healthy new play is an exhilarating professional experience.

The value of new play development (in the narrow sense of the term) can only be judged on a case-by-case basis. Some plays are damaged or ruined; others come into their own and take wing. As the changing political climate in this country makes funding for the arts more elusive and encumbered, the efficacy of new play development will be and should be scrutinized. What started out decades ago as an effort to create and subsidize a "research and development" arm of the not-for-profit theater industry has proven itself as a viable model—one of many—for helping playwrights and creating better plays. At moments, though, it also seems to represent the institutionalized ambivalence of American society toward theater as an art form.

How To Do It:
A Brief History Of Professional Advice
by **Stephen Weeks**

STEPHEN WEEKS is an Assistant Professor of theater at Lewis & Clark College in Portland, Oregon. He has a PhD from Stanford University and has worked as a dramaturg at the Los Angeles Theatre Center and at A Contemporary Theatre in Seattle. He has also taught theater at Brown University, Reed College, and the University of Washington.

It is certainly easier to tell you that there are no principles, no rules, no guidelines, no discipline in the art and craft of playwriting. Some theorists tell you that modern writing is freewheeling, that the concept of "action" is out of date, and that the works of some modern writers prove that great plays can be written without dramatic tension, conflict, or action. Those opinions are—let's be blunt—products of muddled, wrongheaded thinking.
LOUIS E. CATRON, *THE ELEMENTS OF PLAYWRITING*, 1993

It seems hardly possible today for books to be written with titles like
The Elements of Drama. *. . . The encroachment of avant-garde performance theater . . . over the past forty years has significantly challenged our perceptions of how theater can and ought to function.*
MICHAEL VANDEN HEUVEL, *PERFORMING DRAMA/DRAMATIZING PERFORMANCE*, 1991

When I first learned to write for the theater, I was told that a play had a beginning, a middle, and an end. . . . It was only when I dropped that idea that I allowed myself . . . to see it as I felt it rather that as I thought it should be written.
MASANI ALEXIS DE VEAUX AT THE FIRST INTERNATIONAL
WOMEN PLAYWRIGHTS CONFERENCE, 1988

Little about the theater today is immune to controversy, but the proposition that good playwriting is extremely difficult might be. Great plays—the ones with the longest stage life and the highest regard as literature—often seem the product of an impenetrable alchemy that combines genius, opportunity, and favorable historical circumstances. Yet many would argue an additional ingredient, one that lessens the mystery of greatness considerably: craft. Craft suggests the ability to construct an effective vehicle for the stage that accomplishes its intended effect with economy and precision. Without craft, it is said, opportunity, historical circumstance, and even genius are of little consequence. Craft is the indispensable support, the muscle and the sinew, of all dramatic writing, enabling good plays and great ones alike. In this view, Shakespeare must be seen not only as a literary genius, but as a master craftsman, possessing intimate knowledge of every tool and every procedure useful to dramatic writing.

If one sees the playwright as a "wright" first of all—as a craftsperson—the notion of apprenticeship must follow. The principles of craft should lend themselves to explication and be transmissible from one generation to the next. This has been a persuasive notion, and neither the dramatist nor the dramaturg need look far for manuals of the trade. *How Plays Are Made, Writing a Play, The Art of the Playwright, The Elements of Playwriting*: these are the titles of four recent books all of which purport to give how-to advice to prospective dramatists. The titles differ little from those in the next group, all of which date from the first part of this century: *The Art of Playwriting, The Technique of Drama, Playmaking: A Manual of Craftsmanship.* Although one could argue that how-to advice has been integral to Western theater since Aristotle's *Poetics,* the tradition really began to bloom in the late nineteenth century, and it now represents a quite substantial body of writing.

Is so much advice available because there is so little agreement? Or does how-to writing lend itself to the continuous restatement of basic principles? Certainly these basic principles do not seem fully settled. Even a brief sampling of our late twentieth-century air—as in the last two quotations above—indicates widespread dissatisfaction with received wisdom regarding playwriting. This is nothing new, of course. Impatience with received wisdom, with authority, with anything that smacks of dogma, is thoroughly embedded in theatrical history. It was Molière who famously rebelled against the strictures of neoclassicism with the line: "I would really like to know whether the great rule of all rules is not to please, and whether a play that has attained its purpose has not followed a good path." However appealing this simple wisdom may be, many scholars, observers, and critics of the theater have found it insufficient. How-to writing is born of the attempt to map this good path in detail and to supply a more exacting enumeration of fundamental principles than "to please" provides.

The first part of my inquiry is historical and examines the roots of the how-to tradition, both in Europe and in this country. The second part is analytical and aims to understand the extent to which how-to books make similar recommendations. I consider whether a consistent model of practice emerges from these recommendations. The third part of my inquiry focuses on the limitations of the how-to tradition and the challenges it poses to the contemporary dramaturg.

I. THE HISTORY OF HOW-TO

The founding document of Western dramatic criticism is Aristotle's *Poetics* (c. 350 BC). Aristotle not only articulated a theory of tragedy but commented brilliantly on dramatic structure. Renaissance dramatic theory revived his influence, and he has scarcely seemed less important since then. In *Hamburg Dramaturgy* (1769), G. E. Lessing—often considered the founder of modern dramaturgy—sought to dismantle the emphases of French neoclassicism, but without abandoning Aristotle altogether. Indeed, Lessing believed that the errors of the French were based not on their appropriation of Aristotle but on their misunderstanding of him. When Gustav Freytag, writing nearly one hundred years later, in *Technique of the Drama* (1863), sought to update Lessing's observations on dramatic structure, he turned, once more, to Aristotle. Freytag had great regard for Shakespeare as well as Sophocles, but he had little patience for the English poet's violations of Aristotelian principles. For Freytag, Shakespeare was doubly reliable: through both his evident successes and his irksome failures, he could be called upon to illustrate the usefulness of Aristotle.

Freytag's book was the first of a number of nineteenth-century contributions to the explication of dramatic structure and the "technique" of the drama. These were not occasional essays or production reviews, but books, like Freytag's, of dramaturgical analysis. Where once Aristotle and Lessing stood as the twin pillars of the playwright's craft, now many took up the burden of advice and analysis. Many factors account for this surge. Freytag's book was influential, and it generated some direct responses—for example, Elisabeth Woodbridge's *The Drama: Its Law and Technique* (1898). In addition, there was the enticement of accommodating Aristotle's invincible wisdom to the actual dramatic output of the age, which little resembled Greek tragedy. Consider the French well-made play. A genre that depends upon an ingenious, commercially successful pattern of plot development (later disparaged as formulaic), the well-made play contributed to the notion that good playwriting was not mysterious, but the product of basic principles skillfully applied, that is, of craft. But what sort of craft? Did the wisdom of the *Poetics* still apply? The success of the well-made play stimulated theorists and critics to reconcile classical notions of structure with contemporary practice. Exponents of craft from Freytag onward made this project of reconciliation central to their work.

The difficulty of the project was compounded by the sensitivity of the age to historical change and variety. Dramatic literature had undergone any number of revisions since the Greeks, and the first sentence of Freytag's *Technique of the Drama* underscores this variability: "That the technique of the drama is nothing absolute and unchangeable scarcely need be stated."[1] By itself this sentence might appear to undermine the basis for his own book and to make quixotic his attempt to sketch out a universally applicable dramatic structure (which he does quite literally in his famous graph of the dramatic pyramid).[2] He goes on, however, to note that "we should not scorn to seek, and intelligently to use, the technical rules of ancient and modern times, which facilitate artistic effects on our stage," thereby affirming the existence of "technical rules," ancient and modern, that transcend their historical roots.[3] It is a paradox he does not fully elucidate, and it remains a vexing issue within the tradition he helps to inspire. With little more hesitation than the opening line, his book comes to embrace "universal" techniques.

Francisque Sarcey, perhaps the most influential French theater reviewer of the nineteenth century, wrestled with the same problem:

> When the eyes of the audience change, the conventions invented to give the illusion of life should change also, and the laws which the technique each epoch has promulgated and which it has in good faith believed to be universal and unchangeable are destined to fall. . . . What are the universal conventions, those that have their root in all humanity? What, on the other hand, are the temporary conventions?[4]

Like Freytag, Sarcey both denies and affirms a "universal" dramatic technique, first noting the relativism of history, then appealing to a universal "humanity" upon which universal "conventions" rest.

In America, the playwright Bronson Howard examined the issue at a Harvard lecture in 1885. In discussing the Greeks, he noted that

> they did not create the laws of dramatic construction. Those laws exist in the passions and sympathies of the human race. They existed thousands of years before the Father of the Drama [Aeschylus] was born: waiting, like the other laws of nature, to be discovered and utilized by man.[5]

A more recent critic describes this problem as the "ontology of structure."[6] Put simply, do the structural principles of good drama inhere in the material— or in ourselves—or do we just impose them? Howard proposes a world of *a priori* dramatic laws waiting to be discovered and explicated, and in this notion we hear the strong echo of Enlightenment ideals: an unshakable faith in order complemented by an equal faith in the ability of man to apprehend that order. If there is dissatisfaction with how-to writing on drama today, it may stem in part from our disenchantment with such ideals. His suggestion that dramatic laws are analogous to natural ones carries with it the promise that a Newton of drama might appear to formulate with precision what great playwrights do by instinct. This Newton might be a critic, a theorist—or a dramaturg.

Howard influenced numerous American academics in his period. Alfred Hennequin—one of the first teachers of playwriting in this country— published *The Art of Playwriting* in 1890 and dedicated it to Howard. In 1919, Brander Matthews, the first professor of dramatic literature in any English-speaking university, quoted Howard directly:

> These principles however have been obeyed unwittingly by all the great dramatists, ancient and modern. The Rules laid down tentatively or arbitrarily by the theorists of theater are but groping efforts to grasp the

> **undying principles** [emphasis added] which we can seize only unsat-
> isfactorily, which "exist in the passions and sympathies of the human
> race," and which are never completely disclosed to anyone. . . . No
> doubt, this is just as true of painting and of sculpture as it is of the
> drama.[7]

Matthews may have despaired of finding a Newton of dramaturgy, but this
hardly deterred him. Like his predecessors, he set out to explain those "undying principles" himself, in a series of books starting with *A Study of the Drama*
in 1910.

George Pierce Baker was a student at Harvard in 1885 when he heard the
Howard lecture. In his *Dramatic Technique* (1919) he defines three layers of
craft. "Universal" technique refers to the "essentials which all good plays . . .
share, at least in part." "Specific" refers to the technique of a period, and "individual" refers to the methods of a particular playwright. "The chief gift of the
drama of the past to the young playwright . . . is illustration of what is essential in drama. This he safely copies."[8]

Much the same language can be found in one of Baker's source books: *The
Technique of the Drama* by William T. Price (1892). Price undertook to "state
such obvious and accepted principles as underlie the drama—principles that
are known, or should be known, to every literary worker, and that are antecedent to the tricks of the trade."[9]

What we find is a remarkable consistency. Examples of "Freytag's hesitation"—the idea that history demonstrates the impossibility of an ABSOLUTE
dramatic technique—abound, but they are subsumed by an impulse to reveal
a core of essential principles. Historical differences relate to these principles
as a mere overlay, a temporary obscurity. The pursuit of drama's "universal,"
"fundamental," and "essential" laws drives the creation of the how-to tradition.

This pursuit might be identified with one of the central projects of modernism: the reduction of each art form to its purified and defining essence.
Note that Matthews speculates on the existence of "undying principles" for
sculpture and painting, as well as drama. Yet the how-to tradition can by no
means be unambiguously identified with modernism, a defining feature of
which is the disinclination to work within established traditions. How-to writing on drama, to the extent that it views as its central project the unification
of ancient principles and modern practices, embraces tradition, ratifies its
value to playwrights, and underscores its essential continuities. Modernism's
taste for innovation, with the exception of realism, has been notably difficult
for how-to to assimilate.[10] The avant-garde movements early in this century
destabilized traditional notions of craft, and how-to writing found little reason
to adjust to these experiments or to view them as a necessary critique.

The development of the how-to tradition in this country owes a great deal
to the institutionalizing of culture within the university system. Hennequin,
Woodbridge, Matthews, and Baker were academics, and the story of how-to in
this country must be understood in the context of the legitimation of the

study of dramatic art within the academy. Baker's career was exemplary. He was perhaps the most influential teacher of playwriting and dramatic art we have seen in this country and our first real dramaturg. His students included George Abbott, Sidney Howard, Eugene O'Neill, S. N. Behrman, Philip Barry, and Elia Kazan. Baker wanted to develop a native American drama equal in quality to that of Europe—"a drama of American conditions which shall have permanent value."[11] To create "a genuine American drama" Baker put theater and the craft of playwriting on the agenda of American education and helped to legitimize what we now refer to as academic theater. His book *Dramatic Technique*—as well as the many entries in the field by the American professoriate—should be seen as a gesture of that legitimation.

He began to teach his first class in dramatic composition at Radcliffe in 1904. His course books included: Aristotle (of course), Meredith's *The Idea of Comedy* (1877), Freytag's *Dramatic Technique,* Hennequin's *The Art of Playwriting,* Woodbridge's *The Drama: Its Law and Technique*, and William T. Price's *The Technique of Drama.*[12] Aristotle, Freytag, and even Meredith seem predictable choices; the other three books had all been written in the 1890s and were similar to the one he himself would write in 1919. In 1905 at Harvard, he began to teach English 47, The Technique of Drama, which was a refinement of his course at Radcliffe. He taught that course for twenty years.[13] By 1919, Baker's work was widely known and imitated. In 1913, he founded "47 Workshop," a laboratory in which to test experimental plays, but it had no official relationship with the university. When Harvard refused to let him build a true university theater he went to Yale in 1925. He organized that institution's first drama department and built his theater there. At Yale, he worked with Donald Oenslager and Stanley McCandless, two of the country's most influential designers, and was succeeded by the renowned scholar Allardyce Nicoll. And so the ripples of Baker's faith in educational theater, and the kind of American theater he wanted it to foster, continued to spread.

When Baker died in 1934, Eugene O'Neill wrote a letter to the *New York Times* that said, in part:

> Only those of us who had the privilege of membership in the drama class of George Pierce Baker back in the dark age when the American theater was still, for playwrights, the closed shop, star system, amusement racket, can know what a profound influence Professor Baker, who died last Sunday, exerted toward the encouragement and birth of modern American drama.[14]

This letter touches an important point. The American theater, at least until the end of the nineteenth century, was predicated upon commercial appeal. For its more culturally minded critics, theater was tawdry and disreputable. Alfred Hennequin based his playwriting book on the proposition that the commercial stage might help one acquire "a taste for small theatrical artifices,

hackneyed phrases and forced, unmeaning situations,"[15] but not sound principles. A more intractable problem was the state of American literature at large.
In the influential essay "Our Literature," written in 1887, James Russell Lowell
discussed the failure of a genuine literature to take root in this country. Baker
echoed him in 1899: "There is no American drama and never has been. . . . "[16]
For Baker the remedy lay in the audience, and he hoped for one that would
demand art as well as entertainment. Because such an audience needed to be
created, he looked to the possibilities for innovative theater within colleges
and universities. Brander Matthews saw drama in evolutionary terms, with
"unliterary drama" marking the earliest stages of civilization and drama that
has been "lifted into" literature marking the latest and highest stage. Genuine
playwrights had to be "men" of letters. What was at stake was not simply dramatic craft but the development of American culture.

Both Baker and Matthews had been influenced by Matthew Arnold, the
great apostle of high culture in nineteenth-century America. Arnold had argued for the high seriousness of criticism, for culture as the "best that has
been known and thought in the world," and for the diffusion of culture to the
"general electorate." Armed with these ideals, and with an acute sense of the
American theater's impoverishment, the American how-to tradition, as we see
it in its earliest stages here, set out to discover the first principles of drama
and to lay the groundwork for a more authentic culture upon them.[17] In this
way, drama, like literature in general, entered into a long struggle to authenticate American "civilization," and became in the process an area of specialty,
and then a discipline, within the American academy.[18]

II. THE HOW-TO TRADITION AND THE ANALYSIS OF CRAFT

We have seen that the work of the how-to tradition in the late nineteenth and
early twentieth centuries was animated by a search for first principles or fun-
damentals. This "essentializing" impulse sought the laws of dramatic technique
that were immune to, or prior to, historically relative conventions. It will perhaps not be surprising that some of these laws appear inextricably bound to
the cultural assumptions of the period in which their advocates wrote. For example, Bronson Howard in his 1885 lecture, despite claiming that dramatic
laws were to be found in the "passions and sympathies of the human race,"
talked of changing the plot of one of his plays because of the "principle" that
a woman of virtue cannot die whereas a woman who has turned to sin must.[19]
Or we might look at Brander Matthews' claim that "Orientals have no vital
drama because they are fatalists, because they do not believe in that free will
without which drama cannot exist."[20] Or Freytag's claim that tragic effect depends upon the masculine qualities of the writer. These principles are neither
self-evident nor universal, but exemplify hegemonic discourses having everything to do with culture, not nature. The process by which one period's

universal principles reveal themselves in time, as dubious, narrow, and culturally relative is an ineluctable fact of history. Two key questions remain, however. First, does the fact that *some* first principles seem historically relative
prove that *all* first principles are culturally relative? Second, to what extent do
the various books of the how-to tradition agree with another?

I will return to the first point in the next section. With respect to the second point, the general answer is that there is a surprising degree of agreement
among these books. Some of this consensus may be attributed to the somewhat self-enclosed nature of the tradition. One writer refers to a predecessor
or several predecessors, each of whom refers to another predecessor or predecessors. Everyone refers to Aristotle. This is the meaning of how-to as a tradition.[21] Taken as a whole, the recommendations of how-to cluster around a
few key points. The sources are diverse enough to offer points of disagreement and a range of formulations, but they are not so diverse as to prohibit
the emergence of a basic model.

To begin, we should note the pervasive presence of Aristotelian ideas—by
any measure, an extraordinary phenomenon within the Western dramatic tradition. Aristotle's emphasis on plot, for example, is a recurring theme of how-
to. This is not a matter of simple transcription. Many of the how-to books
elaborate Aristotle's beginning-middle-end into the "well-made" structure of
the nineteenth century. William Archer's *Playmaking: A Manual of Craftsmanship* (1912) divides into four books. Books Two through Four discuss dramatic structure and are subtitled *The Beginning, The Middle,* and *The End.* In
Book Two *The Beginning,* he discusses exposition and the first act. In Book
Three *The Middle,* he discusses plot complications through a consideration
of Sarcey's "obligatory scenes,"[22] Aristotle's reversal (what Archer calls
"peripety"), and recognition. In Book Four, *The End,* he deals with climax, an-
ticlimax, and the denouement.[23] Archer does not utilize every term associated with the well-made play tradition, and he quarrels with some of the terms
he does use. But his interpolation of nineteenth-century concerns and language into the basic Aristotelian framework is instructive because it is a recurrent pattern.[24]

Aristotle insists on the "laws of probability and necessity" that join the gross
plot divisions of beginning, middle, and end. Hennequin, in 1890, paraphrases
Aristotle as follows: "The cause of every incident must be apparent in some incident that has preceded it and serves as a motive for it. Every event must
grow naturally out of what has gone before, and to lead naturally to what
comes after." To take a later example, Stuart Griffiths (*How Plays Are Made,*
1982) writes

> The principle of causality is essential to drama. It must not be an unre-
> lated succession of incidents or episodes. . . . A good play . . . has a logi-
> cal chain of cause and effect, with one scene leading on to another, in a
> sequence which . . . will carry [the audience] along in a strong current
> to the conclusion.[25]

The principle of cause-and-effect is a staple of how-to. The major exception to the Aristotelian/well-made emphasis on plot manifests itself in how-to's frequent obeisance to "rounded" or "psychological" characterization. William Archer and George Pierce Baker both inveigh against character types and assert that "great" plays always rely upon the psychology of character. Kenneth MacGowan (*A Primer of Playwriting*, 1951) argues for the "co-equal status" of character and plot, and refers to an array of other how-to writers for support. His prescription for characters is that they be both believable and consistent. Indeed, within the tradition of realism, consistency comes to define credibility, so that "believable" dramatic characters experience change only within the limits imposed by environment and psychology. Realism and its attendant view of character has many sources—Freud in psychology, Stanislavsky in directing, Ibsen and Chekhov in drama—each of which strongly influenced the tenets of how-to.

Aristotle suggests that a plot "must be an imitation of an action that is one and whole"—that is its unity. Unity becomes one of the central principles of how-to. Brander Matthews asserts that unity of action, which Aristotle discusses in relation to tragedy, should apply as well "to every work of art, tragic or epic, pictorial or plastic. Every work of art ought to leave a direct and simple impression, which it cannot make without a concentration upon its theme and without a rigorous exclusion of all nonessentials."[26] George Pierce Baker holds that unity of action is of "first importance"—a principle that he expands to include "artistic unity," by which he means—following the neoclassicists—purity of genre.[27] As a later example, Sam Smiley (*Playwriting: the Structure of Action*, 1971) writes: "Unity is one attribute that brings beauty, comprehensibility, and effectiveness to any work of art. Each of the art forms has its own proper kind of unity. . . . Unity of action is dramatic unity; it is a quality of plot."[28]

The principle of conflict is central to how-to, and although one can find justification for its importance in Aristotle, the idea was given a particularly strong formulation in 1893 by Ferdinand Brunetière, who viewed the "law of drama" as the action of the will in conflict with appropriate obstacles.[29] Theories of conflict that derive from Brunetière often focus on the trials of a single hero. Brander Matthews discussed the way audiences love "to sympathize with some strong, central character battling against odds, with whom for the moment we may even identify ourselves. . . . "[30] Other writers deny the necessity of the central protagonist, recognizing it as premodern historical construct; still others, starting with George Pierce Baker, question Brunetière's absolutist position; but nowhere does one find the suggestion that dramatic work can do without "conflict" or "crisis" or "complication" or "opposed forces." And even in contemporary how-tos one often finds a stark paraphrase of Brunetière, as in Louis E. Catron's *The Elements of Playwriting*, 1993: "Conflict is so essential for effective plays that a 'law of conflict' is a recognized permanent part of successful theatrical writing."[31]

Clarity is a goal for playwrights in how-to. Modernist writing may prize fragmented or open-ended plots and ambiguous imagery, but particularly in the earliest portions of how-to clarity was indispensable. George Pierce Baker: "When an audience does not understand who the people are with whom the play opens and their relations to one another, no amount of striking dialogue or stirring situation will create lasting interest."[32] Brander Matthews records approvingly the following advice (supposedly from an old stage-manager to the playwright Planché):

> If you want the British public to understand what you are doing, you must tell them that you are *going* to do it; then you must tell them you *are* doing it; and after all you must tell them you *have* done it. And then, confound them, *perhaps* they will understand you.[33]

Early teachers of playwriting within the universities, such as George Pierce Baker, had taught rhetoric, and the techniques of argumentation were often linked to dramatic construction. As William T. Price records: "A drama must deal with accepted facts or definitely prove a given proposition."[34] If dramas were seen as offering proof of a proposition, then clarity of strategy would need to be foremost on the playwright's mind. Later how-to writers do not give this notion so much prominence, but it still has currency. MacGowan talks about the clarity of relationships, William Packard about clarity of action; Louis Catron about the playwright's "clear vision of characters and story."

What emerges from the varied formulations of these principles is a structural model that first of all stresses the mechanics of plot-making (despite praise of "deep" character). Plots require a certain rhythm (the natural rhythms of breathing, seasonal change, or sexuality have been suggested), and diagrams can be handily employed to visualize those rhythms. Plots also require a certain sequence which, from Aristotle onward, has been identified as the logic of cause and effect. The model also calls for unity of action (or effect or mood), for plausibility, for consistency, for clarity, and for conflict and the creation of suspense (through complication). Many other features could be adduced, but this short list will suffice for an outline.

III. THE LIMITATIONS OF HOW-TO AND THE CHALLENGE TO THE DRAMATURG

I have suggested that the how-to tradition failed to respond in any meaningful way to currents of modernism (realism excepted). Certainly most twentieth-century experiments in antirealism go unaccounted for. French surrealism, German expressionism, and postwar absurdism, no matter how problematic these labels may be, nonetheless represent the twentieth-century trend away from plot-making based on cause-and-effect logic, principles of clarity and consistency, action (as it is usually defined), unity, the realistic presentation of character, and from the word itself as the primary basis of theatrical creation. Antirealist playwriting has extended the boundaries of dramatic practice by exploring illogic, instability, chance, and disruption in ways that seem to escape Aristotelian analysis.

The elevation of the visual in relation to the word has created particular problems for the tradition of how-to. George Pierce Baker's biographer recites the following incident: when Sheldon Cheney sent a presentation copy of *The New Movement in the Theatre,* Baker wrote in the margin, opposite a discussion of Gordon Craig's elevation of the visual: "Is this the way? Let us keep our reason."[35] Through his devotion to the written script, and his lack of feeling for the visual and decorative aspects of the theater, Baker became the guardian of the dramatic text at the point when the text was increasingly looked upon as a single component of the theatrical performance, rather than its very center. Baker's conservatism on the matter typifies the how-to tradition as a whole.

Later how-to theorists would look for ways to preserve the basic model while making room for innovation. Sam Smiley, for example, discusses "vertical" plays, dominated by "adventitious, or noncausal" structures, as well as plays with "configurative" structures, which can include "curved patterns of action."[36] Still, his attraction to a universal model based on Aristotle is powerful, and he plainly asserts that "most of the innovative new plays have to do with how the principles are used rather than discovery of absolutely new principles."[37] As we have seen, the strongest impulse of the how-to tradition is to find support for a "universal" dramatic structure that binds together the great plays from every age. Such a quest depends upon a faith in a timeless human nature that responds fully to timeless dramatic laws. Modern thought does not always support the notion of a fixed and timeless human nature, and the countless statements attesting to it within the how-to tradition take a controversial proposition for granted.

When Smiley notes that *Waiting for Godot* has no more structural dissimilarity from *Oedipus the King* than any other classic text has, whether a play by Shakespeare or Goethe or Strindberg, he takes the risk of collapsing centuries of cultural difference in order to validate his generalizations about the nature of drama. There are enormous differences between these dramatic texts. To name just one, *Godot* has a "circular" structure in which the second act of the play reprises the structure of the first. *Oedipus* has one of the greatest "linear" structures ever written, in which an inexorable chain of logic leads to a final devastating discovery. If the basic model of structure as articulated by how-to holds for such disparate works it may lay claim to universality, but this is by no means self-evident. The minority position within how-to is the historicist position—the notion that different periods of history produce different assumptions about human experience and those assumptions produce different kinds of dramatic structures.[38] This is Freytag's original hesitation.

If the how-to model does not incorporate modernist innovations with much enthusiasm or accuracy, it seems far removed from several important strands of contemporary practice as well. Feminism has taught us to be wary of assumptions built into the language of "universal" experience. Accordingly, some critics find the rhythm of well-made plots to reflect the rhythms of male sexuality with uncomfortable exclusivity. One can see the point if one reflects on the following sentence from Stuart Griffiths' *How Plays Are Made*: "There is a concept of dramaturgy called 'the lighting of the fuse', the moment when the play really begins, the entry of an exciting force when the play takes off and rises to its climax."[39] Feminist criticism is suggesting new models of plot-making and character drawing that interrogate the usual recommendations of how-to.[40] The modernist and feminist critiques of traditional play structures are not simply formal, but political as well. The how-to model at its most narrow, it is said, simply fails to provide the means to expose the contradictions within the discourses of the dominant culture. It enshrines the status quo and limits the ability of the stage to suggest alternative ways of seeing and experiencing reality.

Postmodernists also work against the grain of how-to. They tend to regard Aristotelian ideas of unity and causality as outmoded; instead they favor juxtaposition, contrast, and irony. Even twentieth-century science is implicated in the debate about postmodern dramatic structure. Newtonian science, it is suggested, gives us clarity, causality, and mechanism; post-Einsteinian science gives us indeterminacy, chance, and the interlinking of the observer to the observed. As Michael Vanden Heuvel has said:

> In truth, we need a new language to describe what takes place in modern theater, an idiom that captures some of the inconsistency, indeterminacy, and downright counterintuitive strangeness of the unstable relationships that form between . . . literary [that is, text-based] and performative [that is, non-text-based] modes of expression.[41]

Heuvel writes from an academic/theoretical perspective. One of the features of the how-to tradition is that it has spoken to the general reader and to the aspiring playwright with the aim of dispensing practical advice. There is a great deal of academic commentary regarding modernism, postmodernism, feminism, and other strands of contemporary theory and practice, but little directed at the audience how-to has traditionally targeted. In this sense there is no such thing as how-to for postmodernism. Still, if the how-to tradition is to continue in any viable form, it will need to respond to the objections that have been lodged against it and move to embrace new forms of dramatic practice. The tradition has shown little evidence of that flexibility and would probably have to abandon its allegiance to a universal model of practice if it did so.

Can we flatly deny that there may be widely, if not universally, applicable principles of dramatic writing that emerge from the fundamental conditions of theatrical performance? I don't think so. Yet these principles, if they do exist, are few in number and general enough to permit the incredible range of theatrical activity that history has furnished. The how-to tradition, even at its most cautious, overstates the case for a universal technique, and consistently manages to overlook the importance of both historical variability and avant-garde innovation. "What works" on stage is always responsive to local conditions, and local conditions are in turn responsive to the endless shuffling of history and culture. The point rarely surfaces in how-to. The consequence has been a failure to develop alternative vocabularies that might more sensitively describe the dramaturgy of plays that fall outside how-to's range of acceptable practice; this failure, in turn, has created difficulties for today's dramaturgs.

How-to has played a powerful role in establishing norms for good drama and good dramaturgy. The "undying principles" it attempts to codify set goals for theatrical writing and specify procedures for reaching them. How-to provides a vocabulary of playwriting instructions, and within that vocabulary it identifies a range of "problems" that can be addressed with a corresponding range of solutions. We should remember that Shakespeare was a rather messy artist for Freytag and that he did not always fit comfortably within the range of his recommendations. Some apparent solutions posed by how-to writing would in fact do damage to undeniably great plays.

Dramaturgs are frequently required to "explain" plays—sometimes to artistic directors, sometimes to other dramaturgs, sometimes to playwrights themselves. To what extent should the dramaturg make use of the formidable how-to vocabulary, range of reference, and historical aura? The tradition is a valuable tool, a cogent distillation of certain forms of theatrical wisdom; it may also be a cul-de-sac. Can alternative road maps be found to facilitate communication between playwrights and dramaturgs traveling along unfamiliar pathways? The dramaturg is sometimes called the playwright's advocate. By what principles will this advocacy be conducted? We have moved well beyond the mechanisms of nineteenth-century dramaturgy into brave new worlds of modern and postmodern performance. Dramaturgs must take the time to question their own assumptions about playwriting otherwise it may be too easy to follow the wake of an aesthetic mission that was defined in the nineteenth century, that was institutionalized in our country in the early part of this century as part of a larger project of cultural validation, and that has consistently found greater affinity with commercial success than avant-garde experiment. Playwriting may be one of the most difficult feats of the human imagination, and the stage certainly demands craft, but craft may be a more slippery beast than how-to depicts, with levels and facets undreamed of. If so, future how-to writing might display more caution and less bravado with respect to its history and its own claims.

Mea Culpa, Nostra Culpa

by **Leon Katz**

This essay was originally published as a part of Portland [Maine] Stage Company's Scholars on Stage Humanities series, which was funded by a major grant from the National Endowment for the Humanities and sponsored in part by grants from the Maine Humanities Council and UNUM Charitable Foundation.[42]

That playwrights have been abused in the name of fostering their development by the academic and nonprofit theater industry is an old and sad story. But it's one not often told except by the victims who, licking their wounds, confide in one another in shrugs and whispers, not wanting to rock the boat since it's the only boat they have.

All those funds for contests, artists' grants, workshops, opportunities for staged readings, centers, institutes, summer retreats, new play series dedicated to launching the playwright—all those funds for these enterprises are funneled now through resident theaters and university departments. The academic and nonprofit theater establishment is now, for all practical purposes, the one usable conduit for the half dozen, out of the thirty thousand or so plays written every year in the United States, to climb, finally, in slow and tortuous stages, to full-stage commercial production on, let's say, Broadway.

Is that still the goal? Only metaphorically. The playwrights' real goal, apart from earning a living by writing, is less tangible and less focused—a dream. To be heard, so to speak, by multitudes, and to share a very personal vision. What's wrong with Broadway, we used to say, as distinct from the regionals and Off- and Off-Off-Broadway, is that on Broadway, if you were lucky enough finally to get there, the chance of sharing the vision intact was nil. Box office, play doctors, money-grubbing producers—they didn't care about the vision; they cared about what "worked." Not so the regionals, the away-from Broadway tiny temples of art and the theater departments that devoted their resources to nurturing the dream, breastfeeding the infant playwright until he or she was strong enough to climb (again to mix the metaphor) the mountain alone.

Sadly, no. Looked at closely, there is little difference between the old-time play doctor who laid violent hands on the playwright's offspring and "made it work," and the army of experts now swelling the theater art scene—the play readers, the literary managers, the directors, the artistic directors, the program directors, the dramaturgs, the department heads, the playwriting faculties, and the helpful ministrations of fellow playwrights who in critique sessions batten on the failings of their peers. Little difference, but some: he was one, they are many; he knew, they rarely do; he didn't obfuscate, they specialize; he did brutal surgery knowing why; they, guessing, bring multiple critical scalpels to draft after draft after draft, nicking away at the body of the play, knowing certainly that, given the playwright's abject surrender of the last vestige of ego resistance, they could excavate that thing they see shyly peeping out from underneath the layers of draft after draft—a play that "works."

I too have sinned, and sin, along with the multitude, and sinning, live with the disquieting reassurance that retribution for this folly is not paid for by the sinner but by the victim. That play that works, if it does, is still being made to work like every other play. The model is reductive and sycophantic, toadying as much to nostalgia for the familiar as that knowing play doctor ever did. It "works," the play does, when it becomes the same as yesterday's.

Is that bad? For the playwright's dream, it couldn't be worse. The story we tell ourselves, we sinners, is that all we're doing is helping playwrights learn their craft, lighting the lamp for them to glimpse the drama's eternal verities. But that's our deepest sin—those verities. When you come right down to it, they've remained the same as that brutally pragmatic play doctor's. And if the playwright truly listens and learns, and stays the course to the end under the guidance of that army of supportive well-wishers, and the play finally dragged out of the sixth draft is one that everybody agrees really works, then the second half of the dream is as thoroughly lost as the first. Because it works for everybody—audience, producers, critics, guiding mentors—only when it squares with those eternal verities that are not remotely eternal, nor remotely veracious.

In recent years, I've had the hideous but instructive experience of working on a collection of five thousand plays produced in the American theater from roughly 1800 to 1950, and ranging from the stillborn to the dazzling hits of their day. Leafing through the smash hits of yesteryear, it becomes embarrassingly obvious that every decade or so, there's a subtle shift in the pious verities that control the psychology, the morality, and the very structure of acceptable, not to speak of hugely successful plays. The movement from one set of verities to another is glacial, but over the course of 150 years, it is glaringly detectable. What is equally glaring is that the controls of any period, while pretending to answer to the basic needs of drama, have in fact little to do with drama itself, but answer to another need—to see reflected in popular plays the specious wisdom of the moment as it has solidified in the cliché marketplace. The "craft" that is taught to playwrights in any period including our own, and before which playwrights are supposed to cower, is little more than a translation into critical stricture of the moral, social, psychological, and political pieties of the moment. The play doctors of a while ago and the frankly market-oriented playwrights didn't and don't hesitate; it's their intention to answer that need. They can be applauded for their honesty of purpose if not for the gleam of their truth. We, in this new institutionalized way of helping playwrights, can be applauded for neither.

Still, there are, in the dark corners of the industry, virtuous resident theaters, intelligent dramaturgs, and sometimes helpful faculties. They are the ones that pay attention to, look hard for the unique voice, the personal and not the lock-step view of life now and life in general.

There is a story, a true story, of the Kansas City slaughterhouse that sends an army of pigs through a declining ramp fitted with sets of barrier-locks preventing the pigs from backing up and losing ground. Once in a lock, they're committed; lock after lock, they're committed more and more, and can't retreat. But now and then, there's a pig who gets close to the last barrier, hears the terrified squealing of his brothers who are being slaughtered en masse, and decides, no. Turning around, hunching his way through the oncoming pack, slipping and sliding through the whips of the cattle hands along the route, he gets close to the end of the run. But not out. Every once in a great while, there is one like that, and when the rest of the pigs are all in the slaughterhouse, the cattle hands come back and take this one back alone, lock by barrier-lock. Either way, he ends up dead, but the hands, for all their trouble, acknowledge and remember the courage of this one, a hero among the pigs.

They're our real and only hope: the pigs who say no and run for dear life the other way.

Morgan Jenness Tells the Truth to Paul Selig:
An Interview

MORGAN JENNESS has spent the major part of her professional career associated with the New York Shakespeare Festival at the Joseph Papp Public Theater. She started as a part-time intern in 1979, then became a script reader, dramaturg, and literary manager. She left in 1988 to serve as Associate Artistic Director at the New York Theater Workshop and then as an Associate Director (in charge of project development) at the now-defunct and lamented Los Angeles Theater Center. She has worked as a free-lance dramaturg and developmental director in theaters and developmental programs all over the country, including New York Stage & Film and The Young Playwrights Festival, the University of Iowa, Brown University, and New York University, and has been honored to work with an incredible range of theater artists. She returned to the Public Theater in 1993 as Director of Play Development and was named an Associate Producer in 1995. She has recently returned to free-lance work and is currently exploring the possibilities of dramaturgy in new media.

PAUL SELIG'S work for the stage has been performed throughout the United States and the United Kingdom. His solo work *Mystery School* will be produced in New York by En Garde Arts, and is included in the anthology *The Best Short Plays of 1995–96. Never Enough,* his collaboration with Shapiro and Smith Dance will be seen at the Joyce Theater in 1997. His play *Sideshow* was included in Marathon '96 at the Ensemble Studio Theatre (New York). *Three Visitations,* his trilogy of chamber operas with composer Kim D. Sherman premiered recently at The New Music-Theater Ensemble in Minneapolis. Other plays include *Terminal Bar* (published, *Best Short Plays of 1988–89, Gay Plays 3*), *The Pompeii Traveling Show* (New York Drama League Award), *Body Parts,* and *Moon City.* The former Education Director for The Young Playwrights Festival, he developed a model for the teaching of playwriting currently being utilized by educators nationwide. He has taught playwriting at The Playwrights Horizons Theater School, The Poetry Center at the 92nd Street Y, The 42nd Street Collective and Marymount Manhattan College and has worked extensively as a dramaturg on new plays by emerging playwrights. He currently serves on the faculty of New York University's Tisch Scool of the Arts Dramatic Writing Program and the Goddard MFA in Writing Program. He is a graduate of the Yale School of Drama.

Paul Selig: How did you wind up a dramaturg?

Morgan Jenness: Totally by default. I was always interested in theater. I was a performer when I was younger. I did musical comedy. When I stopped doing that, I wanted to remain in the theater. Also, at seventeen I was with an original theater company in Ohio called Magic Theater for Madmen Only, and several members of the company were writers. People would bring me their plays and we'd talk about them. When I came to New York, I

tried to be a performer but decided I just didn't have the stamina. Then I
got a part-time clerical job down at the Public Theater in the literary office. People were coming in to read scripts for Robert Blacker[43] and Lynn
Holst,[44] who were working for Gail Merrifield Papp.[45] One day I said to
Bob, "I'd really be interested in reading scripts and reporting on them." He
pointed to a script and said, "Look at that and tell me what you think of it."
So I read it and told him. Evidently, he decided that I made an intelligent
response, so he gave me more scripts and I did more reports. He told
Gail I was sensitive to what was good in the writing and where the obsta-
cles were.

I had always looked at a play as a living thing or as a moving entity. I
tried to feel where the flow was, where the dams were, almost as if it were
a river that surged and eddied in different paths. Where something seemed
to block that flow, wherever the energy was stopped, that was the obstacle
to what was possible, what needed work. It was not some sort of mechani-
cal edifice to fix according to a rule book. Milcha Sanchez-Scott said to me
once about the way I worked, "Morgan, you put the play on like a coat, and
you live inside it like another skin, and you say, 'Oh, this feels tight here,'
and speak from inside the play." I had never known there was this creature
called a dramaturg. I thought it was terribly presumptuous of me to talk to
anyone about his or her work. I learned about dramaturgy at the Public
and that it could be practised by a lot of people without that specific title.
Joe Papp himself could be a tremendous dramaturg. I sat in on rehearsals
as much as possible, and listened to writers talk. That's how I got started. It
seemed perfect because I wanted to have a life in the theater, but wasn't
sure how. It may or may not have been a good thing that it happened so
easily; I might have done other things. I sometimes wonder about that. But
I love it because I am deeply honored by it. I have gotten to go on so many
journeys I would never have otherwise been able to go on.

Selig: What's an ideal production experience?

Jenness: The ideal experience is that everyone has the same core take on
the play, but different thoughts of how to get there, and that all of those
thoughts challenge and inspire one another.

Selig: I am not one of those people who warns students about directors, but
I have also been on the other side of the relationship. A play *is* like a living
thing. You have to find out what the work itself is trying to be. But I have
sometimes experienced what I call "The Cookie Cutter School of Dramaturgy." A playwright writes something that's a fabulous mess; it doesn't necessarily understand itself yet. The dramaturg or director sometimes tries to
stamp it out so that the play resembles an already existing form. . . .

Jenness: . . . Something they already know how to handle—a very human
trait. It's so American to ask, "Do you have a formula?" It's a fear of chaos,
a desire for immediate answers, this "instant breakfast" mentality. We are
so terrified of wandering through the very swamp that we often must go

through to find something valuable. It's so tempting to say, "But of course, you can have the protagonist do this because it happened that way in other established works. It's tried and true, so it works." Certainly, it could work, but it's not necessarily this particular writer's voice or what he or she is after. And the solution you find *that* way is perhaps much less interesting than the breakthrough that might have otherwise been found. But it's also about having time enough to go through that process.

Selig: I had a friend who went to the O'Neill[46] the first time with a play. It was comprised of about fifty short scenes and was beautiful—directed almost as Noh theater. There was a tremendous sense of space, with people out in the desert calling to each other. But when the play was produced in New York, after its incarnation at the O'Neill, it was done essentially as backwoods drama; the collage had been totally streamlined. As a teacher, I get students before they go into production, and I try to prepare them: "Be wary when you go into rehearsal for the first time and you look at your script and all your stage directions are crossed out."

Jenness: . . . Which is what actors are taught to do.

Selig: . . . And what directors are often told to do, because they are trained to work with dead playwrights. They assume that the play is essentially the property of the director, . . .

Jenness: . . . And that the playwright doesn't know what to do with stage directions or images, just writes dialogue but has little sense of anything else, which I think is incredibly arrogant. Some writers don't have a strong sense of the theatrical life, but many have a total awareness of theatrical possibilities. I once worked on a production of Eugene O'Neill's *Moon for the Misbegotten*. We took out all of the stage directions, but we found that not only were we going back to refer to them, but also that they were coming back up organically.

To me, it seems odd to talk about dramaturgy, because sometimes I think that the role of a dramaturg these days is often a "bandaid" solution. Because the economics of theater in America today is so ridiculous, dramaturgs often pick up responsibilities that other people should carry. Dramaturgs read plays and make recommendations to the producer or artistic director, who ideally should also have a strong knowledge of what's out there in the field, should be seeing things, should be reading a lot, should have a hands-on understanding. Now, hardly any artistic director or producer in nonprofit theater can do that, because most of them are too busy being administrators and fundraisers, or directing productions themselves. So, in a way, the dramaturg fulfills part of their function.

In order to make a living as a free-lance director in this country, you have to do four or five shows a year. The most sought-after directors work constantly, opening one show and going into rehearsal for the next a couple of weeks later. There is little lead time to sit down with the writer who has a new play in process, and discuss it over an extended pre-production period. Also, when I was free-lancing, sometimes I would go in on a classical project to do the research and to help suggest a possible artistic take. Now, that's fine and good, but it seems that directors would benefit more from a period of time in which to discover that for themselves, and then perhaps have someone to bounce ideas around with. Because of the economics of putting on a play, especially for untried writers, play development tends to include a lot of readings, where everyone sits down and has conversations. Instead of putting the play on its feet, so to speak, you have "workshops in the mind." The dramaturg can provide a level of knowledge, especially in conversations with people who have little production experience. This can be useful, but it doesn't take the place of putting a work up, of being in rehearsal with a director and actors, of having an audience respond.

Selig: What would you tell a first-time dramaturg going into production on a new play by a first-time playwright?

Jenness: I would never put a first-time dramaturg in alone with a new playwright. That dramaturg should have first been an assistant to somebody for several productions, and should have watched a variety of processes. People tend to go to school for a few years and work with some student writers, and then to make—or run up against—this assumption that they can go straight to work with anybody in any situation and somehow have all the answers.

Selig: What's the best experience one can have as a beginning dramaturg?

Jenness: To be in a room with people who know what they're doing and just learn and observe. To be an assistant, do research, listen, take in those conversations. That's the way I really learned. And then I went off and read every book I could get my hands on. A lot of this happens in the schools, but when students get out of school they often think, "Oh, why can't I get a job right away?" But as what? To work with a writer who's been in the business for fifteen years? What are you going to tell them?

Selig: Often playwrights don't have a vocabulary for their own work. It has come out on the page, and they sort of understand what they've done. Then it's about translating the vision to others. You have a reputation as being a real champion of the writer.

Jenness: Or of the play. . . . I really do see it that way, because I'm not there to be the playwright's personal friend. At a certain point the piece of work develops its own life to which everybody, including the playwright, is responsible. Sometimes the playwright wants to keep a kind of control over something that's getting larger. The director might have an idea that totally explodes the work to another level, but the playwright might be afraid to let go, to not own or control it any more. The collaborative sense that you are allies on a journey of discovery is important. Those negotiations start early on. It's a shared contract that's constantly renewed and reexamined.

Selig: I know from our talks that you have a real vision of what the role of theater can be.

Jenness: My view of the theater goes back to its ancient roots, to the theater as a form of ritual, a kind of experience that enables a group of people who might not be linked in any other way to journey together and have a similar catharsis. Not that it necessarily happens specifically as Aristotle said, but people feel pity and fear and sorrow and joy.

Selig: As a dramaturg, what do you look for in recognizing and realizing a gift?

Jenness: It's like hearing music. Sometimes I think it's better for playwrights to study music composition rather than traditional playwrighting, because music composition deals with many tenets that apply to all art: balance, harmony, tension, release. . . . What I search for is the voice as an ear. Does this writer have an ear? A sense of rhythm? A sense of orchestration? A sense of harmony? What's the melodic line like? This translates into how language is used, into whether or not there is emotional subtext or dramatic action. The structure of the overall play is the last thing I look for. The structure is where the dramaturg can come in. You can't teach someone to have an ear for dialogue. You can't teach someone how to have a gift for language, and you can't teach someone sensitivity—although you can help strengthen all these elements. Having a voice is the primary concern. You can find structure. (Ed. note: Compare Peter Stone's brief note on structure in the appendix, "Dramaturgy: A Compendium of Quotes.")

Selig: You once told me something helpful: that Aristotle had some good things to say, but that he's been dead for a long time. I have repeated that to students who were in a panic that their writing would not fulfill some formula.

Jenness: You must do what Picasso did with painting. You need to know it so you can throw it out. I don't believe you should *not* know it. The knowing is useful: it's a bedrock. I teach it, and then I say, "Okay, now we're going to break all the rules in particular ways." But it's a *deliberate* breaking of the rules. Picasso's early paintings are totally realistic—then he moved on.

Selig: When my students first enter production, they get a lot of differing feedback from a lot of people on their plays. Students have actually come to me and said, "What do people want to see, what should I write?" That's a sad and scary thing. What I say is, "There is a soul to a play, and that is the one thing you must protect with your life."

Jenness: Absolutely. It's finding its heartbeat. In some dramaturgical discussions everyone argues how many legs this creature of the play has or what color its fur should be. I find this absurd. The issue is, is it alive? Can it move? Can it soar? Not, "I think it should have three horns and not two." I say, "Get away, go write your own play."

Selig: Are there specific things that you do as a dramaturg working with a playwright?

Jenness: It depends on where you are in the process. Early on, during the first draft or even before the first draft, the dramaturg's function can be to explode things, to challenge, to ask, "What if . . . Then what . . . Why?"

Dropping depth charges into the psyche: "What would happen if two characters you never considered might have a scene together had a scene together?" Anything that explodes the terrain of possibility. That's very different from conversations in the later stages of production, when it's about results—and often about money.

Selig: Are there specific things that don't work in dramaturgy—ways you should not work with a playwright in production?

Jenness: I'm wary of offering playwrights specific solutions. I think questions are much more effective.

Selig: How so?

Jenness: Offering solutions can keep writers from their own explorations—especially young writers. I'll never forget one young playwrights' festival. I was working with a young writer on a play that was having problems; it had repetitive scenes that needed to be cut. I kept talking to the writer about it, but we were heading into previews and the people producing the festival said, "Well, just make her do it." I nearly flipped out. Basically, they were saying, "Use your power and say 'Cut this, or else,'" without her truly understanding why. She would have been resentful and upset and hurt, but she would have done it because she trusted me. I believed she had to get to the point where she could say, "You know what? I need to cut this because. . . ." And ultimately that's what happened. We went through some really grim performances and she watched the audience going dead during a couple of scenes and then said, "Yes, let's do this, and I see why." She needed to know why, and once she understood why, she could take that to the next play—which she did. She's still out there writing.

Selig: Occasionally you get writers who don't really understand what they've done or why changes were made.

Jenness: That happens a lot at the beginning stages; often, if you're deep into primary writing, you don't know why you write certain things. I don't think you need to in the first drafts; there should be that mystery for awhile. One writer with whom I've worked hates the idea of a workshop or reading at an early stage of a play, because he's trying to hear that voice and the rhythms he's after in his own head. If anybody else comes in strongly with their own impulses, that fragile voice he's after can be obliterated.

Selig: You begin to mistrust your initial choices.

Jenness: That's why I often ask writers later in a process to go back and read their very first draft to reconnect with their initial impulses.

Selig: I have gotten phone calls from playwriting students saying, "The director has asked me to cut the monologue in the middle of the play," when the monologue was the centerpiece of the play. They believe it needs to be there but don't have the vocabulary to explain why.

Jenness: If we had a healthier theatrical environment, none of these issues would matter so much. There would be leeway to explore those questions fully during the performance process—where cuts really reveal themselves. In the sixties, there were all those hole-in-wall places where you could just put a work up without a lot of bread, out of a harsh judgmental spotlight—try it out, and learn something from it. And the audience would be truly interested in that process. That breeding ground still exists somewhat. I see people in their twenties developing in young companies. It takes ten years. You get a group of people with whom you feel simpatico and you try it out. That's the most valuable thing in the world.

Selig: Now there's a shift toward careerism.

Jenness: The expectation of "I'm going to write my play, and the Manhattan Theatre Club can produce it and move it to Broadway, and then! . . ." The first time out! Sometimes that does happen, and sometimes you're trashed and you don't write for ten years because you've been so badly damaged. It's better to do as much work as possible early on, in a nonpressured situation. That can also happen in the schools.

Selig: Ideally, but actually a lot of schools are outfitting their students for careers.

Jenness: But really, how many people have actual viable careers in the theater? It does boil down to why people are in it—to do what? The whole NEA funding question plays into that. On the one hand I can say, "Oh my God, we *must* have the NEA; the arts should be supported in this country." On the other hand, I think, "Well, if the funding goes away, art is not going to be killed. Writers are still going to write if they are writers. Artists with real passion and vision are not going to be stopped by lack of government funding, and if they are, then what are they made of?" Think of the countries in Latin America and Eastern Europe and the Middle East where your life is really on the line for what you write.

Selig: Do you think that funding mentality breeds a sense of entitlement as well?

Jenness: I sometimes think so; that the artist feels somehow above the rest of society. That elitist attitude has turned society against the artist. In fact, a lot of people I know in the theater have little contact with the world outside theatrical circles. We tend to live isolated little lives with "golden problems," as my Yiddish grandmother would have said.

Selig: I have come from real privilege in the theater: I went to the institutions that were correct at the time, but when I was flat broke, I went and taught at a high school in the South Bronx. I walked into a room of forty students, mostly African American, and I said, "What's the last play you saw?" The whole room looked at me as though I were insane. It turned out the only play any of them had seen was, *Mama, I Want to Sing* because it had been produced above 125th Street. That exploded my reality of what the theater is and how to make it accessible. That became part of the reason I began to teach about the empowerment of the individual voice.

Jenness: We all know how in Shakespeare's day, a huge range of people would go to see plays. These days I think the key to broader access and appreciation might be linked more to people discovering the artist in themselves.

Selig: What do you mean by that?

Jenness: When they find out what it is to write a scene, to express them-selves, to make characters, go after actions, have confrontations—when they understand that process and how they too can participate in that process. Once they have attempted to write (or act in) a play, they might be more interested in seeing a play, because they have greater ownership of it.

Selig: How can institutions facilitate this?

Jenness: By connecting to the communities, connecting to education, bring-ing in kids, bringing in new audiences, acknowledging other realities and values. Brustein rants and raves that theaters are not supposed to be social institutions, but I don't agree. Our theaters too often offer narrow perspec-tives for one class of people. I got interested in musicals because I sang songs from musicals. If the butcher in a small town plays Stanley, he's going to be more interested in seeing a production of *Streetcar* or maybe even another Tennessee Williams play. I value the amateur—in the true "for love of" sense of the word—and community and educational orientation. I don't necessarily see it as a bad thing if money sources, especially public ones, say, "No, we're not going to give some middle-class writer money to sit and write a play—they have to go and teach sixteen-year old kids in order to get it." I guess it's because I don't come from that kind of middle-class sensibility; I always thought that being an artist meant you'd be fifty with a hot plate. Others think, "Oh, my God, I'm going to be fifty with a hot plate! That's failure." That's this system's definition of failure, but not mine. I've seen success by this society's definition destroy artists, and it's painful to see. If you are an artist, it seems to me you are more effective not swept up in "success" or the norm or totally embraced by the system. That's why some of our strongest writing often comes from people who have been pushed outside the mainstream, who have been ostracized because of gen-der, race, sexual orientation, economics, or sensibility. There's tremendous potency in being able to observe.

Selig: Do you ever think that theater is just preaching to the converted?

Jenness: Yes. That's why my roommate, Keitryn, who is rewriting Bible sto-ries from a feminist point of view, is taking her work out to women's church and community groups. The women (and men) laugh, and some-times are scandalized, and have discussions that they wouldn't normally have. To Mr. Brustein, that wouldn't be art.

Selig: What is art?

Jenness: Yikes! For me, art is an expression of who someone is and the manifestations of how that person reacts in their deepest places to the world around him or her. Hopefully, it's so deep and so true that it rings; it sets up a sympathetic vibration in other people.

Selig: As you know, I've gotten into the idea of the spiritual theater, which is, I think, in accordance with what you were saying about catharsis and rit-ual. One of the things that moved me toward this was a story you once told me about your potential journey to India. I've repeated it to all my students. Do you want to tell the story?

Jenness: When I was in my early twenties, I was still working part-time doing computer entry and working at the Public a couple days a week. I had been trying to perform and was wondering what my life in the theater was really about. I decided it was all nonsense and that I really wanted to do something more meaningful with my life. So, I got it into my head I was going to join Mother Teresa's Sisters of Mercy in Calcutta and that I was going to pick up dying people off the streets, and own nothing but a sari and a bucket, and give my life to service. I was right in the middle of trying to figure out how I was going to get to India when it turned out that Mother Teresa was making a trip to New York. Then I was beside myself trying to figure out how to meet her. I called up her place in the Bronx, but they didn't know her exact itinerary. I checked the papers and called up places she had visited, but nobody knew where she was going next. One of the people at my computer job suggested I call the Indian Consulate. I thought, if her convent doesn't know, why would the Indian Consulate? But I called, and the person who answered the phone said, "Yes, as a matter of fact, she's going to be at the Consultate in about an hour to address the staff here." Bingo.

I believe it was late spring . . . a beautiful day. I remember saying to everyone around me, "That's it. I'm going. I'm going to meet Mother Teresa and I probably won't be back. Bye!" I dashed there—it was off Fifth Avenue in the '60s or '70s. A guard was standing outside, and I asked him if Mother Teresa had come yet. He said she hadn't. About three minutes later two cars pulled up. She got out of the first one, with these tall men, and a whole flock of nuns got out of the second one. They came walking up the street toward me. I was now practically hearing choirs of angels in my head. She was tiny and had these eyes like burning coals. She looked at me and motioned for me to follow them in. I followed the entourage into the lobby and up these beautiful long stairs—Mother Teresa, then these big tall men, then her nuns, and then me at the end, like the errant little duckling in the Chinese story. We went into this big room packed full of all kinds of dignitaries—serious looking men, women in gorgeous saris. She spoke, and she was really tough and funny and not at all stiff or prissy as you'd think such a religious icon might be. She was amazing.

One person got up and said, "Well, Mother Teresa, they say it's better to teach people how to fish rather than to just give them fish." She replied, "Most of the people that we work with can't even stand up, but I'll make a deal with you: I'll give them fish until they are well enough, and then *you* teach them" I was thinking, "Oh, this is Kismet." Her talk ended, and they were about to take her off for some private reception. I flung myself past people at her, and she stopped and gently said, "What can I do for you?" And I babbled, "Oh, Mother Teresa, I want to come with you; I want to come to India; I want to be part of your order; I want to pick up dying people in the street, please, please. . . ." And she asked, "You need to do this?" And I said, "Yes, yes, I need to do this!" and I thought, "She understands me, she understands this hole in my heart that I need to fill." She gazed at me and she said, "No, you cannot come." I was devastated. The angels stopped singing. Everything became painfully real. I had been rejected by Mother Teresa! It was terrible. She didn't even know me and she rejected me. Then she looked at me and said, "When you are so filled with love for these people that you cannot bear to be away from them for another minute, then you can come." Just the implication of that was staggering! Here I was talking about my need, and it wasn't at all about that. I was crestfallen.

She asked, "What do you do?" and I answered, "I'm in the theater," like confessing this horrible, paltry, putrid occupation. She smiled, nodded, and said, "There are many famines. In my country there is a great famine of the body. In your country there is a great famine of the spirit. That's what you must feed." Then she turned around and went into the reception room. Well, that kept me going for quite awhile, and still does.

Selig: Do you see what you're doing as a form of service?

Jenness: That's the only reason I can bear doing it. You do everything, and anything, to keep that fire in people going. A lot of times dramaturgy is not about your actual suggestions to people about structuring their plays. It's about just being there with them, nearby, in that lonely, sometimes devastating, terrifying place. It's about being a spotter. Remember in high school when you jumped on the trampoline? There were spotters around you, so you could try a somersault, leap as high as possible, without worrying about breaking your neck, because you figured someone was there to catch you.

Selig: Is that what dramaturgs actually do?

Jenness: I don't know. I have such mixed feelings about it all. Here I am, one of the few people who has consistently made a living at dramaturgy, and yet I'm not sure I totally embrace the notion of it. I believe I still don't fully understand what I'm doing. I have a certain background, knowledge, and experience behind me, but every circumstance is different. Every artist is a different journey. Every time, you go in with a Zen beginner's mind. A lot of writers are hostile toward dramaturgs because they don't have to put themselves on the line. Oskar Eustis used to joke, "Being a dramaturg means never having to say you're sorry." There's a lot of truth in that.

Selig: What do you not embrace about dramaturgy and dramaturgs?

Jenness: There's often an arrogance in us—the dramaturg who is smug and superior and pretends to have all the answers. I really hate that. We are in such an information age, but I don't think we are in a real knowledge age. There's a difference. A lot of dramaturgs come with information but not knowledge. Ultimately, I think if one believes in God creating humans in

God's image, then God made human beings able to create. That, to me, is the bottom line. We have an ability to make something out of nothing; that is the spark. It gets clouded by lifestyles and careers and ego and all the little rewards, but what you're ultimately after is truth and your own expression of that truth.

Selig: Some might accuse you of being idealistic.

Jenness: I note that you do refer to it as an accusation. You're damn right, I'm idealistic. The day I stop being idealistic is the day I hope I drop dead because for me to live without some spark of idealism is like living with Pandora's box without that final creature in it. You can accept things not being ideal if you can imagine a future where they are, which is hope. And beyond hope is faith, *knowing* that they will be. I'm not quite sure I'm there yet, but that's where I'd like to be.

The Dramaturgical Dialogue:
New Play Dramaturgy At Actors Theatre of Louisville
by **Michael Bigelow Dixon**

MICHAEL BIGELOW DIXON has been the Literary Manager at Actors Theatre of Louisville since 1986. He oversees dramaturgy for the Humana Festival of New American Plays, Classics in Context Festival, Flying Solo and Friends Festival, National Ten-Minute Play Contest, and the theater's regular season and apprentice projects. He has also been the Literary Manager at Alley Theatre in Houston, Literary Associate at South Coast Repertory, and a Fellow of Theater Management at the National Endowment for the Arts. He has taught at North Carolina Central University, University of California Riverside, Rice University, and Action Theatre in Singapore. He has coedited ten volumes of plays and criticism as well as several monographs from the Classics in Context Festival.

Whatever its manifestations—script analysis, research, consultation—new play dramaturgy at Actors Theatre of Louisville implies a dialogue, the supportive exchange between our theater community and a playwright working on a play. In that description the term dramaturg is conspicuously absent, for new play dramaturgy is best understood in our circumstance as a process, not merely a position. That process, in which many partake, is characterized by the give-and-take of ideas, inquiries, and interpretations, and its purpose for all concerned is to gain the most expansive and penetrating understanding of the dramatic text vis-à-vis the playwright's intentions. Sometimes that ongoing exchange may prompt a playwright to revise a script for clarity and effect, or to integrate new ideas inspired by conversation, but revisions are never the *a priori* goal for such discussions.

The heart of our dramaturgical dialogue is the search for harmonic interpretations among collaborating artists—initially in terms of the playwright's ideas regarding the text, then in terms of other artists' responses to the structure, style, images, and thematic resonance. Once initiated, that conversation invariably sets in motion a dialectic that raises numerous issues but should ultimately delineate central and secondary metaphors to provide a unity for the collaborative process. Some playwrights want to be involved in that dialectic; others don't, which is always their prerogative. Yet when playwrights choose not to participate in discussions that can influence interpretations of the text, they cede responsibility for choices that determine the literal and metaphoric values of production to other artists. Because many playwrights wish to convey *something* specific via the performance of their plays—call it meaning, call it experience, call it theme or what you will—the dramaturgical dialogue proves an effective means by which to articulate that something and refine both the text and its interpretation accordingly.

During the past decade, the importance of our dramaturgical dialogue has been underscored by two principles that have emerged as guideposts for new play development and production across America: first, the playwright controls what belongs in the script; and second, the playwright has the right to be consulted on all major creative decisions. Now contractually binding through The Dramatists Guild, those two articles of playwright empowerment have vast ramifications for theater budgets and methods of collaboration. Take one example: casting. Consultations with the playwright are nearly meaningless if that playwright is not privy to auditions, which requires not only travel expenses but a decision-making process based on consensus.

Moreover, as playwrights confer on casting, design, and other production considerations, we find room at the conference table for someone titled "dramaturg," whose role it is to concentrate on the dramatic text: its thematic possibilities, its structural characteristics, its sources and references, its history and development, and its expression and fulfillment of the playwright's ideas. Like other collaborating artists around the table, the dramaturg serves as a resource, a sounding board, and a contributor. But unlike other collaborators, the dramaturg purposefully facilitates discussion in the interests of thematic clarity and coherence, which emerge only when the various artists' interpretations of the text begin to harmonize.

At Actors Theatre of Louisville, dramaturgs have come with disparate backgrounds—playwriting, design, administration, and graduate studies in dramaturgy—yet we've arrived at a common approach to the dramaturgical dialogue. Speaking on behalf of my colleagues, Liz Engelman and Val Smith, the Actors Theatre methodology begins by reading the script several times, taking notes of those invaluable first impressions never to be had again, and discussing the play with other staff people. Feeling vastly underprepared—a feeling that *should* accompany forays into the unknown—I then contact the playwright. After explaining what I admire in the script and why I chose to work on it, I set out to find what the playwright knows about the play that I don't. These questions addressed to the playwright can reveal important clues to the playwright's intentions and process, which in turn can inform text analysis, the dramaturgical dialogue, and production choices:

- Why was it written and when was it started?
- How many drafts are there and would it be a good idea for me to read earlier versions?
- Have there been readings or workshops, and what was learned from those?
- What should I read and whom should I talk with to understand more about the world of the play?

Then I inquire if the playwright has questions or uncertainties regarding any aspect of the play. (They usually do, and this is often the first time my opinion is solicited.) Do they need assistance of any kind in preparation for rehearsals and residency? (They always do, and we quickly learned that taking good care of playwrights increases their confidence in our overall process.)

Those initial conversations serve partly to learn more about the play and partly to learn more about the playwright. Every artist speaks her or his own jargon, and it's extremely useful to place dramaturgical issues in the framework of a writer's own vocabulary and concerns. It's equally useful to find out what kind of help a playwright doesn't want, because dramaturgical discussions can't be forced upon a playwright.

This brings up our first rule of new play dramaturgy: Take your cue from the playwright. Playwrights are guided by their own methods, preferences, and bêtes noires, and it's invaluable to learn early on what those are, for the practice of new play dramaturgy consists not only of experience and analysis, but of diplomacy.

This raises our other rule of new play dramaturgy: Avoid irrevocable mistakes. Dramaturgical collaboration in the development of a new work is a matter of privilege and trust, and when trust is compromised, the privilege is difficult to recover. In this regard, it's wise to consider the playwright the indisputable authority on the text. There's no need then to make assumptions that might be accurate or erroneous, because you can always ask the playwright. Your questions and the playwright's answers begin the dialectic that defines our dramaturgical dialogue.

As long as we're on the subject of diplomacy and trust, here are a few other tips:

- Although praise is always welcome in generalities or specifics, critical inquiries should be narrowly targeted and framed as questions.
- Discussing process relieves anxiety. Playwrights should be fully apprised of theater schedules and should discuss the director's plans for rehearsal, so that vital textual questions can be addressed in time to make adjustments, if necessary.
- While articulating what a playwright wants to achieve, it's also helpful to find out what the playwright wants to avoid in production. New plays tend to pose original problems, the solutions to which aren't always clear. So sometimes a process of elimination proves useful. For example, here's a question that elicits valuable insights: "What's your idea of a nightmare production of your play?"

When I've followed up on the homework assignments from our initial discussions—and hopefully by then some give-and-take has begun—the dramaturgical dialogue can turn to more penetrating issues. The questions below, which dramaturgs might use to analyze the text, can lead to further, more specific conversations with playwrights.

- How does structure facilitate the progression of action?
- Is the structure efficient?
- Is the sequencing effective?
- Are arguments, motivations, revelations, images, and turning points clear? Or, if desired, are they clearly ambiguous rather than vague?

Of course, specifics need to be dealt with in terms of the playwright's thematic sense of her or his play. The point here is, it's nearly impossible to discuss elements of a play in progress without some agreement as to the play's unifying metaphors, themes, or ideas. However, because many playwrights recoil from requests to explicate the "meaning" of their texts, thematic discussions may more easily evolve from an analysis of character journey or the development of style, event, or structure, whichever's most appropriate to the dominant theatrical quality of the text and to the playwright's intention.

As the director and designers join the conversation, the dramaturgical dialogue turns more production specific—what images, what actors, what sounds and movement help fulfill the playwright's vision? While the production takes shape in minds and on paper, the playwright, director, and dramaturg must vigilantly assess what remains to be learned about a new play and when is the optimal time to learn it—discussions, rehearsals, or performances? When rehearsals begin, I shift gears and begin sharing research that may prove useful to the cast in the form of image murals, information packets, and slide presentations. Later, while observing play run-throughs, I consider what remains unclear, what's extraneous, what's missing—becoming somewhat of an early audience member. My notes to the playwright and director focus on structure (an efficient length and effective sequence of scenes) and interpretation (Is what I'm experiencing in the rehearsal/performance what the playwright and director wish to convey?).

As literary representative of the theater, it's also my responsibility to ensure that the playwright feels fully supported. Therefore, in any playwright–director or playwright–producer impasse I back the playwrights when their arguments can be supported by the text. Those discussions are seldom simple, and passions become heated at times, but breakdowns in communication are usually resolved by our clear priorities: productions of new work at Actors Theatre of Louisville should be true to both the playwrights' text and intentions. Outside the rehearsal hall, there are other dramaturgical duties. At Actors Theatre of Louisville, dramaturgs pen brief publicity descriptions of plays in consultation with playwrights, who generally take great interest in these "blurbs," because they affect audience expectations and ticket sales. Passing condensed play descriptions by a playwright for approval can also help a dramaturg fathom how the playwright hopes others will perceive the play. Dramaturgs are responsible, too, for newsletter articles and community discussions, which provide context and forums for audience response. We oversee audience surveys, which solicit public opinion as to what "works" and what "remains problematic" with plays in progress. And finally, dramaturgs assist playwrights and their agents in efforts to interest publishers and producers. This final endeavor completes the cycle of encouragement and support for playwrights at our theater, while hopefully buying them time to write their next new plays.

How we arrived at our dramaturgical approach has been the work of twenty years by trial and error, lessons learned and adjustments made, networking, listening, and incrementally funding the necessary policies and practices. Throughout that journey our objective has remained constant: to forge an effective and flexible artistic process that simultaneously serves the production, the play, and the playwright. Over the years, as our methodology with new plays evolved, so has the role of the dramaturg. The following thumbnail history of the Humana Festival of New American Plays, the centerpiece of our new play program, illustrates past stages in an ongoing evolutionary process.

At Actors Theatre of Louisville, the new play program became a permanent part of the season in 1976 with the founding of the Humana Festival of New American Plays by producing director Jon Jory. Concerned about the limited repertoire of new work emanating from commercial venues in New York, Jory ventured into the development and production of new plays. Early on, Jory articulated a vision that continues to define the theater's mission for the Humana Festival: to encourage and support the American playwright; to identify, develop, and produce plays of quality each year; and to broaden the spectrum of work seen on the American stage.

The first years of any theater's commitment to developing and producing new dramatic literature must emphasize the first half of the dramaturgical cycle—the collection and evaluation of new scripts. For instance, once initiated, the Humana Festival had no reputation to attract plays, nor was there any effective mechanism in the mid-1970s for the national circulation of new scripts. So literary manager Elizabeth King devised her own methods of script solicitation, and in her first attempt succeeded in collecting more than three hundred plays, a number that swelled to four thousand within a few years. For Actors Theatre, the great motivator of play submissions became The Great American Play Contest, with its lure of money and full production. That contest not only caused plays to be sent, it also caused plays to be written. In setting up the literary office, King also created a system for reader reports that doubtless will serve Actors Theatre through the turn of the twenty-first century. (Yes, Actors Theatre has reader reports for more than sixty thousand plays dating back to 1976.) By the end of King's five years as literary manager, the Humana Festival had premiered several Pulitzer Prize-winning plays and had become a home for American playwrights. The festival promised annually to produce eight to twelve plays that were original in content, style, perspective, and voice. It would encourage new writers and celebrate their works in fully staged, fully costumed productions for review by national and international critics and producers. And to assist in those endeavors, the theater would assign a representative of the literary department—not yet called "dramaturg"—to facilitate the writer's participation in production.

What the playwright's involvement would be and how that would be facilitated, given budget restrictions, and ever-shifting artistic priorities, were not always clear. In the early years of the Humana Festival, the most significant dramaturgical question may have been, "Who has the final authority regarding production—the producer, director, actors, designer, or playwright?" Finding ways to share that authority by encouraging collaboration through conversation has resulted in our obsession with the dramaturgical dialogue.

By the time Julie Beckett Crutcher became literary manager in 1980, questions regarding the playwrights' place in the process were persistent: Should they attend all rehearsals? Do they have to rewrite? Who pays for their residency? So Crutcher set forth to clarify the theater's policies. Her advocacy, along with pressure from agents and playwrights themselves, led to fully funded residencies throughout the rehearsal period, with the theater paying for travel, housing, and per diems. Those funds enabled the playwrights to be in the room during critical periods of decision making, which in and of itself immeasurably advanced the cause of the dramaturgical dialogue. Having made the choice to produce new plays, that financial commitment to the playwrights' presence was the most important expression of the theater's serious commitment to the process of new play development and production.

Having outlined the basics of the dramaturgical dialogue by 1985, when I came on board, Actors Theatre of Louisville began to experiment with its approach to new plays—and for the first time referred to its literary staff as dramaturgs, a title that had been sufficiently demythologized from the status of Germanic demigod to be accepted as a legitimate position in American theaters. In 1986, Jory announced that the Humana Festival would thereafter include second productions as well as premieres. The advantages of that new policy were several: the number of scripts available to the theater for consideration increased, support would increase for playwrights whose work was ignored by theaters interested only in premieres, and the significance of the dramaturgical dialogue beyond first productions was established. In fact, that last discovery—our dramaturgical process remains valuable to productions and scripts regardless of their developmental status—set the stage for a revolution in dramaturgy at Actors Theatre of Louisville. In a five-year period, the dramaturgical dialogue became an integral part of production for all plays contemporary and otherwise, which generated an entire new festival titled the Brown-Forman Classics in Context Festival. But that's another article.[47]

The theater's venture into docudrama, from 1984 to 1991, repositioned the fulcrum between dramaturg and playwright. Following the Actors Theatre of Louisville premiere of Emily Mann's *Execution of Justice* in 1984 (commissioned by the Eureka Theatre), Jory launched a series of docudramas focusing on America's farm crisis, homelessness, and victims' rights. Each of those projects began with the literary staff conducting research, including tape recording and transcribing interviews. Those materials, often thousands of pages, were then handed over to a playwright who was commissioned to create a dramatic text by editing and adapting the interviews, trial transcripts, and other documents. Because the research had been guided by the dramaturg's understanding of the passions, personalities, and issues, the dramaturg provided not only a critical perspective, but became a key contributor to the structure, metaphors, and themes of the dramatic event. That contribution was carried to a logical extreme by Julie Crutcher, who had worked as dramaturg on the farm crisis project. Following three years of research and script editing, Crutcher shared playwright credit with commissioned author Vaughn McBride for their collaboration on *Digging In,* a dramatized community forum that voiced opposition to the economic and human injustice of this nation's farm policies in the 1980s.

In 1991 Jory initiated a series of experiments in the ensemble creation of new work. To inaugurate that project for the Humana Festival, director and adaptor Paul Walker was commissioned to create a performance piece about the nineteenth-century antipornography crusader Anthony Comstock. That production occurred amidst the debate over government funding of the Robert Mapplethorpe exhibit in nearby Cincinnati. With the aid of his cast and dramaturg Chiori Miyagawa, Walker deconstructed the published writings of Comstock and others. Their method imposed meanings on Comstock's text that differed radically from almost anything he might have intended. The result, ironically, was an entertaining performance that consciously distorted Comstock's words to show how he had purposefully twisted the words of his censorship victims.

The following year designer John Conklin used ideas he'd gleaned from working with Robert Wilson to guide an ensemble performance inspired by issues inherent in Mt. Rushmore: public art and patriotic monuments on Native American lands, public funding of art, and the environmental impact of labor and tourism. Dealing with those problems and more, Conklin, the cast, and dramaturg Deborah Frockt created the text by intercutting monologues extracted from *The Carving of Mount Rushmore* with the poetry of William Carlos Williams. Through their extraordinary effort, the text attained a choral effect of fragmented sentences accented by compositions of Eric Satie. The overall performance flirted with hallmarks of Robert Wilson's work: a nonlinear construction, simultaneous action, and sense impression as a structural guide.

As Frockt became immersed in the creative endeavor of interweaving words with movement and sound, the project raised an important issue regarding a dramaturg's role: What happens to the dramaturg's critical function when the dramaturg becomes a collaborator? Because dramaturgs at Actors Theatre work both inside and outside the collaborative process—we endeavor to understand the creator's intent and then offer constructive analysis—becoming a collaborator on the text and performance threatens overexposure and attachment that may undermine critical distance. In fact, as Frockt began to believe she was losing her broad perspective on the play, she called in dramaturgical associates to watch and comment on the work afresh. Though the issue of "inside" and "outside" is one of overlapping grey areas, ensemble creation certainly challenges the dramaturg to find ways to clarify thematic intent and question choices without inhibiting the creative process.

In recent years, two other versions of ensemble creation have provided further insights for myself and my former associate Michele Volansky, now literary manager at Steppenwolf Theatre Company. In her dramaturgical dealings with playwright and director Tina Landau on a created piece titled *1969,* Volansky discovered that Landau's unconventional, improvisational methods could still benefit from conventional dramaturgical analysis. Though Landau develops work through actor assignments and group improvisations, the main difference between hers and a pre-scripted experience, according to Volansky, was that the performance and text were being simultaneously created and interpreted in rehearsal. Hence questions of intent, selection, and meaning had to be addressed in a dramaturgical shorthand based on Landau's favorite aphorism: Information overload equals pattern recognition. By discussing "patterns" as a pathway to theme, character, and structure, Volansky demonstrated how a dramaturg can utilize the idiosyncratic parlance and methods of a playwright—rather than classical terminology to address traditional dramaturgical issues.

When director and adaptor Brian Jucha and his cast created an ensemble performance dealing with murder, love, and purgatory, *Deadly Virtues,* we faced yet another novel approach. The hard fact learned during Jucha's residency was that his unique process could not incorporate our dramaturgical dialogue, since he created the text intuitively and individually with each actor. As the nominal dramaturg assigned to the project, I simply took the advice of *Village Voice* critic Michael Feingold, which I keep posted on the wall above my desk:

> ***Art is only a semirational process. Based on an unconscious need,***
> ***it drives the artists into choices that cannot be explained rationally;***
> ***they just seem to be right. At the same time, there's a second stage***
> ***to the process, a shaping and selecting instinct which some artists have***
> ***naturally and others do not, and a lot of potentially fine work***
> ***gets wasted because it hasn't been refined to reveal its own shape.***[48]

While Feingold makes the case that some playwrights can benefit from dramaturgical assistance in the "shaping and selecting" phase, he also leaves room for playwright/creators who work best on their own or with those they've come to trust over time. By logical extension, some ensemble processes can incorporate a dramaturg from the beginning, while others are so intuitive that they preclude the involvement of a dramaturg altogether. Following our firs rule of new play dramaturgy, I took my cue from Jucha and simply offered whatever technical or personal support the literary department had to offer.

In addition to the intelligence, experience, passion, and sincerity of artists who participate in the dramaturgical dialogue, several other factors are vital to the successful outcome of the process. The first is time: If conversations with the playwright are not initiated well in advance of decision deadlines, it is unlikely that subterranean truths revealed through discussion will be reflected in the landscape of production. Second, all theater is a local event, and so it has proven an advantage at Actors Theatre of Louisville to employ a resident dramaturgical staff who can provide local context for visiting artists.[49] Local context includes the theater's mission, its past experience with new plays and its relationship with various communities, all of which can and should inform production choices.

Because of obvious costs related to time and staffing, the third element essential for the success of any resident dramaturgical process is institutional support. Regardless of which particular theater is being discussed, wherever new play dramaturgy thrives there is a producing entity who values the integrity of the dramaturgical dialogue and its pursuit of thematic clarity and coherence. At Actors Theatre of Louisville that entity is Jon Jory, who as producer and as a director has, over the years, become a great proponent of dramaturgs. As he writes for this article:

> *The director suits the word to the action. The dramaturg finds*
> *the structure for the word. The process succeeds because*
> *in most forms of analysis two minds are better than one.*
> *Dramaturgy is no more optional in the theater than ignition*
> *is to internal combustion engines. You gotta have it.*[50]

A Conversation With Mame Hunt, Dramaturg-Artistic Director, and Susan Mason, Dramaturg-Academic, 19 August 1994, Oakland

Mame Hunt, Artistic Director of the Magic Theatre in San Francisco and the Bay Area Playwrights Festival, has a distinguished career in dramaturgy and new play development. She has worked with some of the most innovative playwrights in the United States including Thomas Babe, Jon Robin Baitz, Neena Beber, Neal Bell, Nilo Cruz, Migdalia Cruz, Quincy Long, Donald Margulies, Heather McDonald, José Rivera, Marlane Meyer, Anna Deavere Smith, Darrah Cloud, and Clair Chafee. Before moving to the Bay Area, she was Literary Manager and Director of New Play Development at the Los Angeles Theatre Center, where she served as dramaturg on the world premieres of Darrah Cloud's *The Stick Wife* and Marlane Meyer's *Etta Jenks.* She designed and co-produced LATC's New Works Project and has worked on new plays at South Coast Repertory Theatre, the Denver Center, Victory Gardens, and the Goodman Theatre. She has been a consultant for the National Endowment for the Arts (NEA), the Rockefeller Foundation, the California Arts Council, and the Nordic Theatre Committee in Reykjavik, Iceland.

Susan Mason is Associate Professor of Theatre Arts and Dance at California State University, Los Angeles, where she teaches dramatic literature, criticism, history, research, theory, acting, and voice. She was a Fulbright lecturer in Utrecht, The Netherlands, in 1993, where she worked as Dramaturg on *On the Edge,* an international collaborative theater project on immigration in The Netherlands. She has recently completed a term as an Honorary Fellow in Theatre and Film Studies at Victoria University in Wellington, New Zealand, and a three-year term as Performance Review Editor of *Theatre Journal.* She spent a post-doctoral year studying dramaturgy and criticism at the Yale School of Drama in 1983–84 and subsequently worked as Literary Associate at the Los Angeles Theatre Center from 1985–90 where she was Dramaturg for The Women's Project, directed by Mame Hunt, and Publications Coordinator assisting Norwegian dramaturg Halldis Hoaas. She is an Ibsen scholar and has published performance criticism on productions of both classical and contemporary plays.

Susan Mason: How would you describe what a dramaturg does?

Mame Hunt: I break it down into three different areas: institutional dramaturgy, process dramaturgy, and production dramaturgy. Institutional dramaturgy is the voice of the writer in an institution, whether it's the voice of Molière at the Guthrie[51] or Marlane Meyer[52] at the Magic. Because writers don't work in the institutions, a sensibility is missing if someone is not speaking for them and representing their issues. Institutional dramaturgy also involves lobbying the artistic director to produce the work of a certain writer or to produce a certain play. It has to do with forming the aesthetic of the institution, being the link between the artistic community and the core artistic person at that institution. Process dramaturgy is what is done at the O'Neill Theatre Center, the Bay Area Playwrights Festival, and the Sundance Institute[53] where dramaturgy involves the development of a work before marketing, publicity, and casting decisions need to be made. The focus is specifically on the work itself, and on helping the writer to find his or her fullest expression of the world of that play. Production dramaturgy is after the play is selected—doing, among other things, research. Production dramaturgy is what is mostly taught in schools. I don't think that people are teaching a lot of process and institutional dramaturgy.

Mason: You need to be in a theatrical institution to learn institutional dramaturgy. Academic programs do sometimes train dramaturgs to work on process with playwrights, but production dramaturgy translates most easily into an academic program. Of course most dramaturgical training is relatively new, and we keep developing new classes and exchanging ideas about how to do it at the Association for Theatre in Higher Education (ATHE) and Literary Managers and Dramaturgs of the Americas (LMDA) conferences.

Hunt: Production dramaturgy in schools seems to focus mainly on production research and how to write dramatic criticism, which is not at all the same as dramaturgy. If people are only trained for production dramaturgy, then when their theater needs process work they won't know how to go about it. For example, leading a postplay discussion is a specific skill. The best postplay discussion guy I know is Jerry Patch, because he doesn't let anyone trample on the writer; he sets boundaries.[54]

Mason: I heard him tell an audience: "There are three basic human instincts: eating, sex, and rewriting other people's plays." So how can you learn institutional dramaturgy?

Hunt: You pay your dues: when I first got out of graduate school, I read and reported on five scripts a week for the Goodman Theatre in Chicago at five dollars a pop.

Mason: So training in institutional dramaturgy is an apprenticeship.

Hunt: When I was at the Goodman Theatre in 1980, I managed to get an interview with Greg Mosher[55] and said, "I want to direct." He said, "A good way to start directing here . . ." (Ha, ha, ha!) ". . . is to read scripts from the literary office." He sent me down the hall to meet with the literary manager, Peregrine Whittlesey. One of the first scripts I read was Emily Mann's *Still Life.*[56] I came back into the office with a big, fat directorial interpretation, and Peregrine said, "No, no, no. You're going to have to do a critique, not a concept. You have to talk about structure and character; you don't talk about interpretation here. You do that someplace else."

Mason: Now that you're an artistic director, you're in a position to bring in young people to apprentice in dramaturgy or literary management. How do you do that?

Hunt: Well, we had a young playwright working in the literary office last season who could have been an extraordinary dramaturg, but she quit midseason. When I asked her why, she said she likes to get paid for what she does. She was about twenty-five! I worked for quite a few years without getting paid, apprenticing as a dramaturg, learning how to communicate with playwrights. At one point, I had three jobs: I was selling tickets to *Evita* at the Shubert over the phone, house-managing at Northlight Theatre in the evenings, and critiquing plays for the Goodman.

Mason: I did about three years reading scripts at Yale,[57] at Playwrights Horizons for Eric Overmyer,[58] and then for you at the Los Angeles Theatre Center (LATC).[59]

Hunt: I think it is generational; young artists aren't willing to train. I don't know why they don't come into my office and say, "We don't have a staged reading program, and I'm a director and I would like to do some readings."

Mason: No innovation? No entrepreneurial spirit?

Hunt: Exactly. At the Theatre Center I remember going to Bush[60] and saying, "What we need is a festival. We need to compete with Louisville."[61]

He said, "Okay, do it."

"How much money do I have?" I asked.

He said, "Zero. Get a grant."

Well, we actually did it. We got the grant and we did the New Works Project.

Mason: What about play selection in institutional dramaturgy?

Hunt: I remember an LMDA meeting here in San Francisco. I think it was Eduardo Machado[62] who said it would be a good idea if artistic directors paid more attention to the recommendations of their literary staff. Literary people always have some glorious play that the artistic directors are not paying attention to.

Mason: Do you think because you've come out of literary management, you're more inclined to listen to what literary people tell you?

Hunt: Probably not. I'm waiting for them to go to the wall for something. When it happens, I respect it greatly.

Mason: But it doesn't happen very often?

Hunt: I was spoiled; LATC had four spaces, so I had fifteen opportunities a year to go to the wall for something.

Mason: If you were to go back into literary management would you be a better literary manager and dramaturg, with your experience as an artistic director?

Hunt: I'm not sure. I'd be more respectful of the pressure that the artistic director is under. But maybe I know too much now to be a really great dramaturg. I know how much things cost now; I know about cash flow and boards of directors now. To be a good dramaturg, you need to be ready to lose your job at any moment. You have to campaign relentlessly for a play or a writer or a new lab.

Mason: Do process dramaturgy and new play development work?

Hunt: New play development doesn't work. New playwright development
works. You can work with a playwright and foster a playwright's work. You
have to understand that the Bay Area Playwright's Festival (BAPF)[63] is
about developing new work *and* the writer. For example, Migdalia Cruz[64]
is just over thirty years old, and she has been painting on a small canvas—
deeply personal stories such as *Miriam's Flowers* and *Lillian,* about characters and their journeys. Now, with the last two plays, *Cigarettes and
Moby Dick* and *Latins in LaLa Land,* we've gone from Frida Kahlo–sized
portraits to murals. They're huge and political; they're social and public.
Latins in LaLa Land is a collection of stories and images about Latinos in
mainstream culture. The purpose of the Festival is to see where Migdalia
needs to go as an artist and to say, "Okay, we're going to help you get there."

Mason: By letting her have the opportunity to see her play and people's responses to it?

Hunt: Exactly. That may be new play development, or it may not be. The
point is that as a dramaturg I am familiar with Migdalia's body of work and
I see what she's trying to do next. I'm helping her take herself to the next
level of fulfillment. Somebody else, who's been painting murals, might
want to paint on a smaller canvas. And that's where process dramaturgy
comes in.

Mason: How does BAPF work? What is the process?

Hunt: They're readings, staged only to the level of entrances and exits. The
most important thing about new play development is flexibility. At BAPF
the structure includes various levels of directorial input, dramaturgical
input, actor input. We tech the readings in an hour or two, so our design
work is minimal. Each playwright and his or her creative team has a certain number of rehearsal hours, two presentations in front of an audience,
two postplay discussions at which the playwright may or may not be present (their choice). We get two hundred scripts submitted every year to
BAPF, so we have to think about what's worthy of our attention but also
whether the structure that we have in place can help that particular
writer at that point in his or her growth. Every year we get one or two
plays that are finished. We don't select them, because they are done, or
they will be finished in a rehearsal process. They don't need the kind of
attention that we can provide.

Mason: How long is the break between the two readings?

Hunt: An average of five days. They go up one weekend, then they come
down and have another eight hours of rehearsal, and then they go up
again.

Mason: I remember you described how Roberta Levitow[65] worked on a
play at Denver[66] one year, and between the first and second readings the
playwright completely rewrote the second act. Is that a good idea under
all that pressure?

Hunt: I don't think so, which is why I don't want to give the writers too
much rehearsal time. They only have a few hours between the first reading

and the second, so they can't do a lot of damage. They can't react in an overly emotional way. They can't overhaul.

Mason: Do you dramaturg at BAPF?

Hunt: I do, but I have to confess not very well. When I work as a dramaturg, I like to travel the journey the same way as the director and the playwright. But I usually can't, because I get pulled out of rehearsals to tend either to the Magic's needs or to other Festival tasks. As artistic director of BAPF, taking care of the artists is a large part of my job. They may need to change their housing, or photocopy a new scene, or find a sweatshirt—because no one is ever prepared for how cold it is in San Francisco in the summer—a lot of things can prevent writers from doing their best work. In a pedantic way, that's my job as artistic director—to make sure they can do their best work.

Mason: And that's not a dramaturg's job?

Hunt: It is the dramaturg's job to ask creative questions that can lead the writer to write the perfect last scene, but not to deal with the logistics of hotel rooms and fundraising.

Mason: I don't think dramaturgs have the power to do that usually.

Hunt: No they don't. As artistic director I can say, "It's more expensive to do it this way, but this is the way we're doing it." Dramaturgs can't say that.

We had a wonderful playwright, Brighde Mullins, who wrote a play we selected for the Festival, but when she got to the retreat the play felt old to her. She had another play that was starting to take shape in her mind, and she asked me if she could switch. Well she hadn't actually written it yet; she didn't know how many characters it would have, but I said, "Yes, as long as you have a script on the first day of rehearsal, go ahead."

Mason: What is the idea behind the retreat?

Hunt: Well, the Festival has a retreat six weeks before rehearsals begin where the playwrights, directors, and dramaturgs all gather together and the playwrights read their scripts out loud. What you learn from hearing them read by the writers is amazing.

Mason: That's a nineteenth-century concept, maybe older. French playwrights read their scripts aloud at the first rehearsal.

Hunt: You hit the ground running. We've all heard the playwright's interpretation, the energy level, the pitch, the rhythm, the level of comedy and irony, and the pacing, and we've heard it all from the primary source. The experiences of the playwright reading the play out loud are some of the most vivid that I've had.

Mason: We've talked about gender issues before. When you work as a dramaturg with playwrights on developing scripts, is it different working with male and female playwrights?

Hunt: When I was first hired as the Literary Manager at the Los Angeles Actors' Theatre,[67] I went to a meeting of the playwrights lab, and there were twenty male playwrights and three women. There was a reading of one of the women's plays, and the central character was a woman. All of the guys criticized the motivation of the central female character. It wasn't believable to them. I understood it just fine.

Mason: In an essay on gender, Linda Jenkins wrote that there is male language and female language.[68] Because the dominant culture is male, women learn male language as well as their own. I suppose this would apply to all non-dominant-culture people. Minority individuals speak both languages; they have to to survive. This is a broad generalization, but may explain why women can, perhaps, more comfortably cross over and dramaturg for men than the reverse.

Hunt: Dramaturgy is to a huge extent a supportive role.

Mason: Is it a nurturing role?

Hunt: In some ways it is. I don't like to call it a nurturing role because society at large looks down on that.

Mason: So do you think dramaturgy—especially new play development—is more "natural" for women given the way females are socialized?

Hunt: I don't know if dramaturgy is more natural for women or not, because it's so hard to make distinctions around why women practice dramaturgy. In my case, I turned to dramaturgy when I couldn't get directing work, but, then, it was Chicago in the early 1980s—that was a pretty masculine theater town then. But more than that, dramaturgy is a middle-management job, and that's where women were then. I remember at the 1989 LMDA conference in San Francisco, Bush said he hired women into middle management because he knew they'd work harder for the money than men. But now women are emerging from middle management and are becoming artistic directors. In the San Francisco area you can't avoid it: five out of six major theaters are headed by women.

Mason: When you work with minority writers, as you often do, are there problematic issues because the dramaturg and playwright have different ethnic backgrounds?

Hunt: If you're a good dramaturg then you're asking the questions that will allow writers to fulfill *their* visions. You couldn't find two people more different than Migdalia Cruz and I. I grew up in Long Beach, California, and I'm seven years older. She grew up in the South Bronx, and she's Puerto Rican. What we have in common is that we're two really smart women who like each other a lot. Maybe it's like marriage. You can marry or cohabitate with someone who's not like you and it doesn't mean that you can't be together. Even though I will never be able to go where Migdalia has been, I've suffered some discrimination as a woman. If you've been locked out of something against your choice, then you know.

Mason: Do you think there's any relationship between ethnicity and structure?

Hunt: Content and structure go hand in hand. I remember that Edit Villarreal[69] spoke on a panel and discussed how everybody was always complaining that writers of color—particularly Latino writers—have trouble with endings. And she said, "We're immigrants. We don't want to think about endings. We just got here. I don't want closure. I want everything to be a beginning." Edit likes to talk about the beginnings of things, and the middles. There is that interplay between content and structure, the source of your material and the manifestation. Marlane [Meyer] is a perfect example. She's half Polynesian, half Swedish, some part Cherokee, and comes from San Pedro, California. Who does she write about? She writes about everybody.

Mason: When I worked with Anna Deavere Smith on *Piano*,[70] I understood the cultural and class aspects: the serving class in a Cuban household right before the Spanish American War, the juxtaposition to the wealthy household. I worked with her on structure. She had such a big story to tell, and it was a matter of clearing the path because there were so many scenes, each packed with so much material. I loved that play!

Hunt: It's important to love them. I fall in love with these plays.

Mason: I'm still in love with *Harvest Moon*;[71] I'm still in love with *Increase After Completion*.[72] But I fell in love with dead playwrights first—Ibsen, Chekhov, Büchner.

Hunt: But you can't have lunch with them! I can call Marlane.

Mason: Is that one of the questions to ask, "Do I love this play?"

Hunt: The first thing you always say to a playwright is what you love about his or her play.

Of course, all of this is prefaced by establishing some kind of relationship with the playwright in the first place. And that's up to you to do.

Mason: How?

Hunt: You eat with them. My relationship with Marlane started over lunch in L.A.

Mason: So, besides "Do I love it," what else should a dramaturg ask?

Hunt: I like to ask questions about the playwright's intention, although I don't usually state it that way. It's good to ask them what kind of music they hear or what it looks like—those questions are a way of getting into the play graciously. Talking about what you love is a good way to get around to places you don't love so much. It's also good to take responsibility for your own responses and questions by saying, "This doesn't work for me," instead of "This doesn't work."

Mason: What about commissioned work?

Hunt: The only commission that makes sense to me is to say, "Here's this amount of money. Go create."

Mason: But sometimes a grant will come along for a play about frontier life in Sacramento, or California history, and you think, "We'd like this grant."

Hunt: That's bad grant-making.

Mason: Don't you think a major work could ever come out of that?

Hunt: I doubt it. Major work is blood on the page and you can't dictate that. I don't see how you can commission a play on specific subject matter. I wouldn't.

Mason: Anna Deavere Smith was commissioned by the Mark Taper Forum to do her piece on the L.A. riots—*Twilight Los Angeles* (and had about four dramaturgs![73]). But her *On the Road*[74] series is always commissioned. Maybe her work is unique, although this kind of documentary theater seems to be becoming more popular. When I was in The Netherlands in 1993, I was the dramaturg on a similar kind of piece based on interviews with immigrants that was created to be part of a month-long symposium on marginalized people. When the playwright (who had been brought over from the United States to "craft" this piece) got away from the subject, I believed my responsibility as a dramaturg was to steer him back to the issues of immigration. A lot of community-based theater that is funded locally and created on paper as a grant proposal can't be entirely organic for the playwright, because it is usually delineated by its subject.

Hunt: It's interesting to look at Emily Mann,[75] who writes entirely from existing material, inspired by real events and conversations, some from tape recordings.

Mason: Like Anna's [Deavere Smith] work. Or what you did with your play, *Unquestioned Integrity,* about Anita Hill and Clarence Thomas.[76]

Hunt: In my case it was transcripts. I got the transcripts on disk. I attacked the three hundred–page transcript with my different pens.

Mason: And you're the playwright? Not the editor or the dramaturg?

Hunt: I didn't just edit. My structural idea for the play was that once Thomas gave the speech about the hearing being "a high-tech lynching," the logic of the hearings disintegrated. The senator sits across from them, the way you saw it on TV, until that speech. Then all bets are off. The thing you see and hear after that speech is a senator who can't complete a sentence. I built out of all the transcript materials, a soliloquy for Anita. After the senator says, "I don't know what to do. . . . We'll adjourn—slam!" And suddenly there's Anita, in the empty hearing room, telling us how she feels.

Mason: Do you think there is a regional ethos of playwriting? Do you recognize a West Coast sensibility? When Marlane's play *Moe's Lucky Seven* was done as a reading at the Mark Taper Forum, I thought it was wonderful. But when it opened in New York, it did not get good press there. And *Kingfish* didn't get good press in New York, but you're doing it at the Magic. Why will it work at the Magic and not in New York?

Hunt: I think the reason her aesthetic works in one place and not in another has to do with space. West Coast people relate to space differently. When we moved *Etta Jenks* from LATC to the Women's Project in New York, it was to a smaller stage. It was so icky watching the actors stand that close to each other, because these characters are not people who can stand close to each other without your skin crawling.

Mason: So, a different kind a play would develop in the East from in the West?

Hunt: Maybe it has to do with the cultural differences. In California we're a young group of people in terms of our attachment to space.

Mason: When I was at Yale, it irritated me that my professors thought that we were hicks because we came from the West, that if you weren't from New York you couldn't really know about the theater.

Hunt: That still exists, especially with agents. The corollary of the attitude of "If you can make it there, you can make it anywhere," is "If you haven't made it there, you haven't made it." So your whole frame of reference and all of your professional experience on the West Coast—that's just sandbox? But also I do think the aesthetic is different; the audience is different, and the audience forms the aesthetic.

The Asian population here has a different kind of influence on "mainstream culture." The immigration from Mexico has a deep effect on the way we process language. We have a whole different Latino population on the West Coast than on the East Coast. We don't have as many Caribbean people on the West Coast. . . . Also, most of us in California spend much of our time outdoors as opposed to indoors. The challenges of the weather are different.

Mason: Stella Adler said we couldn't be creative in California because the weather is too nice. On the other hand, Chekhov's plays work in Seattle and Dallas and New York.

Do you think dramaturgy is a gift or an acquired skill?

Hunt: There's nothing rarefied about it, but it is an art. It's composed of craft and art. Certain aspects of it can be taught. What Marlane says about playwriting is that you have to be able to live by the rules; you have to know what the rules are before you break them. The same thing is true of directing, and the same thing is true of dramaturgy: you have to be able to do fairly pedantic research before you can do what I usually do, which is more improvisational dramaturgy. It's not rooted in the library. It is where the dramaturg really becomes a collaborator with the director and with the playwright and with the producer. Sometimes at conferences I listen to people on panels talk about plays, and I don't understand the relevance of what they're saying to the plays in rehearsal, in performance, or even in the classroom, other than as an intellectual exercise. It doesn't treat the play like a living thing; it treats it like a dead thing.

Tuesday, we had a rehearsal for *Tongues* and *Savage/Love,* originally created in 1978 at the Magic Theatre by Joe Chaikin[77] and Sam Shepard; they wrote and performed them together. Now Chaikin is directing them with two different actors and Sam's not involved. At the first read through of the play, I said to Joe, "You just spent time with Sam in New York. Did Sam say it's okay if you want to change the words." Joe shrugged, so I said, "Why don't you call him and have him come and hang out and then he can change things exactly the way he wants, and we won't have to go through any of this telephone shit."

He said, "Yes, fine." There was a pause, and I began to understand and I said, "You want *me* to call Sam Shepard?" Joe says, "Yes." As if that's the easiest thing in the world to just call Sam up on the phone and have a little dramaturgical chat. But what Joe was saying is so true: when you need information you might as well go to the source.

The Dramaturgy of Reading:
Literary Management Theory
by Tim Sanford

TIM SANFORD is the Artistic Director of Playwrights Horizons. Prior to his appointment to this position he served as the theater's Literary Manager for eleven years.
Under the artistic directorship of André Bishop for seven years and Don Scardino for
four years, he helped develop and produce writers as diverse as Jon Robin Baitz, Neal
Bell, Michael Henry Brown, Migdalia Cruz, David Greenspan, Adam Guettel, A. R. Gur-
ney, Peter Hedges, Kevin Heelan, Christopher Kyle, Tina Landau, Marion McClinton,
Marlane Meyer, Peter Parnell, Regina Porter, Jonathan Marc Sherman, Lynn Siefert, Nicky
Silver, Steve Tesich, Kathleen Tolan, and Wendy Wasserstein. From 1994 to 1996 he was
Co-President of Literary Managers and Dramaturgs of the Americas. He has a BA degree
from Occidental College and a PhD in directing and dramatic criticism from Stanford
University.

In 1984, when I began working as a reader in the literary department at Playwrights Horizons, I felt little qualified by my recently earned PhD in dramatic
literature from Stanford to attend to my theater's specialty, the development
of new plays by American authors. My dissertation on Pinter, Beckett, and
Proust had given me little background in American drama, and the absence of
plays written after 1970 on my department's required reading list left me
equally uninformed about contemporary theater. I found it wisest, therefore,
to leave my preconceptions at the door and use instincts and analysis to look
at each play individually. Fortunately, this approach meshed with the working
philosophy of Playwrights Horizons, whose mission is to nourish and produce
American playwrights with strong, distinct voices.

I was also fortunate to serve my on-the-job apprenticeship under André
Bishop, one of the first American artistic directors to begin as a literary manager. I've remained in this field ever since because I believe the vitality of the
American theater depends upon the strength of its new plays and new writers. Yet I've also wondered more than once how someone with my background developed such an affinity for the field. And I began to wonder how
other literary managers are trained.

Most graduate dramaturgy programs do not emphasize literary management training. Perhaps they do not consider literary management a species of
dramaturgy. In fact, the name of our professional organization, Literary Managers and Dramaturgs of the Americas (LMDA), seems to indicate a theoretical
or definitional distinction between the two functions. Certainly the definitions of "dramaturgy" are legion. I prefer an etymological definition that starts
with its Greek root, *ergon,* which means "work." Because we see drama at
work most effectively in production, dramaturgy is usually defined first in

terms of its relation to production. The work of the literary manager, on the other hand, evaluating scripts and corresponding with writers, generally precedes production. Yet reading, the essential skill of literary management, is fundamental to all dramaturgy. Only a careful reading of a dramatic text can make it come alive.

Over the years, I've developed an appreciation for the trickiness of this endeavor. My experiences in directing, writing, acting, and theater history have certainly given me tools to help me read plays more fully. Interestingly enough, however, it is my background in critical theory that has provided the foundation for how I read. All of the key questions of literary management—the definition of style, the relation of form and content, and the relation between writer and reader or audience—stand at the center of literary and dramatic theory. So while a literary manager needs a range of theatrical experience to assess a writer's voice, craft, evolution, and importance, a foundation in critical discourse can help put these qualities in perspective.

CULTURAL STYLE: REALISM

The question of style often serves as a starting point for literary managers, dramaturgs, and directors to enter a play. Style, however, is an extremely slippery concept because it has so many connotations. Artistically it refers to both a writer's individual voice and to a work's genre and influences. Style also refers more generally to the customs and fashions of a culture. In theater, we usually only consider this aspect of style in the contexts of period pieces, which summon up impressions of antiquated eras with obsolete fashions and artificial manners. In *Style: Classical Theatre and Modern Realism,* Michel St. Denis argues against this notion.

> In each country the theater addresses itself to the public of its time,
> which in due course will become a "period." Each period has its own
> style even though we are not conscious of it as we live. . . . And this
> style influences everybody.[78]

According to St. Denis then, the differentiation between works of "style" and "realism" is artificial. All works will reflect their period in some ways, and this absorption of the style of the times actually constitutes a play's realism.

In contemporary theater, however, we tend to characterize a playwright's style in terms of its resistance to realism. We often equate realism with verisimilitude and the reality it reflects seems to pertain as much to the social sciences as to aesthetics.[79] No wonder social critics from Plato to Newt Gingrich have debated the role of artists in society. In book ten of Plato's *Republic,* Plato banished artists from his model of utopia because he defined artistic endeavor as an imitation of reality, which is itself just an imitation of the ideal, so it is two levels removed from the truth. In *Poetics,* the scientist Aristotle counters the poet Plato by asserting the superiority of poetry to history. He says poetry's very unreality, its fictiveness, frees it to wrestle more directly with philosophical truths. The fictiveness of realism allows the artist to imitate reality but imbue it with philosophy and art. In other words, realism sets up a tension between reality and the artist's imagination, and this tension delineates the artist's style.

Literary analysis does not address this tension when it simply breaks down a work's themes. Themes comprise the content of a work. Its style lies in its form. In *The Act of Reading: A Theory of Aesthetic Response,* the German critic, Wolfgang Iser, develops a theory of reading, *Rezeptionsästhetik* (Reception Theory), that emphasizes the formal, aesthetic character of literature's progressive response to the social and cultural deficiencies of its time. A truly original work, he says, does not just slavishly reflect its culture's conventions, rather it sets up its own parameters on "the borderlines of existing systems" in order "to activate that which the system has left inactive."[80] In other words, progressive artists set up their stories realistically to reflect existing social conventions, but then use the dramatic power of the storytelling to expose the fallacies behind these conventions and the ideals that escape them. Ibsen became famous largely for his ability to break apart the moral precepts of his time. In contemporary dramatic literature, August Wilson pushes different social boundaries in *Joe Turner's Come and Gone.* In a boardinghouse in turn of the century Pittsburgh, he assembles a representative cross-section of "the sons and daughters of newly freed African slaves, . . . cut off from memory, having forgotten the names of the gods and only guessing at their faces."[81] Wilson places these culturally alienated descendants of the African diaspora in his artistic crucible and alchemically transforms them by confronting their histories, "activating" buried race memories, and opening a new horizon for them. Ibsen and Wilson are both often thought of as realistic writers, but both use realism not just to imitate reality, but also to transfigure it. Realism is their style.

LITERARY STYLE: GENRE AND INFLUENCE

Most often, when we think about style, we think in terms of periods or movements (for example, neoclassicism, romanticism, impressionism, expressionism, absurdism). Our tendency to look for influences and echoes of other writers is unavoidable and can be helpful. Taken out of context, however, such assessments can prove reductive or parochial. Iser's theory provides a larger context by depicting art's relationship to reality as a dialogue with its culture. As such, works of art not only interact with the traditions and conventions of their times, they also react to them. Iser groups these worldly and literary conventions together as the "repertoire" of the text, which may consist of "references to earlier works, or to social and historical norms, or to the whole culture from which the text has emerged."[82] Literary allusions, therefore, can also broach the parameters of existing cultural systems, and in the process both subsume and decontextualize the worldview of the source material. The resulting literary resonances might therefore run a gamut between irony and homage. Gerhart Hauptmann, for example, arguably Germany's most important modernist playwright (1862–1946), confronted his theatrical traditions in his masterful, little-known naturalistic tragicomedy, *The Rats.* Its main plot about a grieving mother's attempts to procure an out-of-wedlock baby after her own child's death commences only after a scene with her employer, a blustery theatrical actor-manager, a scene that brilliantly parodies Schillerian acting techniques and simultaneously contrasts with the compelling atmospheric detail bestowed upon the primary story. Stoppard's *Rosencrantz and Guildenstern Are Dead* finds in Shakespeare's minor characters absurdist embodiments of latter-day everymen, both blithe and anxious, who are barely aware of the tumultuous and, for them, almost inscrutable events that sweep them away. Stoppard clearly has fun with *Hamlet,* assuming *a priori* reverence for its fullness of detail in order to spin out his parallel literary universe from it. Even Wendy Wasserstein's *The Sisters Rosenzweig* consciously evokes Chekhov's *Three Sisters.* The moody tableau of its penultimate scene imbues these three sisters with a certain gravity of lyrical longing even while it sets up a tongue-in-cheek contrast of tone. When the following climactic scene brings each sister precipitous fulfillment, the play does not change gears just to satisfy the comedic demands of Wassersteinian form, it also gives each sister a ticket to her respective metaphorical Moscow—with a wink.

STYLE: VOICE

In the cases cited above, style stems from artists' absorption of and resistance to their culture. Literary managers, however, usually attempt to define style more individualistically. Our parlance refers to the "voice" of the writer. No one more fluently defines this subjective impetus of style than Marcel Proust.

> . . . [S]tyle for the writer, no less than color for the painter, is a question not of technique but of vision: it is the revelation . . . of the qualitative difference, the uniqueness of the fashion in which the world appears to each one of us. . . . Thanks to art, instead of seeing one world only, our own, we see that world multiply itself and we have at our disposal as many worlds as there are original artists. . . .[83]

There are as many original styles as there are original artists. Only through style can we enter the world of the work and the author. In this regard, Proust's discussion of style echoes Iser's. For even though Proust emphasizes subjective vision whereas Iser delineates a text's cultural repertoire, both form and style reflect content.

FORM AND CONTENT

Critical theory perpetually wrestles with the idea of the unity of form and content. We discussed previously the relation of art to reality in aesthetic terms. Actually, the roots of the dichotomy run deeper into philosophy which defines it as the separation between the subject (consciousness) and the object (things or thoughts). Even the Proustian epiphany above, although it seems purely aesthetic, actually turns on a cruel paradox steeped in this division. For most of his life, Proust struggled with the seemingly inviolate inscrutability of other people. Philosophically speaking, other people are subjects too, but the mind apprehends them as objects. The seminal Prussian philosopher, Immanuel Kant, probably gives the most rigorous and influential philosophical explication of this objectification. According to Kant, the scope of consciousness is limited by reason, and the scope of reason is limited by the tools of perception. We can never consciously escape our consciousness, yet humans continually long to transcend their subjectivity. Art represents one such form of subjective longing. Kant's aesthetic theory reminds us that while we impute an objective universality to our aesthetic judgments, the foundation for our judgments is subjective and has no real cognitive objective foundation.[84] The only real objectivity present in the artistic transaction lies in the artistic object itself.

The repercussions of these concepts in literary theory lead to the principle of the irreducible unity of form and content. "New Criticism," the preeminent American literary movement in mid-twentieth century, championed this unity. New Criticism insisted on an analytical methodology that begins and ends with texts alone, and inveighed against attempts to extract "meaning" from texts. At times, New Critical approaches seemed narrow, and more recent theories such as Iser's have sought to contextualize art within the world by stressing another aesthetic unity, the unity of expression and reception. In the current political climate, however, no aesthetic unity seems sacrosanct. The political right routinely pries images from artistic contexts in order to impute onto them a subversive content of their own devising, while readers of liberal conscience unblinkingly impute political incorrectness in the work they evaluate. Such discussions reduce art to the level of pamphleteering.

FORM AND CRAFT

The unity of form and content does not preclude independent analysis of artistic form. Ultimately, an artist must work with the materials of form to create the artistic object. This formal work can be defined as "craft," and artists cannot find their true style without mastering their craft. Playwrights are no different from musicians who rigorously practice scales, arpeggios, harmonics, and chromatics before attempting to compose or improvise. Craft becomes the language of expression. Analysis can isolate and evaluate the craft of a text, but it rends and changes its quality if it overlooks style in the process. In this regard, the nature of artistic form resembles the nature of light as conceived in quantum theory. Form is comprised of a style/craft duality, just as light is comprised of a wave/particle duality. When one looks at form as style, it behaves like style. When one looks at form as craft, it behaves like craft.

For some, the original critic of craft is Aristotle. In fact, Aristotle's detractors might call him the original dissector of craft, breaking tragedy down into six elements, with a rather self-evident and linear accent on plot. As a literary manager, I have learned to defend Aristotle's emphasis on plot and action. There's a reason every prominent theory of acting since Stanislavski stresses action. (Ed. note: Compare Weeks on this point.) Plays need a motor. While plots need not be linear, characters need playable actions. In my work, however, Aristotle's four secondary categories—thought, diction, spectacle, and music—serve as even more valuable tools for differentiating the styles of individual dramatists. (Ed. note: See also Devin on Artistotle in section three.)

"Thought," which Aristotle describes as the ideas expressed by the characters, suggests the play's ideas and point of view. This point of view translates directly into its organic language, or "diction." For example, the piercing intelligence, unyielding principles, and passionate lust for experience in David Hare's work is reflected by its elliptical subtextual leaps, its acerbic wit, and distinctively frosty outbursts.[85] The droll, enigmatic, lonely world of Neal Bell's work finds expression in relentlessly clever and heartsick characters who by turns elbow each other to interject one last quip, or drop emotionally laden subjects like hot potatoes.[86] The late Harry Kondoleon's "sad, scary, funny" world pits characters who are both obsessively delighted by worldly ephemera and gnawed at by an insatiable hunger for ever elusive spiritual clarity.[87] His language concomitantly spins out effortlessly hilarious bon mots, stops on a dime, and drops all masks with utter, forlorn simplicity, before hurtling feverishly off into orbit again.

"Spectacle," that most maligned category, need not only refer to the cheap visual thrills generated throughout the history of theater from *deus ex machina* to the sudden appearance of a live bear chasing a character off stage, or through a crashing chandelier or on-stage helicopter landing.[88] The burst of fireworks that goes off with the presentation of Big Daddy's birthday cake in *Cat on a Hot Tin Roof* provides an expressionistic descant that accentuates his Zeus-like stature in the play. The appearance of the sole leaf on the tree in the second act of *Waiting for Godot* casts a mysterious expectancy over events that otherwise seem to degenerate slowly through repetition. But spectacle need not refer only to a play's scenographic elements. It also suggests the presentness of the actors on the stage and illustrates the ability of great dramatists to theatricalize. Mother Courage's silent scream when she learns of the death of her son, Swiss Cheese, and "denies him three times" to save her own skin, and Ruth's sensual crossing and uncrossing of stockinged legs in *The Homecoming,* and the powerful image of fecundity and refuse evoked in *Buried Child* when Tilden heaps corn on Dodge's lap—are all examples of unique theatricalization, physicalized by the actors.

"Song," the final Aristotelian category is usually ignored or considered relevant only to the novelty forms of opera and musical theater. However, just as spectacle can refer to the visual aspect of the performed play, so can song refer to the aural aspect of the performed play, as in the troll-like eruptions emitted by Goober's children in *Cat On a Hot Tin Roof,* or the forlorn broken string near the end of *The Cherry Orchard,* or even performed music itself, as at the conclusion of the Pericles/Marina reunion scene in *Pericles.* Beyond this, great plays also have an almost instinctive orchestral shape and innate musicality based on tone, rhythm, and tempo. Obviously, the choral odes, solo arias, and stychomythic interchanges in Greek tragedies bear musical features, even though they are rarely sung these days. But these principles apply just as readily to modern dramatic literature. *Three Sisters,* for example, achieves a symphonic sweep because of the distinct, movement-like tone of each of its acts. (The restrained, dark lyricism of act 2 and the febrile vivace of the fire-driven third act provide classic models of second and third symphonic movements). In the same way, the contemplative, fragmented effusions in *Play,* Beckett's bottled, boulevard *menage à trois,* or the theme-and-variations playfulness of Mac Wellman's *Terminal Hip* invite musical as much as textual analysis.

FORM AND PROCESS

In all these examples, the fusion of worldview, inspiration, and craft creates style. This creative process is complex and sometimes a little perverse. Each writer and each work develops individually and organically. Problematic areas in a writer's work may constitute part of the style that enables the form as a whole to take flight. Edmund Wilson's seminal collection of essays, *The Wound and the Bow,* examines prominent writers from this perspective. His final chapter on Sophocles's *Philoctetes* provides the book with its central image. Wilson finds in the character of the afflicted archer a compelling metaphor for the maladjusted artist, the person whose wizardry with bow and arrow is a direct outcome of a festering, hobbling foot wound: "The victim of a malodorous disease which renders him abhorrent to society and periodically degrades him and makes him helpless is also the master of a superhuman art which everyone has to respect and which the normal man finds he needs."[89] Without his wound, Philoctetes would not have cultivated his archery skills. In works of art, problem areas or "weaknesses" sometimes activate the voice of the work and determine its design.

Albert Innaurato's *The Transfiguration of Benno Blimpie,* for example, tested the ingenuity of early producers because of its jolting shifts in tone and its seemingly uncastable title role. In the play, the grotesquely obese Benno sequesters himself in his South Philadelphia apartment and recalls his harrowing childhood while eating himself into nonexistence. The tone shifts between exaggeratedly harsh reenacted memories of his truculent parents and his benign but lecherous grandfather's craving for a neighborhood girl, and Benno's dark, rhapsodic odes of spiritual pain and yearning. The present tense of the play seems to carry no action whatsoever. Benno does not move. In fact, when he talks, he refers to himself almost solely in the third person. The dramaturgical problems of this play proved insoluble by attempts to finesse its extremity or its disjunctions. The reductive naturalism of the first production with an overweight actor in the title role proved disastrous. The memory scenes seemed earthbound and merely unpleasant, and the monologues seemed forced and static. It seemed clear that Benno's transfiguration could occur only if his girth seemed almost impossibly mountainous. The subsequent Playwrights Horizons studio production attempted to solve this problem by casting a normal sized actor and putting him in a fat suit. The falsity of the suit underlined the breach in Benno's self-image and the almost zen self-abnegation in the lyrical monologues. This not only contextualized the ugliness of Benno's memories, it also led naturally to a stunning, integral climax (unnoted in the published version of the text). When Benno unzipped his fat-suit and stepped free from himself, he was literally transfigured. In this way the production embraced and exaggerated the seeming "problems" of grotesqueness and inaction in the text and tempered them with artifice and beauty. This *coup de théâtre* would not have happened if its "reader," producer André Bishop, had failed to understand how the potential greatness of the play came directly out of its apparent flaws.

THE READER'S RESPONSE

The reader, then, must actually become a producer of the text. The core of Iser's Reception Theory hinges upon this problem of the reader's response.

> [T]he literary work has two poles, which we might call the artistic and the aesthetic: the artistic pole is the author's text and the aesthetic is the realization accomplished by the reader. In view of this polarity, it is clear that the work itself . . . must inevitably be virtual in character, as it cannot be reduced to the reality of the text or to the subjectivity of the reader, and it is from this virtuality that it derives its dynamism. As the reader passes through the various perspectives offered by the text and relates the different views and patterns to one another he sets the work in motion, and so sets himself in motion, too.[90]

In point of fact, this polarity begins during the process of creation. Artists are also readers of their own work, and the work remains "virtual" until they "realize" it. In Proust's terms, the act of artistic creation is really an act of discovery of a pre-existent truth.[91] The aesthetic response of the reader depends upon an analogous process of discovery. Undoubtedly, Proust had something like this in mind when he said, "In reality every reader is, while he is reading, the reader of his own self."[92] Reading activates the text. Roland Barthes takes this idea one step further: "The goal of literary work . . . is to make the reader no longer a consumer, but a producer of the text."[93] It goes without saying that the very essence of dramatic art depends upon this subsequent production of the text by actors, directors, designers, and audience In fact, Barthes's articulation of an ideal reading process as a continual rereading of the text that "multiplies it in its variety and its plurality," and requires not "consumption, but play,"[94] seems a prerequisite to the reading of dramatic texts. What is the rehearsal process if not a continual rereading of a text and a discovery of its depth and multiplicity?

But because of the virtual character of the dramatic text before it reaches production, and because of the multiplicity of readings required to realize it, its development is a fragile process. Proust, Iser, and Barthes write primarily about finished, nondramatic literary texts. In drama, however, producers, actors, directors, and designers give their own subjective responses to the text while it is still developing. Yet for a play to "work," we must hear just one voice—the playwright's. And although formal analysis can break a play down into its parts, the question of style unites them all. Similarly, although a reader must produce a play inwardly and assume the roles of director, designers, and actors to activate it, the reader begins by trying to enter the world of the playwright. Plays usually start with a writer alone in a room, following an impulse, shaping an internal vision, listening to voices, and formulating questions. A literary manager's first responsibility is to that writer.

In fact, few of the scripts literary managers read actually get produced. The real job of a literary manager is not to find production-ready scripts but to discover writers with distinctive voices. Literary managers read work by writers who are still developing. Playwrights never spring up ready made without flaws. Some writers develop slowly, some make quantum leaps, some write the same play over and over. The literary manager is bound to read an entire spectrum of writers. It helps to put these writers in an evolutionary perspective, as Proust did when describing artistic dilettantes and enthusiasts as "the first attempts of nature in her struggle to create the artist, . . . as touching to contemplate as those early machines which tried to leave the ground and could not, but which yet held within them, if not the secret, . . . at least the desire of flight."[95] Geniuses do not emerge from a vacuum. Artists toil alone but receive inspiration from and react against the artistic climate. The broad spectrum of writers that submits scripts to a theater is a necessary part of this artistic climate.

CONCLUSION

In the end, a literary manager must be able to integrate a variety of responses and perspectives to activate a work fully. The broadest range of these responses seems to demand a paradoxical combination of encyclopedic perspective on the entire culture, and ardent humility to listen to the voice of the text and to hear it even in its most problematic and unformed state. Critical theory can help literary managers broaden their perspectives and deepen them. It can also help them see the parts of a text more clearly: the coherence of a piece's dramatic action, the depth and consistency of characterization, point of view, language, physicality, musicality, social context, and literary antecedents. Yet literary theory also reminds the critic not merely to inventory a text's parts but also to keep sight of its unity, its style. Furthermore, the ability to analyze plays intellectually and historically does not preclude the ability to respond to them emotionally and subjectively. Theory is analogous to craft for the artist. It gives the reader the means to find the text's multiplicity. In fact, theory provides a foundation for the reader's subjective response to the text. In the end, reading is an art unto itself, an organic combination of objective and subjective responses. Literary managers need every tool at their disposal to broaden their perspective, deepen their understanding, and open their heart.

New Play Development and the "New" Dramaturg:

The Dramaturg's Approach to the First Draft

by **Paul C. Castagno**

PAUL C. CASTAGNO, PhD, is director and dramaturg of the New Playwrights' Program and heads the MFA program in playwriting and dramaturgy at the University of Alabama. His articles on the new dramaturgy of Mac Wellman, Len Jenkin, and Eric Overmyer have appeared in *Theatre Topics* and *New Theatre Quarterly.* He served as editor of "Voice of the Dramaturg," a joint effort between LMDA and the journal *Theatre Symposium* (1985). He has written on *commedia* for the *Journal of Dramatic Theory and Criticism* and is the author of *The Early Commedia dell'Arte (1550-1621):The Mannerist Context* (Peter Lang, 1994). Dr. Castagno is on the advisory board of the Southern Writers' Project. His text on the new dramaturgy, *Playwriting 2000,* is under review by several major publishers.

How can dramaturgs, especially those not experienced in new play development, ensure that their interactions with playwrights start positively, then proceed in an enriching and fulfilling manner? A crucial factor is likely the dramaturg's ability to understand the creative process of the new playwright.

While most seasoned dramaturgs recognize certain "problems" in early drafts as by-products of a playwright's process,[96] the new dramaturg itches to fix "mistakes" in the play. What may result is either a breakdown in communication and trust or, an implicit struggle over possession of the work. A better knowledge of what is really happening during the making of a play will give the dramaturg confidence to interact constructively quickly and continually throughout the development process. Certain practices and techniques can be learned and then modified to meet the given situation.

Communication Skills. If you are a dramaturg who is not a writer you are best off to join a playwrights' workshop to experience firsthand the anxieties, doubts, and emotional investment involved in writing a play and to develop through practice an articulate, concise feedback style that will serve well in interactions with playwrights.[97] Attending play readings followed by feedback sessions provides opportunities to closely observe the manner of each respondent (adjudicator or spectator). How do they begin? How is each approach received by the playwright? What is central to their feedback style? How were your comments received and, what was your affective response to the exchange?[98] For better or worse, you must also familiarize yourself with the peculiar cant of play development; use these sessions to get as much practice as you can.

In a classroom setting, roleplay conversations between playwright and dramaturg. Observers should take notes dealing specifically with the interaction, not the content or form of the scene or play. Key in on body language, transitions, balance between nurture and critique, listening, subtexts, and nature of questioning. Discuss with playwright and dramaturg how they felt during the interaction, note blocked areas, others that could be improved. Reenact interactions that were strained or difficult. The dramaturg may need to modify inadvertent natural behaviors or physical mannerisms that would otherwise go unchanged. Similarly, the dramaturg can gauge receptivity through the playwright's nonverbal signs or body language. Strive for high-intensity listening, and pay attention to use of clichés or jargon, which sometime substitute for clearer understanding.

Understanding the Creative Process.   In any first draft a moderate to substantial proportion of the writing will be for the playwright's benefit. This may take the form of extra scenes developed to get the writer from point A to point C: a three-page monologue that details the protagonist's epiphany or moment of peripeteia, the extrapolation of subtext into the dialogue, or the enumeration of minor characters. There may also be a pronounced shift across genre or idiom, for example, from absurdism to conventional realism.

The early draft of a script represents an explorative, not definitive creative step, so the dramaturgic approach should accommodate several potential strategies for development. The dramaturg, in the first meeting with the playwright, should attempt to find out where the playwright "is" in the play or what the playwright senses about the play, and the playwright's relationship to the subject matter: personal, researched, journalistic, subjective, or idea-based.

The dramaturg should realize that structure is not usually a conscious concern even for experienced playwrights, particularly when they are actually writing the play.

While chairing the Southeastern Theatre Conference (SETC) New Play Project, I directed a staged reading of the 1992 winner, *Locked Doors and Lightning Bugs.* I mentioned to the playwright that my key to the play was its structural transitions from realistic interactive scenes to private dream-like passages, which explored the psychology of the female protagonist. She confided that the structure of the play had become apparent to her only after public readings and feedback sessions—a year after her initial drafts were penned. While a sense of the structure is implied in the first drafts of a playscript, not until later in the development of the play should it assume primary focus. Dramaturgs should not impose "school-taught" paradigms on the playwright. (Ed. note: See Weeks in this section.)

Voice.   Often, the "voice" of a script from an inexperienced playwright relates directly to what is influencing that writer at the time. A new playwright may try to affect David Mamet's stylized dialogue only to get stuck in trivializing profanities; or become enamored of Pinter's laconic rejoinders only to succumb to its potential for vagueness and inanity—fascinated by the surface effects on the page while failing to examine the complete context through which the language operates. Verbal imitation or posturing is generally one step in a beginning playwright's journey toward self-definition. The dramaturg can mitigate dialogue problems by emphasizing language as strategy or by touting character-specific speech.

Redundancy. Dramaturgs need to understand how to deal with redundancy, as when scenes or segments of speeches are repeated throughout the script. A common species of redundancy is the parallel scene, in which one scene follows another, interrupted by a blackout. Certain characters may change, but "the givens" (time of day, setting) and emotional horizon remain the same; and so, the sequence lacks contour. The playwright may be focused on problems other than time or place, neglecting the environmental givens. Significant change in time of day, sense of occasion, or physical state of the characters can *promote* a shift in the emotional horizon of the play. Altered conditions can motivate action, provide contour, and develop characterization, while enhancing the theatrical values in the script. On the other hand, the dramaturg should be aware of redundancy that might be a dramatic strategy. In Mac Wellman's Obie-Award winning *Sincerity Forever* subsequent scenes in act 1 repeat almost verbatim the lines spoken by a changing retinue of characters. Redundancy as a structural device calls attention to the artifice behind such traditional conventions as linearity, character-specific speech, and emotional through-line.

Point of Attack. "The beginning is not always the beginning." Dramaturgs should recognize that a playwright needs to get started—somewhere, anywhere. Robert Small, director of the Shenandoah Arts Play Development Workshops, posits that most new plays "do not get going at all until about the twenty-fifth page."[99] This moment becomes the real starting point of the work. In "workshopping" a new script, Small emphasizes flexibility in determining the optimum starting point. The play's point of attack is a prime target of revision; most modern plays start somewhere in the middle of the action, often with a strong sense of theatricality to initially attract the spectator. The dramaturg should describe at what point they truly became interested in the play, and that point's relationship to the point of attack. Consider possible strategies for handling exposition or character development that would alter in revision. Generally, reducing exposition about matters of theme or character allows the audience to develop these conclusions on their own.

Endings. Many first drafts contain no ending whatsoever or just cease abruptly in midstream. A weak or absent ending may indicate problems in conceptualization or ambivalence about the direction of the narrative, or it may simply be an outgrowth of the word processor—you boot up the computer, open your document, and there you are—act 1, scene 1. The writer starts revising scene 1 instead of completing the fledgling draft.

In a 1993 playwrights' workshop at the Kennedy Center with Pulitzer Prize-winning playwright Robert Schenkkan, the question arose, "How do you get to the end of the first draft when you need to stop at some point before you finish?" Schenkkan answered that he picks up where he left off the day before, in the midst of an unresolved segment or scene, maintaining continuity by not finishing the scene he is working on. Other playwrights and dramaturgs have used actors to improvise possible endings.[100] Taping the session may be useful to the playwright. If the play needs more work in its final, underdeveloped scenes, then schedule them early in the rehearsal process when time for experimentation or exploration is more available. Another option is to schedule two or three scenes together to allow exploration of continuity. Finally, it is important to assess how much the playwright can effectively revise between workshops or rehearsals. It is advantageous to leave in a workshop schedule as many open dates as possible where major revisions are anticipated.

Character Conception.   Often, in the rush to create, the new playwright can cease to "hear" the voice of each individual character. The result is character voices that are interchangeable in the play. The playwright may also have difficulty focusing on a major character's development across consecutive scenes, or may flesh out minor characters so thoroughly that they vie with main characters.

The question, "Whose play is this?" becomes crucial during development because occasionally a different character might emerge from what the playwright originally intended. This shift can resist detection, which is why the dramaturg should examine each character carefully to determine who is at the center of action, who is making things happen, and when the main character appears passive or is acted upon. Characters that seem flat, two dimensional, or stereotyped, usually signal a lack of specificity in dialogue, behavior, or relationship to the surroundings.

One solution to character development concerns emerged a few years ago, when I dramaturged a student's prize-winning play for the American College Theatre Festival (ACTF) short play division. After reading the first draft, it was clear that the so-called protagonist was neither interesting nor dramatic. Several rehearsals followed as members of an acting class improvised actions based upon the characters' fictionalized biographies, which were composed by the writer. The biographies served the dual functions of establishing a central character and strengthening all of the characters in the play.

The dramaturg also may need to recognize connections the play makes to the playwright's life. Where there is a personal stake underlying the dramatic one (say, a given character is based upon the playwright's father), it is best to maintain a dramaturgic focus by exploring the "what ifs" of the character in a playful, subjunctive way and encourage the playwright to transcend the factual with the *fictional*.

Theme. Many young playwrights place theme or ideas before dramatic action or characterization. As a result, characters may function as mouthpieces for the playwright's ideas or be reduced to symbolic entities or ciphers with little individuality or humanity. Some playwrights feel compelled to clarify statements or polarize them among characters to create contrast. In either case, the writer is emphasizing themes and ideas, while neither creating a dramatic situation or event that exhibits their unfolding nor defining a tangible world of the play for an audience.

Often, discussions with the playwright will seemingly contradict or rationalize how the play actually reads. "The play now exists only in the playwright's head, not on paper," is an exchange common to playwrights' workshops. Ideas do not create the dramatic, rather the dramatic generates ideas.

Risks. Where is the "gold" in the first draft? Where the playwright *risks* is where the interest lies. Dramaturgs should recognize and encourage these moments in a script, even if they somehow seem contradictory in and of themselves. It may be a character's impulsive action that, while seemingly inconsistent with what preceded, "works" in dimensionalizing the sense of role. It may be the point when the play seems to take over and manifest its "will."[101] Often, risk is centered in monologue when we see the effect of the language and situation seemingly transforming the characters as they speak—a kind of unexpected, unmasking takes place.

Dialogue. After several initial readings of the script, the dramaturg might discuss aspects of the dialogue that seem subtextual, then question how much can be subsumed as actor's work, and what should remain in the play? Locate where dialogue becomes explanatory; audiences do not need to be told what they can already see.

Goals. If this is the playwright's first production, then set two or three attainable goals to be accomplished during the workshops. If the dramaturg takes on or says too much, nothing of value will be accomplished. Be specific about the strategy being used. Strive for improvements, but tolerate imperfection. Whatever progress you can accomplish in the readings and workshop by the time rehearsals begin you need to have settled upon a revision cutoff point.

Cutting. Cutting the script is a phase of revision that best takes place in later drafts. It should be a means to specific ends: greater clarity, sense of rhythm or punch, continuity, and improving the sound of the script. Effective cutting can tune the playwright's "voice," and enhance the rhythmical quality of the scene. Earlier we dealt with the dramaturgic term, point of attack, in regard to the start of the play. Here, simply transfer that concept to the line of dialogue. The beginnings of speeches can often be trimmed. Go into the speech as much as possible, even if you eliminate the subject, or sacrifice the complete sentence. Eliminating compound or conditional verbs, for example, increases the *presence* of the spoken dialogue. The dramaturgic function, whether carried on by playwright, director, or dramaturg, is to extract the simplified essence of each line, determine what the key intent of each line is, and build rhythmically toward that point. A more invasive form of revision is called segue cutting. Here, the dramaturg attempts to target extraneous lines or beats of a dialogue in order to sharpen a sequence or provide a more rhythmic build. Where the transitional material that took the playwright from point A to point C seems superfluous, a segue cut of B may sharpen the sense of transition and sequence essential to the play's structure, while enhancing the overall rhythm, attack, and sense of pace.

Aftermath.   At the end of any development session the operation and outcomes should be assessed and evaluated. Though elements in the play's development may have failed expectations in production, this is not necessarily a cause for deep concern. Dramaturgs should review their methods and ask themselves when and where they intervened or backed off, how they were received, and their feeling at the time. It is useful to visualize and replay each interaction step by step, without self-criticism over failed opportunities. Dramaturgs develop in a gradual, organic process interspersed with glimmers and breakthroughs. Furthermore, the dramaturg who understands and nurtures the playwright's creative process will facilitate the development of both play and playwright.

The Once And Future Audience:
Dramaturgy And Children's Theater
by Suzan L. Zeder

SUZAN L. ZEDER has been recognized nationally and internationally as one of the nation's leading playwrights for family audiences. Her plays have been performed and published in all fifty states, Canada, Great Britain, Japan, Australia, Germany, Israel, and New Zealand. She is a three-time winner of the AATE Distinguished Play Award, a recipient of the Charlotte Chorpenning Playwriting Cup, and a member of the College of Fellows of the American Theatre. Dr. Zeder is a professor at the University of Texas at Austin and is the first holder of the Endowed Chair in Theatre for Youth/Playwriting, the first endowed chair in theater for youth in the United States.

Once upon a time there was an audience: gray of hair, failing of vision, hearing best what it had heard before. This audience, armed with assumptions about the true nature of art, was on a quest for confirmation rather than challenge, for validation rather than innovation, and was content to laugh and cry and applaud aesthetic anesthetic in the guise of entertainment. Once upon another time, there may come another audience—an unruly bunch of individuals, rainbow-haired, fresh of vision, and delighted by what they have never heard before. This audience, armed in ignorance of the true nature of art, will be questing for adventure, for new languages of expression, for ideas that overturn expectations, and images that reflect a world of contradictions.

The fate of the American theater rests in the hands of those who will make the plays of the future and those who will, or will not, come to see them. In the current climate of political hostility toward the arts and dwindling economic resources, the audiences of "once upon a time" are defining and shaping public perception of the state of the arts. In most communities, new plays are considered to be risky business, rather than the lifeblood that constantly renews the art form. The delicate balance of our cultural ecosystem depends upon finding informed, intelligent audiences, receptive to new work and enthusiastic about experimentation. For many theaters it is a life-and-death matter of survival. Unless we can develop strategies to cultivate the audiences of "once upon another time" there may not be another time.

All over the country, theaters look to their education and outreach programs to address the needs of developing audiences in new and dynamic ways. Dramaturgs, education directors and literary managers scramble to select seasons that appeal to previously untapped sectors of society. They devise extensive outreach efforts to smooth paths of access and promote continuing relationships with school groups and special populations. Dramaturgs in increasing numbers find themselves coming out of the library and rehearsal hall and into the classroom. Allen Kennedy's fine article, "Professional Theater and Education: Contexts for Dramaturgy," details efforts of several major theaters to provide young people with exposure to professional theater through programs that actively involve them in a variety of preshow and follow-up activities. (Ed. note: See Kennedy's article in section three of this volume.) These programs are noble in intent, pedagogically sound, and undoubtedly effective, but most offer relatively short-term solutions to a much larger problem.

Many outreach programs are either season- or production-specific, rather than on-going.[102] They also tend to involve older students in junior high or high school, an age group whose cultural perceptions and habits are largely established by the time these programs reach them. Most outreach initiatives deal with strategies that bring young people to regular offerings of the theater's mainstage season and surround these experiences with activities that build bridges between the play, the theater, and students. These programs are excellent examples of dedicated theater professionals finding a place for young people within the home of an essentially "adult" theater. Young people are invited guests, rather than family members with their own rooms. I do not negate or diminish any of these fine programs, but they cannot do the trick alone.

If theatergoing is to become a life-long habit, children and young people must be fully franchised participants in the theatrical event, not necessarily as performers, but as audience members who see their lives, their concerns, their perceptions and points of view reflected on the stage. Plays must provide opportunities for young people to find something of themselves within the dramaturgy, and must make those depictions intellectually challenging and stylistically interesting. Our task, as playwrights, dramaturgs, and directors, is to make theater as exciting as sports, as accessible as television, and as relevant as one's own reflection in a mirror—for all ages of our audience.

Before we can engage in meaningful discussion of issues related to children and theater, we must first clarify terms and clear up misconceptions. To many, the term "children's theater" conjures up visions of young children traipsing around in tights, dressed up like vegetables, performing plays about the eight basic food groups before audiences of adoring parents. To others, the term calls forth images of hyperkinetic apprentice actors dressed in colored jumpsuits performing fractured fairy tales on sets consisting of colored cubes. Both visions are a far cry from the reality of professional theater for young people today.

According to a survey undertaken by Harold Oaks, past president of the United States Center of the Association Internationale du Theatre Pour L'Enfance et la Jeunesse, ASSITEJ/USA,[103] there are more than one hundred professional children's theaters in the United States. Oaks surveyed ninety-three theaters and received responses from forty-seven companies. In that group alone, combined attendance figures exceeded nine million in a single season.

According to Oaks, budget sizes vary widely from multimillion-dollar organizations to shoestring operations held together by passion and persistence. An astonishing 16 percent of the responding theaters have operating budgets in excess of five million dollars.[104] The average budget of the surveyed companies was more than a million dollars. Theater facilities vary from gleaming new complexes complete with multiple stages, classroom and shop spaces, and offices that would be the envy of many regional theaters, to touring companies with administrative offices in the back seat of a Volkswagen bus. More than half of the companies tour to schools and perform in school settings, braving ungodly early performance times, and less than ideal spaces to bring art to the "cafetorium" floor. Many companies also have their own home theaters where productions are staged and children are brought in large yellow buses to see daytime performances with their teachers and parents. Most also schedule weekend and evening performances for family audiences. Despite their diversity, all of these companies share a common commitment to bringing the living art of theater to audiences often overlooked and undervalued by their peers in the "adult" theater world.

Until recently the field of children's theater was often ignored by the larger dramaturgical community. Children's theater was either dismissed as something done by children, with or for other children; or mystified as a special art form—an important, worthy endeavor, performed by specialists with a kind of missionary zeal. Whether it was deemed too insignificant or too holy to be discussed, the results were the same: a critical lack of discourse about the nature of the work and the dynamics of the audience.

Many theater professionals and educators assume that children's theater focuses entirely upon a narrow population of children and young people. Indeed the term, "Theatre for Young Audiences (TYA)," promotes this limited view. Although this term is widely used and accepted among professional children's theaters as well as their adult counterparts, it tends to reinforce the notion that these plays and productions are intended only for children. In recent years many professional companies have witnessed a startling increase in the number of adults attending performances, with or without children. A subtle but important shift in perception of how the field defines itself is reflected in a recent change in the mission statement of ASSITEJ/USA, the primary service organization for children's theater professionals. Since its founding in 1965, the mandate of ASSITEJ/USA has encouraged "the development of professional theater for audiences of young people and their families." In the revised mission statement of 1995, the organization seeks to "promote and develop professional theater concerned with the unique perspective of young people."[105] This redefinition places emphasis on the development of art rather than the age of the audience and calls upon both the organization and the field "to widen its frame of reference to include all theaters, artists, and educators who seek to explore the domain of the child world in the multiple languages of theater."[106]

Within the organizational structures of many professional children's theaters, there has been enormous growth and change in the past decade. An increasing number of companies including Seattle Children's Theatre, Stage One: The Louisville Children's Theatre, The Minneapolis Children's Theater Company and School, and the Omaha Children's Theater have added dramaturgs to their staffs or have designated an associate director or literary manager/education director to undertake duties that mirror those of dramaturgs in "adult" companies. These same individuals usually coordinate outreach activities similar to those described by Kennedy in his study. Because most young audiences are made up of school groups, extended families, and special populations, outreach is the primary thrust, rather than the secondary effort, of virtually all children's theaters. In addition to outreach and educational activities, dramaturgs are increasingly concerned with production dramaturgy and new play development.

These are exciting times in children's theater. In the past five or six years an unprecedented number of serious and significant plays have been created by major playwrights for companies specializing in work for young audiences. Some are veteran writers of plays for young people such as the late Aurand Harris, James Still, and myself. Others have been drafted from the ranks of the regional and Off-Broadway Theaters. New plays by Mark Medoff, Connie Congdon, Tina Howe, Jim Leonard, Mac Wellman, Eric Overmyer, Y York, and Steven Dietz have recently been commissioned and produced by children's theaters. For many of these writers the opportunity to write for younger audiences has been a profoundly moving experience. In May of 1995, I chaired a panel discussion that featured Overmyer, York, Dietz, and Still.[107] All spoke eloquently of how their work for young audiences had challenged their notions of craft and widened the horizons of their art. This wellspring of activity is partially due to major funding initiatives by the National Endowment for the Arts, the Lila Wallace Reader's Digest Foundation, and generous support from private foundations such as the Bonderman and Eccles Foundations and the Theater for Youth Chair at the University of Texas at Austin.[108]

As the canon of dramatic literature for young people deepens and improves, the need for effective production dramaturgy also increases. Higher commission fees and increased production resources are not the only forces attracting playwrights to write for young people. There is potential allure in the material itself. According to Oaks' survey, folk and fairy tales and legends comprise more than one quarter of the plays staged for young audiences in a given year, and adaptations of classic and contemporary children's literature accounts for a third of the works produced.[109] While the motivations of many companies are undoubtedly more commercial than dramaturgical, playwrights have much to mine in the creation of new work based upon old sources.

The books and stories that touched us deeply as children often have similar power to reach us as adults on a different but no less potent level. Myths, legends, and fairy tales date back to an oral tradition, to a time before the in-

vention of childhood as a social construct and were intended for the entertainment and instruction of the whole community. When these stories are
treated with respect and plumbed for their depth and complexity, they speak
to adults on the level of archetype and metaphor. The raw "stuff" of myths, legends and tales reaches into the deepest part of our collective unconscious
and serve as the touchstones of our cultural identities. The best children's theater, like the best children's literature, speaks to the widest possible audience
of human beings who have in common the fact that they were once children.

Avant garde theater artists are keenly aware of the power of these timeless,
ageless sources. Works such as *Warrior Ant* by Lee Breuer and Mabou Mines,
the cross-cultural experimentation of Peter Brook, the theater/movement
work of Martha Clarke and Pina Bausch, draw their inspiration from mythic
sources. Dramaturgs have been vitally important in these creative collaborations. The success of many experimental ventures is due, in large part, to the
analytical and historical contributions of gifted dramaturgs working closely
with visionary directors and choreographers. I do not suggest that all or any
of this specific work is appropriate for children, but I do look to the depth of
their dramaturgical investigations as potential models. There is no less need
for dramaturgical integrity when these same sources are tapped to create
plays for younger audiences.

The problem with many plays for children based upon myths, legends, and
fairy and folk tales, is that they fail to find the complexity within the simplicity
inherent in this material. From the Brothers Grimm to Disney, well-meaning
adults have felt the need to simplify, sanitize, pasteurize, and moralize these
tales into a pabulum suitable for children. They wrongly assume that young
people need one-dimensional characters, linear plots, and themes that can be
summed up in simple homilies. It's not children who require these changes,
but their adult caretakers: the parents, teachers and school administrators who
buy tickets, book shows, and approve field trips. In an attempt to appeal to
children while not offending adults, myths are domesticated into shadows of
their former selves. Folk tales and legends are fractured into cartoons, as their
larger than life heroes are turned into buffoons. Fairy tales, robbed of their
psychological complexity and contradictions, become moral lessons fraught
with cultural and gender stereotypes. There is a critical need to find dramaturgs who are familiar with the historical and cultural perspectives of the
material and are armed with some understanding of child development and
psychology to assist both playwrights and directors in their journeys through
the rich wonderland of these not-so-simple sources.

There is also much to be explored in contemporary themes and original
plays that put young people at the center of the drama. Even a cursory glance
at any newspaper, on any day, in any city of our nation will provide ample evidence of children in crisis in a world seemingly out of control. Our society is
poised in paradox as children represent our worst fears and best hopes
for the future of civilization. Behind the screaming headlines about juvenile

violence, apathy, and despair are the quieter voices telling stories about the wit and wisdom, the courage and compassion of children. Theater is ideally suited to tell both positive and painful stories, to examine critical issues and choices, to offer cautionary tales and to celebrate the survival skills of young people in a hostile world.[110]

Some of the most interesting work of this kind is being done by children and teenagers through programs such as the excellent work of Young Playwrights Inc. (YPI) in New York. Originally founded in 1981 by Steven Sondheim, YPI "introduces young people to the theater and encourages their self-expression through the art of playwriting."[111] This Obie–award winning organization sponsors a variety of playwriting workshops and competitions to "identify, develop, and encourage playwrights aged eighteen or younger, and to develop new work for the theater, and to aid in the creation of the next generation of professional playwrights."[112] Each year this program receives hundreds of submissions from all over the country from writers under the age of nineteen. Several semifinalist scripts are chosen by a blue-ribbon panel of experts,[113] but each submission is given a full dramaturgical critique by carefully screened and selected readers. Semifinalist plays receive a developmental workshop in New York, with full support from dramaturgs and directors chosen from some of the leading names in the Broadway and Off-Broadway theater. From these offerings, three or four festival plays are selected to be given full Off-Broadway productions and a highly-publicized run at Playwrights Horizon.

Programs based upon the Young Playwrights Inc. model are springing up all over the country. In Austin, the Texas Young Playwright's Festival offers playwriting classes and workshops in high schools and community arts centers, and sponsors an annual competition based upon the New York model. Because there is a critical need for dramaturgical support and guidance to provide encouragement within a context of craft, I teach a graduate seminar in new play dramaturgy at the University of Texas at Austin. As one assignment for this course, students serve as dramaturgs for semifinalist and finalist plays for the Texas Young Playwrights Festival. Student dramaturgs find their work with these young writers to be among the most personally rewarding and satisfying experiences of their graduate school careers. Some of the most thoughtful, insightful work I have ever seen from student dramaturgs has been done in these mentoring relationships. The playwrights seem to feel comfortable with a dramaturg closer to their own age than their teachers or drama coaches. The voices of these young writers are often raw, their messages often angry, but they must be listened to—not just for the potential they may hold for the future, but also for the unique perspective they offer of our present condition.

In professional new play dramaturgy for children's theater there has been a surge of activity in the past decade. Since 1985 four major national programs have brought teams of playwrights, directors, dramaturgs, actors, and resource people together with the express purpose of developing new work for young audiences in intensive workshops and residencies. Children's theaters have always commissioned and produced an enormous volume of new work. Indeed, one of the problems of the field has been the tendency for theaters to commission new work rather than produce plays created by other theaters. This has resulted in a mentality where new plays are hastily created and produced only to vanish as soon as the set of the original production is struck. This practice is changing as shown by the programs described below. Never before have there been so many places to workshop and develop new plays for young people.

In 1985 Dr. Dorothy Webb[114] founded the National Youth Theater Playwriting Competition and Symposium at Indiana University/Purdue University at Indianapolis, (IUPUI). This event was the first of its kind in the United States. It combined a new play competition that solicited manuscripts from beginners and seasoned professionals, with a symposium where the "winning plays" would be produced. Runners-up would be given staged readings before an invited audience of publishers, producers, playwrights, directors, students, and others interested in new plays for young people. The symposium also included panel discussions, a key note address, and opportunities to network with leaders in the field.

After the first year of this biennial event, the format was revised to change the emphasis from production to development. Scripts were in relatively early drafts and the focus on production rushed both playwrights and directors to make choices that would assure a good showing. Just at the time when scripts needed exploration and opening up, many directors felt the need to get results . . . fast! With the elimination of full production of one script, four scripts could be selected to be given week-long workshops culminating in readings and public discussion. In 1993 dramaturgs were added to the mix. At present, teams of playwrights, directors, and dramaturgs are selected from all over the country to begin work by phone, fax, or face to face, weeks before the spring rehearsal period in Indianapolis.

According to Webb, "At IUPUI, dramaturgy is now a very important part of the process. The dramaturg works within a structure defined by the playwright. . . . If a playwright refuses the assistance of a dramaturg, the play will not be workshopped."[115] Webb hastens to add that it is "important to choose dramaturgs very, very carefully. I look to colleagues to find someone who is a teacher; a humanist; a gentle, clear communicator; someone who can lead a playwright with good questioning to new realizations."[116] In past years Webb has involved professional dramaturgs such as Janet Allen and Andrew Tsao from the Indiana Repertory Theater, but she has also generously provided training opportunities to advanced graduate students who were sufficiently experienced to handle this delicate assignment. As The National Youth Theatre Playwriting Competition and Symposium has evolved over the years, it has helped to educate the field of children's theater about the ways dramaturgs, directors, and playwrights can successfully collaborate in a new play's growth process.

Another model is provided by the Sundance Children's Theatre that evolved out of the highly prestigious Sundance Playwright's Lab. Since 1981, the Playwright's Lab, under the visionary leadership of David Kranes, has provided the adult theater world with a safe haven for the development of new work. Some of the most important plays in the contemporary dramatic literature have come from this program including: *Miss Evers' Boys, Tales of the Lost Formicans, The Day Room, Angels in America,* and *The Kentucky Cycle.*

The Sundance Children's Theater (SCT), was founded by Robert Redford in 1990 as part of the Sundance Institute in Utah. According to its mission statement, SCT intends to "develop a new body of children's literature for the stage and the screen." In pursuit of that mission, SCT activities include "the commissioning and development of new plays, production of children's plays, adaptations for film and television, and publication."[117] During the summer residency period of the Playwright's Lab, scripts for young audiences receive the same dramaturgical treatment as the scripts intended for adults. Resource teams consisting of a director, dramaturg, actors, and artists from a variety of disciplines, are assigned to each project. According to Artistic Director, Jerry Patch, "Playwrights are encouraged to hold fast to their vision and to be open to new ways of working and of thinking about the realization of that vision."[118] Daily work sessions might include scene rehearsals, readings, improvisation, consultation with musical or dance resources, and discussions with affiliate artists such as storytellers, historians, scientists, visual artists. These resource people contribute a unique perspective to illuminate the writer's work to the writer. Intense one-on-one interaction with the dramaturg is on-going throughout this experience. "Dramaturgs have always been part of this process. They are there to assist the playwright, but the playwright is the bus driver."[119]

Toward the end of the workshop, the plays are read to the group, but outsiders who have not been part of the process are not permitted to attend the readings. This is in contrast to the symposium at IUPUI that invites a national audience to the readings. After the readings at Sundance, discussions are focused around the specific concerns of the playwright. The leadership at Sundance is emphatic that the safety of the laboratory experience not be compromised by a public showing that places the emphasis on marketing and networking works in progress.

Combining the national conference aspect of the IUPUI model with the intense focus on workshop from Sundance, yet another new play development project takes places every other year at the John F. Kennedy Center for the Performing Arts in Washington D.C. "New Visions/New Voices" was founded in 1991 by Carol Sullivan, then producing director of the Kennedy Center Theater for Young People. The purpose of this program is to "aid and assist in the process of developing new plays for young audiences."[120] According to Kim Peter Kovac, current program manager for youth and family programs, the focus of New Visions/New Voices is a bit different from the contest format of IUPUI, in that a professional theater, or university theater department, proposes a specific project that they hope to premiere in an upcoming season. Included in this proposal is some indication of a creative team of playwright, composer, director, and perhaps a dramaturg. The proposal may center on an idea for a play rather than a formal script. "The idea can take many different forms: a story, a scene, an incomplete script, or a full script."[121] Kovac notes that one of the things that makes New Visions/New Voices unique is that every project is in different stages of process. Some projects start as a short story or a fragment of a story, while others are almost finished and have had previous readings or workshop productions. Some projects focus upon the integration of music, not rewriting the text. "We hope it's all about process" says Kovac. During the week-long rehearsal period, six to eight new plays are workshopped. Resources provided include actors, dramaturgs, and technical support, if so desired. "Our hope," says Kovac, "is that after a week, a play is better and the playwright has learned something. . . . [The play] doesn't have to get to a specific place."

Despite Kovac's assurances about a process-over-product philosophy, the plays are presented as staged readings before a national conference similar to the IUPUI symposium. Following each reading is some form of discussion that involves an evaluative and analytical response to the work. Over the years these discussions have taken many forms. In 1991, one person commented on all shows. In 1993, the discussion was led by a four-member panel that included a dramaturg, a playwright, and a director. In 1995 an eight-member panel included a discussion leader, a music director, a booking agent for professional theater, a presenter, and four young people ages 11–17. The whole process of providing playwrights with feedback in a responsible, constructive manner is an important aspect of virtually all developmental programs. New Visions/New Voices is still exploring ways to accomplish this.

The role of the dramaturg at New Visions/New Voices also has evolved. In 1991, dramaturgs were not included in the process at all. In 1993 and 1995, Robert Small, director of Shenandoah Playwright's Retreat in Staunton, Virginia, served as a resident dramaturg for anyone requesting his services. According to Kovac, before rehearsals began none of the workshop teams seemed interested; but by the time the playwrights and directors were actually working, five of the seven groups solicited his insights and help. Dramaturgical support is not a required part of the New Visions/New Voices process as it is at IUPUI. Often, the director acts as a dramaturg. Kovac believes that offering the services of a dramaturg is an appropriate resource, and that dramaturgs need to be involved before the workshop by phone or fax. Next year Kovac hopes to include two consulting dramaturgs before and during the workshop week.

The final program to be discussed is one I have developed at the University of Texas at Austin. Five years ago, when I was offered an Endowed Chair in Theater for Youth/Playwriting, I was asked to name the most pressing need in the field of theater for young audiences. I believed then, and still do, that providing on-going dramaturgical support and developmental resources to new plays and playwrights working in nontraditional forms is of primary importance. I was also aware of the need to train dramaturgs and directors in techniques of new play development, and the only way to do this was to insist that the developmental experiences became a living laboratory for students in direct and tangible ways.

Each year the Department of Theater and Dance enters into a creative partnership with a professional theater to design a series of developmental experiences for a new play that will eventually premiere at the "home" theater. Like New Visions/New Voices, projects may be at early stages of development, but our commitment to dramaturgical support may last for as long as two to three years and carry a project from scenario and early drafts through full production. The nature of the developmental experience is not pre-determined by an established workshop structure or schedule. Although three of the four projects we have undertaken so far have included one- to two-week rehearsal periods, some projects might be better served by smaller-scale work sessions between playwrights, composers, choreographers, and a few students to assist and observe in a less structured environment. In addition to student actors, UT faculty directors, movement specialists, designers, choreographers, librarians, and technical personnel have also served as consultants or workshop participants.

Our first project, undertaken in 1991, was David Saar's *The Yellow Boat*. This play is based on the true story of David's son, Benjamin, the first child in the state of Arizona to be diagnosed with the AIDS virus. After Benjamin's death at eight years of age in 1987, David and his wife Sonja looked back at the literally hundreds of drawings, paintings, and sketches Benjamin left behind and realized that his entire life was reflected in his art work. There, in a child's eloquent iconography, were images of his battle with AIDS, depictions of the fear and prejudice he encountered from a frightened community, and a chronicle of the spiritual journey that transformed his life and death into an inspiration for all who knew him. As Artistic Director of Childsplay, Inc., a professional children's theater in Tempe, Arizona, David knew that the tragedy of his own life held a triumphant story of courage for all children and adults. He was joined in this conviction by Carol North Evans, Artistic Director of Metro Theater Company, who came to Childsplay as a guest director a few months after Benjamin's death. These two artistic directors joined forces to create this play for both their companies and invited me to join the team as dramaturg.

The initial development of this play took place at the first New Visions/New Voices at the Kennedy Center in May of 1990 as a week-long improvisational workshop based on fragments and images from Benjamin's life and a fantastical narrative created by both David and Carol prior to the rehearsal period.

The following fall, David and Carol came to UT for the first of eight visits over a three year period. In that first residency the creative team held an open seminar for interested students. They told Benjamin's story, shared slides of his art work, and outlined the project. During the next three days, the creative team of playwright, director, dramaturg, student dramaturg, and a variety of resource people including designers and a movement specialist worked nearly around the clock and created a visual scenario for the play comprised of images from Benjamin's life and art work. The scenario consisted of drawings made by the team on nearly twenty-five feet of computer paper. Armed with these images and the input of many points of view, David wrote the first draft of *The Yellow Boat.*

David and Carol made five more trips to Austin over the next three years. In the first visit they conducted movement workshops and cast a company made up of graduate and undergraduate students from all program areas including acting, directing, design, playwriting, and children's theater. In the second residency, we workshopped the first and second drafts of the play with the student company augmented by professional actors from both the Childsplay and Metro companies. Three additional drafts resulted from this residency, conference calls, and faxes. An additional visit brought David back to Austin just to escape the daily pressures of being the artistic director of a major professional company. The greatest service the UT program could provide at that moment was time to write. My primary dramaturgical function was to answer the phone and cook for David.

Over the next two years, the creative team, including the student dramaturg, continued work on the script during rehearsal periods for the professional productions at both Childsplay in Arizona and Metro Theater Company in St. Louis. Gina Ojile, a student actress from the UT workshop, took a semester away from her graduate program and joined the Metro company on an internship that included both rehearsal and ten weeks of touring. The rehearsals were quite different in form and content from the freewheeling creative explorations of the developmental workshops.

Now, production problems needed to be confronted head-on. The boundless goodwill and creative euphoria of process hardened into the need for results. The opportunity for unlimited options had expired, it was time to solve problems once and for all. Rewrites were no longer hypothetical what if's, but determined, sometimes desperate attempts to find something . . . anything that worked. Tempers flared and were soothed. Problems arose and were solved. The contrast between workshop development and production preparation were night-and-day contradictions for the students and for the creative team. Although it was difficult at the time, in retrospect this was probably the greatest lesson to be learned: the final formation of the script did not happen in the luxury of the laboratory, but in the crucible of production.

For two years after the developmental period, the Performing Arts Center at the University of Texas brought the Metro Production of *The Yellow Boat* into their facilities as a regular "booked" event. The entire Austin community had the opportunity to see the fruits of our labor made manifest in a dynamic, powerful play for young audiences and their families. For each run, we developed outreach activities including study guides for school and family audiences, an art exhibit of Benjamin's actual drawings and paintings, and a special symposium focusing on issues related to pediatric AIDS. *The Yellow Boat* stands as the most extensive project we have undertaken, but the techniques we developed in that first venture have fueled successful projects in later years. Subsequent productions of *The Yellow Boat* without the participation of the initial creative team have further developed this play, which will be published in both touring and home-theater versions next year.

All projects in the UT New Play Development Program have both a professional and student dramaturg involved at all times. I have served as primary dramaturg for two projects, David Kranes from the Sundance Playwright's Lab and Deborah Frockt, dramaturg from Seattle Children's Theater, have come to campus as guest dramaturgs. Student dramaturgs are included in all meetings, rehearsals, and as many private conferences between collaborators as possible. It is my hope and intent that student dramaturgs will continue to participate in the projects after the projects leave the university and are produced by the home theater. UT PhD student Judy Matetzschk who served as associate dramaturg on *The Yellow Boat,* was involved in both professional productions of this script. In addition, Judy has written her dissertation on the subject of new play dramaturgy and theater for young audiences using *The Yellow Boat* as a case study.[122]

Borrowing from the Sundance model, the UT program makes use of resource artists. Our 1993 project was to work with Seattle playwright, Ed Mast, on his script, *Wolf-Child: The Conversion of Joseph.* This play was developed in association with the Coterie Theatre in Kansas City. Although *Wolf Child* is based on true stories of feral children raised by wolves, it is truly an examination of education systems. It asks young audiences to consider what happens when native cultures are destroyed through the well-intentioned cultural imperialism of prevalent educational systems. In order to provide Ed with specific information about the "native culture" of his play, we found a local breeder of hybrid wolves and arranged for company members to spend an afternoon in movement improvisations with his animals. Although our afternoon of dancing with wolves most probably had little influence on the script, the play's eventual director, Jeff Church, found the experience invaluable to his later production at the Coterie.

Our 1993–1994 project focused on an adaptation of Kay Gibbons' prizewinning novel, *Ellen Foster* by playwright Barbara Bates Smith. The story concerns a young girl's struggle to overcome a past of physical and emotional abuse and possible incest and to find a home for herself within a foster family. After the week-long experimental rehearsal period of *Ellen Foster,* I believed that the whole experience had opened more options than the playwright could deal with effectively. The script, which came to us in relatively fragmentary shape, was even more splintered and disconnected at the end of the workshop. To have left this project at this stage would have been a disservice to the play, the playwright, and the novel. I was deeply concerned that the developmental process might have actually done more harm than good. I decided to cancel a new project for 1994–1995 and to commit the developmental resources for that year to a full production of this piece in our Theater Room series. Smith and Kranes returned to campus for portions of the rehearsal period, and extensive rewrites were undertaken throughout the rehearsal process. With a gifted graduate student director at the helm and a cast drawn from both graduate and undergraduate programs, the University of Texas production of *Ellen Foster* brought the loose ends together and allowed Smith to finalize her vision of the script in a concrete form.

The UT New Play Development Program is based on the notion that the best learning takes place in the real world, on projects that will influence the field of theater for young audience as a whole. The concept of reciprocity is the cornerstone of all projects. Student participants receive important training experiences throughout the process. In return, all of the students involved give the project the gift of their developing talents and unbounded energy, enthusiasm, and dedication.

So far, our track record has been strong. *The Yellow Boat* has been produced by major theaters throughout the country. *Wolf Child: The Conversion of Joseph* enjoyed a successful run at the Coterie Theatre in Kansas City and has been produced by important theaters such as Berkeley Rep, Syracuse Stage, and the Group Theatre in Seattle. *Ellen Foster* has been produced by UT and the Barter Theatre in Virginia. My own script *The Taste of Sunrise* will be our next venture. This play will include a bilingual cast of deaf and hearing actors and will require the student company to learn sign language. This play is just beginning its dramaturgical journey, but will be produced in 1996 by Seattle Children's Theatre.

The other new play development programs described in this article have had similar successes. At IUPUI, sixteen of the twenty plays workshopped have been published, most have received some professional production, and five have been awarded the Distinguished Play Award from the American Alliance of Theater and Education.[123] Sixty to sixty-five percent of the plays developed at Sundance go on to professional production elsewhere.[124] Virtually all of the plays featured at New Visions/New Voices have been produced by their host theaters. This is a record to be reckoned with!

There is both a history of dramaturgy in theater for children and a need for greater depth and integrity in all aspects of the work. Ample opportunities exist for dramaturgs to work within present structures or to break away to establish new paradigms of collaboration with artists dedicated to finding a cultural voice for young people in our society. The survival of live theater as an art form depends on the care and aesthetic nourishment of young audiences.

But all this talk of art and culture really doesn't matter a damn in the face of the larger questions of our survival as civilized beings on this planet.

In his essay "A Plea for Radical Children's Literature," progressive educator Herbert Kohl states:

> I believe that what is read in childhood not only leaves an impression behind but also influences the values and shapes the dreams of children.
>
> It can provide negative images and stereotypes and cut off hopes and limit aspirations. It can erode self-respect through overt and covert racism and sexism. It can also help young people get beyond family troubles, neighborhood violence, stereotyping, and prejudice . . . and set their imaginations free. . . .[125]

The power of live theater is an equally potent force to the power of reading. Some child development experts believe that the personal identification that occurs during a live theatrical performance has even greater power to transform thought and perceptions as it engages young people simultaneously on visual, aural, kinesthetic, and emotional levels. So much of what children and teenagers are exposed to in the media celebrates stupidity and models mediocrity. How can we be shocked by brain-dead audiences of adults when we have trained these audiences to be complacent and resistant to change?

But there is hope. The antidote to the everyday is the force of imagination. Again, I turn to Kohl for comfort:

> The power of the imagination comes from our ability to entertain alternatives to what we have experienced or have been told. The existence of imagination is perhaps the originating force of the ideas of freedom, choice, and the possibility of personal, social, and political change.[126]

The role of the dramaturg in theater for children can be so much more than a need or an opportunity. It can be a mission. The impact of the dramaturg upon the development of new work and upon the reenvisioning of timeless sources into timely themes is there for the doing. If the audience of "once upon a time" is ever to be transformed into "once upon another time" there must be the vigilant watch-persons reminding playwrights, directors, and administrators of the larger picture, deepening the conversation, challenging assumptions, paving the path for outreach and access. There must be education directors and dramaturgs inviting young people to join with artists of the highest caliber to build a theater worthy of the once and future audience.

Making Theater From A Queer Aesthetic
by **Susan Finque**

SUSAN FINQUE is an actor, director, and educator who spent ten years in the Santa Cruz and San Francisco area working and studying before relocating to Seattle. She was for nearly a decade the Coartistic Director of the Alice B. Theater, Seattle's Gay and Lesbian Theater for All People, where her work was distinct for the development of ensemble new work, her commitment to communities of color and young people, and for the level of excellence and risk for which Alice B. earned its renown. Her solo movement performance about female-to-male transsexuality, *T.S./CROSSING*, was critically acclaimed and toured nationally. Finque has guest directed for the Pomo Afro Homos, toured with a vaudeville circus, taught and performed in women's prisons, and has received numerous awards, grants, and residencies from government and private institutions. She is on the faculty of Antioch College and spends part of the year in Yellow Springs, Ohio.

PART I: AUTOBIOGRAPHY OF THE SELF AND THE OTHER

In order to create a training environment in the studio that explores deeply the experiences of the new young community of would-be theater artists, we directors, dramaturgs, and teachers have to shatter our own ideas about the nature of men and women and their vastly different sexualities and gender behaviors. In order to do this, we cannot wait for a new generation of playwrights to provide us with the scripted material we need for these explorations. Theater training must allow students to create experiments and performance that tell the stories of their own lives, and it is imperative and beneficial that the growing numbers of queer students be included in this equation. We will need to break through the image we may have of ourselves as *interpretive* artists and begin to conceive of our work in the theater as *generative*: that of *making work*.

To guide young theater artists forward, acting teachers need dramaturgical skills; directors need to learn the language of actors; and dramaturgs need a comprehensive understanding of the performer's physical, emotional, intellectual, and interpersonal training. That the craft of the theater is driving with determination down the road of interdisciplinary approaches bodes well for artists and would-be artists of a queer identity. Gay, lesbian, bisexual and gender-fluid identities give us lives that are intrinsically interdisciplinary as we grapple with our "otherness" in this heterosexually defined world. As more of us come to the theater, the craft will change and the methodology of training must also change.

My aesthetic and my personal cultural language are driven by my sense of otherness, of being queer, and it makes me keenly aware of the struggles of communities of color and others who are not of the "dominant culture."[127] My lesbian identity empowers my teaching, my ability to make new work with young people, and helps me to reconceive ideas about physical training. In sharing some specific stories and ideas about making autobiographical work and cross-gender performance in theater training, I hope the reader will begin to understand my argument that if we as theater artists truly engage our differences and our *selves,* we cannot help but make new work, even as we are interpreting a three-hundred-year-old play for the many thousandth time.

During my tenure as the coartistic director of the Alice B. Theater in Seattle, I spent nearly three years working with queer youth, teaching classes and eventually developing a performance piece entitled *Contents Under Pressure.* Collaborator Deb Parks-Satterfield and I set out to develop an ensemble of racially diverse youth who were queer-friendly. The final ensemble of ten performers were diverse in their sexual orientation, and amongst them gender identity was fluid. They spent a year in classes with Deb, an African-American woman whose background as a writer and performer in such ensembles as At The Foot Of The Mountain, uniquely prepared her to act as the playwright-in-residence, and with myself, a Jewish white woman with training and experience in directing ensembles.[128]

During that first year we had multiple objectives. We wanted to build a trusting studio environment, one that encouraged risk and outrageousness. We also wanted to employ a wide range of performance skills including acting, writing, movement, and mask technique. In the beginning, we were not intending to create a play, we just believed in theater skills as life skills. We wanted to give the participants firm footing in skills of self-expression, personal focus and discipline, knowledge of their bodies, and in abilities necessary to work in collaborative ways with people from different backgrounds. We found these young people partly through cosponsorship of the classes by the American Friends Services Committee, an organization with a more than one-hundred-year history of serving disenfranchised populations and that since the mid-'80s had specifically dedicated itself to "at-risk" youth. Statistics show that gay and lesbian-identified youth are disproportionately represented among the numbers of homeless, drug-addicted, depressed, and suicidal young people in America today. Though the emergence of a gay and lesbian culture makes it possible for young people to come out at a younger age, the world that greets them is arguably no less hostile than it was for their gay ancestors. Often high school is a hostile if not dangerous place to come out. Lesbian and gay youth are frequently the victims of violent attacks and systematic harassment. If condemned by their parents, churches, or peers, queer youth struggle intensely with isolation and self-hatred. So the risk is real on many levels.

I am in conflict about that expression, "at-risk." In the world at large, the term is used to refer to people (usually young) who are vulnerable, who might fall off the "edge" of safety. Yet in the theater we often use the word "risk" to describe a *desired* state of being. Risk evokes chance-taking, stepping out of a comfortable range of choices and extending past "safe" or familiar ways of responding to a given moment. Few acting teachers or directors want their actors to risk their lives or well-being when they talk about physical or emotional risk in theater work. When I use the term, I am encouraging my collaborators and students to go down the path of the unknown, to find and explore the edge of danger or expression—to *find* the edge, not fall off of it.

With the class that would eventually evolve into the performance ensemble of *Contents Under Pressure*, exploration of the meaning and embodiment of risk became central to our work. This was enormously empowering both to those who had lived on the street, were HIV positive, or had other high-risk life realities, and to others who had never taken a risk in their lives. Risk began to become about the *discovery* and *exposure* of truth, to the *witnessing* of others. The young people's mixed racial backgrounds and sexual identities gave them a keen consciousness of being the Other and made real-life risk a daily negotiation. Risk was at the heart of our process, and perhaps should be at the heart of all theater-making.

As we worked, Deb and I became clear that we wanted to make a show with this remarkably gifted and willing group of young people. We agreed no extant script would do justice to the diversity and depth of their stories, and that it would be inadequate for Deb to go away and write the material independently, in the traditional manner of a playwright. At the beginning of our second year of work, we agreed that the life stories, and "lifemaps" of the ensemble members gave us a wealth of dramatic material from which we could shape a performance. We used the term "lifemap" to refer to a graphic and experiential plotting of the path one has walked through in life. The map includes what *has* happened, and the *imagined* happenings along the way; the present tense response to the memories, and the opinions about the response. All the stuff of great theater.

Even before we had decided to make a play, while we did extensive warm-ups, situational improvisations, trust exercises, and physical training designed to expand range of motion, *material for a performance piece had already begun to emerge.* Now I began to deliberately craft exercises for our process that were geared toward the development of material from these lifemaps and life visions, and their resulting text and movement ideas. My dramaturgical concerns became organic to the process of constructing these exercises. For example, after a particularly compelling improvisation where one actor recreated a memory of her mother and herself in a dialogue about freedom, we structured an exercise that entailed all of the ensemble creating a facial "mask" representing "Authority".[129] This fantastic museum full of immobile silent faces then came to life as each actor let go of the mask and confronted their own nightmare of authority, as did the first actor whose autobiographical experience triggered the ensemble event. In talking about the exercise, the young people shared the images they had in their minds about who their authority mask represented, each in her or his own improvisation—for one a parent, for another a rapist, for another a clergyman.

The next day I took the physical improv another step and tried to develop the voices for these masks. We donned the masks again and the actors moved around the room, finding relationships with each other in the physical space. It was only when we began to take some of the masks off, so that the Authorities were interacting with the "Selves" that the text began to emerge. Deb had to understand what we were doing physically in order to inform her own dramaturgical process of organizing the text. As the director, I had to understand the possibilities for creating *context* for the text being improvised. How would solo work sit in relationship next to duet or ensemble events? What did the autobiographically based memories have in common? In conflict? How could we handle making exciting improvisations, virtually unrepeatable, viable in performance? Did the rehearsal techniques themselves, that is, the *form* of our work, directly *inform* the content of what would finally become the play? How would all of the stuff hang together? Could it? All of us—the actors, Deb, and I—required a dramaturgical consciousness in the studio, both in the moment of the risk-taking improvisation and months later when we were all grappling with the task of putting our wealth of material together to make a single, coherent play.[130]

In a process such as this, all the participants own the dramaturgy of play development. They are conscious of what they each bring to the process, and what they must generate creatively in order to meet the text that exists, or to create the words themselves. They begin the process of unraveling their life experiences, and finding *dramaturgically conscious* ways of using their stories and visions for source material in every exercise and every encounter in the studio. They are not blank slates for the director and writer to draw upon, but rather are consciously making theater with us, empowered in the task by the experiences of their own lives.

After months of generating enough material to make a hundred hours of performance, we began the task of inventory. Deb and I began to edit the material, first grouping the "good stuff," all material that was most compelling to us in studio performance. Then we looked for common themes, successful partnerings, a good combination of word-based work and sections that were more physical. To be honest, a lot of our early outlines were utterly arbitrary. That seemingly random order allowed us to examine material both on the page and on the stage. We saw connections that didn't exist in our minds before, certain juxtapositions yielded gaping holes, others revealed brand new ideas about the content. Sometimes the holes, or lack of transitions, caused us to throw sections away; other times they created great opportunities to see the material in new ways. By the final piece, transitions were no longer just a mechanism for getting from one place to another; they became the very location where theatrical transformation occurred and the story-line emerged.[131]

In the final script, the central theme of *Contents Under Pressure* centered on surviving in this world, and how the intricate personal conning of masks inhibits or enables that life struggle. We built actual masks out of cloth, and these masks played a key role in establishing the theatricality of the final work. Sometimes the cloth masks were used; sometimes the actors' faces transformed before us. But the piece was not merely a collection of solo autobiographies in which each performer directly addressed the audience telling his or her story, just as our developmental process did not focus on the solo act of sitting and writing in an isolated fashion. The piece was a reflection of our process, which was often physical and ensemble oriented. Solo moments ended up being woven into ensemble sections that took one person's experience into a group dynamic. Let me offer some examples of events in the final piece and attempt to describe the processes that led to them.

One young woman's story about her butch identity and the cruelty it had provoked took on the physical life of a jungle gym. The company built a physical structure with their bodies that she could climb, and the set design supported this further by providing a weight-bearing steel sculpture. The jungle gym came alive with the voices of her tormentors as she struggled to get through it: "I think. . . . No! No! Don't think! . . . Okay. . . . Don't worry your pretty little head. Can you walk? Hey, what is it? Is it a boy or a girl? It's an IT! Let's call it an IT! Hey! This is the Women's Room! You say you're a girl? Prove it!"[132]

The voices demanded she be one gender or the other, they eventually became violent. She climbed over and through them, her physical agility and defensiveness evoking a mask of competence, masculinity, and anger. When she broke free of the maze, she removed her mask and told us about her discoveries; her sexuality, and her mechanisms for survival. She revealed a multigendered and incredibly resilient person who had begun to understand the roots of her rage. For her, the risk was in exposing a self that was vulnerable and battered.

In the studio we had to do the physical work of weight bearing, carrying, shifting, climbing, and combat. Trust exercises were necessary for this conflict to have deep theatrical resonance and for the performers to develop confidence in weight exchange. The dramatic action of wearing a mask and then removing it to reveal truth and self became a task universally important to every performer and a unifying element critical to the dramatic arc of the final piece.

Another example of how an individual story took on an ensemble context was in another actor's story about his Blackness and growing up in an all-White community. He reenacted a meeting with a street drunk he had encountered one day when he was hurrying to work. The drunk fellow was also African American and, though in a blurred and messed-up state, was acutely aware of the younger man's well-dressed look, and it pissed him off. The actor played *both* himself and his confronter. The older man told him to stop acting so white, being so white, and to look at his skin," . . . you so Black you could be a African prince!"[133] When the actor removed his mask he told us:"I do think about the pain, the injustice. Regardless of how I dress, I still know my heritage, I still know my family. And I've managed to not let the past make me prejudiced or make me go out there whacking people like some gang member. I know who I am. I know where I'm from. An African prince. Hmmmmm. Well, that might have been true two hundred years ago, but what I was, right then, was a Black man who was late for work."[134] *Both* characters were "masked," and the actor's true self lay in his discovery of the space between the masks. This solo section then segued into a chaotic group section of simultaneous action and text about oppositions: Black/White, rich/poor, sober/drunk, old/young, directed/directionless. Accompanied by Thelonius Monk's music, the actors physically embodied this confrontation by holding their masks out in front of them, "meeting" their opposite, and then slipping into the mask, losing the gestures of their selves. This work was a direct recreation of our exercises in the studio, now given dramatic context by being juxtaposed to one actor's story.

Another section of the piece wove two of the actors' autobiographical sketches together. For one man and one woman sex was the central risk in their lives. She had started work in the sex industry at the age of fifteen and currently worked as a table dancer. She mourned the loss of love, of never having had it in the first place, of feeling like sex was work. He had worked as a prostitute at the same early age, serving exclusively male clients, and now struggled with his HIV-positive status, the fear of death, and the seemingly unavoidable link between sex and mortality. Both were of mixed-race heritage, he was adopted and had experienced much abuse at the hands of his adoptive mother. They shared multiple experiences of alienation: brown in a white world, gay in a straight world, parentless in a world designed for families. Both felt old before their time, and that their time was running out. In rehearsal, these two performers often worked together physically with a lot of trust, and within exercises they often mirrored each other's movements and voices. Their brown skin was nearly the same shade, and when moving abstractly, they were eerily alike. We began to shape material building from this mirror work and develop it into a section of the play that exposed their common yet distinct histories, while touching on moments of blurred gender and exposure of truth.

The ensemble wove the two autobiographies into one section in the performance. Even though the material was solo-driven in its development, the performance became a duet. The style of text was poetic, interwoven, and rhythmically hypnotic. The text was a barrage of sex talk: the pick-up, the business deal, the promises between lovers, the fighting, the battering. The actors were restricted in a Beckett-esque manner to two chairs, and changed their gender fluidly with voice, body, and the changing and removing of masks. The audience barely knew who was playing female or male and when or if the gender had changed. The two played different masks of themselves; they played their customers, their attackers, their lovers. They played each *other's* lovers, too, which made for a dynamic and demanding interchange of sexual assumptions on the part of the audience. Who was queer? Who was straight? Whose lover was what gender? The tension of changing characters made the scene sexy and at times frightening:"I don't know what it was. I don't know what it was that made sex . . . so . . . dull. . . . You should be used to this. This isn't going to take very long. Just a little while longer, okay? OK? Just to feel the closeness? It was really exciting when I first was out on the street. I got this rush as I watched the men drive by. Do you know what it's like to have someone want you? They'd wink. . . . Really want you? They pay me once, and they think they own me. I'm not very comfortable. You can stand to be a little uncomfortable. Just to feel the closeness. I'm paying you enough. You need to learn to respect me. You can have the money back. Just do it. Do it."[135] At the end, both masks were removed in a slow, ritual unveiling. The performers created a moment of recognition between them; eye contact, touch, release of the mask's physical impact on their whole bodies. The players released tension, the Selves, (or storytellers) realized their lives were paralleled and that there was a strong bond between them.

Great stuff. The material was driven by the life stories of all the ensemble, focusing sex issues into the intense personal histories of two individuals. It included many of the actors' own words, shaped dramatically by the playwright. The scene's choreography and blocking were composed of much of the performers' own idiosyncratic movement, then shaped theatrically by my direction. My job became to choreograph it all into a whole dance—one coherent piece of theater with its source in autobiography and yet with many stories to tell.

Autobiography and autoperformance in theater training are not just a means toward the end of producing a whole new crop of solo performers. Nor is making plays with at-risk populations merely to serve their healing process. The ensemble of *Contents Under Pressure* was not in therapy sessions with me; they were studying the craft of theater and in the *process* reconciling the struggle of their own lives. It is too easy to dismiss using life experience and autobiography as work for psychotherapists and their clients, or to suggest that only "performance artists" should be writing their own stories. The generative process of making theater and using participants' own stories—real and imagined—may be absolutely essential for a curriculum of theater training. This work gives voice to students' lives along with grounding them powerfully in their own creative and experiential roots. Not only will we as practitioners of our craft have our minds expanded by the life stories of the diverse populations that are the future of theater, but we will also be laying the groundwork for artists' development from a place of truth, self, and risk. This autobiographically based work is one of the best ways I have experienced to explore the nature and diversity of human beings; the nature of Self and Other. The playing field is made level when the material comes from the students themselves. Given that our craft is beginning to more accurately reflect the true diversity of American culture, the white, straight, male student can no longer perceive his story as the central one; now he too must finally confront his "otherness."

Though I don't suggest this kind of training replace the study of classic and contemporary texts, nor that it alone provides sufficient physical training, I do argue for a contemporization of our training for theater artists so that they can be ready for the changes in our field. The color, language, style, sex, and discipline of the theater is changing. The next generation of artists are part of these changes. They will be fluid in their sexuality and gender, cross-cultural in their consciousness, and interdisciplinary in their thinking about making art. Artists are emerging from different parts of society, and being informed by a whole new canon of classics generated by theater-makers such as Anna Deavere Smith, Bill T. Jones, Bill Irwin, Anne Bogart, and Split Britches. Are we now adequately preparing theater students for this future—a future they passionately want? We need to examine how we teach, what we teach, and to whom. We need to acknowledge our students' and our own identities, and begin to include them into the alchemy of the theater studio.

PART II: DRAMATURGY OF THE BODY

Toward these ends I am developing coursework in cross-gender performance at Antioch College. Behind this class is my deep interest in cross-gendered work; the conviction that the reinterpretation of classic texts invigorates the material for contemporary audiences; and the desire to make new work from queer perspectives. The class, a midlevel acting course, has at its center three assumptions:

- Essential to character study and development is the understanding of gender construction, behavior, and desire.
- The skill of crossing from one's own gender to another (with some stops along the way) will be increasingly in demand given the direction of contemporary theater.
- The ancient, historical, and multicultural traditions of crossing gender in performance merit in-depth study.

The syllabus includes a section of time devoted to the investigation of one's own gender construction and how it expresses itself in terms of physical pattern, gesture, and movement. We tackle extreme gender stereotypes using our own iconography and scenework from twentieth century writers such as Tennessee Williams, Lillian Hellman, and Bertolt Brecht. We investigate Shakespeare's "breeched" and "gartered" roles such as Viola, Rosalind, and Malvolio. We dig into the work of writers of camp, queer and lesbian/gay texts such as Charles Ludlam, Holly Hughes, and Split Britches, studying how they reflected and departed from the past. We look at excerpts from nearly one hundred videos, of film and live performance, to gain perspective on how drag and cross-gender performance has evolved throughout many cultures.

In this class, we have talked about the different challenges for biological men and women in doing this work, and the questions were jarring: What does it take for drag performance by men to rise above the insulting and exaggerated—the quick and cheap laugh? How does the work of Charles Ludlam differ from Vegas performers in the La Cage revues? How did Katharine Hepburn's portrayal of a girl disguised as a boy in *Sylvia Scarlett* precede Anna Deavere Smith's approach to the men in her solo docudramas? What is the actor's task when the cross-gendered character is about illusion? When it's commentary? Is the actor asking the audience to believe he is one gender, or is the actor sharing a secret? How do political performance techniques, Brechtian in their roots, interplay in this commentary and other kinds of camp performance? And how does this work connect back to one's own autobiography?

All acting students come to class with a physical vocabulary that is a diary of their lives. Those who were hit as kids often hunch and protect their faces. Those who lack self-confidence may be slow to speak slowly or to respond physically. Those who are afraid of their emerging sexuality, whatever the orientation, may have caved-in chests, legs with no range of movement, arms that won't reach above their heads. Those who manipulate their sexuality, whether or not they are sexually active, often walk leading from the groin, breasts, or hips. These movement patterns are not chosen; they are imprinted. Any acting teacher who has tried to get students to "stop" tugging at their shirt, rolling their eyes, or looking at the floor, can testify how strong a brick wall it is that protects these gestural patterns. Good training must include learning to recognize personal physical patterns and finding a path toward neutrality. Neutrality may not necessarily *exist,* but the *pursuit* of neutrality allows actors to gain an objectivity about who they are, and *where they might be able to go.* To help performers develop a vocabulary that will enable them to choose from a wide range of body types and gestural expression, I have to radically alter assumptions about what is true or possible for men, women, and everyone in between. Examining theater through the lens of gender identity and construction lends patterns of movement and ideas about masculinity and femininity a whole new richness.

I use words such as masculine, feminine, male, and female with caution because, as I have discovered through my own queer identity and in my theater work, these polarized binaries are incredibly inadequate when grappling with the complexities of human beings. Take for example the tomboy and or butch-identified lesbian actor. Her physical patterning, when examined in theater exercises, is far more "masculine" than "feminine" in nature. Maybe her voice is low and her chest broad and strong, like a male athlete. When she inventories her own body, she discovers that in the challenge of crossing gender she has much further to go in inhabiting the stereotype of the most feminine female, the iconography of a Marilyn Monroe. This woman student could more easily tackle the characterization of a James Dean. To study one's own gender and its crossing we all need to *count higher than two.* Queer-identified artists have an edge here, maybe even a gift because in struggling with these challenges we are already dealing with unique mixes of gender identity and gender behavior in our own lives.

I am not talking about "gender-blind" casting or even drag performance; I am suggesting whole new ways of imagining how the interplay of gender and sexual orientation can affect studio work, character development, performance style, script interpretation, and the development of new material. All of these areas pose new challenges for dramaturgs and dramaturgy. Our work in the training studio becomes about *meeting* scene work, not just interpreting it. All of us: actors, directors, writers, teachers, and dramaturgs, become playmakers together as we reexamine texts through the light of gender construction and desire.

In my recent production of *As You Like It,* a grunge-rock version set outdoors with a live band, Orlando was cast as a boyish young woman, and Phebe as a back-to-the-land young gay boy. The end of the play gave us four loving couples that looked very much more like the young lovers of today's world. Some other gender flipping went on, including adapting Corin the shepherd, given as an aging country fellow full of simple wisdom about the folly of love, to a matriarchal presence, an earth goddess of sorts, whose wisdom and clever ironies rang ever-so-true in our contemporary setting. We took Shakespeare's gender reversal a few steps further, meeting the play in its own integrity. This required vigorous dramaturgy, not to "make the idea work," but to help us keep up with the new resonances exploding out of the text. We felt as if we were doing *As You Like It* for the first time. I hope to have that wonderful feeling every time I work on a show.

In the cocreation of autobiographic performance, in the development of acting technique in gender-crossing, and as a director of all kinds of theater, dramaturgy is essential to my work. I am constantly looking at invention: the performer meeting the material; the Self meeting and sometimes becoming the Other; the artist crossing from the world of the familiar to the world of the unknown. First, we make work about what we know, and then we make work about what we don't know. How can I possibly expect to keep my lesbian identity and queer aesthetic out of the studio? And why would I want to? One's otherness, however it is identified, is what draws one to a sense of identity, and the theater has at its heart first the exploration of one's own identity and then of "crossing" to otherness or otherworldliness. When one's sense of self is firmly intact, one can proceed with absolute integrity along a theatrical journey that may alter or transform the Self completely. Theater artists then can carry a deeper understanding and compassion for cultures, people and times, and most importantly, know how to get back home. Considering the fragility of the artist's self-esteem, this sense of center is perhaps one of the most critical gifts we can give to each other. Whether exploring other-worlds is about immersion into character; the world of the play; time period; nonnaturalistic performance styles; or crossing race, gender, class, sexuality, even planetary affiliation: the creation of character and the task of play-making has this work of the Self and the Crossing at its heart.

Gender & Sexuality is a good way 2 compare that other-ness a dramaturg needs 2 have. I don't think there need to be any separate study of gender and sexuality in-order to gain a better understanding of the "other" it is important to have a concept of the "other" but be completely of the whole.

Tony Kushner's *Angels*

An Interview With Tony Kushner Conducted By **Susan Jonas**

TONY KUSHNER'S plays include *A Bright Room Called Day*; *The Illusion*, freely adapted from Corneille; *Angels in America, A Gay Fantasia on National Themes, Parts One: Millenium Approaches*, and *Part Two: Perestroika*; *Slavs!: Thinking about The Longstanding Problems of Virtue and Happiness*; and adaptations of Goethe's *Stella*, Brecht's *The Good Person of Sezuan*, and Ansky's *The Dybbuk*. His work has been produced by theaters around the United States, including New York Theatre Workshop, the New York Shakespeare Festival, the Mark Taper Forum, Berkeley Rep, Steppenwolf Theatre, and Hartford Stage Company; on Broadway at the Walter Kerr Theatre; at the Royal National Theatre in London, the Abbey Theatre in Dublin, the Deutsches Theatre in Berlin; and in over thirty countries around the world.

Angels in America has been awarded the 1993 Pulitzer Prize for Drama, the 1993 and 1994 Tony Awards for Best Play, the 1993 and 1994 Drama Desk Awards, The 1992 Evening Standard Award, two Olivier Award nominations for best play of 1993 and 1994, the 1993 New York Drama Critics Circle Award, the 1993 Los Angeles Drama Critics Circle Award, and the 1994 LAMBDA Literary Award for Drama, among others. *Slavs* was awarded a 1995 OBIE award.

Mr. Kushner is the recipient of grants from New York State Council of the Arts and the National Endowment for the Arts, a 1990 Whiting Foundation Writers' Award, and an Arts Award from the American Academy of Arts and Letters, among others.

A collection of recent writings, entitled *Think About The Longstanding Problems of Virtue and Happiness*, has been published by Theatre Communications Group.

Mr. Kushner was born in Manhattan and grew up in Lake Charles, Louisiana. He has a BA from Columbia University and an MFA in directing from New York University, where he studied with Carl Weber. He lives in Manhattan.

Susan Jonas: I have before me the two lists of acknowledgment—official and unofficial dramaturgs you credit in the published versions of *Angels in America* and *Perestroika*. Did all of these people influence the development of these scripts?

Tony Kushner: Kim [Kimberly Flynn] had the biggest impact on the script of anyone. I've written in detail about her contribution in the afterword to *Perestroika*, both in the specific ideas and lines of dialogue she contributed, and the harder-to-define, profoundly shaping influence of our intellectual friendship, in which she's been mostly the leader and I the follower. None of it is conventional dramaturgy. With both plays, Ellen McLaughlin helped a lot in terms of cutting, which is a process that I find very difficult. With *Millennium*, Roberta Levitow was tremendously helpful in terms of reading through the script with me several times and making cuts. Because Ellen is a writer, I weighed her suggestions differently, and sometimes discarded them. When writers help you cut your material, they start unconsciously to make it sound like their material. When Philip Kan Gotanda was at the first rehearsal of the workshop of *Millennium*, he was tremendously encouraging and, in several instances, urged me to keep things that I would have been persuaded to lose. Connie Congdon did an analogous thing with Eileen Nugent; she watched a couple of times and said things like, "I liked this. . . . This didn't work" very general suggestions.

Jonas: You've been recognized by dramaturgs as a great advocate of dramaturgy. You are one of the few playwrights who doesn't mind saying, "A lot of people influenced me and my work changed a lot."

Kushner: A lot of that has to do with Kim. I have been instructed through ten years and more of pitched battles over intellectual ownership and giving people credit. I really have to give credit to her for whatever generosity I seem to manifest. It's not something that comes naturally to me. It's basically the result of being called on the carpet by somebody who points out that, politically, it's deeply suspect that writers—especially male writers—feel that they have to produce everything completely on their own, and that the act of writing becomes in part an act of denying that one is in any way reliant on other people. I've thought that maybe other writers simply don't need other people's help as much I do, or maybe I'm just a bad writer. I suspect that some people are more solitary, and really dredge it all out of their own souls. But even there, there may be ways in which other people are feeding them about which they're not aware. Kim and I have really struggled with this for a very long time. I benefited a lot from that struggle. And I've survived; I haven't been diminished by admitting that other people have participated.

Jonas: What about when you're on the other side. *You* were the dramaturg on Anna Deavere Smith's play, *Twilight?*

Kushner: Well, Kim and I *both* were. She has not been given nearly enough credit. Kim did much, much more on the piece than I did. It's a weird feeling to have an idea absorbed into a piece. I've worked on plays as the director with writers and as a dramaturg with writers, and I've fed them lines that they've used. It requires a certain magnanimity of spirit that nobody is completely capable of in this "fame-crazed" society. It's hard to feel totally great about that, and I don't think anybody does. Oskar Eustis has a great understanding of the pain of it, and the necessity of being able to not mind too much that we get absorbed.

Jonas: From everything you've said, Oskar was extraordinarily instrumental.

Kushner: Definitely. He's brilliant and spectacularly articulate. It was complicated with Oskar in *Angels*. He wasn't in any ordinary sense a dramaturg. I wrote the play specifically for Oskar to direct. Then, at the end of a very difficult and complicated process over five years, we decided to go our separate ways with it. We felt that in order to preserve a very, very important relationship, we needed to part company. It was insidiously difficult, especially for him, because he left the play at the moment at which it took off. And that's taken years of work afterwards to. . . .

The play was really begun in conversation with him. Certain features of my politics and his politics are similar, and we have always enjoyed talking about that. The title and the events and Roy Cohn and all that stuff was my idea. At the point when I started working on it, I was in New Hampshire directing *Mother Courage,* and I had just finished reading the [Nicholas Von Hoffman] biography of Roy Cohn, because I already knew I wanted to make him one of the characters in the play that Oskar had commissioned.[136] I called Oskar, and we had a wonderful conversation about the American Right. It was a fifty-fifty conversation, but it was one of those moments of. . . . Well, for example, Prelapsarianov's monologue at the beginning of *Perestroika* is my writing, but it was Oskar's idea. Oskar and I were screaming and yelling at each other on the phone, about what Perestroika meant—in the early days of Perestroika. Oskar's feeling was, "It's not going to work because it doesn't have a theory." Because I don't completely agree with him, but also because I thought it was a very smart thing to say, the monologue is a kind of joking tribute to Oskar; it's Oskar's speech.

Jonas: You said in the notes from the British production that a lot of the play was written as an imaginary argument with Oskar.

Kushner: Exactly.

Jonas: You say that Oskar was not a dramaturg in any ordinary or traditional sense. What is a dramaturg in the ordinary or traditional sense, and does anyone on this list fit that bill?

Kushner: Well, I would say all of them in one form or another. The dramaturgy that every playwright fears is the play editor. Ellen's a very close friend as well as a writer I greatly admire. She helped me in terms of just talking through problem points and giving me insights. In the middle of *Perestroika,* which is the hardest thing that I ever had to write, she said, "One thing you should recognize about the character of Harper," which is a character Ellen always loved, "is that she's always at her best as a character and she's always most dramatically interesting when she's on stage with Joe." That was a small but incredibly important insight.

I had the best and the most dangerous thing that can happen with dramaturgy. The play was fed into by an astonishing number of incredibly smart people. George Wolfe is completely brilliant. Without George, I would not have had the nerve to rewrite *Perestroika* as completely as I did for Broadway. With George in your corner, you feel you're protected against anything, because George is so tremendously powerful a person. We were closing *Angels,* a show that was completely selling out, that had won the Pulitzer and four Tony Awards. We were going to do four-performance weeks in the middle of a completely sold-out summer and then close for four weeks to put up *Perestroika,* a play that had not gotten good reviews when it went up in L.A. The play was not yet finished. It was long and difficult and complicated, and it could have easily sunk at once. It was literally back-breaking; I mean, I couldn't sit in a chair . . . and George

Understanding of dramaturgy?

made it okay. And the financial pressures were on him, in terms of the money that we were losing and so on. It was just staggering, and he was huge and indomitable. To me, that's a kind of dramaturgy. Also George is a writer, and he made incredibly smart suggestions. He could reconfigure things in his mind without even putting them on paper—come up with a whole new design for a scene. I hated one of the new scenes in *Perestroika,* but George loved it and said, "We're keeping it no matter what you say." It turned out to be an incredibly important scene in the play. The work on the Belize character, which was difficult for me, was greatly facilitated by the fact that George, who is black, was directing the play. I felt that he was keeping me from making stupid mistakes.

Jonas: Did you feel that you were making any concessions to the venue?

Kushner: No. By the time it ended up on Broadway, the play was longer and more difficult than it was at the Taper. The big mistake—dramaturgically—was to listen to a number of people to whom I never should have listened. But then again, maybe it was right to have listened, because we needed to try it. When I wrote *Perestroika,* it was a five-act play, but we all thought that it should be more like *Millennium,* so I turned it into a three-act play by the time it opened at the Taper. It was not and never should have been a three-act play. It had a totally different rhythm. It's not "bum, bum, bum." It's five acts; it has a more rolling structure. I let myself be talked into it in part because of the concern about intermission breaks, which is something that I shouldn't even have been thinking about. I learned a big lesson. Rewriting, which dramaturgy has a lot to do with, is tricky—to be smart enough to recognize what it is in the original impulse that makes the work yours and makes the work good—if it is good. It's difficult to be brave and daring in rewriting, while not being foolhardy or betraying that original impulse. That's the impossible, terrifying thing. People kill things with rewrites all the time. They also kill things by not being able to rewrite.

Jonas: What did Leon Katz do?

Kushner: Leon wrote me wonderful long letters full of suggestions. It's hard to separate out the specific influences of so many people, and it's been a long time. Sometimes he was quite critical, but after he saw the first performance of *Millennium* at the Taper New Works Festival, he was rapturous. That meant the world to me, because I knew who he was, and I was somewhat in awe of him. After he saw *Perestroika,* he came backstage and said, "I have a lot of problems with what this is right now, but it doesn't really matter because no one's writing like this in this country." Whether that's true or not, hearing it was really lovely. It made me feel, "Well, even if I fuck up, I'm still doing something that moved somebody."

Jonas: This points to the other use of the word "dramaturgy." One of the critics said the play's dramaturgy, its actual structure, was "audacious."

Kushner: I think that some of the formal structures, which seem innovative **are** close to original, and some of them are not. I wrote in the introduction to Connie Congdon's book that I saw *Tales of the Lost Formicans* while I was working on *Angels* and it had a big impact. Caryl Churchill's work also had a huge impact on me.

The most unusual thing about *Angels* is that so much of the stage time is occupied. Well, first of all, the length of it . . . I had no idea if it would work, but it just had to happen. The size and ambition of it. . . . I think the subtitle *A Gay Fantasia on National Themes* may be one of the most important things about the play, because it announces immediately that it has immense ambition. Of course it's pretentious, and of course it's grandiose, but that's part of the fun of it. It's reclaiming something American. My favorite writer is Herman Melville, and part of what I adore about him is that he makes it *a trope* to be oversized and outrageous and much bigger than anyone could possibly be, and to say, "I will write this book and incorporate all of Thomas Browne and Shakespeare and opera and sailing and the entire globe and whales. . . . And of course it's going to fail. Of course it's going to collapse under its own weight. But isn't it great that we're doing this?" I think that's very American. O'Neill did it, and a lot better than I.

Jonas: There is a great deal of criticism directed against the way that new play development is done in this country. Many charge that in the process, dramaturgs and others do a lot of damage trying to normalize the play, using their own preconceived notions of play structure. Yet with all this input, plays survived, and they are absolutely and gloriously **not** normalized.

Kushner: The person I always quote when I talk to playwrights is Maria Irene Fornes, who thinks that you should do your own dramaturgy yourself. As with so many other things, she's right in a certain sense. Of course, there are a lot of very smart people around and the theater is a collective enterprise. Because it has a tradition of collective creation, playwrights should—and if they're smart they will—take advantage of the community sense of it. It's not like writing a novel; you're not stuck in a room alone with your brain. You're out in the world and a lot of voices can contribute to what you're doing. But I also think that you should be "Fornesian" about saying it's yours. You have absolute final responsibility for it. It is your work, and if you don't know how to fix it, don't touch it.

Jonas: It is a common and fundamental mistake on the part of dramaturgs to assume artistic responsibility in the making of plays, and a common and fundamental mistake on the part of writers to abnegate or deflect responsibility by being influenced in that way.

Kushner: There are a lot of people in this country who are dramaturgs because they weren't able to write plays or direct well enough to have careers. They wind up being damaged by the jobs that they're given—by becoming literary managers and having to sift through hundreds and hundreds and hundreds of bad plays every year. And being a person without power or respect within an organization also diminishes you. As a writer, you have to be careful of these people. The nightmare age of dramaturgy is finally over, but when it was this new thing, artistic directors would literally say, "We are paying this person on our staff to be a dramaturg. You take their suggestions or get out of our theater."

Jonas: It seems that because you have a strong sense of self, you can afford to hear these suggestions and negotiate with them, without losing your impulse, your vision or yourself.

Kushner: Well, I've been doing it for ten years now. It's a process that develops slowly. It's hard because of painful episodes, like taking a five-act play, doing all the work necessary to turn it into a three-act play, and then realizing in the middle of one of the scariest try-out situations in American theatrical history, that you've made a terrible mistake and you have to turn it into a five-act play again. I've learned something from that. I'll never make that mistake again. And you become more familiar with yourself. You learn whether you're the sort of a writer like Whitman, who should never have rewritten anything because his first drafts were always best (Every time he rewrote *Leaves of Grass* he fucked it up even more.), or whether you're the sort of writer who writes very, very slowly and needs to sort of grope his way. Most of us are in between. It's just a matter of becoming familiar with yourself. And of being wary and recognizing that people with the best hopes in the world for your work can fuck it up very, very badly.

Jonas: You trained as a director. Did you have the intention of writing plays as you were training?

Kushner: I think I always wanted to. I'm a very fearful person and I was very afraid of writing—and writing badly.

Jonas: And directing seemed less scary?

Kushner: Much less. You're not alone. You're not starting from nothing. I do think it's harder to be a playwright than anything else. But then it's much easier for me to be a playwright than to not be one. Maybe other writers don't find it so hard.

Jonas: I don't know any of them.

Kushner: I don't either. Everybody struggles terribly. Creating something from nothing is hideous. Theater, as tough as it can be, always has the world of the rehearsal room, which is a chance to be an artistically creative person, but not do it in isolation—to be part of this wonderful crazy family, and you really want to do that. Playwrights live halfway between what writers usually are, which is isolated and lonely, and are also denizens of a garrulous, promiscuous and wonderful place—the theater. There are many things that destroy playwrights. One of them is to become sucked into that whole world, which, on the one hand, you rely on entirely and have to know incredibly well, but then on the other hand, you have to avoid like the plague. If you want to do really serious work, you have to be alone with your books and your pens and your thinking, or in the real world, trying to understand it better.

One of my biggest grouses about dramaturgy, especially when it starts to bleed into what playwrights do, is the kind of research that dramaturgs do in this country, which is absent of ideology and partisan politics. It's too sociological and too ethnographic. I don't think that art comes from that. I think it comes from places in the spirit that are inimical to that; it's completely subjective and completely unfair and completely judgmental and closeminded and prejudicial and prejudiced in advance. I see dramaturgs from the La Jolla model say, "Here's a table of all of our research," then do the *Cherry Orchard* and not talk about Bolshevism and what's in this play. I think playwrights sometimes pick up that model of research.

Jonas: What I'm hearing is that there should be more discussion of ideology and an ideological basis for all the participants, and that art is not merely a function of history, sociology, or other things that can be researched.

Kushner: Right. Art comes from interrogating yourself as to what you want to say with this work of art, not from pretending that you're going to recapitulate some kind of objective truth about existence. As an actor, as a dramaturg, as a set designer, as an associate assistant wigmaker, you are doing this because you want to say something to an audience. What the hell is it that you want to say? We so rarely ask that. Instead you find out what a Russian middle-class intellectual would eat for breakfast in a highway hotel room halfway between Moscow and St. Petersburg—that kind of boring, detailed, unimportant homework. I don't think you need that shit to do Chekhov. What you need to find out is: What is this play saying? What is this passionately partisan, political, harsh play saying about life that I want to say. Some research is necessary, but when actors do *Angels in America,* they spend too much time studying valium addiction, studying Mormonism so that they can cite all one hundred and eighty-five articles of faith, when it is utterly unnecessary.

Jonas: If you were counseling someone who's dramaturging an extant script, what would you say?

Kushner: I would say, "Look at what Kim does when she works dramaturgically with a director." She's done it for me when I've directed. When I did *Fen,* she laid the bedrock for that whole production. She did not go out and say, "Here's how Fen women pick potatoes: they stick their hand here, and they do this with their elbow. And here's the history of the potato and the history of all of that stuff," that Caryl Churchill obviously already did—to the extent that playwrights do it. Brecht says in his journals that playwrights don't know anything about what they're writing about, and the great thing about being a playwright is that you can know so little and sound like you're an expert, and it's all fake. And it is; it's theater; it's completely fake. We forget that, so we expect this person on salary to go to the library and clean out eight shelves, put it all in the back of the car, and bring it to the rehearsal room. And there it is—this great unappetizing lump.

What Kim does is she reads the play, then analyzes it as a work of literature and, because she's an immensely political person, as a work that comes with ideological baggage and with an ideological design. She presents research and reading materials and thinking about the deepest core of the play in terms of what it means as a work of art. That creates in the rehearsal room a sense of the immediate importance of what one is doing, rather than creating a museum era sort of thing. Actors, because they are badly trained in this, think their job is to do all this research. They hate doing it; they read about halfway through any book you give them. But they don't know *why* they're up on stage, and they don't *want* to know, because soon they're going to go and play Joe and Jane Doe, and do commercials trashing national health insurance, so it's best *not* to ask. Dramaturgs *should* be the intellectuals. That's what they *should* do.

Jonas: What if someone is doing this kind of dramaturgical "take" on *your* work? It's not Chekhov; it's *your* play? Is it weird to hear it?

Kushner: No, because it means somebody's performing an act that we should all be performing. Even if it's wrong, it starts the process. Kim is enormously smart, so when she came in and talked to these women about *Fen*, she brought in a vast amount of digested information about British socialist feminism, which you need to know if you're going to approach Caryl Churchill's world. And all of those issues are electrifying. Every single woman in this room responded, "This is my life." They read this stuff and they were turned on by it. Then ideas start to get fun, and people start to own the play in a way that's deep and important and real. That's what directors don't understand. They think that they should come in with this pre-first-reading chat about what the play means: "Why *I'm* doing this play and you people are all lucky to be in *my* vision of this play." But dramaturgs should not have an official place in the rehearsal room process. Dramaturgs should be as welcome in the rehearsal place as anyone, which is on the sufferance of the director. The relationship between the playwright and the director should not be intruded upon by anyone. Dramaturgs who feel they are getting in the way should know that if they *do* get in the way, they are probably going to do vast damage to the rehearsal, and consequently to the production. There are very famous dramaturgs who are nightmares, because they believe their job is to forcibly insert themselves in between. Their job is to absolutely never, ever get in between. The director and playwright have to talk to one another, or the playwright has to go away. I've done that.

Jonas: Who goes out for a drink with the dramaturg after rehearsal?

Kushner: The dramaturg should have the right to be an absolutely loathsome person, because what you want in a dramaturg is an absolutely brilliant mind. They don't need to know anything about the theater at all. They need to be able to come in and take the play and say, "This is what this is, and this is what this person is trying to do." Theoretically, it would be best if they didn't hate the play and could say, "This is why this is exciting."

Jonas: But with no conversation with the playwright?

Kushner: That's what my idea of what a dramaturg is. I'm incredibly prolix as a playwright and need help from somebody to say, "Cut this, cut this, cut this," but I would never go into a theater with a new script and sit down with someone I just met and let that person do that with me. It's much too scary because I'm suggestible enough. I would go and find Roberta Levitow or Ellen McLaughlin or K. C. Davis, or Oskar, although I know that Oskar isn't great about cutting. He's a sissy about it; he doesn't like losing words. He loves words, which is why he's great as another kind of dramaturg. He has very articulate suggestions about what he thinks you're trying to do, but Oskar isn't a great editor because he doesn't mind having an audience sit for eight hours. So if I need cutting, I go to people I think can cut. I have to know them and trust them, otherwise I don't want them around.

Scary dramaturgy asks, "What's *wrong* with this play?" Every writer has a list of people whom he or she can trust. They shouldn't trust them too much. I don't entirely trust Kim, who is my closest friend in the whole world, when she makes a suggestion. I think about the suggestion. I think about it very seriously. But she didn't write the play, and nobody but I will know if it's the right thing. You should be open to everybody and listen, but you should be armed to say, "Okay, that's interesting, but it's not this play." How do you train for that kind of thing? I don't know.

Jonas: It sounds like, whether or not you take their suggestions, you enjoy the conversations.

Kushner: It's great. Great things come out of it. After working for three and a half years on the angel's antimigratory epistle in *Perestroika,* I finally figured out what I was trying to say with it, at Joe Allen's at three o'clock in the morning in a conversation with Ellen McLaughlin, Jeffrey Wright, Stephen Spinella, George Wolfe, and Kimberly. We sat around and said, "What does this mean? What is this trying to say?" We came up with a couple of lines as a result of that conversation. We cracked the spine of the problem it presented, and I did a rewrite, but *they* made it work dramatically. Another time I was doing *The Illusion,* and there was something missing. Mark Lamos came over during previews and said, "Jerry, Mark's lover, watched the play last night and said, 'What am I watching? Why am I watching this play?'"

My first reaction was, "Well, I'm a very postmodern playwright. I don't give the audience that kind of moment. You have to figure it out for yourself." Then I thought, "What a bullshit defensive stance to take." I said, "I don't know how to write that." And Mark said, "I think you absolutely do. And I think you just have to ask yourself what is this play about for you? There has to be this moment towards the end where the penny drops, and the audience goes, 'Oh, I get it.'"

Connie Congdon loved the line where the father finds out that the kid is still alive, which was passed over rather quickly. She said, "I wish there was more of that moment, because it's very moving when you suddenly realize that his son is alive." So I repeated several times, "He's alive." I expanded it until it became the emotional center of the play.

One of the actors said to me early on in rehearsals, "Well, of course, what the play is saying is that there are many kinds of illusion. One is love, because what is love after all? You can say it exists; it's an illusion." It's an obvious point, but I never thought of it in that way. So I took that idea and I wrote it down. Then I had this great dream with Mark Lamos in a chef's suit, cooking something in a big white bowl. I woke up the next morning and I thought, "What a peculiar dream. What is that?" I was agonizing over how to write this moment. We didn't have any previews left and I had to get it written and I suddenly realized, "Oh! It's the Emperor of Ice Cream in the Wallace Stevens poem. . . ." You know . . . "Out with the maker of big cigars, the row of big cigars, the person who's whipping concupiscent curds in a bowl. . . ." Then I thought of the last line of that moment—the finale of the scene. I went for a run at the Hartford gym and literally wrote that speech while I was running around—the speech that the wizard had in the end about love being an illusion. It's about the nicest thing I ever wrote. All of those people fed into that. And that's why in the play's introductory material, I refer to Mark as "The Emperor of Ice Cream." That kind of process comes from a community of people focusing on one thing over and over and over again.

Jonas: I noticed in one of the interviews you gave, you said that you liked to be referred to as "a gay playwright."

Kushner: I said that partly because I always hate it when I read a gay playwright saying in an interview, "Well, I'm not a **gay** playwright. I'm a person and I'm a playwright and my plays aren't gay." It always feels like denial. "You're a **gay playwright.** You're gay, and you're a playwright." It feels like, "Don't reduce my market share by making me. . . ." I believe that there's a gay sensibility, and that my work participates in and partakes of it fully, and it's **my** sensibility. In the same way, I would never in any way balk at being called a Jewish playwright, because my sensibility is very Jewish.

Jonas: But you don't write for a Jewish audience, or a gay audience?

Kushner: Oh, I do in a way. I write for people like myself. You preach to the converted. That's what you're there to do. You envision an audience that's every bit as smart as you are, every bit as culturally knowing as you are, as far advanced evolutionarily as you are. Generally speaking, audiences are smarter than theater people, so we have to assume that and run to keep up with them, rather than go slow so they can "learn"; that's the worst kind of teaching. Your challenge comes from trying to keep *those* people entertained. It would not be a challenge to keep Jesse Helms entertained, because the man doesn't know anything!

Jonas: I look in *American Theatre* and every year see the same ten plays being done at all the regional theaters around the country. I'd love you to suggest to the dramaturgs, directors, teachers and playwrights who read this conversation some plays and playwrights that you really love, that aren't being read and done, so that they'll continue to be circulated.

Kushner: Suzi-Lori Parks is the most exciting playwright in America today. I think that her work will be done very widely. It better be, or there's no point in doing theater. Phyllis Nagy is a remarkable playwright who has not yet had a fair hearing in this country, but probably will very soon. A young woman, Naomi Wallace, whom I taught at University of Iowa and whose play I just directed, just won the Susan Blackburn Prize. She's extraordinary. Ellen McLaughlin is phenomenal. Her huge play, *Infinity's House,* is a masterpiece, and nobody's touched it. I think David Greenspan is remarkable and ought to be done a lot more. Fornes is an immensely important writer. I would love to see a great deal more attention paid to her, because she's neglected. There's a lot of interesting Adrienne Kennedy that should be reexamined. I would love to see someone give Amiri Baraka's work a reexamination. Even though politically he's sometimes very difficult, and sometimes he says things that are really sexist and homophobic, within those plays there are things that are hair-raisingly great. I'd love to see people dig into Richard Foreman's body of work, because I think he's a genius, and that isn't a term that I use lightly. I'd love to see more Gertrude Stein done. There's a lot of early John Guare that I think needs to be reexamined, like *Landscape of the Body.* It's become neglected, and it's so prescient. What's going to happen is the British are going to do it first. Why do they always get to that stuff first?

Jonas: How would you feel if in ten, twenty, thirty years, you looked at *Angels* and said, "You know what? Its time has come and gone?"

Kushner: You always run that risk. I would love it if *Angels in America* were still of value twenty years from now. But I think the worst thing, besides trying to write for everybody, is to write for immortality. It's impossible and a mistake.

Dramaturgy On The Road To Immortality:
Inside The Wooster Group

A conversation between Wooster Group dramaturgs **Norman Frisch** *and* **Marianne Weems**

NORMAN FRISCH was an associate member of The Wooster Group from 1983–1989. MARIANNE WEEMS has been an associate member of The Wooster Group since 1988. ELIZABETH BENNETT has worked as a dramaturg at Arena Stage and the Yale Repertory Theatre.

Frisch: Okay, the tape is rolling.

Weems: Here we go.

Frisch: So, Marianne.

Weems: Norm.

Frisch: Right up front I'll say that The Wooster Group is one of the more accomplished and longest-lived experimental theaters in America, and that during the past decade both you and I, at different points in time, have worked in it . . . on it . . . with it.

Weems: Right.

Frisch: Back in the mid-'80s, I used to say to people, "I work with The Wooster Group." "Oh, cool," they'd say. "The Wooster Group's fabulous. What do you do?" "Well, I played Allen Ginsberg in *L.S.D.,* sitting down at the end of the long table." "That was you?! Oh, yeah."

"Yup. And also I'm The Dramaturg." (So now I'm expecting them to be deeply impressed. But a funny look crosses their faces.) "The Wooster Group has a dramaturg?! What does a dramaturg do with The Wooster Group?" Or (even better), "The drama-what?"

Weems: Exactly. And what would you say to them?

Frisch: Well, I'm sure my answer changed over time. I came to The Performing Garage on Wooster Street in Manhattan, which is the Group's base of operations, first as a manager, having been a friend of the company for several years—to organize fundraising, touring, things like that. But I had dramaturgical and (at that time) directorial ambitions, and some experience, and soon Liz LeCompte found a role for me in rehearsals. At that time, *L.S.D.* was in its early stages of development, and there was written and recorded material which had been collected and generated for almost a year before I arrived, and an enormous amount of stuff that was not used in the previous show (*Routes 1&9*). And it was all—all this paper, these films, these books, these photos, these recordings—all this stuff was laying about everywhere in the Garage. Upstairs and down—every surface was littered with it. So for the first year or more, my primary role was as the keeper of all these precious and discarded materials. Therefore, at first, when I had to explain what a dramaturg does at The Performing Garage, I think I used to focus on the tasks of handling all of this material and of constructing the script. I would say something like, "The Wooster Group make their shows out of many, many bits of text and recordings and visual materials, drawn from a great many sources. Everyone is bringing them in all the time—performers, the director, designers, friends, technicians, the bookkeeper, the babysitter . . ."

Weems: It's true!

Frisch: I know! And I'd say that the dramaturg's function is to keep track of all that material and to work with the director in constructing a performance text. Or words to that effect. But I know that I changed my little rap over time, because I was inadvertently giving the impression that we were writing a script, so to speak. And, of course, we were not. At that time, and for that show—*L.S.D.* (which was also known as *The Road to Immortality, Part Two*)—each Wooster performance was quite unique, incorporating large amounts of improvised action and randomly timed events. So what we had was a rigid scenario for a performance, but never a set text. Or rather, it was a score—like some enormous jazz masterwork, recognizable as itself from night to night, but ultimately just a container for that night's jam. The Wooster texts—in their published or publishable forms—were in those days (during the Seventies and Eighties) always created long after the first performances of a production, usually toward the end of its touring life as a document and an artifact of the production, never as a guide for the actors. And any written transcription could only have reflected a single night's performance—so it would have been entirely arbitrary. It was not until into the third year of performing *L.S.D.*, for example, that we began to have a comprehensive text on paper. But I think you worked rather differently on the later shows, after my time, no?

Weems: Yes and no. But when did you actually start work there?

Frisch: In late 1983, I think. That whole part of my life is a bit of a blur. I'm forty-one now, and I started out twenty-two years ago as a stage manager and assistant director in summer stock and in regional theaters. Then I landed in the management program at the drama school at Yale, and in that same year—1977—met Jerzy Grotowski in New York. And the coincidence of those two influences, the tension created by this double life of the mind, really began to radicalize me. And then a sort of earthquake erupted: at one of the New Theater Festivals in Baltimore I stumbled into a performance of The Wooster Group's *Rumstick Road,* and there was no turning back. My real commitment to theater dates from that performance, I'm quite sure. Because for the first time, a piece of theater had changed my life, raised my consciousness by two notches and forever in the space of ninety minutes. And I then had to believe what I had been reading about for years—that this transformative experience was actually possible, not just in theory, but in practice.

Weems: That happened to me when I saw *L.S.D.*

Frisch: But The Wooster Group, I surmised then, was a closed shop—
certainly to some kid like me. At that time, I couldn't imagine what I
could bring to such a group, what I could contribute. But I had to find
out. My talks with Grotowski had drawn me toward Europe. And when an
invitation came to join one of the final paratheatrical projects being
mounted in Wroclaw, I knew that I couldn't forego the opportunity.

My poor parents. I left Yale to travel to Poland—which is not something
nice Jewish boys are expected to do. And when the project in Poland
wrapped up, I ended up as a dramaturg with a theater lab in Cardiff,
Wales—which in the late Seventies, alongside the Polish Lab and Odin
Teatret and Theatre du Soleil, was one of the more happening places in
Europe. That was the apex of the "third theater" movement, as Eugenio
Barba had termed it. The "first theater" being the worlds of commercial
and national theaters—industrial theaters, so to speak. The "second theater" being the institutional avant garde, existing within the boundaries of
the art world and its own systems of commodification—a sort of reac-
tionary response to developments within the first theater. And the third
theater being the manifestation of a genuinely worldwide counterculture
or subculture of itinerant performers and shamen, be they traditional theater practitioners or experimentalists or religious people or carnies, whose
mere existence recalled the mysteries that gave rise to a theatrical culture.
So I was extraordinarily lucky to have my first real dramaturgical experiences in this context, among people who took history and politics and
cultural identity and issues of training and one's relationship to one's audience very, very seriously. I'm not sure where I might have found this in the
States, although I know little pockets of such work existed.

Weems: And did you ever think of going back to Yale?

Frisch: Never. It never seriously occurred to me. In Wales I met Spalding
Gray, who was the first Wooster member I came to know well. He came
through performing one of his early monologues, together with a guy
named Bob Carroll, driving in a van together across Europe. *The Salmon
Show* was Bob Carroll's thing—did you ever see that? Carroll was one of
the first stand-up performance artist/storytellers. Completely queer. And
connecting with them, hearing about what was going on back at The Performing Garage, rekindled my sense of my own American-ness, and the
need for American centers as focused and as serious as these in Europe,
and made me want to be back in New York.

At that time, in 1979, The Wooster Group, Mabou Mines, Bob Wilson,
Foreman's group (Ontological-Hysteric), Ludlam, Serban, Squat, Bread and
Puppet, Meredith Monk, the remnants of the Open Theater, and Andre Gre-
gory's troupe—all those folks were still working in the city. Performance
Space 122 was just getting off the ground over in the East Village, and I had
connected with some of those P.S. 122 people over in Poland. My friend

Peter Sellars, whom I had met just before leaving the States, was about to graduate from Harvard, and we formulated a plan to both move to New York later that year—he from Cambridge and I from Cardiff. We just wanted to be around that scene together, and to be working in those spaces. And Peter had some early supporters, including Ellen Stewart at La MaMa, who were willing to showcase his work. Of the people of my own age, my own generation, there was no question in my mind that Peter was going to be one of my important professional partners. I knew that from the first time we began to work together, or even before that, when we met and had just begun to talk and to correspond—I think he must have been nineteen, and I was three years older.

So I arrived in New York penniless, not knowing many folks—my classmates were still in their last year at Yale and Peter was still up at Harvard—and Spalding took me in and let me live in his loft on Wooster Street while he was out on tour with his monologues. And there I met Liz and Willem, who lived at the same address, and the rest of The Wooster Group, and began hanging out at the Garage. *Routes 1&9* was the show in development at that time, and I was completely fascinated by it. Shaken to the core. I was sure it was the most elegantly structured, gorgeously performed, aesthetically brave work of theater I had ever witnessed, even in its early, unfinished state. Actually, I still think that, almost twenty years later. So when Peter arrived in the city, it was the first show I brought him to see. And he despised it, was literally nauseated by it. So right at the beginning of our working relationship, I was sure it was over—I thought I couldn't possibly work closely with someone who didn't see the beauty of *Routes 1&9*. And he thought my new art-heroes, my new friends, were deeply twisted sickos. So Peter and I had this rather serious falling out over *1&9*.

I really needed a job. And back in 1979, nobody really knew much from dramaturgs (believe it or not). So I managed, through my Yale friend Michael David, to get a job as an assistant to Des MacAnuff.

Weems: No.

Frisch: Oh, yes. He had just recently moved down from Canada and was making a real name for himself out in Brooklyn. And he was tremendously kind to me. Des knew all about sex and drugs and rock and roll, and I desperately needed to know about that stuff if I was ever going to do cool theater. Des even lived on St. Marks Place—that's how hip he was. And, indeed, decades later, he ended up staging The Who's *Tommy,* so that proves it.

Weems: But you did end up working with Peter, of course.

Frisch: Well, again, thanks to the Woosters. The next year, they mounted one of their retrospectives. And Peter came back with me to see all three or four of the productions being revived. And when he saw *Routes 1&9* again, alongside *Nayatt School* and *North Atlantic* and *Hula* and whatever else was on that season, he finally got it—the complexity and radiance of those shows, that dense language of references that underlay *1&9*—and became one of the Group's most articulate supporters. And so we were reconciled. By then his directoral career was taking its first very strange turns. He had been fired from *My One and Only,* the Gershwin musical that he had conceived for Tommy Tune, and won his MacArthur grant, and done his first important work on the Handel and Mozart operas in Boston and at the Pepsico festival. And he came back from a trip to Russia wanting to establish an ongoing company—to commit himself to moving forward artistically within the framework of a permanent ensemble—which was my ambition, as well.

That's when we reconnected professionally. He and I ended up back in Boston with The Boston Shakespeare Company and mounted a season there that included Peter's productions of *Pericles* and *A Midsummer Night's Dream,* some Beckett plays, and *The Lighthouse* by Peter Maxwell Davies, Tim Mayer's production of *Mother Courage* with Linda Hunt, and Joann Green's staging of Schubert's "Winterreise." Bill Rauch and other Harvard students who later founded Cornerstone Theater were our interns. But the dream of a permanent company, which had been inspired by the Woosters and the Russians—that whole Boston venture—survived for just one year, then crashed and burned. Peter was being courted from so many directions that he simply couldn't focus on it. And he hadn't nearly enough money to work with, to his way of thinking. So before that first season was over, he decided to go to Washington to become the director of the American National Theater at the Kennedy Center. And I had the chance then—because Jeff Jones, the Wooster's manager, had left to concentrate on his own writing and directing—to join The Wooster Group. And that's when I was plunged into the construction of *L.S.D.* and the whole intense Wooster culture—right around 1983.

Actually, the Boston Shakespeare experiment had one last after-effect. Peter and I had Flaubert's *The Temptation of Saint Anthony* in our minds for our second season in Boston, which never occurred. In fact, we had applied for and received a grant from the Massachusetts Arts Council to mount it as a collaboration with The Wooster Group. And Peter and I— despite the mutual sense of betrayal and abandonment surrounding the collapse of the Shakespeare season—really did recognize in one another a shared aesthetic approach that was too rare to turn our backs on. So we decided to carry on our collaboration with one another through Liz—

Weems: That's an odd way of putting it.

Frisch: —or through our mutual admiration for The Wooster Group's work; so we began to mount an early draft of the Flaubert, with Liz and Peter both directing the Wooster performers independently of one another, and myself functioning as the go-between and reconciler of the two rather opposing visions of the text. Peter brought The Wooster Group, now including myself, with him to The Kennedy Center as artists-in-residence for a long stretch of time—several months. And there we did a run of *North Atlantic,* a run of *L.S.D.,* and produced a great deal of the early version of *St.Antony.*

It was a crucial gesture of affirmation for the Woosters just then, Sellars' invitation to play at The Kennedy Center. We had just come through a gruesome year of legal hassles with Arthur Miller, who had barred us from using the text of *The Crucible* in *L.S.D.,* and succeeded in painstakingly remaking the show by substituting a text by Michael Kirby that mirrored the Miller dialogue syllable for syllable. And *North Atlantic* was a brilliant work—a military-cowboy-musical by Jim Strahs—a sort of *South Pacific* as staged by William Burroughs—and had been panned by the New York critics, dismissed as childish obscenity. But the Washington audiences adored both shows, the staff of the NEA became our unofficial hosts and groupies, all kinds of presenters were flying in from Europe to arrange future touring, and we were accomplishing a great deal of work on the next production, *St.Antony.*

Peter staged several scenes from the Flaubert text as ballets, with musical and textual overlays. And Liz videotaped the first drafts of the "Channel J" sequences (which featured the Wooster performers in the nude improvising an impressionistic rendering of Flaubert's text as if on a late-night, soft-porn cable television talk show). And we premiered some of Ken Kobland's video sequences, and began to experiment with integrating them into the stage action, alongside stagings of dialogue lifted from Ingmar Bergman's *The Magician.* And we all lived happily ever after—except that Peter's company at The Kennedy Center also crashed and burned. And all the material that he developed with the Group for *St.Antony* was eventually jettisoned. And after several years, Liz and I began to get on each other's nerves in a pretty serious way.

In '87, we were playing *L.S.D.* in the Los Angeles Festival, and Peter was out there, considering whether or not he wanted to take on the directorship of this Festival, which was one of the largest in the country—an outgrowth of the Olympic Arts Festival in 1984. Peter and I talked for a long time about what that festival could be, and when he accepted the position, he invited me to coordinate the curation of the festival, which we did together for six years. We mounted two very large festivals, one in 1990 and the last in 1993. And from '87 until 1990, I continued to tour with the Woosters in *L.S.D.* from time to time. By 1990, of course, Flaubert's *The Temptation of Saint Anthony* had been fully transformed into The Wooster Group's *Frank Dell's The Temptation of St.Antony.* But even from a distance, I could see that completing the show was an agonizing process and seemed to be nearly killing the Group.

Anyway, anyway . . . that's how I became the dramaturg for The Wooster Group.

Weems: It's a mysterious process—the way people find their place at the Garage.

Frisch: It is.

Weems: It *is.*

Frisch: At some point within my first few months of work at the Garage, although I had come to New York to fill in for the Group's manager, I had moved increasingly from the upstairs office down into rehearsal and actually into the performances, and we had begun to replace me in many aspects of the Group's management. And we simply realized that we had to in some way formalize my unique function in the Group's process. And I started saying on grant applications or to journalists that I was the dramaturg, hoping that nobody in the Group would say, "No you're not. We don't have a dramaturg." And they never did.

Weems: I think that Liz understood the tie to the European model. Certainly most American companies at The Wooster Group's level didn't have a dramaturg at that time. Dramaturgy was still this obscure European thing.

Frisch: And there was no one really filling that function with the Group— no single person, anyway. Kate Valk was the person up until then who had really been in charge of the texts. She was the person who would keep track of everything: the books and the transcripts and so on. And indeed Kate was the person, along with Ron Vawter, who was most interested in what was happening textually—in what was being said. Liz in those years was working so much as an architect that she seemed most of the time to be quite unconcerned with what people were saying. She was far more concerned with the construction, the building blocks of the piece, and the texture or the type of material being introduced, rather than with the specific textual material of each piece. So this gave me a great deal of freedom to work directly with the performers on what it was that they were interested in saying, within the framework that Liz was gradually designing around them. There were these various planes of fabrication going on simultaneously, with different people focused on different elements in the same moment. So this became my primary function eventually, as the dramaturg—to reconcile these many and varied, sometimes compatible, sometimes mutually exclusive, approaches that twelve or twenty Wooster Group members were pursuing alongside one another every single day in that windowless space.

For example, while we were making *L.S.D.,* Liz was very much concerned with the actual skeletal theatrical structure, as manifested in the set and sound design, the way the acts unfolded one into another, and in diagramming all this in her notebooks. Her notebooks are amazing documents. Or in the play of amplified and unamplified voices. Or in the juxtaposition of textiles on stage. But she had no interest in plot. And she doesn't construct "themes," as such, she rather just observes them as they emerge, if they emerge, out of what the actors are thinking and doing.

Whereas Kate Valk, who was trained by Stella Adler and is a "real" actress, was deeply interested in the construction of character—characters

within the pieces. At that time—I'm thinking now of the early development of *L.S.D.* and on into the making of *St. Antony*—Liz was hardly concerned with that at all. Character was a completely fluid notion to Liz. She
didn't like that too-close identification of any actor with any single character. Lizzie loved it, for example, when two or three actors would be playing
the same role simultaneously. When Willem Dafoe as John Proctor was replaced by Jeff Webster (while Willy was shooting *Platoon*), and then Steve
Buscemi began shadowing Jeff (because one of Jeff's parents was ill and
he might have needed to leave the show in midtour); and then eventually
all three of them were on stage in varying combinations from month to
month, all in the same role—well, Liz was in heaven. Absolute heaven.

So while Liz was revelling in these experiments with theatrical form,
my function became that of supporting the performers in their efforts to
fill the forms with meaning. For example, during the making of *L.S.D.,* Ron
Vawter was concerned with the performance of the source materials
themselves—the Timothy Leary and Gordon Liddy materials, the Arthur
Miller text, the spiritual investigations of Arthur Koestler and Alan Watts
and Allen Ginsberg. Peyton Smith and Nancy Reilly were particularly interested in eyewitness and firsthand accounts of people who had been
involved in various psychedelic scenes, and who had been at Millbrook.
Michael Kirby had an enormously strong connection to the Burroughs and
Ginsberg texts, which had been such important artistic reference points in
his own life at the time they were first published.

In fact, for most of The Wooster Group, all these materials really were
the stuff of their own growing up and coming out and coming to New
York, and were tied up with what brought them to theater in the first
place, and to experimental theater in particular. And they really wanted it
treated. So there were all of these people—twenty people—with various
agendas, each of whom were bringing their own "stuff" into rehearsal. And
my role as a dramaturg really was to function as a kind of traffic cop, to
help all of these people get as much of their "stuff" as possible into the
process, simultaneously, and without obscuring one another.

L.S.D. was about looking back on the utopian revolutions of one's youth
from the perspective of middle age. It was about the people who joined
Schechner's Performance Group for *Dionysus in '69* or *Tooth of Crime* in
their early twenties looking back at that time as they turn forty. It's about
Allen Ginsberg watching his friends and lovers die, one by one, and deciding to live on and write on. It's about Timothy Leary's children remembering their childhoods, the wild weekends, and the prison cells. It's about
shooting your wife at a drunken party and living with the consequences of
that, or perhaps escaping the consequences of it, for decades and decades
to follow. It's about starting out as a Green Beret recruiter and ending up
as a famous faggot actor—which was Ron's story. I mean, like all of the
Wooster shows during that period, it was just about the members of the

Group, and where their heads were at in that year, at that moment, as focused through Liz. And that was its great, great accomplishment, I'm sure.

One of the things that I've always most loved about The Wooster Group's work is that at any given point in time you can look at what's happening in rehearsal or what's recently been performed and see a kind of encoded chronicle of the group's life during the previous year. There's no question in my mind that one can read *L.S.D.* and *St. Antony* and almost all the other Wooster works as diaries of what the Group members were living through during the years in which those pieces were made. The pieces are public manifestations of these private conversations going on inside The Performing Garage.

Certainly *St. Antony* was initially all about constructing a piece around Ron in bed following his collapse back in 1986, during the revival of *Routes 1&9* at the Kitchen, when he came near to dying. It was Ron who really embraced *St. Antony* as a subject matter and refused to let it go, even when Liz was kind of done with the collaboration with Sellars. Because for him it was a resolution of his religious calling. Remember, Ron had been in a seminary during part of his military career. And that impulse toward the priesthood has turned out to be the first step for him toward theater, and toward coming out and coming to terms with his true individual nature.

Weems: So everyone was bringing source materials into rehearsals?

Frisch: In that case, during the making of *L.S.D.,* the material was pouring into the rehearsal room. The books, the drugs, the films, the transcripts, the props from the earlier shows, the record albums. . . .

Weems: And how much of the actual source material did you bring to the process?

Frisch: Oh, almost none. It was all being brought in by the cast members. Some of it was in written form. Obviously, *L.S.D.* was a very booky show and there were eventually piles of books on the stage, directly reflecting the construction process and rehearsals. People were picking up these books, free associating off of one anothers' materials, finding a reference from one line of source material that would corroborate or counterpoint another. And films—the Kennedy assassination films, the Lenny Bruce performance film, Donna Sierra and the Del Fuegos. . . .

Weems: Wasn't that left over from *1&9?*

Frisch: It must have been, because they had already done a lot of work on it by the time I arrived. But that, I think, is the way that all of the Wooster pieces have begun—out of the refuse, the material that was cut out of previous productions and things that people, for one reason or another, are just not yet ready to let go of.

Weems: I think the new piece is always built on the shards of what's left over from the last one. The Group recycles images and icons and architectonic fragments, and that process contributes part of the epic sense of continuity in the work.

Frisch: Certainly in the transition from *L.S.D.* to *St.Antony* that was the case. The Lenny Bruce material, the little nightclub act in Miami—all of that was clearly heading somewhere that was not resolved in *L.S.D.* In fact, there was a big overlap period between the completion of *L.S.D.* and the beginnings of *St.Antony,* as I said before. And how did it work on the other end of *St.Antony?* I had left the Group by then to work on the festival in L.A., and you came on board sometime after, in 1988.

Weems: I would say that at the end of *St.Antony* there really was a lot of closure for the Group. That piece was such a struggle that by the time they were done with it, they were really done, and Liz was ready to move on to a new theatrical vocabulary.

Frisch: That is how the performance itself ends, isn't it? I mean, you see that in the show. *L.S.D.* ends with a gunshot in the dark and this strange cabaret having appeared out of nowhere—and you can feel the audience's response: "What? It's over? What happened? That's it?" It's very much like those historic revolutions that the show describes.

Whereas, *St.Antony* ends with a real Hollywood finale—with the actors packing their trunks and loading the van and Ron Vawter (who may or may not be dead) wrapping himself like Gloria Swanson, ready for his close-up—St. Antony's vision of Christ in the sunrise. And one knows without doubt, "This is the end of an era." It was the staging of Ron's death, in which he allowed us to participate, and it was the end of The Wooster Group as it had been anchored by him during his lifetime.

Weems: The piece really transformed the miracle play. Really, it was one long, glorious resolution.

Frisch: Now, I had worked on *St.Antony* for more than a year—almost two—when I left to work on the L.A. Festival. And I know you were on hand for its final stages of development. I remember you at the Garage, but I don't remember us working together, really—at least not as dramaturgs.

Weems: We didn't overlap at all. What happened was . . .

Frisch: Yes? . . .

Weems: Well, like everyone else who has passed through those doors, I came to The Wooster Group by a circuitous path. I suppose it's clear by now that no one who's ended up there has done it by graduating from a theater program, applying for a job, then being handed a job description and a contract.

Frisch: Right. But what about you?

Weems: I grew up in Seattle and fled to New York in the early Eighties, where I began working peripherally with some of the more open-ended downtown types, Meredith Monk, Ping Chong, Charles Allcroft (who was one of Jack Smith's last assistants), and others. I finally decided to finish school at Barnard where I graduated in music composition and comp lit. At the time I had conflicting feelings about the music world, particularly classical musicians, who always gave me the feeling that I was about to be entombed in a mausoleum. And of course I was seduced by the semiotic and deconstructive theory, which was sweeping liberal arts campuses at that time. I was also writing music for various theater groups, and I became much more interested in the processes by which these works were created than in the music itself.

Once I got out of school I worked in education at the Museum of Modern Art, and I was enrolled in the Whitney Museum Independent Study Program, which was de rigeur for all "downtown" visual artists in the Eighties. We worked with Barbara Kruger, Yvonne Rainer, Hal Foster, and many other influential artists and critics. I was one of the few performance people who had ever gone there. So you see I was really cutting my teeth on a kind of cross-media education. I also was a founding member of a performance and study group called The V-Girls. We acted as kind of guerrilla academics, performing panels at which we "presented papers" constructed around feminist critiques of the academy. We appeared at many university gatherings and conferences, museums and galleries throughout the country and Europe during the Eighties. During that time I also helped found and administrate a new foundation called Art Matters. One of my jobs was to make studio and site visits and attend performances around New York, so for five or six years I saw pretty much every "cutting edge," multimedia piece of theater and performance that took place in New York. Of course I had always admired The Wooster Group's work and now I came to revere it, since it threw into stark contrast what else was taking place in the mid-Eighties. Of course there were other exciting artists out there. John Jesurun, John Kelly, and Karen Finley were manifestly productive, and Richard Foreman was still creating wonderful work—but it was abundantly clear that the lack of funding and time and space for rehearsal was forcing the New York performance scene into a kind of "settle for less" mode. And the Group's pieces were grounded in such a deep history, an ongoing, aesthetically coherent body of work—you could feel the weight of that every time you walked into The Performing Garage.

Parenthetically I have to add that Liz and others have always said that, at bottom, The Wooster Group's survival rested on their owning the Garage—their home base. They have always had a solid piece of real estate to fall back on where they could work as long as and whenever they needed to. This base has also contributed to their ability to build a loyal, enthusiastic audience. They really have established an intimate dialogue with a community in New York which has made them independent of critics and other journalists and even advertising to a certain extent. The Group sells out showing their works-in-progress, and the same audiences return to see the work in different stages of development. The Group very, very rarely opens shows to the press because they don't need to. They operate entirely independently of a cumbersome institutional framework. They're one of the few self-producing success stories left in America.

Anyway, I knew some of the administrative people working with the company, and I'd met the rest of them here and there. I worked with Richard Foreman on *Symphony of Rats,* which was a collaboration with some of the Group members: Kate, Ron, Peyton, and Jeff Webster. . . .

Frisch: How did you get that gig?

Weems: I wrote Foreman a letter that started with a long Lacanian joke and ended with a plea to let me sit in on rehearsals. So I met him at his loft amidst all of the posters and props from his old shows. He was sitting there making tape loops, and he stopped long enough for us to talk about what he was reading. After a while he invited me to attend rehearsals for *Symphony of Rats,* which he was just beginning. So I did and was of course completely floored by Ron, and by all of the members of the company, and particularly loved the way that Richard made the dances, so organically and suddenly.

Around this time I also saw The Wooster Group's retrospective at the Kitchen, including *1&9,* and I had seen *L.S.D.* several times at several different stages, and also the Group's brilliant collaboration with Foreman, *Miss Universal Happiness.* I had been developing and directing my own small-theater pieces for about three years, and I decided I was ready to leave the foundation world. I wanted to get closer to The Wooster Group, to find out about their process, and to try to discover how what was so complex and multivalent was actually formed. So this time I wrote Liz a letter.

Frisch: And what did it say?

Weems: That I worshipped her work. You know, the usual.

Frisch: Uh-huh.

Weems: But I meant it, and I met her, and after we talked for a while Liz said "You know, I need a dramaturg." I was surprised, but thrilled, of course. I had assumed that someone had taken up that role since you had left almost a year before, but apparently not. So I jumped right into the thick of *St. Antony,* which was about two-thirds finished, I'd say. The production was at that stage where everyone knew everyone's lines, so no one had bothered to write anything down for about a year. There were fragments of text floating around, but, coming from the outside, I could garner nothing about what had come from where. So the first thing I did was to construct a new script on the computer (a first for The Wooster Group). I couldn't have done it without Kate Valk, who had the patience to correct my many misattributions and guesses. And when I went over the script with Liz she was fascinated and seemed slightly surprised to find that one could actually make this text legible. . . .

Frisch: Well, I don't suppose The Wooster Group had ever created a script before then during the actual rehearsal process. Only after the shows had run for maybe six months or a year were there attempts to organize them on paper.

Weems: Yes, well, when I entered into *St. Antony* there was enough salvage-able material to create a script. Before I arrived, there was a long period where large sections of text were shifted every day, and so many different kinds of material were being displaced that there would have been no point to it. But there always comes a point in the work where things structurally and musically start to fall into place, and that's a good time to start putting things down on paper.

By the way, it's interesting that you say that Liz was working primarily visually, which of course she always does. But I came to believe that first, last, and foremost, she approaches the actual text musically. For instance, during *Brace Up!* (the piece after *St. Antony*, based on Chekhov's *Three Sisters*), if she was trying to tell Joan Jonas how to perform the line "What a miserable goddamn life," she would say, "Joan, it's: What a nana-nanana-na." You know, she would sort of sing the line in this syllabic way that would indicate where it should be placed rhythmically, how it should work musically—but not attach it to the actual . . .

Frisch: Words.

Weems: Right.

Frisch: And *L.S.D.* functioned very much in that way, too.

Weems: Absolutely.

Frisch: It's just one long song that these performers are creating back and forth across the table with one another. And in fact when the Arthur Miller material had to be forcibly removed, it was a tremendous relief to Liz. The audience naturally gets quite attached to a text like *The Crucible*. And so when she had an excuse for taking it away, and for people going "Blblblblblblblblbl!" she was thrilled! It became a more pure musical experience.

Weems: I think that has occasioned a lot of the writing around The Wooster Group's approach to abstraction and narrative. In fact, these are merely small examples of a larger phenomenon, especially in *St. Antony*, where these lines, and the larger narratives they contribute to are eviscerated of narrative sense—they keep the structures of telling a story, but the content of the story is constantly shifting. So one follows all of these different lines that never reach any conclusive reading, that move toward but never reach one meaning.

Frisch: But the performances do depend on the fact that an audience does care about meaning, and the performers do care about it. And I think it's one of the reasons that audiences experience such a sense of bonding with The Wooster Group actors, that they take them so to heart. Because a sense develops in the room that the actors and the audience are really trying to get someplace together. And that, in a way, Liz is creating an obstacle course that obliges the audience to help the actors, and the actors to help the audience, to get to that place that they all seem to want to reach by the end of the evening. And one of Liz's great delights and most effective tricks is to end the show before that moment of mutual satisfaction, which leaves everyone in a state of expectation, or mystery—wondering what that moment would have felt like.

Weems: Absolutely. It's fascinating what Liz chooses to reveal to an audience. Constructing the program notes with her for instance. . . .

Frisch: I spent a great deal of my time with The Wooster Group generating the program materials for the many successive versions of *L.S.D.* and *St. Antony,* both—constructing program notes that would give the audience some handle on what was going on on stage. It was a constant point of tension between Liz and myself, because Liz's tendency is not to want to give the audience anything useful—or rather, to deliberately give them information that is unuseful.

Weems: I'm not sure that it's purposely obfuscating. I think the program has simply become another layer of material in the performance.

Frisch: But people aren't used to dealing with program notes in that way, and so . . .

Weems: For instance, in the *St. Antony* program we added short summaries of what the troupe was doing in each scene. You know, "Onna and Phyllis place a phone call to Frank"—something like that. They were obscure details, but it was something for the audience to identify as it flashed past. Our final version of the program notes had one column of summaries of the episodes of Flaubert's *Saint Anthony,* and another column summarizing events in the life of the troupe in the hotel room, which also functions as a contemporary version of Bergman's *The Magician.* And the audience could read back and forth between the two.

Frisch: Hmmm. Amazing. So you saw *St. Antony* through to its completion, and I was curating the festival in L.A . . . .

Weems: I remember when we brought the production to L.A. during the 1990 festival. We were on the panel together discussing the show. And you said, "Well, when I left New York, I thought this piece was going to kill the Group; but now I realize that the Group has killed the piece." I took that as a compliment, although I don't know if anyone else did.

Frisch: I certainly meant it as a testimonial to their strength. That they had struggled through this dark night of the soul, with the truly demonic forces underlying this work—with death, with illness, with fame, with boredom—and they had survived to perform it all in this one show.

Weems: It's true, they conquered it. And after *St. Antony,* everyone seemed to breathe a conceptual sigh of relief. There really was a break and a new sense of energy. New people were brought in to work on *Brace Up!* (including Joan Jonas and Beatrice Roth). We started with a specific text, Chekhov's *Three Sisters,* in a new translation by Paul Schmidt.

Frisch: And obviously your work as a dramaturg must have been completely different.

Weems: Yes, it was, entirely.

Frisch: Was it anything more like a conventional . . .

Weems: Dramaturgy? It's hard to say. I think that by the end of *St. Antony,* having wrestled it to the page, I had become identified as 'keeper of the text." So I spent a lot of time with Liz and with Kate reviewing the text of Chekhov's *Three Sisters.* It turned out that *Brace Up!* was not about people bringing in an enormous variety of different kinds of material. We started specifically from *Three Sisters* and that's where we stayed for a long time, about two years actually. Paul Schmidt, who did the translation, was present at the rehearsals; he played Chebutykin. So having "the doctor" on call settled a lot of the minor dramaturgical issues that came up.

Of course, we worked with other framing materials. Liz was interested in different kinds of Japanese material. We spent hours and hours looking at tapes of Noh and Kyogen plays with no translation. People would nap, Liz would take notes, and eventually we'd start a little rehearsal. One thing that was distinctly different from previous productions was our absolute adherence to every single stage direction in the Chekhov. The directions became sacrosanct. The setting, every sound effect, the video, the lights, everything was directly influenced by each minute stage direction in the Chekhov. This began as a slightly humorous rereading of the classical Stanislavskian approach, and ended up contributing to a kind of hypernaturalism that Liz was developing.

Frisch: The other thing that I remember observing from a distance was the development of the dances for *Brace Up!,* which I think are gorgeous. Kate Valk had come along with Sellars and me in 1988 on a research trip to Australia, to attend a festival of Pacific cultures, and taken hours and hours and hours of performance video. And I was aware that she and Jeff Webster had begun soon afterwards to work on that material—the dances from Wallis and Futuna, and the other Micronesian and Polynesian dances.

Weems: Kate also played a central role as a "Benshi" in this piece, explaining and elaborating on the story of the *Three Sisters.* We went to see one of the last working Benshis at the American Museum for the Moving Image, and Liz and Kate had recently seen a Benshi perform in Japan, as well. Another central source text was a documentary film called *Geinin,* which was about a Japanese traveling theater troupe who traveled around to low-rent hotels, performing their Western-influenced song and dance routines. And of course that was a continuation of the traveling theater troupe trope from *L.S.D.* and *St. Antony,* but in an Eastern register.

The Geinin troupe emerged again in the transition from *Brace Up!* to *Fish Story*—there's a great deal of seamless overlap between these two pieces, where things that were foregrounded in *Brace Up!* were simply moved to the background for *Fish Story.* And parts of Chekhov's *Three Sisters* that we never fit into *Brace Up!* served as points of departure for *Fish Story*—fragments of Act 4, for instance. And the idea of a Japanese theater troupe who are performing a vaguely familiar Western "classic" was an idea buried deep in *Brace Up!* but is made explicit in *Fish Story.* In any case, another interesting thing about working with Liz on *Brace Up!* was that every day—I'm sure you're familiar with these conversations with her—every day she would produce a story that was the central story to the piece.

Frisch: But a different one every day.

Weems: Sometimes antithetical from day to day! But each one was The Story. And the discovery of these tiny narratives was central to the process, even if they became completely buried, because all these readings eventually are allowed to sit next to each other in a polyphonous way. Each day ended with an account of the narrative that that day had produced (for example, the centrality of the life of the maid, Anfisa or the importance of Masha drinking a glass of water). For a long time I was writing them down and pointing them out as they resurfaced, but then it became clear that it wasn't about trying to sustain and combine them as one narrative.

Frisch: Marianne . . .

Weems: Norm.

Frisch: Let me ask you an odd question: were you ever a "real" dramaturg, before joining The Wooster Group?

Weems: Real dramaturg? No, not at all.

Frisch: You were just a director?

Weems: I was a director, and I had done a lot of work with text in different contexts, but I certainly wasn't trained as a dramaturg.

Frisch: Indeed. I had studied Asian politics in college and was training as a journalist—which in fact is excellent dramaturgical training. But you can't relate your Wooster Group experience to, say, dramaturging Shaw plays at Hartford Stage?

Weems: I'm afraid not. Can you?

Frisch: Maybe. I think our work with a company like the Woosters has both nothing and everything to do with what dramaturgs normally do.

I mean, what dramaturgs are doing in general, I think, is working to reconcile the content of a production, which usually manifests itself as the script—the words, the action, the themes—with the form of the production, which usually manifests itself as the performance style, design elements, and so on. And usually the latter is derived from the former—the form is derived from the content, the production is derived from the script—because most conventional theater is an interpretive enterprise. Everyone involved in a production is referring to the same script. So the job of keeping them in sync is not so overwhelming a task, because the creative partners are more or less starting from the same place and moving in the same direction, and production dramaturgy is usually just a question of keeping them in some sort of healthy, timely relation to one another.

And, needless to say, working with The Wooster Group is nothing like that. I imagine that it's among the most extreme dramaturgical experiences one can undertake. There is no chicken or egg when it comes to questions of form and content, script and production. And people's roles in the processes of both construction and interpretation are highly fluid. At any given point during the creation of a single show, one may be juggling six "scripts" and eight notions of a work's "form," all developing simultaneously, each with its own adherents. And one has to allow each to unfold as fully as possible, because one can never be sure which is going to find its way into the performance, which is going to survive the years-long evolutionary process, which is going to turn out to be important in the end. And even elements that are eventually edited out may turn out to be crucial at a later stage, before the work is finished, or even in the making of the next project. So one can never really let an idea just fall by the wayside. Everything has to be archived in some manner for future reference.

Weems: And you won't ever get to the next step until you've thoroughly explored what's on the board.

Frisch: And this can get extraordinarily exhausting and complicated. Because, although one may pretend that one is attempting to stage some fragment of text—or even an entire play by O'Neill or Chekhov—what is actually being staged in a Wooster production is the life of the rehearsal room. So the material—that life—that one is staging is being manifested in the very moment one is staging it. It is never static. It is never really knowable. The nature of it is rarely, if ever, agreed upon by the players involved. So the dramaturg, in projecting some order or pattern onto all these fluid, disparate, multidimensional elements, takes on a difficult role in interpreting the very private impulses and gestures of one's colleagues. You may think you're making an observation about Masha, or Jones, or Tituba, but if the lines between performer and performance have been intentionally blurred, your observations may be taken quite personally. Likewise, you may know that what someone is working hard on is turning out to be of minor importance, or is on its way to being edited out entirely of the production. But indicating this at the wrong moment would be quite disheartening to that colleague and might derail them from the journey through that material and out the other side of it to something more valuable. It's all dynamite, and it can explode in your face at any moment.

Weems: I think, too, that as a dramaturg with The Wooster Group, you quickly discover that there's no "outside" vantage point from which to view the piece. It's like a physics experiment where your mere presence affects the atoms as they interact—you're part of the process, and so you're implicated in a way that doesn't allow for a kind of clinical dramaturgy. There's no point in stolidly maintaining a scholarly approach. It's not a question of "I was trained as a professional dramaturg, and I can do my job for any production, whether I care about it or not."

Frisch: That is why it always gave me great satisfaction to perform in *L.S.D.* Liz and Ron "cast" me as Allen Ginsberg, which was precisely correct. I mean, what I was doing on stage in *L.S.D.* was exactly mirroring what I did in rehearsal for the Group.

Weems: That's great.

Frisch: And Liz has an enormous talent for . . .

Weems: Framing people.

Frisch: Yes, on stage. So performing the role of Ginsberg, and the role of Earl Sandle (the blind Christian who has been shot in the face), and running the video for the acid sequences (from which all the action onstage is cued)—all helped me to more clearly understand my functions within the Group. Each of these performances was a metaphor for a role I was playing out in rehearsal and in the management of the company.

For example, Ginsberg saw himself as the historian and as the chronicler of the Beat movement, and as the repository of all of his friends' materials. He was a Jew; he was a clown; he was bookish; he was a hero-worshipper; he was an enthusiast; he was an unrequited lover. All of this put him in a certain relationship to his comrades, and kept him in role of the observer—the scribe. And "playing" him contributed enormously to my own ability to communicate to my Wooster colleagues who I was and what I was doing in the room with them.

Weems: I suppose I assumed an analogous position in *Brace Up!* because I too ended up on stage at the back table with the script.

Frisch: You know, I never knew exactly what you were doing back there. And, of course, the audience never can know in a Wooster work what anyone on stage is really doing without seeing the "score" that performer has in front of them. But I always assumed that what you were effectively doing was calling the show to the actors. Like the kind of prompter who usually is obscured by that little downstage shell popping up from the floor.

Weems: Hmm. Well, during the early work-in-progress shows, we were playing a series of games with the Chekhov, timing sections and such that I was in charge of, and later in the process, the performers could drift away from the text, so I was on book in order to get them back on track. But that function has long since passed, and it's sort of a vestigial role at this point. So one becomes a visible symbol on stage of what one did in the process of making the piece.

Frisch: And where has it propelled you, those years with The Wooster Group? Now you're primarily directing again, yes?

Weems: I am, and I'm delighted to be doing so. But before I left, I did some work with Ron Vawter, we created *Roy Cohn/Jack Smith* (with Greg Mehrten and Clay Shirky) and toured Europe, and made a film of that show, and did some other work with Greg Mehrten, who was Ron's lover.

Frisch: In *Roy Cohn/Jack Smith,* you must have been in a more conventional dramaturgical position, because you were staging a text that existed before the commencement of rehearsals, yes? Two texts: the Roy Cohn speech, as imagined by Gary Indiana; and the excerpted audio recording of Jack Smith in performance.

Weems: I ended up doing a lot of research for Gary about Roy Cohn, and we had many lengthy evenings with Gary talking about the angle that Ron wanted to develop, how he wanted to approach Cohn as a character who was both sympathetic and menacing—in order to avoid a completely didactic performance.

Frisch: And how did you then function in rehearsal?

Weems: I became assistant director and producer. I produced the American and European tours of the show, and later coproduced the film version with Good Machine (Ted Hope and James Schamus), which Jill Godmillow directed, and Jonathan Demme executive produced.

Frisch: And what new piece were you working on with Ron and Greg when Ron died in the spring of '94?

Weems: We were beginning a piece called *Dark Victory: The Ascent,* to be directed by Susan Sontag, which was actually more along the lines of beginning a Wooster Group project, because we began with disparate kinds of material that Susan wanted to explore—all around the idea of illness and death in literature and film. The piece was named after Bette Davis' film *Dark Victory*. Susan planned to open the piece with Ron crawling up the stairs as Bette Davis does at the end, and to cast Greg as Bette's helpmate whom she heroically sends away. Susan and I had done a lot of research on different film clips that we'd been kicking around. But one of the reasons we went to Italy, where Ron died, was to settle down in Bellagio and begin creating a script. That never transpired.

Frisch: And now? You're directing.

Weems: Yes, I have an ensemble called The Builders Association that is made up of performance and media artists, including Jennifer Tipton, Ben Rubin, Jeff Webster and many others. The piece that we just completed is based on Ibsen's *The Master Builder.* And it is well within this tradition of placing different texts next to each other to see what emerges and what recedes.

Frisch: And what are those different texts, in addition to Ibsen's play?

Weems: Well, I'm working with some industrial films from the Forties and Fifties about the construction of the home and the maintenance of a happy family. And I'm obsessed with Gordon Matta-Clark's late architectural experiments with splitting houses, and television home-construction shows such as "This Old House."

Frisch: So you function as your own dramaturg when you direct?

Weems: At this point, yes.

Frisch: And does your cast take on a certain dramaturgical function, or do you really retain it yourself?

Weems: I basically try to set where we're going, and then I invite the company to bring in whatever they think might be appropriate, and most of it isn't, but I also see that as part of building an ensemble. If you throw your net wide, somebody's bound to bring in something that will spark the next idea. Some people are good at it, and some people aren't; that emerges over time. Anyway, we're just beginning a production of *Faust* to be produced in Zurich, and hopefully in New York as well. What are you working on now, dramaturgically?

Frisch: Nothing, really. I'm working primarily as a performance curator for various presenting institutions—an outgrowth of my work on the Los Angeles Festivals. I did some research and thinking last year and the year before for a *Merchant of Venice* with Peter Sellars. It was a pretty challenging idea. It posited the absolute antithesis of so-called colorblind casting, whatever you'd call that—tribal casting, I guess. But in the end, by the time we found someone who was actually willing to stage the production, I was up to my ears in curatorial work, so Peter ended up doing it with the staff dramaturgs at the Goodman Theater—Richard Pettengill and his crew—which is where it landed. Later it toured in Europe. Peter's talking about filming it later this year out in L.A., at Venice Beach, and at that point I think I'd like to reinvolve myself in it.

Weems: That's pretty radical.

Frisch: But I don't know when, if ever, I will get back to production dramaturgy. Reza Abdoh, who was a playwright and director, was a close friend of mine. We shared a house together in L.A. And since the late Eighties I had more or less come to think of his work as the future of American theater. His company, dar a luz, existed for only a few years—first in Los Angeles, then in New York, but playing mostly in Europe—and with it Reza was positing a fusion of operatic and poetic ideals with the stuff of American political and pop culture . . . as performed by a tribe of street kids. But since his death in the spring of 1995, I've had difficulty looking around the theater "scene" and projecting any kind of future—either for it, or for myself in it.

Before we end, let me ask about your advice to young dramaturgs. I can't think of anything in my theater training, other than my experiences in the European labs, that really prepared me for the kind of work I was doing with The Wooster Group. I'm not entirely sure how anyone would prepare—although I'm enormously impressed by some of the young university dramaturgs I meet every year at the LMDA conferences who are curious about the Woosters and Reza and so on. But I wonder where they'll work?

One thing I do believe is that the creative partnerships that young people make early on, even in school, should be taken a lot more seriously than they are. I know a lot of the best director–dramaturg teams—and director–designer teams—are people who began working together as graduate students or undergraduates and have been working together for fifteen or twenty years. Those are the dramaturgs that I point to, in many cases, as being really the most creative people in the field. After five or ten years of working with the same colleagues—that's when you really begin to be able to get down to something. It all flows from that shared . . .

Weems: Sensibility.

Frisch: Yes. Let me ask you, did you ever read anything that helped you enormously in thinking about yourself as a dramaturg?

Weems: That's a good question, and there are too many things to mention here. But one thing that was extremely useful during my time with The Wooster Group was W. R. Bion's *Experiences in Groups.* Have you ever read that book? Do you know who Bion was?

Frisch: No.

Weems: He was basically the first psychoanalyst to posit the notion of group therapy. He was Beckett's analyst—much good he did him, you know, he lived with his mother for her entire life. But he was an extremely bright British analyst who, during World War II, theorized a system of group psychology as a rehabilitation program for soldiers. Many people still refer to him regarding ideas of how groups form and reform around leaders; how a leader functions; how a group demands a leader to a certain extent; how certain members within a group help facilitate the relationship between the company and the leader; and in the absence of a leader, the demand to create a new one. It's a brilliant book about group dynamics, and it was interesting while at the Garage to read and reread that. And you?

Frisch: Well, as I said, Allen Ginsberg's journals; and later the annotated editions of *Howl* and *Kaddish* that eventually appeared—these really touched me, with their talmudic structure and their approach to the texts. I think that David Savran's book on The Wooster Group, *Breaking the Rules,* is a fascinating study of how an ensemble functions—the interview material, in particular. It should absolutely be required reading for all university dramaturgs—and actors, as well. Michael Kirby's books on Futurist and Structuralist theater. Stefan Brecht's series on Robert Wilson, Bread and Puppet, and Queer Theater. Warhol's films—every one of them. And Fred Wiseman's documentary filmmaking. Now *that's* dramaturgy. E. Martin Browne's book on the making of T. S. Eliot's plays. All of this was very important to me as a young person. In fact, the Eliot, especially—I loved this book when I was nineteen years old. So I suppose that from such peculiar youthful obsessions, great dramaturgs are born, huh?

NOTES ON THE WOOSTER GROUP

Compiled by Elizabeth Bennett

The Wooster Group is an ensemble of artists who, for twenty years, have collaborated on the development and production of theater and media pieces. The core members of the Group are Jim Clayburgh, Willem Dafoe, Spalding Gray, Elizabeth LeCompte, Peyton Smith, Kate Valk, and Ron Vawter.* Under the direction of LeCompte, the Group, with its associates and staff, has created and performed a large body of work at the Group's permanent home, The Performing Garage, in the Soho district of New York City. The primary activity of The Wooster Group is the collaborative creation and presentation of original work for theater and television. In contrast with conventional practice, The Wooster Group as a whole functions as producer for its new works, each member taking on a number of responsibilities during the course of a piece's development. Wooster Group theater pieces are constructed as assemblages of juxtaposed elements. They combine radical restagings of classic texts, found materials, films and videos, dance and movement works, multi-track scoring, and an architectonic approach to design. Through a process of overlaying, collaging, and sometimes colliding systems, the structure of a piece gradually emerges and the various elements fuse into a cohesive theatrical form. Not afraid of the "noise" of the modern world, the work incorporates the techniques and images of our new electronic age. Overall, The Wooster Group's work has been concerned with themes of paradox and ambiguity, of the collision and integration of cultures, of spiritual transformation and materialism, of social decay and regeneration, and ultimately of the artist's place in society.

From an "Introduction/Brief History" written by the members of The Wooster Group

Wooster Group Theater Productions

The Hairy Ape (1995): written by Eugene O'Neill
Fish Story (1994)
The Emperor Jones (1993): written by Eugene O'Neill
Brace Up! (1991): Source materials included Paul Schmidt's translation of Chekhov's *Three Sisters* and a documentary about the Ichikawa Santuro Geinin troupe.
The Road to Immortality:
> *Routes 1&9* (1981): Source materials included Thornton Wilder's *Our Town,* recordings of Pigmeat Markham performing his comedy routines, and an Encyclopedia Britannica teaching film.

---

*Editor's Note: Ron Vawter died in April 1994.

L.S.D. (. . . Just the High Points . . .) (1984): Source materials included texts and recordings by Allen Ginsberg, Aldous Huxley, Timothy Leary, Jack Kerouac, William Burroughs, and others; recollections provided by Timothy Leary's children and their babysitter Ann Rower; Arthur Miller's play *The Crucible* as rewritten by Michael Kirby as *The Hearing.*

Frank Dell's The Temptation of St. Antony (1987): Source materials included *The Temptation of Saint Anthony* by Gustave Flaubert, Flaubert's *Letters From Egypt,* Ingmar Bergman's film *The Magician,* material by and about Lenny Bruce (particularly Albert Goldman's book *Ladies and Gentlemen, Lenny Bruce!!*), and Geraldine Cummins' *The Road to Immortality.*

Three Places in Rhode Island:

Sakonnet Point (1975): Source materials included recollections of childhood memories shared by Wooster Group members.

Rumstick Road (1977): Source materials included taped conversations between Spalding Gray and his grandmother, father, and his mother's psychiatrist.

Nayatt School (1978): Source materials included T. S. Eliot's *The Cocktail Party;* a 1950s recording of *The Cocktail Party* (featuring Alec Guinness); Jim Strahs' text "The Breast Exam"; the record "Drop Dead" by Arch Oboler; a Folkways instructional record called "The Understanding and Self Examination of Breast Cancer."

Point Judith (An Epilog) (1979): Source materials included Jim Strahs' text *The Rig* and Eugene O'Neill's *Long Day's Journey into Night.*

North Atlantic (1984): written by Jim Strahs.

Dance pieces:

Hula (1981)
For The Good Times (1983)

Collaborations written and directed by Richard Foreman:

Miss Universal Happiness (1985)
Symphony of Rats (1988)

Film and video work:

Rhyme 'Em to Death (1994)
White Homeland Commando (1992): written by Michael Kirby
Flaubert Dreams of Travel But The Illness of His Mother Prevents It (1986)
Rehearsal Tape: Wrong G, Summer 1987

Schema for the The Temptation of St. Antony:

THE ARGUMENT

A Hotel Room in Washington D.C.	Sunset in the Desert
Episode 1: The Monologue In Which Frank Runs His tape, and takes a call from Cubby.	"Enfeebled by prolonged fasting, the hermit finds himself unable to concentrate upon holy things. His thoughts wander; memories evoke regrets that his relaxed will can no longer suppress. His fancy leads him upon dangerous ground."
Episode 2: The Dance Break In Which Frank rehearses the Girls in a dance.	"The scene shifts. The Queen of Sheba descends to tempt the Saint with the deadliest of all temptations. In fantastic obedience to his fancy, the scene changes again."
Episode 3: The Digression In Which Onna and Phyllis Rearrange the hotel room furniture and Frank talks intimately with Sue.	"Under the guise of a former disciple, Hilarion the demon endeavors to poison the mind of Antony. He cites texts only to foment doubt, and quotes the evangels only to make confusion. And Hilarion grows taller."
Episode 4: The Party In Which Frank Takes a Rest and Onna practices some verbal routines. They convince the hotel maid and the bartender to join in.	"Hilarion induces Antony to enter with him into a spectral basilica. The hermit is confounded. By this hallucination the tempter would prove to the Saint that martyrdom is not always suffered for the purest motives."
Episode 5: Old Times Remembered In Which Dieter Reveals Himself and the Troupe prepares to perform as Frank takes another call from Cubby.	"The tempter assumes the form of a Hindu Brahmin, terminating a life of the wondrous holiness in self-cremation. Then he seeks to shake Antony's faith in the excellence and evidence of miracles."
Episode 6: The Magic Show In Which Onna and Phyllis Recall the Cotton Bandage Test, "The Invisible Chains," and the Catalepsy Test. The Performance Ends Abruptly and the Troupe Packs Up.	"Hilarion reappears, taller than ever, growing more gigantic in proportion to the increasing weakness of the Saint. He evokes deities; phallic and ithyphallic; fantastic or obscene. Venus displays the rounded daintiness of her nudity. Hilarion towers to the stars, Antony is lifted upon the mighty wings and borne away above the world."

Episode 7: The Monologue Continued
In Which Phyllis Leaves, Onna Finishes
Packing and Frank Hears Again from
Cubby.

"Antony comes to himself in the
desert. The tempter returns as the
Spirit of Lust and the Spirit of Destruction. The latter urges him to suicide,
the former to indulgence of sense.
Antony feels a delirious desire to unite
himself with the Spirit of Universal
Being. The vision vanishes. The Temptation has passed. The face of Christ is
revealed."

—from *The Temptation of Saint
Antony*, Modern Library Edition, 1911.

The schema for *The Temptation of St. Antony*, written by Liz LeCompte and Marianne
Weems, was previously printed in the program for the production.

FOR FURTHER READING

Aronson, Arnold. "The Wooster Group's *L.S.D. (. . . Just the High Points . . .). The
Drama Review* 29 (1985): 65.

Arratia, Eurydice. "Island Hopping: Rehearsing The Wooster Group's *Brace Up!" The
Drama Review* 36 (1992): 121-141.

Barba, Eugenio, and Nicola Savarese. *The Dictionary of Theatre Anthropology: the secret art of the performer.* New York: Routledge Press in association with the Centre
for Performance Research, 1991.

Champagne, Lenora. "Always Starting New: Elizabeth LeCompte." *The Drama Review*
25 (1981): 19-28.

Foreman, Richard. *Plays and manifestoes.* New York: New York University Press, 1976.

Foreman, Richard. *Unbalancing Acts: Foundations for a Theater.* New York: Theatre
Communications Group, 1992.

Fuchs, Elinor. "*North Atlantic* and *L.S.D.*" *Performing Arts Journal* 23 (1982): 51-55.

Grotowski, Jerzy. *Towards a Poor Theatre.* New York: Simon and Schuster, 1970.

Kirby, Michael. *A Formalist Theatre.* Philadelphia: University of Pennsylvania Press,
1987.

Kirby, Michael and Victoria Nes Kirby. *Futurist Performance.* New York: PAJ Publications, 1986.

LeCompte, Elizabeth. "Who Owns History?" *Performing Arts Journal* 16: 50-53.

Mee, Susie. "Chekhov's *Three Sisters* and the Wooster Group's *Brace Up!" The Drama
Review* 36 (1992): 143-153.

Rabkin, Gerald. "Is There a Text on This Stage: Theater/Authorship/Interpretation."
Performing Arts Journal 9: 142-159.

Savran, David. *Breaking the Rules: The Wooster Group.* New York: Theatre Communications Group, 1988.

Savran, David, "The Wooster Group, Arthur Miller, and *The Crucible*," *The Drama Review* 29 (1985): 105.

Schmidt, Paul. "The Sounds of *Brace Up!* Translating the Music of Chekhov." *The Drama Review* 36 (1992): 154-158.

Shank, Theodore. *American Alternative Theatre.* London: The Macmillan Press, Ltd., 1982.

Vanden Heuvel, Michael. *Performing Drama/Dramatizing Performance.* Ann Arbor: University of Michigan Press, 1994.

SECTION NOTES

1. Gustav Freytag, *Technique of the Drama,* trans. Elias J. MacEwan (Chicago: S. C. Griggs & Company, 1895) 1.

2. This famous formulation included five steps: Introduction, Rising Action, Climax (the apex of the pyramid), Falling Action, and Catastrophe. It borrows from Aristotle the emphasis on plot, the focus on a single hero, the causative nature of dramatic action, and the inevitable demise or fall of the hero. Freytag's structure also bears close relation to the basic pattern of the French well-made play: exposition, complication, climax, and denouement.

3. Freytag 4.

4. Francisque Sarcey, "A Theory of the Theatre," *Papers on Playmaking,* ed. Brander Matthews (New York: Hill and Wang, 1957) 125.

5. Bronson Howard, "The Autobiography of a Play," *Papers on Playmaking,* ed. Brander Matthews (New York: Hill and Wang, 1957) 25.

6. Jackson G. Barry, *Dramatic Structure* (Berkeley: University of California Press, 1970) 14.

7. Brander Matthews, *The Principles of Playmaking* (New York: Charles Scribner's Sons, 1919) 5.

8. George Pierce Baker, *Dramatic Technique* (Boston: Houghton Mifflin, 1919) 3.

9. William T. Price, *The Technique of the Drama* (New York: Brentano's, 1892) iv.

10. See Jürgen Habermas, "Modernity—The Incomplete Project," *The Anti-Aesthetic: Essays on Postmodern Culture,* ed. Hal Foster (Seattle: Bay Press, 1983) 3-16.

11. Wisner Payner Kinne, *George Pierce Baker and the American Theatre* (Cambridge: Harvard University Press, 1954) 2.

12. Ed. note: Readers may find it interesting to compare this list of books with Mark Bly's in section two and John Lutterbie's in section three.

13. In 1911 Harvard granted its first advanced degree in creative writing, courtesy of the MacDowell Fellowship in Dramatic Composition. The fellowship made it possible for writers such as Eugene O'Neill and Thomas Wolfe to attend English 47 as graduate students.

14. Kinne 287.

15. Alfred Hennequin, *The Art of Playwriting* (Boston: Houghton Mifflin, 1890) viii.

16. Kinne 68.

17. Playwrights do have to try to make a living, though, and commercial considerations would never be entirely separable from the how-to tradition. Fanny Cannon published *Writing and Selling a Play* in 1915; Arthur Edwin Krows wrote *Playwriting for Profit,* an especially direct title, in 1928; Louise Howard and Jeron Criswell offered *How Your Play Can Crash Broadway* in 1939, and there have been many successors. It is fairly routine for contemporary books about

playwriting to include marketing information, and the continuum of emphasis suggested in the title *Writing, Producing and Selling Your Play* (Louis E. Catron, 1984) is typical of recent work. The notions of culture that underlie the dramatic prescriptions of men such as Baker and Matthews couldn't hope to triumph completely over American commercial ethos.

18. See David R. Shumway, *Creating American Civilization: A Genealogy of American Literature as an Academic Discipline* (Minneapolis: University of Minnesota Press, 1994).

19. Howard 33.

20. Brander Matthews, *A Study of the Drama* (Boston: Houghton Mifflin, 1910) 96.

21. See Kenneth MacGowan, *A Primer of Playwriting* (New York: Random House, 1951). MacGowan was a student of George Pierce Baker in English 47, so it is not surprising that *Primer* owes a good deal to *Dramatic Technique*. Still, MacGowan is eclectic in his borrowings, and he moves easily from Lessing to Freytag, to W. T. Price, to Archer, and to later how-to theorists such as Marian Gallaway, John Howard Lawson, and Lajos Egri. MacGowan's book is notable, in fact, for its wide-ranging familiarity with the how-to tradition and for the precision of its commentary on individual writers.

22. An "obligatory scene," part of the vocabulary of the well-made play, is any scene that MUST be written and presented by the dramatist, because the structure of the play and the expectations of the audience demand it.

23. William Archer, *Play-Making: A Manual of Craftsmanship* (Boston: Small, Maynard and Company, 1912).

24. Sam Smiley in *Playwriting: the Structure of Action* (1971) begins his remarks on structure by affirming the universality of Aristotle's dictum that a play is an action "as qualified by imitation, powers, magnitude, and completeness . . . these principles, and those to come, apply to any play. They function as fully in epic or absurdist drama as they do in realistic or well-made plays." It is the rare book in the how-to tradition that substantially avoids or refigures Aristotelian terms. Jackson Barry's *Dramatic Structure* (1970) offers a valuable critique of traditional terminology and posits a fresh way of looking at structure as weaving together of that which feels patterned and that which feels improvisational. But in the main, the how-to tradition cleaves to its original aim of aligning Aristotelian principles with the dramaturgy of the nineteenth-century theater, particularly with ideas of "well-madeness."

25. Stuart Griffiths, *How Plays Are Made* (London: Heinemann Educational Books, 1982) 17.

26. Matthews, *A Study of the Drama* 277–8.

27. Kinne 111.

28. Sam Smiley, *Playwriting: The Structure of Action* (Englewood Cliffs, N.J.: Prentice-Hall, 1971) 61.

29. Ferdinand Brunetière, "La loi du theatre," *Annales Du Theatre Et De La Musique* (Paris: 1893) xi.

30. Matthews, *A Study of the Drama* 103.

31. Louis E. Catron, *The Elements of Playwriting* (New York: Collier Books, MacMillan Publishing, 1993) 22.

32. Kinne 154.

33. Matthews, *A Study of the Drama* 120.

34. Price 23.
35. Kinne 172.
36. Smiley 74.
37. Smiley 74.
38. Barry 21.
39. Griffiths19.
40. As an introduction to feminist theories of dramatic form, see Sue-Ellen Case's "Toward a New Poetics," the final chapter of her *Feminism and Theatre* (New York: Routledge, 1988).
41. Michael Vanden Heuvel, *Performing Drama/Dramatizing Performance* (Ann Arbor: University of Michigan Press, 1991) 18.
42. Ed. note: For a brief biography of Leon Katz see "The Compleat Dramaturg" by Leon Katz in section two.
43. Associate Literary Manager of the Public Theater in late 1970s, early '80s. More recently Associate Artistic Director at the La Jolla Playhouse.
44. Literary manager at the Public Theater in the 1970s, early '80s. Most recently Director of program development for PBS's "American Playhouse."
45. Director of play development and key force at the Public Theater for most of its existence.
46. The National Playwrights Conference at the Eugene O'Neill Theater Center in Waterford, Connecticut.
47. The Brown-Forman Classics in Context Festival, founded in 1985, celebrates and examines classical drama within the political, biographical, social and aesthetic context of its creation. The festival surrounds productions on stage with films, lectures, exhibits, and discussions. Over the years it has featured performances by the Moscow Art Theatre, the Berliner Ensemble, the Picolo Teatro di Milano and individual artists such as Jacques Lecoq and Bill Irwin.
48. This quote was typed and tacked to our bulletin board by my literary manager predecessor, Julie Crutcher, sometime prior to my arrival at Actors Theatre of Louisville in 1985. Michael Feingold acknowledges that it reads like something he may have written and continues to write, but is unsure of its exact source— probably a play review in *The Village Voice* from the early 1980s.
49. Those who continue to work as part of the resident dramaturgical staff, in addition to myself and assistant literary manager Liz Engelman, are Val Smith, Marcia Dixcy, Julie Crutcher, and Bellarmine College Scholar in Residence Jim Valone. Other literary staffers who have contributed to the development of our process over the years are: Michele Volansky, Deborah Frockt, Chiori Miyagawa, Kathleen Chopin, Nancy Beverly, and Elizabeth King. Guest dramaturgs in recent years have included Elizabeth Wong, Tom Szentgyorgyi, and Victoria Norman Brown.
50. A serious advocate of dramaturgs, Actors Theatre of Louisville producing director Jon Jory wrote this statement for this article in 1993. In addition to his support for the dramaturgical process at Actors Theatre, it's also worth noting that Jory sponsored a National Contest for Dramaturgs in 1986, which was won by Dr. Felicia Londre, Professor at the University of Missouri at Kansas City and dramaturg at Missouri Repertory Theatre. Her proposal for a festival focusing on the French Romantics provided a blueprint for the 1987 Classics in Context Festival that included more than thirty arts and cultural organizations in Louisville. The prize was $1,000, and Dr. Londre was commissioned to create an evening of Ro-

mantic poetry, *Wanderers,* performed by a cast of four. The National Contest for Dramaturgs ended after one year, when officers of a new organization, Literary Managers and Dramaturgs of America, voiced their objections to the idea of a national competition for dramaturgical proposals.

51. The Guthrie Theater in Minneapolis.
52. Marlane Meyer is a Los Angeles playwright, currently living in New York City. Mame Hunt has worked as a dramaturg on several of Marlane's plays and has championed her work for several years, most recently producing *Kingfish* at the Magic Theatre. Hunt was also the dramaturg on the world premiere of *Etta Jenks* at the Los Angeles Theatre Center in 1988.
53. See *The Dramatists Sourcebook* (New York: Theatre Communications Group, each year) for information on these and other playwright development programs.
54. Dramaturg at South Coast Repertory Theatre in Costa Mesa, California.
55. Former Artistic Director of the Goodman Theatre in Chicago.
56. *Still Life* (New York: Dramatists Play Service, 1982) is Emily Mann's documentary drama taken verbatim from interviews.
57. Yale Repertory Theatre. Dramaturgy students at the Yale School of Drama read scripts for Yale Repertory Theatre as part of their course work.
58. A playwright and former literary manager of Playwrights Horizons in New York City.
59. The Los Angeles Theatre Center, a four-theatre complex in downtown Los Angeles from 1985 to 1991 under Producing Artistic Director Bill Bushnell. Also referred to as LATC and The Theatre Center, it was created when the LA Actors' Theatre, also run by Bill Bushnell, expanded.
60. Bill Bushnell, former Producing Artistic Director of The Los Angeles Theatre Center.
61. The Actors Theatre of Louisville has had a new play festival every spring for eighteen years.
62. A New York-based Cuban-American playwright, raised in Los Angeles. His major plays include the Floating Islands trilogy, *Broken Eggs* and *Rosario and the Gypsies.*
63. Founded in 1976 by Robert Woodruff who was Artistic Director of the festival until 1982.
64. A Puerto Rican–American playwright based in New York. Her play *Miriam's Flowers* was published in *Shattering the Myth: Plays by Hispanic Women,* ed. Linda Feyder (Houston: Arte Publico Press, 1992).
65. Roberta Levitow is a Los Angeles–based director and one time artistic staff member of the Los Angeles Theatre Center. She directed the premiere of *Etta Jenks* at LATC and is a frequent participant, both as director and dramaturg, in new play development including with the Bay Area Playwrights Festival.
66. The Denver Center Theatre.
67. Los Angeles Actors' Theatre developed into the larger Los Angeles Theatre Center in 1985.
68. Linda Walsh Jenkins, "Locating the Language of Gender Experience," *Women and Performance* 2 (1984): 5–20.
69. Playwright and associate professor of theater, film and television at UCLA. The panel was on ethnic writing and Edit's paper was "Self Identity, Selective Memory."

and the Will to Speak Out: Playwriting and Cultural Pluralism" at the Atlanta ATHE Conference in 1992.

70. *Piano* by Anna Deavere Smith (New York: TCG Plays in Process, 1989). *Piano* was developed in the Women's Project at the Los Angeles Theatre Center where it was given a staged reading in 1987. In 1989 it was produced by American Conservatory Theatre in San Francisco.

71. By Jose Cruz Gonzalez, published by Rain City Projects, Seattle. *Harvest Moon* was workshopped in 1991 and later premiered at the Group Theatre in Seattle. Jose Cruz Gonzalez is associate literary manager at South Coast Repertory Theatre, where he created the yearly Hispanic Playwrights Festival.

72. By Mira-Lani Oglesby. Developed in the LATC Women's Project and given a staged reading at the Los Angeles Theatre Center in the Festival of New Plays, 1989.

73. Anna Deavere Smith had four production dramaturgs: Elizabeth Alexander, Oskar Eustis, Dorinne Kondo, and Hector Tobar; and one physical dramaturg: Merry Conway, who worked with her on accurate physical expression of the thirty plus people she was portraying.

74. Anna Deavere Smith interviews people (usually diverse people involved in a race or gender incident or issue) and creates a one person performance where she portrays, verbatim, the people she has interviewed. She calls this series of interview performances which she has been creating since 1985, *On the Road.* The largest and most widely publicized have been *Fires in the Mirror* at the Public Theatre in New York in 1992, and *Twilight Los Angeles* at the Mark Taper Forum in 1993. Others include *Chlorophyll, Postmodernism and the Mother Goddess: A Converse-ation* (1988) and *Gender Bending: On the Road/Princeton* (1989).

75. Playwright, director and Artistic Director, Emily Mann's *Still Life* and *The Execution of Justice* are documentary dramas. *Still Life* is taken verbatim from interviews and edited together; *The Execution of Justice* is taken entirely from court transcripts.

76. Published in *Voicings: Ten Plays from the Documentary Theatre,* ed. Atilio Favorini (Hopewell, N.J.: The Ecco Press, 1995).

77. Founded the Open Theater in New York in 1963 with Peter Feldman. In 1978 he and Sam Shepard collaborated on a piece, *Tongues,* first performed at the Magic Theatre; they collaborated again on *Savage/Love.* Both were revived at the Magic Theatre in 1994.

78. Michel St. Denis, *Theatre: The Rediscovery of Style* (New York: Theatre Arts Books, 1960) 48–49.

79. There is some precedent for this empirical approach to realism. Literary typologists often link the emergence of realism to the rise of naturalism in the late nineteenth century, a movement whose scientific objectives were championed by Émile Zola in *The Experimental Novel.*

80. Wolfgang Iser, *The Act of Reading: A Theory of Aesthetic Response* (Baltimore: Johns Hopkins University Press, 1978) 72.

81. August Wilson, Preface to *Joe Turner's Come and Gone* (New York: Penguin Books, 1988).

82. Iser 69.

83. Marcel Proust, *Remembrance of Things Past,* trans. C. K. Scott Moncrieff and Andreas Mayor, 2 vols. (New York: Random House, 1970) 2:1020.

84. Immanuel Kant, *The Critique of Judgment,* trans. J. H. Bernard (London: Hafner Publishing, 1931).

85. Cf. *Plenty, Map of the World,* and *Racing Demon.*

86. Cf. *Two Small Bodies, Raw Youth, On the Bum,* and *Ready for the River.*

87. Quoted from bookjacket, *Self Torture and Strenuous Exercise* (New York: Theater Communications Group, 1991). Cf. *Christmas on Mars, The Vampires,* and *Anteroom.*

88. Respective references are to moments in *The Winter's Tale, Phantom of the Opera,* and *Miss Saigon.*

89. Edmund Wilson, *The Wound and the Bow,* (New York: Oxford University Press, 1965) 240.

90. Iser 21.

91. Proust 2: 1008.

92. Proust 2: 1031.

93. Roland Barthes, *S/Z,* trans. Richard Miller (New York: Farrar, Straus and Giroux, 1974) 4.

94. Barthes 16.

95. Proust 2: 1017.

96. Of course, the experienced dramaturg can assess early on in the reading of a play, the craft level of the playwright. In this essay we are discussing the relatively inexperienced playwright at the student level.

97. Interesting to note that the Italian word *dramaturgico* means playwright.

98. These sensitivity concerns underscore one of the major shortcomings of the postreading or postproduction session, in which spectators are invited to fire away at the playwright. The sheer weight of the verbiage soon renders numb the suffering playwright, who strains to "grin and bear it." Rather than recycle the already apparent problems, it is usually more productive to hand out a two-question sheet and serve refreshments. Two questions I have found most useful: What did you respond to most strongly in the play? What would you like to see more of, or what was unclear about the play?

99. Panel Presentation "Marketing and Developing your Script," chaired by author, Southeastern Theatre Conference (SETC), Washington D.C. (March 1993).

100. This method is effective because young playwrights often conceive endings thematically, rather than as outcomes of behavior.

101. Stanley V. Longman, "The Dramaturgy and the Will of the Play," *Theatre Symposium* 3 (1995): 55-62.

102. There are notable exceptions to this, including the fine work of the People's Light and Theatre Company in Malvern, Pennsylvania. Allen Kennedy's article in section three of this volume describes this work in detail.

103. The initials ASSITEJ stand for Association Internationale du Theatre Pour L'Enfance et la Jeunesse, (International Association of Theater for Children and Young People).

104. Harold Oaks, "What's Happening in Theatre for Young Audiences?" *TYA Today* 9.2 (March 1995): 11.

105. *ASSITEJ/USA White Paper,* ASSITEJ/USA, (Seattle: distributed to ASSITEJ/USA membership at One Theatre World Conference, 12 May 1995).

106. *ASSITEJ/USA, White Paper.*

107. "Lila Wallace Reader's Digest Foundation, New Generation Playwright's Forum." This event took place as part of One Theatre World, an international theatre

symposium jointly sponsored by ASSITEJ/USA, The Seattle International Children's Festival, and The Seattle Children's Theatre, on May 13, 1995.

108. National Endowment for the Arts/Lila Wallace Reader's Digest Foundation: New Generation Play Project, 1988. Lila Wallace Reader's Digest Foundation: New Works for Young Audiences Program, 1991–1995. Support from the Bonderman and Eccles Foundations are on-going to fund The Bonderman/IUPUI National Youth Theatre Playwriting Competition and Symposium and the Sundance Children's Theatres respectively. The Theatre for Youth Chair at the University of Texas is an endowed chair provided by an anonymous donor that funds the New Play Development Program at the University of Texas at Austin on a yearly basis.

109. Oaks 11.

110. Y York's adaptation of Janet Taylor Lisle's novel *The Afternoon of the Elves,* commissioned by Seattle Children's Theatre in 1991 is an eloquent example of this kind of play. This script focuses upon the friendship of two young girls, as one of them struggles to hide her mother's increasingly incapacitating mental illness.

111. *About Young Playwrights Inc.:* Fact sheet and informational material distributed by Young Playwrights Inc. (New York: 1995).

112. *About Young Playwrights.*

113. YPI Committee has included Christopher Durang, Ruth Goetz, Carol Hall, David Henry Hwang, Albert Innaurato, Marsha Norman, Mary Rogers, Alfred Uhry, and Wendy Wasserstein among others.

114. Dr. Dorothy Webb is professor of theater and chair of Communications Studies at Indiana University/Purdue University at Indianapolis.

115. Dorothy Webb, personal interview, 14 September 1995.

116. Webb.

117. *Program Descriptions:* Fact sheet and informational materials circulated by Sundance Children's Theatre (1995).

118. Jerry Patch, personal interview, 15 September 1995.

119. Patch.

120. *Mission Statement, New Visions/New Voices:* Fact sheet and informational materials circulated by Youth and Family Programs, John F. Kennedy Center for the Performing Arts. (Washington, D.C.: Sept. 1995).

121. Kim Peter Kovac, personal interview, 15 September 1995.

122. Judy Matetzschk, "Contemporary New Play Dramaturgy: Structures and Techniques. A Report of Current Practices in the Field of Theatre for Young Audiences." dissertation, University of Texas at Austin, in progress.

123. Webb interview.

124. Patch interview.

125. Herbert Kohl, "A Plea for Radical Children's Literature," *Should We Burn Babar?* (New York: The New Press, 1995) 62.

126. Kohl.

127. For me, terms such as "minority," "otherness," "marginalized," and "dominant" have inherent problems in their usage. If I live in a gay community, make gay theater, and have a credit card that is financially connected to a gay funding organization, haven't I created for myself a dominant culture, at least in my own circle? So I use these words with a grain of fruity salt.

128. At The Foot of the Mountain was the long-lived, Minneapolis-based women's theater. Deb is currently Artistic Director of Four Big Girls.

129. These were not masks in the *commedia* or masquerade sense, not made of papier mâché or any other material. Rather, they were facial expressions imprinted and frozen through sculptural movement on the actors' own faces. In the finished work, both these facial masks and masks made of *papier mâché* were used.

130. Our process was perhaps not so different from that of the Open Theater nearly thirty years ago, where writer Megan Terry was present at the ensemble process led by Director Joseph Chaikin during the development of various projects. The very act of witnessing the actors work *before the text was made,* must have profoundly informed Terry's writing process. Just as she was learning the language of actors, the performers were learning that they were *generating* material, not merely *interpreting* an exercise or monologue. The director's and playwright's task encompassed the skills of dramaturgy, text development, play-making and perhaps most critically, learning the actors' languages. Though we have many theatrical ancestors who have paved the way for this kind of process, we still had the fortune of feeling as if it was our very own discovery.

131. I think perhaps there is no such thing as a transition, really. If an actor thinks they are in one, they probably have not made a necessary link between what they are doing in one moment and then another.

132. From the script of *Contents,* by permission.

133. *Contents.*

134. *Contents.*

135. *Contents.* The sex and gender roles were constantly changing between the two actors, so please try to imagine that almost every line is spoken by a new voice, with four characters emerging: the boy hooker, his trick, the girl, her boyfriend. Both the actors, one woman, one man, played all four parts at different times during the section.

136. Nicholas Von Hoffman, *Citizen Cohn,* (New York: Doubleday, 1988).

APPENDIX

This section contains a variety of resources for individuals interested in dramaturgy: first of all, a brief glossary and some relevant dates along with an extensive compendium of quotes on dramaturgy and related subjects. Victoria Abrash, dramaturg and former president of Literary Managers and Dramaturgs of the Americas (LMDA), describes organizational efforts that have done much to give dramaturgy a sense of identity and direction. She also reviews several important services that LMDA offers students, teachers, and professionals.

Anne Cattaneo has made available a series of exercises she uses with students to explore theater history, dramatic criticism, and a variety of dramaturgical strategies. Teachers or students planning independent study projects in dramaturgy may find it useful to borrow her exercises in part or whole. Jane Ann Crum's interview with Cattaneo further clarifies her approach. Of course, these ideas are only suggestive of the many ways in which a dramaturgical sensibility is being nurtured in various graduate and undergraduate theater programs. For further materials on teaching and dramaturgy, individuals should consult *The LMDA Source Book: Resources on the Teaching of Dramaturgy*, edited by Susan Jonas with the assistance of LMDA members: a compilation of syllabi, curricula, articles, exercises, and other tools useful in teaching dramaturgy available through the LMDA offices. (See section five, "Addresses," in the bibliography at the end of the appendix.) Some dramaturgy syllabi and teaching materials may also be found on the "dramaturgy northwest" web page (www.ups.edu/theatre/dramaturgy/index.htm). Finally, one of the best forums for information on education and dramaturgy is the annual University Caucus Pre-Conference held on the day before LMDA's annual conference. For information on upcoming pre-conferences, the reader can contact the LMDA offices or the editors of this volume.

Deborah Torres and Martha Vander Kolk kindly share their guide to theater resources on the Internet. Their guide offers the reader many excellent online starting points.

Finally, a comprehensive bibliography provides numerous suggestions for further reading and exploration.

‖ Glossary

AATE: The American Alliance for Theatre and Education.

ASSITEJ: Association Internationale du Théâtre Pour L'Enfance et la Jeunesse (International Association of Theater for Children and Young People).

ATHE: Association for Theatre in Higher Education; the professional organization for university and college teachers of theater.

LMDA: Literary Managers and Dramaturgs of the Americas; the professional organization of dramaturgs and literary managers; for an account of its history see Victoria Abrash on page 527.

LOG: a dramaturg's regular diary of observations about the production process.

THE O'NEILL: The National Playwrights Conference at the O'Neill Theater Center in Waterford, Connecticut; one of the major venues for the development of new plays; a pioneer in the use of dramaturgs as part of the developmental process.

PROTOCOL: as described by Leon Katz in "The Compleat Dramaturg" (this volume, section two), is a "four-part pre-production study of a play— together with a glossary of the text, for the information of the Director and possibly of the rest of the company. The parts consist of (1) relevant historical, cultural, social or other pertinent background of the play, (2) relevant biographical information concerning the playwright, (3) a critical and descriptive production history of the play, and (4) a critical analysis and breakdown of the play. The glossary consists of a script with facing notes explaining all unfamiliar or questionable terms and references in the play"; similar to a CASEBOOK (see Bly in this volume).

TCG: Theatre Communications Group; founded in 1961, TCG is the national organization for nonprofit professional theater.

TDR: *The Drama Review;* a journal with a focus on contemporary theater; has published on dramaturgy along with Yale *Theater* (formerly *yale/theatre*) and other journals.

‖ Some Relevant Dates

1767: Gotthold Ephraim Lessing becomes resident critic at the Hamburg National Theatre; he writes a series of essays that will become the *Hamburg Dramaturgy*.

1905: George Pierce Baker begins to teach English 47, The Technique of Drama, at Harvard; over the course of his career, his students will include Eugene O'Neill, George Abbott, Sidney Howard, S. N. Behrman, Philip Barry, and Elia Kazan.

1908–1910: John Corbin at the New Theatre in New York becomes one of America's first literary managers.[1]

1925: George Pierce Baker moves from Harvard to Yale and organizes that institution's first drama department.

1920s: Bertolt Brecht serves as one of Max Reinhardt's dramaturgs.

1920s and 1930s: John Gassner and Francis Fergusson are literary advisers to the Theatre Guild and the American Laboratory Theatre. (See below an excerpt from Francis Fergusson's letter to the administration of the American Laboratory Theatre.)

1931: Harold Clurman with Lee Strasberg and Cheryl Crawford establishes the Group Theatre; Clurman functions in many respects as the theater's dramaturg, although the term has not yet come into use in the United States.

1963: Richard Gilman and Gordon Rogoff work with Joseph Chaikin and the Open Theater.

1969: The National Playwrights Conference at the O'Neill Center institutes a "program for visiting dramaturgs."[2]

1970: William R. Ellwood's "Preliminary Notes on the German Dramaturg and American Theater" (*Modern Drama*): one of the first journal articles to speculate about the potential role of the dramaturg in American theater.

1971: Michael Feingold becomes Yale Repertory Theatre's first full-time literary manager.

1972: Heiner Müller is dramaturg at the Berliner Ensemble.

1977: Yale establishes an MFA/DFA program in dramaturgy and dramatic criticism; New York State Council on the Arts' Theatre Program secures funds for employment of dramaturgs at six New York theaters.[3]

1978: First issue of Yale *Theater* devoted to dramaturgy; Joel Schechter, editor.

1986: Second issue of Yale *Theater* devoted to dramaturgy; special editor, Mark Bly.

‖ Dramaturgy: A Compendium Of Quotes

When Prince Schwarzenberg asked Heinrich Laube, the great director of the
Burgtheatre in Vienna, what a dramaturg *really was, the latter could only*
answer hesitatingly and shrugging his shoulders: "Highness, that is what
no one could tell you in a few words."
GÜNTER SKOPNIK, "AN UNUSUAL PERSON—DER DRAMATURG—UNE INSTITUTION
PROPREMENT ALLEMANDE" [4]

The editors present this compendium of quotes with no attempt at compre-
hensiveness, consistency, or prescription, and in the hope that these opinions
will provide additional places from which to continue the conversation about
the role of the dramaturgy and the dramaturg in American theater. Many of
the individuals cited below have been leaders in the field in Europe or North
America.

Playwright, Ferenc Molnar on the science of dramaturgy: If I were
ever to write a great work on dramaturgy, I would use as my starting-point the
idea that spending the evening at the theater is a punishment.
[Molnar then goes on to describe over thirty torments of attending live theater: being required "to sit in the dark for three hours, rigid and motionless" in
"a narrow seat"; being "forbidden" to leave "the room," get "up," blow one's
nose, cough, sneeze, eat, drink, smoke, laugh of one's "own accord," sleep, read,
write, stretch, yawn, look anywhere "except forward," move "to another seat,"
and so forth. He then poses the following question.]
What then, is dramaturgy? Dramaturgy is that charitable science which has
gathered all the rules for ameliorating the situation of the condemned victim
of bodily torment by tearing down one wall of the hall and showing him something in the gap. And this something must be so attractive that the above-
desired bodily torment becomes first bearable to the victim, then impercep-
tible, and finally desirable. So desirable that the victim is even ready to spend
his hard-earned money for it, and indeed to scramble for the privilege of sitting inside.[5]

**From Francis Fergusson's letter to the American Laboratory The-
atre, 1928:** Keeping our feet on the ground does not seem to me to mean
persuading millionaires by word of mouth that we are good. It seems to mean
evolving drama which shall be vital and comprehensive to a public large
enough and rich enough to support a small theater full of frugal artists. I am
thus constitutionally incapable of selecting plays that will support the box office. I haven't time to pursue bad plays and debate whether we had better revive some former Broadway hit. I assure you that I shall never find time for

that, and that if I remain as playreader, you can confidently expect me to look for and bring plays which seem to me significant according to the criteria outlined above, and **only** such plays."[6]

Martin Esslin on the the dramaturg in the eighteenth and nineteenth century: [T]he resident playwright who wrote his own plays for the actors in the troupe, or found foreign plays, which he translated, say, from the French or Italian, or produced cut versions of classical plays that required a cast too large for the restricted number of actors available to his particular troupe.[7]

Joel Schechter on dramaturgy and the audience: [A] number of major German dramaturgs, including Lessing, Johann Tieck, Otto Brahm, and Bertolt Brecht (one of Max Reinhardt's dramaturgs), advocated theatre forms that were initially unpopular and later found an audience.[8]

William R. Ellwood on dramatury and geography, part 1: The Dramaturg does not exist to any large degree in theatres west of Germany, but rather east of the Rhine in Poland, Czechoslovakia, Hungary, Russia, Germany, and the Scandinavian countries.[9]

William R. Ellwood on dramaturgy and literature: In short, the Dramaturg is primarily responsible for the dramatic and literary, as opposed to the theatrical aspects of the theatre.[10]

Herbert Blau on dramaturgy and the Text: There used to be a time, as with the Sacred, when we could go back to the Book and check our interpretation. The Text was the inseminating source to which we were to show fidelity, line perfect, deferring to the Author as if he were God the Father.[11]

Patrice Pavis on dramaturgy as an attribute of the playscript: Dramaturgy: action, story, fable, catastrophy, rules, unities, etc.; . . . [the] treatment of time and space, the configuration of characters in the dramatic universe, the sequential organization of the episodes of the Story.[12]

Eugenio Barba and Nicola Savarese on dramaturgy as a weaving-together: The word text, before referring to a written or spoken, printed, or manuscripted text, meant "a weaving together." In this sense, there is no performance which does not have a "text."

That which concerns the text (the weave) of the performance can be defined as "dramaturgy," that is, **drama-ergon,** the "work of the actions" in the performance.[13]

German director Peter Stein on dramaturgy and doubting: I believe that the basic requirement for all rehearsal work at the Schaubühne is primarily a kind of doubting process . . . a doubting and questioning of the theatrical means and also of the traditional themes.[14]

Anne Cattaneo on dramaturgy and practical experience: I have found a good deal of directing and acting experience to be as essential for a dramaturg as a background in literature, playwriting, or theatre history.[15]

Peter Stein on dramaturgy and research: We use a great many aids which other actors and theatre people do not use since they don't see the necessity to use them, such as readings, literary studies, scientific works, political analysis, films, paintings, etc.—actually things which are quite normal, but the difference is that we conduct this research in a relatively extensive and rigorous fashion. Then, during rehearsals, we start to push ourselves and to express things which we have grasped, understood, or sensed, by using our bodies and making some movements.[16]

Lila Wolff-Wilkinson on dramaturgy and the liberal arts: A liberal arts theatre education should teach text analysis, research, writing, language, and organizational skills; appreciation of cultural (not just theatrical) history and current events; artistry; critical acumen; responsibility and interpersonal skills. I believe any liberal arts education, particularly theatre, is capable of increasing the student's self-esteem and therefore the student's ability to function optimally in a complex and interdependent world.

Production dramaturgy includes . . . text analysis, research, and writing. It demands organizational skills. It fosters ability to work collaboratively and sensitively with others. But it must also be considered an art, because it involves, as well, exercise of the creative imagination and aesthetic judgment. It is a microcosm of the entire liberal arts experience.[17]

Peter Hay on dramaturgy and questioning: The reluctance to accept dramaturgy and dramaturg as English words reflects a deeper resistance to thinking about the theatrical process as a whole. . . .

The main job of a dramaturg is to keep asking why. Why are we doing this play? Why this season? Why here? Why does our theatre exist? Why do we exist?

[E]verybody . . . concentrates on the mechanics of how to get it done, hoping that the "why" will take care of itself. Yet, as Dr. Victor Frankl has pointed out, it works exactly the other way around. He observed that only those survived the Nazi concentration camps who knew why they wanted to live; those who could not find meaning in their life died faster than those from whom they stole bread. In order to find the "how," we must first know the "why."

Meaning is central to human existence and art.[18]

James Leverett on dramaturgy and physics: To talk about a dramaturg and dramaturgy, perhaps we ought to resort to physics. A dramaturg can be a particle or a wave. When we expect one, we always get the other. In recent history, he, she, or it tends to be a "particle" because the wide spectrum of functions rests in one person or one identifiable group of people who call themselves dramaturgs. This is a fairly recent phenomenon.

Dramaturgy is also a wave because it's always been there as a force in the theatre. It's not an innovation. It's not an interloper. The function, the impulse, the need, the action has always been there. . . . In other words, we know perfectly well that this critical function is necessary in the theatre and that it has to get accomplished. How it gets accomplished is perhaps our subject.[19]

Charles Marowitz on dramaturgy and developing new work: A dramaturg who cannot propose remedies for remediable scripts and who, like the Auschwitz railway doctor, merely gestures to the right for salvageable or the left for expendable, seems to me to be an unnecessary luxury in a theatrical institution.

The dramaturg's most valuable function is to help create new material in collaborations with others—writers, directors, actors, and designers. This presupposes a dramaturg who is not merely a PhD graduate from an Ivy League university or a jumped-up journalist, but a person with literary and theatrical skills who can function not only as editor, but as writer as well.[20]

David Copelin on dramaturgy and semiotics: If you put our profession in historical perspective, though, things don't look so bad. We've only been around the American theatre (consciously, as dramaturgs) for twenty years or so, and we've made some real progress. When you consider that many people still don't know what a theatre is for, their ignorance about dramaturgy is scarcely surprising. But this is no cosmic state which we must endure, it's a situation which we can help to change. If part of the problem is semiotic, perhaps part of the solution is as well. As Michael Bigelow Dixon, literary manager of Actors Theater of Louisville says, "The word 'dramaturg' is like the word 'fuck.' They'll get used to it."

They'll get used to us, too.[21]

Tim Sanford on dramaturgy and love: A script comes in at my theatre, and I'm the first one who is apt to fall in love with it. . . . [S]ometimes there's no director for that play yet. Okay now, I may not choose the director, but the fact is, once it goes into production I have had the longest relationship with that play of anybody at that theatre.[22]

James Leverett on dramaturgy and geography, part 2: You can often tell by where the dramaturg's office is. If it's near the artistic director, that's one thing; if it's around the corner down the hall behind the air conditioning unit, that's another.[23]

James C. Nicola on dramaturgy and memory: It's ... an enormous asset to have somebody who can not only speak in terms of history but also understands the form, who understands that any play written today is descended from a series of traditions of form and can remind me as I am working that this form exists: "Do you want to follow those rules? Do you want to break those rules? What do you want to do?" It's somebody that challenges me to articulate what I feel and think, which in the heat of doing things, you don't always stay in touch with.[24]

Jayme Koszyn on dramaturgy and journeying: The play asks a question. A great play asks more than one. The job of the dramaturg is to help all the artists and the audience to ask the same question of themselves. The journey of the theater is self-discovery.[25]

Harriet Power on dramaturgy and the writer: Working with a playwright as a dramaturg is the most intimate experience outside marriage that I've encountered.[26]

Lenny Pinna on dramaturgy and puppetry at the Second Annual Puppetry Conference, O'Neill Theatre Center: The most clear demonstration of how a dramaturg could potentially function in a puppet theatre was offered through the actual process of working on George Latshaw's *The Bonsai Boy. The Bonsai Boy* began as an original idea of Mr. Latshaw's which he sought to develop into a structured performance text. Pre-conference I met with Mr. Latshaw in order to catch hold of his vision. At the conference, I was able to help him organize his images and to begin working toward a structured narrative framework. In order to facilitate the collaborative process amongst the participants in the most expedient manner, it became necessary for me to also serve as an informative liaison between Mr. Latshaw and the participants, so that everyone could invest their energies into developing their particular aspects of the vision.[27]

Peter Stone, musical "book doctor" and original book writer on dramaturgy and musical theater: I am far from the best writer in the theatre, but I see myself as a first-rate structuralist. Without structure nothing will work—not the songs, not the dialogue, not the characters. You can fix all those in rehearsals in no time at all. But if you don't have the structure right, whatever fixing you do on the other things, the musical simply is not going to work.[28]

Denise Fujiwara, Canadian choreographer, on working with dramaturg, D. D. Kugler: Throughout the creative process, Don [Kugler] challenged me by asking questions that I attempted to answer through the choreography. He created a supportive environment which allowed ideas to emerge and evolve. He helped me to organize the ideas that came intuitively into the structure of the piece. He was objective when I was subjective, and logical when I was intuitive.

Is this what a dramaturg does? If so, the dramaturg can play a significant role in helping the choreographer to create more potent dance.[29]

Dramaturgy, the absurd, and Jan Kott: My office as Chief Dramaturg was located in a separate wing with a separate flight of stairs. The word office is far too modest to describe it. A padded door (intended, no doubt, to protect the dramaturg's secrets from spreading to the outside) led from an ante-room to an apartment complete with a bedroom and a kitchen. There was a cupboard with a china service for four, a supply of coffee, tea, and even a bottle of cognac. The study was furnished with four club armchairs, two sofas, and a huge desk with two telephones, one black, one white. The white one was dead and always disconnected, and nobody ever called me on the black one except my wife. And that happened rarely.

And nobody ever visited me there either except the caretaker, who punctually at 11.35 would bring me the daily newspaper, and on Mondays the illustrated weeklies.[30]

Jim Lewis on *The Dramaturges of Yan*:

Jim Lewis at the Guthrie Theatre sent us (the editors of the LMDA Review) the following book cover for his regular column on dramaturgy in the popular culture:

John Brunner, (Author of the stunning science-fiction classic *STAND ON ZANZIBAR*) *DRAMATURGES OF YAN.* The Greatest Show on Yan! Yan was the home of an old culture where the humanoid natives walked in the shadows of immense artifacts, the dramatic legacy of a history long forgotten. Only myths remained to tell of the dramaturges, the great heroes of ancient Yan. *DRAMATURGES OF YAN* is available from Ballantine books.[31]

Dramaturgy, *Sports Illustrated*, and basketball: ... the two teams shot a combined 61 percent, and Laettner, Duke's senior star, launched twenty shots on the evening, ten from the field and ten from the line, bottoming out each one. **Dramaturges** couldn't have scripted anything more compelling than the final 31.5 seconds: Five times the ball changed hands, and each possession resulted not only in a score but also in a lead change."[32]

Robert Parker on dramaturgy and murder: (Spenser to the AD of the Port City Theater Company:) "Any reason you can think of why someone would follow you? Disgruntled actor? Embittered dramaturge?"
Susan glanced at me. The "dramaturge" was showing off, and she knew it.[33]

Literary Managers and Dramaturgs of the Americas
by Victoria Abrash

VICTORIA ABRASH has worked in the literary offices of The Second Stage, Manhattan Theatre Club, The Women's Project and Productions, and the Philadelphia Drama Guild. She has been a production dramaturg at the New York Shakespeare Festival, the Acting Company, Young Playwrights, Inc., and many other theaters, on plays ranging from classics to performance art. She has served on panels for New Dramatists, the Playwrights' Center, and elsewhere, consulted for the National Endowment for the Arts and the New York State Council on the Arts, and taught at Williams College, SUNY-Stony Brook, Temple University, and the University of the Arts. Ms. Abrash is a board member and past President of Literary Managers and Dramaturgs of the Americas.

In the 1970s, the dawn of the modern era in American dramaturgy, a handful of trailblazing dramaturgs worked at New York City theaters doing exciting new work. Anne Cattaneo of the Phoenix Theater, Steve Carter of the Negro Ensemble Company, André Bishop of Playwrights Horizons, Jonathan Alper of Manhattan Theatre Club, B. Rodney Marriott of Circle Rep, and others helped to usher in a heyday of the new American play. They commissioned and cultivated such daring young writers as Lanford Wilson, Charles Fuller, Samm-Art Williams, Christopher Durang, and Wendy Wasserstein. And they got together to exchange ideas and information. These early meetings were informal lunches at which the dramaturgs swapped scripts, names information, and stories. If someone loved a script that his or her theater couldn't produce, it was passed on to another theater. If someone needed an assistant or a translator, the lunch meetings were sure to produce a personal recommendation.

The ranks of dramaturgs continued to swell throughout the 1970s and into the 1980s. More and more universities began to offer degrees in dramaturgy. Theatre Communications Group (TCG) held conferences on dramaturgy in 1979 and 1981. The informal lunch meetings continued, but by the 1980s, dramaturgs at theaters across the United States and Canada who couldn't make a lunch meeting in New York still craved colloquy with their colleagues. The time had come for a service organization to meet the profession's growing needs.

In the spring of 1984, Alexis Greene and C. Lee Jenner both dramaturgs, critics, and scholars, spearheaded the drive to transform the ad hoc lunch meetings into a professional service organization. They spread the word, rallied constituents, found meeting and office space, and generally toiled to bring Literary Managers and Dramaturgs of America (LMDA) into being.

The first meetings were held at New Dramatists in New York, which generously donated space and support. Lynn Holst and Susan Gregg hosted, Alexis Greene and C. Lee Jenner organized, and enthusiasm ran high.

LMDA, established in 1985 to "affirm, support and broaden the role of dramaturgs and literary managers in the American Theater," now has more than three hundred members in the United States and Canada and a wide variety of programs to serve its membership and the field. But the organization, like the profession it serves, grew out of what was already happening in the field. LMDA provides the kind of networking and information sharing that dramaturgs have always done informally, but in a more organized and effective way.

LMDA initially focused on fostering communication within the profession and understanding beyond it. The original programs included lunch meetings, announced by postcard and able to accommodate the twenty or more people who were likely to show up. A national conference was instituted to allow far flung dramaturgs to gather each year to exchange ideas, experiences, and news. The *LMDA Review* newsletter provided a forum for information about LMDA's activities as well as thoughtful articles about the profession. Originally, it even included Laurence Maslon's dramaturgical cartoons, such as one in which a dramaturg chides Sophocles, "With his own mother? No one will believe it."

LMDA continued to grow over the years. Under the presidencies of Alexis Greene, C. Lee Jenner, and David Copelin, membership and activity continued to increase. In 1988, LMDA set up offices at the Center for Advanced Studies in Theater Arts (CASTA) in the doctoral program in theater at the City University of New York (CUNY), with the generous help of Edwin Wilson. The conference, originally based in New York City, moved to a different part of the country each year, bringing in new members and focusing on the artists and issues of that region. Anne Cattaneo added many new programs and expanded LMDA's funding base during her tenure as president. She also instituted a system of regional vice-presidents to make LMDA's activities more accessible for all its members. In 1989, LMDA's name changed to Literary Managers and Dramaturgs of *the* Americas, to reflect growing membership outside the United States. During my own term as president, I focused on outreach, particularly to our Canadian members.

LMDA's officers all are working dramaturgs, and its programs all were initiated and are run by members. LMDA's extensive list of programs and services now includes:

The *LMDA Review* newsletter, with articles and listings of general interest and import to the membership.

The annual **LMDA Conference** draws participants from across the United States and Canada, as well as from Europe, Australia, and elsewhere. The conference is usually held in June and has traveled to many cities, including New York, Chicago, Minneapolis, Seattle, Los Angeles, Atlanta, Montreal, and Toronto, always featuring the theater and issues of that region. Panels, performances, and presentations explore topics such as new play development, approaches to the classics, and season planning, and highlight the work of innovative theater artists. Workshops and exercises give practical insight into diverse production methods, and lunch tables and caucuses offer opportunities for more intimate discussion of issues of particular interest.

LMDA's **University Caucus,** founded by Susan Jonas, Geoff Proehl, and John Lutterbie, organizes the University Pre-Conference and other events to explore and expand the relationship between professional theater and academia. This book, in fact, was initiated through the University Caucus Pre-Conference activities.

Regional Meetings have now replaced the original New York City lunch meetings. LMDA's regional vice-presidents bring together the literary managers and dramaturgs of their area for discussion, refreshment, and special events.

The **LMDA Job Phone** offers members a toll-free telephone listing of current job opportunities for dramaturgs in professional theater and university settings.

The *Script Exchange,* created and edited by member Lynn M. Thomson, is a publication through which members share scripts and recommend and discover playwrights.

The **New Dramaturgs** program identifies, encourages, and supports newcomers to the profession, offering meetings on a range of topics; introductions to theater professionals; free theater tickets; conference scholarships; and a network of information and support.

The **Production Diaries Project** was the brainchild of member Mark Bly, who is its editor and program director. This project commissions dramaturgs to keep diaries documenting the conception, planning, research, and realization of selected theater productions, offering a rare window into the creative process and into working models of collaboration. The first four casebooks—Jim Lewis on *The Clytemnestra Project,* directed by Garland Wright; Shelby Jiggetts on *The Love Space Demands,* by Ntozake Shange; directed by Talvin Wilks; Paul Walsh on *Children of Paradise: Shooting a Dream,* by Theatre de la Jeune Lune; and Christopher Baker on *Danton's Death,* directed by Robert Wilson—have been published as a volume by TCG. (Ed. note: See bibliography for full details.)

The **National Theatre Translation Fund (NTTF)** was initiated by Carey Perloff, then artistic director of Classic Stage Company, to foster translations of plays into stage worthy American English. Now administered by LMDA, NTTF commissions translations, supports staged readings, and publishes the *NTTF Translation Sourcebook* to promote productions of high-quality translations.

LMDA's **New York City Special Events** have included panel discussions on collaboration, commissioning, and criticism, and a town meeting on dramaturgy at the Public Theatre. LMDA often collaborates with organizations such as the Dramatists Guild, the Society of Stage Directors and Choreographers (SSD&C) and the City University of New York on presentations.

The **LMDA Bibliography,** edited by Geoff Proehl (and included in this book's bibliography), is an extensive listing of publications about dramaturgy and related subjects.

The *LMDA Source Book: Resources on the Teaching of Dramaturgy,* edited by Susan Jonas, compiles syllabi, curricula, articles, exercises, and other tools useful in teaching dramaturgy.

The *LMDA Guide to Dramaturgy Training Programs* is a listing of more than forty training programs in dramaturgy and related fields, with information on requirements, teaching philosophy, faculty and more.

The *LMDA Guide to Dramaturgy Internships* lists internships available at theaters across the country, complete with information on contacts, responsibilities, and stipends.

Although these LMDA programs are up and running, a few dream projects have proven elusive over the years. A long-planned script-reading service, to provide playwrights with personal feedback and hone dramaturgs' skills, never found the necessary funding and was finally abandoned as too ambitious. Other projects, though, are still underway. LMDA is now connecting its technologically adept members through e-mail. LMDA and the doctoral program at CUNY hope to establish an archive of dramaturgical materials. Other proposals, such as dramaturgy workshops and a mentor program continue to tantalize.

Jayme Koszyn has succeeded Tim Sanford and Erin Sanders as president as LMDA enters its second decade. Many of LMDA's individual programs are now larger than the entire operation was not so long ago. But, just as at those early lunch meetings, LMDA's primary mission is still to provide literary managers and dramaturgs with a stimulating network through which to exchange information and ideas. (Ed. note: For information on how to contact LMDA, see "Addresses" in the bibliography or log on to "dramaturgy northwest" at http://www.ups.edu/cta/theatre/dramaturgy.

Methods Of Dramaturgy:
A Sample Syllabus for a Class in Dramaturgy
by **Anne Cattaneo**

This is essentially a two-quarter class that with some expansion could cover two semesters. The class uses Büchner's *Woyzeck* as a base text and in the course of the semester interprets the text and shapes it for a hypothetical production following the theories of a variety of theatrical approaches.

Because *Woyzeck*'s scene order is historically indeterminate, students can rearrange scenes. No original student emendations are allowed. (NO REWRITING.) Students can, IF DESPERATE, find Büchner material from other plays and texts and interpolate. Interpretations for each unit can be written up as papers, but class discussion to share approaches is a MUST.

My philosophy is to require the students to change as little as possible to realize their interpretation—not to present a jazzy production concept with little grounding in Aristotle's theories or the historical realities of fifth-century staging.

SYLLABUS

Class 1: Work through Büchner's *Woyzeck,* without outside references or information on Büchner, pointing out how text works as theater, elements of music, casting, etc.

Class 2: Read Aristotle's *Poetics* and go through thoroughly.

Class 3: Read *Oedipus Rex* and see how it follows the form of tragedy outlined in *Poetics* (do this technically—where is the parabasis, where is the anagnorisis, is hero high or low? Go through each section).

Class 4: Make *Woyzeck* into an Aristotelian tragedy. Students bring in their approaches. As in class 3, they identify this time in *Woyzeck* each part of tragedy—ultimately to see which are lacking. What can then be done to satisfy Aristotle—what must be added or changed or cut? Students present a production concept a la fifth century that would have pleased Aristotle—staging, acting, etc.

Class 5: Read Dryden's *An Essay of Dramatic Poetry* as a theory of neoclassical theater.

Class 6: Read *Phedre* and *All for Love* and see how they follow Dryden's guidelines.

Class 7: Make *Woyzeck* into a neoclassical tragedy (try French scenes, decorum, etc.). Present production concept.

Class 8: Read Clurman or Strasberg or some preferred Method text and go through thoroughly.

Class 9: Invite acting or directing teacher to class. Read a twentieth-century play that conforms to Method analysis and go through the play breaking it down into beats, find objectives and superobjectives—do a complete technical breakdown according to Clurman's or Strasberg's Method analysis.

Class 10: Make *Woyzeck* into a method play. Students break it down in the same way and see what's there to support this way into the play and what's lacking. Present a production concept for this kind of theater.

Class 11: Read *Brecht on Theatre* and go through Epic vs. Culinary Theater.

Class 12: Read *The Good Woman of Setzuan* or another play by Brecht and see how it fits the definition of Epic Theater.

Class 13: Make *Woyzeck* into an Epic Theater text—what parts would be stressed, what would need to be added (lines from the play as super-titles, music, etc.). Present a production concept Brecht would have approved of. (Historically, I think there is material from the Berliner Ensemble on this.)

Class 14: Read *The Theatre and Its Double* and discuss Artaud's theater.

Class 15: Read a Theater of Cruelty text—*The Cenci* or *Jet of Blood*.

Class 16: Turn *Woyzeck* into a Theater of Cruelty piece—what would be kept, stressed, what added for production concept, how staged, where, etc.

Class 17: Return to an interpretation that honors Büchner himself. Read Büchner's complete works and get biographical information so much as is possible.

Class 18: Present a production concept Büchner would have approved of, in line with his philosophy of theater, playwriting, and politics.

Conversation With Anne Cattaneo
On the Sample Syllabus for a Class in Dramaturgy
by **Jane Ann Crum**

Jane Ann Crum: What struck me initially about your approach was your interest in having students wrestle with text, to learn that a play script can be worked with, played with. You're teaching them how to cut, how to refine, as well as how to find the deep structure of a play.

Anne Cattaneo: That was the most successful part of the course. I wanted to actually teach what the tasks of a dramaturg are, which is to say, to interpret a play along a certain model. Standing in for eight great directors who have come to direct *Woyzeck* are Aristotle, Dryden, Brecht, Artaud, etc. In this way, I was able to do two things—to interpret *Woyzeck*, but also to demonstrate the importance of knowing theater history and different theoretical approaches to the drama.

Crum: Theater history, then, becomes a designer of sorts. The historical realities of a particular period, its staging conventions, becomes the scenography. . . .

Cattaneo: . . . as well as the way in which that theater, be it Greek or Medieval, functioned as a civic institution. For instance, if you did a Greek production of *Woyzeck* (which, by the way, you would never do) you would need to find an American equivalent of a place we come together as a civic unit, as well as using a circular orchestra space complete with chorus, etc.

Crum: What was your students' initial response?

Cattaneo: The students at Columbia took a few weeks to get it. After all, the exercise is relatively technical. Once you come up with a way into a play (which Aristotle and the other theorists provide), then you technically must make it fit, deciding how to clothe it, how to stage it; in the neoclassical section, for example, you must create French scenes. It's the combination of interpretation and workmanship that is needed. The fun part is to find a really inventive solution to figure out how to do it as Artaud or Brecht or Dryden would have done it. If your solution isn't good enough, then you can make parts of it work, but other parts don't. As in any production, if you come up with a great interpretation, a clever, clever way to figure it out, then it will all work. The students got turned on by that challenge.

Crum: You don't mention a particular text in relation to studying the Method. What did you end up using?

Cattaneo: I wanted them to do what all the first year acting students do, which is to read those texts and understand what an objective is, what a superobjective is, to do *Woyzeck* as directed by Lee Strasberg.

Crum: To learn the actor's language.

Cattaneo: Exactly. The best way to handle that section would be to use whatever text the acting students use. It was helpful because it sent the dramaturgs to the actors and the acting teachers. After all, dramaturgs must understand things like given circumstances, logic of action, subtext, images, tempo, beats, because actors are trained to talk about what they do in those terms.

Crum: You begin in a fairly formalistic fashion, then, in the last section, add the details of Büchner's life and politics.

Cattaneo: First I ask them to treat *Woyzeck* as an anonymous text. Then, having read about Büchner, if they make a case to me that he was a political radical, they might want to do a very agit-prop production.

Crum: How many of them had to go to *Leonce and Lena* or *Danton's Death* for additional dialogue?

Cattaneo: A lot of them did. They needed to. But I stressed that the best dramaturgy does the least, so I was not encouraging everybody to throw everything into the pot, which becomes gratuitous. They had to do the tiniest amount to make it work. They couldn't hang fifty thousand lanterns or add a cast of ten thousand. I was very strict with them. I kept saying: "Do what you need to do, but do as little as you possibly can."

Crum: Can you reflect on any particular successes or failures?

Cattaneo: The class got better as they shared concepts and discussed the merits of particular solutions. Students would say: "Maybe what so-and-so did with lighting last week might work." Then they would use that idea on a new unit in a new way. Also, by the end of the class, certain students found they had a knack for this, a gift for it. It's easy to come to a text with a point of view. It's very hard not to force that point of view on a text, and even more difficult to actually complete the work. There's a lot of "first-act" dramaturgy out there, a play being put into a period which has some resonance and then it doesn't go anywhere, doesn't pay off. For that to work, it has to be done honoring the text, to show something new in that text, not just because you want to use Edwardian clothes.

Crum: So how should dramaturgy be taught?

Cattaneo: I learned about it by working with two dramaturgs from Germany, Botho Strauss and Dieter Stürm. It was like jumping into a pool with someone who knows how to do a great crawl. I suppose the best approach is to deal with it on all fronts. You go to a LMDA conference, you read a textbook (like this one), you talk to other dramaturgs, you go to a good graduate school, and you piece it together for yourself.

This conversation took place at Lincoln Center in New York City on June 29, 1994.

Guide to Theater Resources on the INTERNET

DEBORAH A. TORRES is a doctoral student at the School of Information and Library Studies, University of Michigan, Ann Arbor. Her interests include information technology, human-computer interaction, and information needs. She holds a master of information and library studies degree and a bachelor of science degree in journalism. Her interest in the theater is avocational, inspired by participating in drama classes and stage productions when she was a teenager.

MARTHA VANDER KOLK, reared in a small town along the eastern shore of Lake Michigan, holds a bachelor of arts degree in German from Hope College and a master's degree from the University of Michigan's School of Information and Library Studies. She is the coauthor, with Lou Rosenfeld and Joseph Janes, of the *Internet Compendium* series of books, published by Neal-Schuman. She currently works as an Internet specialist for an information management and dissemination firm and resides in Alexandria, Virginia, where she remains connected to the rest of the world via a 2400-baud modem.

Version: 2.1b

Compiled by: Deborah Torres | e-mail: dtorres@umich.edu

Martha Vander Kolk | email: mjvk@sils.umich.edu

School of Information and Library Studies

University of Michigan

Descriptive keywords: drama, performance, theater, theatre

Intended Audience: Theater Professionals, Theater Technicians, Theater Managers, Academic Researchers

1. Introduction

1.1 Scope of this Guide

This guide is intended to provide information on Internet resources pertinent to or closely related to the stage. The intended audience is theater professionals and academics. This guide does not currently include information on resources pertaining to dance. This guide is not intended as a comprehensive listing of resources.

Also, due to the dynamic, changing nature of the Internet we can provide only a "snapshot" of what is offered. New resources may appear after our updates, and old ones may disappear. (Ed. note: This "Guide to Theater Resources on the INTERNET" is no longer available online. Its creators suggest that individuals visit the "Argus Clearinghouse" via the World

Wide Web to explore guides to theater and performance under the category:"Arts and Entertainment." The web address is
"http://www.clearinghouse.net/tree/artent.html."
Readers may also want to explore dramaturgy-related links at the
"dramaturgy northwest" web page:
http://www.ups.edu/cta/theatre/dramaturgy.
Many of the projects described below are now in the process of moving
onto the World Wide Web and might also be located using web search
engines.)

1.2 Organization of this Guide

SECTION 1 contains some introductory information.

SECTION 2 is organized by tool, with some descriptions of the resources.
We include a way or ways to get to the resources and something of what
you will find when you get there.

SECTION 3 lists resources by tool with access information only.

SECTION 4 contains definitions of terms that need clarification or may
be unfamiliar to you.

SECTION 5 contains some miscellaneous information about this guide.

SECTION 6 contains acknowledgements and thanks.

1.3. How to Learn More About the Internet

If you are uncomfortable just jumping in, or are new to the Internet, we
suggest that you get a reference tool of some sort—we recommend: Ed
Krol's *The Whole Internet: User's Guide and Catalog.* (O'Reilly & Associates, Inc., 1992.) $24.95.

But any friendly-looking book about the Internet will do. Krol's book
is somewhat out of date by now, so check out your local library and
bookstore.

1.4 Subscribing to Listservs

To subscribe to a Listserv, send the following e-mail message to
LISTSERV@HOST (where HOST is the part of the address after the @
character: sub <listname> <your name>

IMPORTANT: Leave the subject field blank.

Example: subscribe perform-l deborah torres

To unsubscribe to a Listserv send the following e-mail message to the
same address you used to subscribe:

signoff <listname>

IMPORTANT: Leave the subject field blank.

Example: signoff perform-l

1.5 What's a URL?

A URL is a "uniform resources locator," and it provides a standard way for describing the location of resources available on the Internet. This edition of our guide makes use of URLs for access information for some resources available on gophers or on FTP sites. An example of a URL follows:

gopher://una.hh.lib.umich.edu:70/11/gophers/veronica

The first part of the URL before the colon tells the method of access. The part after the two slashes indicates a host machine. (There also may be some information regarding the port of the host machine.) The next parts, separated by slashes, tell you the path to the resource. The final part is the actual resource.

2. Resource Listings by Tool—with Descriptions

2.1 Listservs:

2.1.1 ARTMGT-L—Arts Management Discussion Group
Subscription addresses:
Bitnet: <listserv@bingvmb>
Internet: <listserv@bingvmb.cc.binghamton.edu>
To post a message send to:
Bitnet: <artmgt-l@bingvmb>
Internet: <artmgt-l@bingvmb.cc.binghamton.edu>
Description:
A discussion group for persons interested in art administration.

2.1.2 ASIANTHEA-L—Asian Performing Arts
Subscription address:
Internet: <probert@uhunix.uhcc.hawaii.edu>
To post a message send to:
Internet: <asianthea-l@uhunix.uhcc.hawaii.edu>
Listowner: Robert Petersen
Description: We received the following message on Nov. 1, 1993:

I would like to invite all theatre scholars, anthropologists, and folklorists to participate in a new mail list, asianthea-l, specifically relating to the issues in Asian Performing Arts. Asianthea-l will be open to conference information and announcements of performances in Asian Theatre.

2.1.3 ASTR-L—American Society for Theater Research

Subscription addresses:

Bitnet: <listserv@uiucvmd>

Internet: <listserv@vmd.cso.uiuc.edu>

To post a message send to:

Bitnet: <astr-l@uiucvmd>

Internet: <astr-l@vmd.cso.uiuc.edu>

Listowner: Peter Davis <padavis@vmd.cso.uiuc.edu>

Description: This forum is used most often for posting questions and answers. The responses to questions asked are prompt and (as far as we can tell) accurate. The questions are research oriented and the list is fairly active. ASTR-L had its first anniversary in fall 1993.

2.1.4 CANDRAMA—Canadian Theater Research

Subscription addresses:

Bitnet: <listserv@unbvm1.bitnet>

Internet: <listserv@unb.ca)>

To post a message send to:

Internet: <candrama@unb.ca>

Listowner: Edward Mullaly <mullaly@UNB.Ca>

Description: Very light activity on CANDRAMA.

2.1.5 COLLAB-L—Collaboration of Theater Artists

Subscription address:

Subscription is not automatic. For more information, send an e-mail message to <sas14@psu.edu>

Listowner: Steve Schrum <sas14@psu.edu>

Description: COLLAB-L is a new discussion list bringing together playwrights, directors, theater technicians, composers, and librettists for the purpose of creating collaboratively new scripts for performance.

2.1.6 COMEDIA—A Discussion of Hispanic Classic Theater

Subscription addresses:

Bitnet: <listserv@arizvm1.bitnet>

Internet: <listserv@arizvm1.ccit.arizona.edu>

To post a message send to:

Bitnet: <comedia@arizvm1>

Internet: <comedia@arizvm1.ccit.arizona.edu>

Listowner: James Abraham <jabraham@ccit.arizona.edu>

Description: This discussion on Hispanic classic theater has light activity with usually only a few postings weekly.

2.1.7 H-COSTUME—Historical Costumes

Subscription address:

Internet: <h-costume-request@andrew.cmu.edu>

To post a message send to:

Internet: <h-costume@andrew.cmu.edu>

Listowner:Gretchen Miller <grm+@andrew.cmu.edu>

Description: This discussion group is fairly active with about five to ten messages per day. The following contains information we received from the welcome message:

This list concentrates on recreating period elegance, from the Bronze Age to the mid-twentieth century. Its emphasis is on accurate historical reproduction of clothing, historical techniques for garment construction, and the application of those techniques in modern clothing design. Other topics appropriate for discussion include adapting historical clothing for the modern figure, clothing evolution, theatrical costumes, patterns, materials, books, and sources for supplies.

2.1.8 PERFORM—On Medieval Performance

Subscription addresses:

Bitnet: <listserv@iubvm>

Internet:

<listserv@iubvm.ucs.indiana.edu.>

To post a message send to:

Bitnet: <perform@iubvm>

Internet: <perform@iubvm.ucs.indiana.edu>

Co-listowners:

Larry Clopper <clopper@ucs.indiana.edu>

Jesse Hurlbut <frejdh@ukcc.uky.edu>

Description: Most messages are from university persons conducting research on various aspects of medieval performance. Light activity; may go for a few days without any messages being posted.

2.1.9 PERFORM-L—On Performance Studies

Subscription address:

Internet: <listserv@acfcluster.nyu.edu>

Listowner: Sharon Mazer: <mazers@acfcluster.nyu.edu>

Description: This consists primarily of students of acting, acting professors, and actors. It is run at New York University, and many of the participants are students there. The discussion focuses on performance-related topics. You need not be officially in performance studies to take part in the list or use the file archive.

2.1.10 REED-L—Records of Early English Drama Discussion

Subscription address:

Bitnet: <listserv@utoronto.bitnet>

To post a message send to:

Bitnet: <reed-l@utoronto>

Internet: <reed-l@vm.utcc.utoronto.ca>

Listowner: Abigail Ann Young <reed@epas.utoronto.ca>

Description: The following is a description of the group from a welcome message sent after we subscribed:

The purpose of this group is to foster discussion of early English drama, music, folk customs, and the myriad other activities documented in REED volumes. This list, however, is not meant to be limiting: we hope that those with interests in early drama, art, and music elsewhere will also contribute from their perspectives.

2.1.11 RENAIS-L—Early Modern History/Renaissance

Subscription addresses:

Bitnet: <listserv@ulkyvm.bitnet>

Internet: <listserv@ulkyvm.louisville.edu>

To post a message send to:

Bitnet: <renais-l@ulkyvm.bitnet>

Internet: <renais-l@ulkyvm.louisville.edu>

Listowner: Unknown.

Description: Contains some discussion relating to theater in the Renaissance period, but be prepared for many postings not on this topic.

2.1.12 SHAKSPER—Shakespeare

Subscription addresses:

Internet: <LISTSERV@ws.BowieState.edu>

Listowner: Hardy Cook <HMCook@boe00.minc.umd.edu>

Description: A discussion of things Shakespearean, this has been highly recommended by both academic Shakespeare scholars and performers. SHAKSPER is not open to automatic subscription, but no one has been refused a subscription. You will receive a message from the listowner containing more information and instructions on how to be added to the mailing list after you send your subscribe message. The following is part of a welcome message we received when we sent a subscribe message:

Thank you for your interest in SHAKSPER, the international electronic conference for Shakespearean researchers, instructors, students, and any others who share their academic interests and concerns. Like the annual Shakespeare Association of America meetings (and the International Shakespeare Association conferences), SHAKSPER offers announcements and bulletins, scholarly papers, and the formal exchange of ideas—but SHAKSPER also offers the same opportunities for spontaneous informal discussion, eavesdropping, peer review, and a fresh sense of worldwide scholarly community.

2.1.13 STAGECRAFT

Subscription address:

Internet: <stagecraft-request@zinc.com>

To post a message send to:

Internet: <stagecraft@zinc.com>

Listowner: Brad Davis <b-davis@zinc.com>

Description: This is just what it says it is: a listserv for technicians. The following contains some information we received regarding STAGECRAFT when we subscribed:

This list is for the discussion of all aspects of stage work, including (but not limited to) special effects, sound effects, sound reinforcement, stage management, set design and building, lighting design, company management, hall management, hall design, and show production. This is not a forum for the discussion of various stage productions (unless the discussion pertains to the stagecraft of a production), acting or directing methods (unless you know of ways to get actors to stand in the right spots), film or video production (unless the techniques can be used on the stage). The list will not be moderated unless problems crop up.

2.1.14 THEATRE

Subscription addresses:

Bitnet: <listserv@pucc.bitnet>

Internet: <listserv@pucc.princeton.edu>

To post a message send to:

Bitnet: <theatre@pucc.bitnet>

Internet: <theatre@pucc.princeton.edu>

Listowner: Rita Saltz

Description: The most active listserv we encountered on theater, THEATRE recently moved from GREARN in Greece to Princeton in the United States. The purpose is to involve those interested in theater in sharing experiences and ideas. Discussion ranges from research-oriented questions to debates on the merits of an MFA degree.

2.1.15 THEATRE-THEORY—Acting-Movement-Voice Theory
To subscribe, send message to the listowner:
Internet: <quijote@mit.edu>
To post a message to THEATRE-THEORY, send it to:
Internet: <theatre-theory@mit.edu>
Listowner: Andrew Q. Kraft
Description: Devoted to discussion of theories of acting, voice, movement, directing, and more. List manager is a theater major specializing in directing. Subscription is not automatic.

2.1.16 WTP-L—Women and Theatre Program Discussion List
To subscribe, send message to:
Internet: <listserv@uhccvm.uhcc.hawaii.edu>
To post a message send to:
Internet: <wtp-l@uhccvm.uhcc.hawaii.edu>
Listowners: Lisa Anderson (Meriel@stein.u.washington.edu)
Juli Burk (Burk@uhunix.uhcc.hawaii.edu)
Description: The following description was contained in the welcome message we received after subscribing:

WTP-L is intended to provide a forum for scholars and artists interested in and across issues of feminism, sexualities, race, class, or gender as they relate to theater and performance. The list gives people an opportunity to ask questions and exchange information about current research, production methodologies, teaching or rehearsal strategies, funding sources, useful texts, films and videos, the availability of performers as guest artists, innovative courses, new plays, or interesting productions. WTP-L also welcomes announcements about and reports on relevant conferences, calls for papers, job opportunities, publications and the like.

2.2 Electronic Newletters/Journals:

2.2.1 ATHE_NEWS ONLINE—Assocation for Theater in Higher Education
Subscription address:
Internet: <athe_news@mailer.fsu.edu>
Listowner: James Thomas <jthomas@mailer.fsu.edu>
Description: The following was received as part of a welcome message to the newsletter:

Welcome to ATHE NEWS ONLINE, a service of the Association for Theatre in Higher Education in cooperation with the School of Theatre and the Academic Computing Network Service at Florida State University. Subscribers to ATHE NEWS ONLINE automatically receive news updates about current or upcoming ATHE activities.

2.2.2 DIDASKALIA: ANCIENT THEATRE TODAY

To subscribe send message to: <didaskalia-editor@classics.utas.edu.au>

Description: A monthly electronic publication to provide listings, previews, reviews, features, and resources pertaining to ancient theater and its modern incarnations. It is distributed from the University of Tasmania, Australia. The ancient Athenians called their records of the performing arts (music, dance, and theater) *didaskaliai.*

2.2.3 POSTMODERN CULTURE

To receive the table of contents for each issue, send the message: sub pmc-list <your name> to <listserv@listserv.ncsu.edu>

Description: We received the following information about this journal:

Postmodern Culture is an electronic journal of interdisciplinary studies in contemporary literature, theory, and culture. We publish writing which ranges from analytical essays and reviews to video scripts and other new literary forms. *Postmodern Culture* hopes to open the discussion of postmodernism to a wide audience and to encourage reconsideration of the forms and practices of academic writing. This journal contains some discussion of theater. It has more than 2,500 subscribers.

2.2.4 *RD*: GRADUATE RESEARCH IN THE ARTS (electronic edition)

Subscription address:

<rd@writer.yorku.ca.bitnet>

To Subscribe: send your name, academic status, and e-mail address.

Description: *RD*: Graduate Research in the Arts is a refereed journal dedicated to publishing the work of graduate scholars in the arts. Papers are accepted from graduate students in the arts, fine arts, and humanities in any of the following areas: language, literature, and other artifacts, constructions of the self, gender, class, and race, the academy itself, and its institutional imperatives. Although based at York University, Canada, *RD*'s editors, editorial board, and readers are made up of graduate students across North America. *RD* is published twice yearly.

2.2.5 *TDR* Journal of Performance Studies

For information on how to subscribe:

URL: telnet://techinfo.mit.edu/Around MIT/MIT Press/journals/arts

To browse the latest issue:

URL: gopher://gopher.internet.com:2100/11/alpha/sz/dr

Description: Although *TDR* is not yet an electronic journal, you can browse through sample articles online, or subscribe through the Electronic Newsstand and via e-mail from MIT. *TDR* is edited by Richard Schechner of the Department of Performance Studies, New York University, and published quarterly by MIT Press. Check out the table of contents.

2.2.6 *TPI* Theatre Perspectives International

To subscribe send this message: <subscribe tpi [your name]>

to: <listserv@lists.Colorado.EDU>

Description: A new electronic journal dedicated to exploring the changing nature of theater around the world as it happens. The first issue was published at the end of March 1994.

2.3 Gophers:

2.3.1 Federal Arts Information

URL:

telnet://gopher.internet.com/Counterpoint Publishing/Federal Register

login: gopher

Description: *Federal Register* information is indexed and searchable on this gopher. You can look for information about the National Endowment for the Arts and the National Foundation on the Arts and Humanities (NFAH) by conducting an agency or keyword search in recent *Federal Register* issues. There is some information regarding grants in the National Endowments for the Arts, but the National Foundation on the Arts and Humanities file is much more comprehensive and wide reaching. Items include meeting minutes, postings regarding grant availability and news releases.

2.3.2 ENGLISH SERVER at Carnegie-Mellon University

URL: gopher://english-server.hss.cmu.edu:70/11ftp:English Server

Description: Choose drama from the menu listing to find a listing of the full texts of plays available, as well as access to the archives of the REED-L listserv. Other menu options may also be of interest, because this is a completely humanities-oriented server, run by graduate students in Carnegie Mellon's English department, and includes sections on poetry, art and architecture, queer resources, and fiction, to name a few. There is also a public forum area where several people can participate in a conversation at once (see "About the English Server" in their gopher menu for particulars). Throughout the few months we have used the English Server, we have grown to like and appreciate it. Of particular interest to us is the "New Things" section. Much of the content of the English Server is not strictly theater related, but might be useful in an interdisciplinary way.

2.4 USENET Newsgroups:

NOTE: The group rec.arts.theatre recently divided into four newsgroups in order to have more focused discussions. The new discussions are as follows.

2.4.1 rec.arts.theatre.misc

Description: Discussion of miscellaneous topics about theater that do not pertain to discussions of plays, musicals, or stagecraft.

2.4.2 rec.arts.theatre.plays

Description: A discussion for fans of all kinds of plays and dramaturgical questions and comments.

2.4.3 rec.arts.theatre.musicals

Description: A discussion for people to share experience, ideas, thoughts, and comments about musicals. It is a place to talk about musicals being performed on Broadway, in community theaters, and college theaters. The most active of the theater newsgroups, with many fans of Sondheim and Lloyd-Webber.

2.4.4 rec.arts.theater.stagecraft

Description: A discussion of all the technical aspects of the theater.

2.5 Archives:

2.5.1 OXFORD TEXT ARCHIVE
URL: ftp://black.ox.ac.uk/ota
Login: <anonymous>
Password: <your e-mail address>
Description: The following information is from an FAQ about the Oxford Text Archive:

The Archive offers scholars long-term storage and maintenance of their electronic texts free of charge. It manages noncommercial distribution of electronic texts and information about them on behalf of its depositors. The Archive contains electronic versions of literary works by many major authors in Greek, Latin, English, and a dozen or more other languages. It contains collections and corpora of unpublished materials prepared by field workers in linguistics. It contains electronic versions of some standard reference works. It has copies of texts and corpora prepared by individual scholars and major research projects worldwide. The total size of the Archive exceeds a gigabyte, and there are about a thousand titles in its catalogue.

2.5.2 PERFORM-L Archives

URL: ftp://acfcluster.nyu.edu

Login: <anonymous>

Password: <Your real identity, e.g. jane smith>

Contact Person: Jeff Chrisope: (Int) <chrisopj@acfcluster.nyu.edu>

(Ph) 212-251-0947

Description: This archive contains bibliographies, syllabi, works in progress, and anything else of interest to the large and fuzzy area of performance studies. Though affiliated with the PERFORM-L mailing list, the files in this archive are available to anyone and everyone. These files can be accessed either by anonymous ftp, or by mailing special commands to the listserver at New York University. Exact instructions on how to access the PERFORM-L archive are made available when you subscribe to PERFORM-L electronic discussion group.

2.5.3 PROJECT GUTENBERG (archives of Public Domain electronic texts)

For Information, send mail to:

Bitnet: <gutnberg@uiucvmd>

Internet: <gutnberg@vmd.cso.uiuc.edu>

Access: Anonymous FTP

URL: ftp://mrcnext.cso.uiuc.edu/etext

[not available between 10 am and 5 pm]

Login: <anonymous>

Password: <your e-mail address>

URL: ftp://quake.think.com/pub/etext

Login: <anonymous>

Password: <your e-mail address>

Description: This is a database of more than three hundred texts in electronic form. The database includes such titles as Sophocles' *Oedipus Trilogy, The Book of Mormon, Paradise Lost, Peter Pan,* and *1990 CIA World Factbook.* The form of some texts are copyrighted, so it is advisable to read any READ.ME files you may encounter to find out about use limits and restrictions.

2.5.4 REC.ARTS.THEATRE FAQ

URLs:

ftp://ftp.std.com/archives/RAT-archive

ftp://quartz.rutgers.edu/pub/theater/rec-arts-theatre-faq-1.gz

ftp://quartz.rutgers.edu/pub/theater/rec-arts-theatre-faq-2.gz

ftp://quartz.rutgers.edu/pub/theater/rec-arts-theatre-faq-3.gz

gopher://quartz.rutgers.edu:70/11/theater

Description: The rec.arts.theatre frequently asked questions (FAQ) information is so long they have divided it into three parts. It contains such tidbits as the history of the spelling of theater/theatre, how to buy tickets to Broadway and Off-Broadway productions, drama-related bookstores. An invaluable resource for any theater lover.

2.5.5 RUTGERS QUARTZ TEXT ARCHIVE, Rutgers University

URL: ftp://quartz.rutgers.edu/pub/theater

Login: <anonymous>

Password: <your e-mail address>

Description: The theater section has many entries, most of which focus on popular theater, particularly in New York City. The rec.arts.theater FAQ is found here. There is also an electronic text section, providing access to Project Gutenberg, Oxford Text Archive, and The On-line Book Initiative. Much of what is in this archive is a lot of fun, so we suggest exploring it—you never know what you'll find, or when it could be useful.

2.5.6 SHAKESPEARE PLAYS, Department of Computing, Imperial College, London

URL: ftp://src.doc.ic.ac.uk/pub/literary/authors/shakespeare/comedies

ftp://src.doc.ic.ac.uk/pub/literary/authors/shakespeare/histories

ftp://src.doc.ic.ac.uk/pub/literary/authors/shakespeare/tragedies

Login: <anonymous>

Password: <your e-mail address>

Description: Includes complete texts of Shakespeare Plays you can download to your own machine. These files are compressed, so make sure you leave off the file extension .z when you get the file you want. These files will be long after they are decompressed. For instance, *Hamlet* was 179k when we downloaded it. Consult Krol's *The Whole Internet,* chapter 6, to learn more about anonymous ftp.

2.6 Databases (Searchable)

2.6.1 Shakespeare Plays File at Dartmouth

URL: gopher://baker.dartmouth.edu:23/8

At command prompt, type: <select file shakespeare plays>

Description: This database at Dartmouth College is the best database of Shakespearean texts that we found for searching on and retrieving portions of texts. It contains thirty-three of the thirty-seven plays (missing are *King Henry VI Pt. 1, Coriolanus, King Henry VIII,* and *All's Well That Ends Well*). It is fairly user friendly and comprehensive, and allows for searching on words, phrases, characters, and scenes, among other options. Commands for searching appear at the bottom of the screen. A word of warning: the print function does not work for non-Dartmouth users.

2.7 Fee-based Communications Service:

CALLBOARD

NOTE: CallBoard is a fee-based communications service for persons interested in the technical aspects of the performing arts. Inclusion in this guide is by no means an endorsement of this service, but does reflect the fact that fee-based services are now being offered to gain access to the Internet. Description: The following contains information sent to us about CallBoard from the operations manager:

> CallBoard is an electronic communications project of the CITT Alberta Section. It began as a small local experiment in Calgary in 1985, and has grown to almost three hundred subscribers across North America. Subscribers include the USITT and CITT boards of directors, technical and production managers from major regional theaters, designers and educators, IATSE members and freelance technicians. We believe that our major attraction lies in the fact that we are a highly targeted service, concentrating solely on the technical production aspects of the performing arts. CallBoard offers the basic BBS services of electronic mail, conferencing and file transfers. There are currently over twenty conference areas on CallBoard, with topics ranging from cadd, to technical and production management, through props and wardrobe. For information on how to subscribe and subscription fees contact: Tim Clinton <clinton@acs.ucalgary.ca>; Operations CITT Alberta CallBoard (403) 220-4905; Fax: (403) 282-7751.

3. Resource listings by Tool—access information only

3.1 Listservs:

3.1.1 ARTMGT-L—Arts Management Discussion Group
Subscription addresses:
Bitnet: <listserv@bingvmb>
Internet: <listserv@bingvmb.cc.binghamton.edu>
To post a message send to:
Bitnet: <artmgt-l@bingvmb>
Internet: <artmgt-l@bingvmb.cc.binghamton.edu>

3.1.2 ASIANTHEA-L—Asian Theater
Subscription address:
Internet: <probert@uhunix.uhcc.hawaii.edu>
To post a message send to:
Internet: <asianthea-l@uhunix.uhcc.hawaii.edu>

3.1.3 ASTR-L—American Society for Theater Research
Subscription addresses:
Bitnet: <listserv@uiucvmd>
Internet: <listserv@vmd.cso.uiuc.edu>
To post a message send to:
Bitnet: <astr-l@uiucvmd>
Internet: <astr-l@vmd.cso.uiuc.edu>

3.1.4 CANDRAMA—Canadian Theatre Research
Subscription address:
Internet: <listserv@unb.ca>
To post a message send to:
Internet: <candrama@unb.ca>

3.1.5 COLLAB-L—Collaboration of Theater and Musical
Subscription address: Subscription is not automatic.
For more information send an e-mail message to <sas14@psu.edu>
Listowner: Steve Schrum <sas14@psu.edu>

3.1.6 COMEDIA—Hispanic Classic Theater
Subscription addresses:
Bitnet: <listserv@arizvm1>
Internet: <listserv@arizvm1.ccit.arizona.edu>
To post a message send to:
Bitnet: <comedia@arizvm1>
Internet: <comedia@arizvm1.ccit.arizona.edu>

3.1.7 H-COSTUMES—Historical Costumes
Subscription address:
Internet: <h-costume-request@andrew.cmu.edu>
To post a message send to:
Internet: <h-costume@andrew.cmu.edu>

3.1.8 PERFORM—On Medieval Performance
Subscription addresses:
Bitnet: <listserv@iubvm>
Internet: <listserv@iubvm.ucs.indiana.edu>
To post a message send to:
Bitnet: <perform@iubvm>
Internet: <perform@iubvm.ucs.indiana.edu>

3.1.9 PERFORM-L—On Performance Studies
Subscription address:
Internet: <listserv@acfcluster.nyu.edu>
To post a message send to:
Internet: <perform-l@acfcluster.nyu.edu>

3.1.10 REED-L—Records of Early English Drama
Subscription addresses:
Bitnet: <listserv@utoronto>
Internet: <listserv@vm.utcc.utoronto.ca>
To post a message send to:
Bitnet: <reed-l@utoronto>
Internet: <reed-l@vm.utcc.utoronto.ca>

3.1.11 RENAIS-L—Early Modern History/Renaissance
Subscription addresses:
Bitnet: <listserv@ulkyvm.bitnet>
Internet: <listserv@ulkyvm.louisville.edu>
To post a message send to:
Bitnet: <renais-l@ulkyvm.bitnet>
Internet: <renais-l@ulkyvm.louisville.edu>

3.1.12 SHAKSPER—Shakespeare
To join SHAKSPER, send mail to: <HMCook@boe00.minc.umd.edu>
Or use this subscription address: <LISTSERV@ws.BowieState.edu>

3.1.13 STAGECRAFT
Subscription address:
Internet: <stagecraft-request@zinc.com>
To post a message send to:
Internet: <stagecraft@zinc.com>

3.1.14 THEATRE
Subscription addresses:
Bitnet: <listserv@pucc>
Internet: <listserv@pucc.princeton.edu>
To post a message send to:
Bitnet: <theatre@pucc>
Internet: <theatre@pucc.princeton.edu>

3.1.15 THEATRE-THEORY—Acting-Movement-Voice Theory
To subscribe, send message to the listowner:
Internet: <quijote@mit.edu>
To post a message to THEATRE-THEORY, send to:
Internet: <theatre-theory@mit.edu>
Listowner: Andrew Q. Kraft

3.1.16 WTP-L—Women and Theatre Program Discussion List
To subscribe, send message to:
Internet: <listserv@uhccvm.uhcc.hawaii.edu>
To post a message send to:
Internet: <wtp-l@uhccvm.uhcc.hawaii.edu>
Listowners: Lisa Anderson (Meriel@stein.u.washington.edu)
Juli Burk (Burk@uhunix.uhcc.hawaii.edu)

3.2 Electronic Newletters/Journals:

3.2.1 ATHE_NEWS ONLINE—Assocation for Theater in Higher
Education
Subscription address:
Internet: <athe_news@mailer.fsu.edu>
Listowner:
James Thomas <jthomas@mailer.fsu.edu>

3.2.2 DIDASKALIA: ANCIENT THEATRE TODAY
To subscribe send message to: <didaskalia-editor@classics.utas.edu.au>

3.2.3 POSTMODERN CULTURE
To receive the table of contents for each issue:
send the message:
sub pmc-list <your name> to <listserv@listserv.ncsu.edu>

3.2.4 *RD*: Graduate Research in the Arts
(electronic edition)
Subscription address:
<rd@writer.yorku.ca.bitnet>
To subscribe: send your name, academic status, and e-mail address.

3.2.5 *TDR* Journal of Performance Studies
For information on how to subscribe to print edition:
URL: telnet://techinfo.mit.edu/Around MIT/MIT Press/journals/arts
To browse the latest issue:
URL: gopher://gopher.internet.com:2100/11/alpha/sz/dr

3.2.6 *TPI* Theatre Perspectives International
To subscribe send this message: <subscribe tpi [your name]>
to: <listserv@lists.Colorado.EDU>

3.3 Gophers:

3.3.1 Federal Arts Information-NEA & NFAH
URL:
telnet://gopher.internet.com/Counterpoint Publishing/Federal Register
login: gopher

3.3.2 ENGLISH SERVER at Carnegie-Mellon University
URL: gopher://english-server.hss.cmu.edu:70/11ftp:English Server
Choose drama from the menu listing.

3.4 USENET Newsgroups:

3.4.1 rec.arts.theatre.misc

3.4.2 rec.arts.theatre.plays

3.4.3 rec.arts.theatre.musicals

3.4.4 rec.arts.theatre.stagecraft

3.5 Archives:

3.5.1 OXFORD TEXT ARCHIVE
URL: ftp://black.ox.ac.uk/ota
Login: <anonymous>
Password: <your e-mail address>

3.5.2 PERFORM-L Archives
URL: ftp://acfcluster.nyu.edu
Login: <anonymous>
Password: <Your real identity, e.g. jane smith>

3.5.3 PROJECT GUTENBERG (archives of Public Domain electronic texts)
For information, send mail to:
Bitnet: <gutnberg@uiucvmd>
Internet: <gutnberg@vmd.cso.uiuc.edu>
URL: ftp://mrcnext.cso.uiuc.edu/etext
[not available between 10 am and 5 pm]
Login: <anonymous>
Password: <your e-mail address>
URL: ftp://quake.think.com/pub/etext
Login: <anonymous>
Password: <your e-mail address>

3.5.4 REC.ARTS.THEATRE FAQ
URLs:
ftp://ftp.std.com/archives/RAT-archive
ftp://quartz.rutgers.edu/pub/theater/rec-arts-theatre-faq-1.gz
ftp://quartz.rutgers.edu/pub/theater/rec-arts-theatre-faq-2.gz
ftp://quartz.rutgers.edu/pub/theater/rec-arts-theatre-faq-3.gz
gopher://quartz.rutgers.edu:70/11/theater

3.5.5 RUTGERS QUARTZ TEXT ARCHIVE, Rutgers University
URL: ftp://quartz.rutgers.edu/pub/theater
Login: <anonymous>
Password: <your e-mail address>

3.5.6 SHAKESPEARE PLAYS, Department of Computing, Imperial College, London

URL:

ftp://src.doc.ic.ac.uk/pub/literary/authors/shakespeare/comedies

ftp://src.doc.ic.ac.uk/pub/literary/authors/shakespeare/histories

ftp://src.doc.ic.ac.uk/pub/literary/authors/shakespeare/tragedies

Login: <anonymous>

Password: <your e-mail address>

3.6 Databases (Searchable)

3.6.1 Shakespeare Plays File at Dartmouth

URL: gopher://baker.dartmouth.edu:23/8

At command prompt, type: <select file shakespeare plays>

3.7 Fee-Based Service:

CallBoard

For information on how to subscribe and subscription fees contact:

Tim Clinton <clinton@acs.ucalgary.ca>

Operations CITT Alberta CallBoard

(403) 220-4905 Fax: (403) 282-7751

4. Definitions of Terms

4.1. BITNET: (Because It's Time NETwork): A cooperative, international, academic network connecting nearly twenty-three hundred hosts in thirty-two countries. Its primary services include mail, mailing lists, and file transfer. Many listservs reside on BITNET.

4.2 Downloading: The act of transferring electronic data from a larger system to a smaller system; for example, from a mainframe computer to a personal computer.

4.3 Electronic Journal/Newsletter: a journal or newsletter in electronic form. It may be only in electronic form, or may be in e-form in addition to the print version.

4.4 E-Mail: Electronic mail allows an individual to post a message to the mailbox of another user. Internet users, or, rather, their mailboxes, have unique addresses that anyone else on the Internet can generally mail to.

4.5 FAQ (Frequently Asked Questions): Part of a Usenet News group file, FAQs are answers to questions or points that have often been discussed. It is advisable to read these files prior to posting a question to the group, because it is likely that the issue has already been addressed. You can also learn a lot about the nature of the newsgroup by reading its FAQ file.

4.6 FTP (File Transfer Protocol): The Internet standard high-level protocol for transferring files from one machine to another. ANONYMOUS FTP lets you access files on a machine without being a registered user.

4.7 Gopher: Public domain software that was initially created at the University of Minnesota. Gopher software uses a hierarchical menu system to allow you to navigate to distributed Internet resources. Because of this menu system, you may hear people refer to burrowing or tunneling through the Internet.

4.8 INTERNET: The worldwide network of networks that uses the TCP/IP protocol suite. These networks consist of foreign, state, local, topical, private, government, and agency networks. The Internet reaches many universities, government research labs, and military installations.

4.9 Listserv: short for Listing Service. A topical mailing list to which anyone on the Internet may subscribe. Any message posted to a listserv is then forwarded to all other subscribers. Hundreds, if not thousands, of listservs exist.

4.10 Mosaic: A software interface for the World Wide Web that has been developed for UNIX and Macintosh computers.

4.11 Newsgroups: (also called USENET newsgroup) similar to a bulletin board service or discussion group, these groups cover many different topics. They are accessible in many ways, mostly through a news reader program.

4.12 TCP/IP: Stands for Transmission Control Protocol/Internet Protocol. TCP/IP is a suite of protocols that people on the Internet agree to use so that their computers can talk with each other.

4.13 TELNET (TELetype NETwork): A software application that provides terminal emulation, and thus remote logon capability from a microcomputer to some remote host. In other words, telnet allows you to connect to and log into another computer system.

4.14 URL: Uniform Resoures Locator. A standard for describing where resources are located on the Internet.

4.15 USENET: A distributed bulletin board and discussion system. Also known as NEWS or NETNEWS. Generally requires access to a computer running the UNIX operating system.

A WORD ABOUT HOW TO ACCESS USENET NEWS GROUPS:

Some USENET news groups are available through gopher systems, but generally you will need to use a news reading software program. Some UNIX-based USENET news readers are called rn (news reader), trn (treaded news reader) and xrn (X-Windows news reader). A Macintosh-based program is called Nuntius. If you are not sure how to access USENET news, ask your computer system administrator if it is available on your system. Also, consult chapter 8 in *The Whole Internet* by Ed Krol.

Because of the informal, discussion-oriented nature of Usenet, we believed it was appropriate to mention that it addresses a wide range of subject areas—particularly the alt. hierarchy, where many off-beat discussion groups exist—and may prove a helpful source of information when doing research for a particular production.

4.16 WAIS: Public domain information retrieval software initially created by Thinking Machines, Inc., which allows users to concurrently search distributed Internet textbases and databases.

4.17 WORLD WIDE WEB (WWW): A hyper-text-based system for finding and accessing resources on the Internet. The interface allows you to "browse" resources.

5. Final Notes, Odd/Ends

5.1 Where/How to contact Us:
Guide organizers:
Martha Vander Kolk: mjvk@umich.edu
Deborah Torres: dtorres@umich.edu

5.2 Origin of This Guide
This guide originated as a team project for a masters-level class offered at the School of Information and Library Studies, University of Michigan, during fall term 1993. The class was ILS 606, Internet: Resource Discovery and Organization. We believe it to be the first class with this particular emphasis regarding the Internet.

6. Thanks and Acknowledgements

6.1 Acknowledgements

Our deepest gratitude to Ken McCoy of Bowling Green State University, Ohio, who shared his own guide to theater and performance studies with us and sent us on our way to resource discovery. You can find the latest version of Ken's guide in the Clearinghouse for Subject-Oriented Internet Guides:

URL: gopher://una.hh.lib.umich.edu:70/00/inetdirsstacks/theater:mccoy

We also wish to acknowledge our two clients for the original version of this guide, whose input along the way was invaluable. They are Mr. Stephen M. Paulsen, assistant to the managing director, Alabama Shakespeare Festival, Montgomery, Alabama, and Mr. David Rowell, production stage manager, Browning Performing Arts Center, Weber University, Orem, Utah.

‖ Bibliography

The editors with to thank members of Literary Managers and Dramaturgs of the Americas who have suggested titles for inclusion here; this bibliography owes much to earlier bibliographies by ROSEMARIE BANK (1983) and LAURENCE SHYER (1978), both cited below.

Section I: Dramaturgy in General and Production Dramaturgy

Bank, Rosemarie. "Shaping the Script: Commission Produces a Bibliography of Dramaturgy." *Theatre News* Jan./Feb. 1983: 124.

—"Interpreters, Dramaturgs, and Process Critics: A New Configuration for American Theatre." In *The 1980 Winners.* Ed. Roger Gross (a monograph published by the UCTA Program in Theory and Criticism of the American Theatre Assn.), 1981, 11–16.

Barba, Eugenio, and Nicola Savarese. "Dramaturgy." In *A Dictionary of Theatre Anthropology: The Secret Art of the Performer.* Trans. Richard Fowler. New York: Routledge, 1991, 68–73.

Benedetti, Robert L. *The Director at Work.* Englwood Cliffs, N.J.: Prentice-Hall, 1985, 29.

Bennetts, Leslie. "Stage Conference Asks What Is a Dramaturge?" *New York Times* 23 June 1983, sec. C:15.

Bentley, Eric. "Stark Young." *Theater* 14.1 (1982): 47–53.

Berc, Shelly. "Theatre in Boston: Lee Bruer's *Lulu.*" *Theater* 12.3 (1981): 69–77.

Bharucha, Rustom, Janice Paran, Laurence Shyer, and Joel Schechter. "Directors, Dramaturgs, and War in Poland: An Interview with Jan Kott." *Theater* 14.2 (1983): 27–31.

Bly, Mark, ed. *The Production Notebooks: Theatre in Precess, Volume 1.* New York: Theatre Communications Group, 1996. Includes: *The Love Space Demands,* produced by Crossroads Theatre Company, dramaturg, Shelby Jiggetts; *Danton's Death*, produced by Alley Theatre, dramaturg, Christopher Baker; *The Clytemnestra Project*, produced by the Guthrie Theater, dramaturg, Jim Lewis; and *Children of Paradise: Shooting a Dream*, produced by Theatre de la Jeune Lune, dramaturg, Paul Walsh.

Booth, Susan V. "Dramaturg in Search of an Axis." *American Theatre* September 1990: 62–63.

Brecht, Bertolt. *The Messingkauf Dialogues.* Trans. John Willet. London: Eyre Methuen, 1965.

Cardullo, Bert, ed. *What Is Dramaturgy?* New York: Peter Lang, 1995.

Castagno, Paul C. "Informing the New Dramaturgy: Critical Theory to Creative Process." *Theatre Topics* 3.1 (1993): 1-6.

Copelin, David. "Ten Dramaturgical Myths." *Call Board* (Theatre Communications Center of the Bay Area) June 1989: 5-9.

Croft, Giles, ed. *Platform Papers: Translation.* London: Royal National Theatre Publications, 1992.

Davis, Ken, and William Hutchings. "Playing a New Role: The English Professor as Dramaturg." *College English* 46 (1984): 560-569.

De Marinis, Marco. "Dramaturgy of the Spectator." *The Drama Review* 31.2 (1987): 100-114.

"Dramaturgy and Physics: panel discussion moderated by James Leverett with James C. Nicola, Richard Dresser, Morgan Jenness, and Tim Sanford." *Journal of the Stage Directors and Choreographers Foundation* 5.1 (1991): 4-21.

Ellwood, William R. "Preliminary Notes on the German Dramaturg and American Theater." *Modern Drama* 13.3 (1970): 254-258.

Hay, Peter. "American Dramaturgy: A Critical Reappraisal." *Performing Arts Journal* 7.3 (1983): 7-24.

— "Dramaturgy: Requiem for an Unborn Profession." *Canadian Theatre Review* 8 (1975): 43-46.

Helbo, André, et al. *Approaching Theatre.* Bloomington: Indiana University Press, 1991.

Hornby, Richard. *The End of Acting: A Radical View.* New York: Applause Books, 1992, 246-247.

Horwitz, Simi. "John Lahr: Literary Lion." *TheatreWeek* 19 February 1996: 20-27.

Kott, Jan. "The Dramaturg." *New Theatre Quarterly* 6.21 (1990): 3-4.

Lessing, Gotthold Ephraim. *Hamburg Dramaturgy.* Trans. Helen Zimmern. New York: Dover, 1962.

Levine, Mindy. "How Does a Literary Manager Manage?" *Theatre Times* Feb. 1983.

LMDA Review: newsletter published by Literary Managers and Dramaturgs of the Americas. See address on page 567.

Loup, Alfred J. "Vienna's Burgtheater in the 1970s." *Theatre Journal* 32 (1980): 55-70.

Maes, Nancy. "Drama-what? Dramaturg—the behind-scenes interpreter." *Chicago Tribune* 23 May 1986, sec. 7: 5+.

McKenna, Maryn. "The Dramaturg: Towards a Job Description." *Dramatics* April 1987: 28-31.

McNuff, Des. "Observations: A Place in the Room for Dramaturgs." *American Theatre* April 1986: 42–43.

Marrance, Bonnie and Gautam Dasgupta, ed. "Special Issue: The Arts and the University," *Performing Arts Journal* 17.2/3 (1995).

Marinelli, Donald, ed. *Arthur Giron's Edith Stein: A Dramaturgical Sourcebook.* Pittsburgh: Carnegie Mellon University Press, 1994.

Napoleon, Davi. "Schoolbiz." *Theater Week.* 22 April 1996: 38–40.

"On Adaptation," *The Dramatists Guild Quarterly* 19.3 (1982).

Paran, Janice. "How to Succeed in Dramaturgy Without Really Trying." *American Theatre* Oct. 1995: 85–86.

Pavis, Patrice. *Languages of the Stage: Essays in Semiology of Theatre.* New York: Performing Arts Journal, 1982. 27–28, 98, 100.

Pinna, Lenny. "Puppeturgy? Puppet Theatre Art from a Dramaturg's Perspective," *The Puppetry Journal* 44.3 (1993): 14–15.

Price, Antony. "The Freedom of the German Repertoire." *Modern Drama* 13.3 (1970): 237–246.

Proehl, Geoffrey S. "Dramaturg" and "Dramaturgy." In *Encyclopedia of English Studies and Language Arts.* Ed. Alan C. Purves et al. Vol. 1. New York: Scholastic, 1994, 409–412.

Schechter, Joel. "American Dramaturgs." *The Drama Review* 20.2 (1976): 88–92.

— "Heiner Müller and Other East German Dramaturgs." *yale/theatre* (now *Theater*) 8.2 and 3 (1977): 152–154.

— "Lessing, Jugglers, and Dramaturgs." *yale/theatre* (now *Theater*) 7.1 (1975/1976): 94–103.

Shyer, Laurence. "Playreaders, Dramaturgs and Literary Managers: A Bibliography." *Theater* 10.1 (1978): 60–61.

— "Writers, Dramaturgs, and Texts." *Robert Wilson and His Collaborators.* New York: Theatre Communications Group, 1989, 87–152.

Skopnik, Günter. "An Unusual Person—*Der Dramaturg*—Une Institution Proprement Allemande" *World Theatre* 9.3 (1960): 233–238.

Slavic and East European Arts 4.1 (1986). Issue devoted to dramaturgy in Russia and Eastern bloc nations; edited by E. J. Czerwinski and Nicholas Rzhevsky; article titles include:
    "The Role of the Dramaturg in Contemporary Romanian Theatre" (Ileana Berlogea)
    "The Dramaturg in Yugoslavia" (Sanja Ivic and Vesna Cvjekkovic)
    "I Love Literature, Great Poetry, and the Keen Intelligence of Writers" (Kazimierz Braun)
    "The Dramaturg: Dreams and Reality" (Andrzej Makarewicz)
    "Dramaturgs in Czechoslovakia" (Zdenek Hedbavny)

"Dramaturgs in Hungary" (Judith Szanto)

"The Dramaturg in the Theatres of Bulgaria" (Aleco Mintchev)

"Responsibilities and Functions of the Dramaturg in West Germany" (Klaus Voelker)

"The Power and Impotence of the Dramaturg: The Image of a Profession and Its Problematic Nature" (Ernst Schumacher)

"Bertolt Brecht as Dramaturg" (Russell E. Brown)

"Sensuality in Brecht" (Alf Sjoberg)

"The American View: The Future of Dramaturgs on U.S. Campuses" (C. J. Gianakaris)

"A Note on Soviet Dramaturgs" (Felicia Hardison Londré)

"Soviet Dramaturgy Today" (Alexey Kazantsev)

"The Program as Performance Text" (Nicholas Rzhevksy)

"Jozef Szajna's *Replika*: Expanding the Scope of Dramaturgy" (E. J. Czerwinski)

Sobieski, Lynn Ann. "The Crisis in West German Dramaturgy." *DA* 47.12 (1987): 4239A. New York University.

Theater 10.1 (1978). Formerly *yale/theatre*; issue devoted to dramaturgy; Joel Schechter, ed.; article titles include:

"America's First Literary Manager: John Corbin at the New Theatre" (Laurence Shyer)

"Dramaturgs in America: Eleven Statements"

"Dramaturgy at A.C.T.: An Interview with Dennis Powers and William Ball of the American Conservatory Theatre" (William Kleb)

"Literary Management at the National Theatre, London: An Interview with John Russell Brown" (Richard Beacham)

"Literary Management at the RSC Warehouse, London: An Interview with Walter Donohue" (Carol Rosen)

"The Role of the Dramaturg in European Theatre" (Martin Esslin)

"Dramaturgy in Berlin: An Interview with Ernst Wendt" (Henning Rischbieter)

"Dramaturgy in Stuttgart: An Interview with Hermann Beil" (Reinhardt Stumm)

"Brecht and Other Dramaturgs" (Joel Schechter)

"Playreaders, Dramaturgs and Literary Managers: A Bibliography" (Laurence Shyer)

Theater 17.3 (1986). Formerly *yale/theatre*; issue devoted to dramaturgy; Mark Bly, special ed.; article titles include:

"American Production Dramaturgs: An Introduction" (Mark Bly)

"Dramaturgy at the Eureka: An Interview with Oskar Eustis" (Mark Bly)

"Dramaturgy at the Mark Taper Forum: An Interview with Russell Vandenbroucke" (Mark Bly)

"Dramaturgy at the Magic and the O'Neill: An Interview with Martin Esslin" (Mark Bly)

"Dramaturgy at Second Stage and the Phoenix: An Interview with Anne
    Cattaneo" (Mark Bly)
"Dramaturgy at Large: An Interview with Arthur Ballet" (Mark Bly)
"Dramaturgy at the Yale Rep: An Interview with Gitta Honegger" (Mark Bly)
"Dramaturgy at the Brooklyn Academy of Music: An Interview with Richard
    Nelson" (Mark Bly)
"Dramaturgy at the Guthrie: An Interview with Mark Bly" (David Moore, Jr.)
"Dramaturgy at the Court and Wisdom Bridge" (Linda Walsh Jenkins and
    Richard Pettengill)
"A Note on Literary Managers and Dramaturgs of America" (Alexis Greene)
"On the Necessary Non-Sense of Production Dramaturgy" (Helmut Schäfer;
    Trans. Mona Meinze)
"Sweepstakes for a Vision: 'Classics in Context' in Context" (Mark Lord)

Theaterschrift. no. 5–6 (1994). "On dramaturgy"; issue devoted to dramaturgy;
    article titles include:
    "Fragments of The Intersubjective Encyclopedia of Contemporary
        Theatre," parts 1–4
    "Speaking about Silence" (Erwin Jans)
    "Towards a Theory of Fluid Groupings" (Josette Féral)
    "Purged of All Falseness" (Interview with Jan Kott)
    "The Politics of Space" (Eda Cufer and Emil Hvratin)
    "On Pub and Kitchen Dramaturgy" (Mira Rafalowicz)
    "Looking Without Pencil in Hand" (Marianne Van Kerkhoven)
    "Just Deal with It!" (Interview with Norman Frisch)
    "A Library of Cultural Detritus" (Interview with Elisabeth LeCompte)
    "Theatre as a Meeting Point of Arts" (Interview with Robert Lepage)
    "Dinner with BAK-Truppen" (Interview with BAK-Truppen)
    "The Passive Spectator Does not Exist" (David Maayan)
    "A Continuing Dialogue" (Interview with Jan Loris Lamers)
    "The Resistance Forced Upon Us by Reality" (Interview with Alexander
        Kluge)

"The Voice of the Dramaturg." *Theatre Symposium: A Journal of the South-
    eastern Theatre Conference* 3 (1995); issue devoted to dramaturgy; Paul
    Castagno, ed. (available from the University of Alabama Press); article ti-
    tles include:
    "Voice of the Dramaturg" (Paul C. Castagno)
    "The Questioning Spirit and the Creative Process" (Mark Bly)
    "Listening: The Art of Collaboration at Theatre de la Jeune Lune" (Paul
        Walsh)
    "Compiling and Shaping the Performance Text" (Anne Cattaneo)
    "Dramaturgy and the Community: Audience Development at the
        Alabama Shakespeare Festival" (Susan Willis)
    "'Mission' and Multiculturalism" (Shelby Jiggetts)

"There Is Clamor in the Air" (Michael Lupu)

"Symposium Discussion with Castagno (moderator), Bly, Cattaneo, Jiggetts, Lupu, Walsh, and Willis

"The Dramaturg and the Will of the Play" (Stanley V. Longman)

"'Komische Welt! schöne Welt!': Georg Büchner's *Woyzeck* as Dramaturgical Proving Ground" (Jay Malarcher)

"Breaking the Silence: Dramaturgy, Multicultural Collaboration, and White Privilege" (Susan C. Haedicke)

"Confronting the Fear of Otherness: Indiana Repertory Theatre's Production of *The Cherry Orchard*" (Janet Allen)

"The Dramaturg, the Past, and the Present: Period Pieces in Contemporary Society" (Thomas Pender)

"The Personality Profile: A Useful Character Analysis Tool for Dramaturgs" (Samuel J. Zachary)

"Improving Director/Dramaturg Collaboration" (Nina LeNoir)

"Performance Practice in a Literary Classroom: Plan, Process, and Validation" (Harry Smith)

Tynan, Kenneth. "A Rehearsal Logbook." *The Sound of Two Hands Clapping.* London: Jonathan Cape, 1975, 119–26.

Wolff-Wilkinson, Lila. "Comments on Process: Production Dramaturgy as the Core of the Liberal Arts Theatre Program." *Theatre Topics* 3.1 (1993): 1–6.

Zeydel, Edwin H. *Ludwig Tieck: The German Romanticist.* New York: Hildesheim, 1971.

Zipes, Jack. "John Lahr, Critic-at-Guthrie Theatre Rehearsals." *Variety* 16 Oct. 1968, 2.

—"Utopia as the Past Conserved: An Interview with Peter Stein and Dieter Stürm of the Schaubühne am Halleschen Ufer." *Theater* 9.1 (1977): 50–57.

Note: Related theoretically to dramaturgy is "dramaturgism," a form of sociological analysis that views social interaction in dramatic and theatrical terms. The approach may have some applications to dramaturgical work in the theater. For an overview of "dramaturgism," see Dennis Brissett and Charles Edgley, eds., *Life as Theatre: A Dramaturgical Sourcebook* (Hawthorne, New York: Aldine de Gruyter, 1990) 1–46. For an overview and a comprehensive bibliography, see Art Borreca, "Political Dramaturgy: A Dramaturg's (Re)View," *The Drama Review* 37.2 (1993): 56–79 (includes a selected bibliography on political dramaturgy).

Section II: New Play Development

Allison, Ralph. "England's National Theatre: An Interview with Kenneth Tynan." *Performance* 1 (1972): 82–86.

Anderson, Douglas. "The Dream Machine: Thirty Years of New Play Development in America." *The Drama Review* 32.3 (1988): 55-84.

Ballet, Arthur. "Fifteen Years of Reading New Plays: Reflection on the Closing of the Office for Advance Drama Research." *Theater* 9.2 (1978): 41-44.

—"Playwrights for Tomorrow: the Work of the Office for Advanced Drama Research." *Theatre Quarterly* 8.29 (1978): 12-28.

Bryden, Ronald. "'Dear Miss Farthingale, Thank You for Your Tragedy...'" *New York Times* 7 Dec. 1975, sec. 2: 1.

Cattaneo, Anne. "Backtalk: Institutionalizing the Blind Date, The Theatre and the Playwright." *Performing Arts Journal* 8.3 (1984): 100-104.

Cohen, Edward M. *Working on a New Play: A Play Development Handbook for Actors, Directors, and Playwrights.* New York: Prentice-Hall, 1988.

Cook, Judith. "John Russell Brown: Head of Script Department." In *The National Theatre.* London: Harrap, 1976, 67-72.

Daniels, Barry, ed. *Joseph Chaikin & Sam Shepard: Letters and Texts, 1972-1984.* New York: New American Library, 1989.

Esslin, Martin. "Giving Playwrights Experience." *West Coast Plays* 2 (1978): 213-216.

—, et al. "Playwrights' Polemic: A Shortage of Themes." *West Coast Plays* 10 (1981): 73-100.

Gibson, William. *The Seesaw Log: A Chronicle of the Stage Production, with the Text.* New York: Alfred Knopf, 1959.

Granville-Barker, Harley. *The Exemplary Theatre.* London: Sidwick & Jackson Ltd., 1922, 185-192.

—*A National Theatre.* London: Sidwick and Jackson, 1930, 40-42.

Hay, Peter. "Canadians at the O'Neill." *Canadian Theatre Review* 21 (1979): 17-26.

Johnstone, Keith. "Notes on Myself." In *Impro: Improvisation and the Theatre.* New York: Theatre Arts Books, 1979.

Kahn, David and Donna Breed. *Scriptwork: A Director's Approach to New Play Development.* Carbondale: Southern Illinois University Press, 1995. See "Developmental Dramaturgy, 1995," 28-72 and "Appendix: Interviews" with Anne Cattaneo, Oskar Eustis, Robert Hedley, Morgan Jenness, et al.

King, W. D. "Dramaturgical Text and Historical Record in the New Theatre: The Case of *Rumstick Road.*" *Journal of Dramatic Theory and Criticism* 7.2 (1992): 71-88.

Lahr, John. "Green Room: I Lost It at the Theatre." *Plays and Players* 20.4 (1973): 12-13.

Leverett, James. "Dramaturgs and Literary Managers: A Major Conference to Define the Role." *Theatre Communications* 2 (1981): 4-5.

LMDA Script Exchange. Edited by Lynn M. Thomson. See address for LMDA on page 567.

Matetzschk, Judy. "New Play Dramaturgy Takes Focus at IUPUI Youth Theatre Playwriting Contest." *LMDA Review* 5.1: 1+.

McNamara, Brooks. "The Shubert Brothers and the 'Box-Office' Play." *LMDA Review* 5.1: 1-5.

Mednick, Murray. "The Playwright as Author." *Newsletter: The Audrey Skirball-Kenis Theatre, Inc.* 1.3 (1992): 7+.

Morrow, Lee Alan, and Frank Pike. *Creating Theater: The Professionals' Approach to New Plays.* New York: Vintage Books, 1986.

Nelson, Richard and David Jones. *Making Plays: The Writer-Director Relationship in the Theatre.* Ed. Colin Chambers. London: Faber and Faber, 1995.

Newsletter: The Audrey Skirball-Kenis Theatre, Inc. (address: 9478 West Olympic Blvd., Suite 308, Beverly Hills, CA 90212).

Trousdell, Richard. "Arts View: New Writers, New Plays: A Dramaturg Measures What's Wrong (and Right) With Them." *Theatre News* March/April 1985: 2, 12.

Tynan, Kenneth. "The Critic Comes Full Circle." *Theatre Quarterly* 1.2 (1971): 37-48.

Wellman, Mac. "A Chrestomathy of 22 Answers to 22 Wholly Unaskable and Unrelated Questions Concerning Political and Poetic Theater." *Theater* 24.1 (1993): 43-51.

—"The Theatre of Good Intentions." *Performing Arts Journal* 8.3 (1984): 59-70.

White, George. "The O'Neill Experience: A Practical Experiment in Helping New Writers." *Theatre Quarterly* 4.15 (1974): 32-53.

—*National Playwrights' Conference: 1965-1969.* A Report to the Rockefeller Foundation.

Windheim, Bennett I. "Tales from the Scripts: Conversations with Literary Managers." *Back Stage: The Performing Arts Weekly* 14 Aug. 1992: 1, 18-21.

Zipes, Jack. "The Mark Taper Forum's New Play Program." *West Coast Plays* 1 (1977): 141-149.

Section III: On the Relationship Between Script and Performance

Ball, David. *Backwards and Forwards: a Technical Manual for Reading Plays.* Carbondale: University of Illinois Press, 1983.

Barthes, Roland. "From Work to Text." In *Textual Strategies. Perspectives in Post-Structuralist Criticism.* Ed. Josué V. Harari. Ithaca: Cornell, 1979, 73-81.

Beckerman, Bernard. *Dynamics of Drama.* New York: Alfred Knopf, 1970.

Carlson, Marvin. "Theatrical Performance: Illustration, Translation, Fulfillment, or Supplement?" *Theatre Journal* 37 (1985): 5–11.

Clay, James H. and Daniel Krempel. "How Does a Play Mean?" and "The Process of Interpretation." *The Theatrical Image.* New York: McGraw-Hill, 1967.

Field, Syd. *Screenplay: the Foundation of Screenwriting.* New York: Dell Pub. Co., 1982.

Kott, Jan. *Shakespeare, Our Contemporary.* Trans. Boleslaw Taborski. New York: Norton, 1974.

—*The Eating of the Gods.* Trans. Boleslaw Taborski and Edward J. Czerwinski. New York: Random House, 1973.

—*The Gender of Rosalind, Interpretations: Shakespeare, Büchner, Gautier.* Trans. Jadwiga Kosicka and Mark Rosenzweig. Evanston: Northwestern University Press, 1992.

Helbo, André, et al. "Pedagogics of Theatre: Analysis of the text; Analysis of the Performance." In *Approaching Theatre.* Bloomington: Indiana University Press, 1991, 135–164.

Hornby, Richard. *Script into Performance: A Structuralist View of Play Production.* Austin: University of Texas, 1977.

Milhous, Judith, and Robert D. Hume. "The Concept of Producible Interpretation." In *Producible Interpretation: Eight English Plays, 1675–1707.* Carbondale: Southern Illinois University Press, 1985, 3–34.

Scanlan, David. *Reading Drama.* Mountain View, Cal.: Mayfield, 1988.

Schechner, Richard. "Drama, Script, Theater, and Performance." In *Performance Theory.* Rev. ed. New York: Routledge, 1988, 68–105.

Scolnicov, Hannah, and Peter Holland. *The Play Out of Context: Transferring Plays from Culture to Culture.* Cambridge: Cambridge University Press, 1989.

Styan, J. L. *The Shakespeare Revolution: Criticism and Performance in the Twentieth Century.* London: Cambridge University Press, 1977.

Thomas, James. *Script Analysis for Actors, Directors and Designers.* Boston: Focal Press, 1992.

Veltrusky, Jiri. "Dramatic Text as a Component of Theatre." In *Semiotics of Art: Prague School Contributions.* Ed. Ladislav Matejka and Irwin Titunik. Cambridge: MIT Press, 1976, 94–117.

Weber, Carl. "On Theatre Directing." In *Master Teachers of Theatre: Observations on Teaching Theatre.* Ed. Burnet M. Hopgood. Carbondale: Southern Illinois University Press, 1988, 119–158.

Williams, Raymond. "Argument: Text and Performance." In *Drama in Performance,* Rev. ed. New York: Basic Books, 1968, 172–191.

Section IV: General References

LMDA Guide to Dramaturgy Programs. Available from Literary Managers and Dramaturgs of the Americas, Box 355, CASTA, CUNY Graduate Center, 33 West 42nd St., New York, NY 10036; 212-642-2657.

Jonas, Susan, ed. *The LMDA Source Book: Resources on the Teaching of Dramaturgy.* 1 (1992): Available from Literary Managers and Dramaturgs of the Americas, Box 355, CASTA, CUNY Graduate Center, 33 West 42nd St., New York, NY 10036; 212-642-2657.

Meserve, Mollie Ann, ed. *The Playwright's Companion: A Practical Guide to Script Opportunities in the U.S.A.* New York: Feedback Theatrebooks, most recent edition.

Osborn, M. Elizabeth, ed. *Dramatists Sourcebook: Complete Opportunities for Playwrights, Translators, Composers, Lyricists, and Librettists.* New York: Theatre Communications Group, most recent edition.

Theatre Directory. New York: Theatre Communications Group, most recent edition.

Theatre Profile. New York: Theatre Communications Group, most recent edition.

Section V: Addresses

Association for Theatre in Higher Education, 200 North Michigan Ave., Suite 300, Chicago, IL 60601-3821; 312-541-2066; e-mail: 71005.1134@compuserve.com

Literary Managers and Dramaturgs of the Americas, Box 355, CASTA, CUNY Graduate Center, 33 West 42nd St., New York, NY 10036; 212-642-2657

Society of Stage Directors and Choreographers, 1501 Broadway, 31st Floor, New York, NY 10036; 212-391-1070

Theatre Communications Group, 355 Lexington Ave., New York, NY 10017; 212-697-5230

The editors of this volume may be contacted through Geoff Proehl at Theatre, University of Puget Sound, 1500 N. Warner Rd., Tacoma, WA 98416 or by e-mail (gproehl@ups.edu) or by phone (206-756-3101)

Section VI: Dramaturgy Web Pages

"Dramaturgy Northwest," a project of the Northwest Region of LMDA and the University of Puget Sound under the direction of Robert Menna, Intiman Theatre Company (Seattle) and Geoff Proehl, University of Puget Sound (Tacoma): http://www.ups.edu/cta/theatre/dramaturgy. This web site contains information on resources for dramaturgs and literary managers, a listing of Northwest theater events, answers to frequently asked questions about dramaturgy and LMDA, and links to other dramaturgy-related web sites. It will include a supplement to this bibliography after the publication date. It also provides a way for readers to communicate with the editors of this book and suggest corrections, changes, or additions for future editions.

Section VII: Dramaturgy E-Mail List

The University Caucus of LMDA maintains an e-mail distribution list.

The "Dramaturgy List" is an informal e-mail distribution list begun in 1994 for dramaturgs, literary managers and individuals interested in dramaturgy with e-mail. An initial goal of this project was to create an e-mail directory. Individuals, however, also use this list to pass on questions, queries, information, or announcements. For information on how to join this list, contact Geoff Proehl: gproehl@ups.edu.

APPENDIX NOTES

[1] Laurence Shyer, "America's First Literary Manager: John Corbin at the New Theatre," *Theater* 10.1 (1978): 14.

[2] Joel Schechter, "American Dramaturgs," *The Drama Review* 20.2 (1976): 89.

[3] Joel Schechter, "Enter Dramaturgs," *Theater* 10.1 (1978): 6.

[4] Günter Skopnik, "An Unusual Person—Der Dramaturg—Une Institution Proprement Allemande," *World Theatre* 9.3 (1960): 233–238.

[5] Ferenc Molnar, "The Science of Dramaturgy," *A Companion in Exile: Notes for an Autobiography,* trans. Barrows Mussey (New York: Gaer, 1950).

[6] Francis Fergusson, from "A Letter to the Administration of the American Laboratory Theatre," 1928.

[7] Martin Esslin, "The Role of the Dramaturg in European Theatre" *Theater* 10.1 (1978): 48.

[8] Joel Schechter, "American Dramaturgs," *The Drama Review* 20.2 (1976): 89.

[9] William R. Ellwood. "Preliminary Notes on the German Dramaturg and American Theater." *Modern Drama* 13.3 (1970): 254.

[10] Ellwood 255.

[11] Herbert Blau, *Blooded Thought: Occasions for Theatre* (New York: Performing Arts Journal, 1982) 28.

[12] Patrice Pavis, *Languages of the Stage: Essays in Semiology of Theatre* (New York: Performing Arts Journal, 1982) 98, 100.

[13] Eugenio Barba and Nicola Savarese, "Dramaturgy," *A Dictionary of Theatre Anthropology: The Secret Art of the Performer,* trans. Richard Fowler (New York: Routledge, 1991) 68.

[14] Jack Zipes, "Utopia as the Past Conserved: An Interview with Peter Stein and Dieter Stürm of the Schaubühne am Halleschen Ufer." *Theater* 9.1 (1977): 52.

[15] Anne Cattaneo 20.

[16] Zipes 53.

[17] Lila Wolff-Wilkinson, "Comments on Process: Production Dramaturgy as the Core of the Liberal Arts Theatre Program," *Theatre Topics* 3.1 (1993): 1.

[18] Peter Hay, "American Dramaturgy: A Critical Reappraisal." *Performing Arts Journal* 7.3 (1983): 13–14; Dr. Victor Frankl, *Man's Search for Meaning: An Introduction to Logoherapy* (Boston: Beacon Press, 1959).

[19] "Dramaturgy and Physics: panel discussion entitled "How to Use a Dramaturg" sponsored by Stage Directors and Choreographers Foundation and the Dramatists Guild on Sept. 25, 1989; moderated by James Leverett with James C. Nicola, Richard Dresser, Morgan Jenness, and Tim Sanford. *Journal of the Stage Directors and Choreographers* 5.1 (1991): 4.

[20] Charles Marowitz, "Frontlines: The Dramaturg's Lament." *American Theatre.*

[21] David Copelin. *LMDA Review* Spring 1989: 5.

[22] Tim Sanford, "Dramaturgy and Physics," 19.

[23] James Leverett, "Dramaturgy and Physics," 12.

[24] James C. Nicola, "Dramaturgy and Physics," 14–15.

[25] Jayme Koszyn, dramaturg, Huntington Theatre Company, in conversation.

[26] Harriet Power, dramaturg and artistic director of Venture Theatre, in conversation.

[27] Lenny Pinna, resident dramaturg, Second Annual National Puppetry Conference (June 1–6, 1992), Eugene O'Neill Theater Center Waterford, Connecticut from "Puppeturgy? Puppet Theatre Art from a Dramaturg's Perspective," *The Puppetry Journal* 44.3 (1993): 14–15.

[28] Peter Stone, *Previews,* 155.

[29] Denise Fujiwara, Canadian choreographer, on her work with D. D. [Don] Kugler, Canadian dramaturg, from "Care to Dance Dramaturge? The Invention of a New Craft," *Theatrum* (fall 1988): 18.

[30] Jan Kott, "The Dramaturg," *New Theatre Quarterly* 6.21 (1990): 3–4.

[31] From the *LMDA Review* 5.1 (n.d.): 4.

[32] Reported by Jim Lewis, dramaturg, and re-printed from *Sports Illustrated* in the *LMDA Review* 4.3 (n.d.): 3; emphasis added.

[33] Robert Parker, *Walking Shadow* (New York: Putman's, 1994).

Index